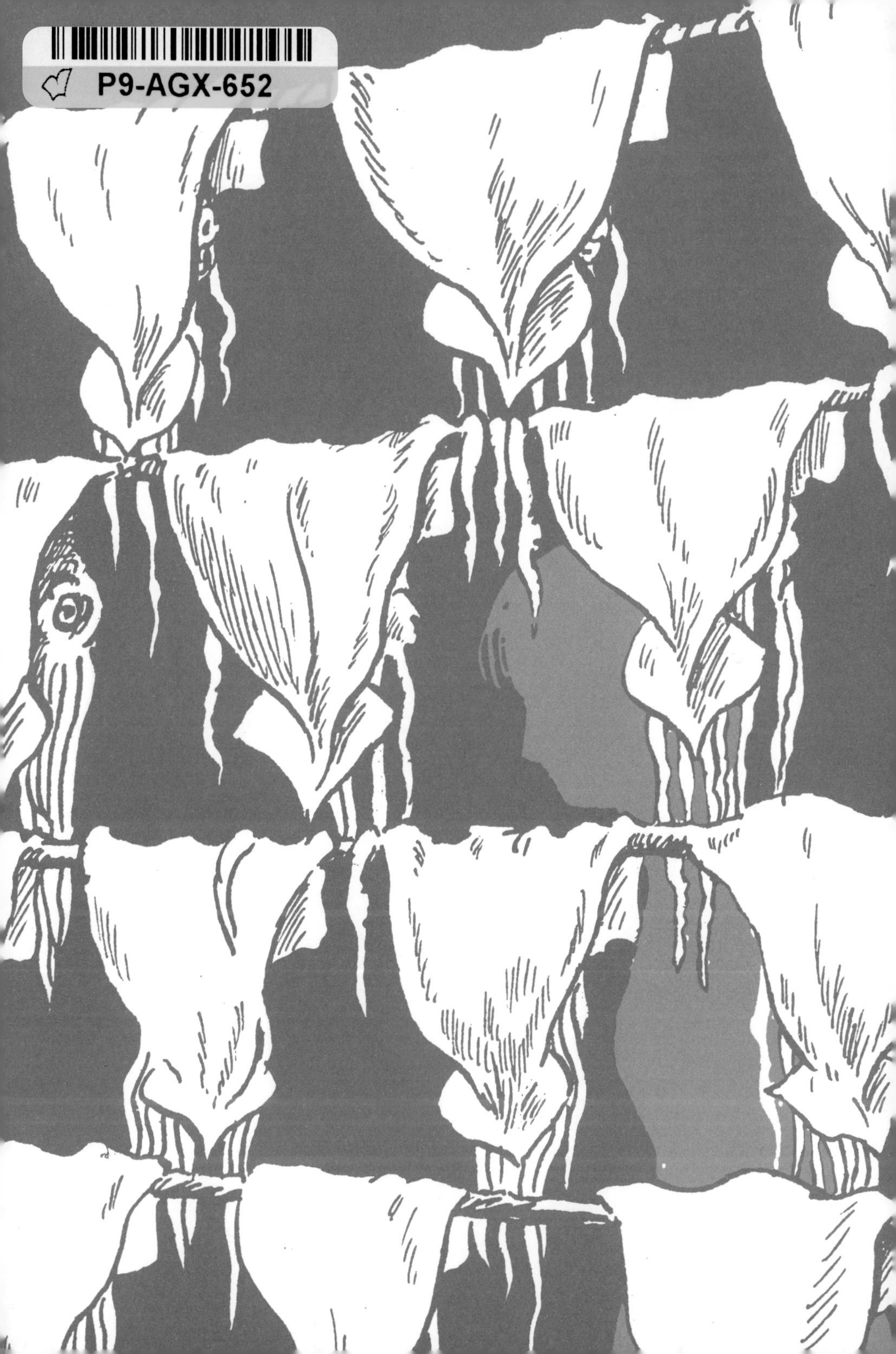

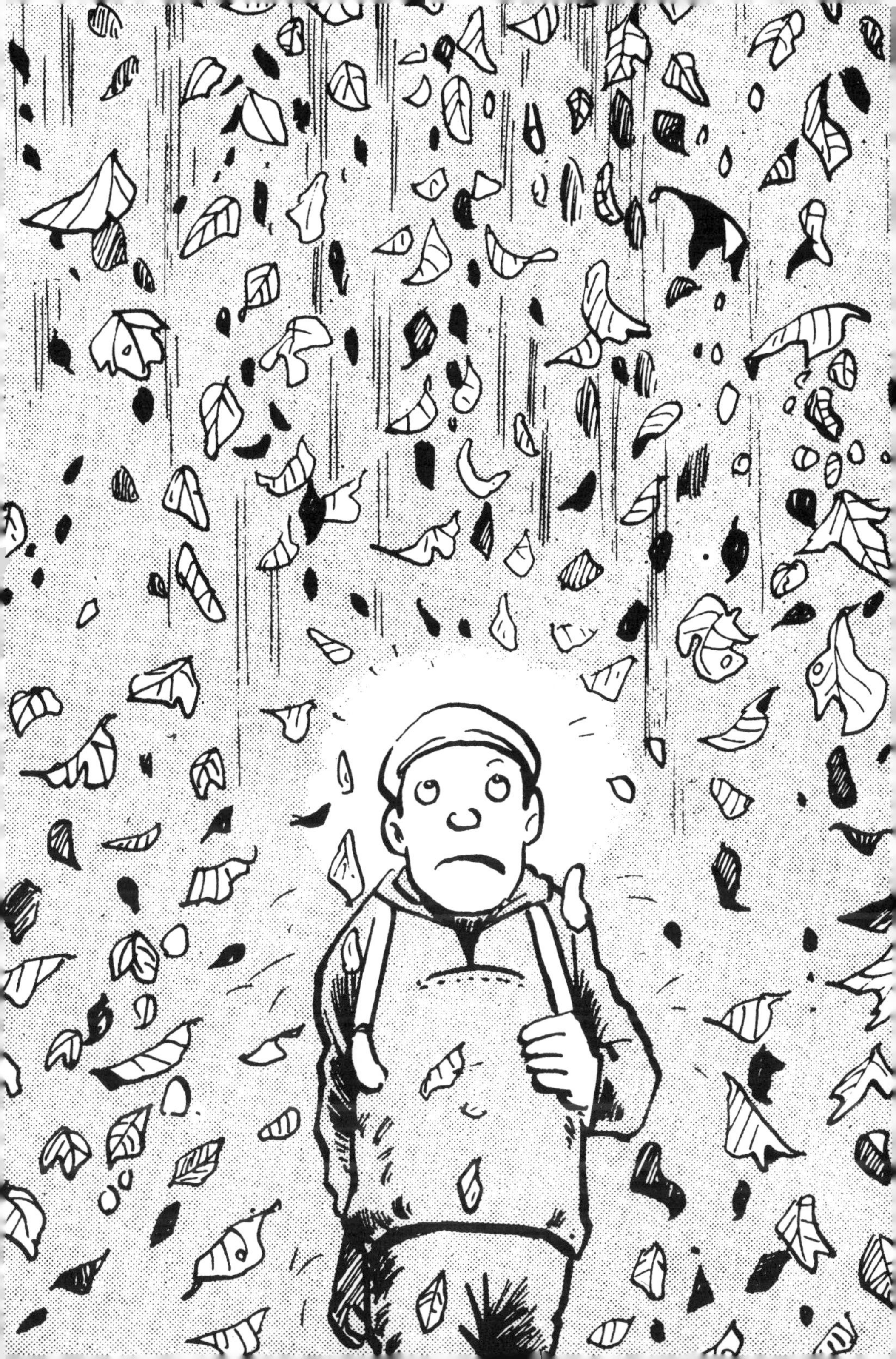

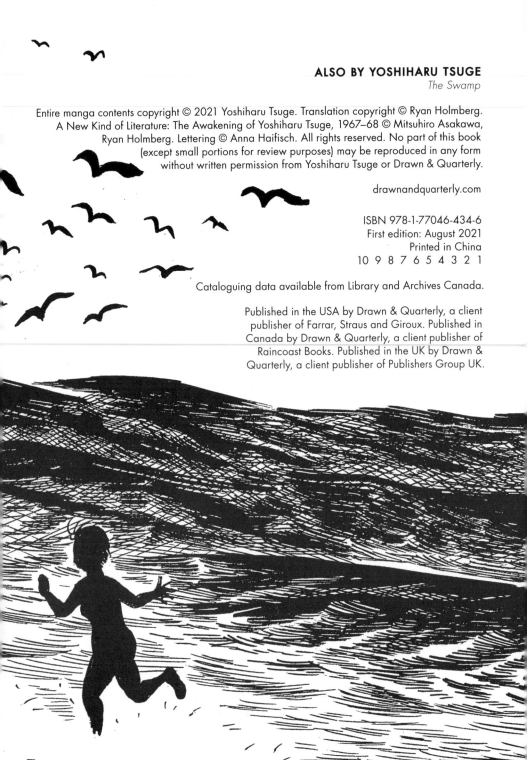

ALSO BY YOSHIHARU TSUGE

The Swamp

drawnandquarterly.com

ISBN 978-1-77046-434-6
First edition: August 2021
Printed in China
10 9 8 7 6 5 4 3 2 1

Cataloguing data available from Library and Archives Canada.

Published in the USA by Drawn & Quarterly, a client publisher of Farrar, Straus and Giroux. Published in Canada by Drawn & Quarterly, a client publisher of Raincoast Books. Published in the UK by Drawn & Quarterly, a client publisher of Publishers Group UK.

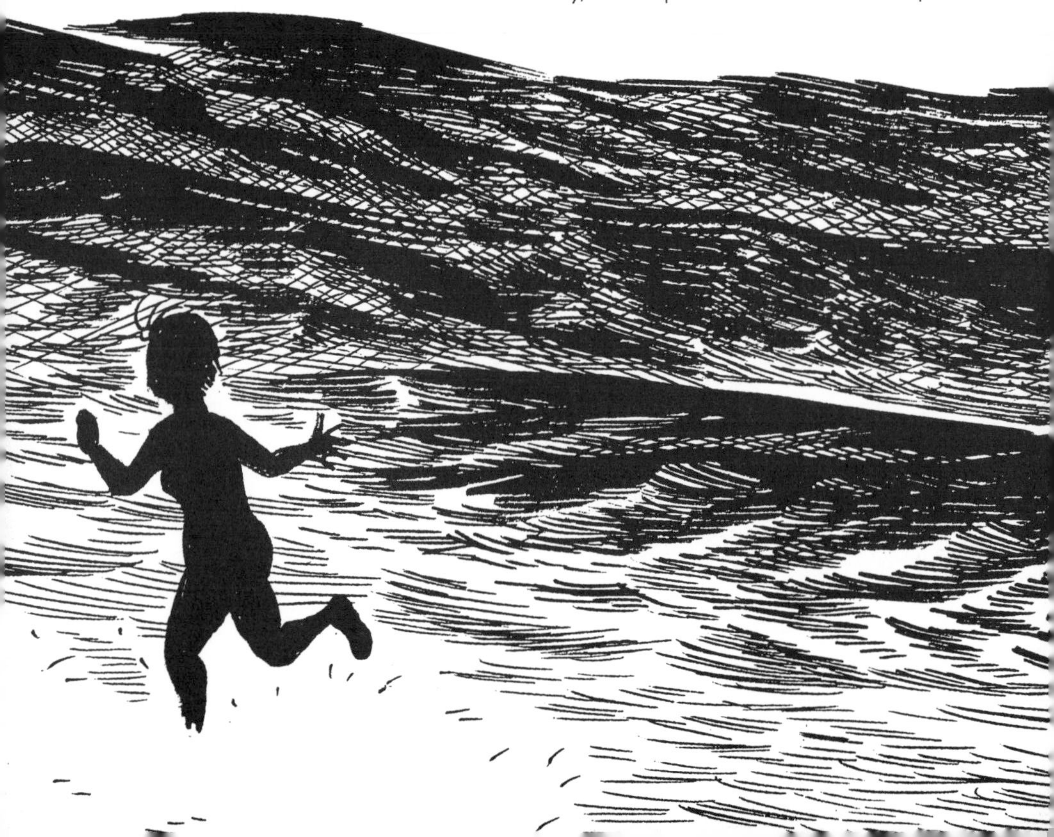

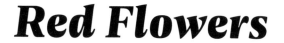

Red Flowers

YOSHIHARU TSUGE

The Complete Mature Works of Yoshiharu Tsuge Volume 2

Series editor and essay, Mitsuhiro Asakawa
Co-editor, translator, and essay co-author, Ryan Holmberg

DRAWN & QUARTERLY

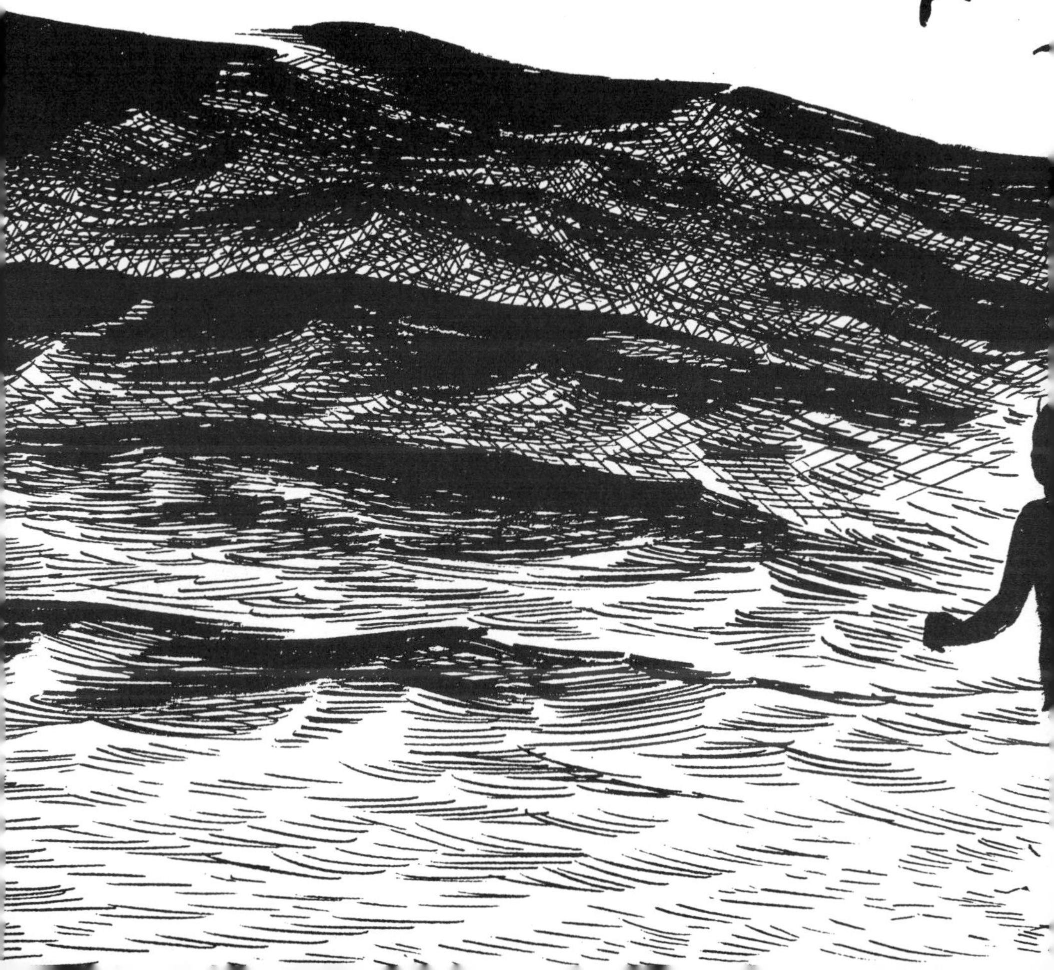

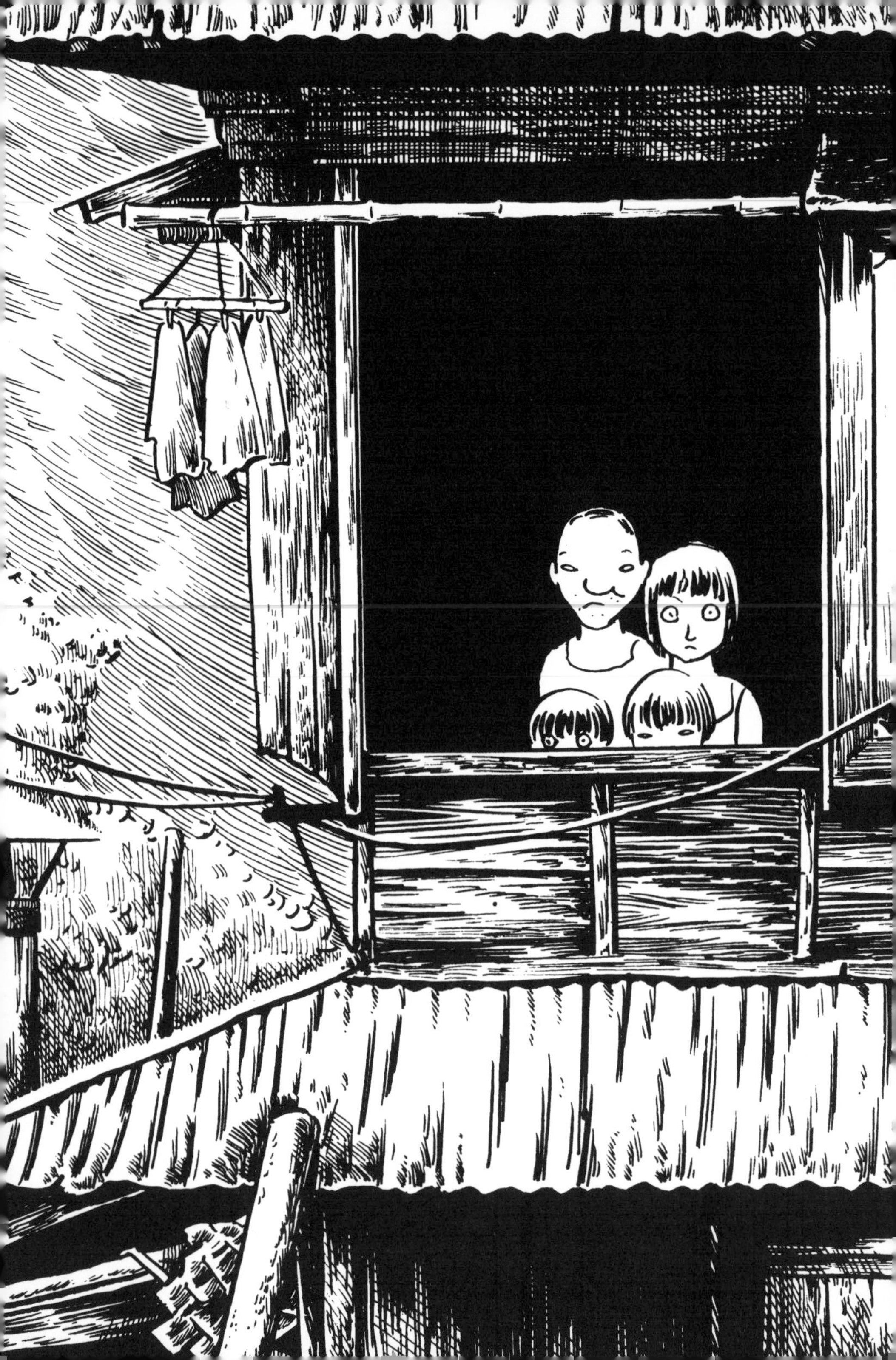

CONTENTS

THE WAKE

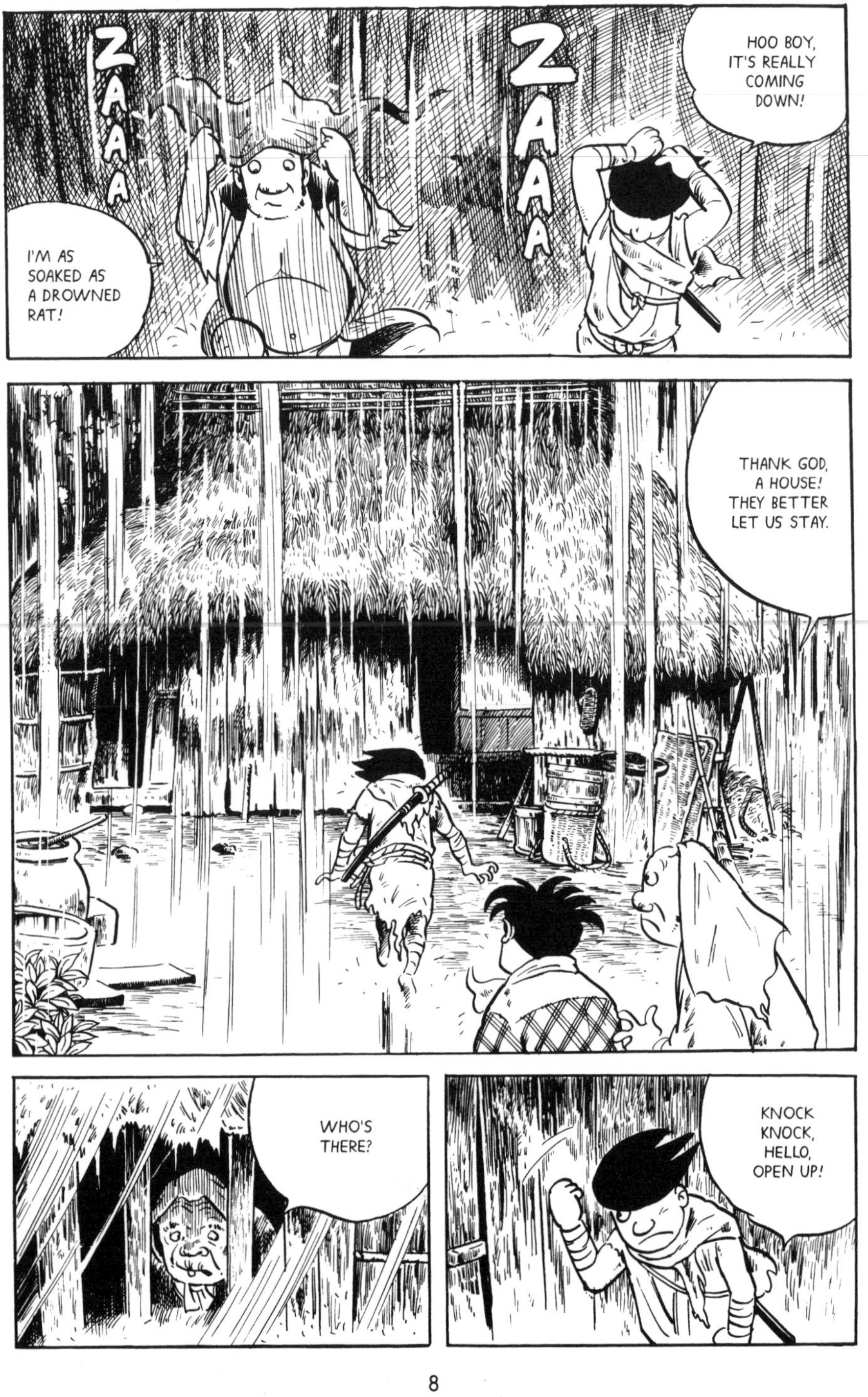
HOO BOY, IT'S REALLY COMING DOWN!
ZAAAA
ZAAA
I'M AS SOAKED AS A DROWNED RAT!
THANK GOD, A HOUSE! THEY BETTER LET US STAY.
KNOCK KNOCK, HELLO, OPEN UP!
WHO'S THERE?

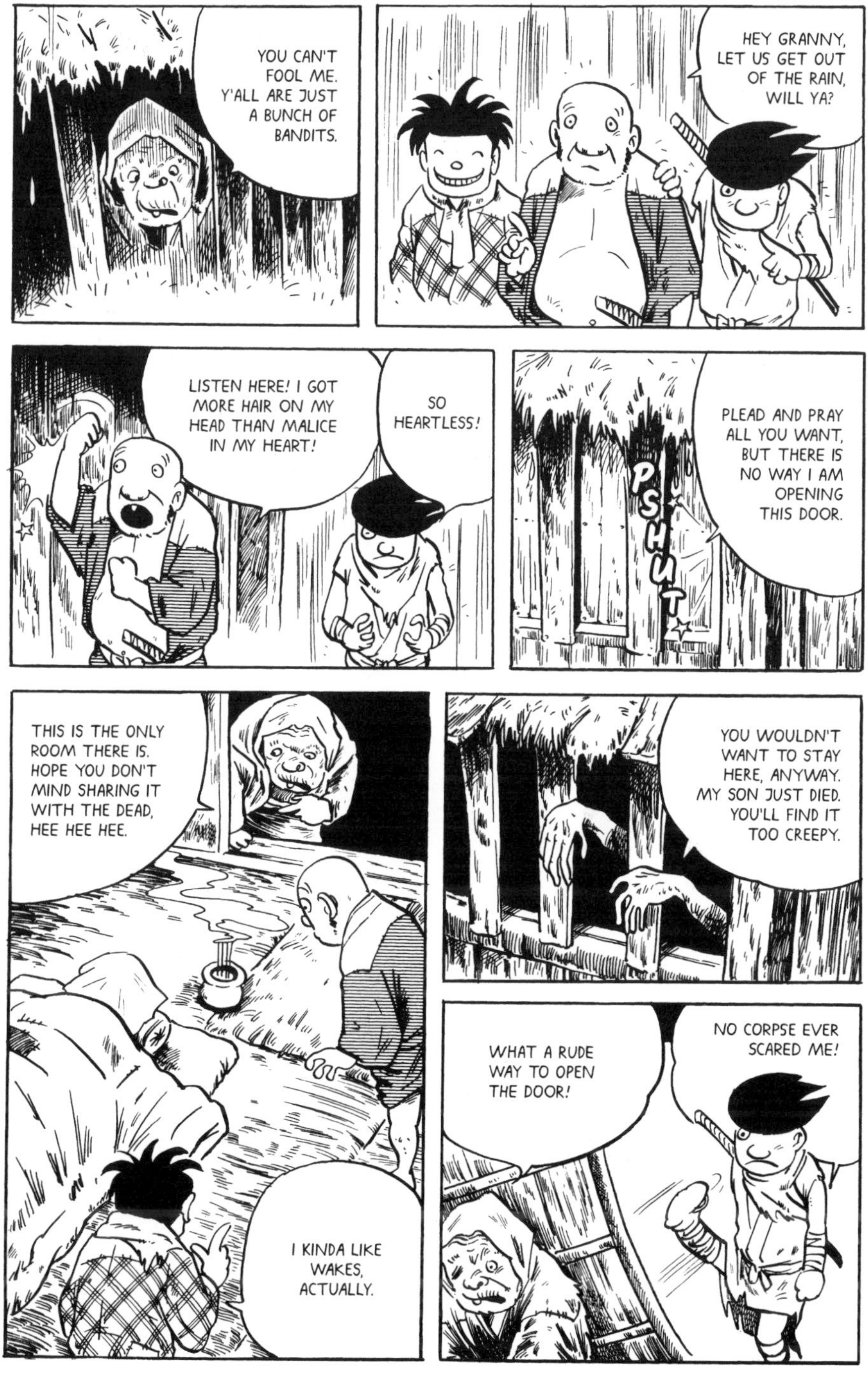
HEY GRANNY, LET US GET OUT OF THE RAIN, WILL YA?
YOU CAN'T FOOL ME. Y'ALL ARE JUST A BUNCH OF BANDITS.
PLEAD AND PRAY ALL YOU WANT, BUT THERE IS NO WAY I AM OPENING THIS DOOR.
PSHUT
SO HEARTLESS!
LISTEN HERE! I GOT MORE HAIR ON MY HEAD THAN MALICE IN MY HEART!
YOU WOULDN'T WANT TO STAY HERE, ANYWAY. MY SON JUST DIED. YOU'LL FIND IT TOO CREEPY.
NO CORPSE EVER SCARED ME!
WHAT A RUDE WAY TO OPEN THE DOOR!
THIS IS THE ONLY ROOM THERE IS. HOPE YOU DON'T MIND SHARING IT WITH THE DEAD, HEE HEE HEE.
I KINDA LIKE WAKES, ACTUALLY.

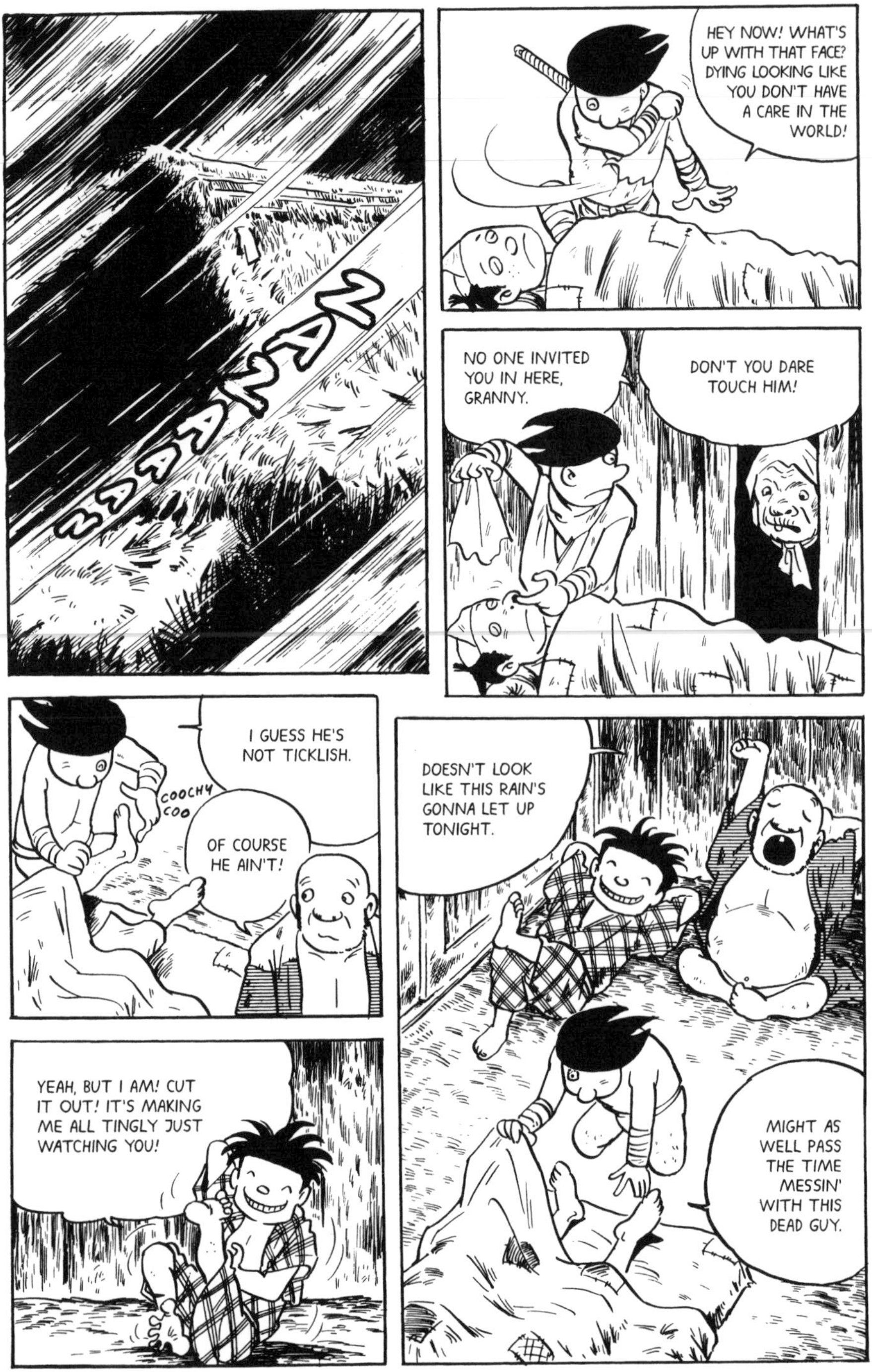
HEY NOW! WHAT'S UP WITH THAT FACE? DYING LOOKING LIKE YOU DON'T HAVE A CARE IN THE WORLD!
DON'T YOU DARE TOUCH HIM!
NO ONE INVITED YOU IN HERE, GRANNY.
ZAZAAAN
DOESN'T LOOK LIKE THIS RAIN'S GONNA LET UP TONIGHT.
MIGHT AS WELL PASS THE TIME MESSIN' WITH THIS DEAD GUY.
I GUESS HE'S NOT TICKLISH.
COOCHY COO
OF COURSE HE AIN'T!
YEAH, BUT I AM! CUT IT OUT! IT'S MAKING ME ALL TINGLY JUST WATCHING YOU!

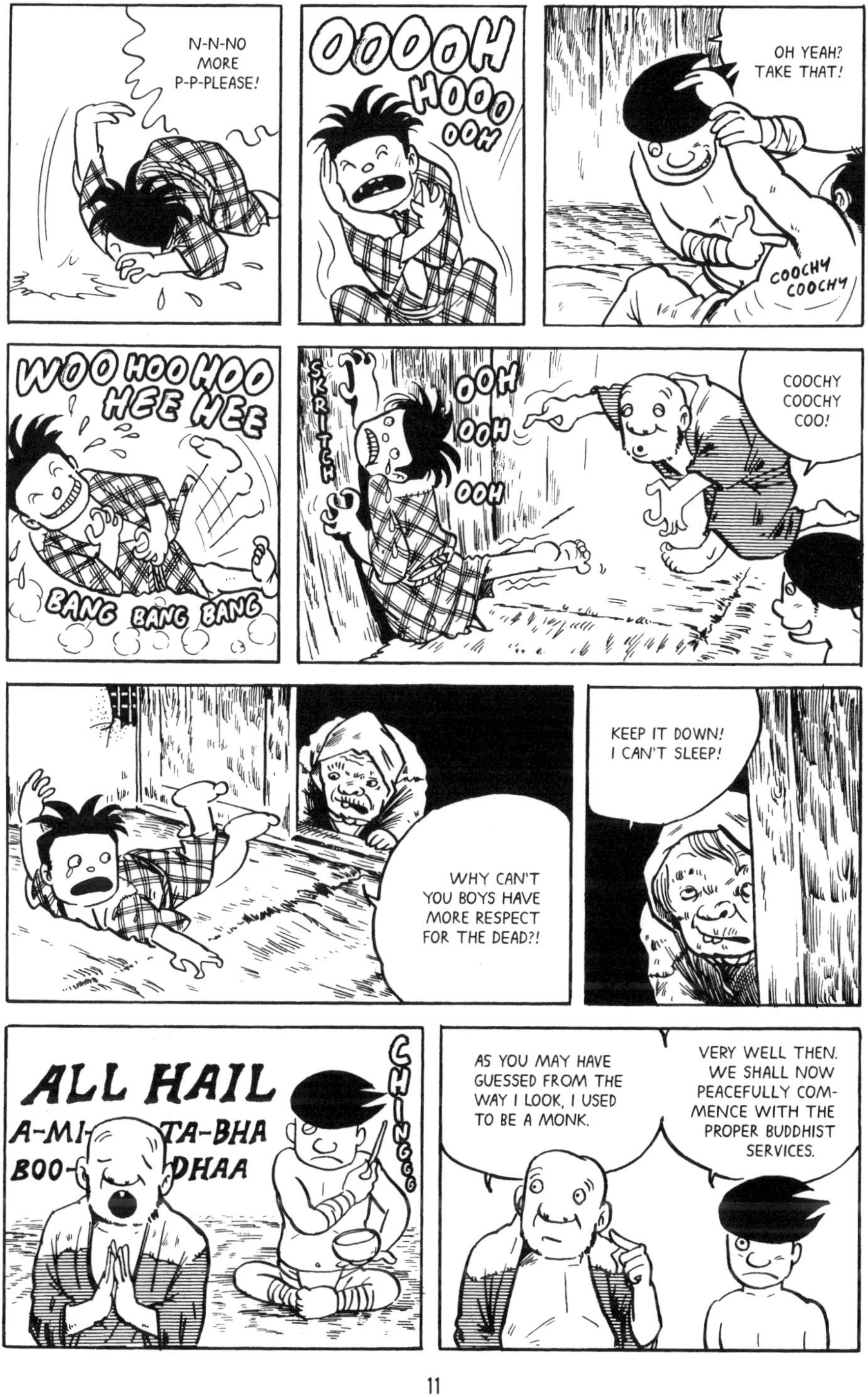

OH YEAH? TAKE THAT!
COOCHY COOCHY
OOOOH HOOO OOH
N-N-NO MORE P-P-PLEASE!
COOCHY COOCHY COO!
OOH OOH OOH
SKRITCH
WOO HOO HOO HOO HEE HEE
BANG BANG BANG
KEEP IT DOWN! I CAN'T SLEEP!
WHY CAN'T YOU BOYS HAVE MORE RESPECT FOR THE DEAD?!
VERY WELL THEN. WE SHALL NOW PEACEFULLY COM-MENCE WITH THE PROPER BUDDHIST SERVICES.
AS YOU MAY HAVE GUESSED FROM THE WAY I LOOK, I USED TO BE A MONK.
CHINGGG
ALL HAIL A-MI-TA-BHA BOO-DHAA

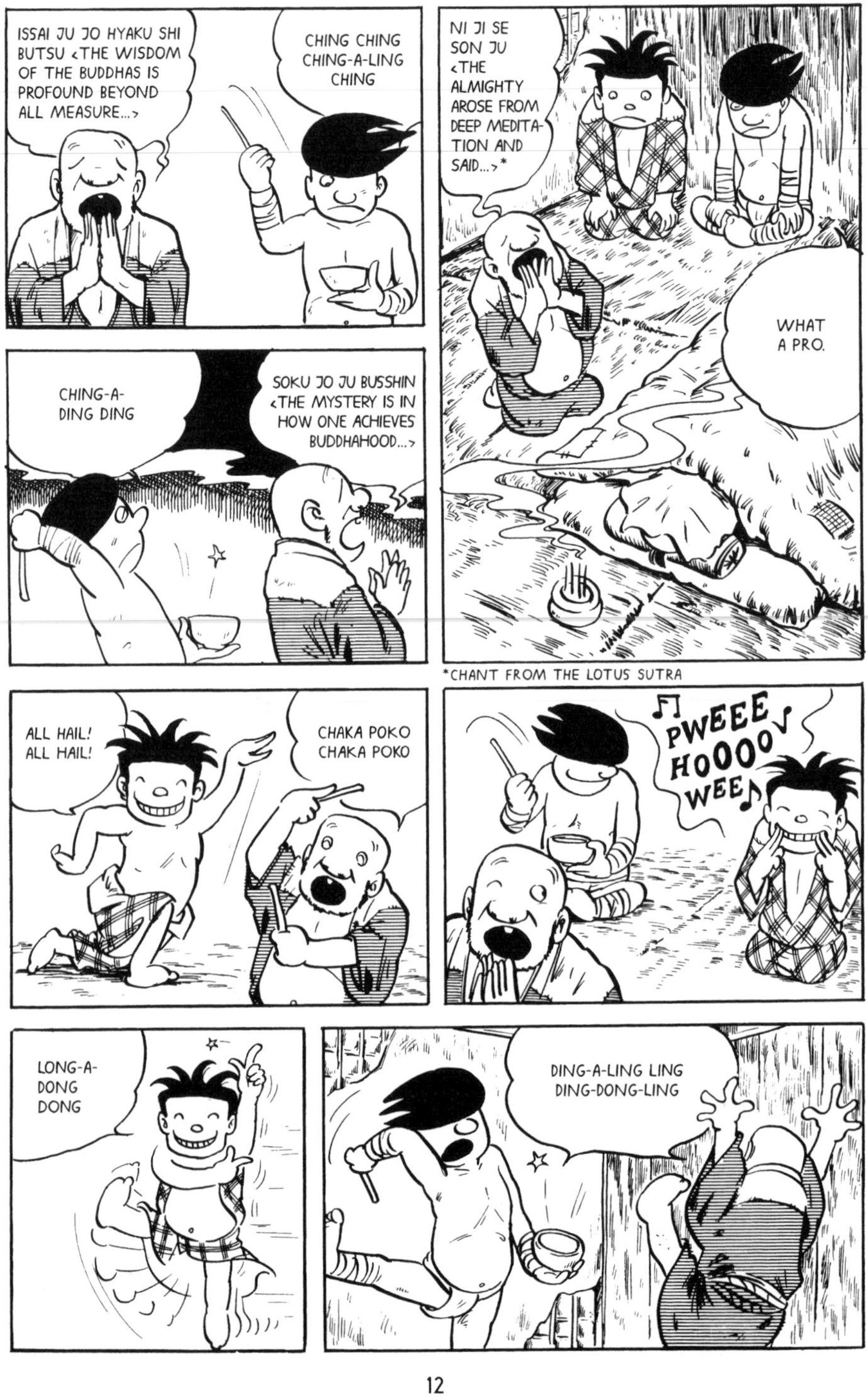
NI JI SE SON JU <THE ALMIGHTY AROSE FROM DEEP MEDITATION AND SAID...>*
WHAT A PRO.
CHING CHING CHING-A-LING CHING
ISSAI JU JO HYAKU SHI BUTSU <THE WISDOM OF THE BUDDHAS IS PROFOUND BEYOND ALL MEASURE...>
SOKU JO JU BUSSHIN <THE MYSTERY IS IN HOW ONE ACHIEVES BUDDHAHOOD...>
CHING-A-DING DING
PWEEE HOOOO WEE
CHAKA POKO CHAKA POKO
ALL HAIL! ALL HAIL!
DING-A-LING LING DING-DONG-LING
LONG-A-DONG DONG

*CHANT FROM THE LOTUS SUTRA

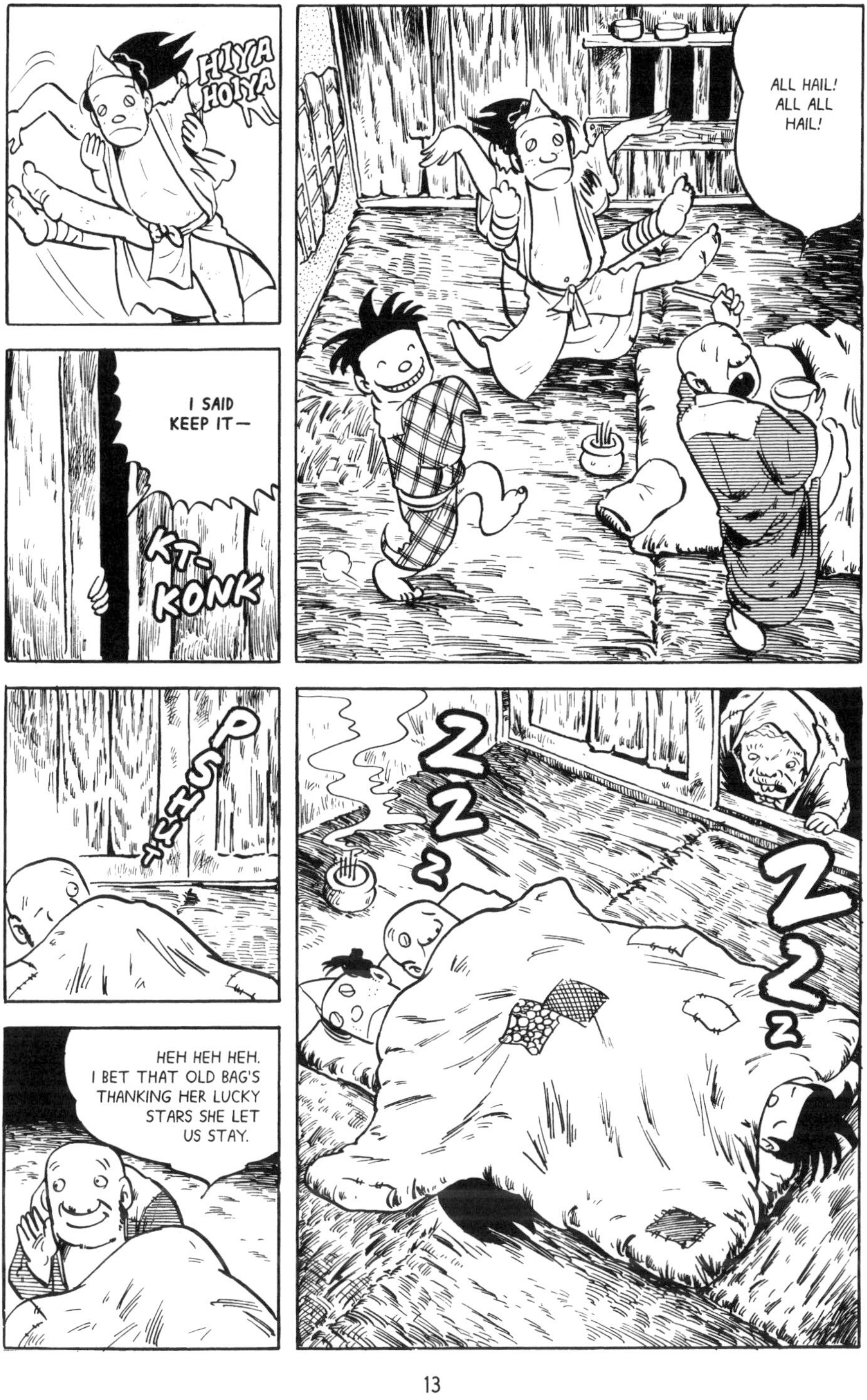

ALL HAIL! ALL ALL HAIL!
HIYA HOIYA
I SAID KEEP IT—
KT-KONK
ZZz
ZZz
PSHHT
HEH HEH HEH. I BET THAT OLD BAG'S THANKING HER LUCKY STARS SHE LET US STAY.

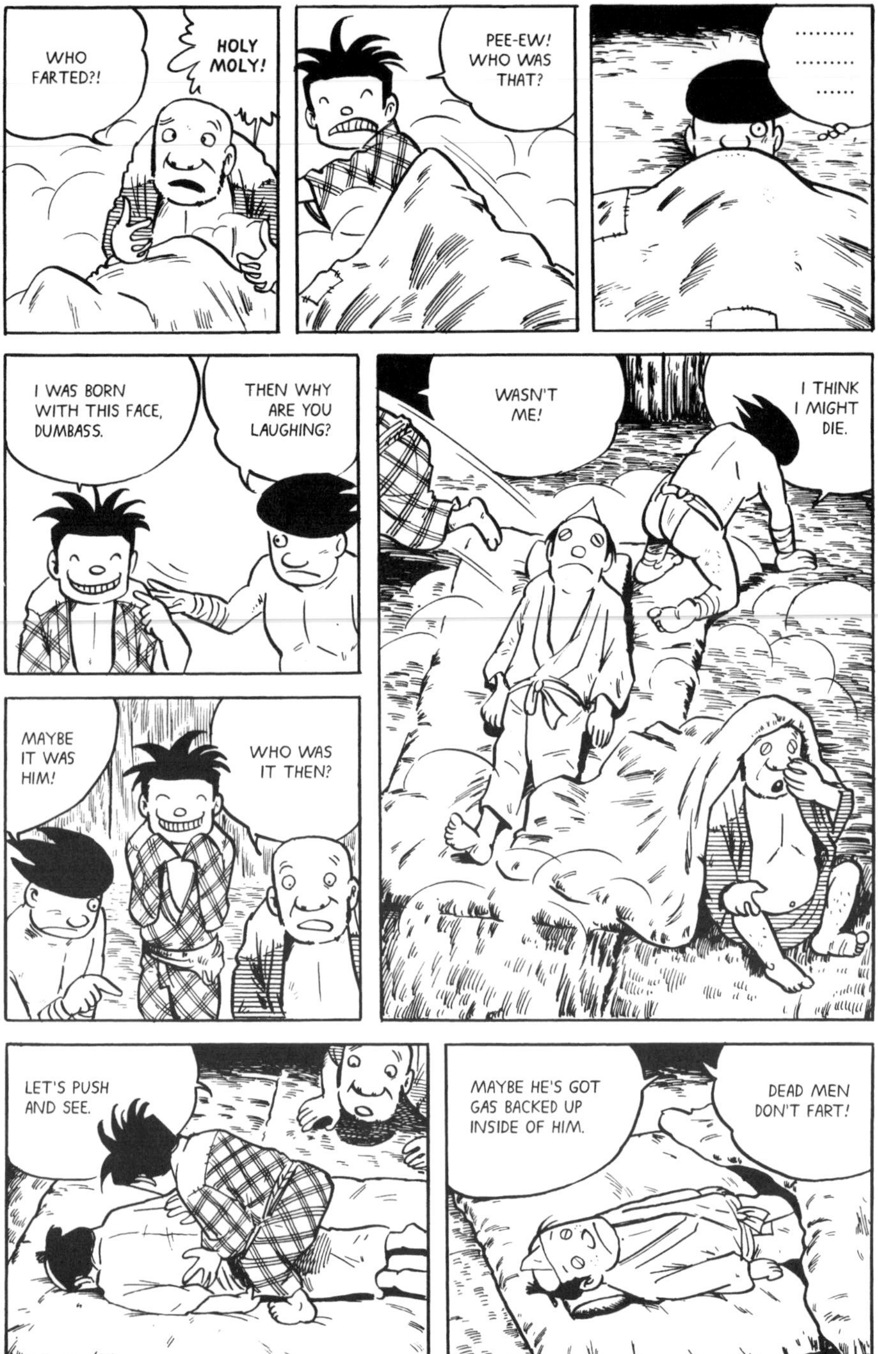
....
....
......
PEE-EW! WHO WAS THAT?
HOLY MOLY!
WHO FARTED?!
I THINK I MIGHT DIE.
WASN'T ME!
THEN WHY ARE YOU LAUGHING?
I WAS BORN WITH THIS FACE, DUMBASS.
WHO WAS IT THEN?
MAYBE IT WAS HIM!
DEAD MEN DON'T FART!
MAYBE HE'S GOT GAS BACKED UP INSIDE OF HIM.
LET'S PUSH AND SEE.

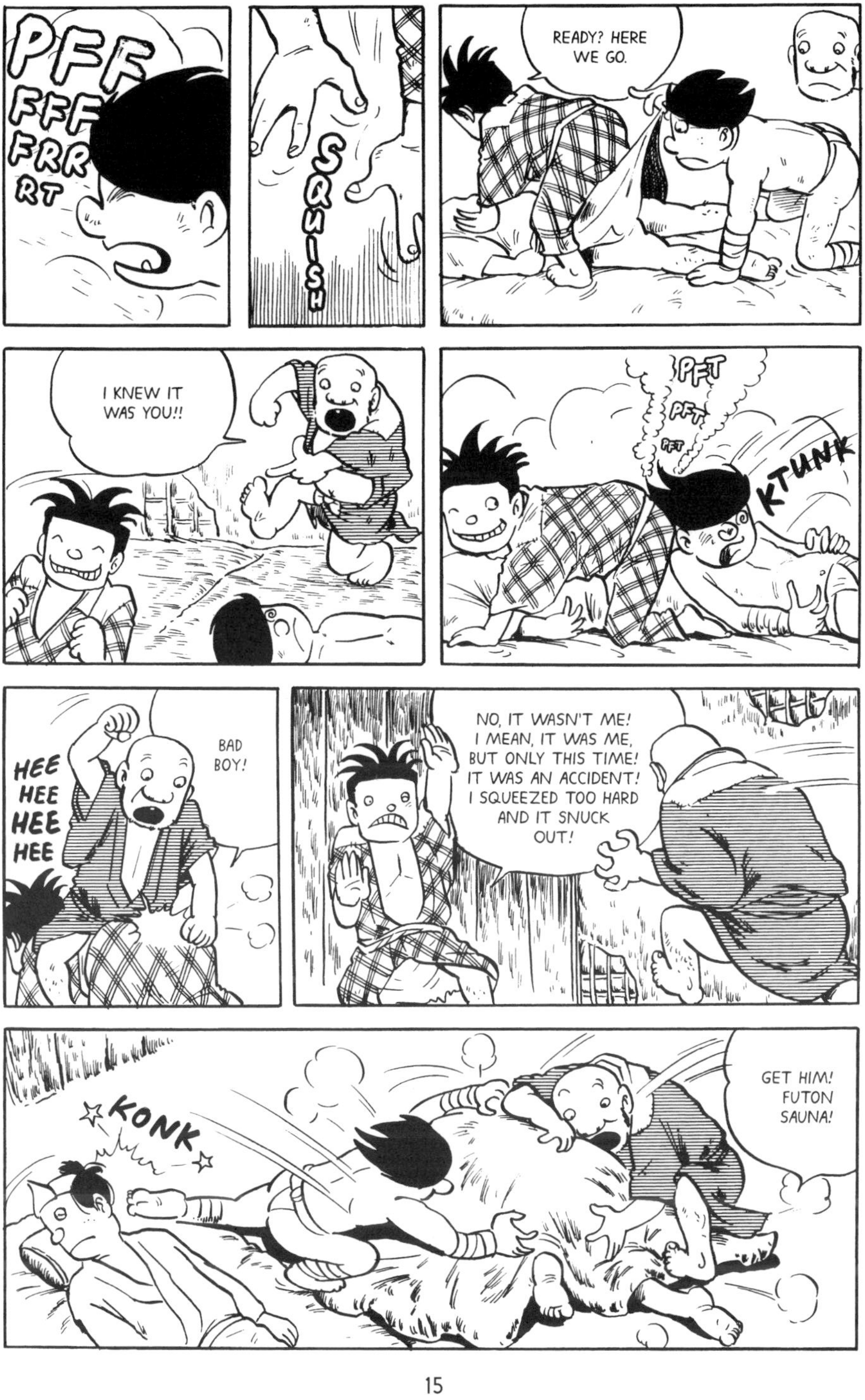
READY? HERE WE GO.
SQUISH
PFF FFF FRR RT
PFT PFT PFT
KTUNK
I KNEW IT WAS YOU!!
NO, IT WASN'T ME! I MEAN, IT WAS ME, BUT ONLY THIS TIME! IT WAS AN ACCIDENT! I SQUEEZED TOO HARD AND IT SNUCK OUT!
BAD BOY!
HEE HEE HEE HEE
GET HIM! FUTON SAUNA!
KONK

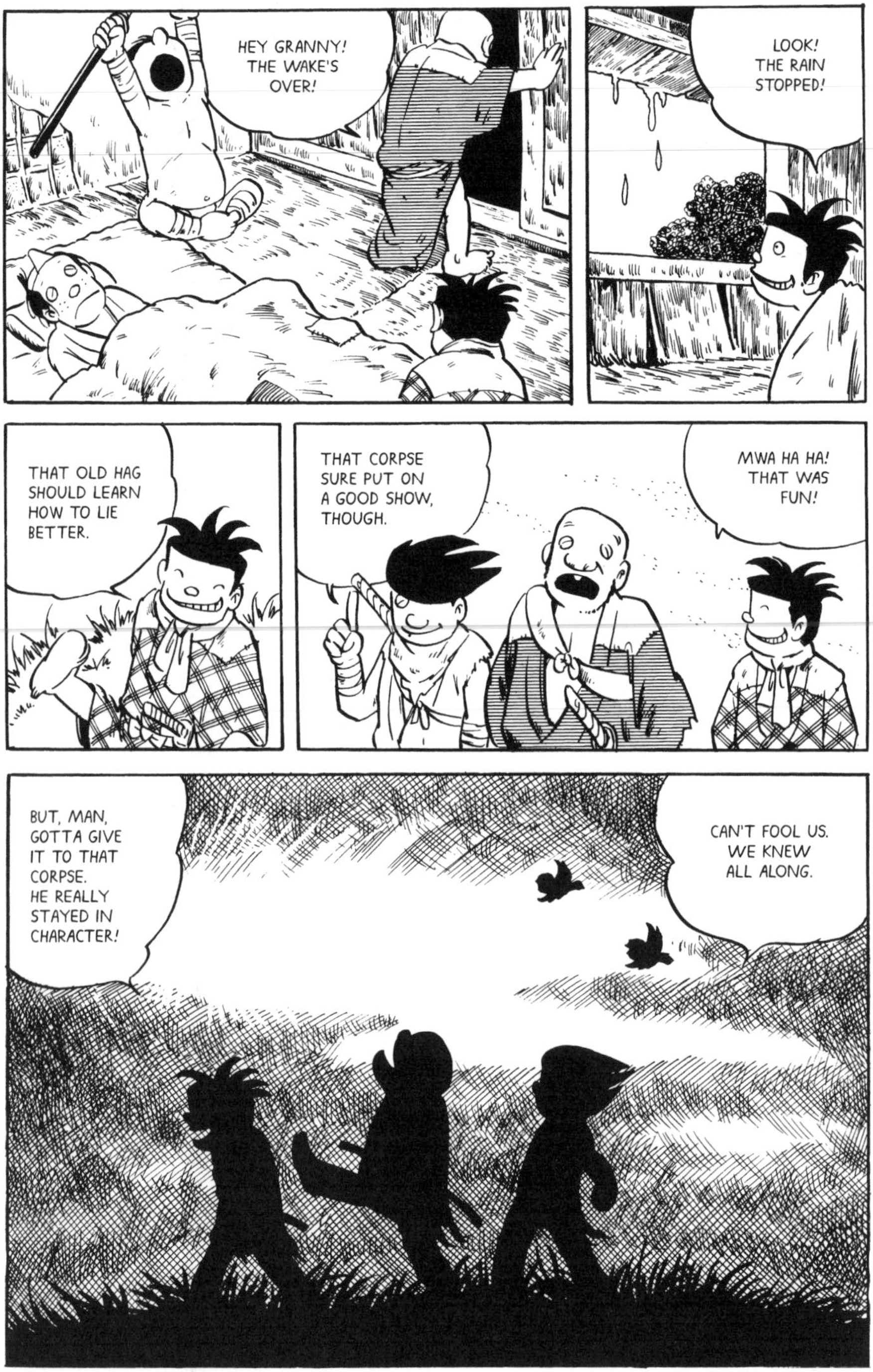
LOOK! THE RAIN STOPPED!
HEY GRANNY! THE WAKE'S OVER!
MWA HA HA! THAT WAS FUN!
THAT CORPSE SURE PUT ON A GOOD SHOW, THOUGH.
THAT OLD HAG SHOULD LEARN HOW TO LIE BETTER.
CAN'T FOOL US. WE KNEW ALL ALONG.
BUT, MAN, GOTTA GIVE IT TO THAT CORPSE. HE REALLY STAYED IN CHARACTER!

THE SALAMANDER

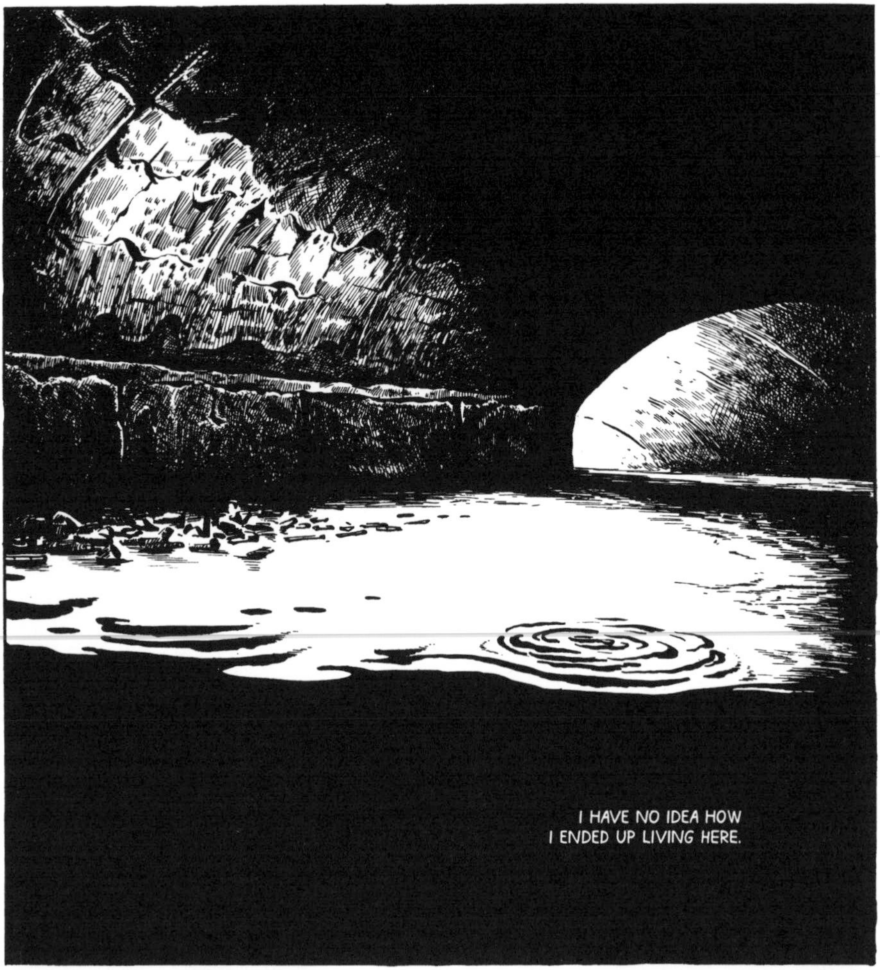
I HAVE NO IDEA HOW
I ENDED UP LIVING HERE.

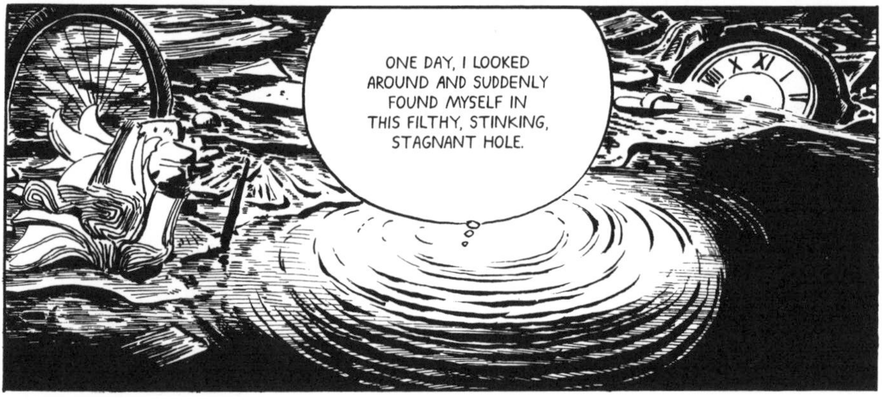
ONE DAY, I LOOKED
AROUND AND SUDDENLY
FOUND MYSELF IN
THIS FILTHY, STINKING,
STAGNANT HOLE.

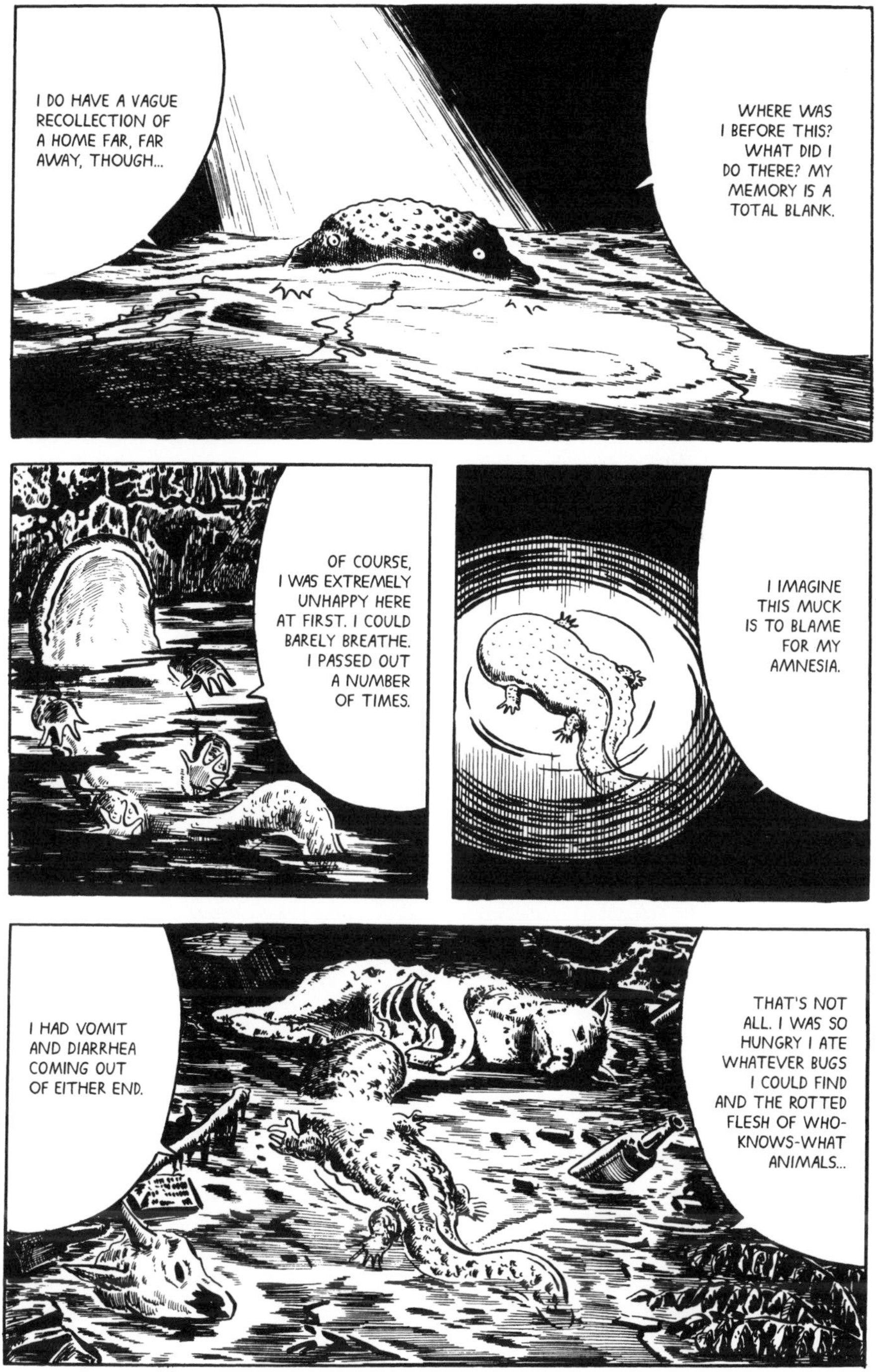
WHERE WAS I BEFORE THIS? WHAT DID I DO THERE? MY MEMORY IS A TOTAL BLANK.
I DO HAVE A VAGUE RECOLLECTION OF A HOME FAR, FAR AWAY, THOUGH...
I IMAGINE THIS MUCK IS TO BLAME FOR MY AMNESIA.
OF COURSE, I WAS EXTREMELY UNHAPPY HERE AT FIRST. I COULD BARELY BREATHE. I PASSED OUT A NUMBER OF TIMES.
THAT'S NOT ALL. I WAS SO HUNGRY I ATE WHATEVER BUGS I COULD FIND AND THE ROTTED FLESH OF WHO-KNOWS-WHAT ANIMALS...
I HAD VOMIT AND DIARRHEA COMING OUT OF EITHER END.

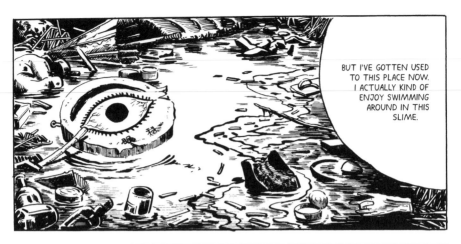

BUT I'VE GOTTEN USED TO THIS PLACE NOW. I ACTUALLY KIND OF ENJOY SWIMMING AROUND IN THIS SLIME.
CHANGE YOUR ENVIRONMENT, CHANGE YOUR DIET, AND YOUR PHYSICAL CONSTITUTION WILL CHANGE IN TURN.
AT SOME POINT, I REALIZED THAT I WAS NO LONGER MYSELF. I HAD TURNED INTO A DIFFERENT CREATURE.
I WEIGH THREE TIMES AS MUCH AS I USED TO. SOMETIMES I LOOK AT MYSELF AND THINK HOW NICELY SHINY AND BLACK I HAVE BECOME.

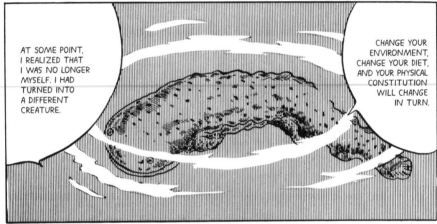

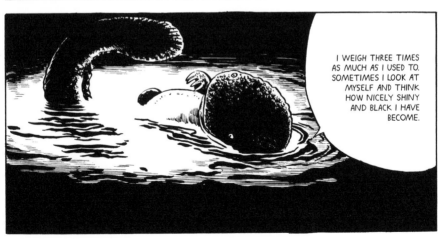

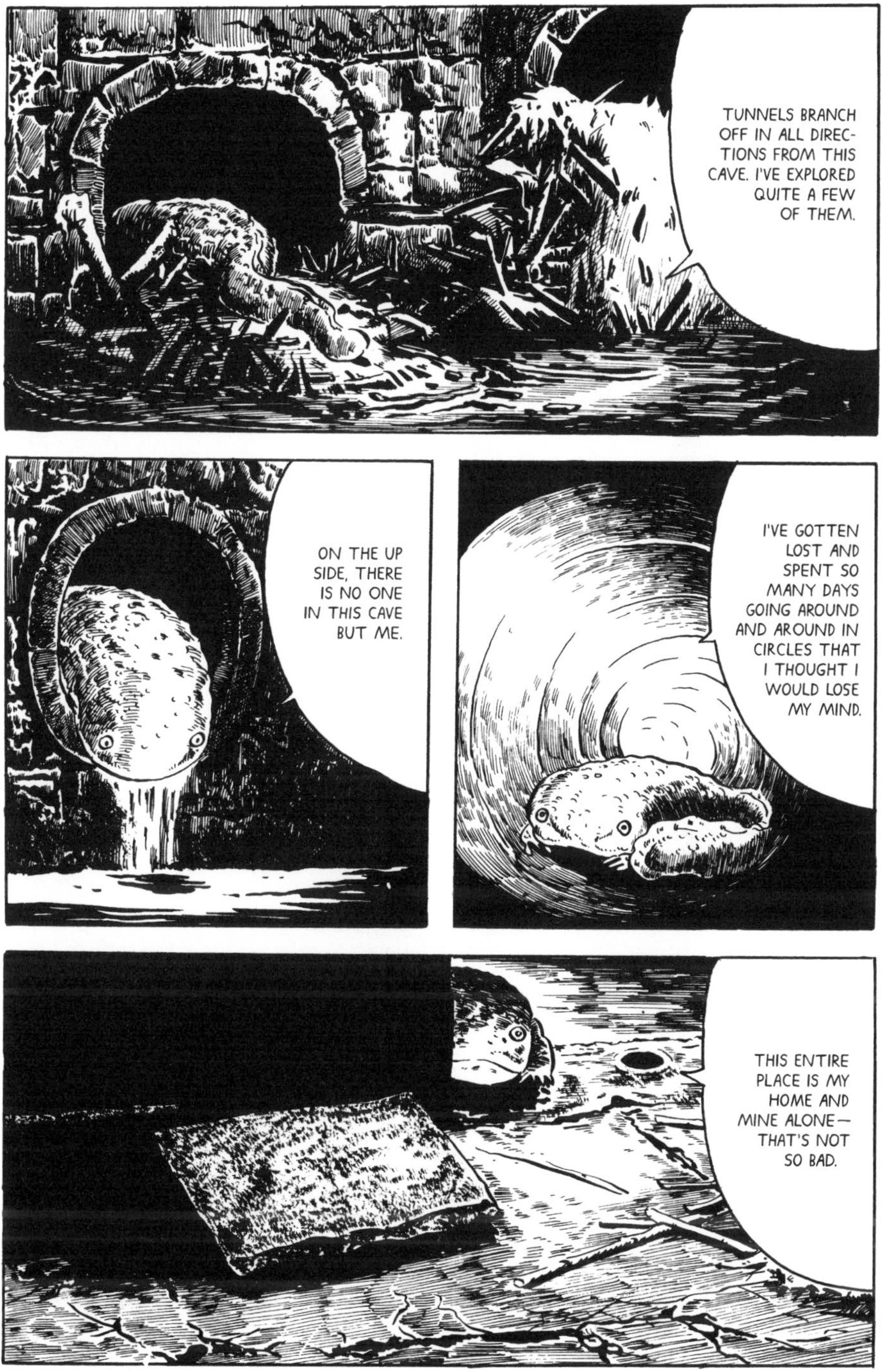
TUNNELS BRANCH OFF IN ALL DIREC- TIONS FROM THIS CAVE. I'VE EXPLORED QUITE A FEW OF THEM.
I'VE GOTTEN LOST AND SPENT SO MANY DAYS GOING AROUND AND AROUND IN CIRCLES THAT I THOUGHT I WOULD LOSE MY MIND.
ON THE UP SIDE, THERE IS NO ONE IN THIS CAVE BUT ME.
THIS ENTIRE PLACE IS MY HOME AND MINE ALONE— THAT'S NOT SO BAD.

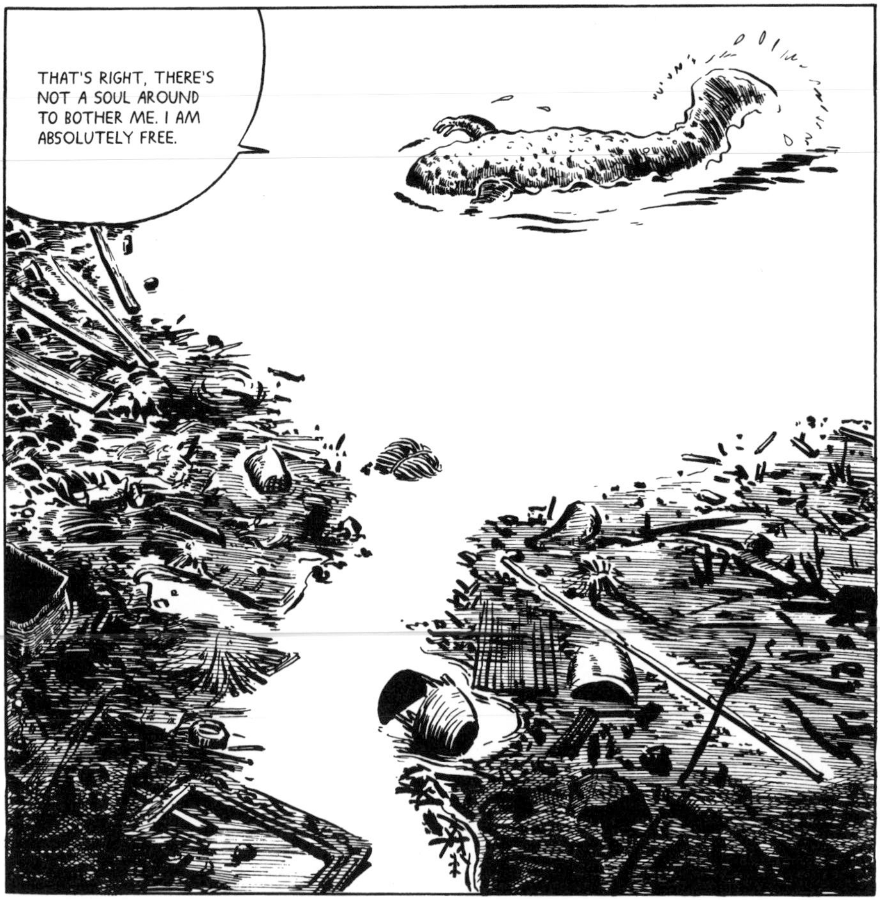
THAT'S RIGHT, THERE'S NOT A SOUL AROUND TO BOTHER ME. I AM ABSOLUTELY FREE.

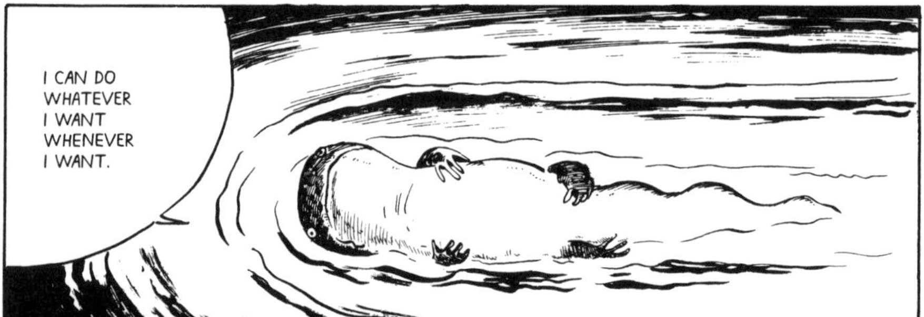
I CAN DO WHATEVER I WANT WHENEVER I WANT.

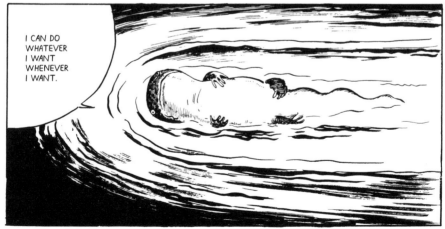

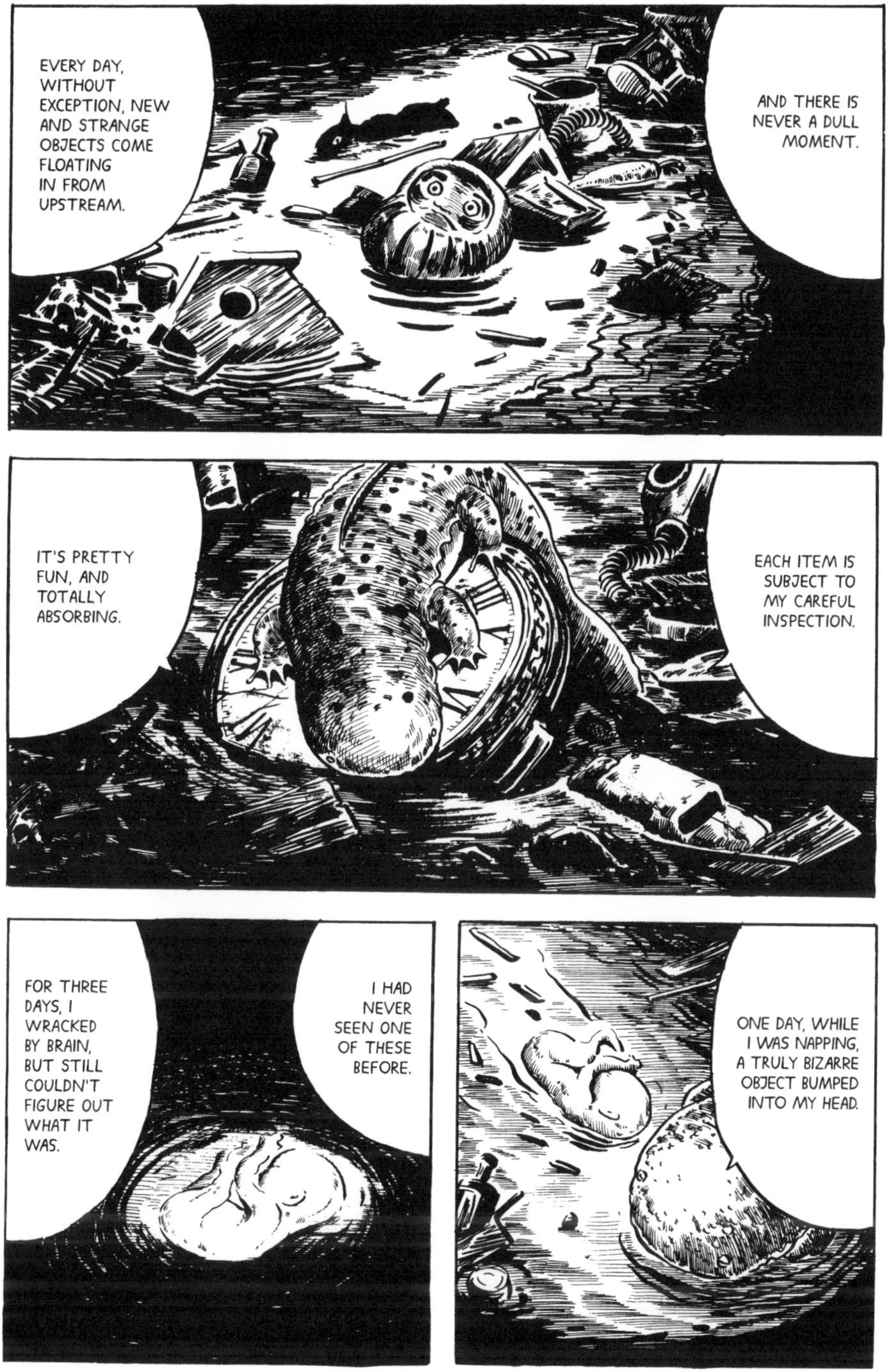
AND THERE IS NEVER A DULL MOMENT.
EVERY DAY, WITHOUT EXCEPTION, NEW AND STRANGE OBJECTS COME FLOATING IN FROM UPSTREAM.
EACH ITEM IS SUBJECT TO MY CAREFUL INSPECTION.
IT'S PRETTY FUN, AND TOTALLY ABSORBING.
ONE DAY, WHILE I WAS NAPPING, A TRULY BIZARRE OBJECT BUMPED INTO MY HEAD.
I HAD NEVER SEEN ONE OF THESE BEFORE.
FOR THREE DAYS, I WRACKED BY BRAIN, BUT STILL COULDN'T FIGURE OUT WHAT IT WAS.

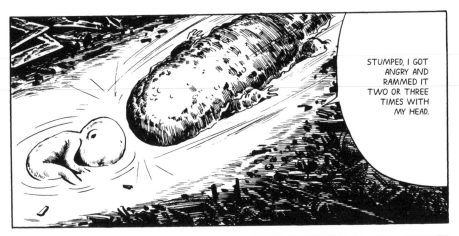

STUMPED, I GOT ANGRY AND RAMMED IT TWO OR THREE TIMES WITH MY HEAD.
THAT'S ABOUT AS WEIRD AS THE THINGS THAT I SEE GET.
I WONDER WHAT WILL FLOAT IN TOMORROW?
I'M SO EXCITED! I CAN'T WAIT!

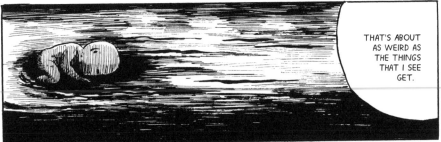

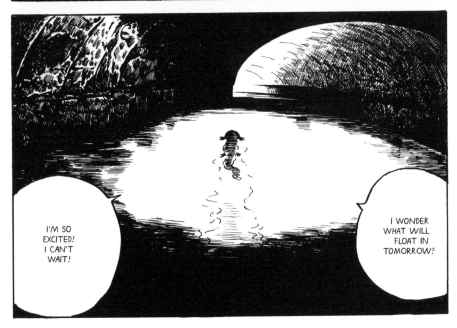

THE LEE FAMILY

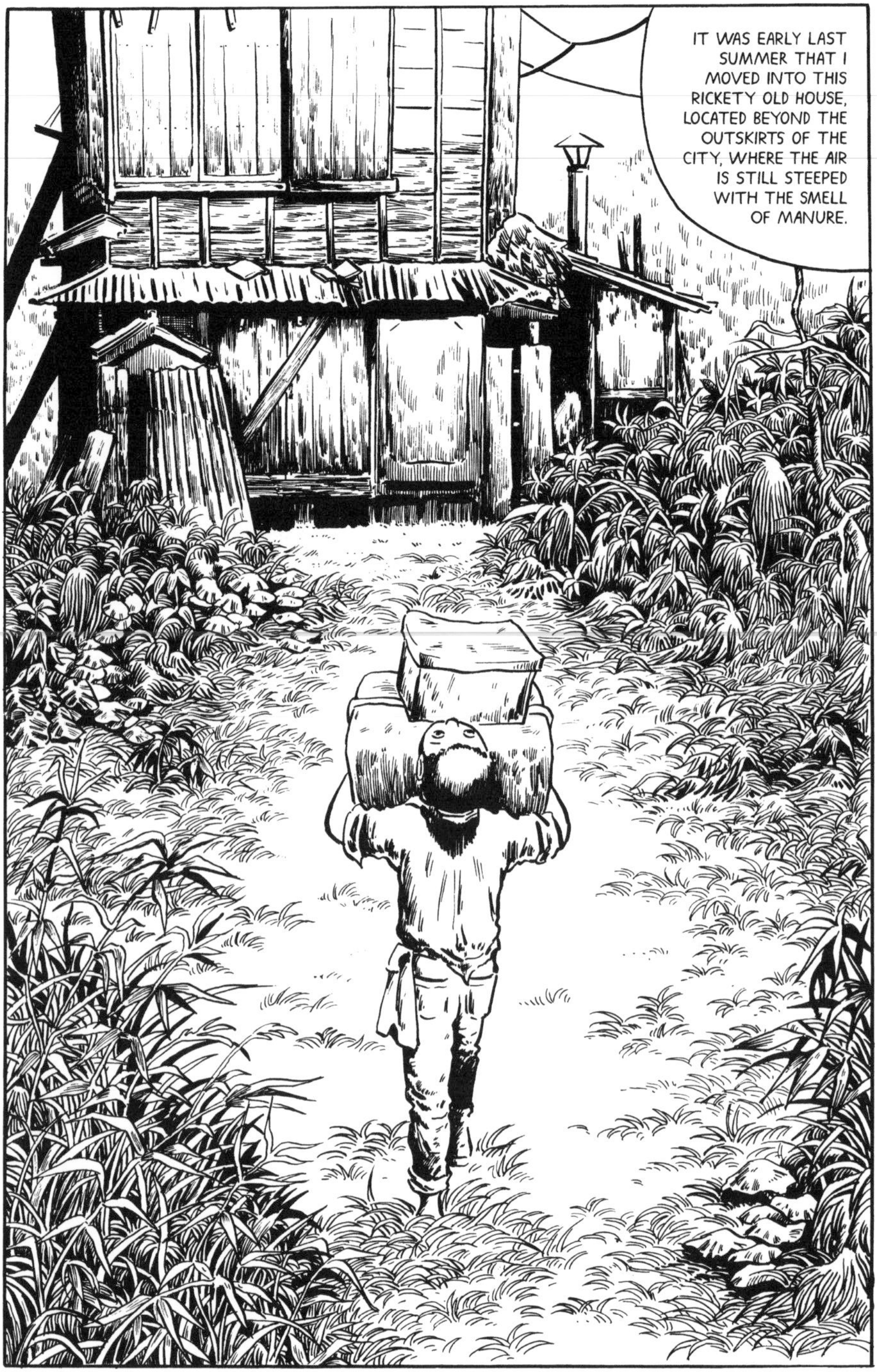
IT WAS EARLY LAST SUMMER THAT I MOVED INTO THIS RICKETY OLD HOUSE, LOCATED BEYOND THE OUTSKIRTS OF THE CITY, WHERE THE AIR IS STILL STEEPED WITH THE SMELL OF MANURE.

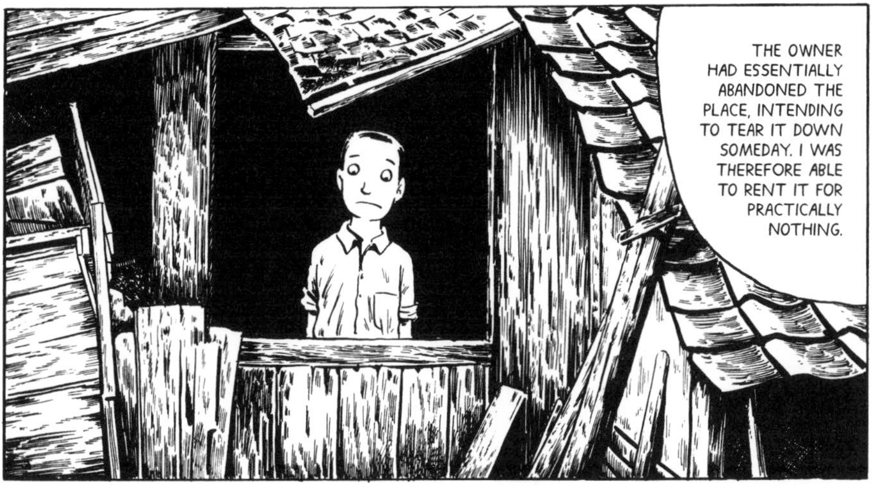
THE OWNER HAD ESSENTIALLY ABANDONED THE PLACE, INTENDING TO TEAR IT DOWN SOMEDAY. I WAS THEREFORE ABLE TO RENT IT FOR PRACTICALLY NOTHING.

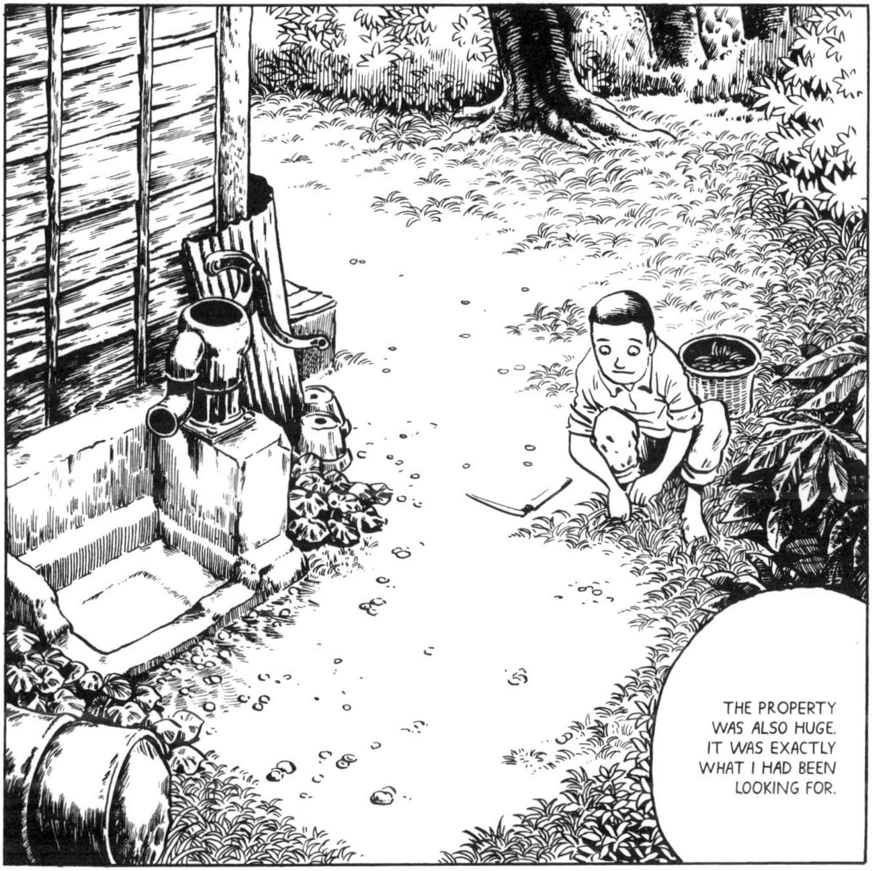
THE PROPERTY WAS ALSO HUGE. IT WAS EXACTLY WHAT I HAD BEEN LOOKING FOR.

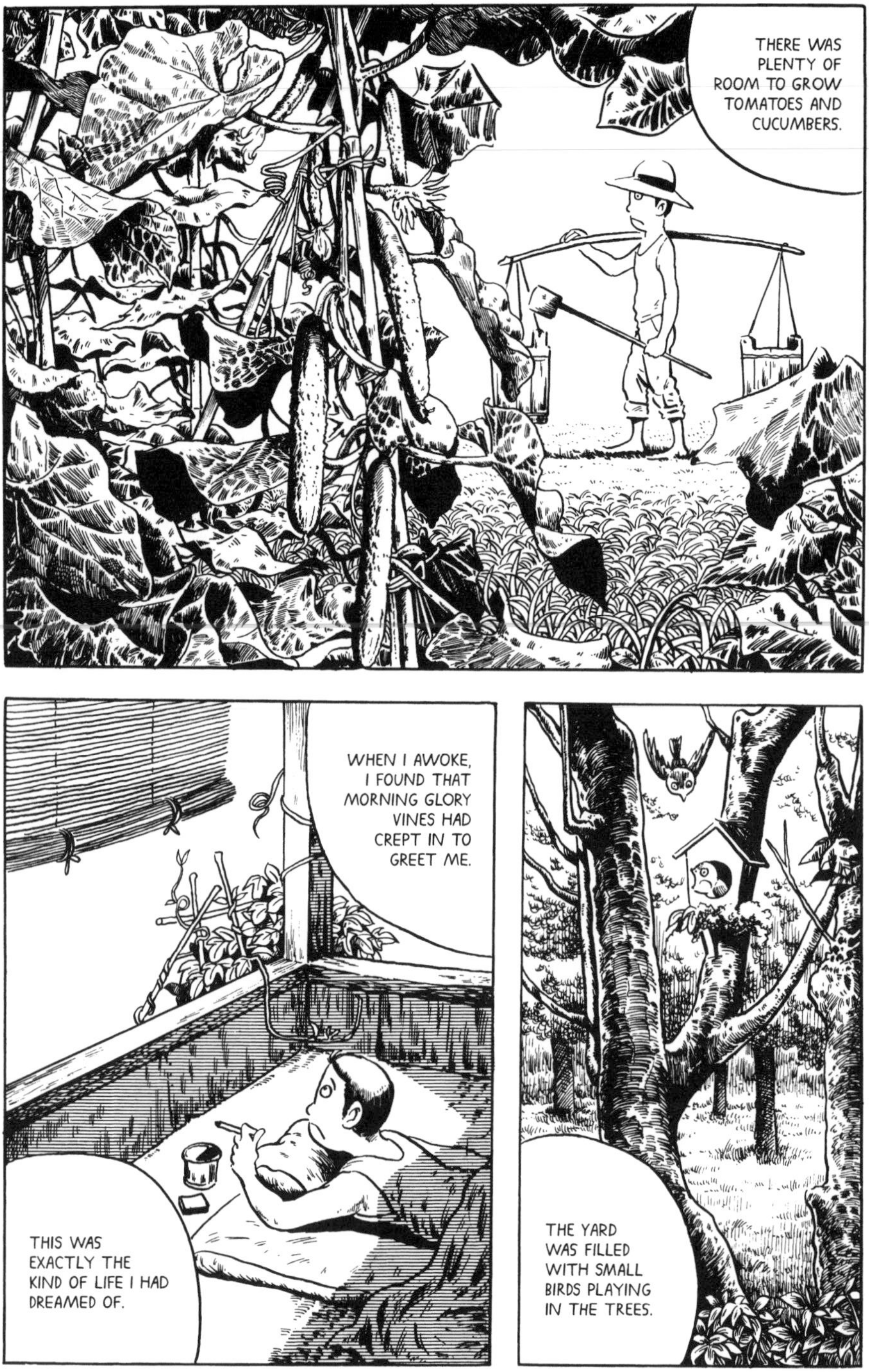
THERE WAS PLENTY OF ROOM TO GROW TOMATOES AND CUCUMBERS.
THE YARD WAS FILLED WITH SMALL BIRDS PLAYING IN THE TREES.
WHEN I AWOKE, I FOUND THAT MORNING GLORY VINES HAD CREPT IN TO GREET ME.
THIS WAS EXACTLY THE KIND OF LIFE I HAD DREAMED OF.

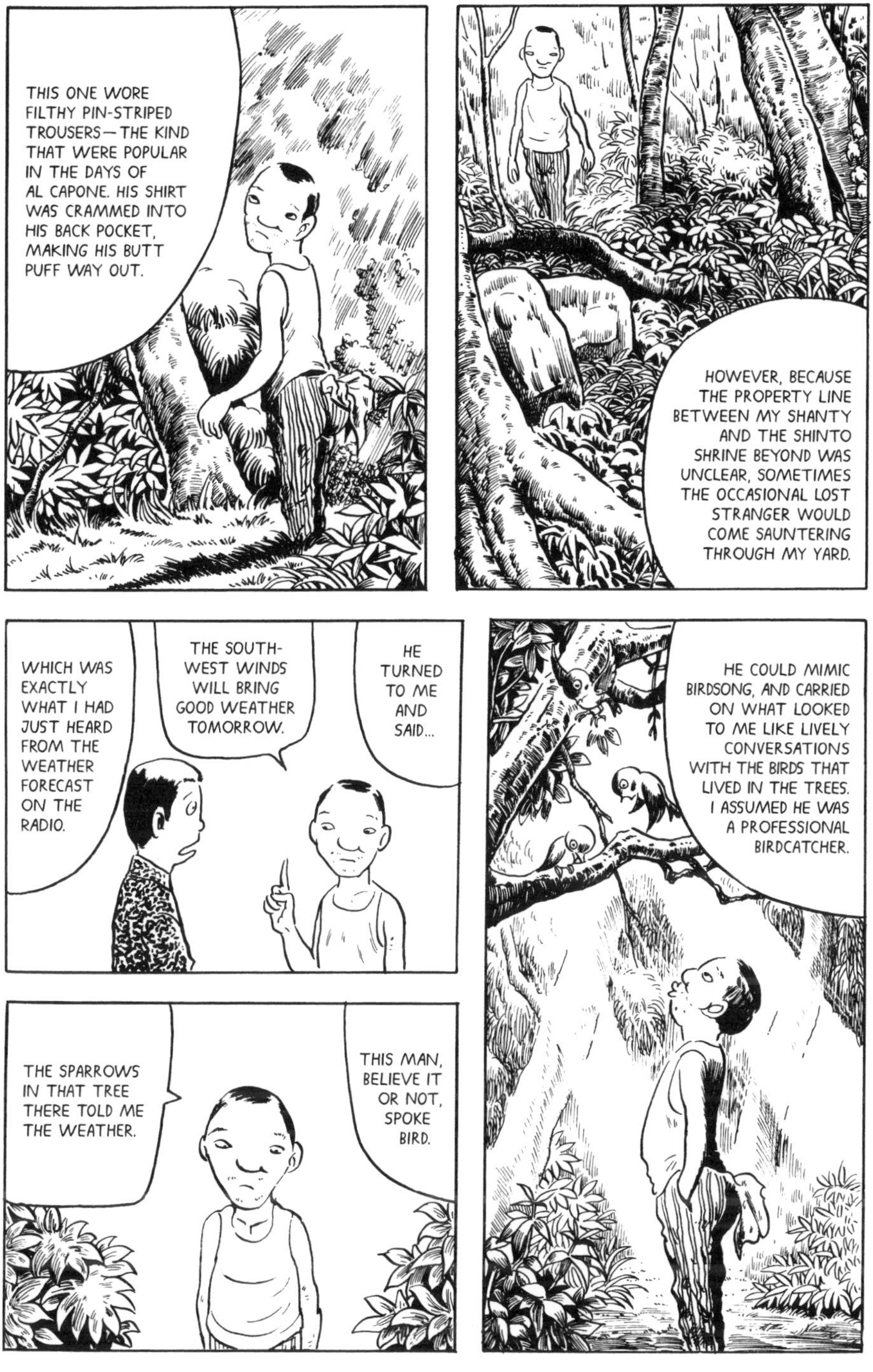
HOWEVER, BECAUSE THE PROPERTY LINE BETWEEN MY SHANTY AND THE SHINTO SHRINE BEYOND WAS UNCLEAR, SOMETIMES THE OCCASIONAL LOST STRANGER WOULD COME SAUNTERING THROUGH MY YARD.
THIS ONE WORE FILTHY PIN-STRIPED TROUSERS—THE KIND THAT WERE POPULAR IN THE DAYS OF AL CAPONE. HIS SHIRT WAS CRAMMED INTO HIS BACK POCKET, MAKING HIS BUTT PUFF WAY OUT.
HE COULD MIMIC BIRDSONG, AND CARRIED ON WHAT LOOKED TO ME LIKE LIVELY CONVERSATIONS WITH THE BIRDS THAT LIVED IN THE TREES. I ASSUMED HE WAS A PROFESSIONAL BIRDCATCHER.
HE TURNED TO ME AND SAID...
THE SOUTH-WEST WINDS WILL BRING GOOD WEATHER TOMORROW.
WHICH WAS EXACTLY WHAT I HAD JUST HEARD FROM THE WEATHER FORECAST ON THE RADIO.
THIS MAN, BELIEVE IT OR NOT, SPOKE BIRD.
THE SPARROWS IN THAT TREE THERE TOLD ME THE WEATHER.

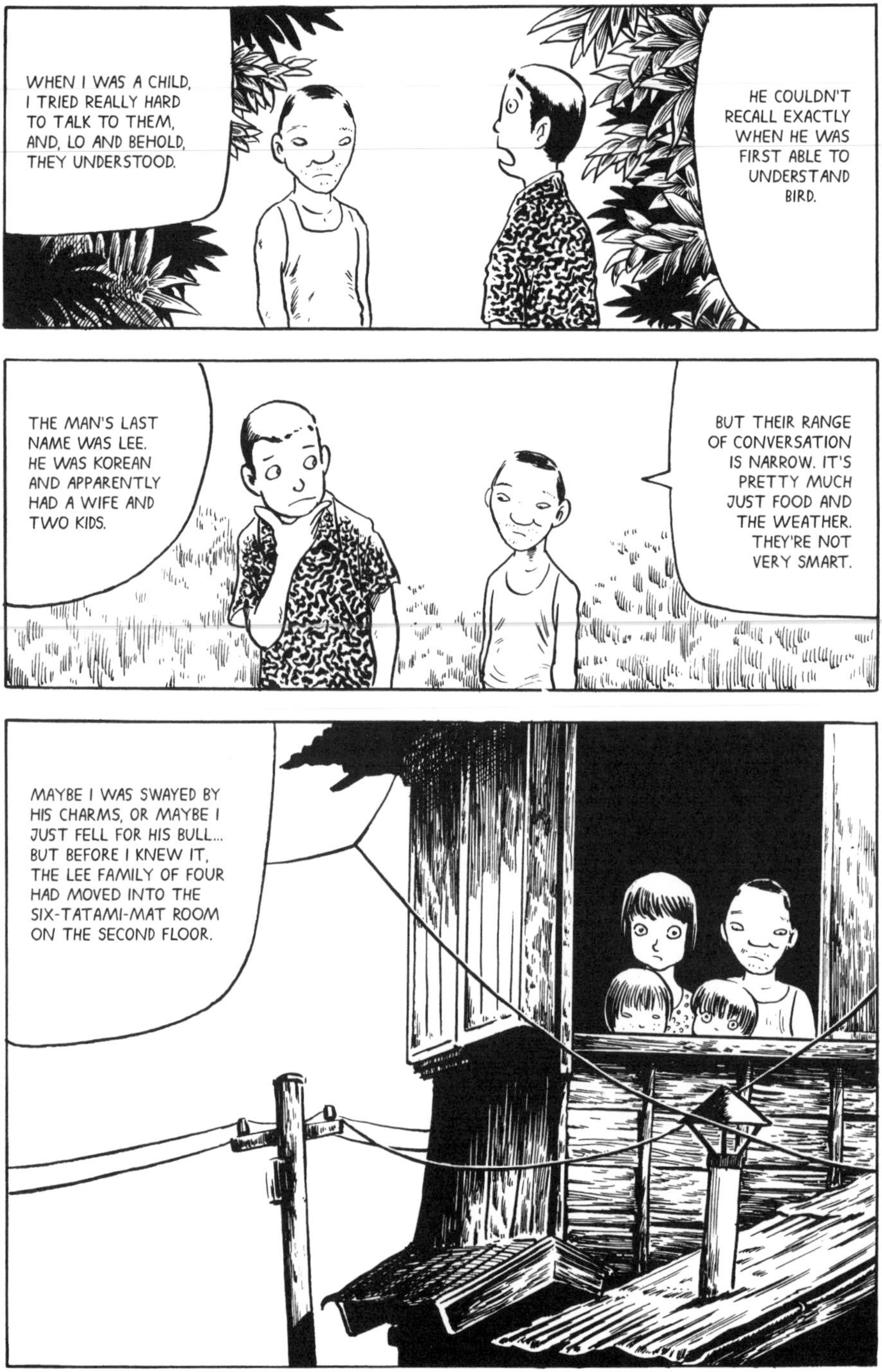
HE COULDN'T RECALL EXACTLY WHEN HE WAS FIRST ABLE TO UNDERSTAND BIRD.
WHEN I WAS A CHILD, I TRIED REALLY HARD TO TALK TO THEM, AND, LO AND BEHOLD, THEY UNDERSTOOD.
BUT THEIR RANGE OF CONVERSATION IS NARROW. IT'S PRETTY MUCH JUST FOOD AND THE WEATHER. THEY'RE NOT VERY SMART.
THE MAN'S LAST NAME WAS LEE. HE WAS KOREAN AND APPARENTLY HAD A WIFE AND TWO KIDS.
MAYBE I WAS SWAYED BY HIS CHARMS, OR MAYBE I JUST FELL FOR HIS BULL... BUT BEFORE I KNEW IT, THE LEE FAMILY OF FOUR HAD MOVED INTO THE SIX-TATAMI-MAT ROOM ON THE SECOND FLOOR.

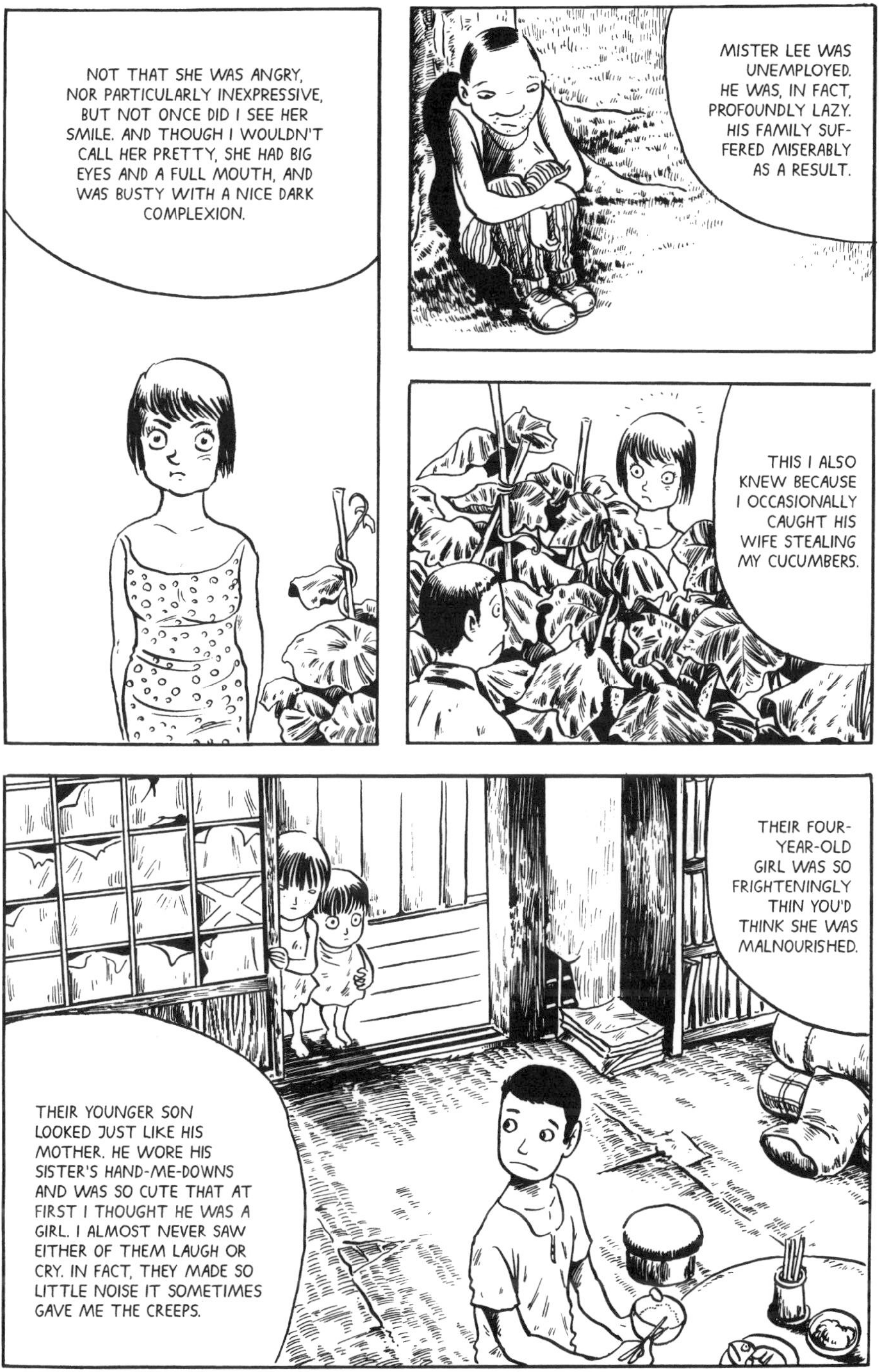
MISTER LEE WAS UNEMPLOYED. HE WAS, IN FACT, PROFOUNDLY LAZY. HIS FAMILY SUFFERED MISERABLY AS A RESULT.
THIS I ALSO KNEW BECAUSE I OCCASIONALLY CAUGHT HIS WIFE STEALING MY CUCUMBERS.
NOT THAT SHE WAS ANGRY, NOR PARTICULARLY INEXPRESSIVE, BUT NOT ONCE DID I SEE HER SMILE. AND THOUGH I WOULDN'T CALL HER PRETTY, SHE HAD BIG EYES AND A FULL MOUTH, AND WAS BUSTY WITH A NICE DARK COMPLEXION.
THEIR FOUR-YEAR-OLD GIRL WAS SO FRIGHTENINGLY THIN YOU'D THINK SHE WAS MALNOURISHED.
THEIR YOUNGER SON LOOKED JUST LIKE HIS MOTHER. HE WORE HIS SISTER'S HAND-ME-DOWNS AND WAS SO CUTE THAT AT FIRST I THOUGHT HE WAS A GIRL. I ALMOST NEVER SAW EITHER OF THEM LAUGH OR CRY. IN FACT, THEY MADE SO LITTLE NOISE IT SOMETIMES GAVE ME THE CREEPS.

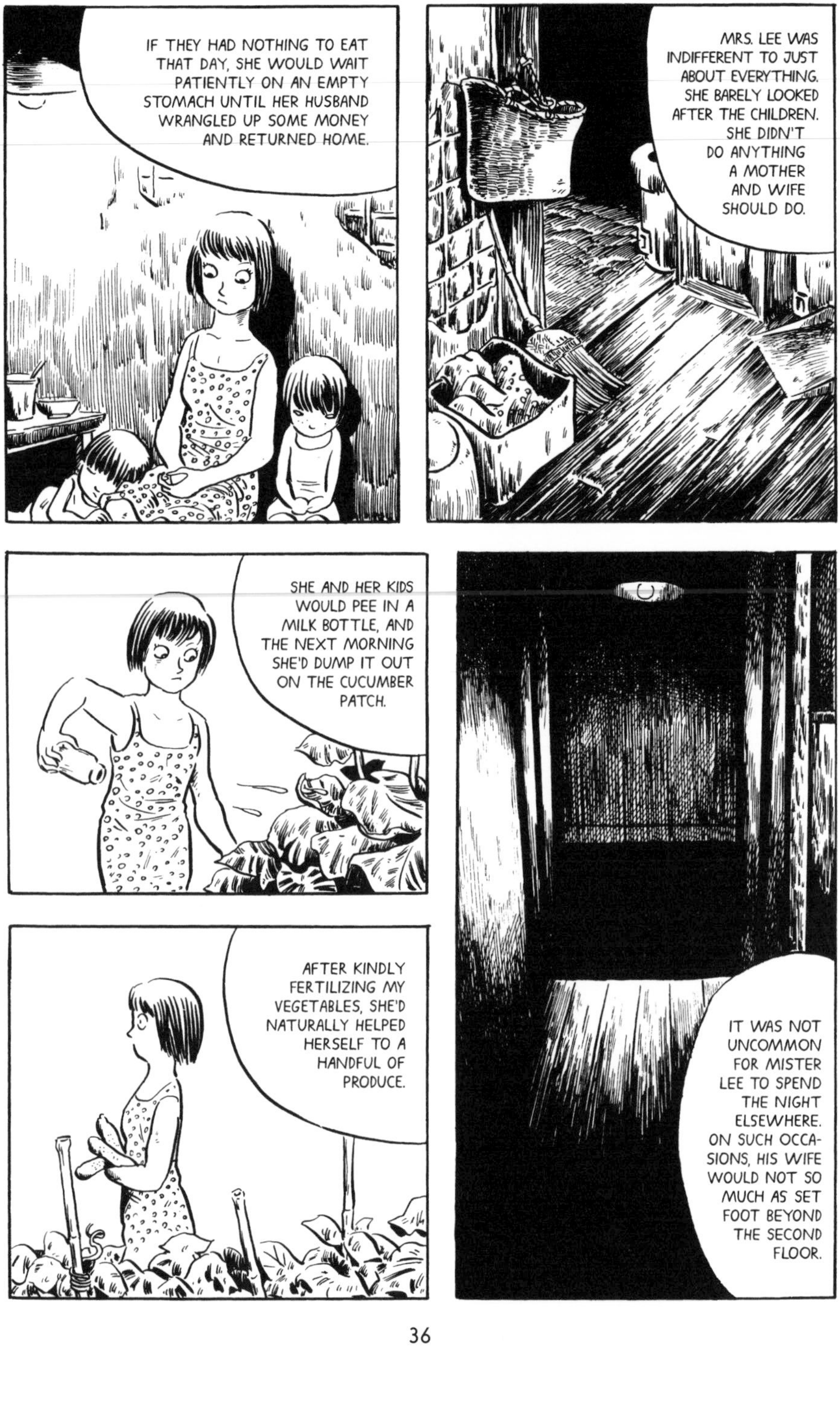
MRS. LEE WAS INDIFFERENT TO JUST ABOUT EVERYTHING. SHE BARELY LOOKED AFTER THE CHILDREN. SHE DIDN'T DO ANYTHING A MOTHER AND WIFE SHOULD DO.
IF THEY HAD NOTHING TO EAT THAT DAY, SHE WOULD WAIT PATIENTLY ON AN EMPTY STOMACH UNTIL HER HUSBAND WRANGLED UP SOME MONEY AND RETURNED HOME.
IT WAS NOT UNCOMMON FOR MISTER LEE TO SPEND THE NIGHT ELSEWHERE. ON SUCH OCCA-SIONS, HIS WIFE WOULD NOT SO MUCH AS SET FOOT BEYOND THE SECOND FLOOR.
SHE AND HER KIDS WOULD PEE IN A MILK BOTTLE, AND THE NEXT MORNING SHE'D DUMP IT OUT ON THE CUCUMBER PATCH.
AFTER KINDLY FERTILIZING MY VEGETABLES, SHE'D NATURALLY HELPED HERSELF TO A HANDFUL OF PRODUCE.

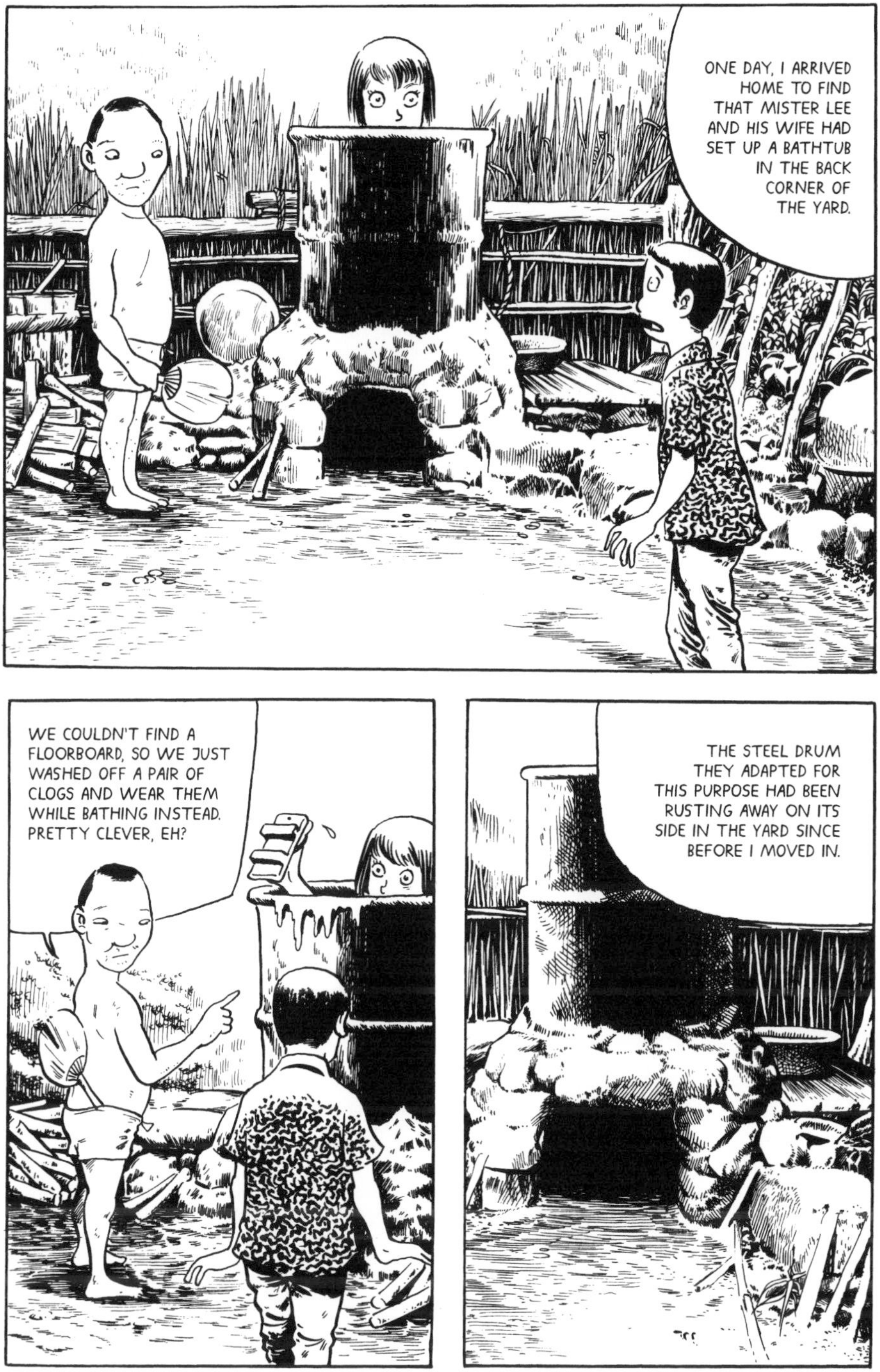
ONE DAY, I ARRIVED HOME TO FIND THAT MISTER LEE AND HIS WIFE HAD SET UP A BATHTUB IN THE BACK CORNER OF THE YARD.
THE STEEL DRUM THEY ADAPTED FOR THIS PURPOSE HAD BEEN RUSTING AWAY ON ITS SIDE IN THE YARD SINCE BEFORE I MOVED IN.
WE COULDN'T FIND A FLOORBOARD, SO WE JUST WASHED OFF A PAIR OF CLOGS AND WEAR THEM WHILE BATHING INSTEAD. PRETTY CLEVER, EH?

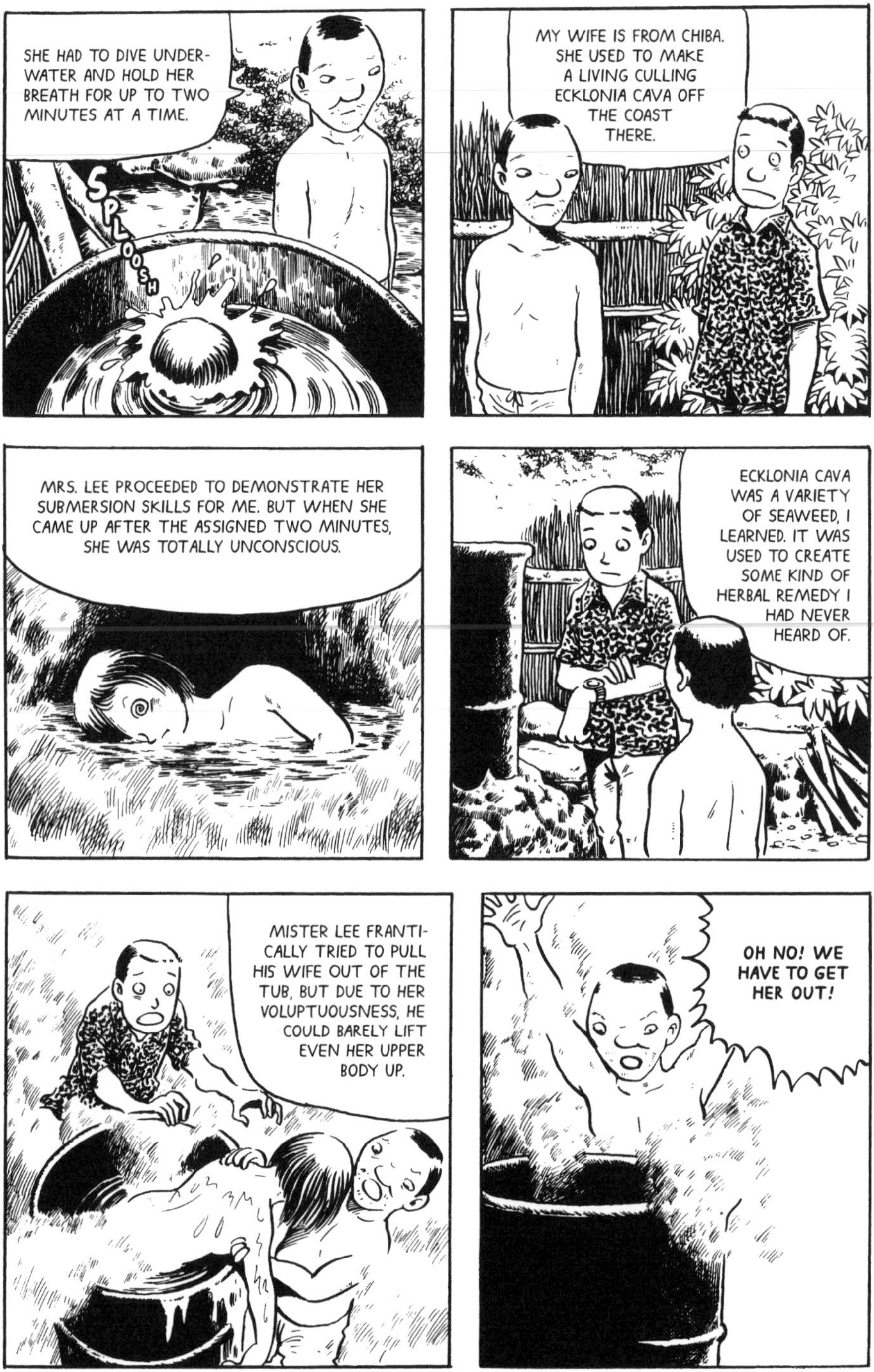
MY WIFE IS FROM CHIBA. SHE USED TO MAKE A LIVING CULLING ECKLONIA CAVA OFF THE COAST THERE.
SHE HAD TO DIVE UNDER-WATER AND HOLD HER BREATH FOR UP TO TWO MINUTES AT A TIME.
SPLOOSH
ECKLONIA CAVA WAS A VARIETY OF SEAWEED, I LEARNED. IT WAS USED TO CREATE SOME KIND OF HERBAL REMEDY I HAD NEVER HEARD OF.
MRS. LEE PROCEEDED TO DEMONSTRATE HER SUBMERSION SKILLS FOR ME. BUT WHEN SHE CAME UP AFTER THE ASSIGNED TWO MINUTES, SHE WAS TOTALLY UNCONSCIOUS.
OH NO! WE HAVE TO GET HER OUT!
MISTER LEE FRANTI-CALLY TRIED TO PULL HIS WIFE OUT OF THE TUB, BUT DUE TO HER VOLUPTUOUSNESS, HE COULD BARELY LIFT EVEN HER UPPER BODY UP.

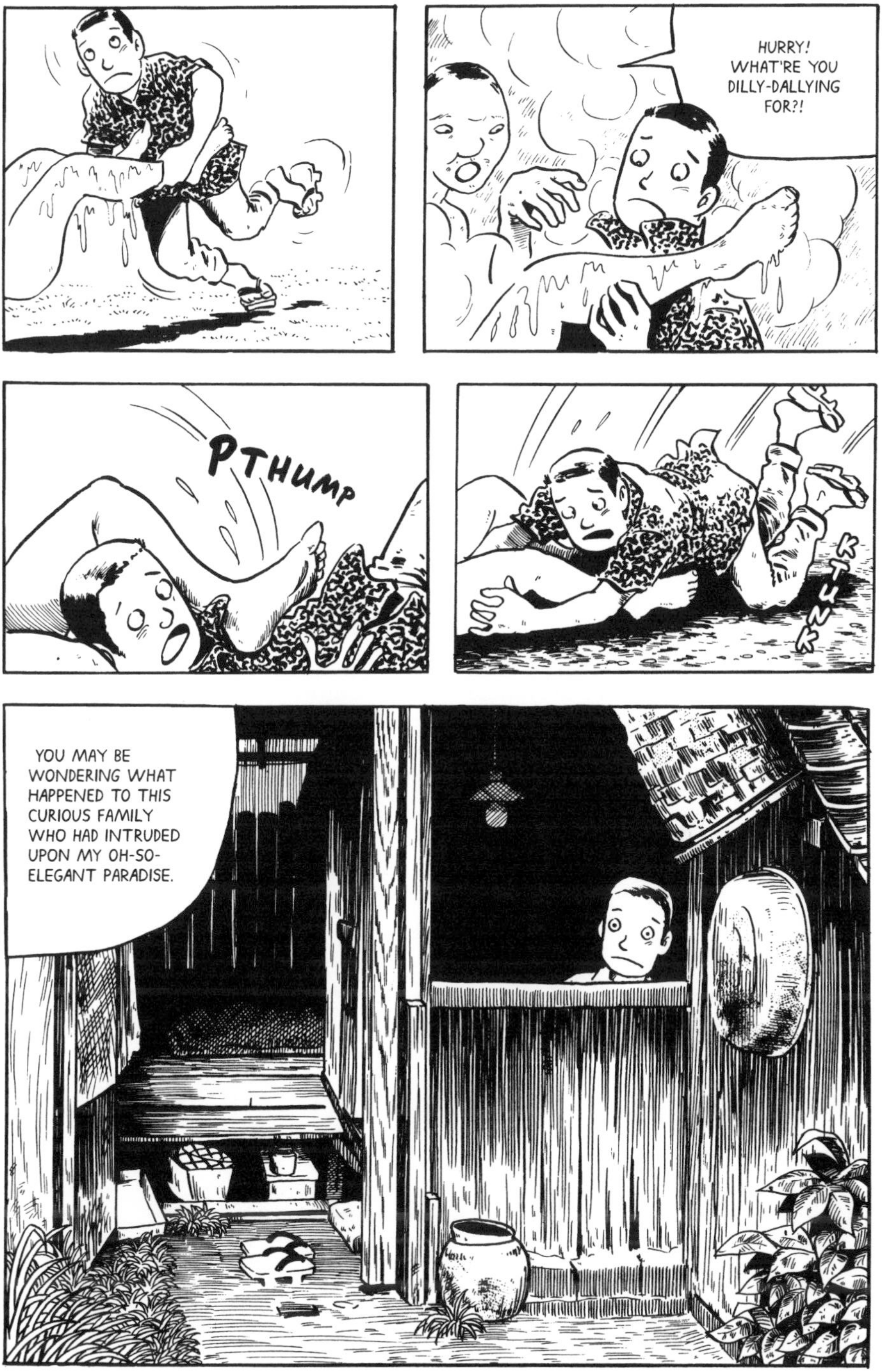
HURRY! WHAT'RE YOU DILLY-DALLYING FOR?!
KTUNK
PTHUMP
YOU MAY BE WONDERING WHAT HAPPENED TO THIS CURIOUS FAMILY WHO HAD INTRUDED UPON MY OH-SO-ELEGANT PARADISE.

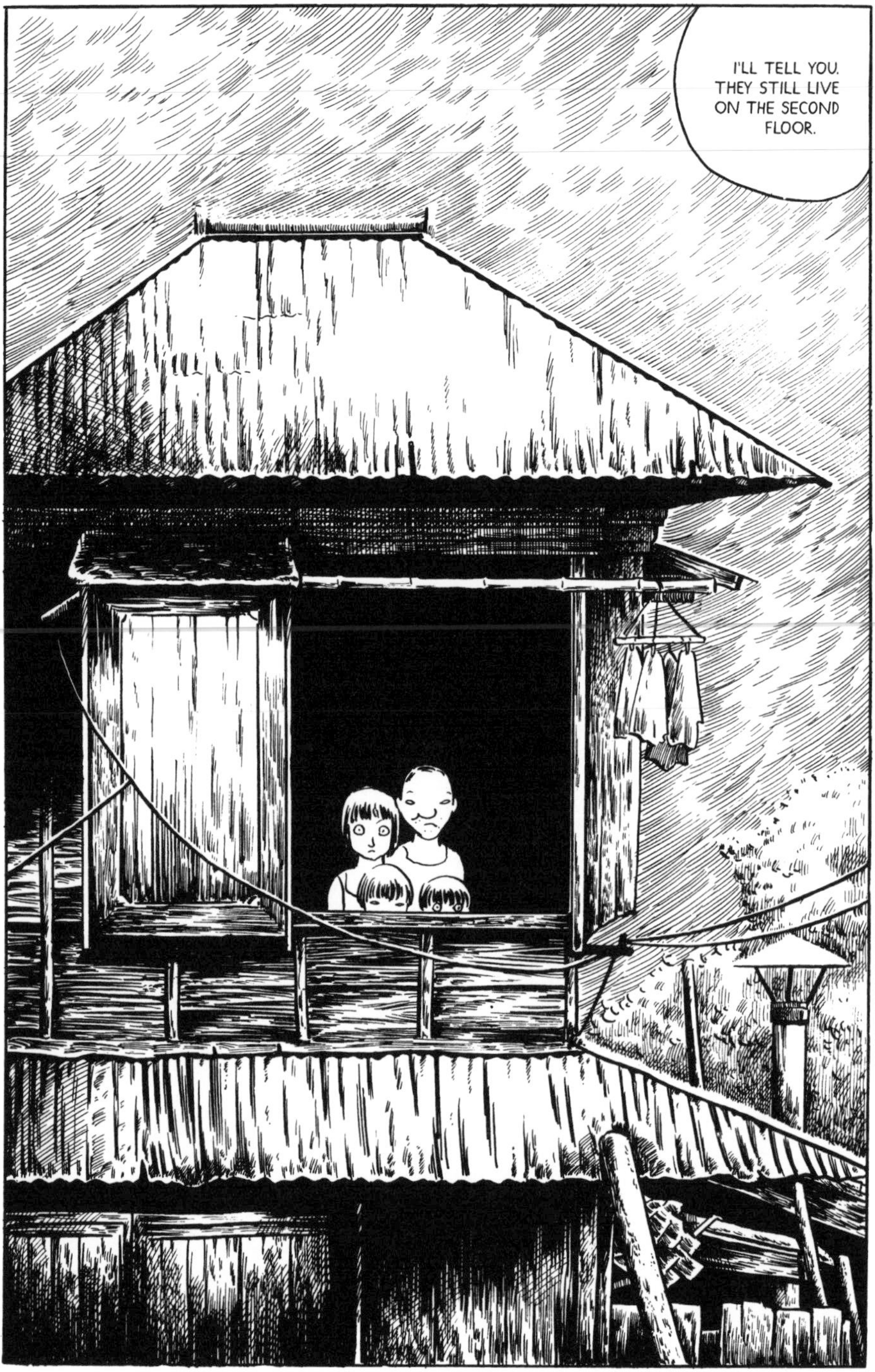
I'LL TELL YOU. THEY STILL LIVE ON THE SECOND FLOOR.

THE DOG FROM
PRAYER PASS

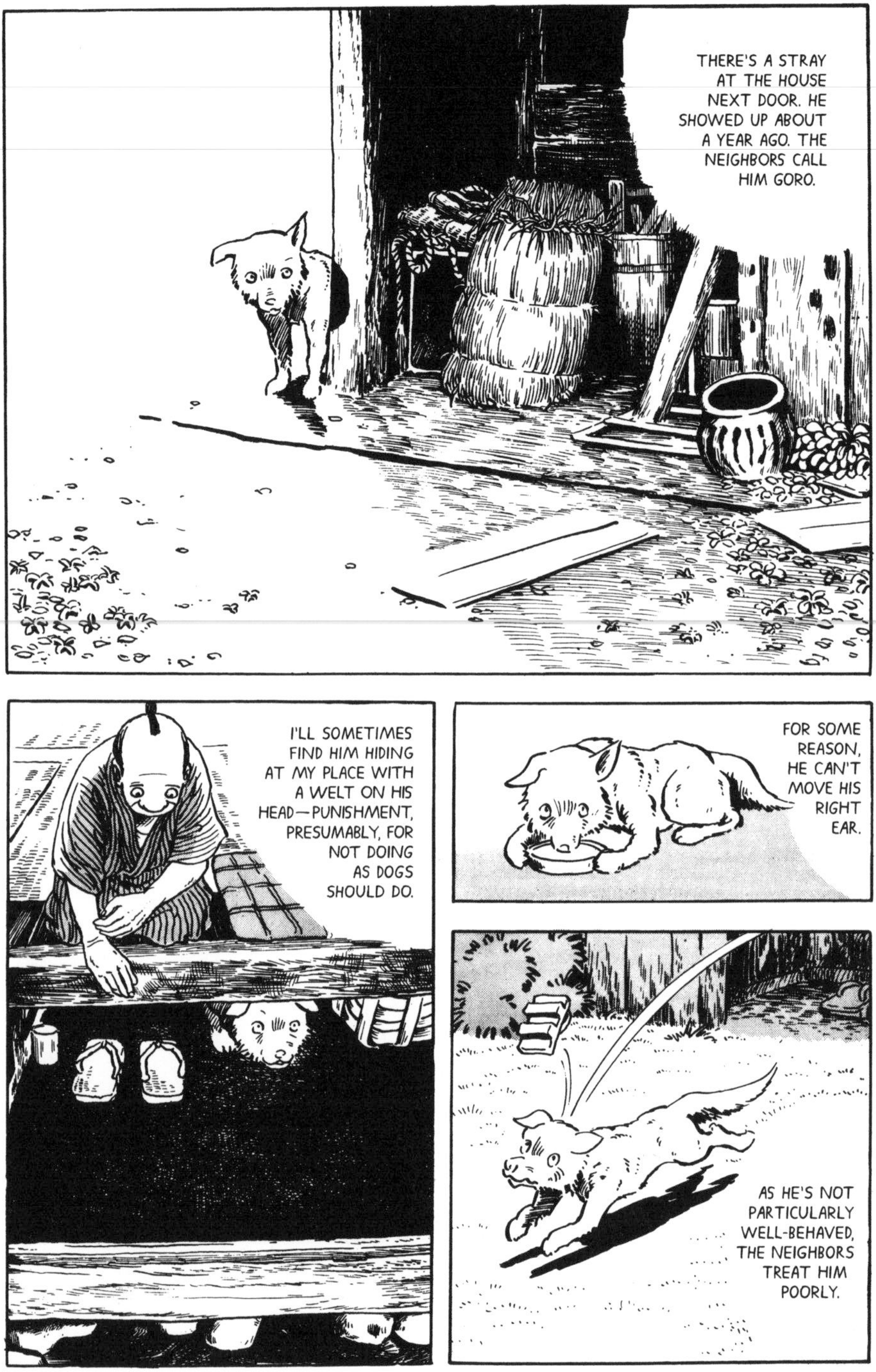
THERE'S A STRAY AT THE HOUSE NEXT DOOR. HE SHOWED UP ABOUT A YEAR AGO. THE NEIGHBORS CALL HIM GORO.
FOR SOME REASON, HE CAN'T MOVE HIS RIGHT EAR.
AS HE'S NOT PARTICULARLY WELL-BEHAVED, THE NEIGHBORS TREAT HIM POORLY.
I'LL SOMETIMES FIND HIM HIDING AT MY PLACE WITH A WELT ON HIS HEAD—PUNISHMENT, PRESUMABLY, FOR NOT DOING AS DOGS SHOULD DO.

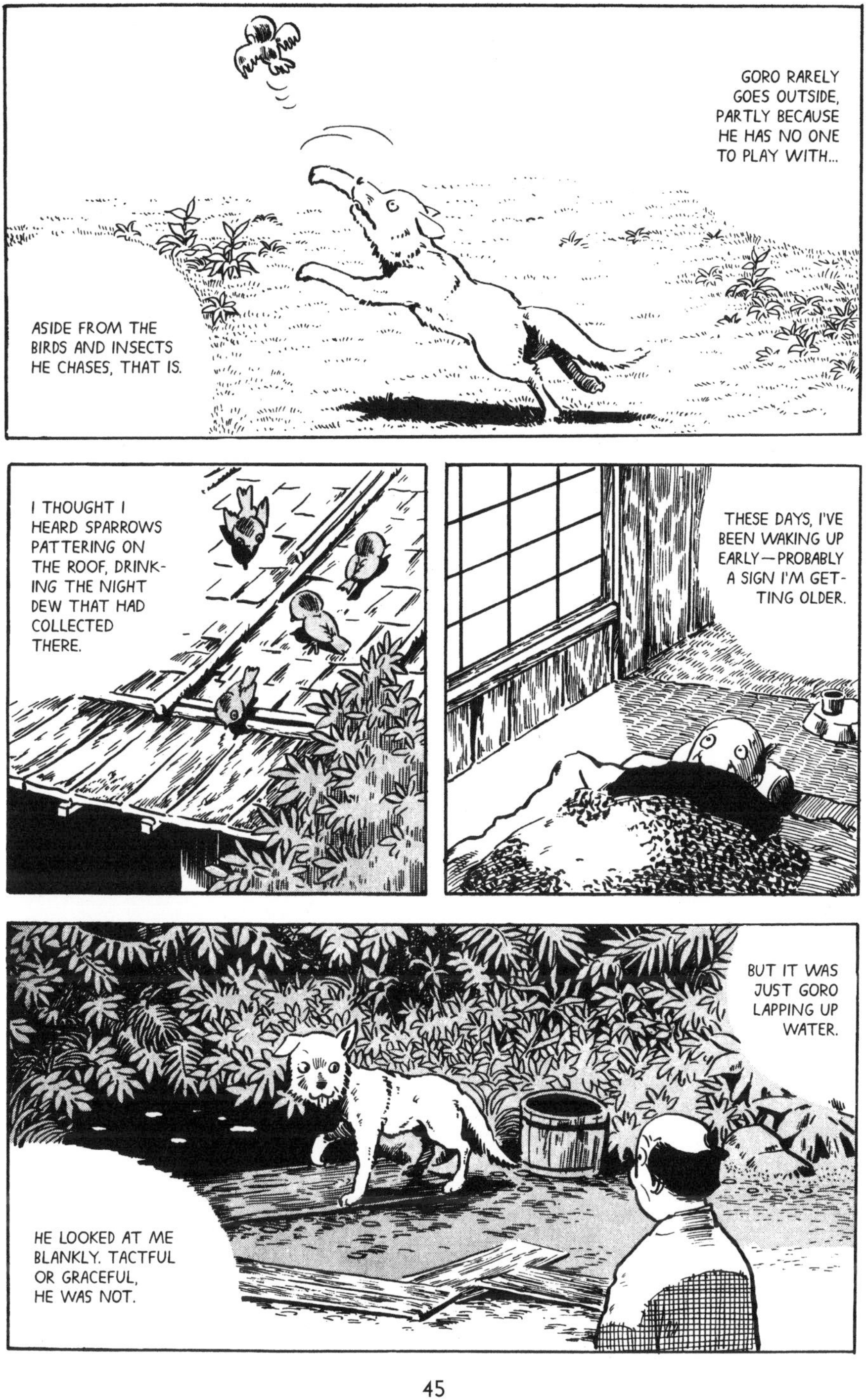
GORO RARELY GOES OUTSIDE, PARTLY BECAUSE HE HAS NO ONE TO PLAY WITH...
ASIDE FROM THE BIRDS AND INSECTS HE CHASES, THAT IS.
THESE DAYS, I'VE BEEN WAKING UP EARLY—PROBABLY A SIGN I'M GETTING OLDER.
I THOUGHT I HEARD SPARROWS PATTERING ON THE ROOF, DRINKING THE NIGHT DEW THAT HAD COLLECTED THERE.
BUT IT WAS JUST GORO LAPPING UP WATER.
HE LOOKED AT ME BLANKLY. TACTFUL OR GRACEFUL, HE WAS NOT.

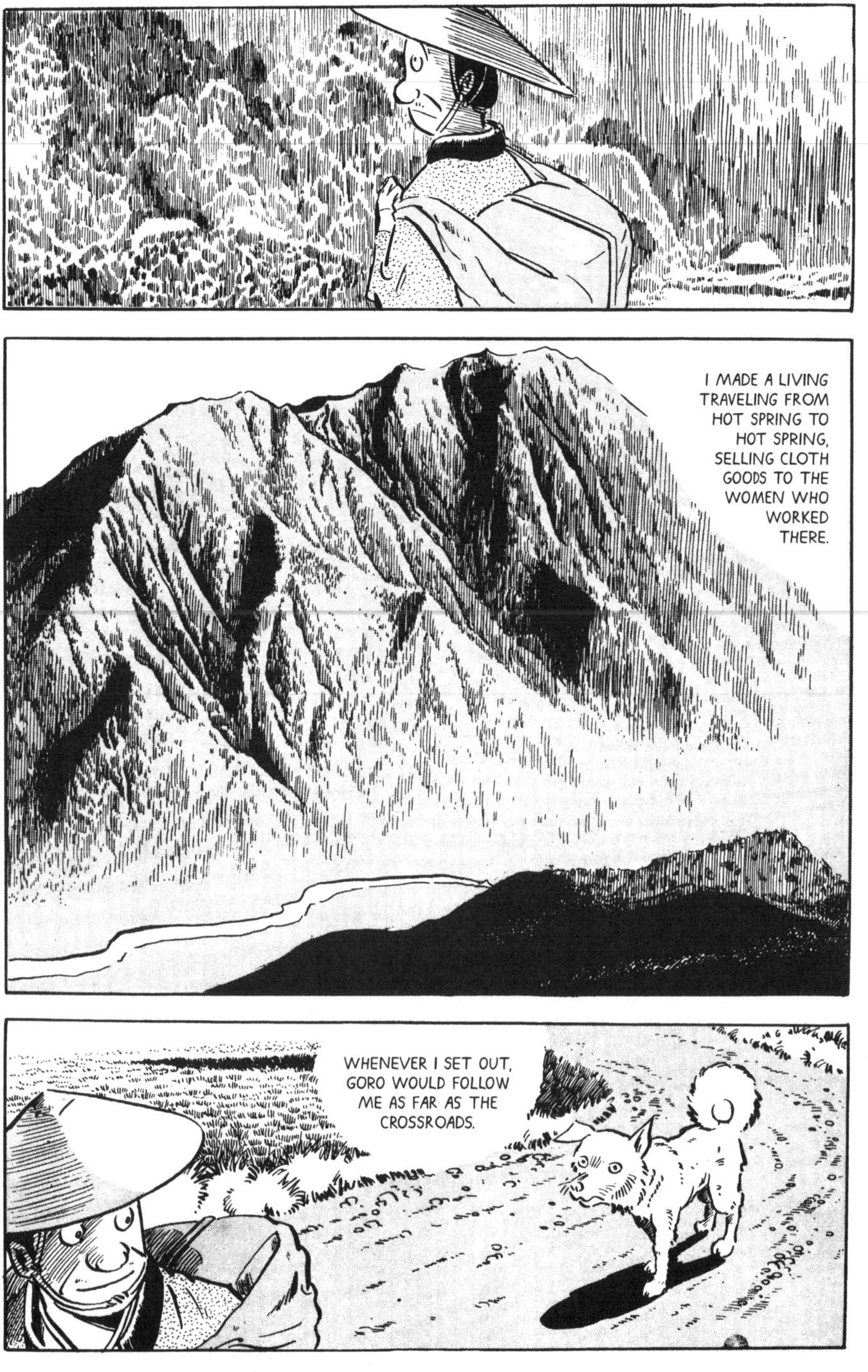
I MADE A LIVING TRAVELING FROM HOT SPRING TO HOT SPRING, SELLING CLOTH GOODS TO THE WOMEN WHO WORKED THERE.
WHENEVER I SET OUT, GORO WOULD FOLLOW ME AS FAR AS THE CROSSROADS.

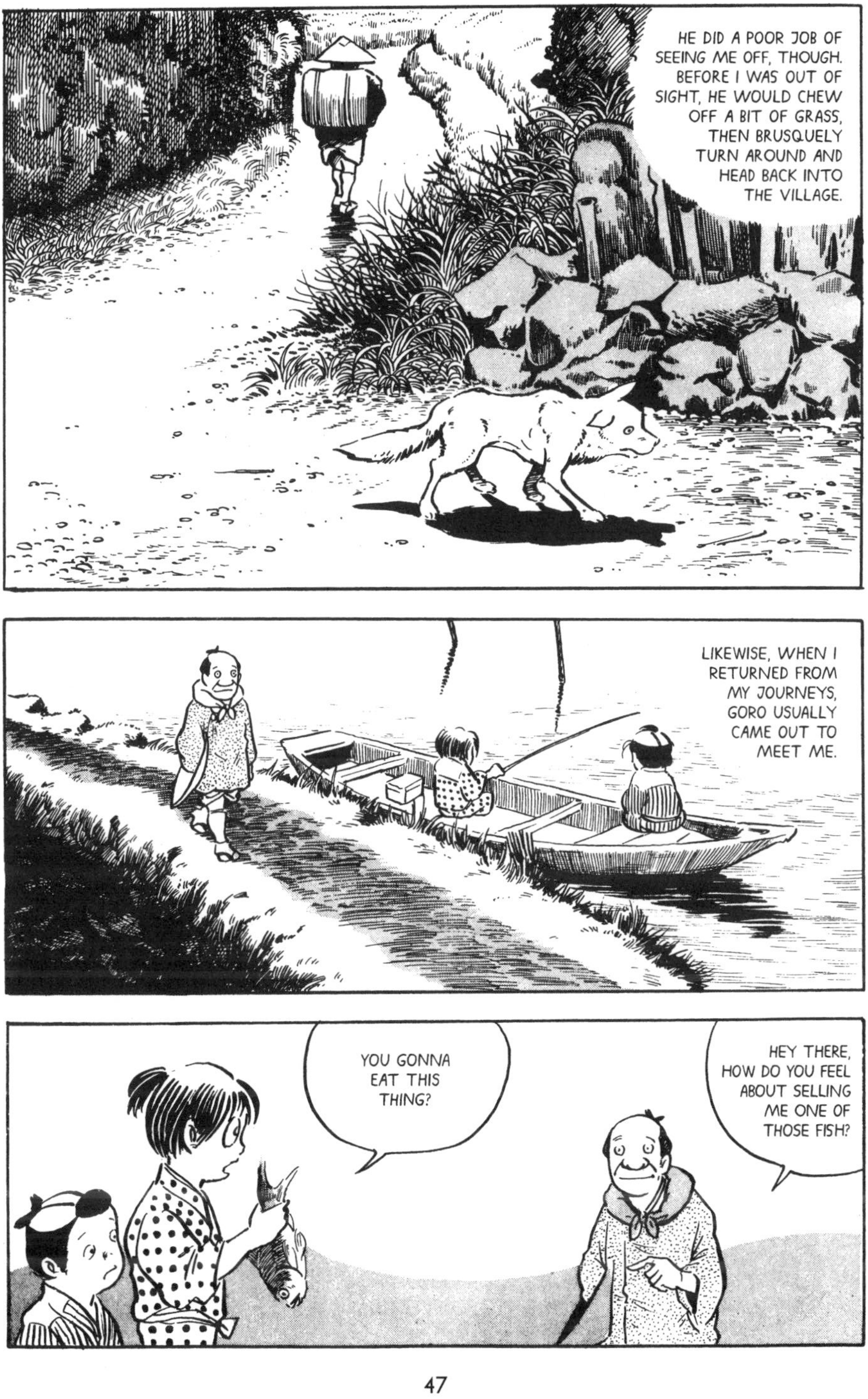
HE DID A POOR JOB OF SEEING ME OFF, THOUGH. BEFORE I WAS OUT OF SIGHT, HE WOULD CHEW OFF A BIT OF GRASS, THEN BRUSQUELY TURN AROUND AND HEAD BACK INTO THE VILLAGE.
LIKEWISE, WHEN I RETURNED FROM MY JOURNEYS, GORO USUALLY CAME OUT TO MEET ME.
HEY THERE, HOW DO YOU FEEL ABOUT SELLING ME ONE OF THOSE FISH?
YOU GONNA EAT THIS THING?

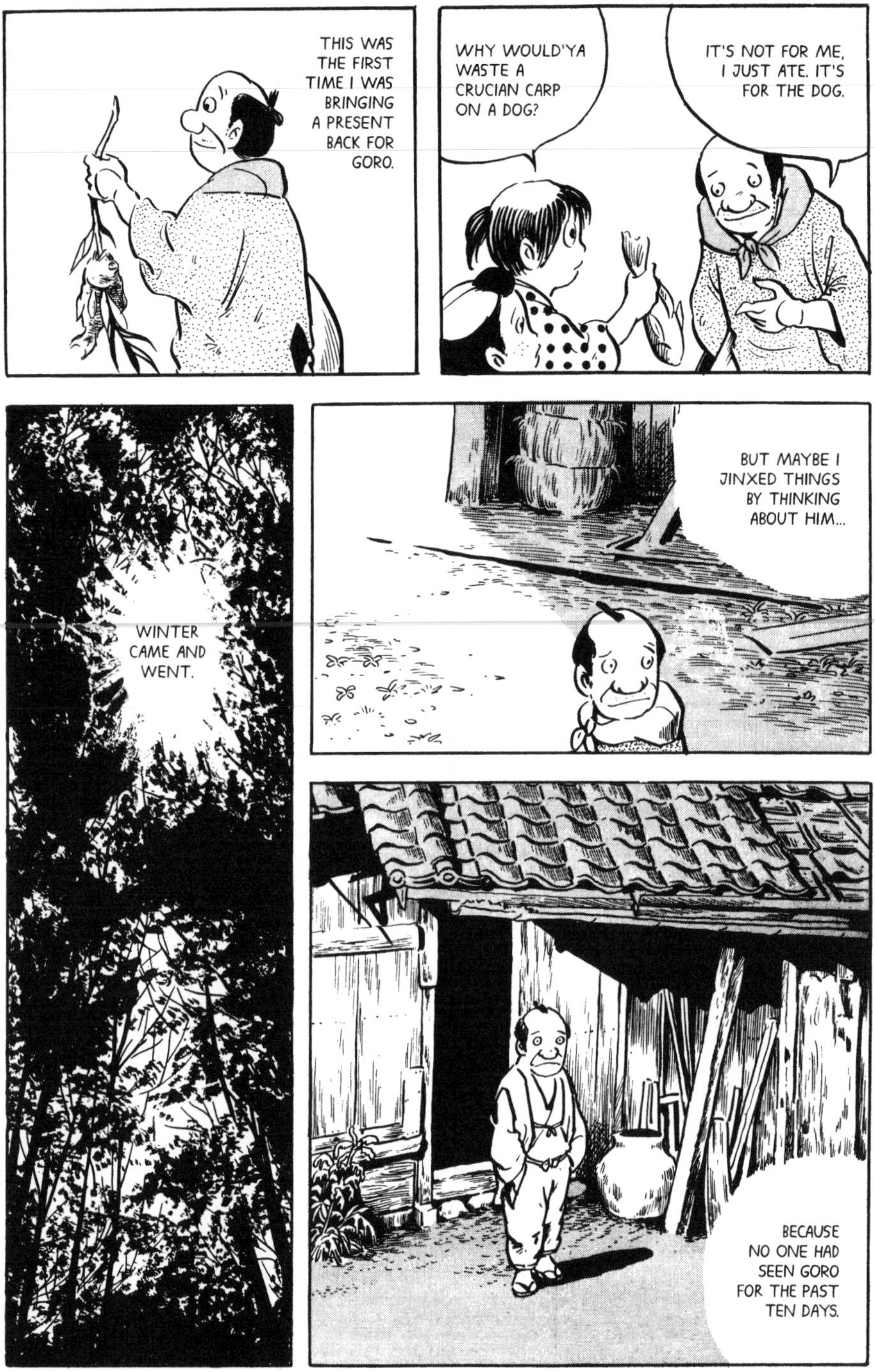
THIS WAS THE FIRST TIME I WAS BRINGING A PRESENT BACK FOR GORO.
WHY WOULD'YA WASTE A CRUCIAN CARP ON A DOG?
IT'S NOT FOR ME, I JUST ATE. IT'S FOR THE DOG.
WINTER CAME AND WENT.
BUT MAYBE I JINXED THINGS BY THINKING ABOUT HIM...
BECAUSE NO ONE HAD SEEN GORO FOR THE PAST TEN DAYS.

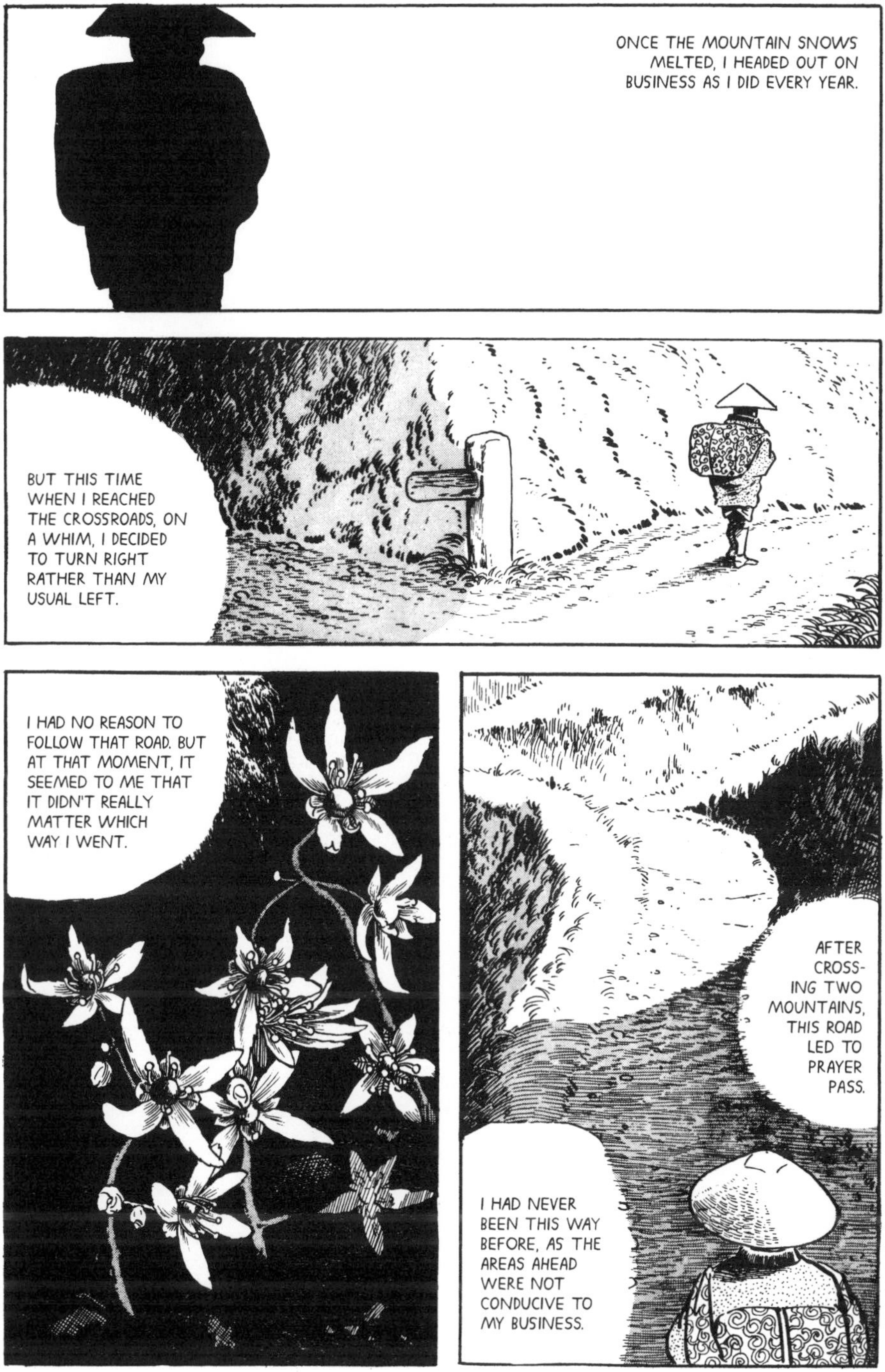
ONCE THE MOUNTAIN SNOWS MELTED, I HEADED OUT ON BUSINESS AS I DID EVERY YEAR.
BUT THIS TIME WHEN I REACHED THE CROSSROADS, ON A WHIM, I DECIDED TO TURN RIGHT RATHER THAN MY USUAL LEFT.
AFTER CROSSING TWO MOUNTAINS, THIS ROAD LED TO PRAYER PASS.
I HAD NEVER BEEN THIS WAY BEFORE, AS THE AREAS AHEAD WERE NOT CONDUCIVE TO MY BUSINESS.
I HAD NO REASON TO FOLLOW THAT ROAD. BUT AT THAT MOMENT, IT SEEMED TO ME THAT IT DIDN'T REALLY MATTER WHICH WAY I WENT.

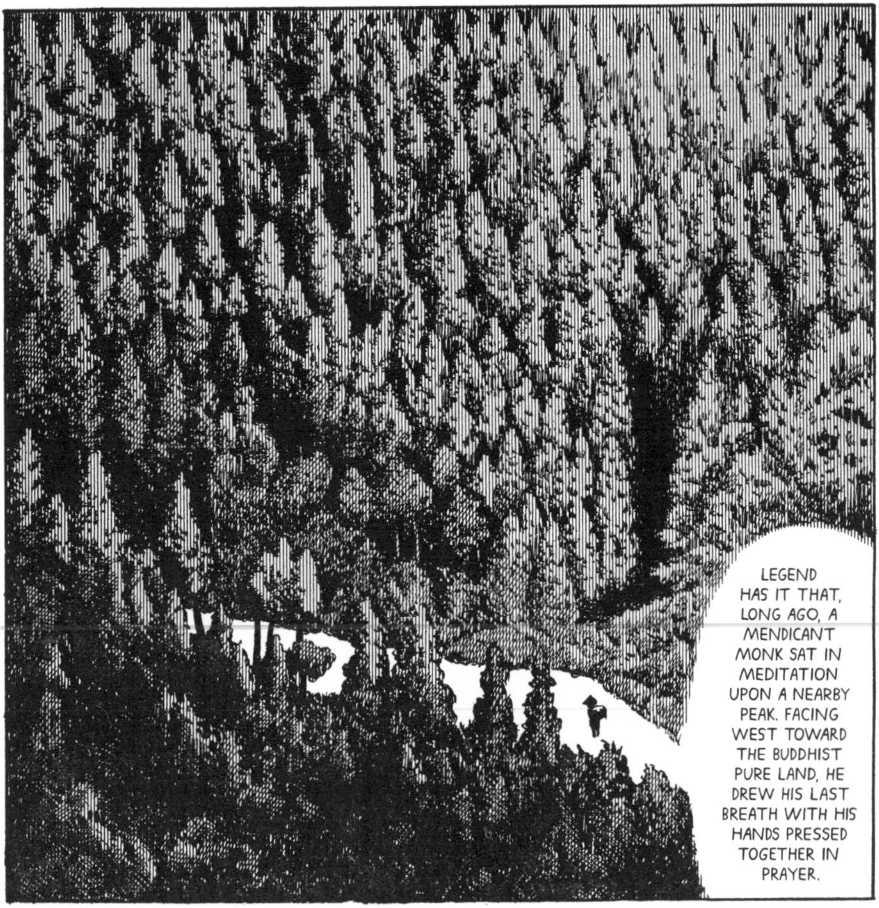
LEGEND HAS IT THAT, LONG AGO, A MENDICANT MONK SAT IN MEDITATION UPON A NEARBY PEAK. FACING WEST TOWARD THE BUDDHIST PURE LAND, HE DREW HIS LAST BREATH WITH HIS HANDS PRESSED TOGETHER IN PRAYER.
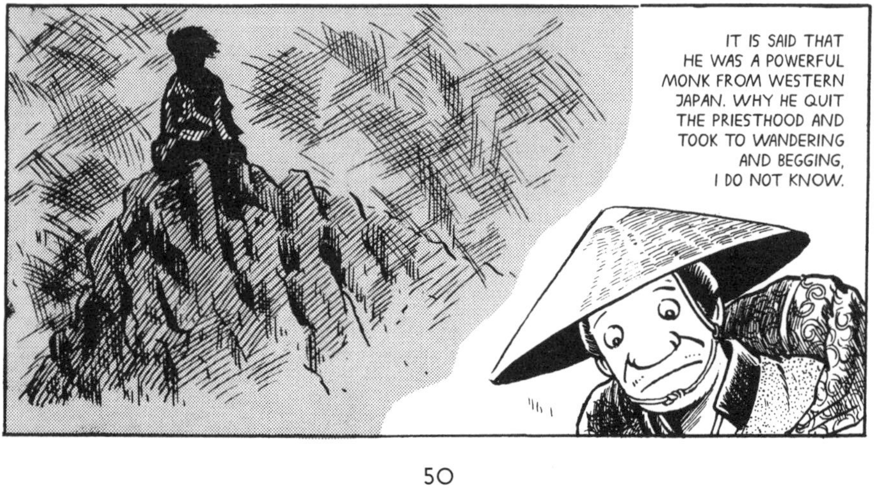
IT IS SAID THAT HE WAS A POWERFUL MONK FROM WESTERN JAPAN. WHY HE QUIT THE PRIESTHOOD AND TOOK TO WANDERING AND BEGGING, I DO NOT KNOW.

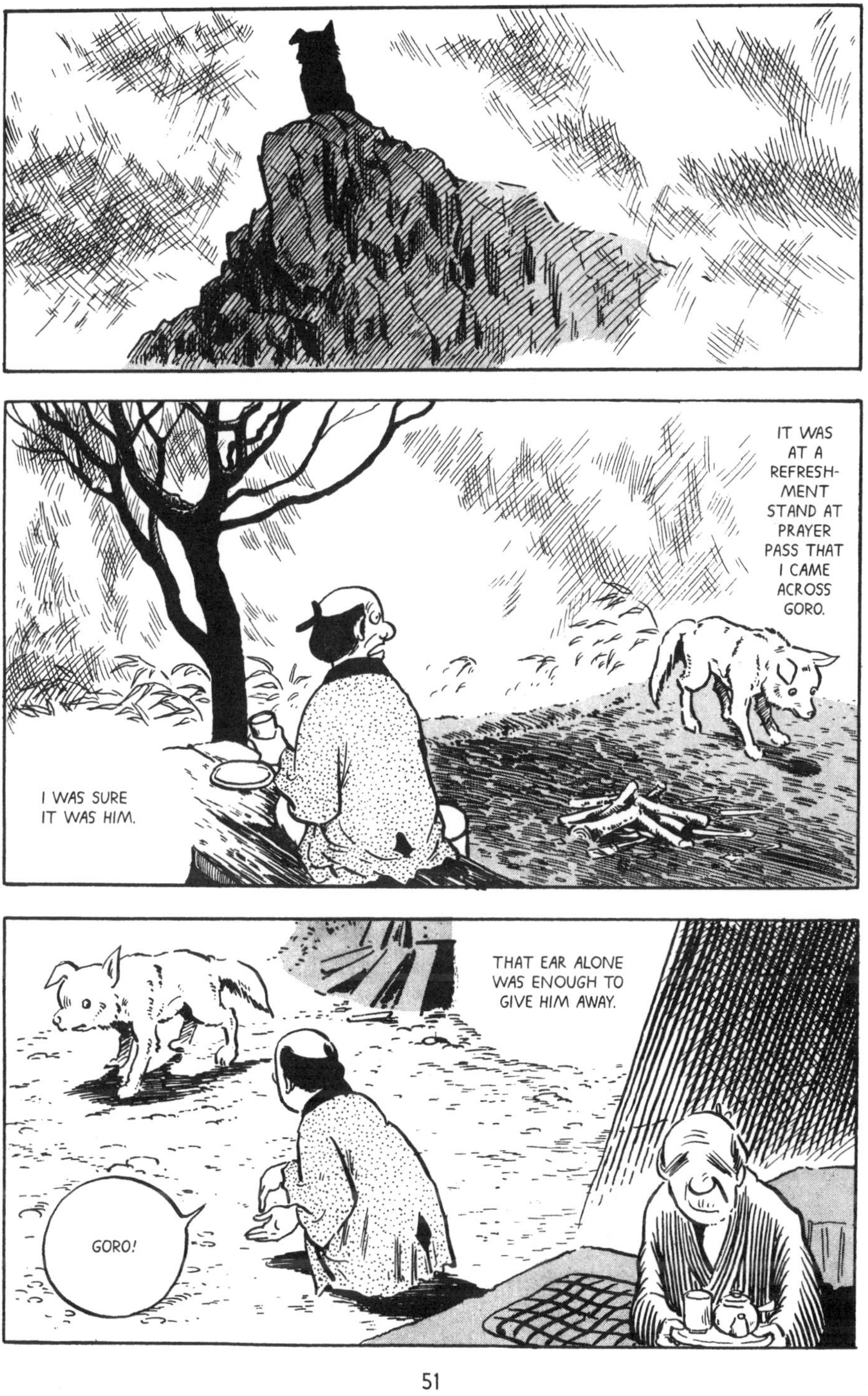
IT WAS AT A REFRESHMENT STAND AT PRAYER PASS THAT I CAME ACROSS GORO.
I WAS SURE IT WAS HIM.
THAT EAR ALONE WAS ENOUGH TO GIVE HIM AWAY.
GORO!

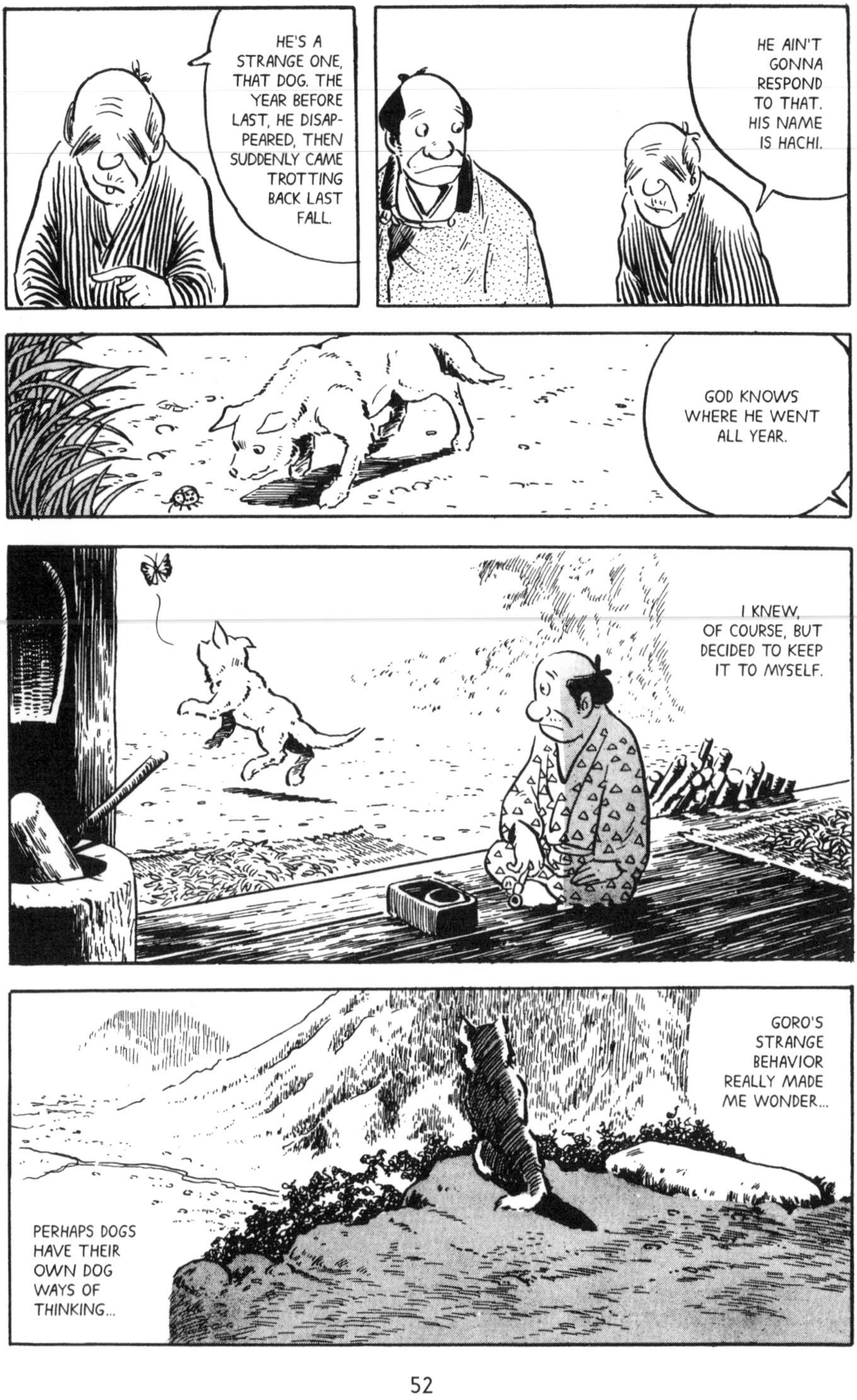
HE AIN'T GONNA RESPOND TO THAT. HIS NAME IS HACHI.
HE'S A STRANGE ONE, THAT DOG. THE YEAR BEFORE LAST, HE DISAP-PEARED, THEN SUDDENLY CAME TROTTING BACK LAST FALL.
GOD KNOWS WHERE HE WENT ALL YEAR.
I KNEW, OF COURSE, BUT DECIDED TO KEEP IT TO MYSELF.
GORO'S STRANGE BEHAVIOR REALLY MADE ME WONDER...
PERHAPS DOGS HAVE THEIR OWN DOG WAYS OF THINKING...

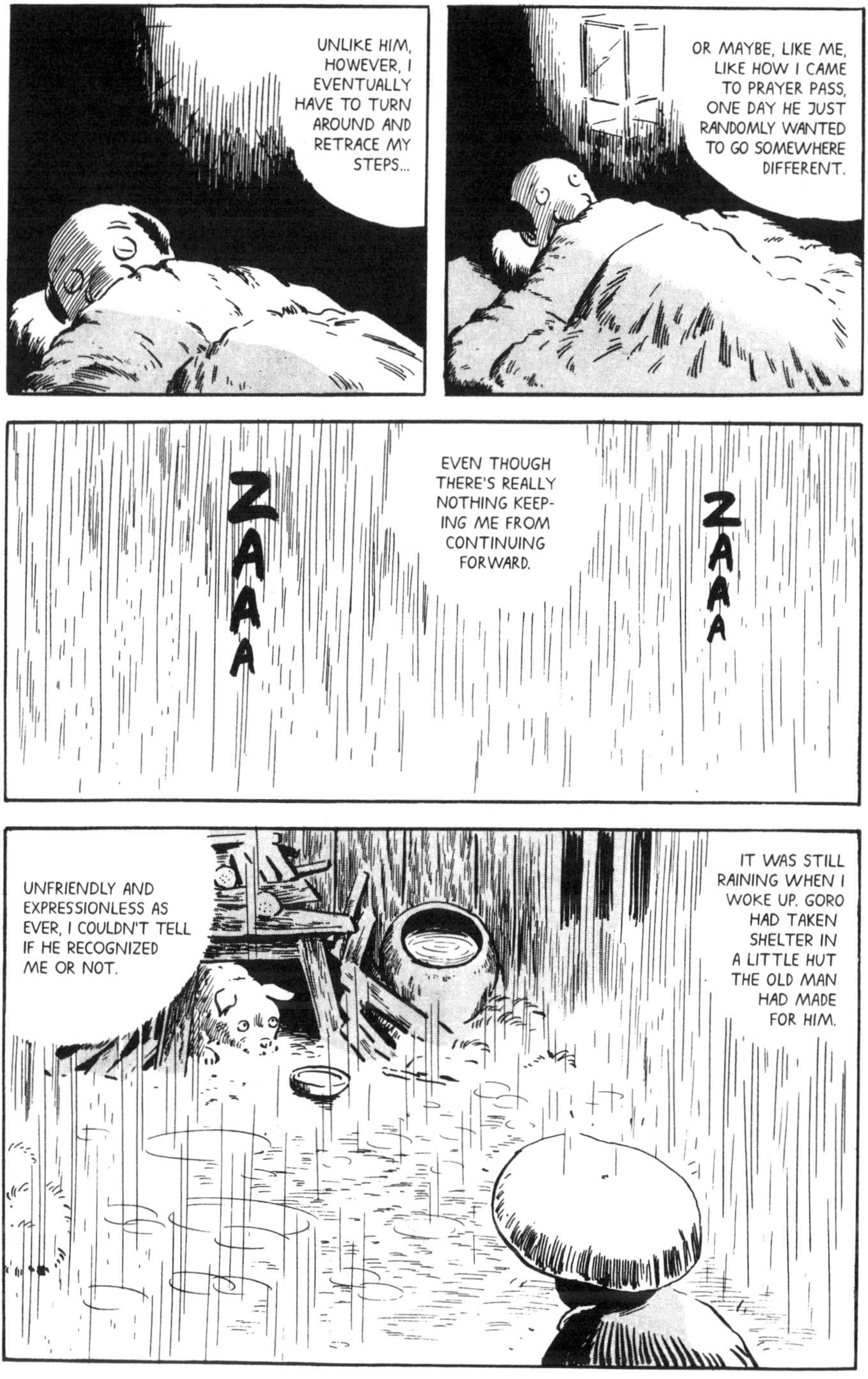
OR MAYBE, LIKE ME, LIKE HOW I CAME TO PRAYER PASS, ONE DAY HE JUST RANDOMLY WANTED TO GO SOMEWHERE DIFFERENT.
UNLIKE HIM, HOWEVER, I EVENTUALLY HAVE TO TURN AROUND AND RETRACE MY STEPS...
ZAAA
EVEN THOUGH THERE'S REALLY NOTHING KEEPING ME FROM CONTINUING FORWARD.
ZAAA
IT WAS STILL RAINING WHEN I WOKE UP. GORO HAD TAKEN SHELTER IN A LITTLE HUT THE OLD MAN HAD MADE FOR HIM.
UNFRIENDLY AND EXPRESSIONLESS AS EVER, I COULDN'T TELL IF HE RECOGNIZED ME OR NOT.

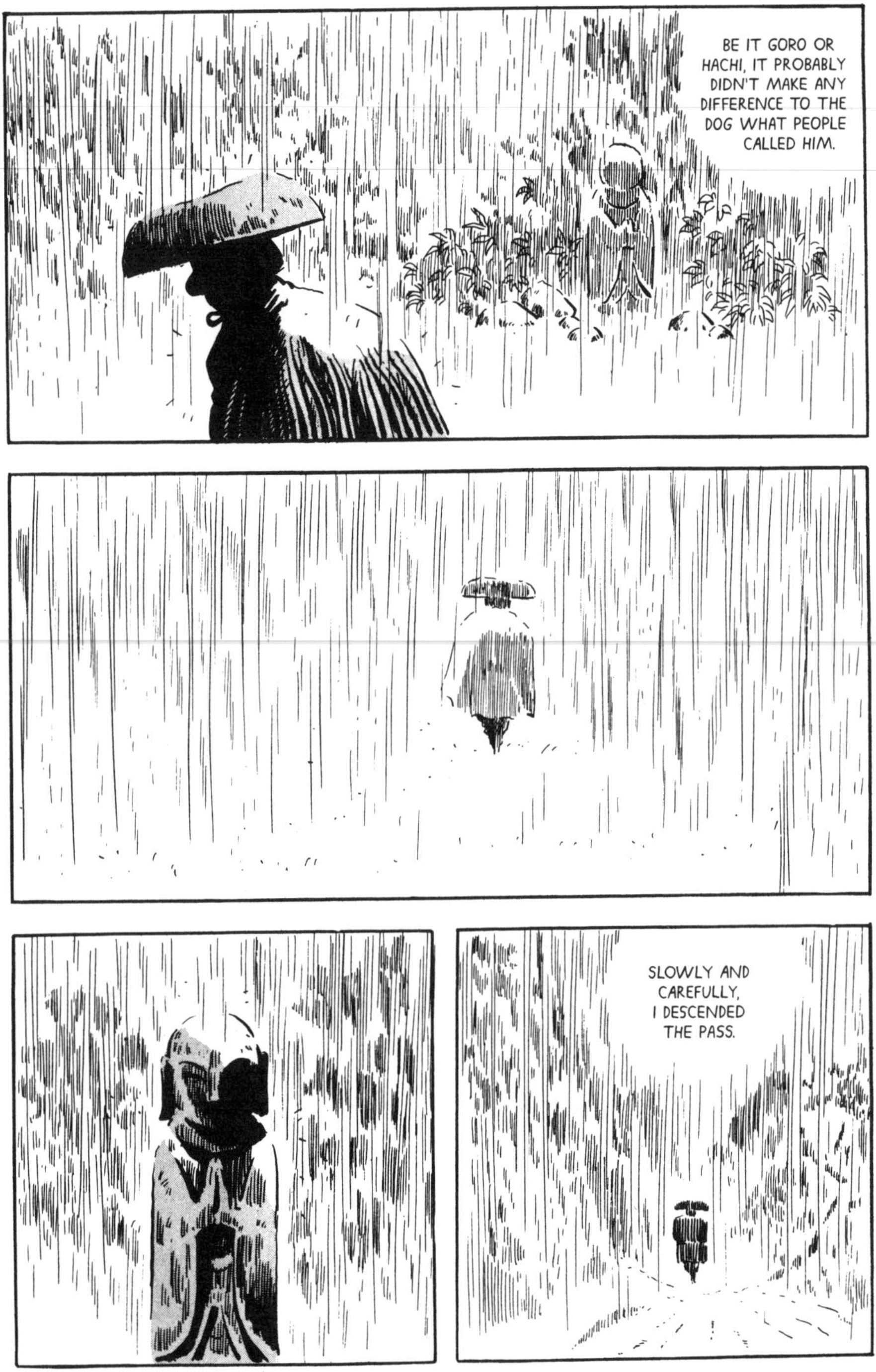
BE IT GORO OR HACHI, IT PROBABLY DIDN'T MAKE ANY DIFFERENCE TO THE DOG WHAT PEOPLE CALLED HIM.
SLOWLY AND CAREFULLY, I DESCENDED THE PASS.

SCENES FROM
THE SEASIDE

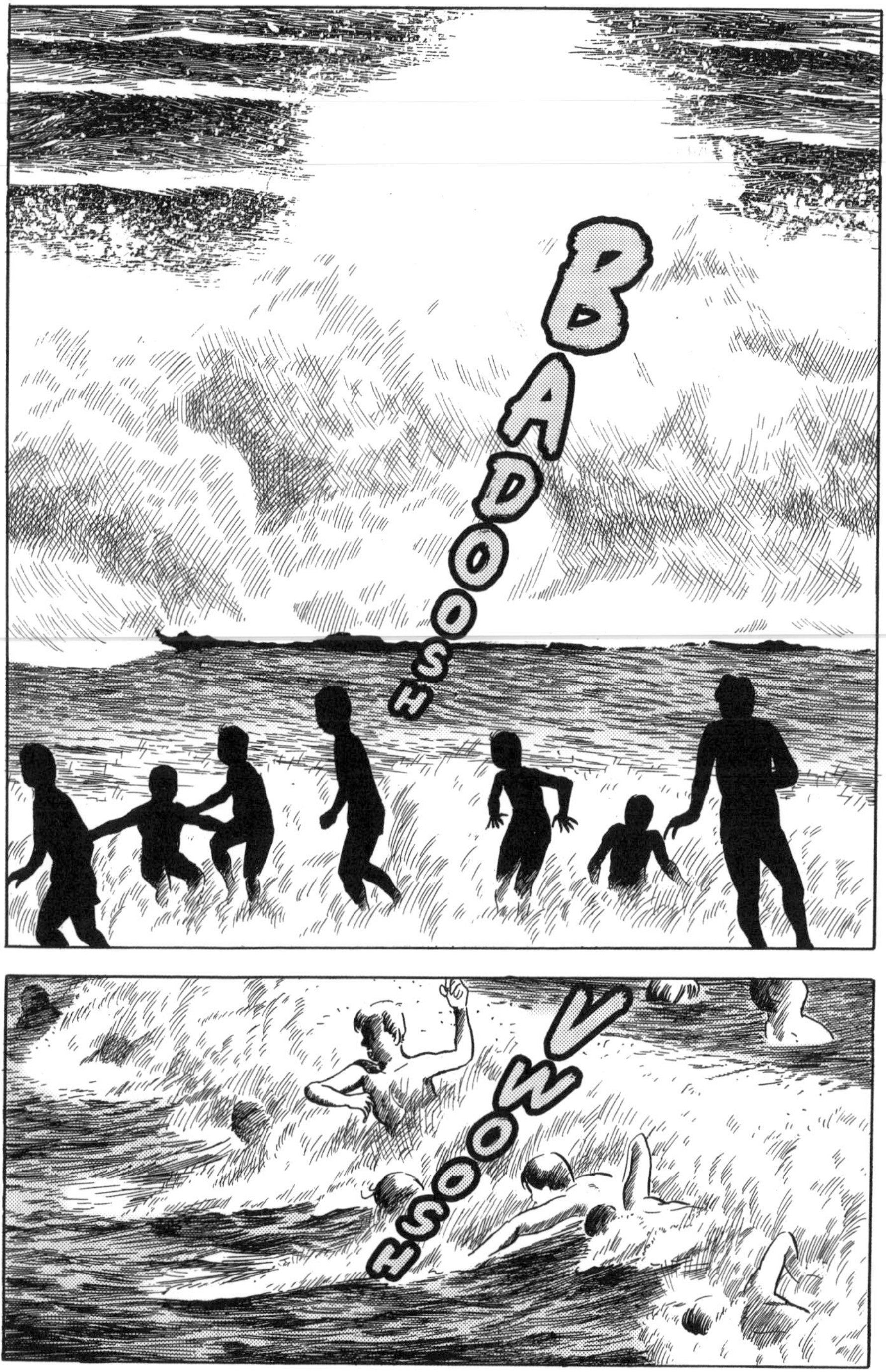
BADOOOSH
VWOOOSH

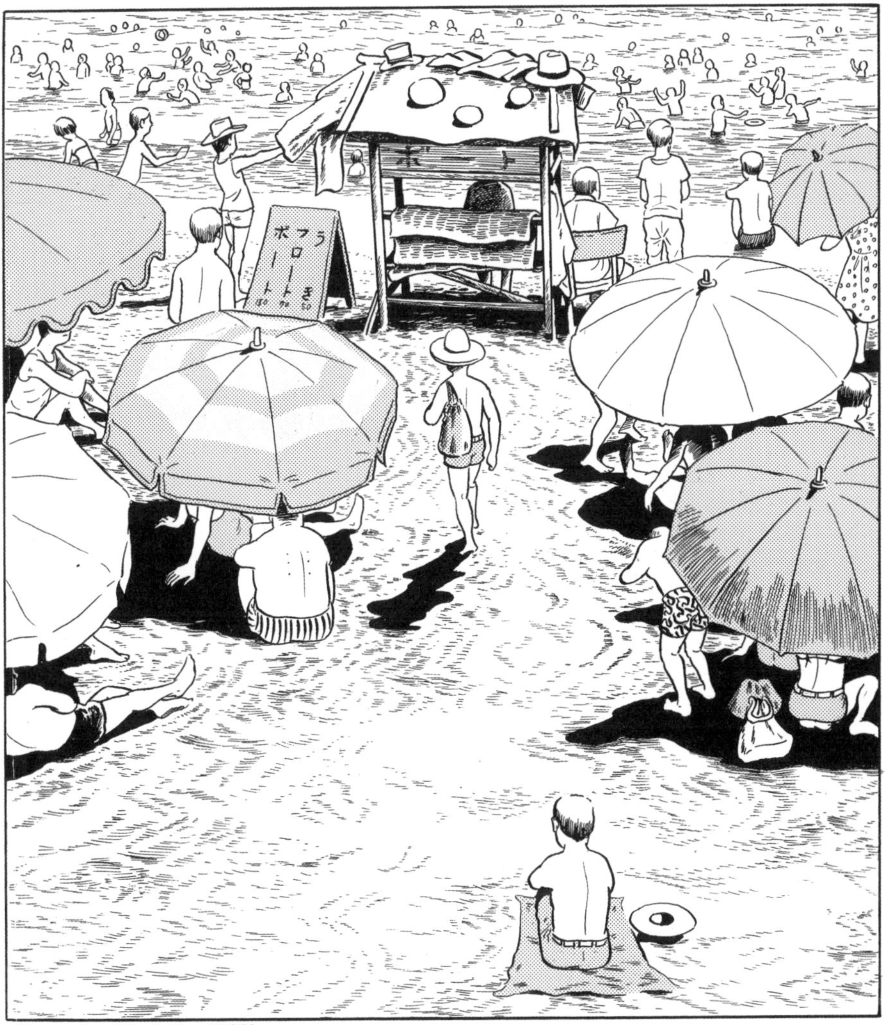

SIGN: BOATS, INNER TUBES, FLOATS

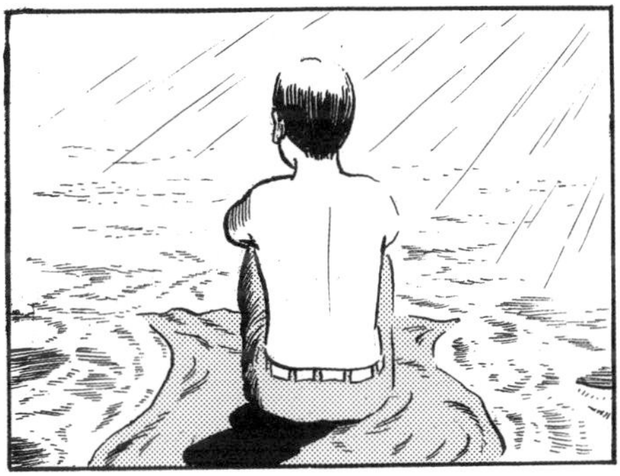

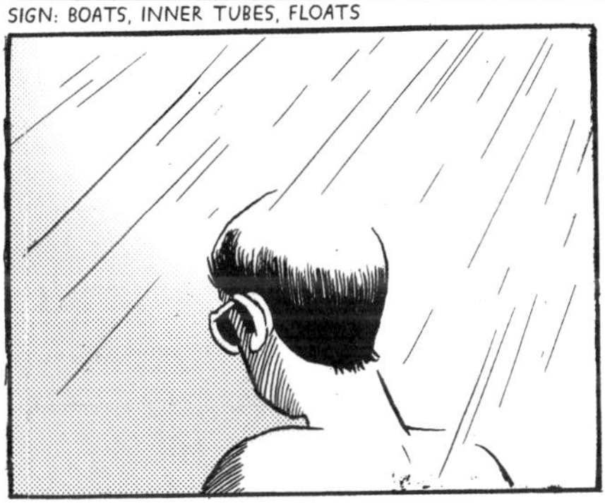

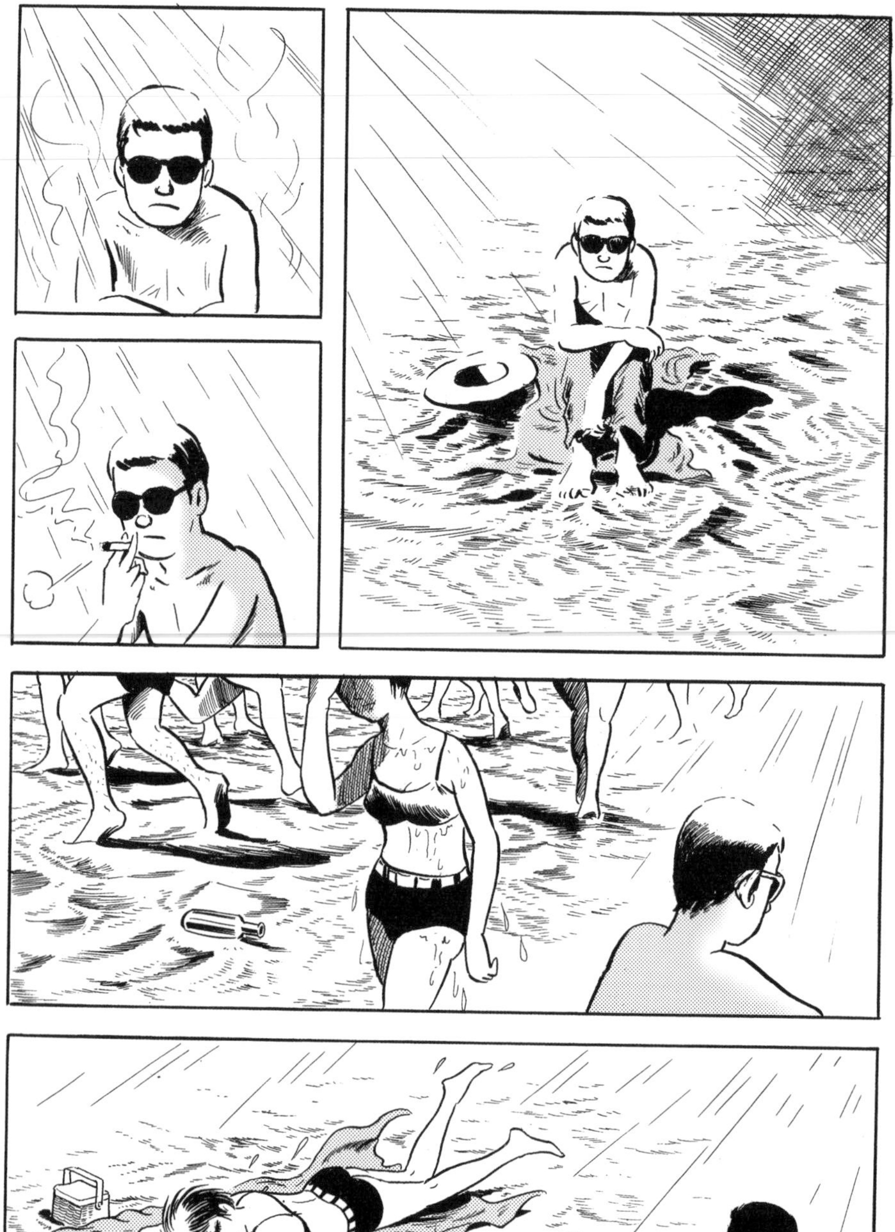

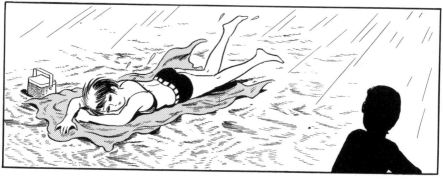

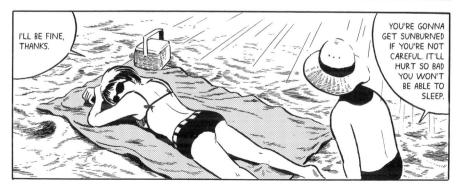

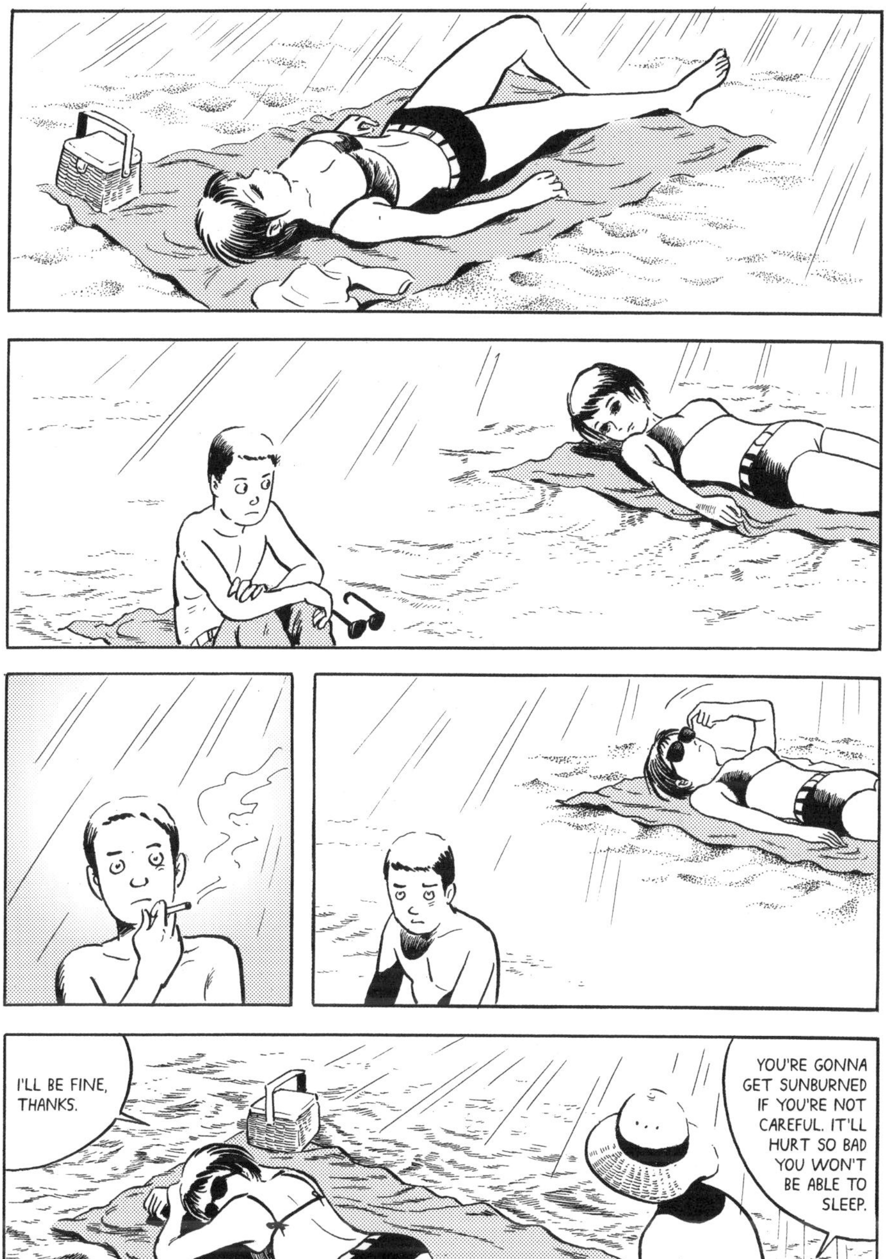
YOU'RE GONNA GET SUNBURNED IF YOU'RE NOT CAREFUL. IT'LL HURT SO BAD YOU WON'T BE ABLE TO SLEEP.
I'LL BE FINE, THANKS.

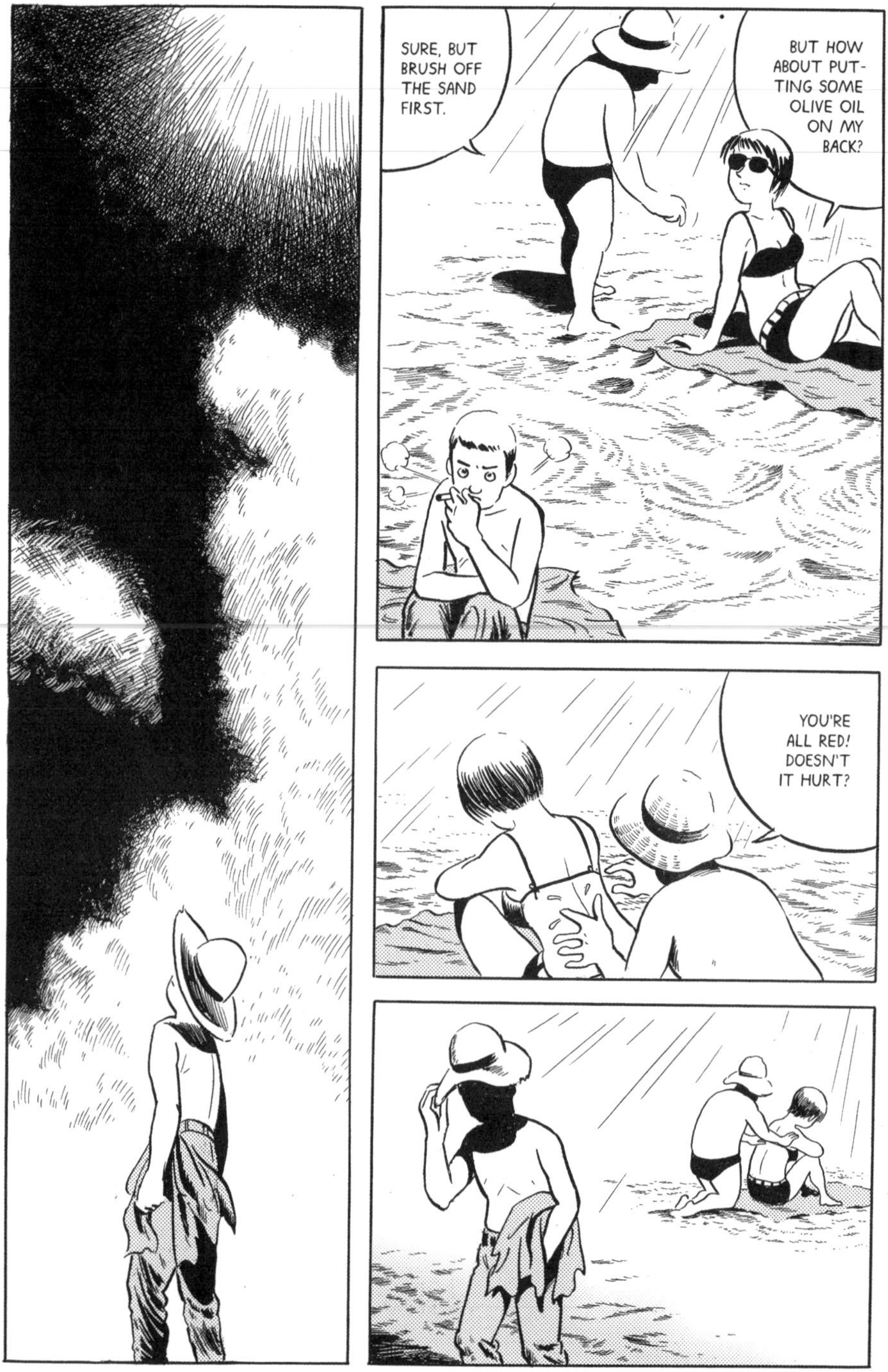
BUT HOW ABOUT PUTTING SOME OLIVE OIL ON MY BACK?
SURE, BUT BRUSH OFF THE SAND FIRST.
YOU'RE ALL RED! DOESN'T IT HURT?

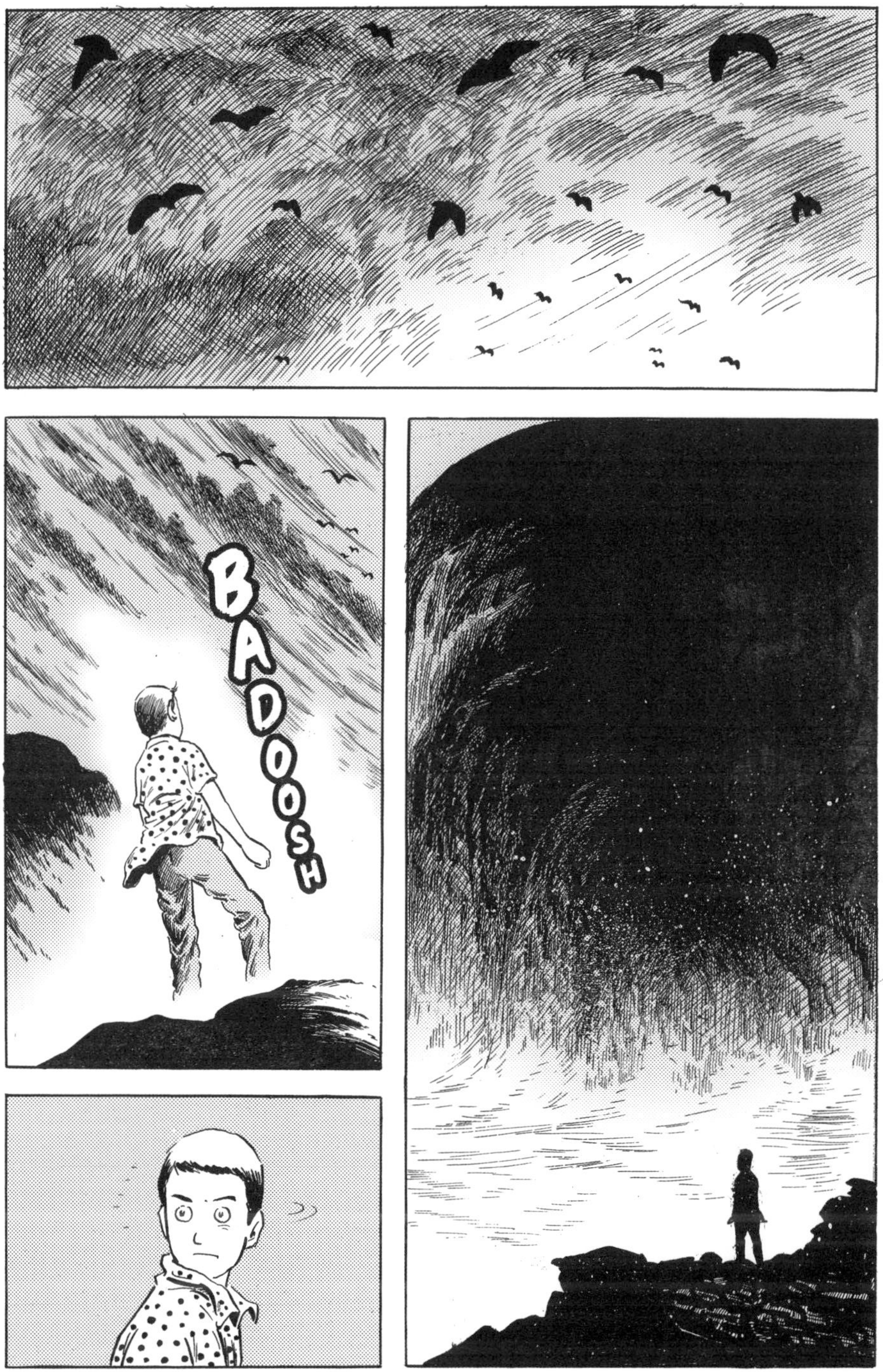
BADOOSH

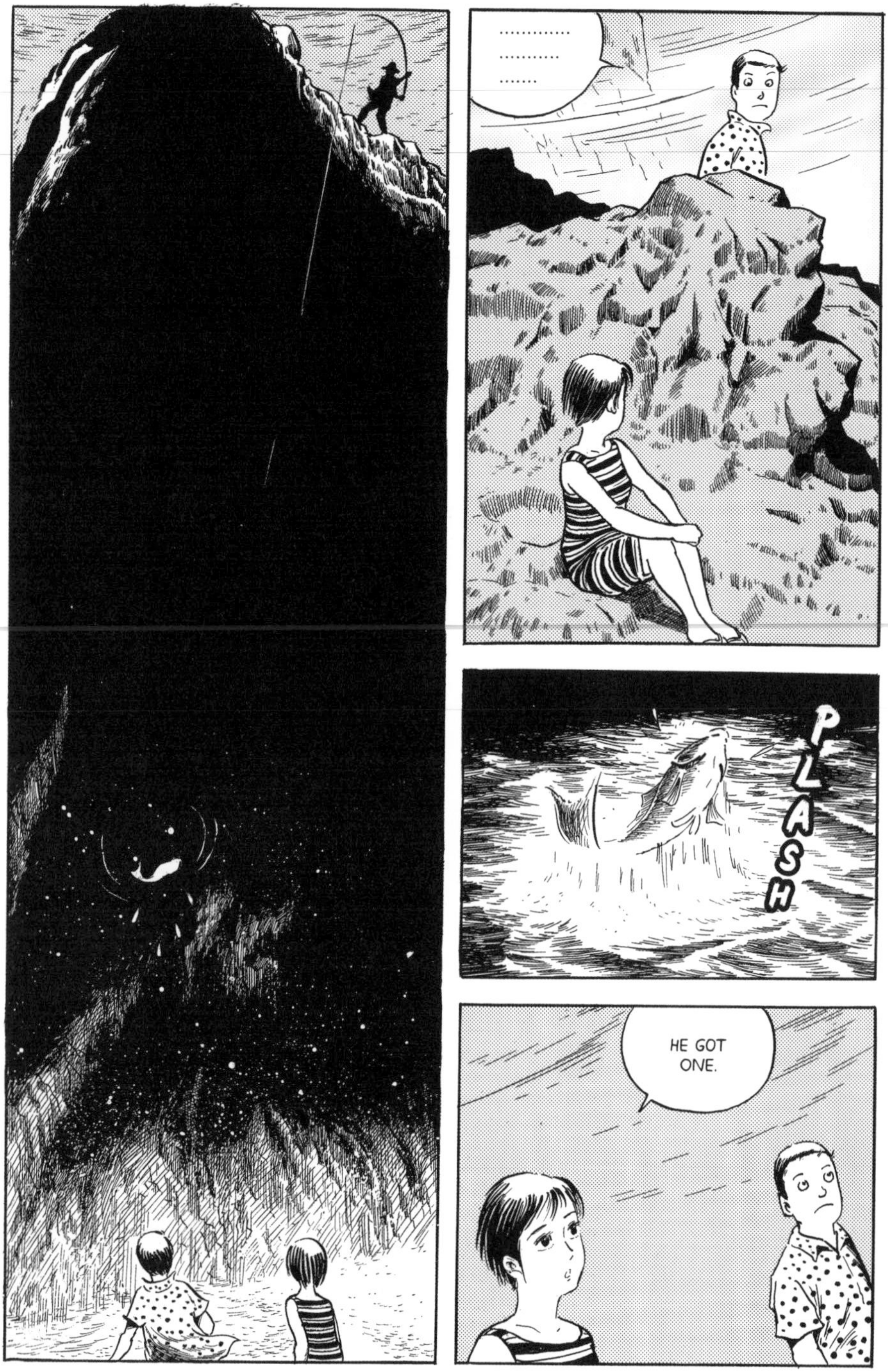
....
....
....
PLASH
HE GOT ONE.

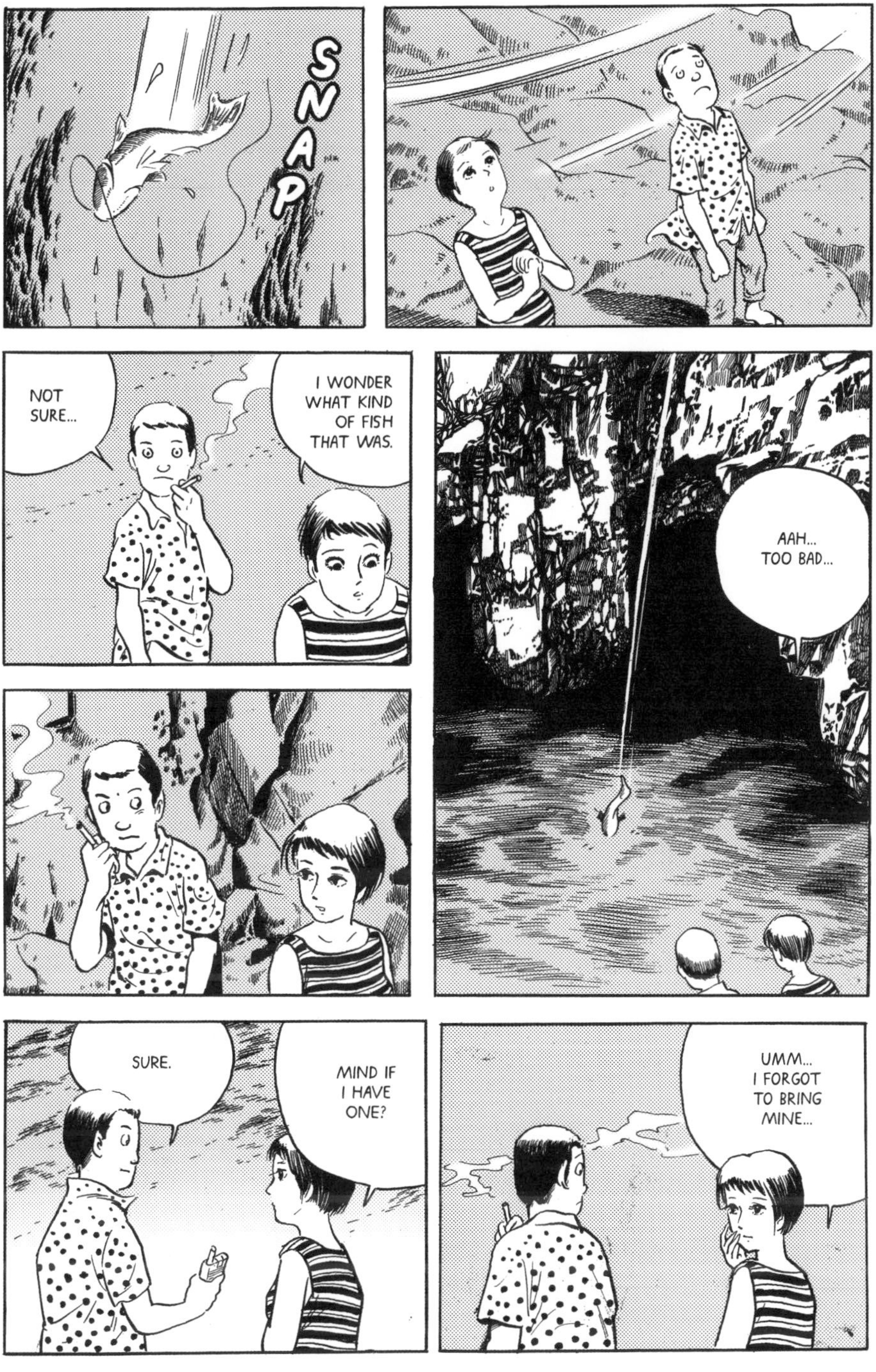
SNAP
AAH... TOO BAD...
I WONDER WHAT KIND OF FISH THAT WAS.
NOT SURE...
UMM... I FORGOT TO BRING MINE...
MIND IF I HAVE ONE?
SURE.

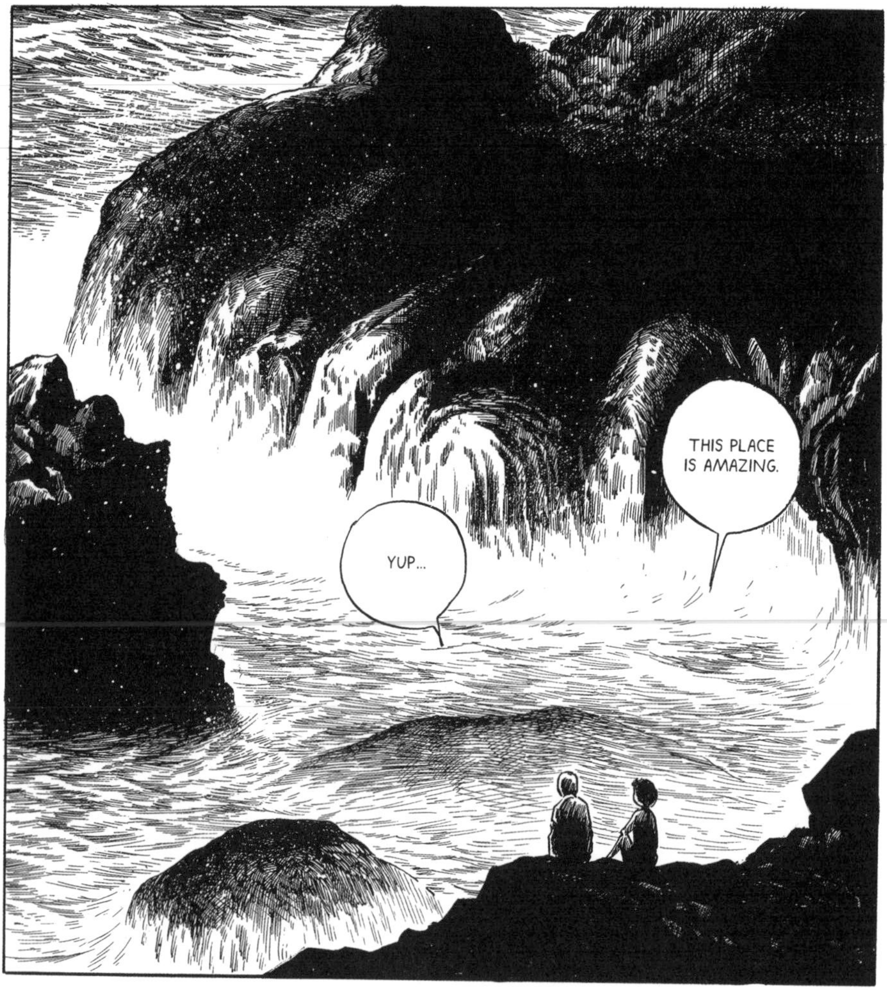
THIS PLACE IS AMAZING.
YUP...

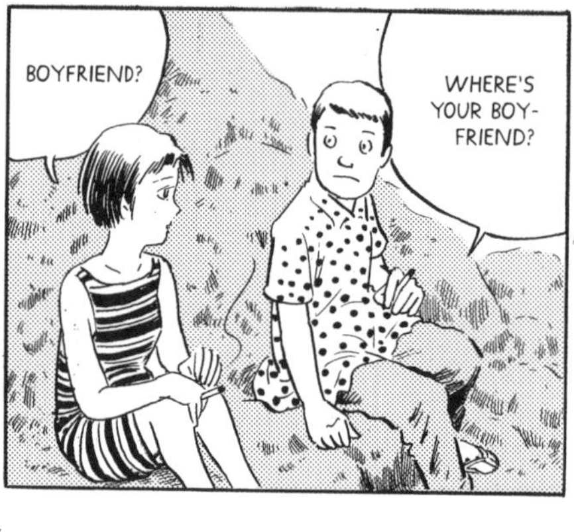
WHERE'S YOUR BOY-FRIEND?
BOYFRIEND?

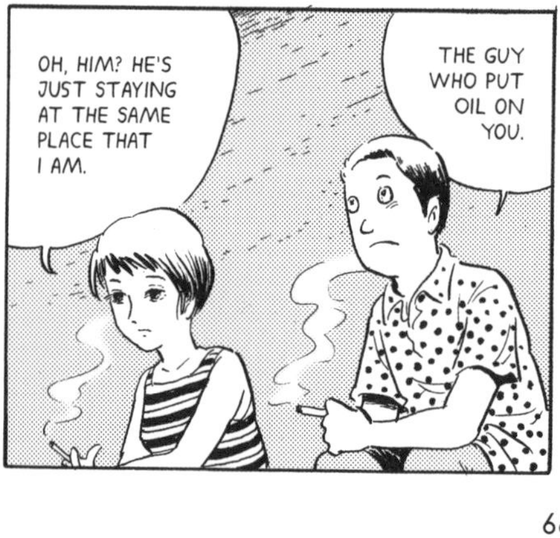
THE GUY WHO PUT OIL ON YOU.
OH, HIM? HE'S JUST STAYING AT THE SAME PLACE THAT I AM.

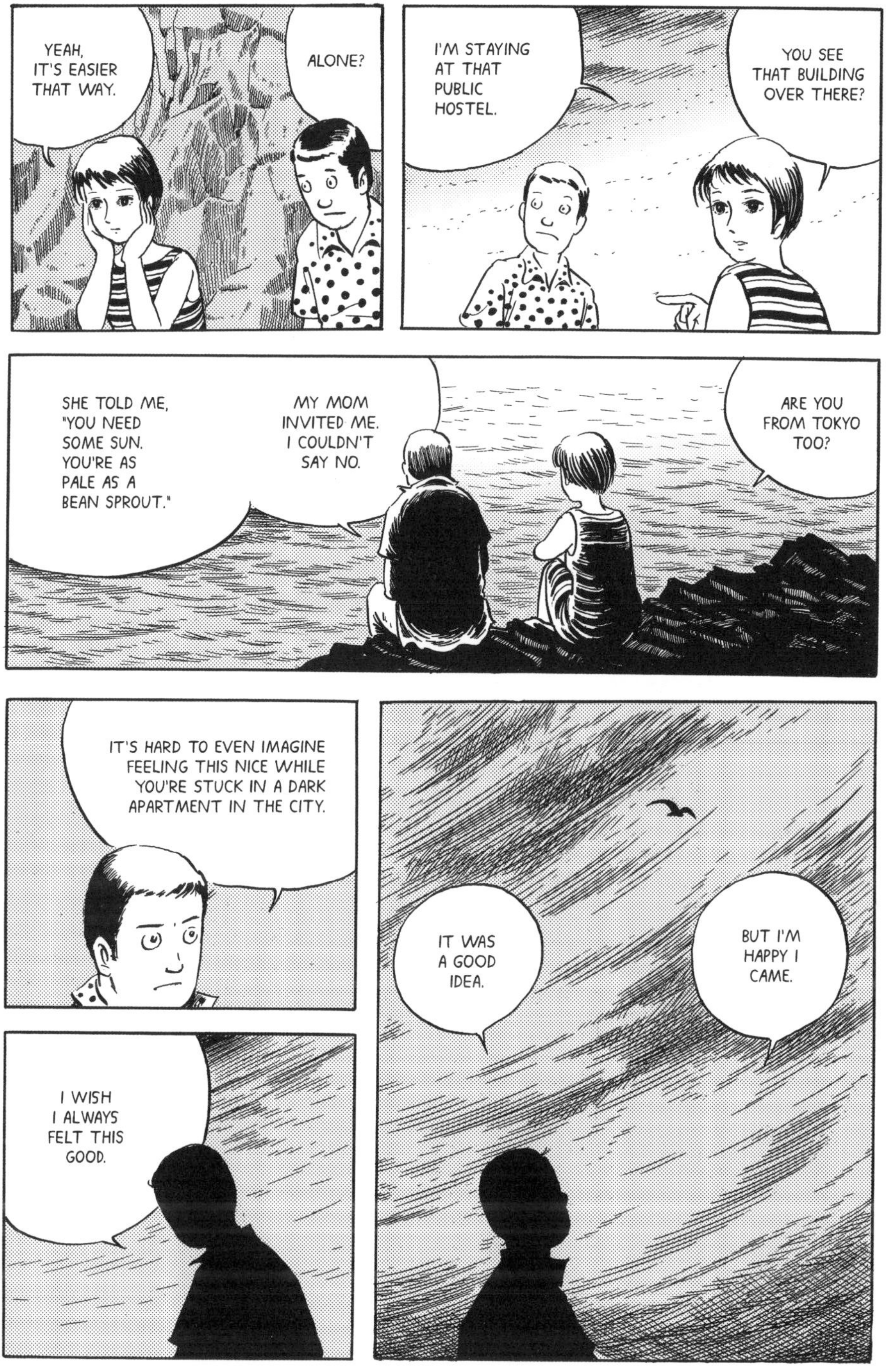
YOU SEE THAT BUILDING OVER THERE?
I'M STAYING AT THAT PUBLIC HOSTEL.
ALONE?
YEAH, IT'S EASIER THAT WAY.
ARE YOU FROM TOKYO TOO?
MY MOM INVITED ME. I COULDN'T SAY NO.
SHE TOLD ME, "YOU NEED SOME SUN. YOU'RE AS PALE AS A BEAN SPROUT."
BUT I'M HAPPY I CAME.
IT WAS A GOOD IDEA.
IT'S HARD TO EVEN IMAGINE FEELING THIS NICE WHILE YOU'RE STUCK IN A DARK APARTMENT IN THE CITY.
I WISH I ALWAYS FELT THIS GOOD.

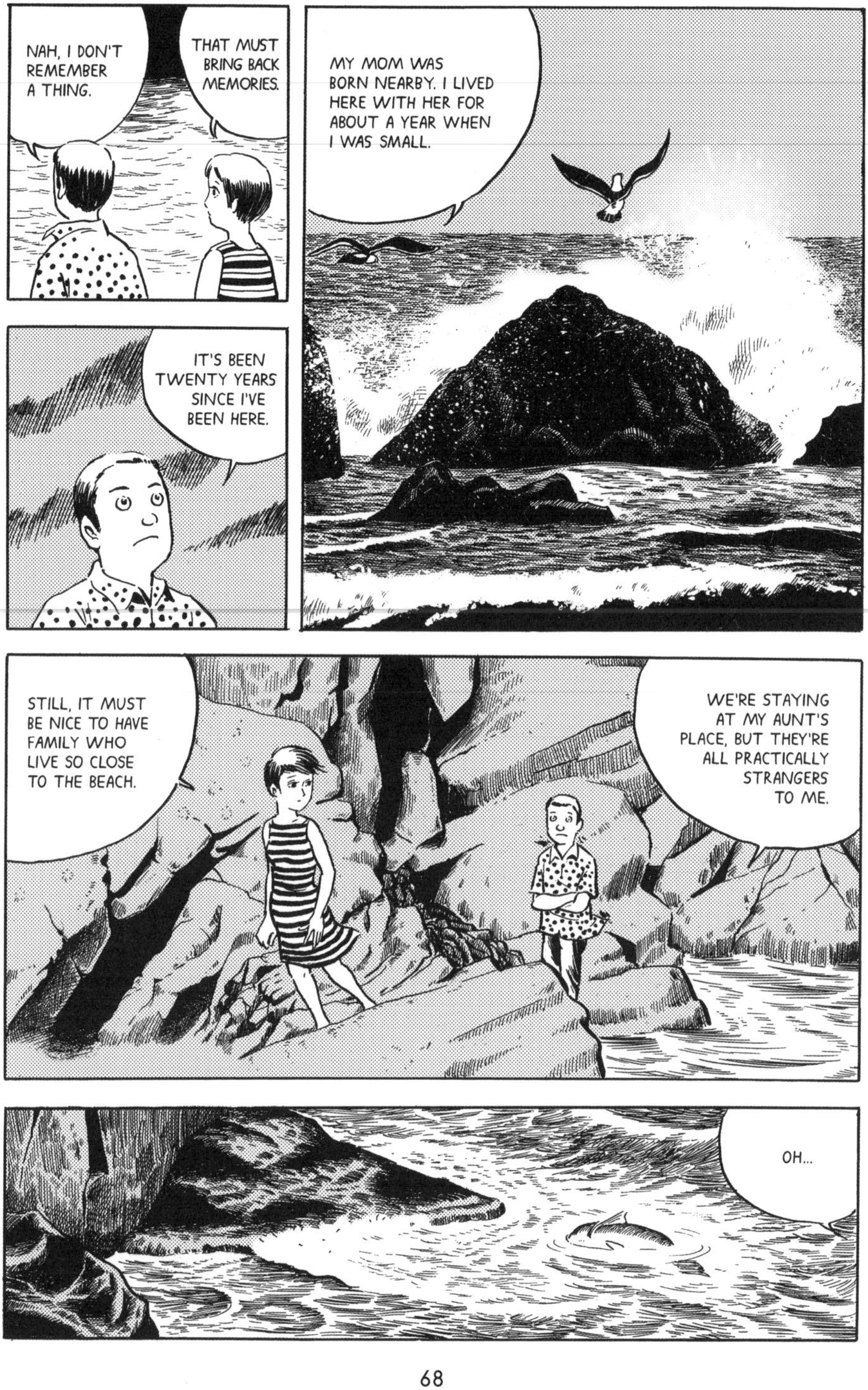
MY MOM WAS BORN NEARBY. I LIVED HERE WITH HER FOR ABOUT A YEAR WHEN I WAS SMALL.
THAT MUST BRING BACK MEMORIES.
NAH, I DON'T REMEMBER A THING.
IT'S BEEN TWENTY YEARS SINCE I'VE BEEN HERE.
WE'RE STAYING AT MY AUNT'S PLACE, BUT THEY'RE ALL PRACTICALLY STRANGERS TO ME.
STILL, IT MUST BE NICE TO HAVE FAMILY WHO LIVE SO CLOSE TO THE BEACH.
OH...

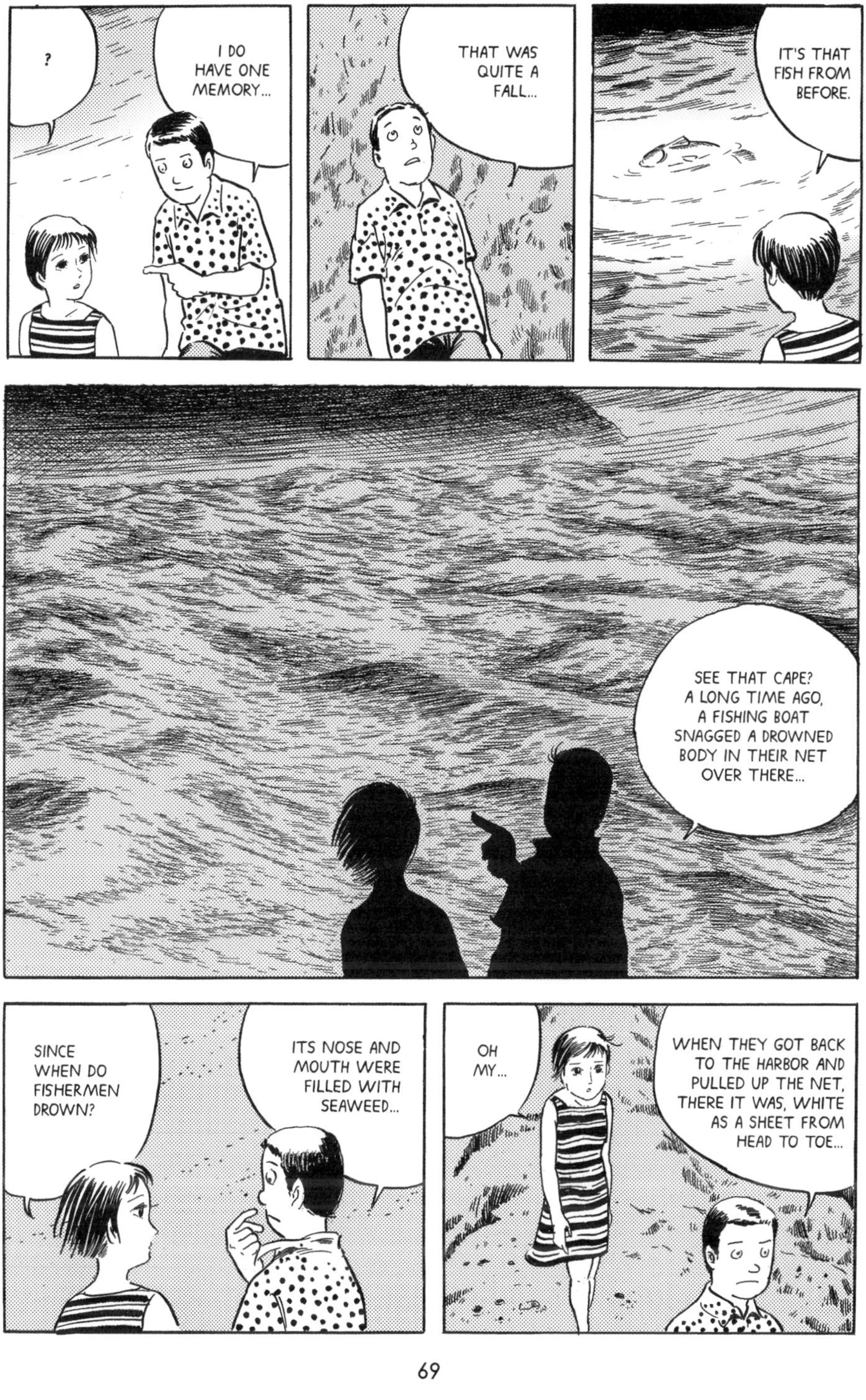
IT'S THAT FISH FROM BEFORE.
THAT WAS QUITE A FALL...
I DO HAVE ONE MEMORY...
?
SEE THAT CAPE? A LONG TIME AGO, A FISHING BOAT SNAGGED A DROWNED BODY IN THEIR NET OVER THERE...
WHEN THEY GOT BACK TO THE HARBOR AND PULLED UP THE NET, THERE IT WAS, WHITE AS A SHEET FROM HEAD TO TOE...
OH MY...
ITS NOSE AND MOUTH WERE FILLED WITH SEAWEED...
SINCE WHEN DO FISHERMEN DROWN?

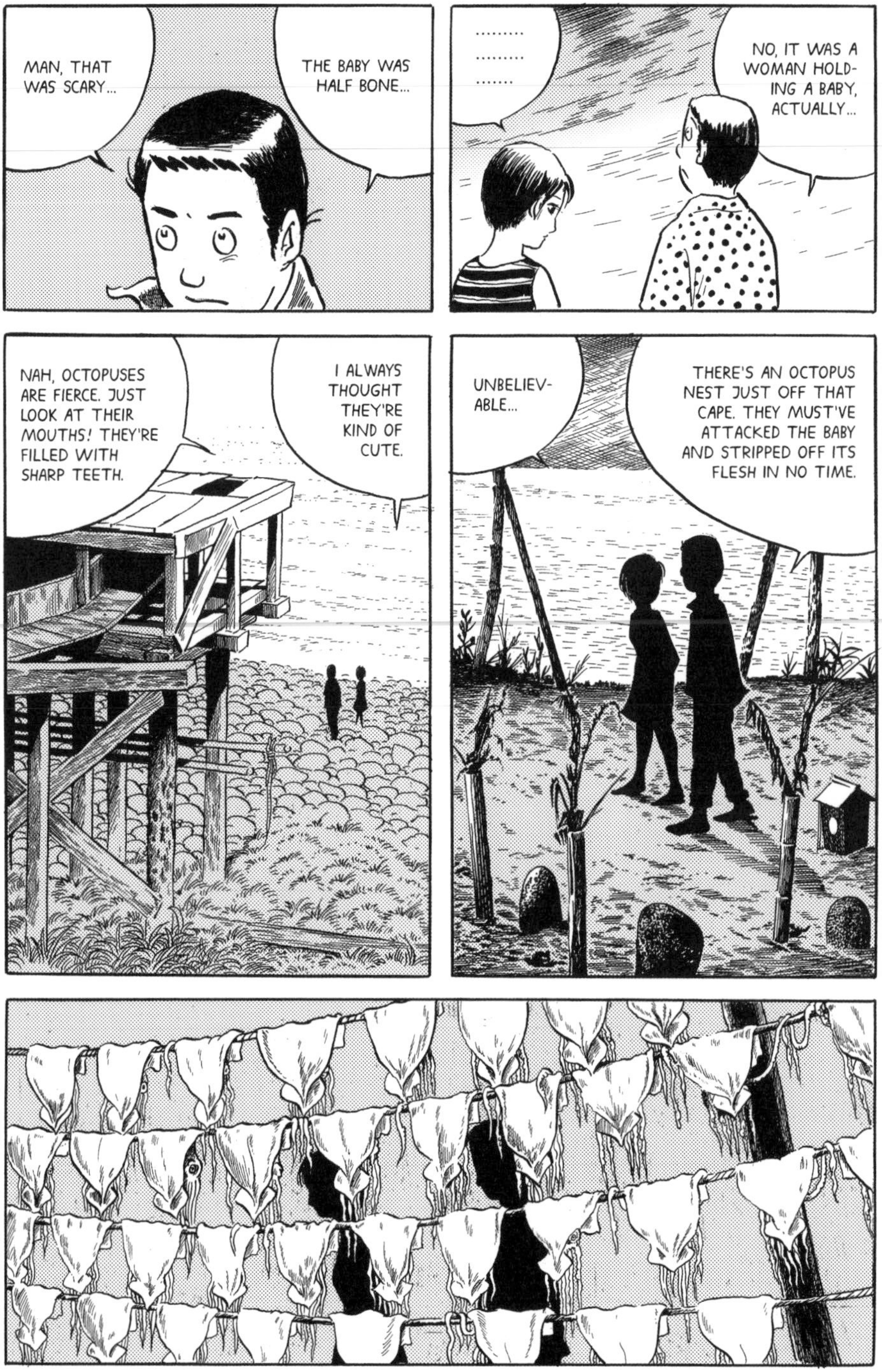
NO, IT WAS A WOMAN HOLDING A BABY, ACTUALLY...
....
....
....
THE BABY WAS HALF BONE...
MAN, THAT WAS SCARY...
THERE'S AN OCTOPUS NEST JUST OFF THAT CAPE. THEY MUST'VE ATTACKED THE BABY AND STRIPPED OFF ITS FLESH IN NO TIME.
UNBELIEVABLE...
I ALWAYS THOUGHT THEY'RE KIND OF CUTE.
NAH, OCTOPUSES ARE FIERCE. JUST LOOK AT THEIR MOUTHS! THEY'RE FILLED WITH SHARP TEETH.

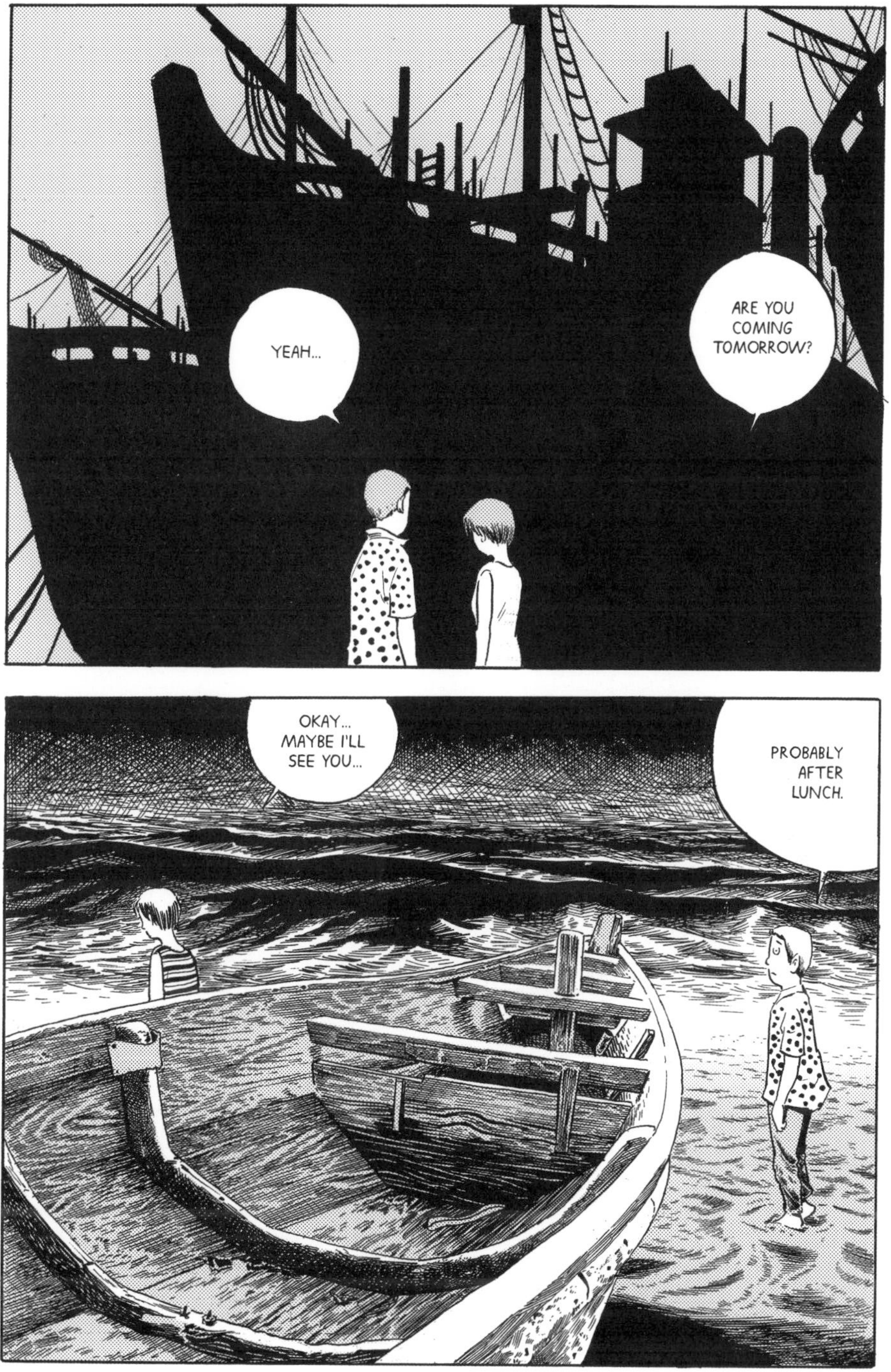
ARE YOU COMING TOMORROW?
YEAH...
PROBABLY AFTER LUNCH.
OKAY... MAYBE I'LL SEE YOU...

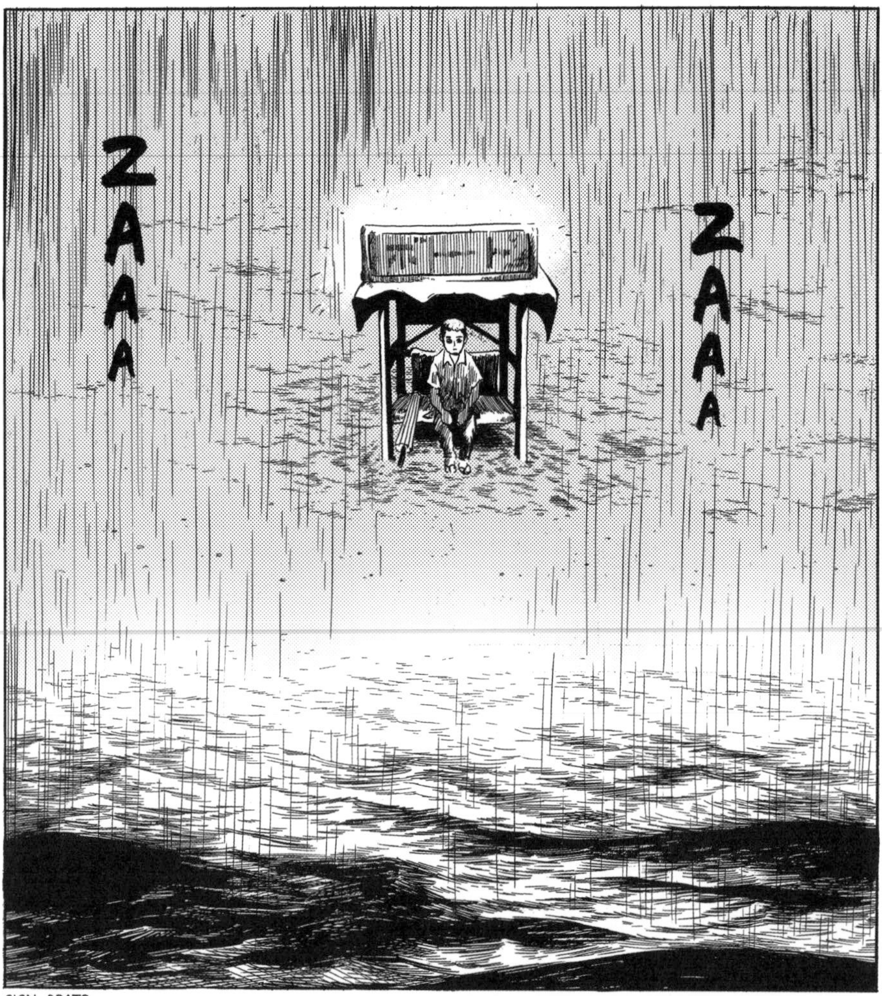
ZAAA
ZAAA
SIGN: BOATS

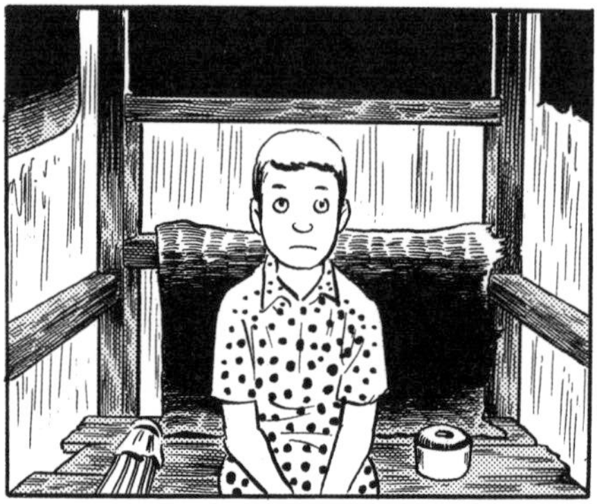

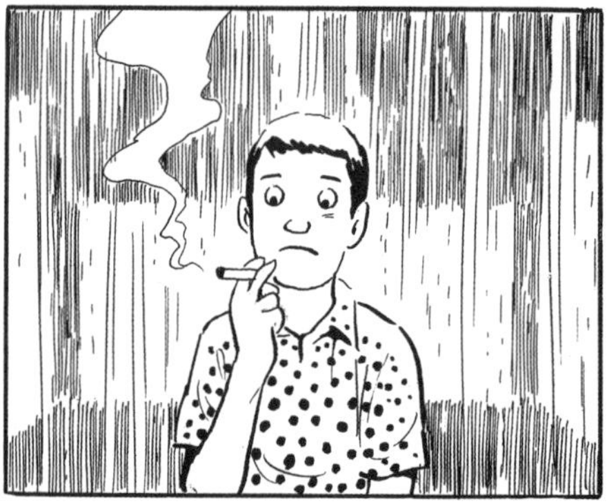

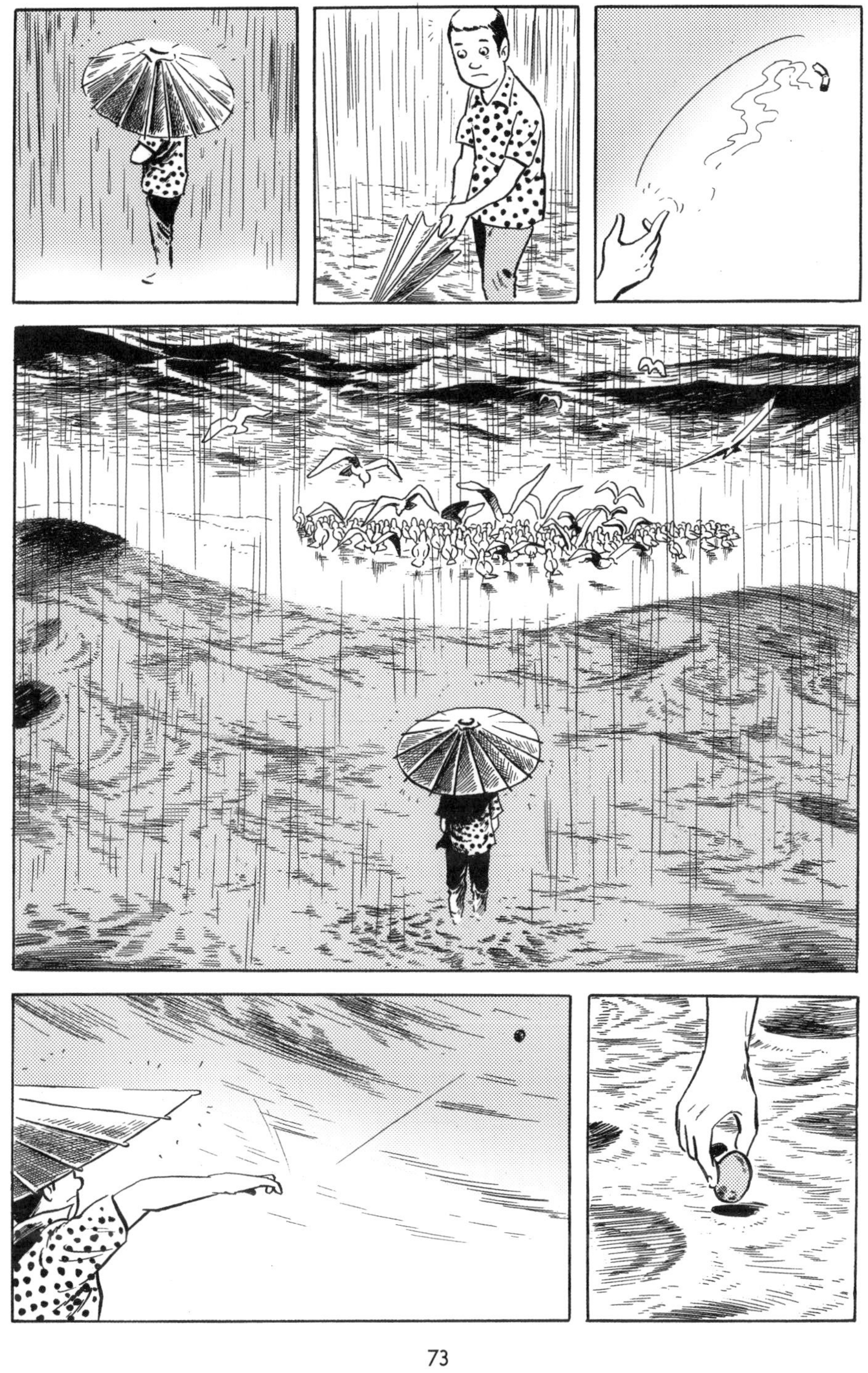

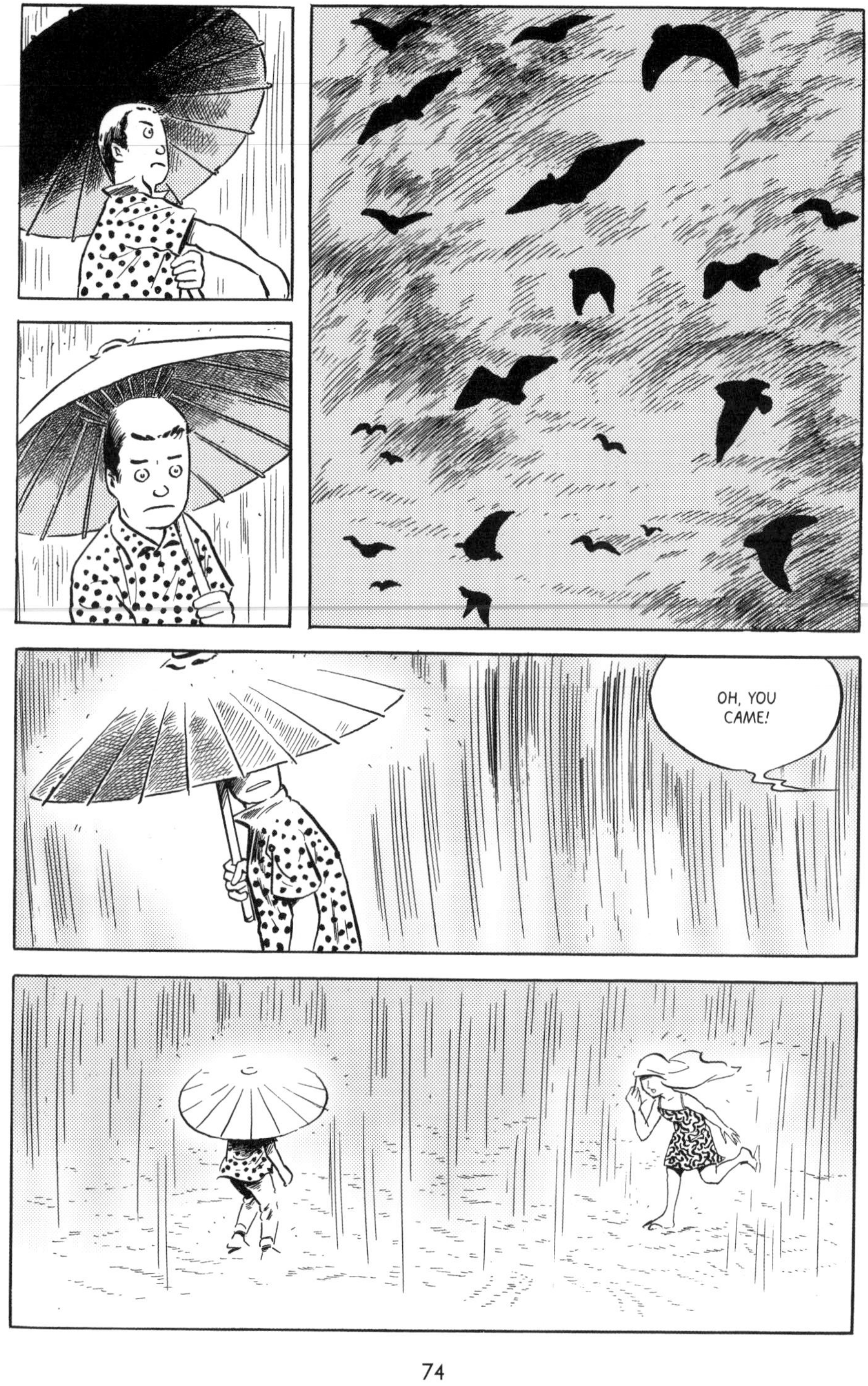
OH, YOU CAME!

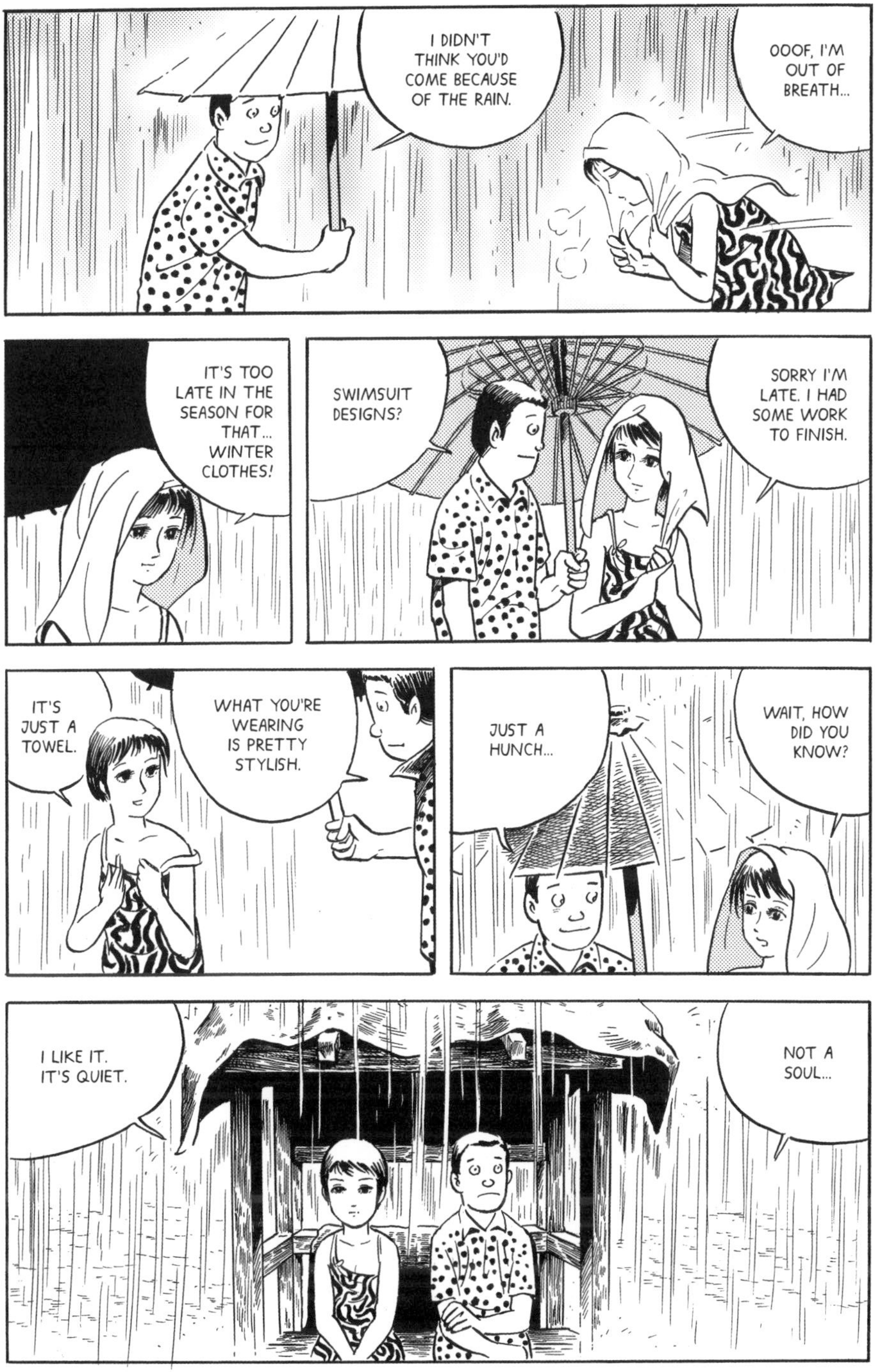
OOOF, I'M OUT OF BREATH...
I DIDN'T THINK YOU'D COME BECAUSE OF THE RAIN.
SORRY I'M LATE. I HAD SOME WORK TO FINISH.
SWIMSUIT DESIGNS?
IT'S TOO LATE IN THE SEASON FOR THAT... WINTER CLOTHES!
WAIT, HOW DID YOU KNOW?
JUST A HUNCH...
WHAT YOU'RE WEARING IS PRETTY STYLISH.
IT'S JUST A TOWEL.
NOT A SOUL...
I LIKE IT. IT'S QUIET.

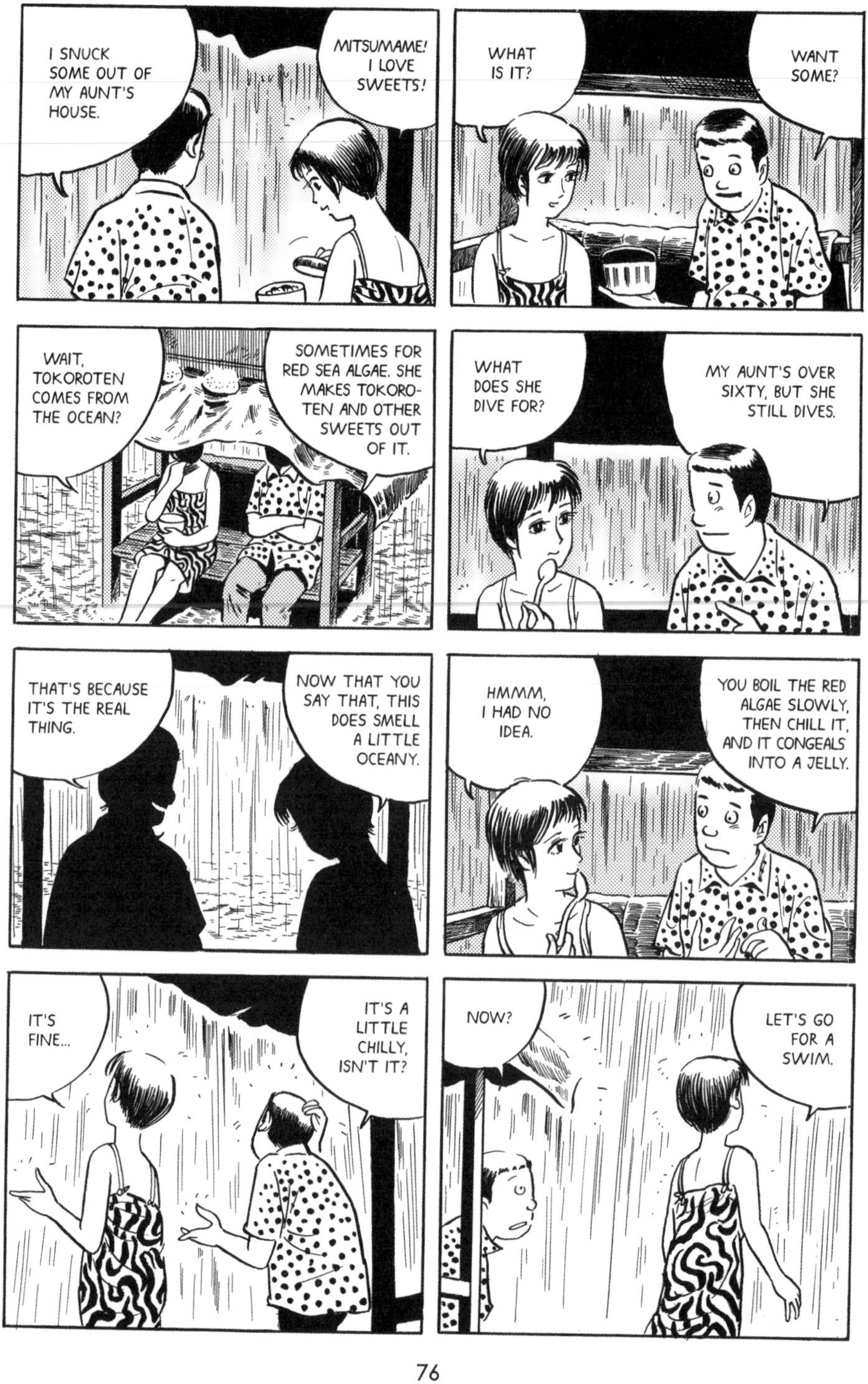
WANT SOME?
WHAT IS IT?
MITSUMAME! I LOVE SWEETS!
I SNUCK SOME OUT OF MY AUNT'S HOUSE.
MY AUNT'S OVER SIXTY, BUT SHE STILL DIVES.
WHAT DOES SHE DIVE FOR?
SOMETIMES FOR RED SEA ALGAE. SHE MAKES TOKOROTEN AND OTHER SWEETS OUT OF IT.
WAIT, TOKOROTEN COMES FROM THE OCEAN?
YOU BOIL THE RED ALGAE SLOWLY, THEN CHILL IT, AND IT CONGEALS INTO A JELLY.
HMMM, I HAD NO IDEA.
NOW THAT YOU SAY THAT, THIS DOES SMELL A LITTLE OCEANY.
THAT'S BECAUSE IT'S THE REAL THING.
LET'S GO FOR A SWIM.
NOW?
IT'S A LITTLE CHILLY, ISN'T IT?
IT'S FINE...

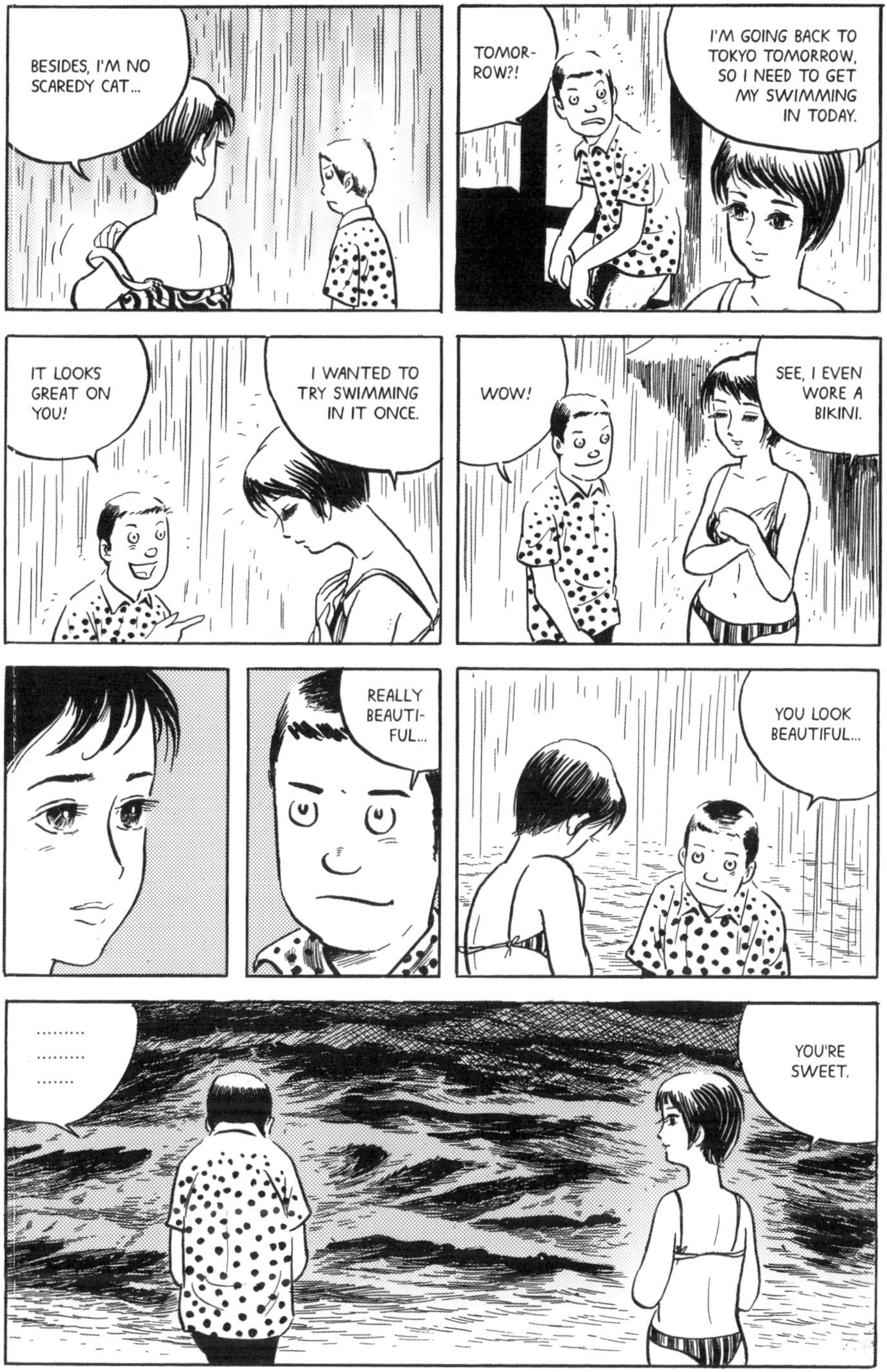
I'M GOING BACK TO TOKYO TOMORROW, SO I NEED TO GET MY SWIMMING IN TODAY.
TOMOR-ROW?!
BESIDES, I'M NO SCAREDY CAT...
SEE, I EVEN WORE A BIKINI.
WOW!
I WANTED TO TRY SWIMMING IN IT ONCE.
IT LOOKS GREAT ON YOU!
YOU LOOK BEAUTIFUL...
REALLY BEAUTI-FUL...
YOU'RE SWEET.
....
....
....

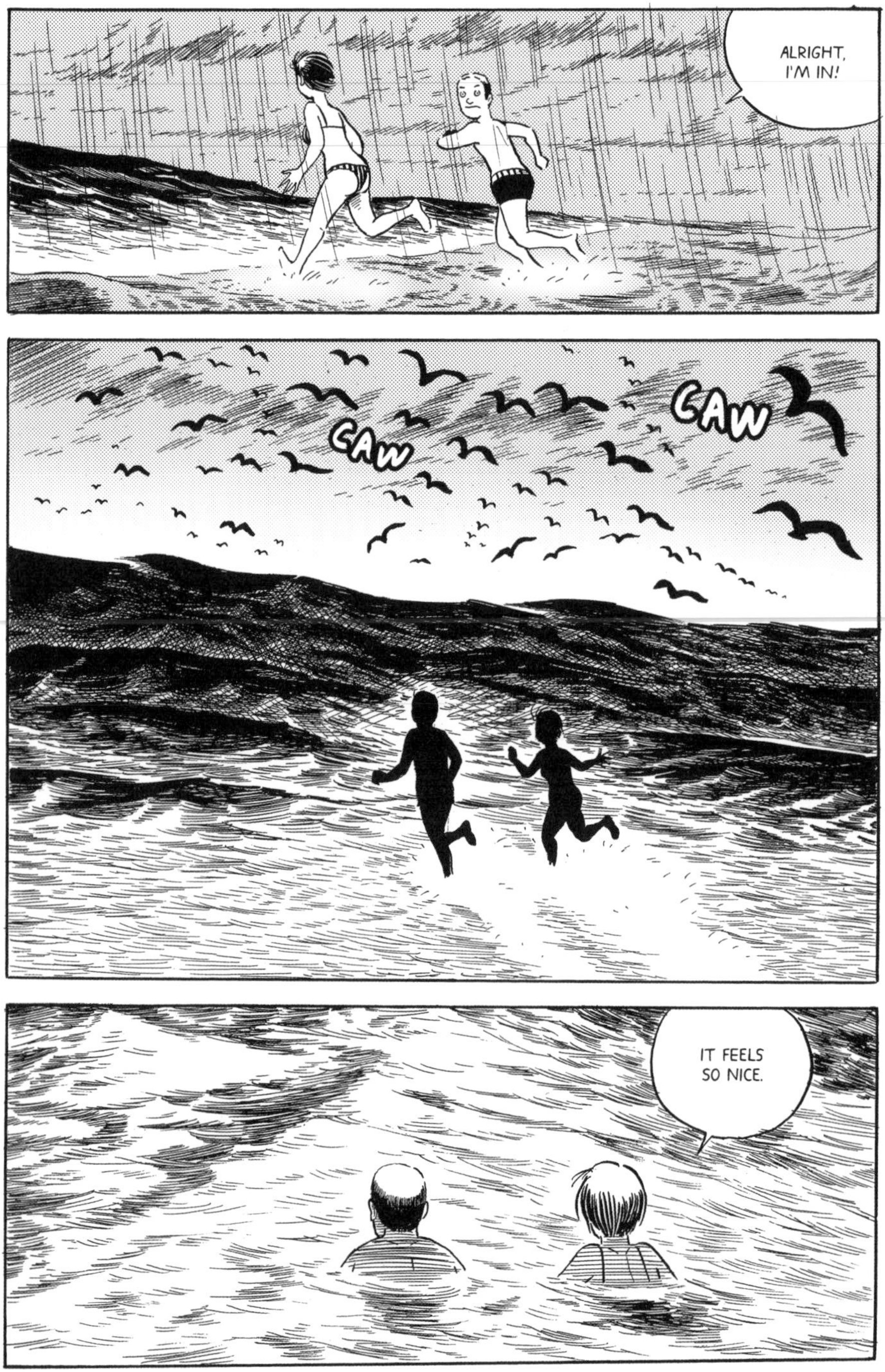
ALRIGHT, I'M IN!
CAW
CAW
IT FEELS SO NICE.

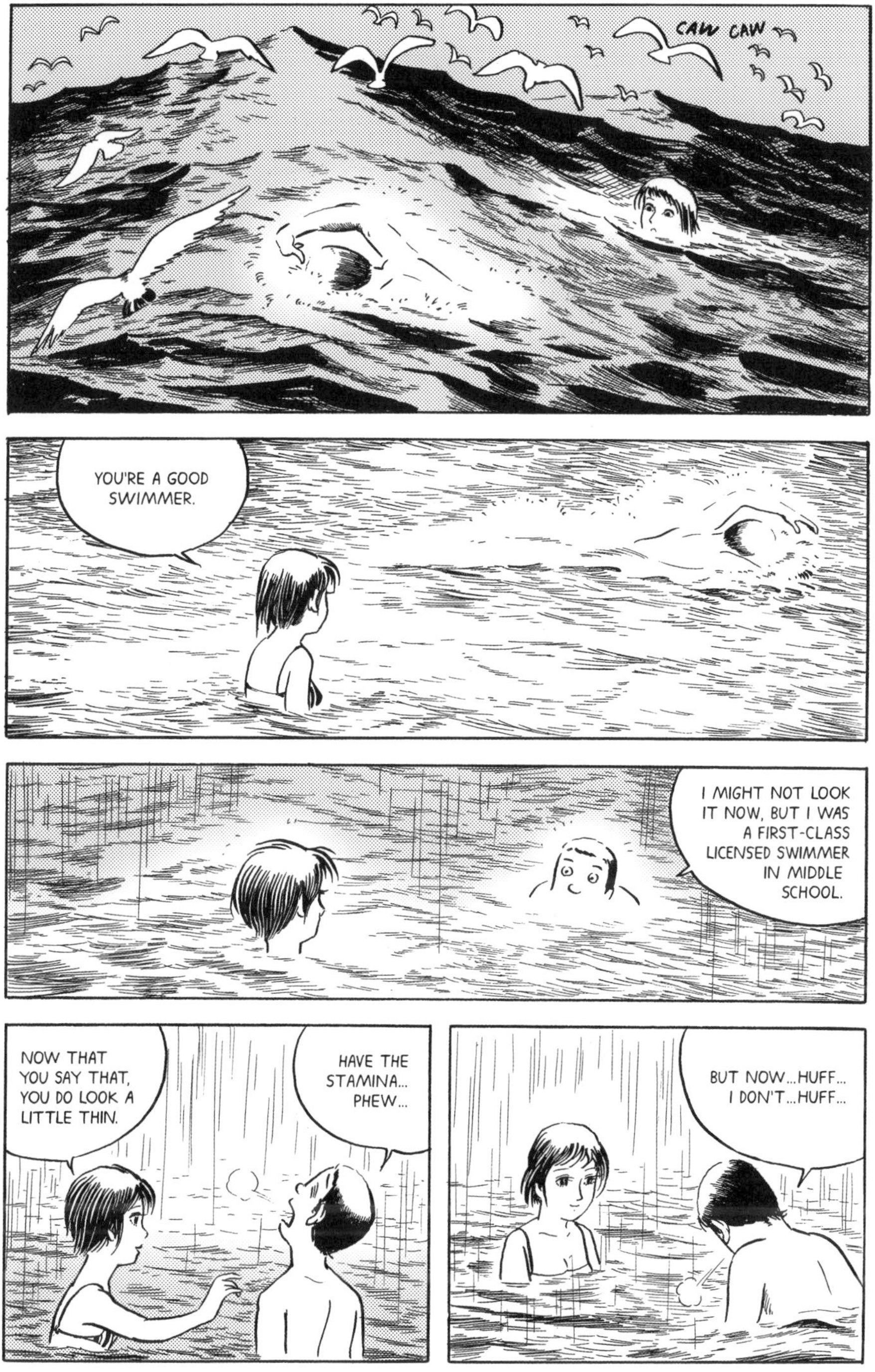
CAW CAW
YOU'RE A GOOD SWIMMER.
I MIGHT NOT LOOK IT NOW, BUT I WAS A FIRST-CLASS LICENSED SWIMMER IN MIDDLE SCHOOL.
BUT NOW...HUFF... I DON'T...HUFF...
HAVE THE STAMINA... PHEW...
NOW THAT YOU SAY THAT, YOU DO LOOK A LITTLE THIN.

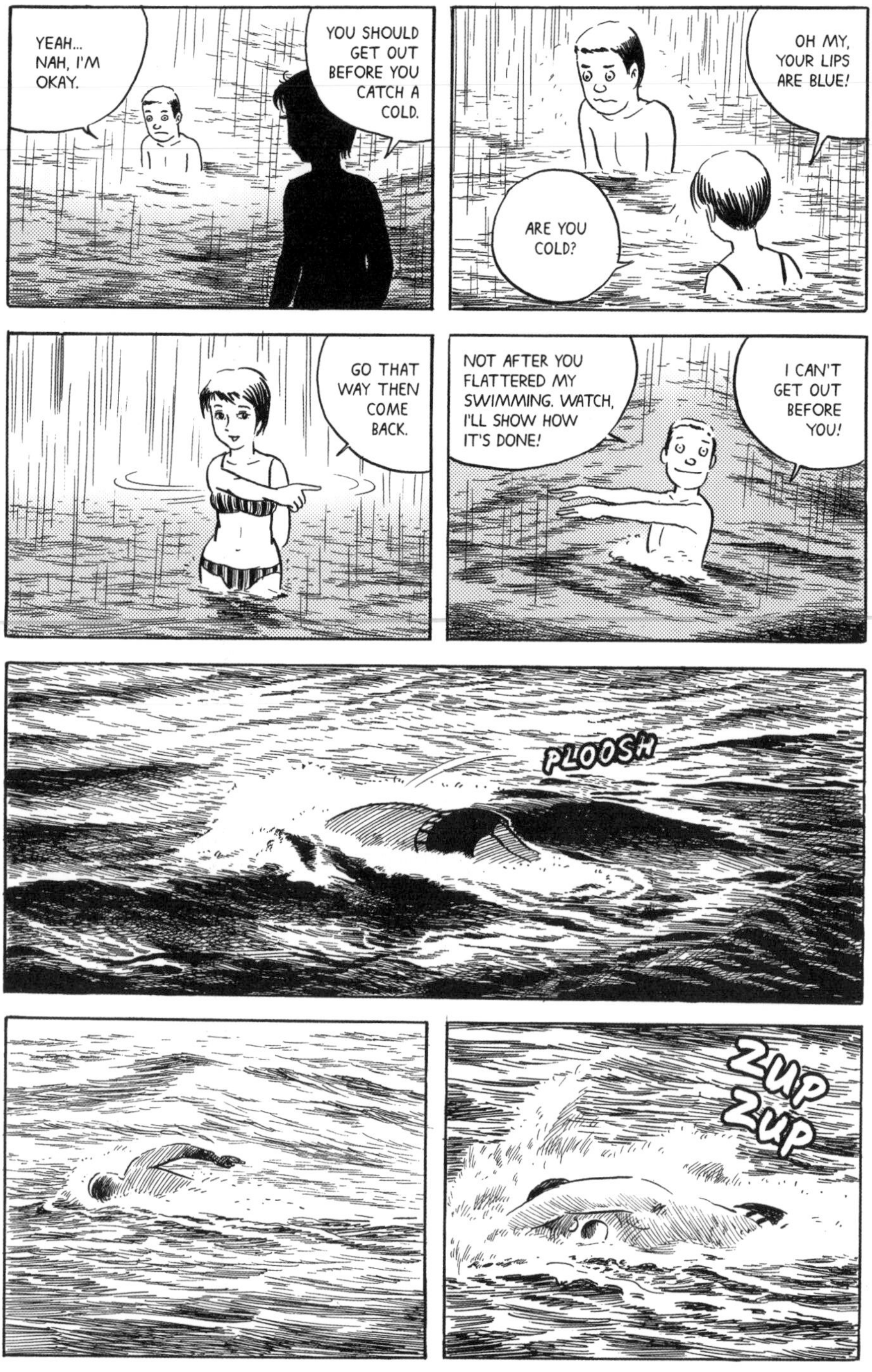
OH MY, YOUR LIPS ARE BLUE!
ARE YOU COLD?
YOU SHOULD GET OUT BEFORE YOU CATCH A COLD.
YEAH... NAH, I'M OKAY.
I CAN'T GET OUT BEFORE YOU!
NOT AFTER YOU FLATTERED MY SWIMMING. WATCH, I'LL SHOW HOW IT'S DONE!
GO THAT WAY THEN COME BACK.
PLOOSH
ZUP ZUP

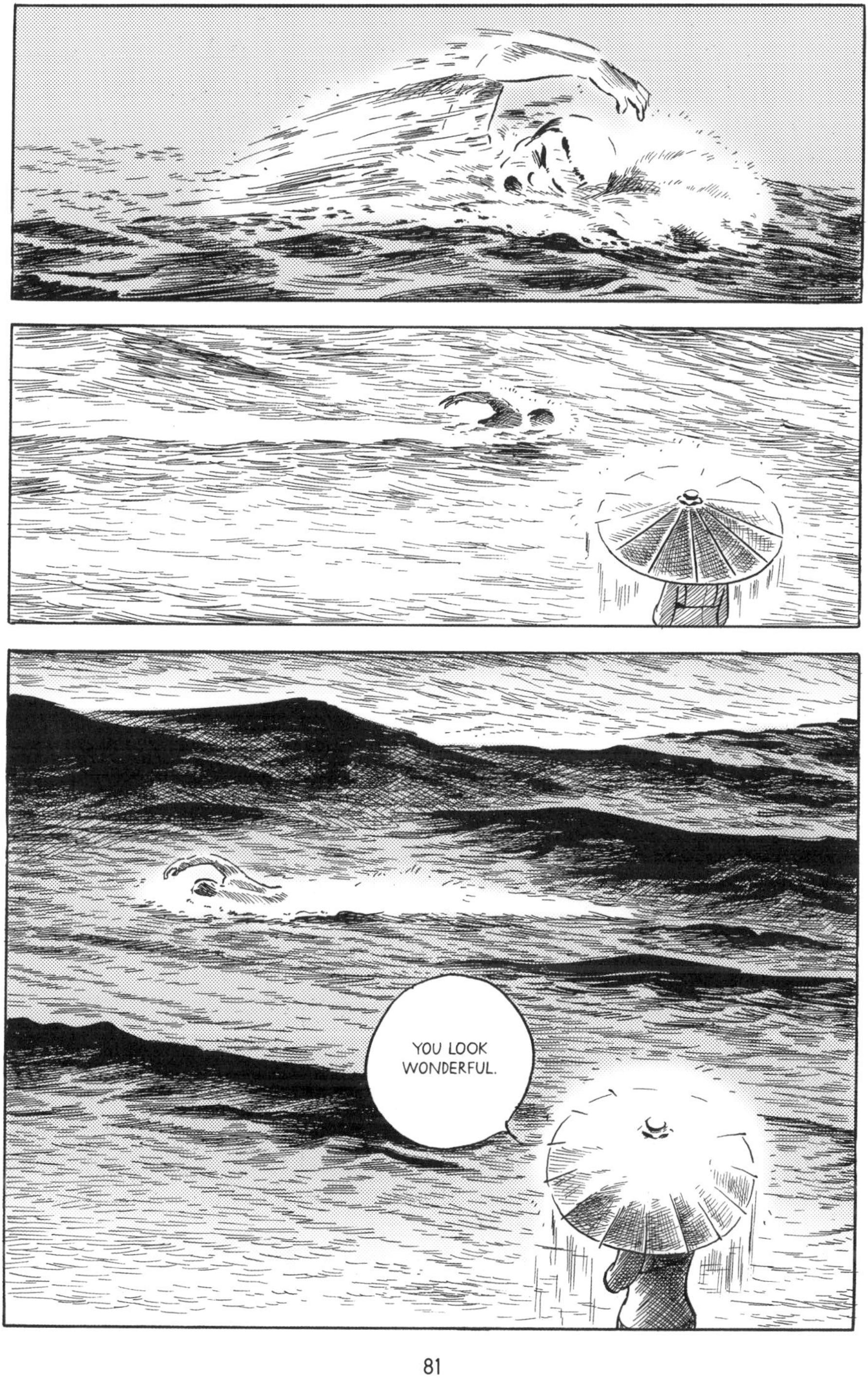
YOU LOOK WONDERFUL.

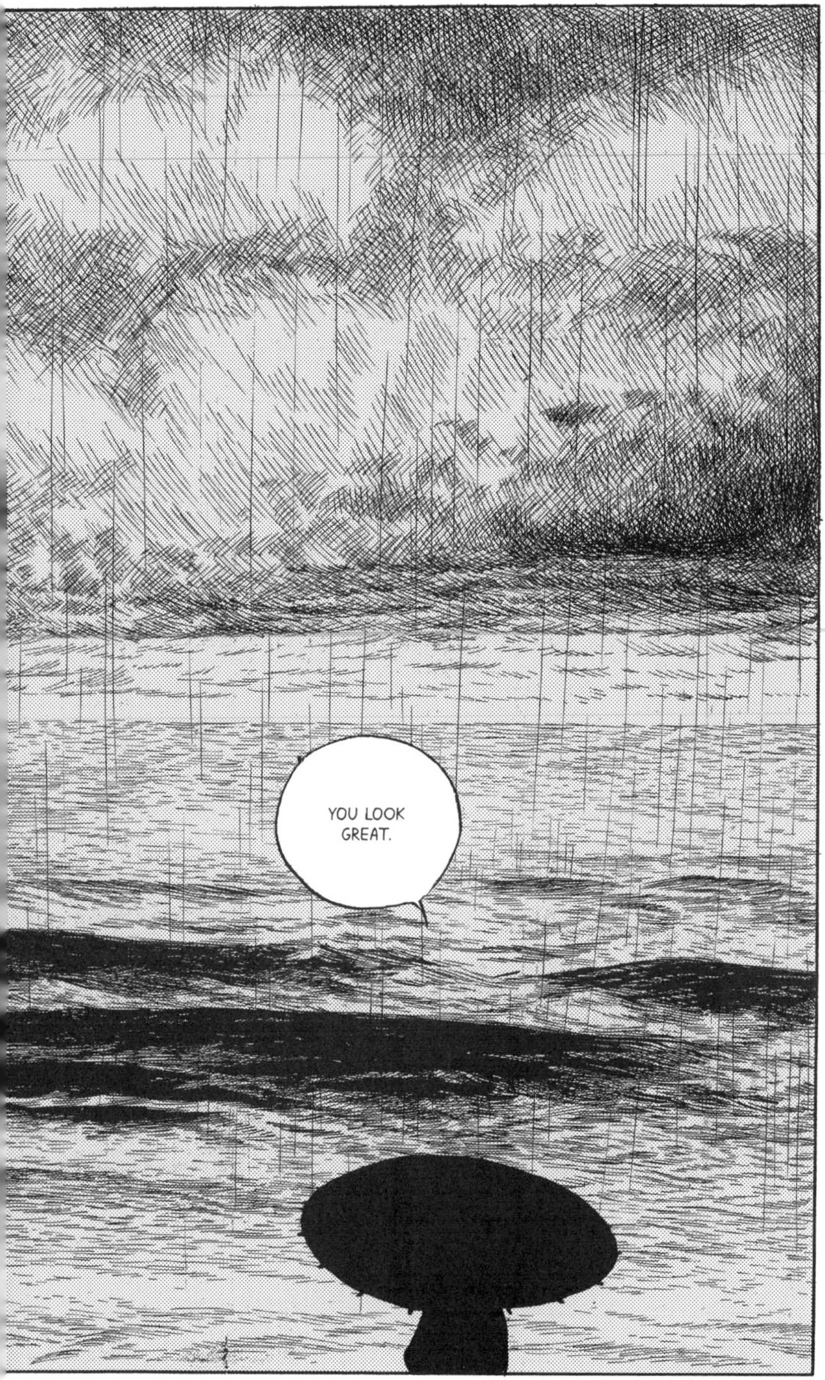
YOU LOOK GREAT.

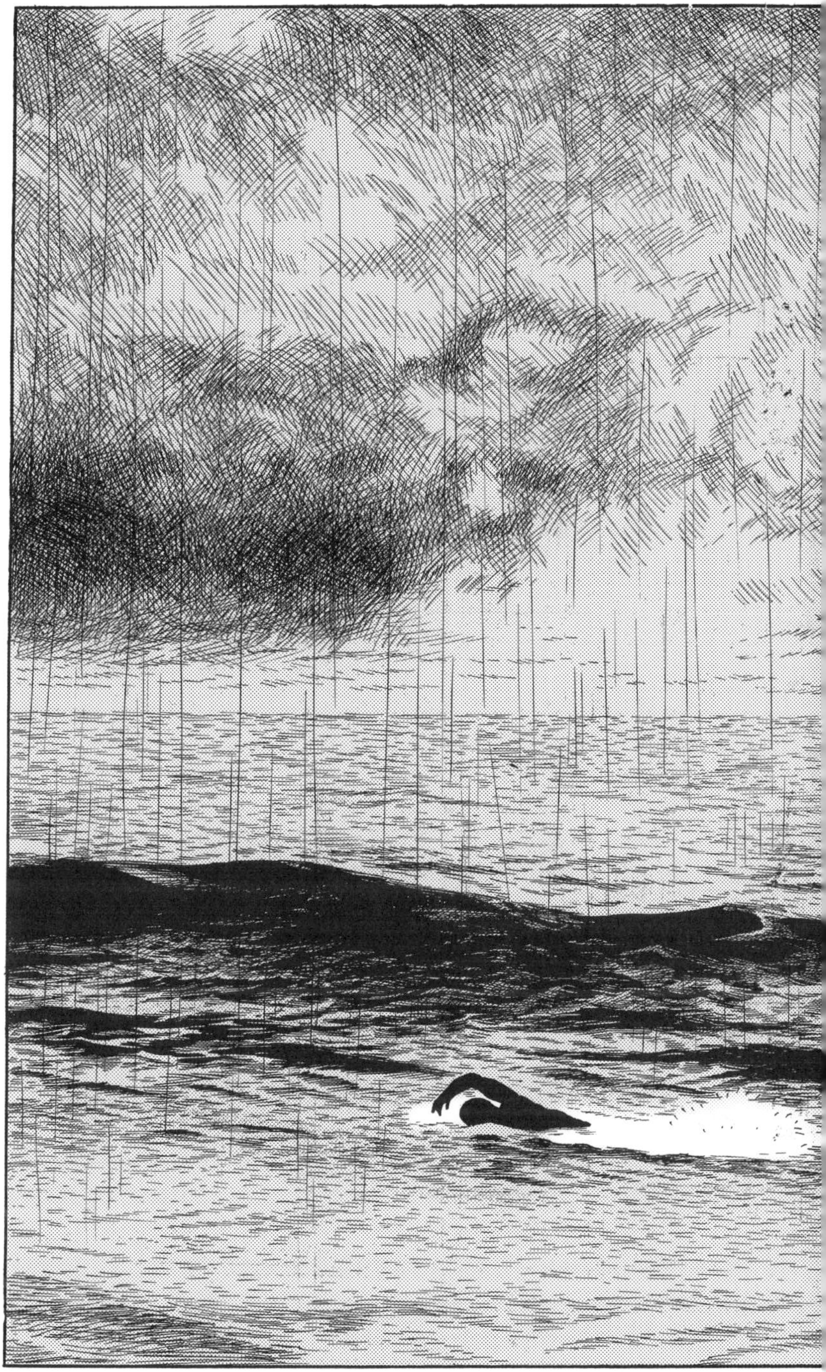

RED FLOWERS

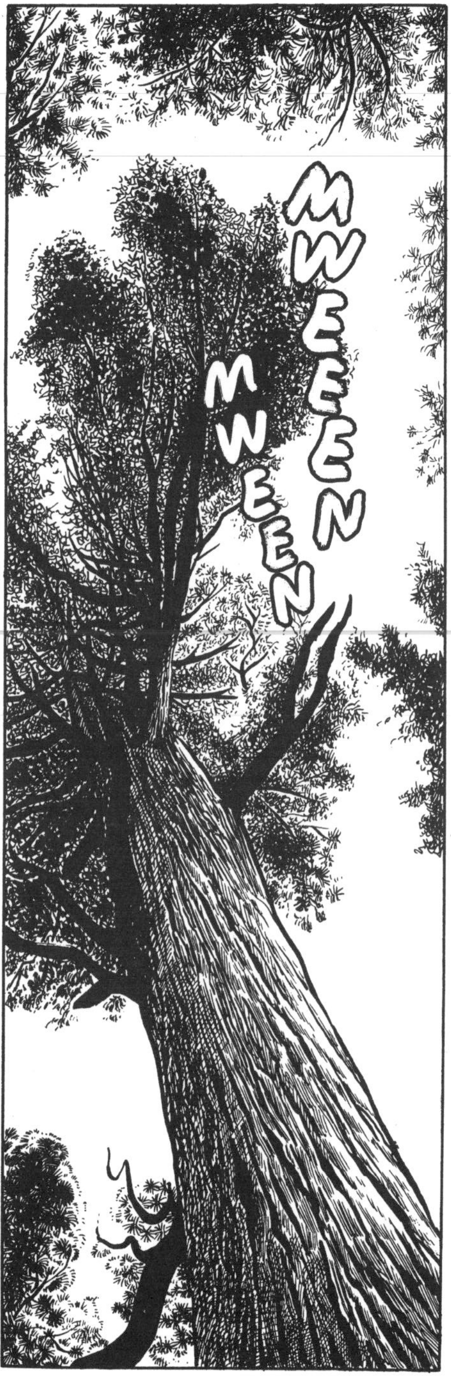
MWEEEN
MWEEN

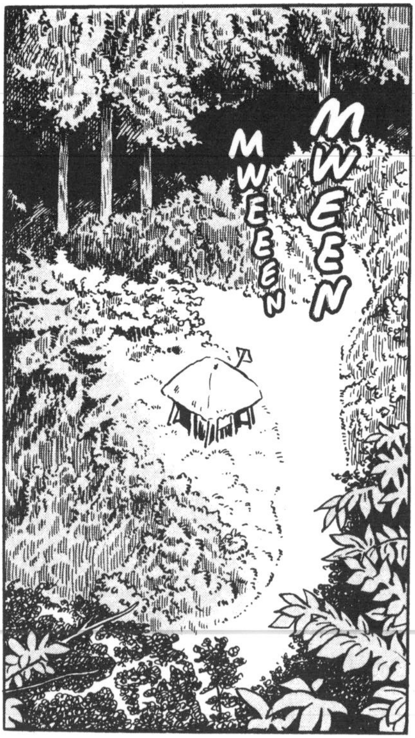
MWEEN
MWEEEN

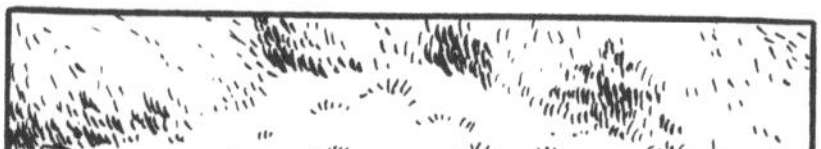
茶

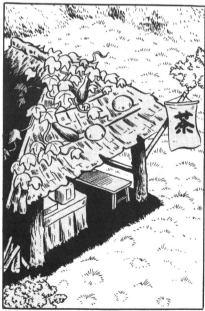

SIGN: TEA

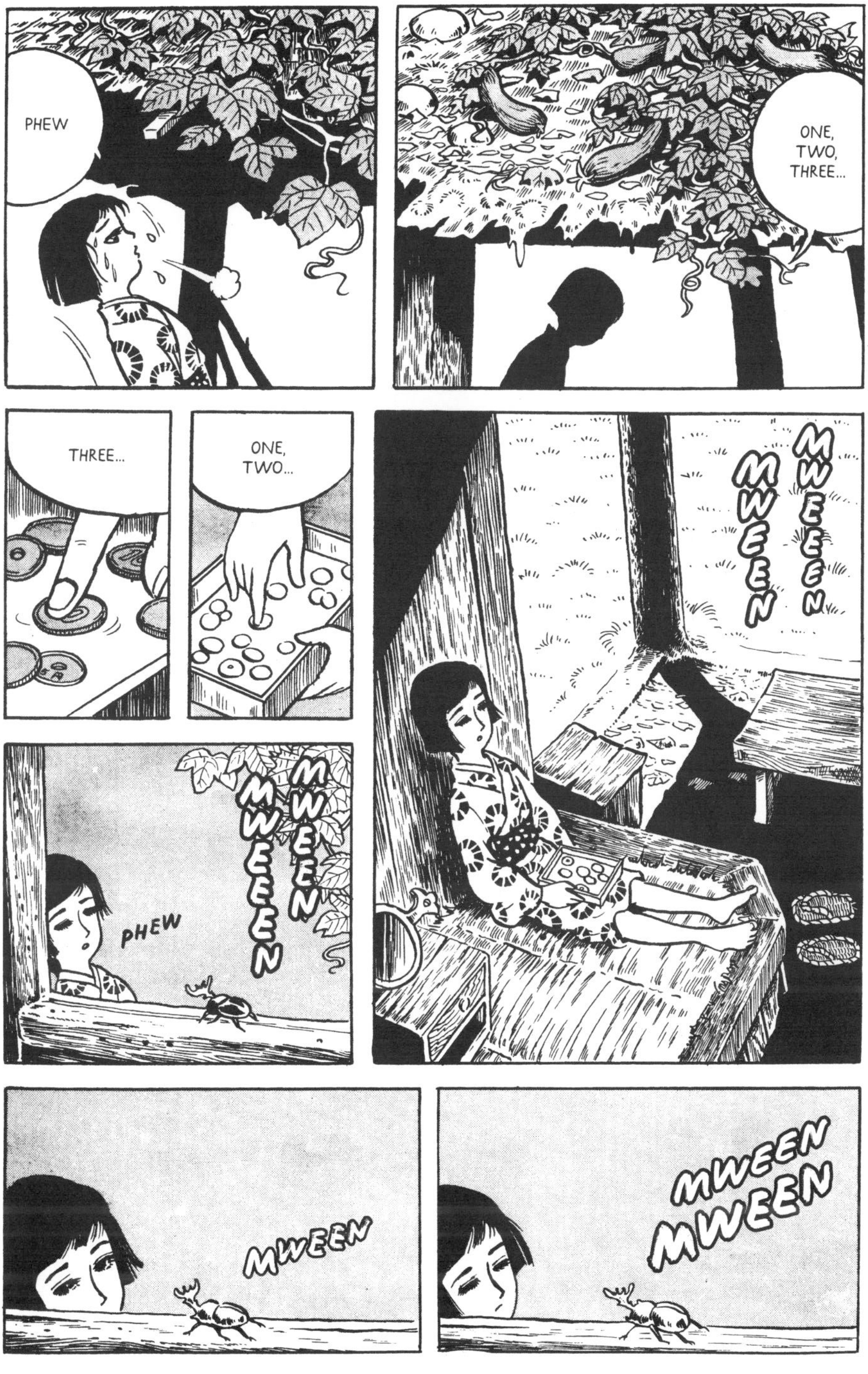

ONE, TWO, THREE...
PHEW
MWEEEN
MWEEN
ONE, TWO...
THREE...
MWEEN
MWEEN
PHEW
MWEEN
MWEEN
MWEEN

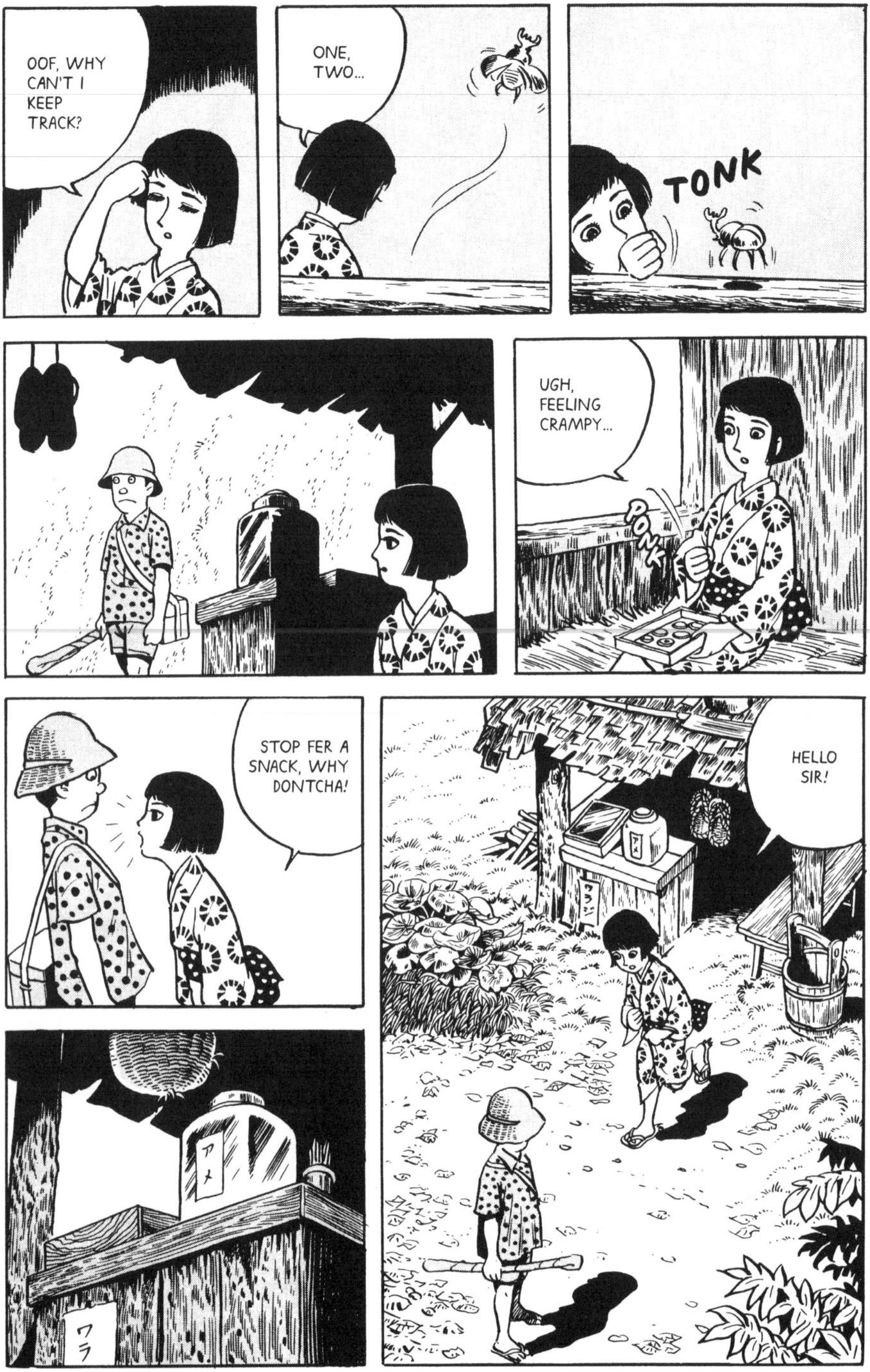
TONK
ONE, TWO...
OOF, WHY CAN'T I KEEP TRACK?
UGH, FEELING CRAMPY...
PONK
HELLO SIR!
STOP FER A SNACK, WHY DONTCHA!
アメ
ワラ
SIGN: STRAW SANDALS / JAR: CANDY

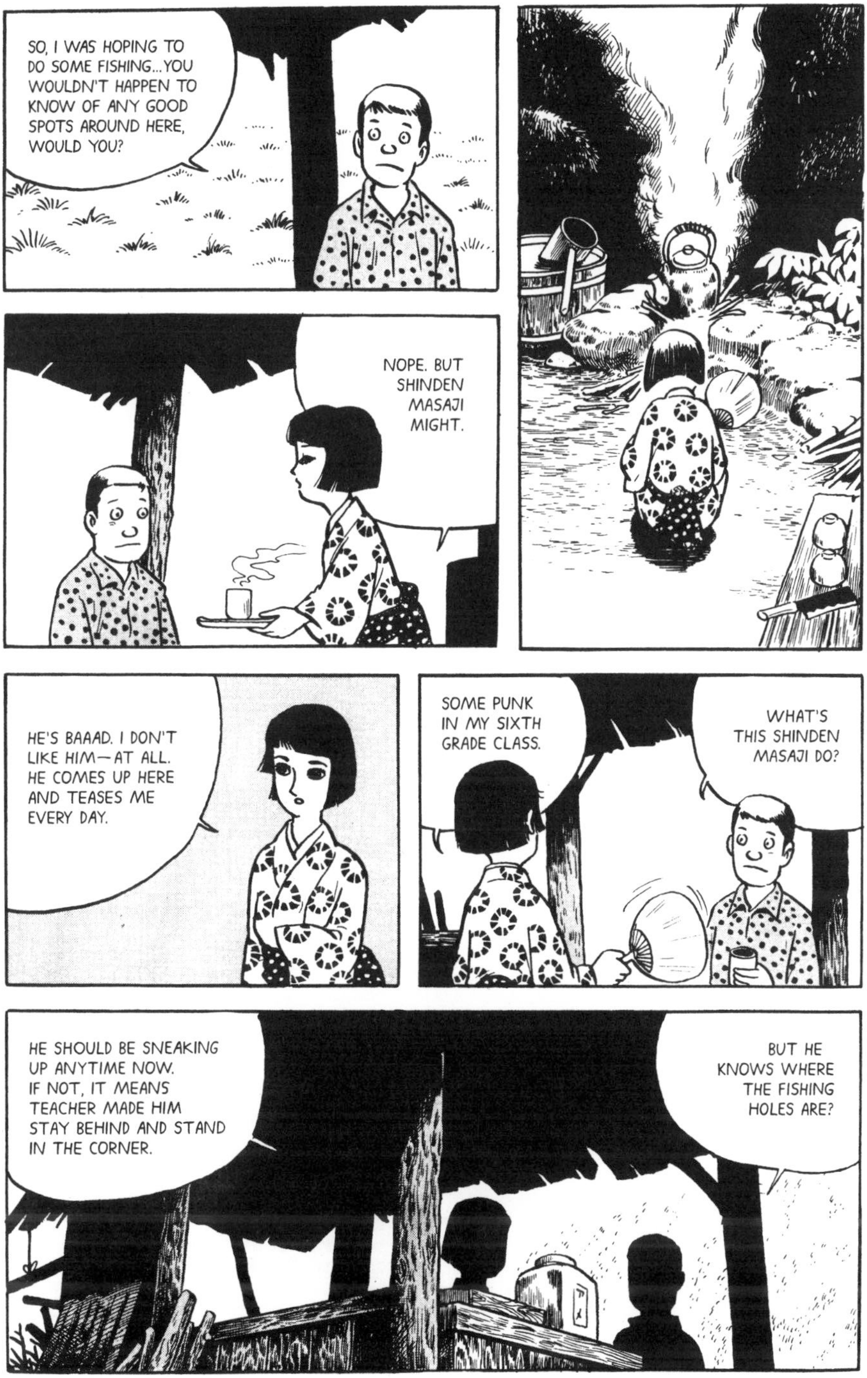
SO, I WAS HOPING TO DO SOME FISHING...YOU WOULDN'T HAPPEN TO KNOW OF ANY GOOD SPOTS AROUND HERE, WOULD YOU?
NOPE. BUT SHINDEN MASAJI MIGHT.
WHAT'S THIS SHINDEN MASAJI DO?
SOME PUNK IN MY SIXTH GRADE CLASS.
HE'S BAAAD. I DON'T LIKE HIM—AT ALL. HE COMES UP HERE AND TEASES ME EVERY DAY.
BUT HE KNOWS WHERE THE FISHING HOLES ARE?
HE SHOULD BE SNEAKING UP ANYTIME NOW. IF NOT, IT MEANS TEACHER MADE HIM STAY BEHIND AND STAND IN THE CORNER.

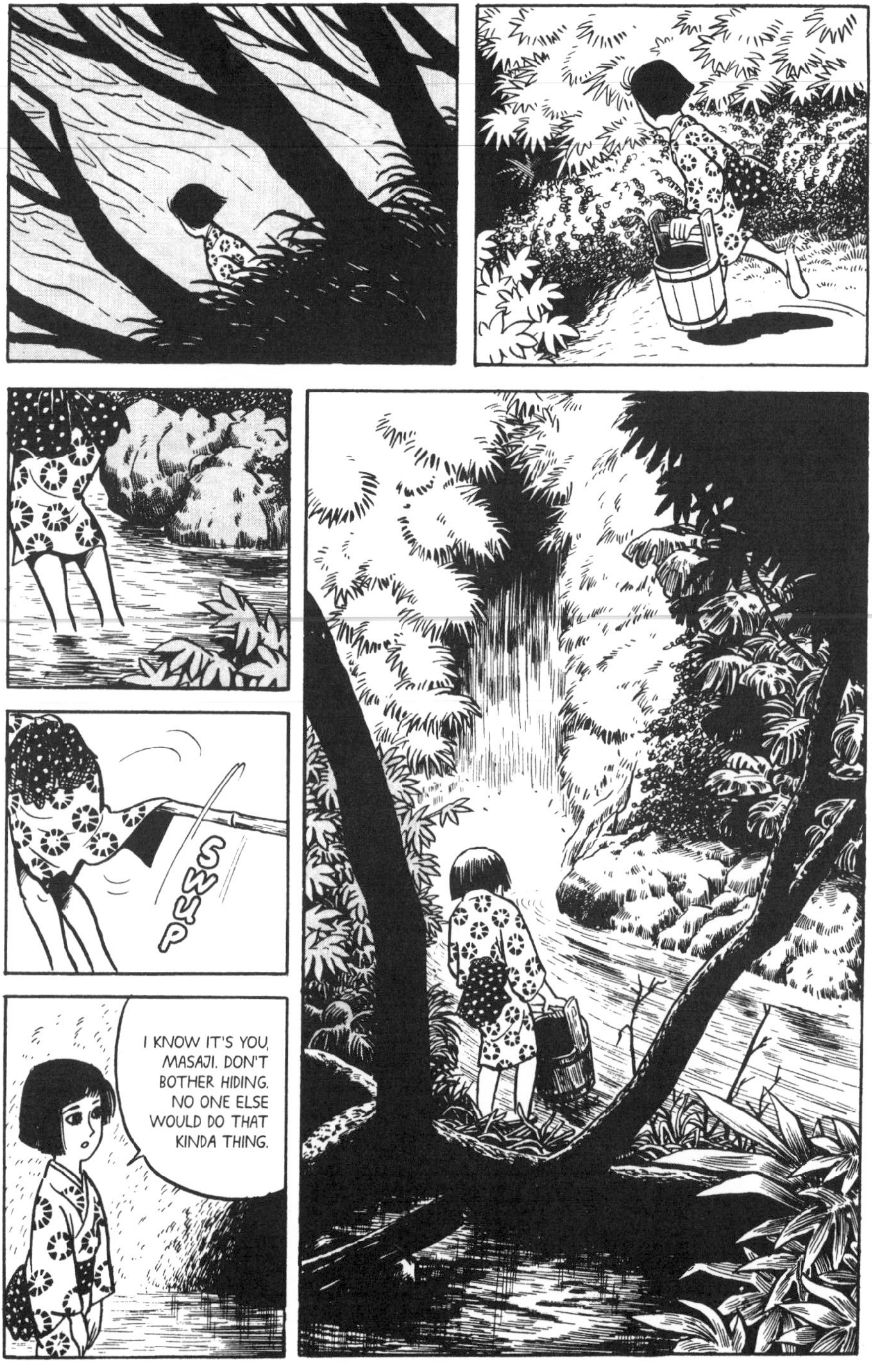
SWUP
I KNOW IT'S YOU, MASAJI. DON'T BOTHER HIDING. NO ONE ELSE WOULD DO THAT KINDA THING.

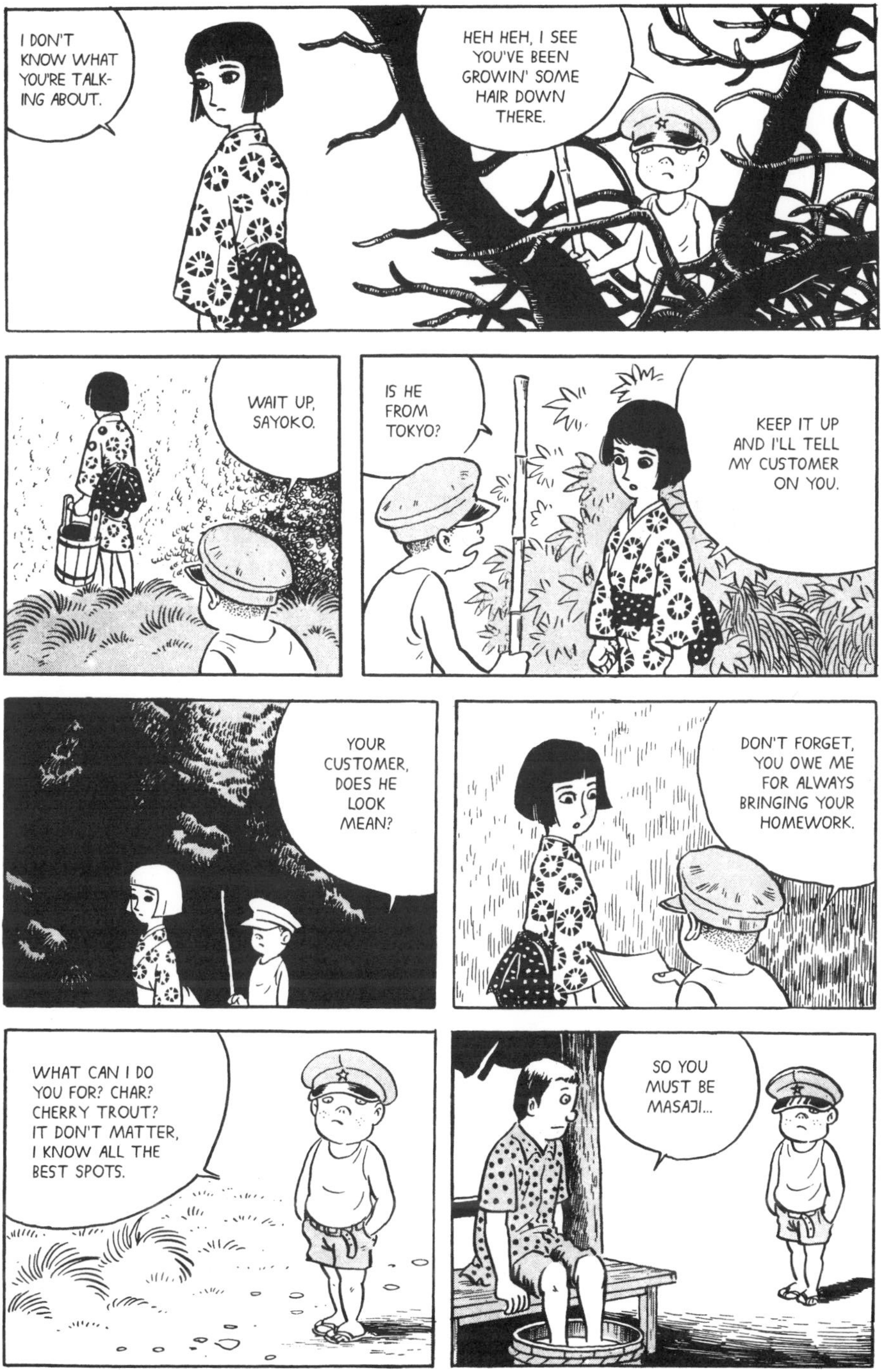
HEH HEH, I SEE YOU'VE BEEN GROWIN' SOME HAIR DOWN THERE.
I DON'T KNOW WHAT YOU'RE TALK-ING ABOUT.
KEEP IT UP AND I'LL TELL MY CUSTOMER ON YOU.
IS HE FROM TOKYO?
WAIT UP, SAYOKO.
DON'T FORGET, YOU OWE ME FOR ALWAYS BRINGING YOUR HOMEWORK.
YOUR CUSTOMER, DOES HE LOOK MEAN?
SO YOU MUST BE MASAJI...
WHAT CAN I DO YOU FOR? CHAR? CHERRY TROUT? IT DON'T MATTER, I KNOW ALL THE BEST SPOTS.

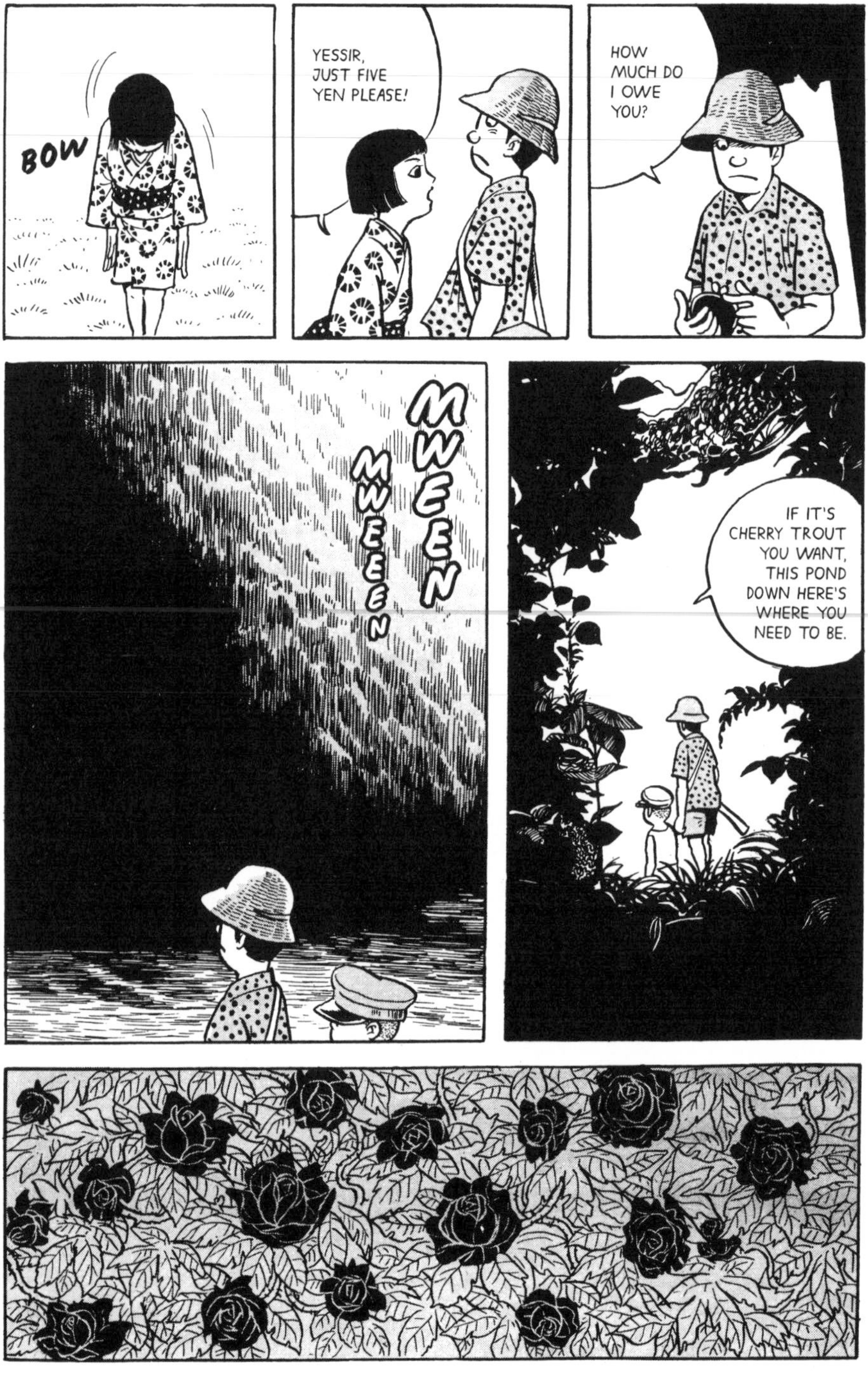
HOW MUCH DO I OWE YOU?
YESSIR, JUST FIVE YEN PLEASE!
BOW
IF IT'S CHERRY TROUT YOU WANT, THIS POND DOWN HERE'S WHERE YOU NEED TO BE.
MWEEN
MWEEEN

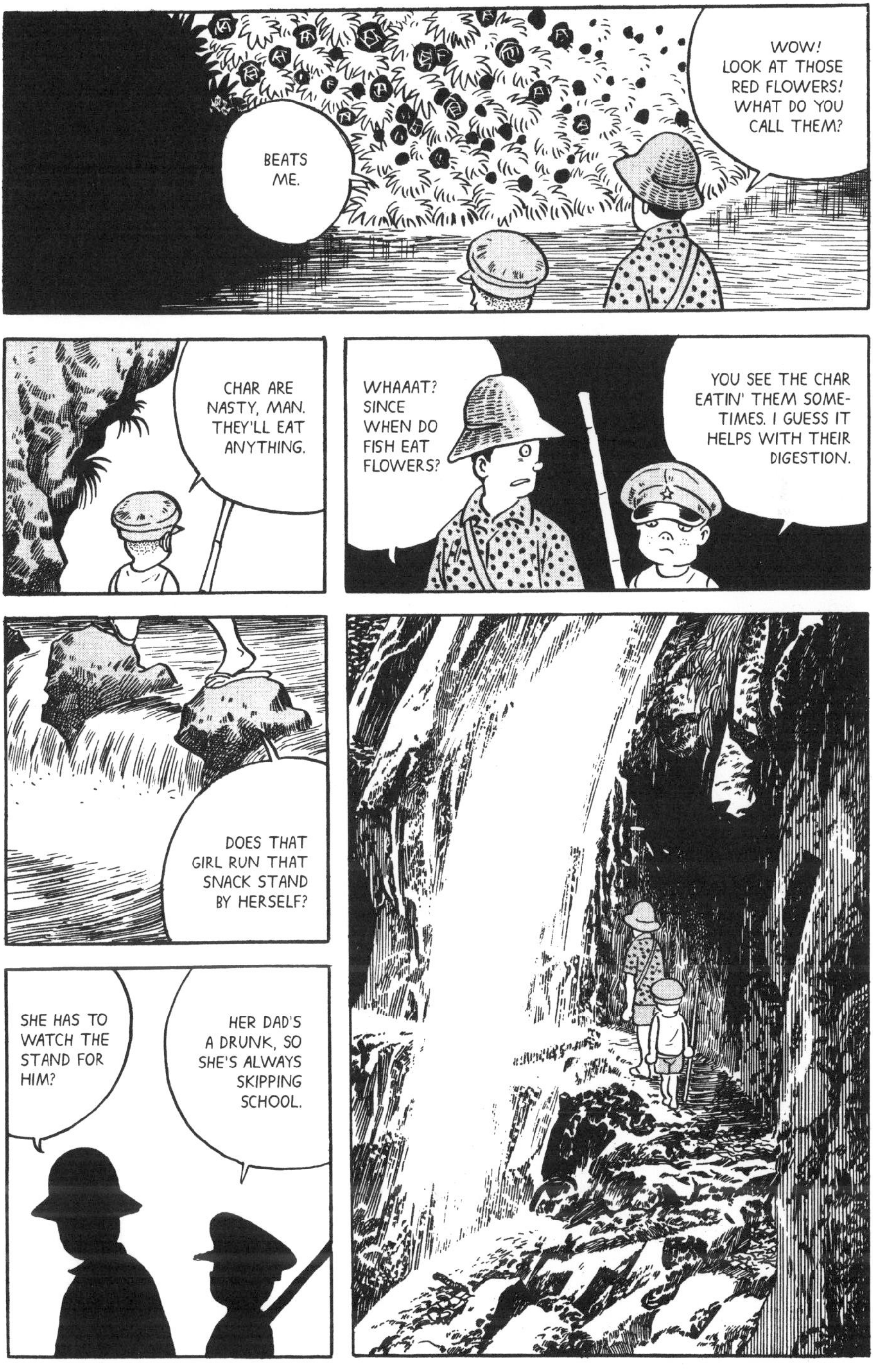
WOW! LOOK AT THOSE RED FLOWERS! WHAT DO YOU CALL THEM?
BEATS ME.
CHAR ARE NASTY, MAN. THEY'LL EAT ANYTHING.
WHAAAT? SINCE WHEN DO FISH EAT FLOWERS?
YOU SEE THE CHAR EATIN' THEM SOME-TIMES. I GUESS IT HELPS WITH THEIR DIGESTION.
DOES THAT GIRL RUN THAT SNACK STAND BY HERSELF?
HER DAD'S A DRUNK, SO SHE'S ALWAYS SKIPPING SCHOOL.
SHE HAS TO WATCH THE STAND FOR HIM?

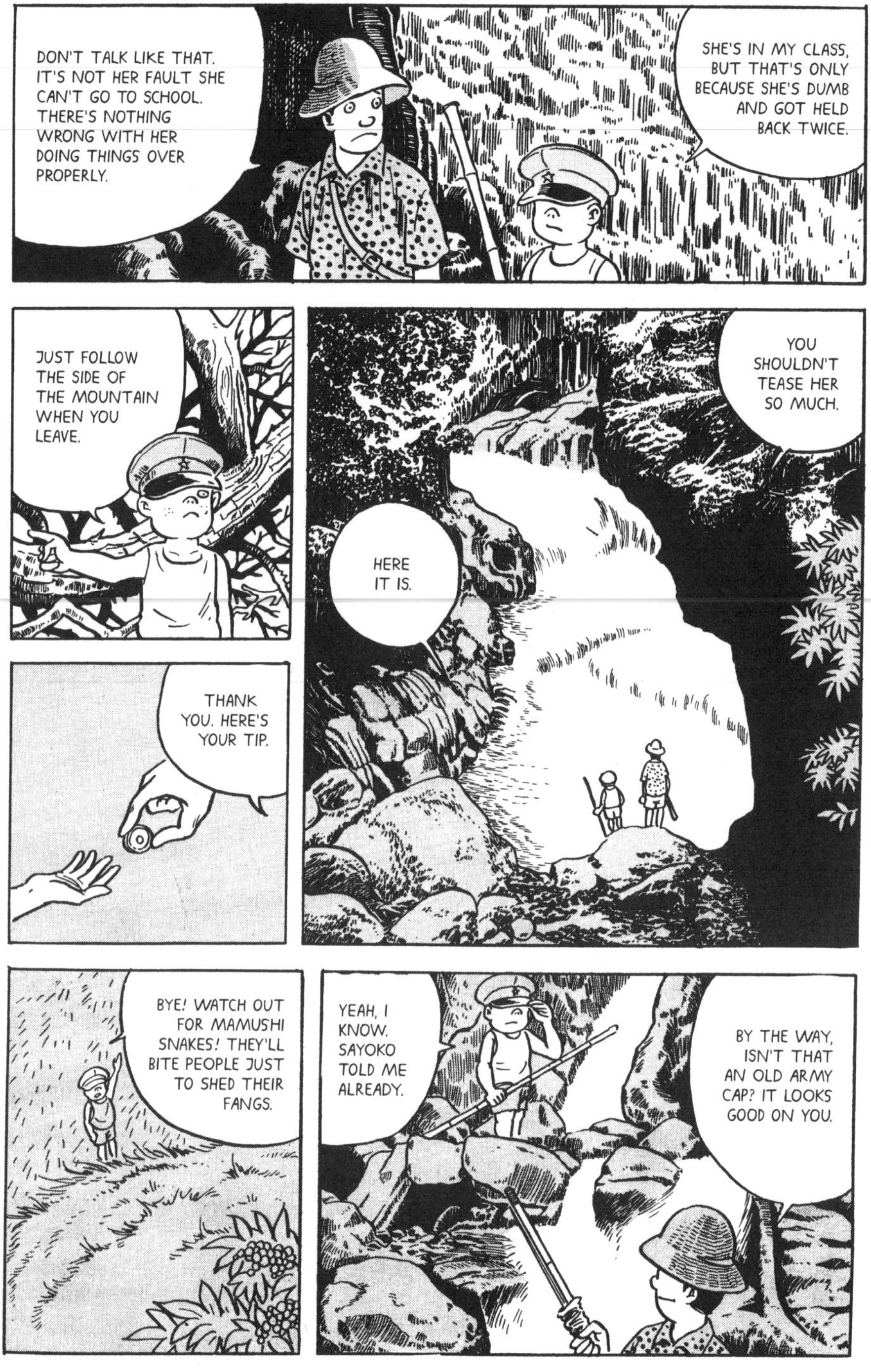
SHE'S IN MY CLASS, BUT THAT'S ONLY BECAUSE SHE'S DUMB AND GOT HELD BACK TWICE.
DON'T TALK LIKE THAT. IT'S NOT HER FAULT SHE CAN'T GO TO SCHOOL. THERE'S NOTHING WRONG WITH HER DOING THINGS OVER PROPERLY.
YOU SHOULDN'T TEASE HER SO MUCH.
HERE IT IS.
JUST FOLLOW THE SIDE OF THE MOUNTAIN WHEN YOU LEAVE.
THANK YOU. HERE'S YOUR TIP.
BY THE WAY, ISN'T THAT AN OLD ARMY CAP? IT LOOKS GOOD ON YOU.
YEAH, I KNOW. SAYOKO TOLD ME ALREADY.
BYE! WATCH OUT FOR MAMUSHI SNAKES! THEY'LL BITE PEOPLE JUST TO SHED THEIR FANGS.

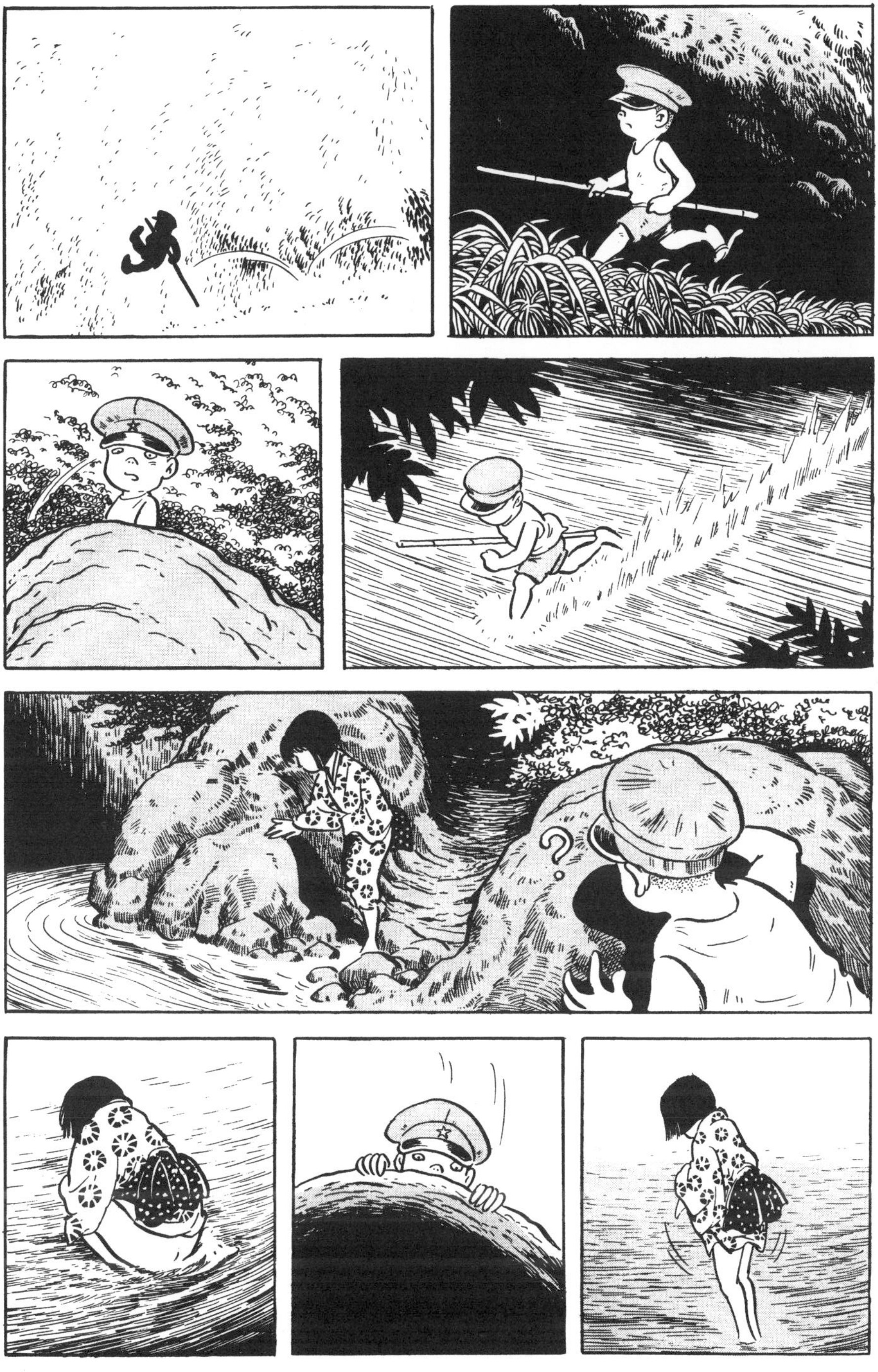

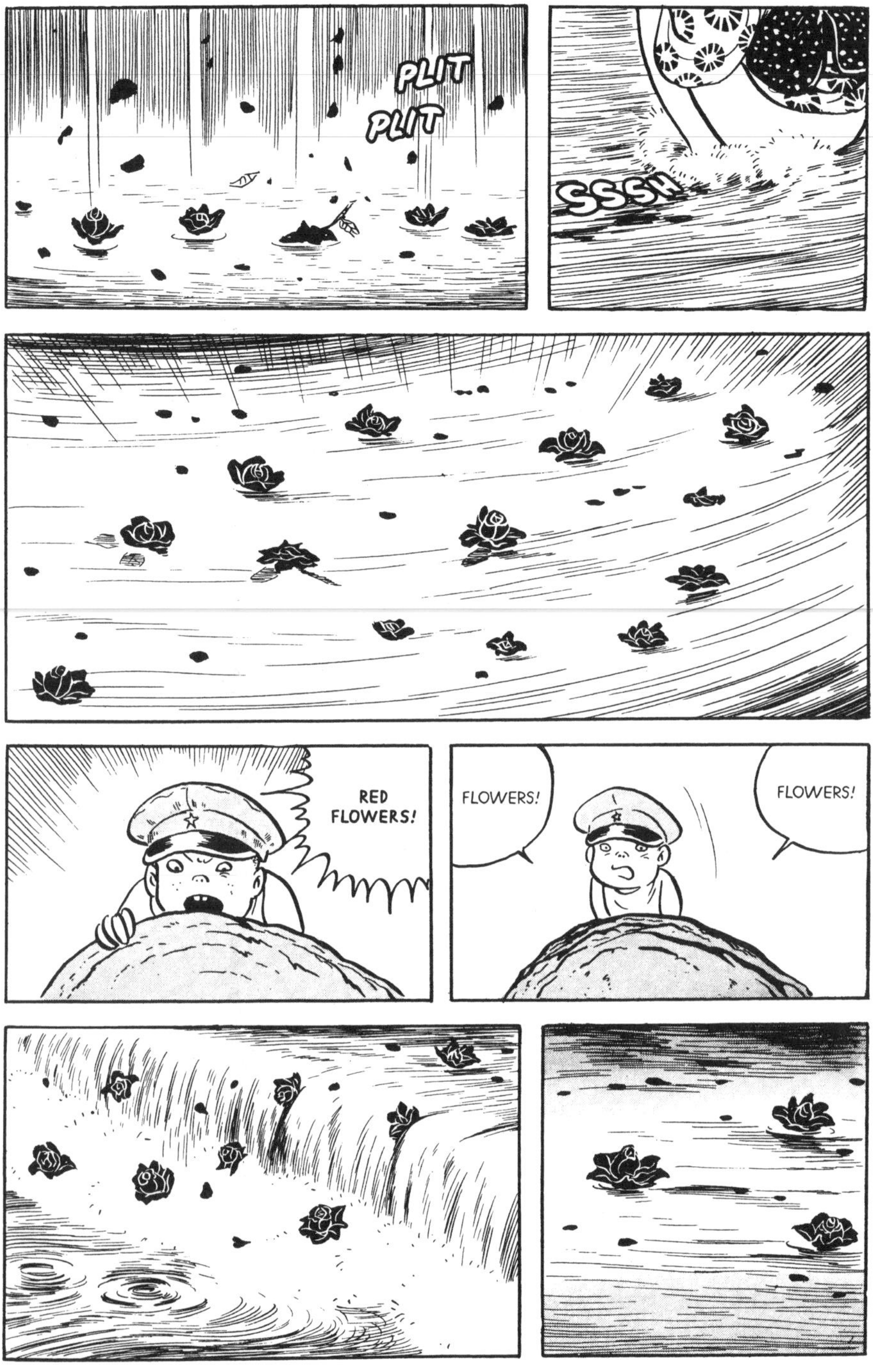
SSSH
PLIT
PLIT
FLOWERS!
FLOWERS!
RED FLOWERS!

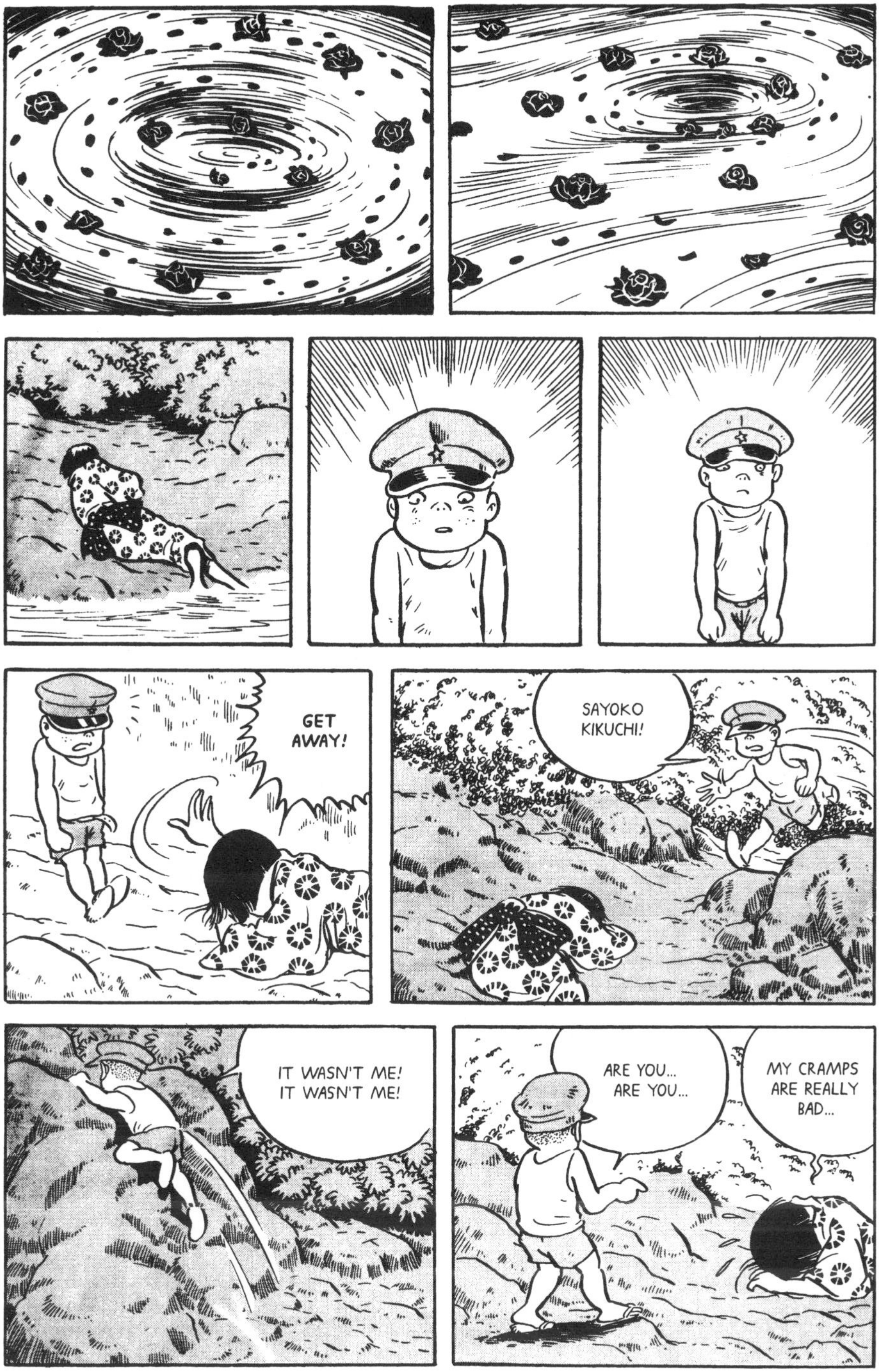
SAYOKO KIKUCHI!
GET AWAY!
MY CRAMPS ARE REALLY BAD...
ARE YOU... ARE YOU...
IT WASN'T ME! IT WASN'T ME!

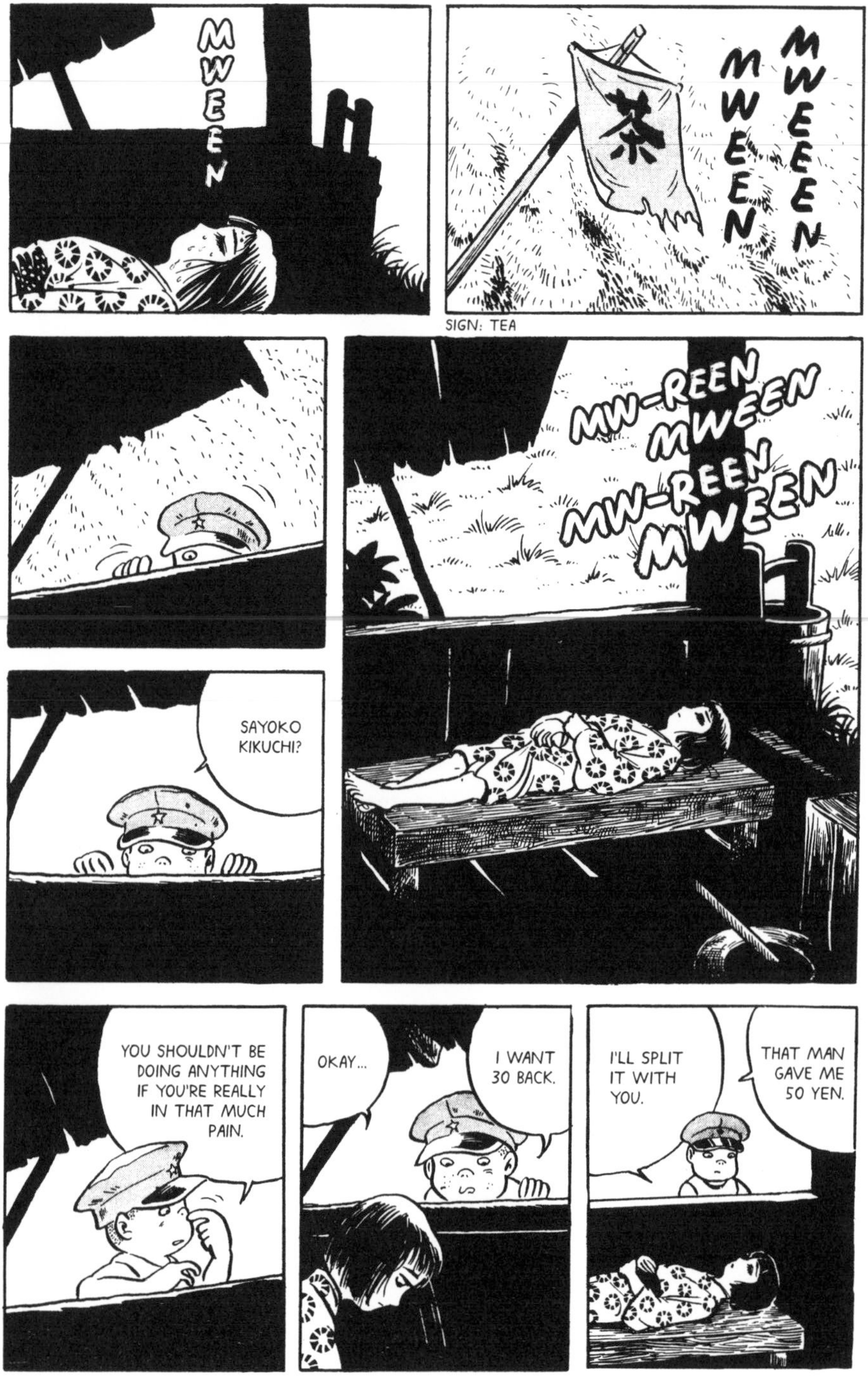
MWEEEN
MWEEN
茶
SIGN: TEA
MWEEN
MW-REEN
MWEEN
MW-REEN
MWEEN
SAYOKO KIKUCHI?
THAT MAN GAVE ME 50 YEN.
I'LL SPLIT IT WITH YOU.
I WANT 30 BACK.
OKAY...
YOU SHOULDN'T BE DOING ANYTHING IF YOU'RE REALLY IN THAT MUCH PAIN.

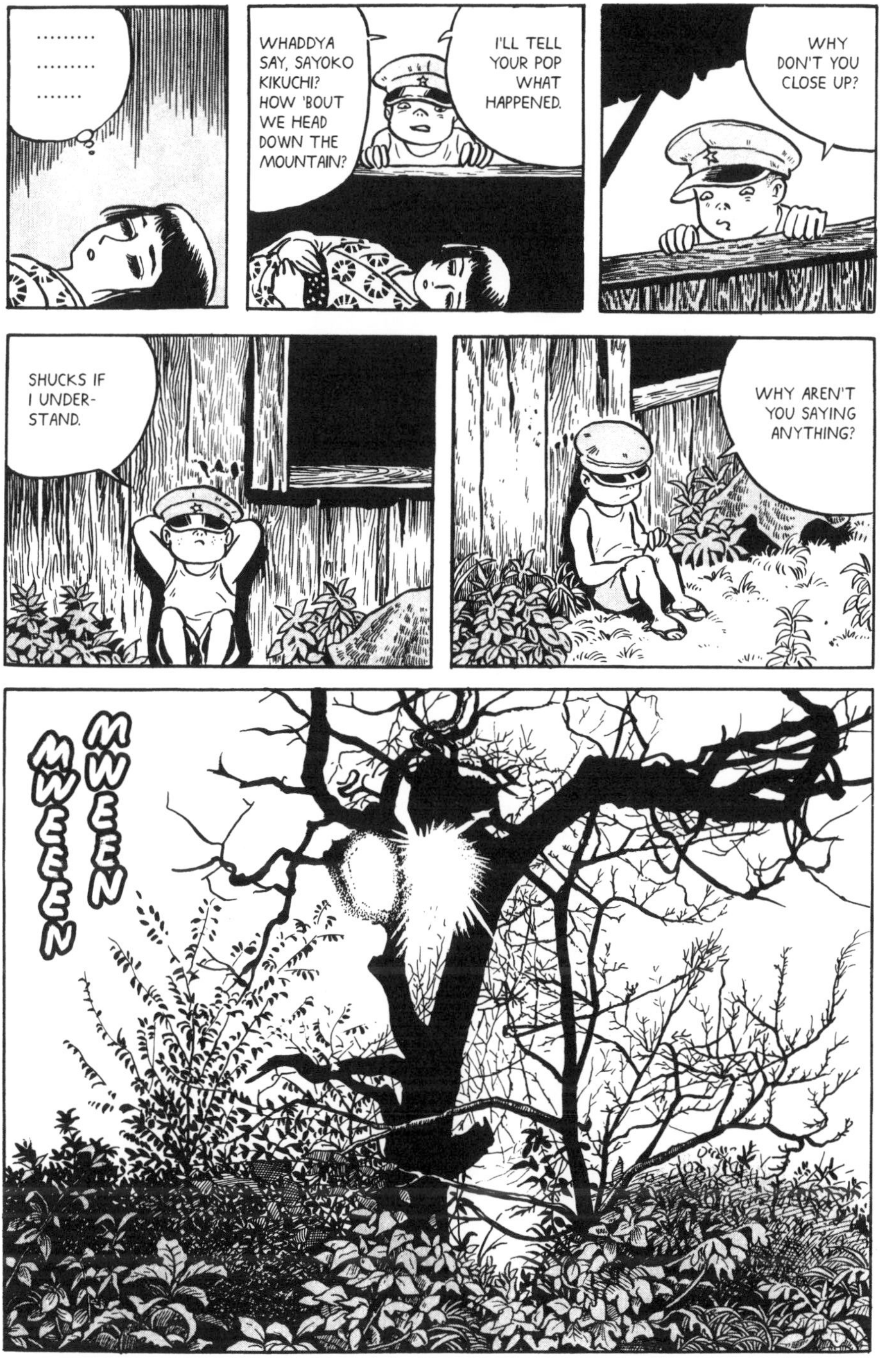
WHY DON'T YOU CLOSE UP?
I'LL TELL YOUR POP WHAT HAPPENED.
WHADDYA SAY, SAYOKO KIKUCHI? HOW 'BOUT WE HEAD DOWN THE MOUNTAIN?
....
WHY AREN'T YOU SAYING ANYTHING?
SHUCKS IF I UNDER-STAND.
MWEEN
MWEEEN

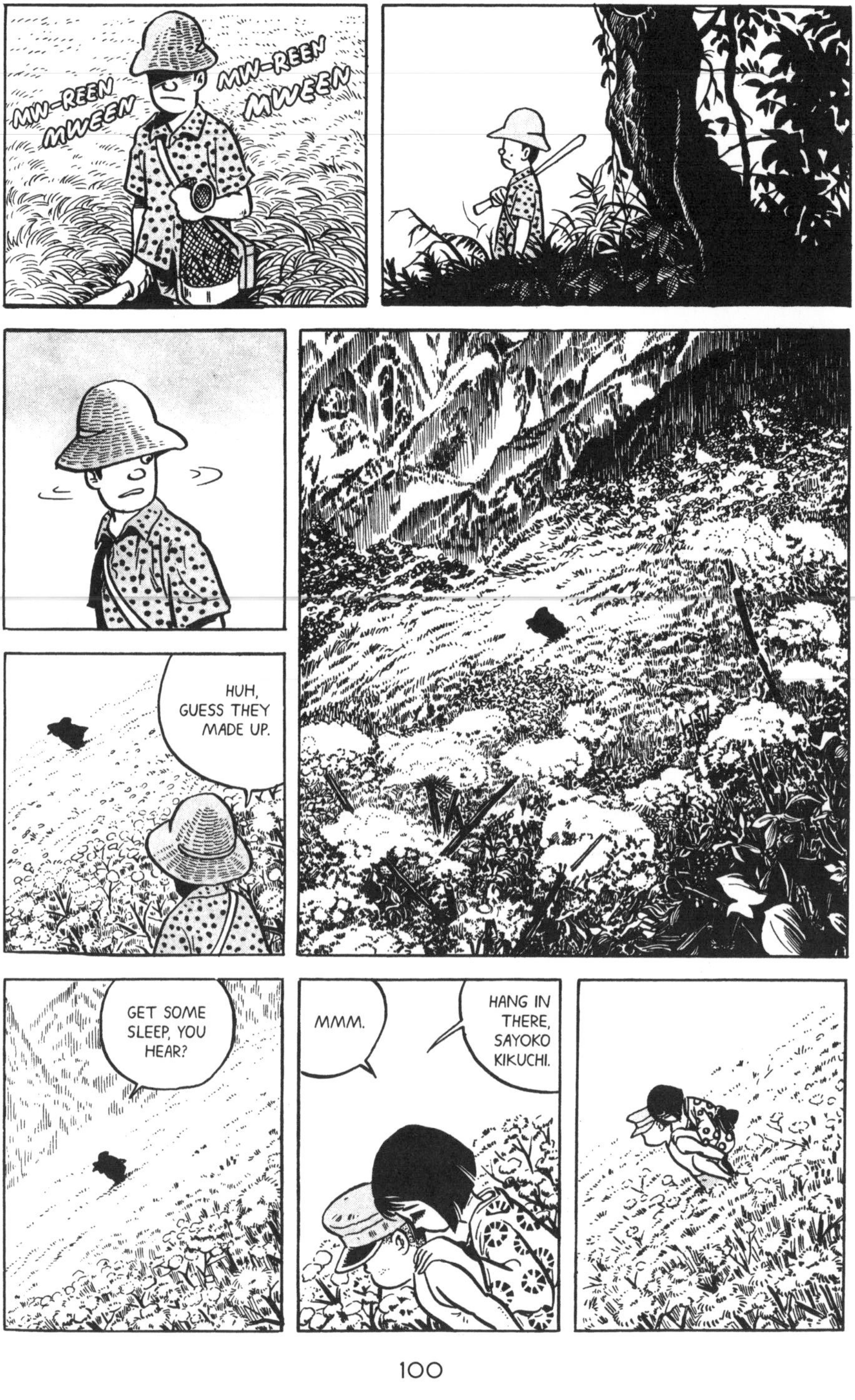
MW-REEN MWEEN
MW-REEN MWEEN
HUH, GUESS THEY MADE UP.
HANG IN THERE, SAYOKO KIKUCHI.
MMM.
GET SOME SLEEP, YOU HEAR?

THE INCIDENT
AT NISHIBETA
VILLAGE

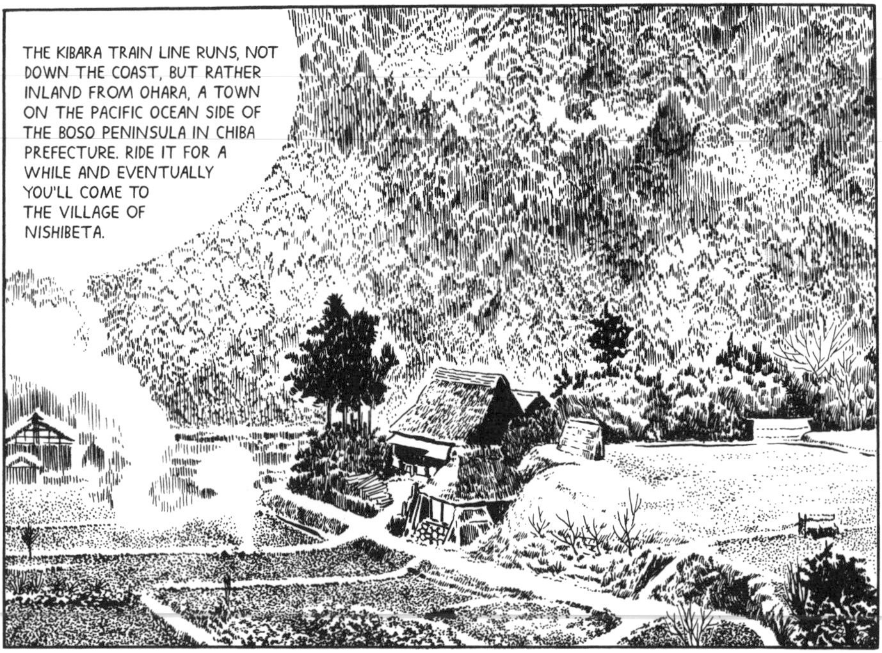
THE KIBARA TRAIN LINE RUNS, NOT DOWN THE COAST, BUT RATHER INLAND FROM OHARA, A TOWN ON THE PACIFIC OCEAN SIDE OF THE BOSO PENINSULA IN CHIBA PREFECTURE. RIDE IT FOR A WHILE AND EVENTUALLY YOU'LL COME TO THE VILLAGE OF NISHIBETA.

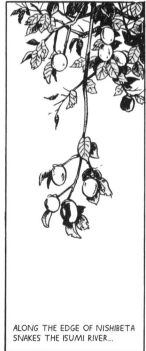

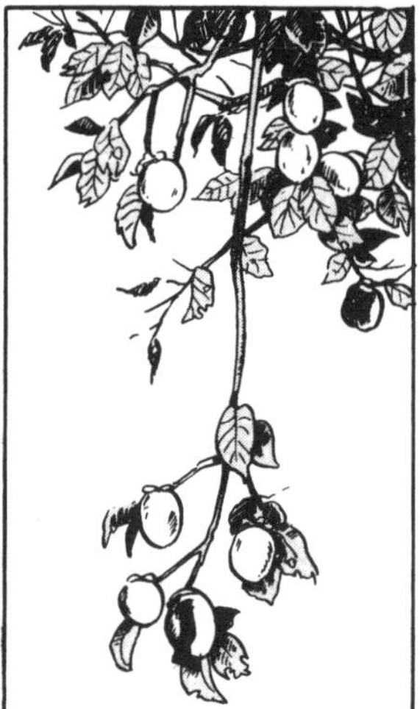
ALONG THE EDGE OF NISHIBETA SNAKES THE ISUMI RIVER...

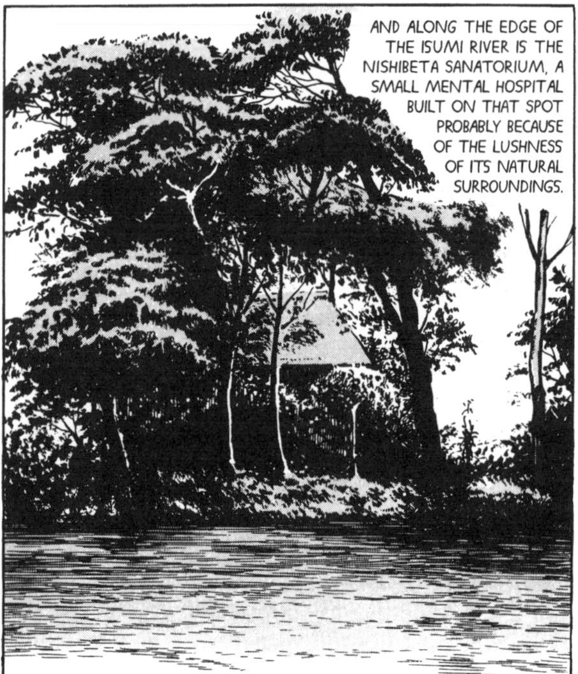
AND ALONG THE EDGE OF THE ISUMI RIVER IS THE NISHIBETA SANATORIUM, A SMALL MENTAL HOSPITAL BUILT ON THAT SPOT PROBABLY BECAUSE OF THE LUSHNESS OF ITS NATURAL SURROUNDINGS.

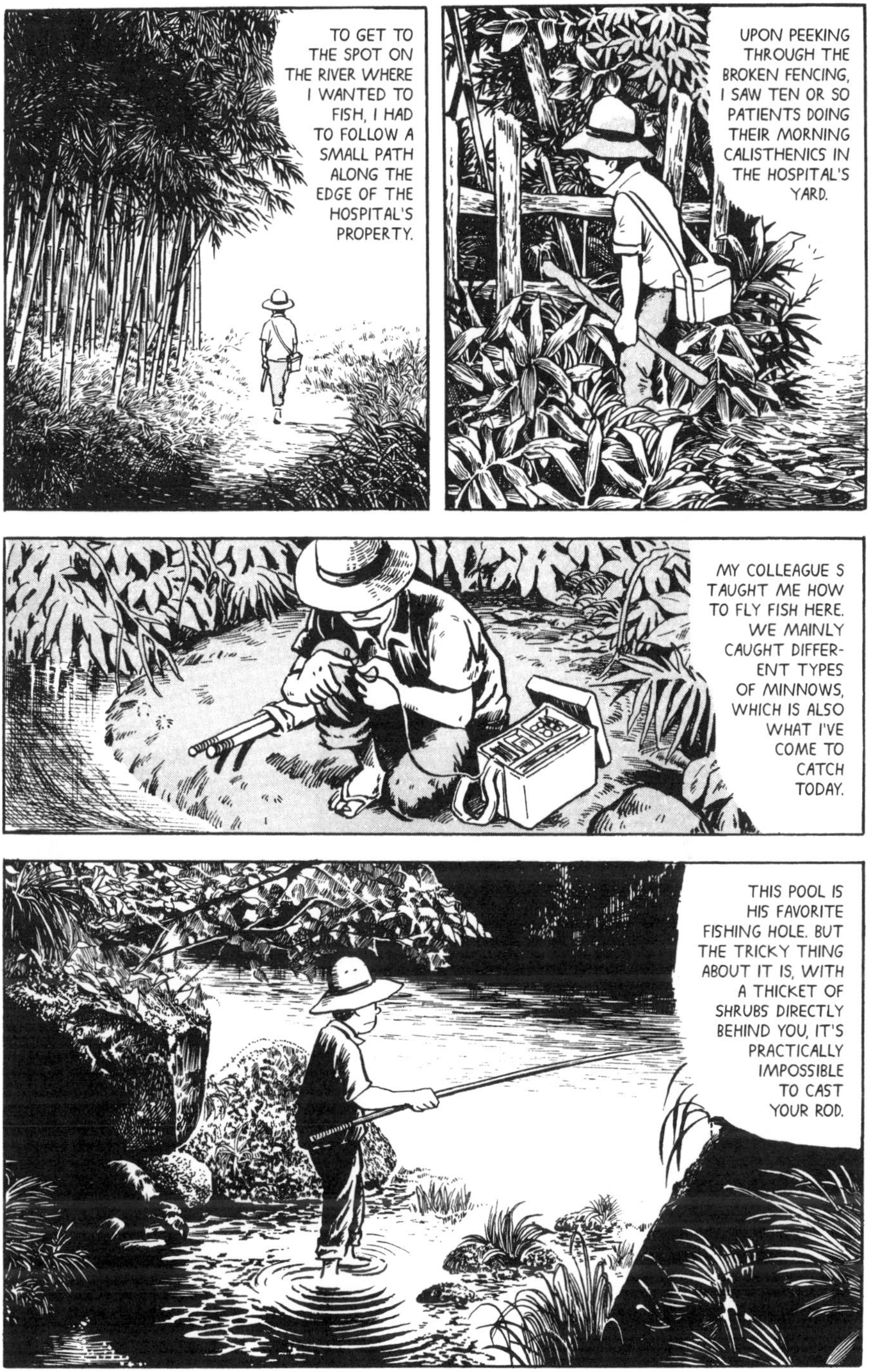
UPON PEEKING THROUGH THE BROKEN FENCING, I SAW TEN OR SO PATIENTS DOING THEIR MORNING CALISTHENICS IN THE HOSPITAL'S YARD.
TO GET TO THE SPOT ON THE RIVER WHERE I WANTED TO FISH, I HAD TO FOLLOW A SMALL PATH ALONG THE EDGE OF THE HOSPITAL'S PROPERTY.
MY COLLEAGUE S TAUGHT ME HOW TO FLY FISH HERE. WE MAINLY CAUGHT DIFFER-ENT TYPES OF MINNOWS, WHICH IS ALSO WHAT I'VE COME TO CATCH TODAY.
THIS POOL IS HIS FAVORITE FISHING HOLE. BUT THE TRICKY THING ABOUT IT IS, WITH A THICKET OF SHRUBS DIRECTLY BEHIND YOU, IT'S PRACTICALLY IMPOSSIBLE TO CAST YOUR ROD.

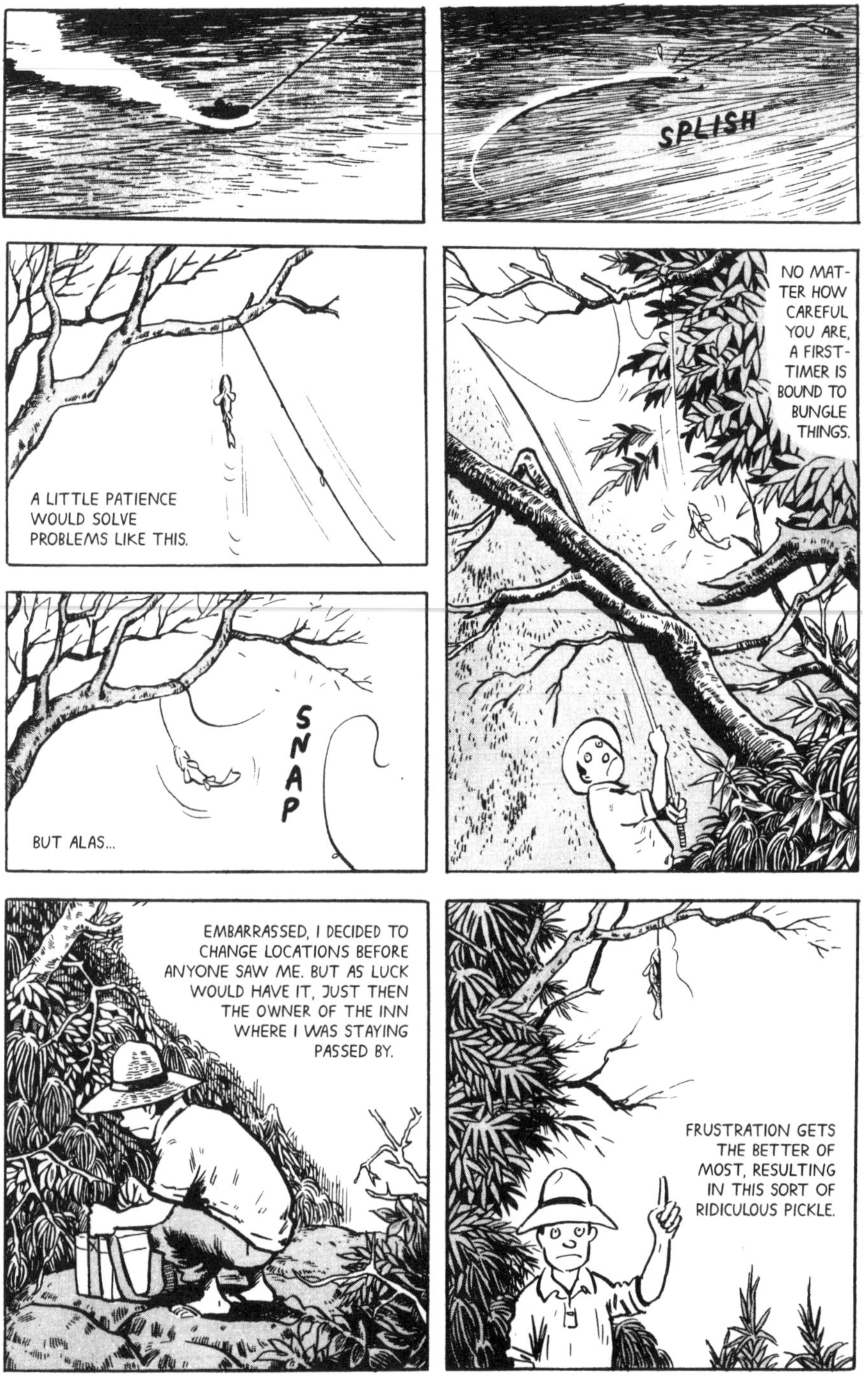
SPLISH
NO MATTER HOW CAREFUL YOU ARE, A FIRST-TIMER IS BOUND TO BUNGLE THINGS.
A LITTLE PATIENCE WOULD SOLVE PROBLEMS LIKE THIS.
SNAP
BUT ALAS...
FRUSTRATION GETS THE BETTER OF MOST, RESULTING IN THIS SORT OF RIDICULOUS PICKLE.
EMBARRASSED, I DECIDED TO CHANGE LOCATIONS BEFORE ANYONE SAW ME. BUT AS LUCK WOULD HAVE IT, JUST THEN THE OWNER OF THE INN WHERE I WAS STAYING PASSED BY.

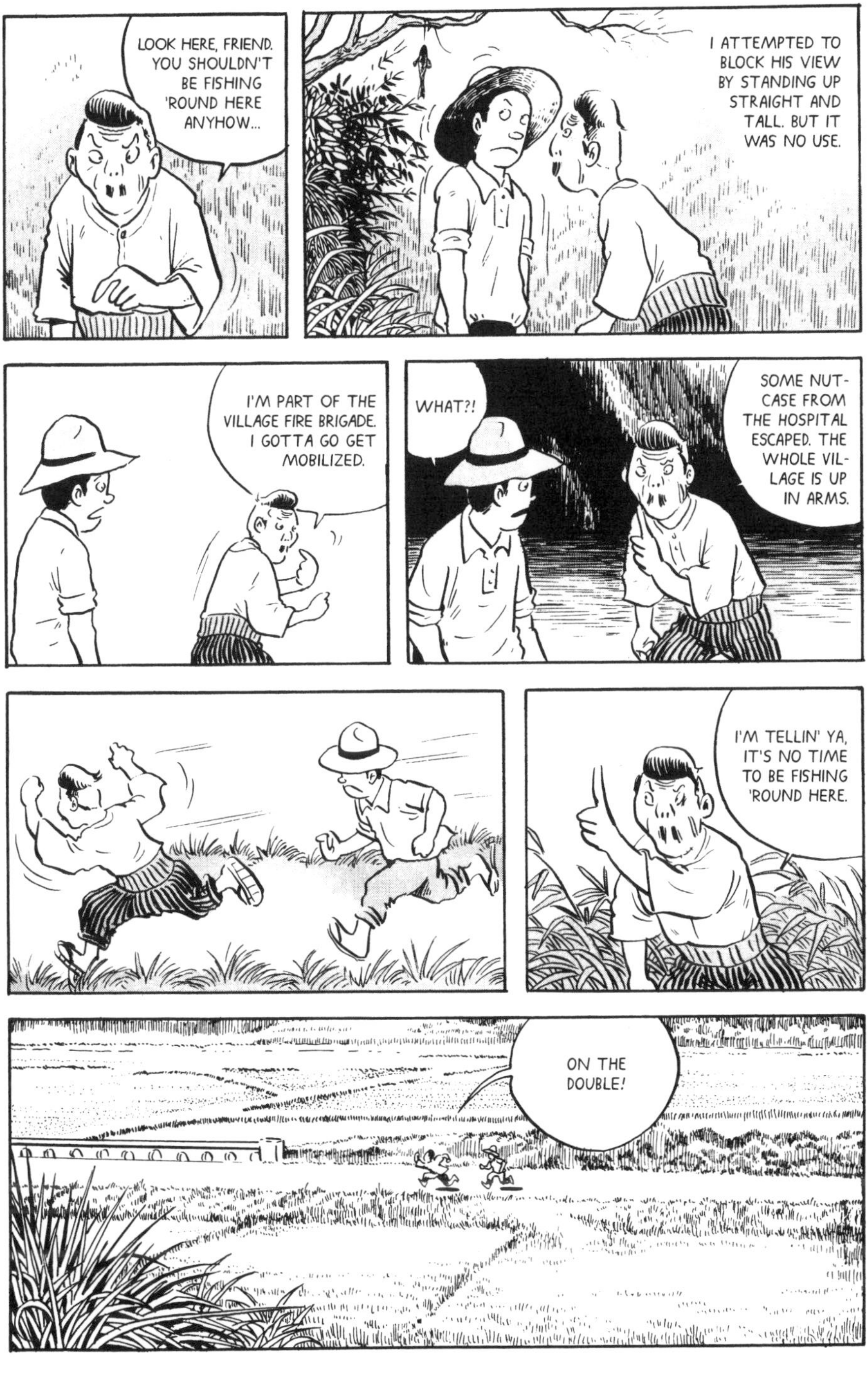
I ATTEMPTED TO BLOCK HIS VIEW BY STANDING UP STRAIGHT AND TALL. BUT IT WAS NO USE.
LOOK HERE, FRIEND. YOU SHOULDN'T BE FISHING 'ROUND HERE ANYHOW...
SOME NUT-CASE FROM THE HOSPITAL ESCAPED. THE WHOLE VILLAGE IS UP IN ARMS.
WHAT?!
I'M PART OF THE VILLAGE FIRE BRIGADE. I GOTTA GO GET MOBILIZED.
I'M TELLIN' YA, IT'S NO TIME TO BE FISHING 'ROUND HERE.
ON THE DOUBLE!

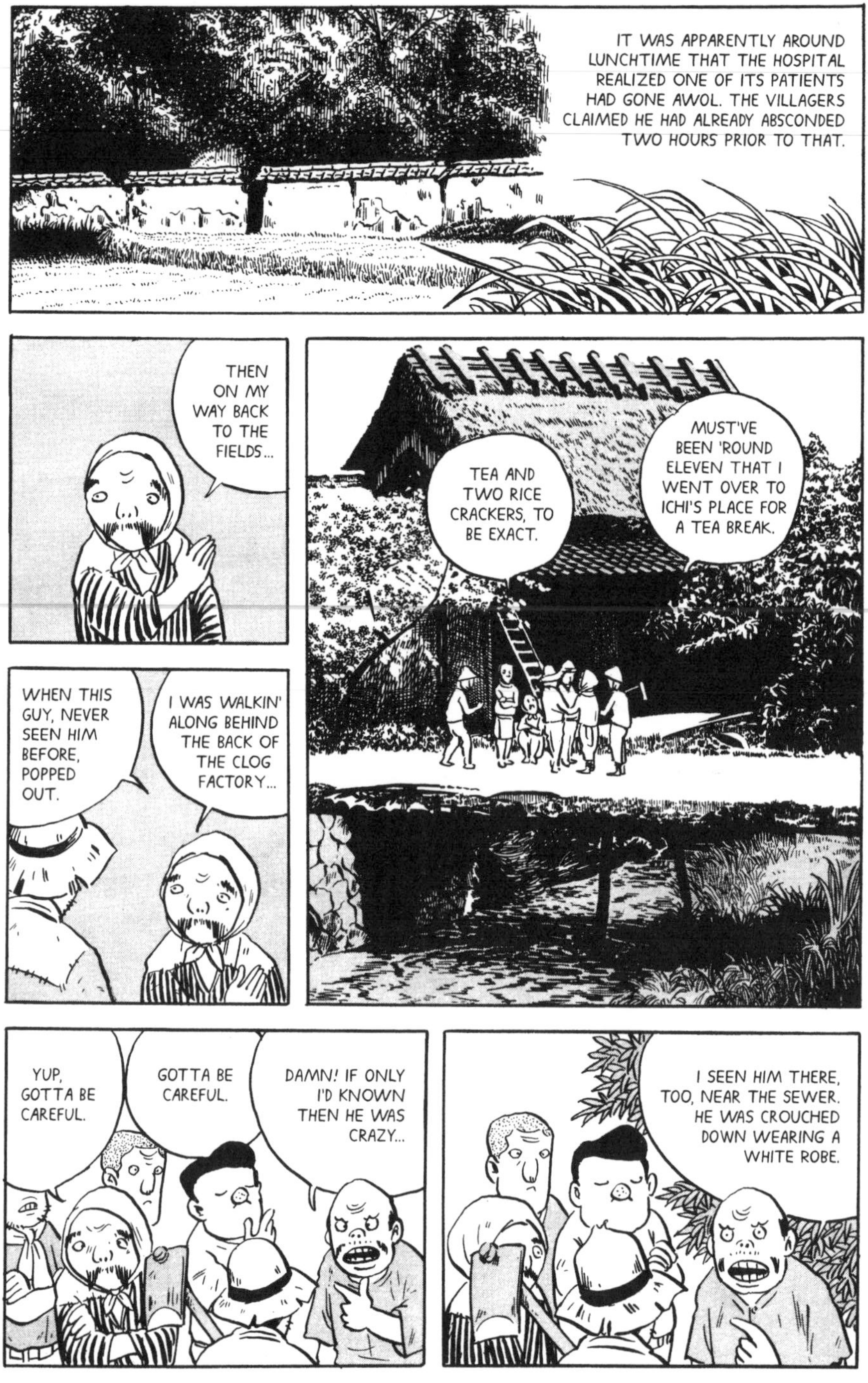
IT WAS APPARENTLY AROUND LUNCHTIME THAT THE HOSPITAL REALIZED ONE OF ITS PATIENTS HAD GONE AWOL. THE VILLAGERS CLAIMED HE HAD ALREADY ABSCONDED TWO HOURS PRIOR TO THAT.
MUST'VE BEEN 'ROUND ELEVEN THAT I WENT OVER TO ICHI'S PLACE FOR A TEA BREAK.
TEA AND TWO RICE CRACKERS, TO BE EXACT.
THEN ON MY WAY BACK TO THE FIELDS...
I WAS WALKIN' ALONG BEHIND THE BACK OF THE CLOG FACTORY...
WHEN THIS GUY, NEVER SEEN HIM BEFORE, POPPED OUT.
I SEEN HIM THERE, TOO, NEAR THE SEWER. HE WAS CROUCHED DOWN WEARING A WHITE ROBE.
DAMN! IF ONLY I'D KNOWN THEN HE WAS CRAZY...
GOTTA BE CAREFUL.
YUP, GOTTA BE CAREFUL.

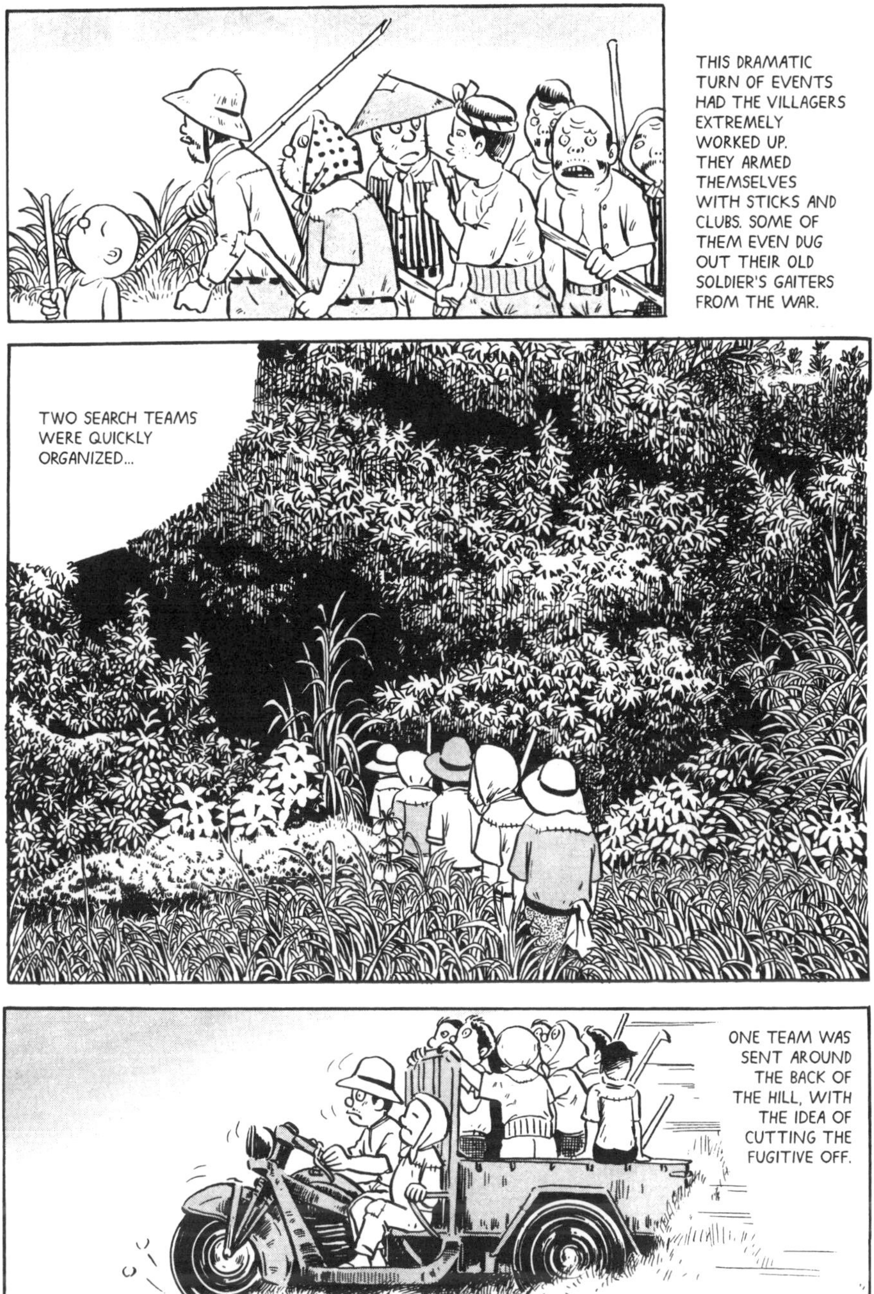
THIS DRAMATIC TURN OF EVENTS HAD THE VILLAGERS EXTREMELY WORKED UP. THEY ARMED THEMSELVES WITH STICKS AND CLUBS. SOME OF THEM EVEN DUG OUT THEIR OLD SOLDIER'S GAITERS FROM THE WAR.
TWO SEARCH TEAMS WERE QUICKLY ORGANIZED...
ONE TEAM WAS SENT AROUND THE BACK OF THE HILL, WITH THE IDEA OF CUTTING THE FUGITIVE OFF.

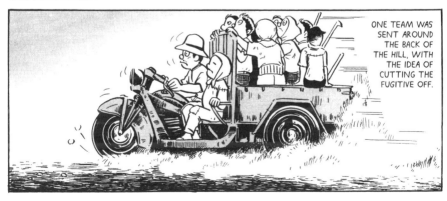

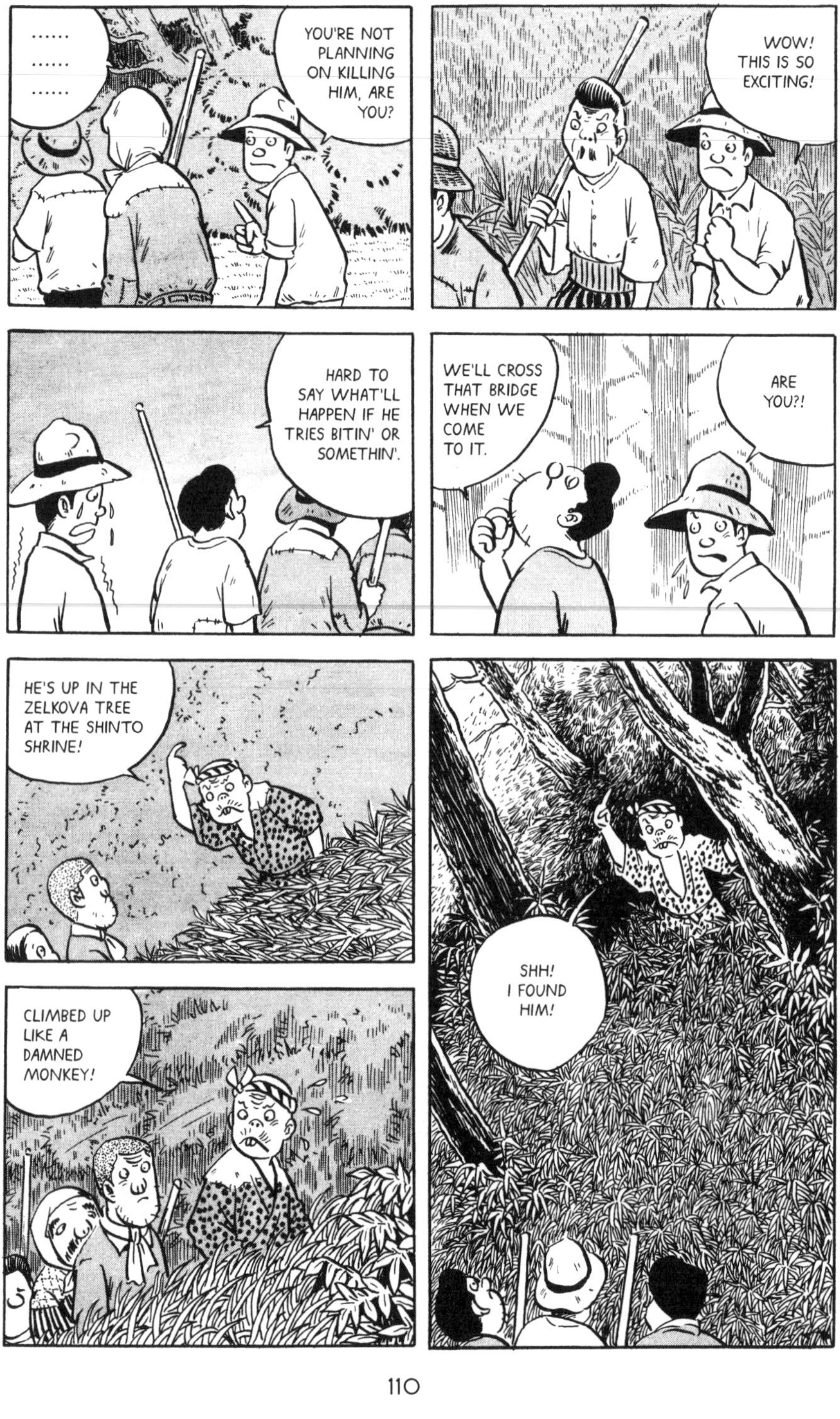
WOW! THIS IS SO EXCITING!
YOU'RE NOT PLANNING ON KILLING HIM, ARE YOU?
......
......
......
ARE YOU?!
WE'LL CROSS THAT BRIDGE WHEN WE COME TO IT.
HARD TO SAY WHAT'LL HAPPEN IF HE TRIES BITIN' OR SOMETHIN'.
SHH! I FOUND HIM!
HE'S UP IN THE ZELKOVA TREE AT THE SHINTO SHRINE!
CLIMBED UP LIKE A DAMNED MONKEY!

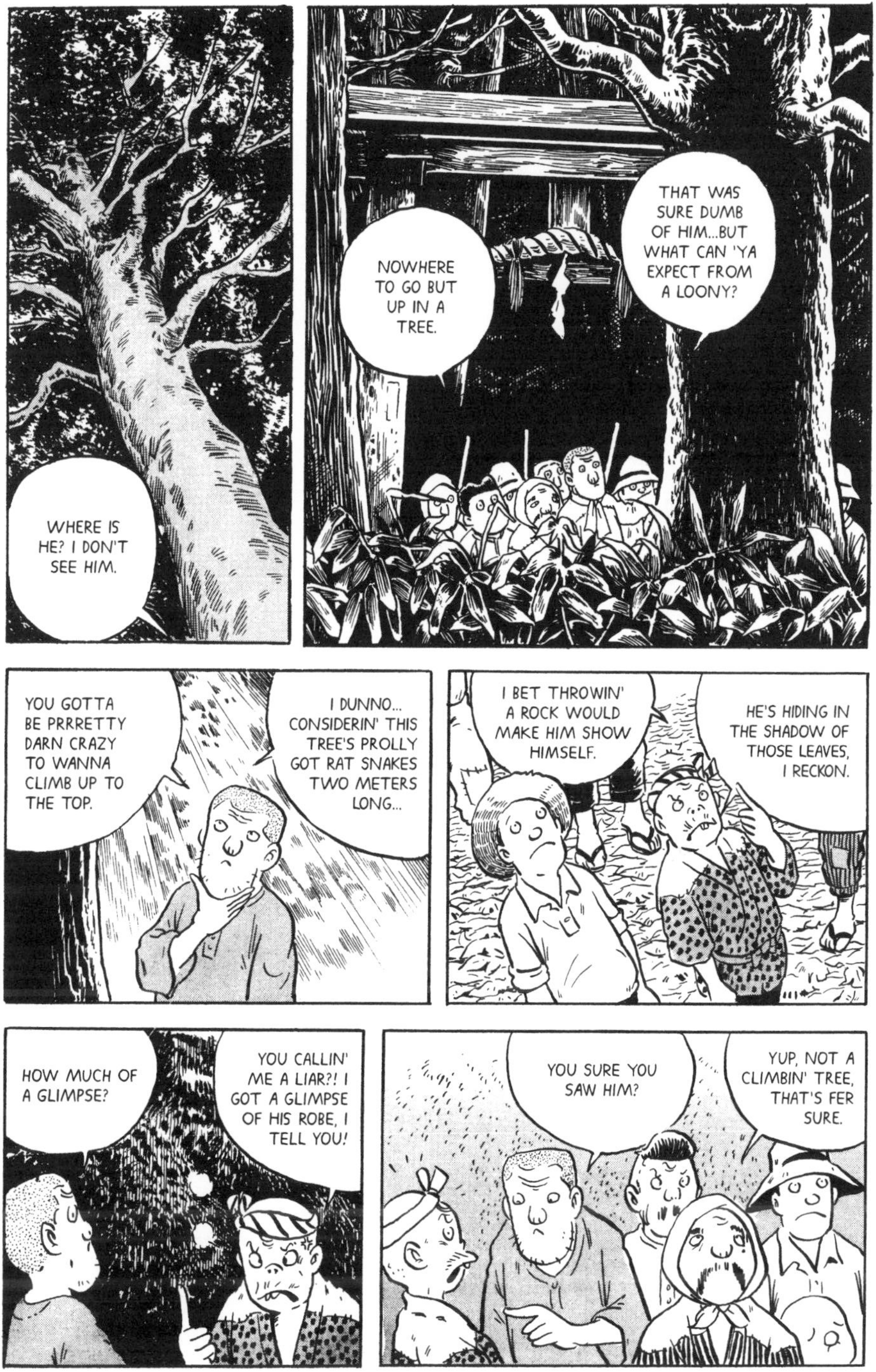
THAT WAS SURE DUMB OF HIM...BUT WHAT CAN 'YA EXPECT FROM A LOONY?
NOWHERE TO GO BUT UP IN A TREE.
WHERE IS HE? I DON'T SEE HIM.
HE'S HIDING IN THE SHADOW OF THOSE LEAVES, I RECKON.
I BET THROWIN' A ROCK WOULD MAKE HIM SHOW HIMSELF.
I DUNNO... CONSIDERIN' THIS TREE'S PROLLY GOT RAT SNAKES TWO METERS LONG...
YOU GOTTA BE PRRRETTY DARN CRAZY TO WANNA CLIMB UP TO THE TOP.
YUP, NOT A CLIMBIN' TREE, THAT'S FER SURE.
YOU SURE YOU SAW HIM?
YOU CALLIN' ME A LIAR?! I GOT A GLIMPSE OF HIS ROBE, I TELL YOU!
HOW MUCH OF A GLIMPSE?

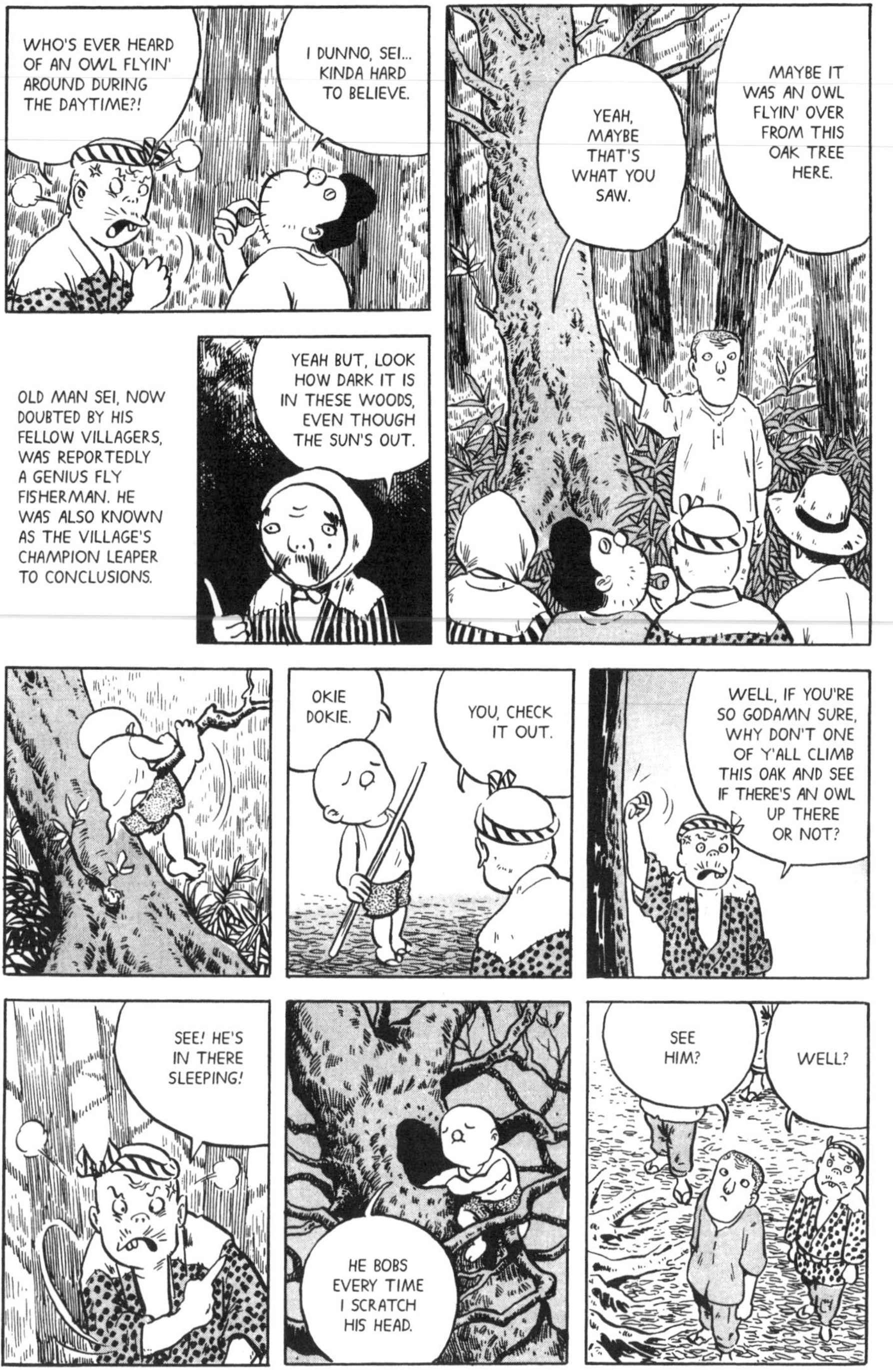
MAYBE IT WAS AN OWL FLYIN' OVER FROM THIS OAK TREE HERE.
YEAH, MAYBE THAT'S WHAT YOU SAW.
I DUNNO, SEI... KINDA HARD TO BELIEVE.
WHO'S EVER HEARD OF AN OWL FLYIN' AROUND DURING THE DAYTIME?!
YEAH BUT, LOOK HOW DARK IT IS IN THESE WOODS, EVEN THOUGH THE SUN'S OUT.
OLD MAN SEI, NOW DOUBTED BY HIS FELLOW VILLAGERS, WAS REPORTEDLY A GENIUS FLY FISHERMAN. HE WAS ALSO KNOWN AS THE VILLAGE'S CHAMPION LEAPER TO CONCLUSIONS.
WELL, IF YOU'RE SO GODAMN SURE, WHY DON'T ONE OF Y'ALL CLIMB THIS OAK AND SEE IF THERE'S AN OWL UP THERE OR NOT?
YOU, CHECK IT OUT.
OKIE DOKIE.
WELL?
SEE HIM?
HE BOBS EVERY TIME I SCRATCH HIS HEAD.
SEE! HE'S IN THERE SLEEPING!

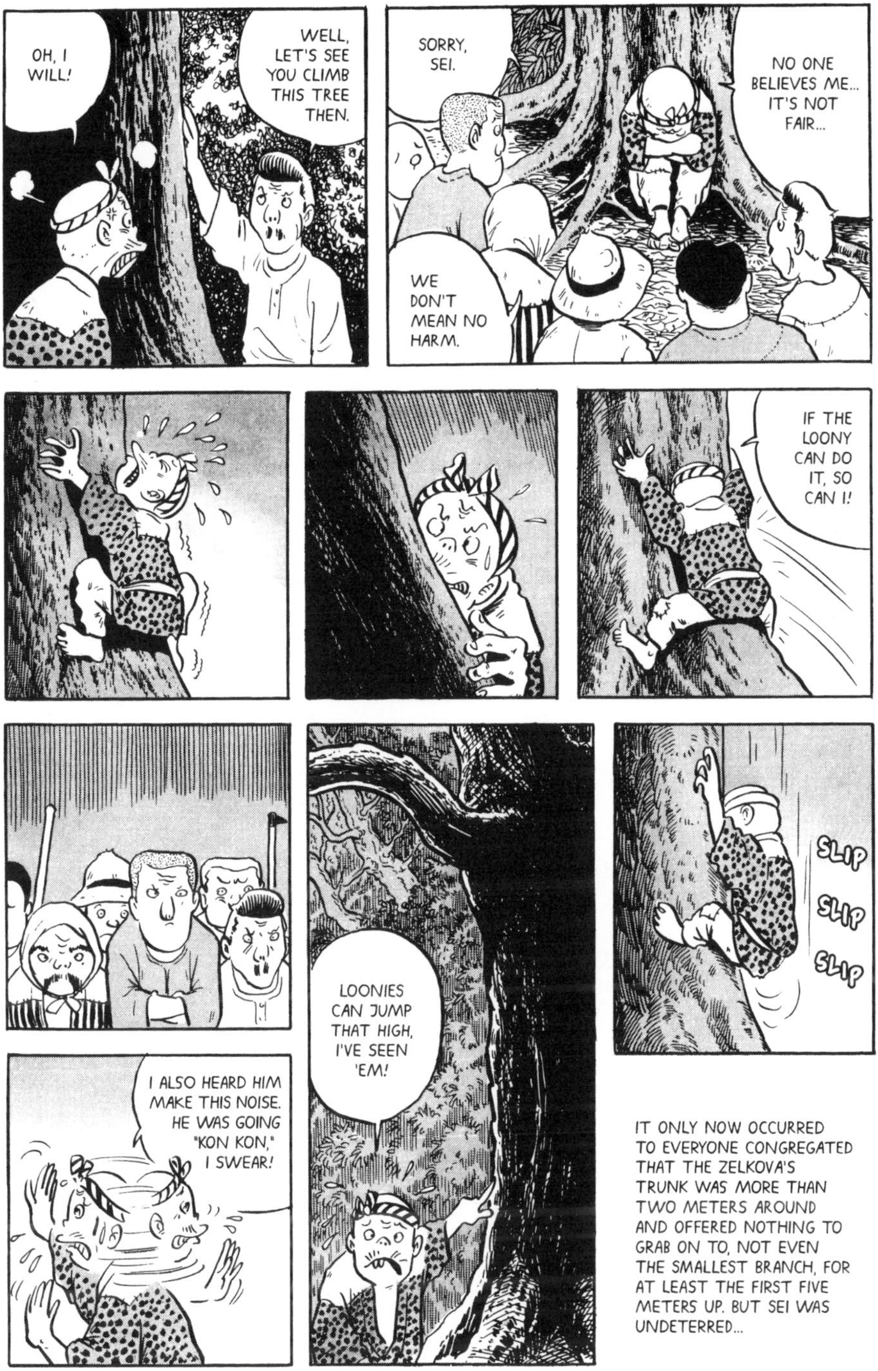

NO ONE BELIEVES ME... IT'S NOT FAIR...
SORRY, SEI.
WE DON'T MEAN NO HARM.
WELL, LET'S SEE YOU CLIMB THIS TREE THEN.
OH, I WILL!
IF THE LOONY CAN DO IT, SO CAN I!
SLIP
SLIP
SLIP
IT ONLY NOW OCCURRED TO EVERYONE CONGREGATED THAT THE ZELKOVA'S TRUNK WAS MORE THAN TWO METERS AROUND AND OFFERED NOTHING TO GRAB ON TO, NOT EVEN THE SMALLEST BRANCH, FOR AT LEAST THE FIRST FIVE METERS UP. BUT SEI WAS UNDETERRED...
LOONIES CAN JUMP THAT HIGH, I'VE SEEN 'EM!
I ALSO HEARD HIM MAKE THIS NOISE. HE WAS GOING "KON KON," I SWEAR!

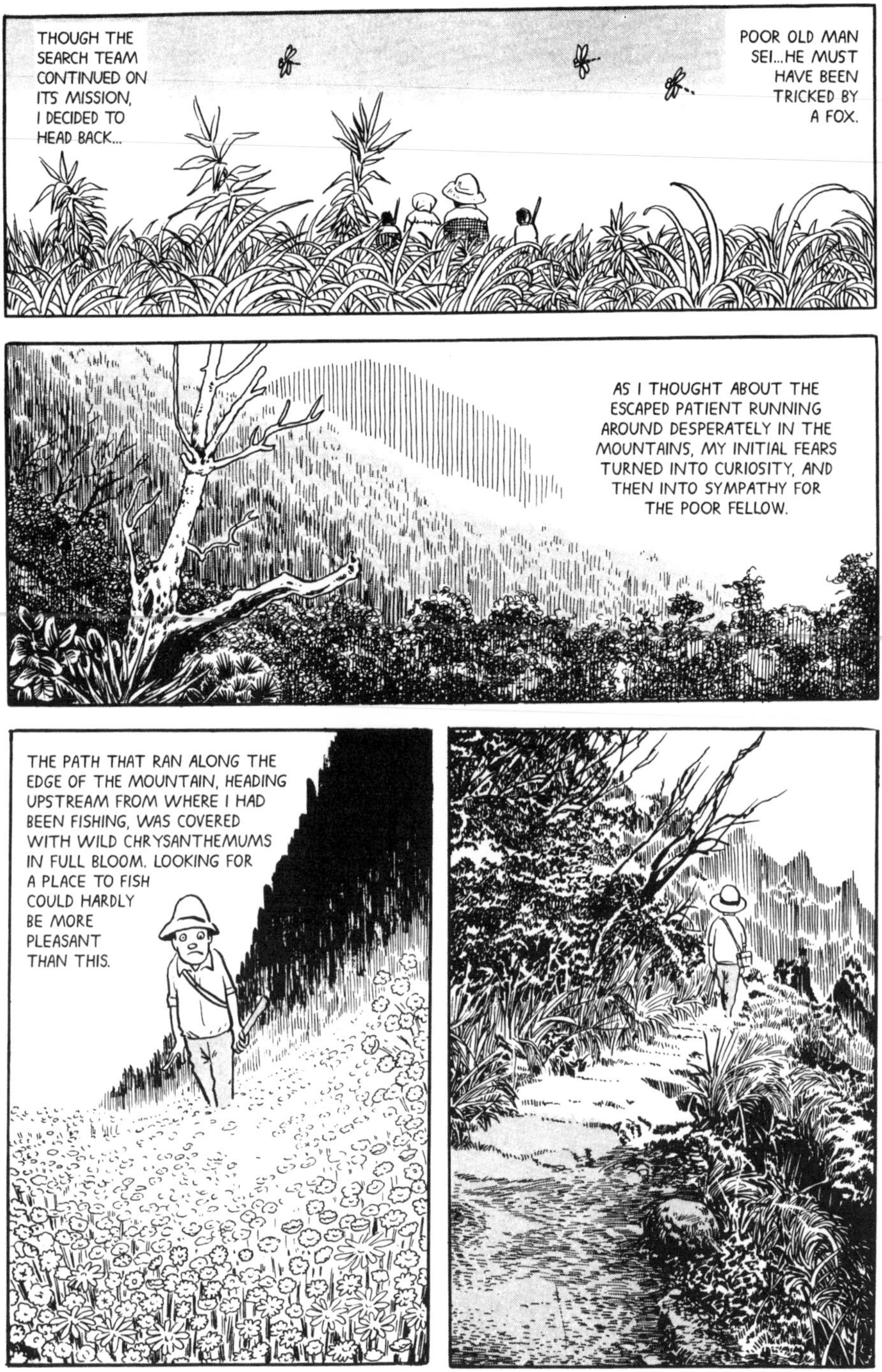
POOR OLD MAN SEI...HE MUST HAVE BEEN TRICKED BY A FOX.
THOUGH THE SEARCH TEAM CONTINUED ON ITS MISSION, I DECIDED TO HEAD BACK...
AS I THOUGHT ABOUT THE ESCAPED PATIENT RUNNING AROUND DESPERATELY IN THE MOUNTAINS, MY INITIAL FEARS TURNED INTO CURIOSITY, AND THEN INTO SYMPATHY FOR THE POOR FELLOW.
THE PATH THAT RAN ALONG THE EDGE OF THE MOUNTAIN, HEADING UPSTREAM FROM WHERE I HAD BEEN FISHING, WAS COVERED WITH WILD CHRYSANTHEMUMS IN FULL BLOOM. LOOKING FOR A PLACE TO FISH COULD HARDLY BE MORE PLEASANT THAN THIS.

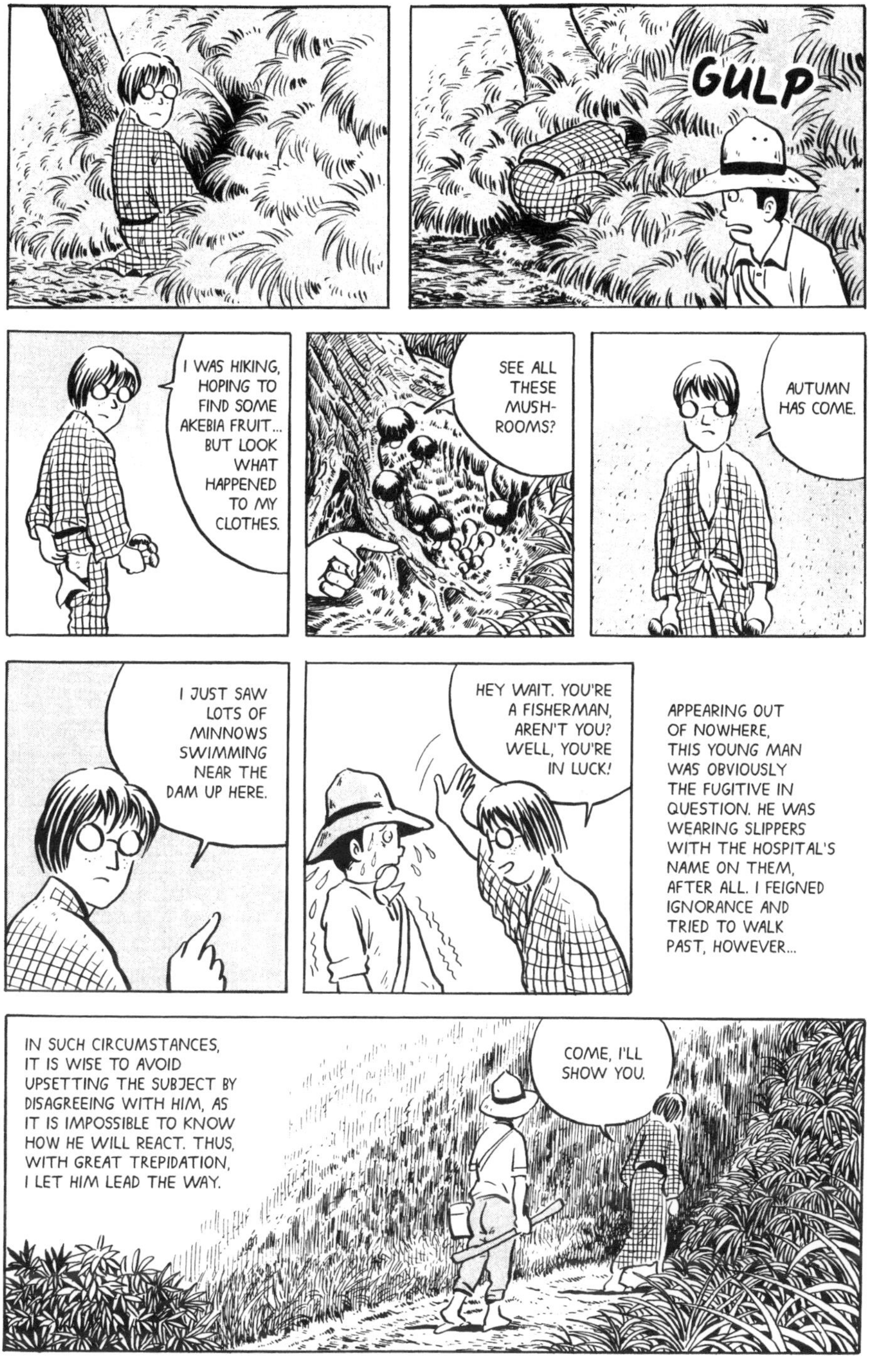
GULP
AUTUMN HAS COME.
SEE ALL THESE MUSH-ROOMS?
I WAS HIKING, HOPING TO FIND SOME AKEBIA FRUIT... BUT LOOK WHAT HAPPENED TO MY CLOTHES.
APPEARING OUT OF NOWHERE, THIS YOUNG MAN WAS OBVIOUSLY THE FUGITIVE IN QUESTION. HE WAS WEARING SLIPPERS WITH THE HOSPITAL'S NAME ON THEM, AFTER ALL. I FEIGNED IGNORANCE AND TRIED TO WALK PAST, HOWEVER...
HEY WAIT. YOU'RE A FISHERMAN, AREN'T YOU? WELL, YOU'RE IN LUCK!
I JUST SAW LOTS OF MINNOWS SWIMMING NEAR THE DAM UP HERE.
COME, I'LL SHOW YOU.
IN SUCH CIRCUMSTANCES, IT IS WISE TO AVOID UPSETTING THE SUBJECT BY DISAGREEING WITH HIM, AS IT IS IMPOSSIBLE TO KNOW HOW HE WILL REACT. THUS, WITH GREAT TREPIDATION, I LET HIM LEAD THE WAY.

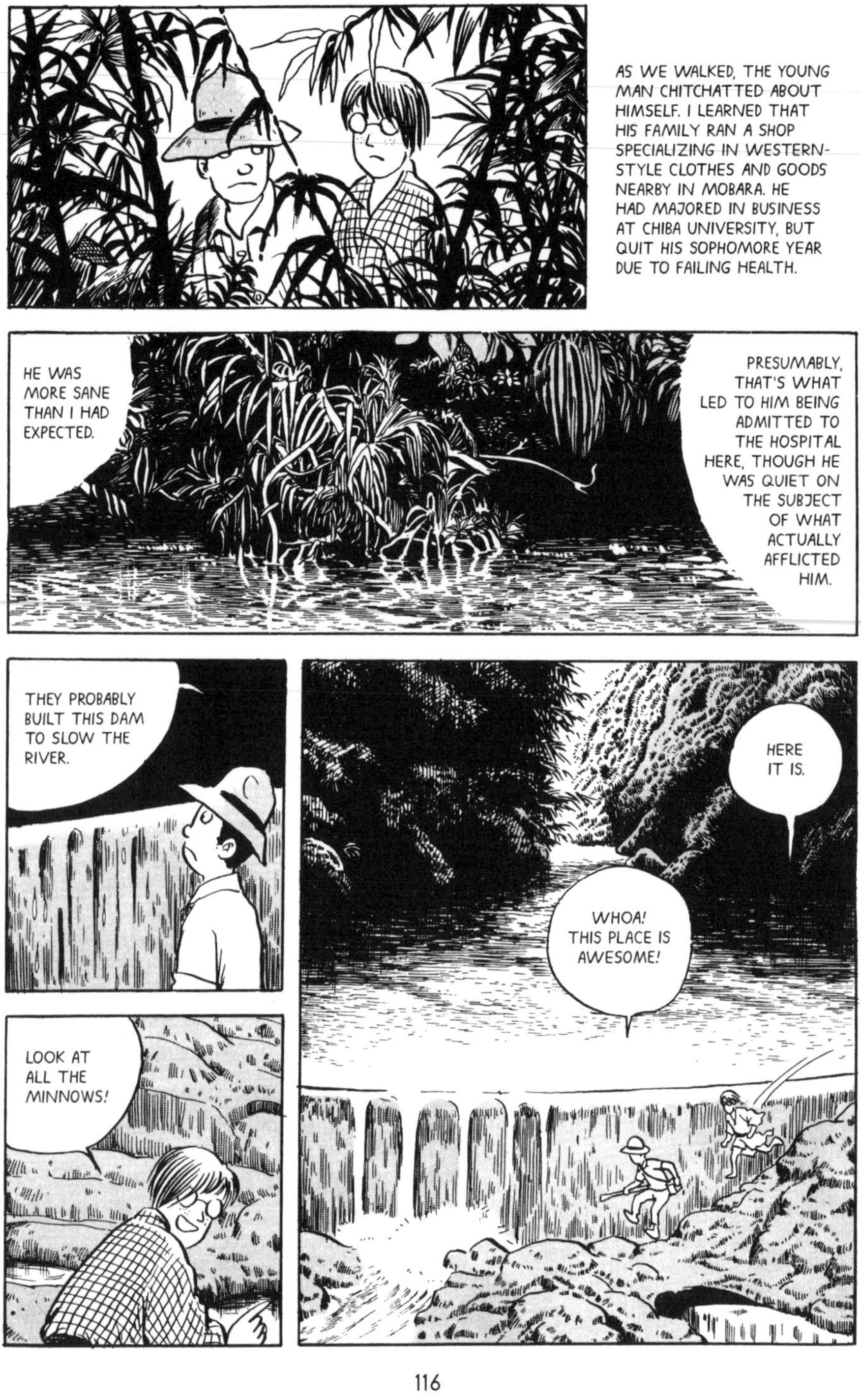
AS WE WALKED, THE YOUNG MAN CHITCHATTED ABOUT HIMSELF. I LEARNED THAT HIS FAMILY RAN A SHOP SPECIALIZING IN WESTERN-STYLE CLOTHES AND GOODS NEARBY IN MOBARA. HE HAD MAJORED IN BUSINESS AT CHIBA UNIVERSITY, BUT QUIT HIS SOPHOMORE YEAR DUE TO FAILING HEALTH.
PRESUMABLY, THAT'S WHAT LED TO HIM BEING ADMITTED TO THE HOSPITAL HERE, THOUGH HE WAS QUIET ON THE SUBJECT OF WHAT ACTUALLY AFFLICTED HIM.
HE WAS MORE SANE THAN I HAD EXPECTED.
HERE IT IS.
WHOA! THIS PLACE IS AWESOME!
THEY PROBABLY BUILT THIS DAM TO SLOW THE RIVER.
LOOK AT ALL THE MINNOWS!

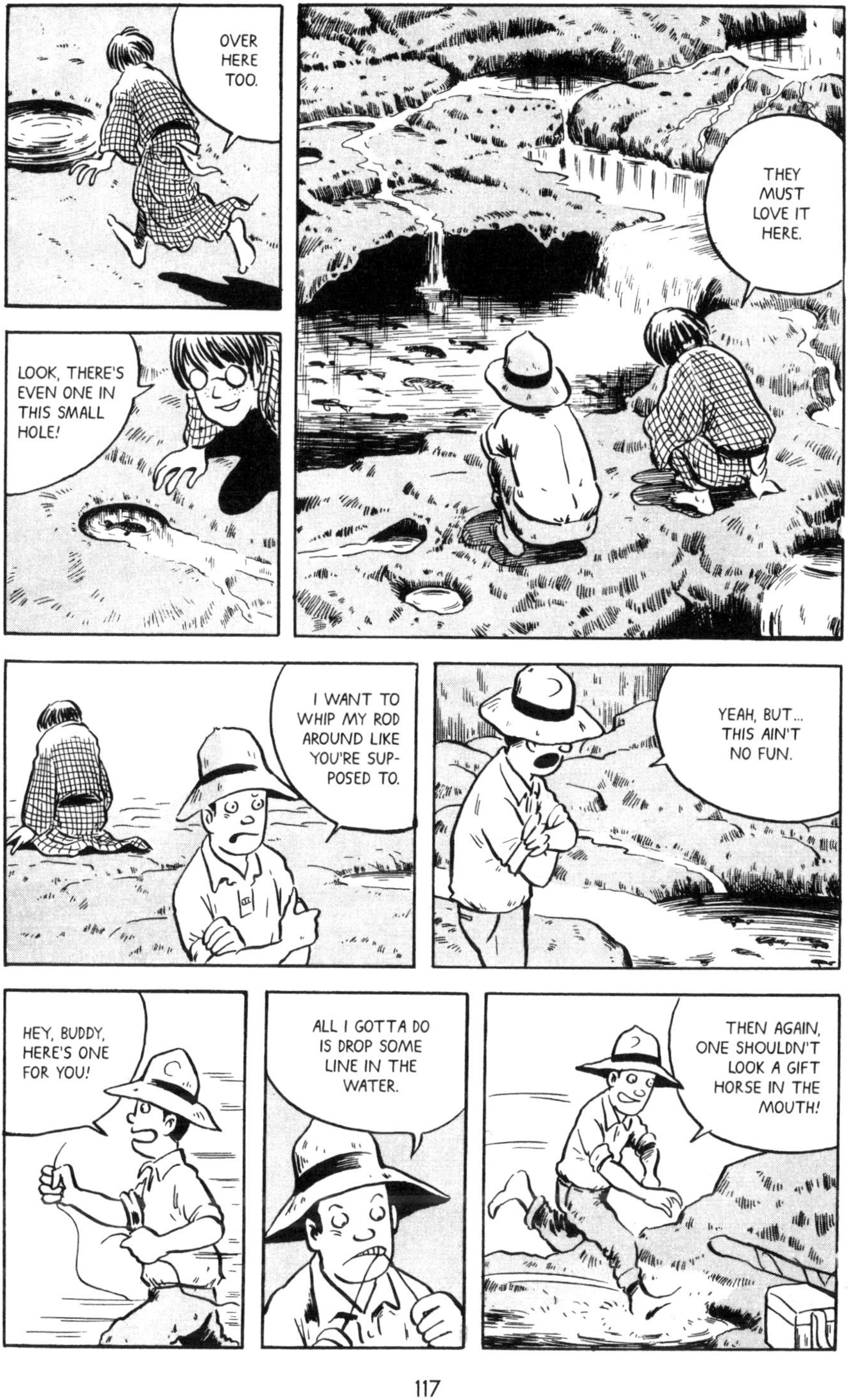
THEY MUST LOVE IT HERE.
OVER HERE TOO.
LOOK, THERE'S EVEN ONE IN THIS SMALL HOLE!
YEAH, BUT... THIS AIN'T NO FUN.
I WANT TO WHIP MY ROD AROUND LIKE YOU'RE SUP-POSED TO.
THEN AGAIN, ONE SHOULDN'T LOOK A GIFT HORSE IN THE MOUTH!
ALL I GOTTA DO IS DROP SOME LINE IN THE WATER.
HEY, BUDDY, HERE'S ONE FOR YOU!

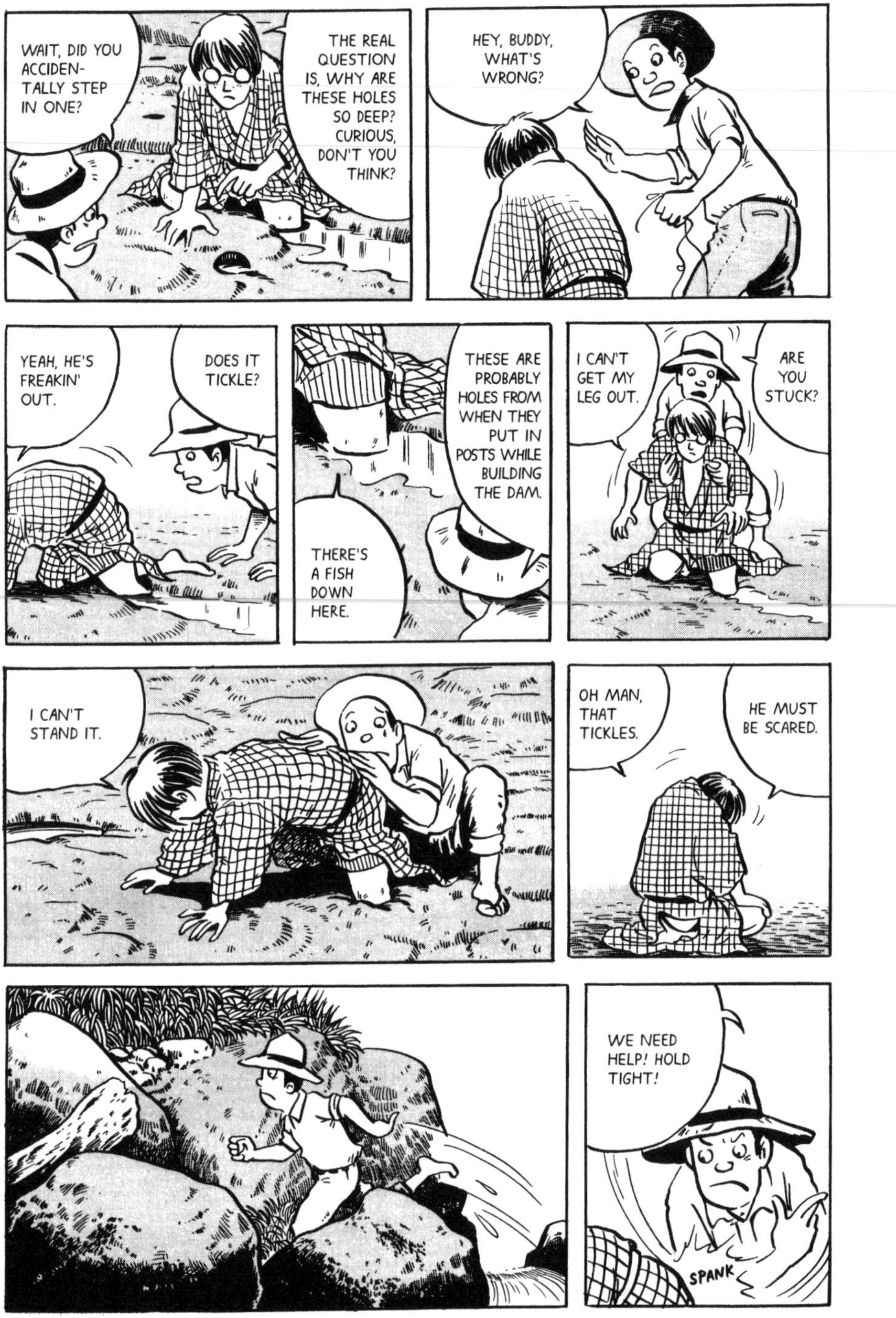
HEY, BUDDY, WHAT'S WRONG?
THE REAL QUESTION IS, WHY ARE THESE HOLES SO DEEP? CURIOUS, DON'T YOU THINK?
WAIT, DID YOU ACCIDENTALLY STEP IN ONE?
ARE YOU STUCK?
I CAN'T GET MY LEG OUT.
THESE ARE PROBABLY HOLES FROM WHEN THEY PUT IN POSTS WHILE BUILDING THE DAM.
THERE'S A FISH DOWN HERE.
DOES IT TICKLE?
YEAH, HE'S FREAKIN' OUT.
HE MUST BE SCARED.
OH MAN, THAT TICKLES.
I CAN'T STAND IT.
WE NEED HELP! HOLD TIGHT!
SPANK

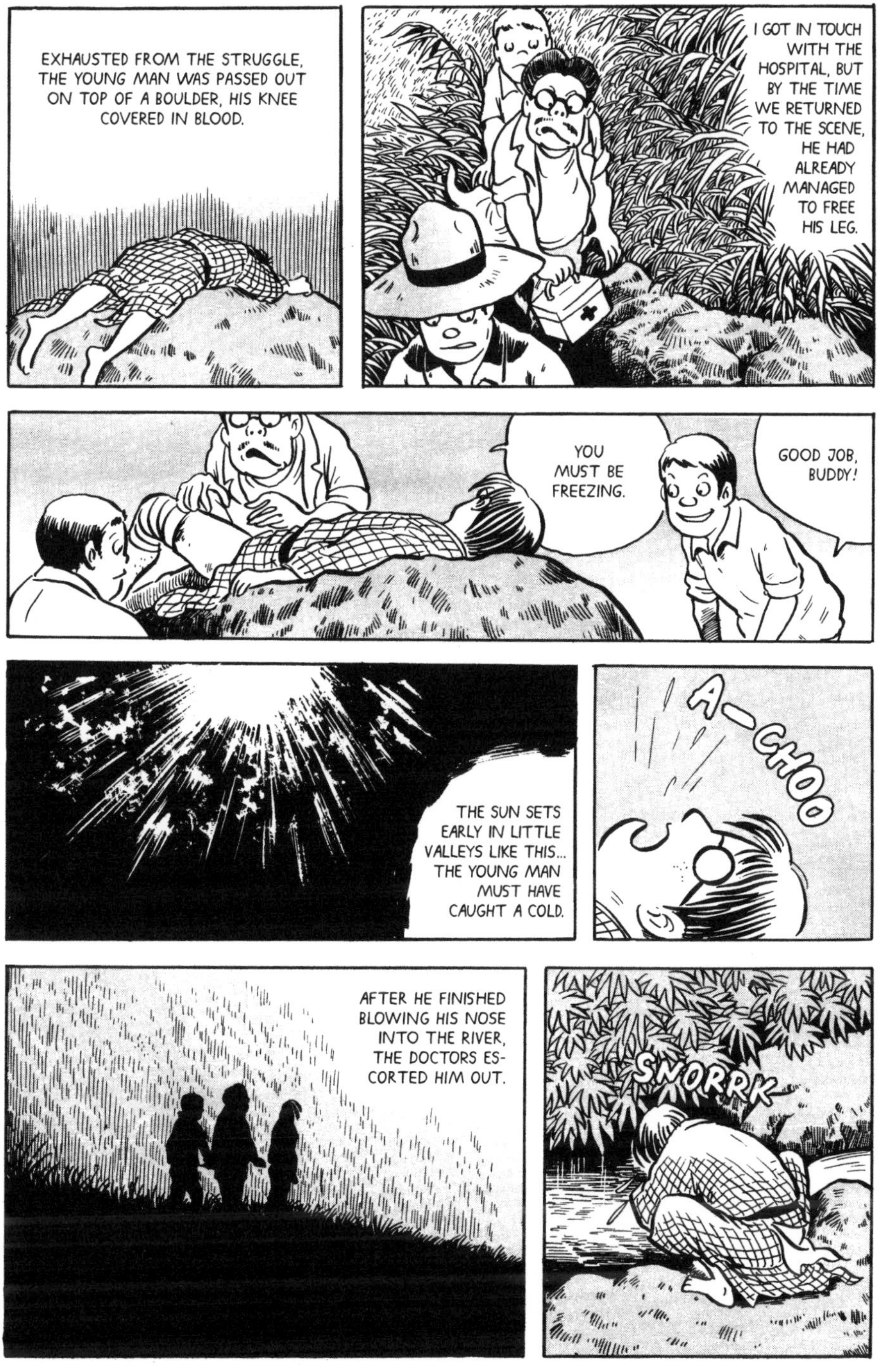
I GOT IN TOUCH WITH THE HOSPITAL, BUT BY THE TIME WE RETURNED TO THE SCENE, HE HAD ALREADY MANAGED TO FREE HIS LEG.
EXHAUSTED FROM THE STRUGGLE, THE YOUNG MAN WAS PASSED OUT ON TOP OF A BOULDER, HIS KNEE COVERED IN BLOOD.
GOOD JOB, BUDDY!
YOU MUST BE FREEZING.
A-CHOO
THE SUN SETS EARLY IN LITTLE VALLEYS LIKE THIS... THE YOUNG MAN MUST HAVE CAUGHT A COLD.
SNORRK
AFTER HE FINISHED BLOWING HIS NOSE INTO THE RIVER, THE DOCTORS ES-CORTED HIM OUT.

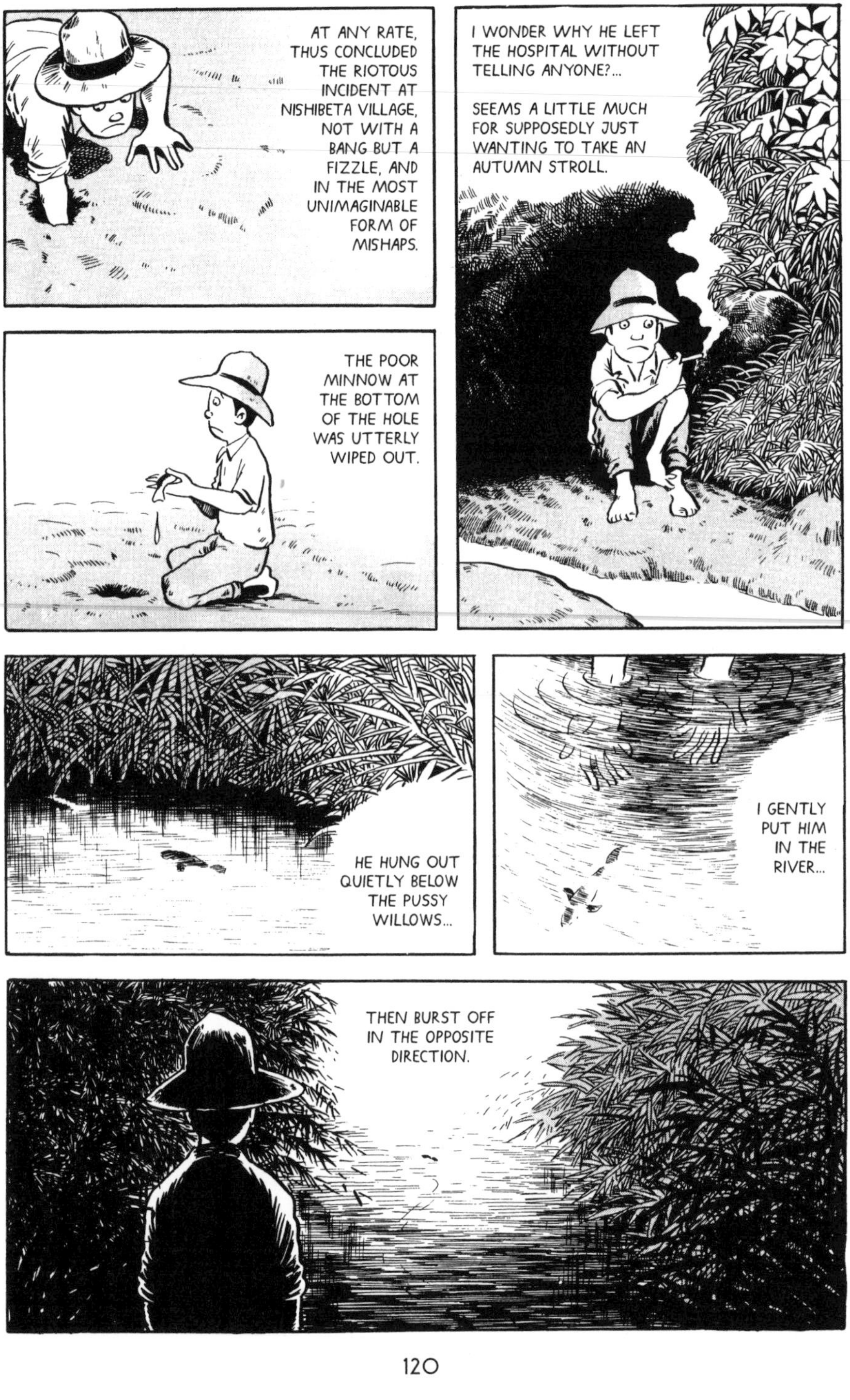
I WONDER WHY HE LEFT THE HOSPITAL WITHOUT TELLING ANYONE?...
SEEMS A LITTLE MUCH FOR SUPPOSEDLY JUST WANTING TO TAKE AN AUTUMN STROLL.
AT ANY RATE, THUS CONCLUDED THE RIOTOUS INCIDENT AT NISHIBETA VILLAGE, NOT WITH A BANG BUT A FIZZLE, AND IN THE MOST UNIMAGINABLE FORM OF MISHAPS.
THE POOR MINNOW AT THE BOTTOM OF THE HOLE WAS UTTERLY WIPED OUT.
I GENTLY PUT HIM IN THE RIVER...
HE HUNG OUT QUIETLY BELOW THE PUSSY WILLOWS...
THEN BURST OFF IN THE OPPOSITE DIRECTION.

CHOHACHI INN

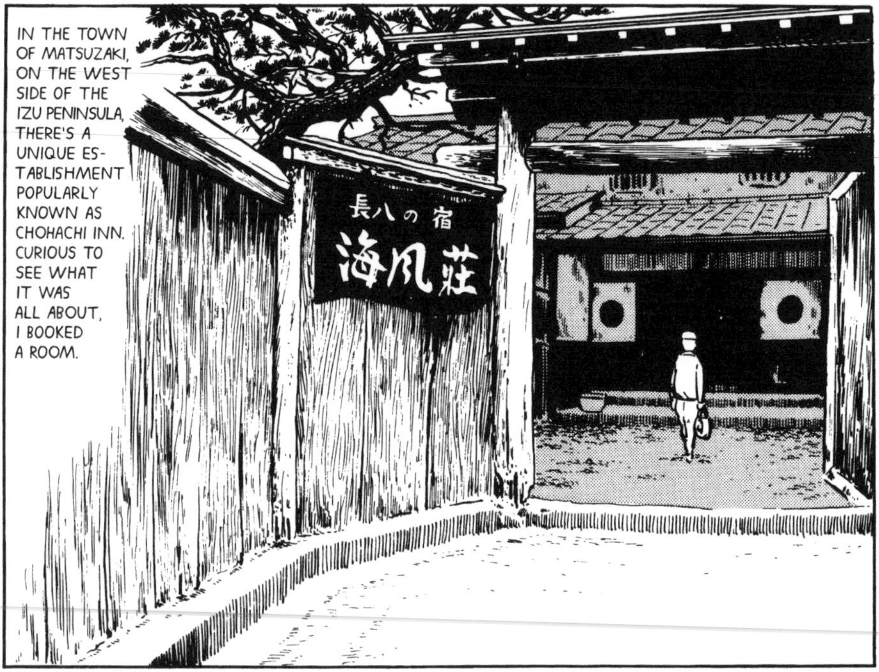
IN THE TOWN OF MATSUZAKI, ON THE WEST SIDE OF THE IZU PENINSULA, THERE'S A UNIQUE ESTABLISHMENT POPULARLY KNOWN AS CHOHACHI INN. CURIOUS TO SEE WHAT IT WAS ALL ABOUT, I BOOKED A ROOM.
長八の宿
海風荘
SIGN: KAIFUSO, CHOHACHI INN

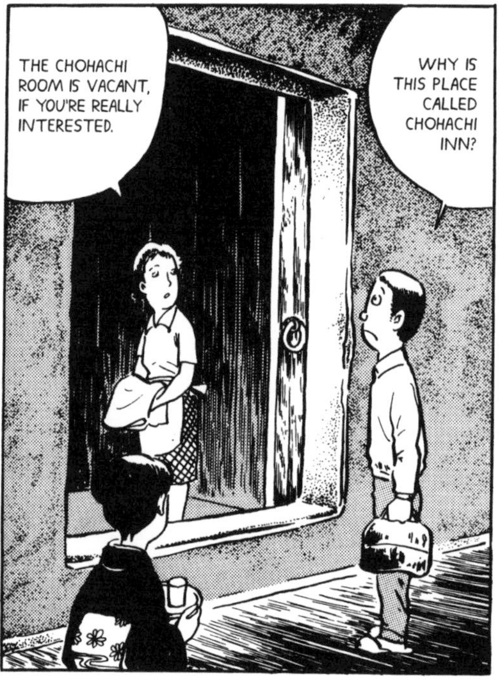
WHY IS THIS PLACE CALLED CHOHACHI INN?
THE CHOHACHI ROOM IS VACANT, IF YOU'RE REALLY INTERESTED.

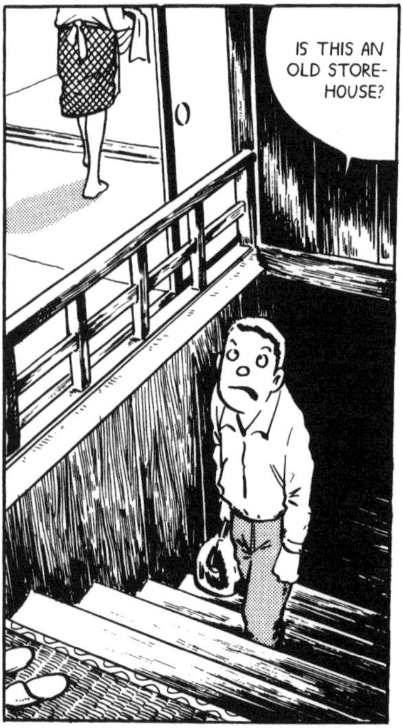
IS THIS AN OLD STOREHOUSE?

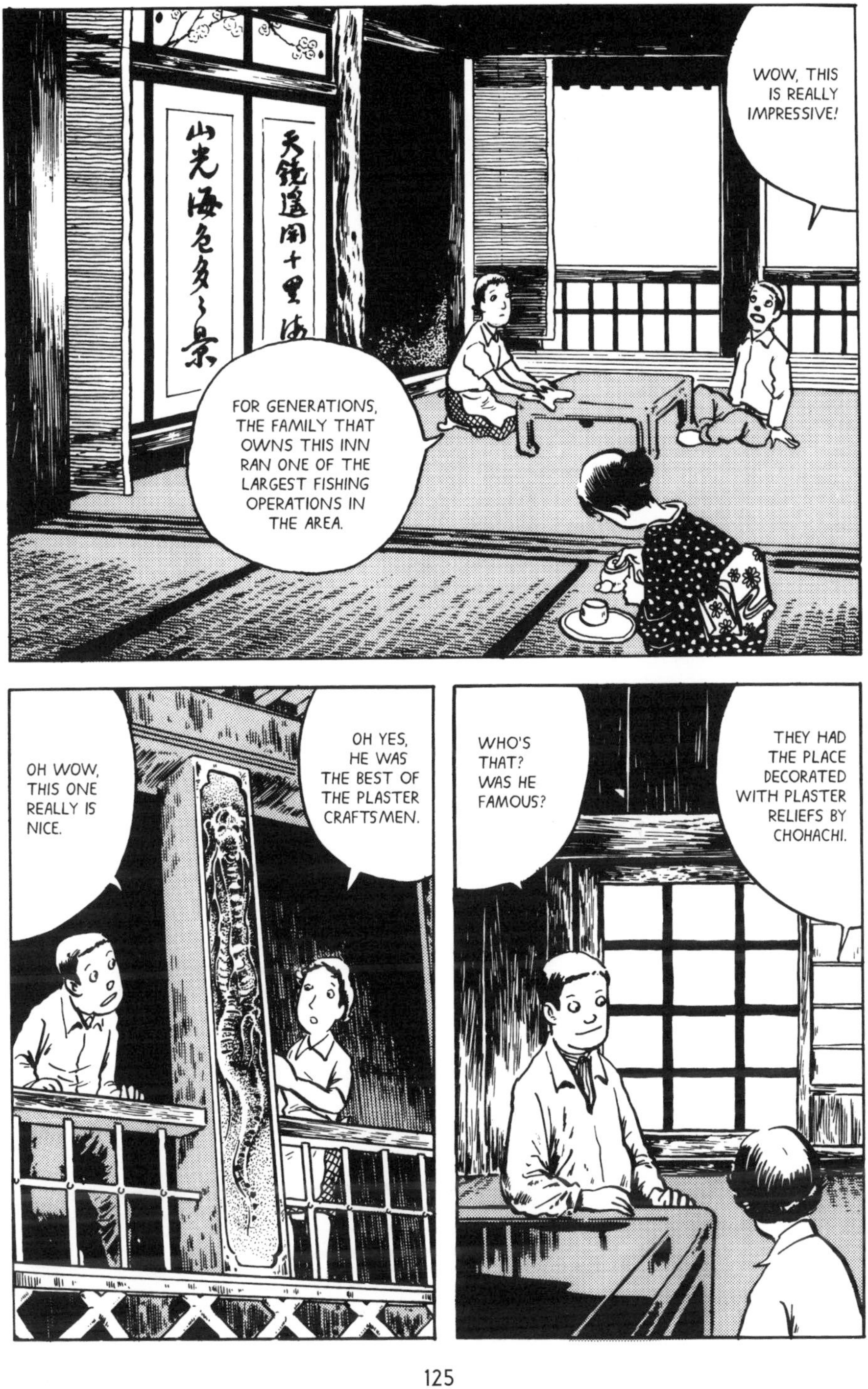
WOW, THIS IS REALLY IMPRESSIVE!
FOR GENERATIONS, THE FAMILY THAT OWNS THIS INN RAN ONE OF THE LARGEST FISHING OPERATIONS IN THE AREA.
THEY HAD THE PLACE DECORATED WITH PLASTER RELIEFS BY CHOHACHI.
WHO'S THAT? WAS HE FAMOUS?
OH YES, HE WAS THE BEST OF THE PLASTER CRAFTSMEN.
OH WOW, THIS ONE REALLY IS NICE.

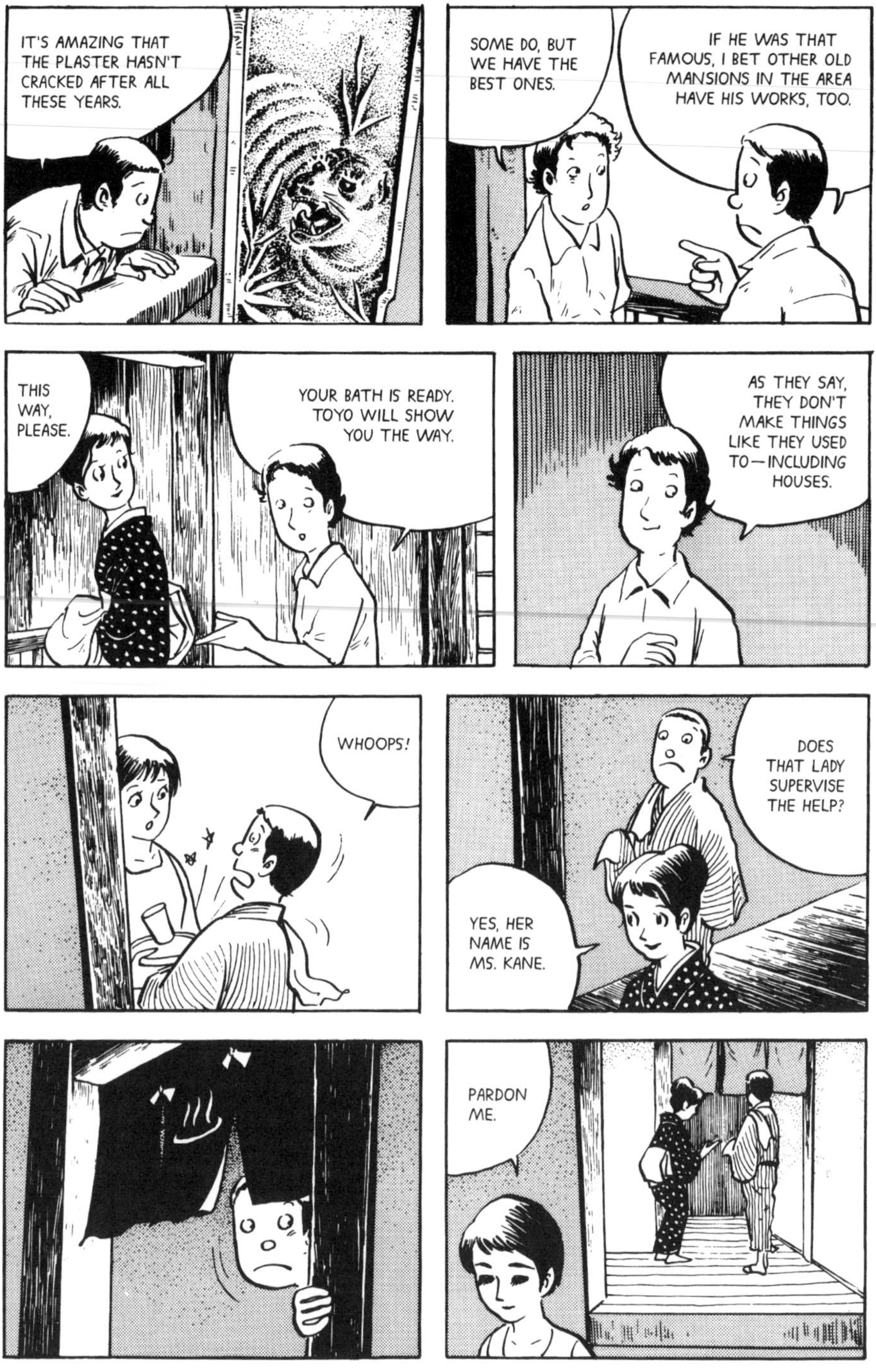
IF HE WAS THAT FAMOUS, I BET OTHER OLD MANSIONS IN THE AREA HAVE HIS WORKS, TOO.
SOME DO, BUT WE HAVE THE BEST ONES.
IT'S AMAZING THAT THE PLASTER HASN'T CRACKED AFTER ALL THESE YEARS.
AS THEY SAY, THEY DON'T MAKE THINGS LIKE THEY USED TO—INCLUDING HOUSES.
YOUR BATH IS READY. TOYO WILL SHOW YOU THE WAY.
THIS WAY, PLEASE.
DOES THAT LADY SUPERVISE THE HELP?
YES, HER NAME IS MS. KANE.
WHOOPS!
PARDON ME.

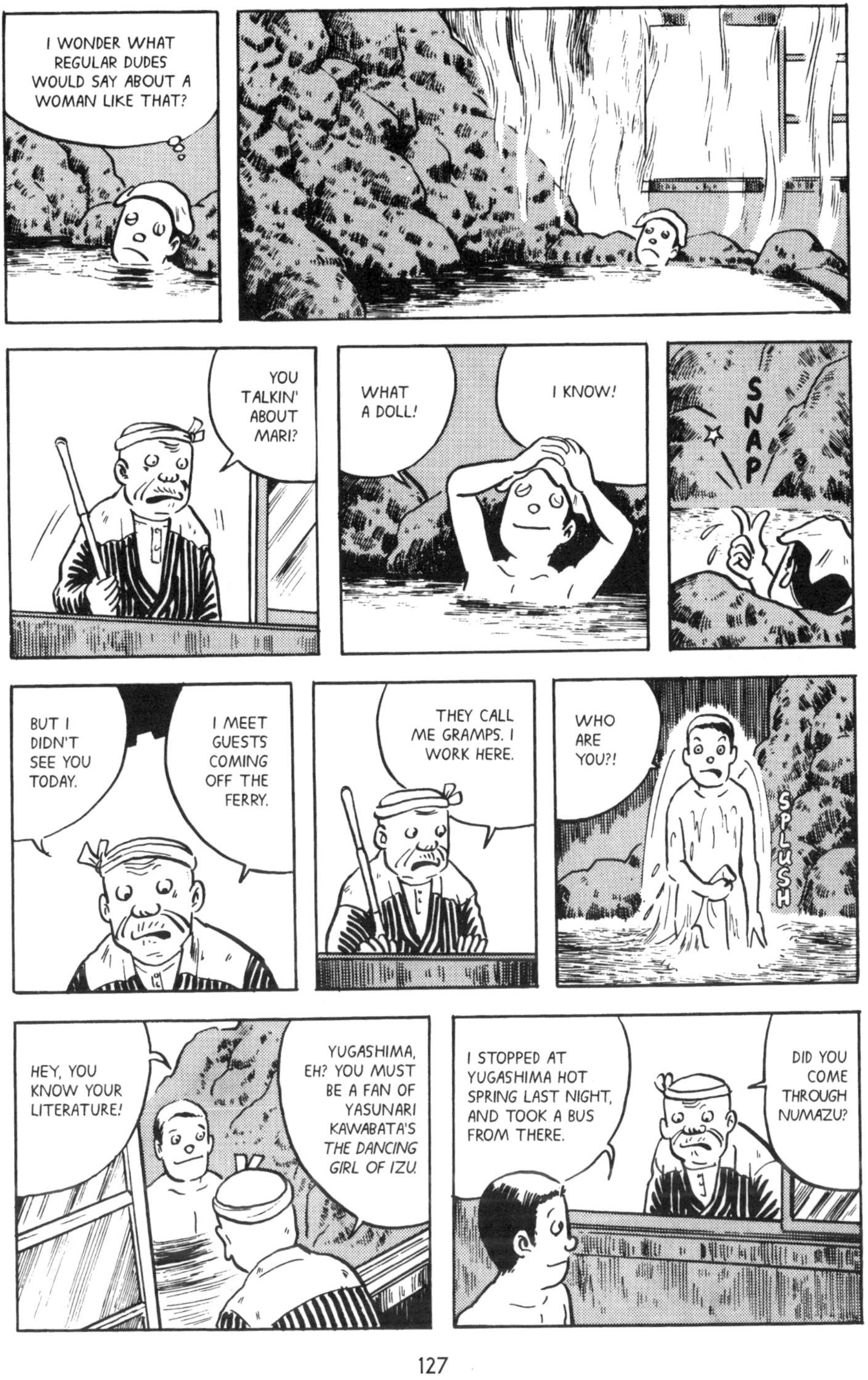
I WONDER WHAT REGULAR DUDES WOULD SAY ABOUT A WOMAN LIKE THAT?
SNAP
I KNOW!
WHAT A DOLL!
YOU TALKIN' ABOUT MARI?
WHO ARE YOU?!
SPLUSH
THEY CALL ME GRAMPS. I WORK HERE.
I MEET GUESTS COMING OFF THE FERRY.
BUT I DIDN'T SEE YOU TODAY.
DID YOU COME THROUGH NUMAZU?
I STOPPED AT YUGASHIMA HOT SPRING LAST NIGHT, AND TOOK A BUS FROM THERE.
YUGASHIMA, EH? YOU MUST BE A FAN OF YASUNARI KAWABATA'S *THE DANCING GIRL OF IZU.*
HEY, YOU KNOW YOUR LITERATURE!

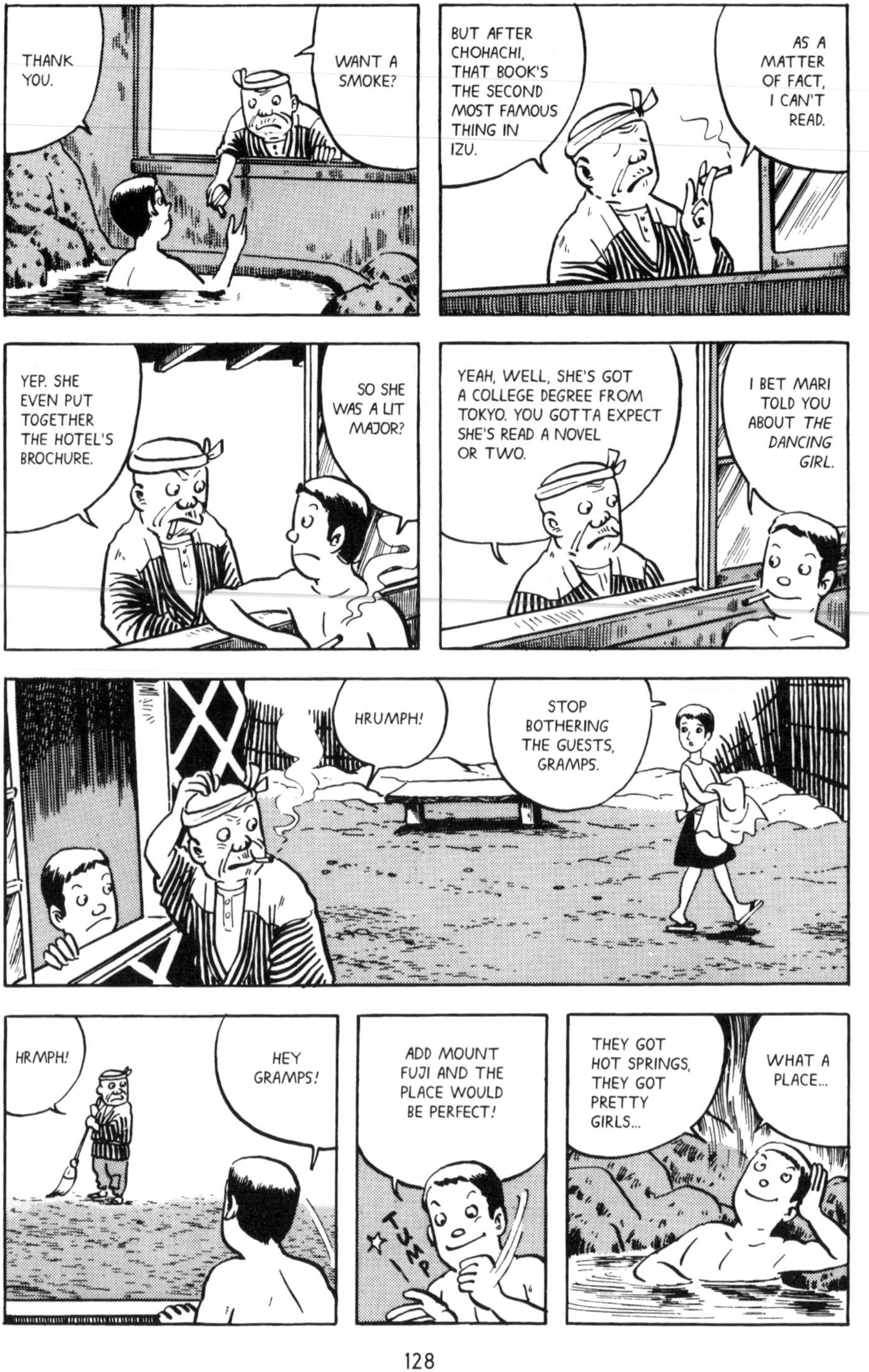
AS A MATTER OF FACT, I CAN'T READ.
BUT AFTER CHOHACHI, THAT BOOK'S THE SECOND MOST FAMOUS THING IN IZU.
WANT A SMOKE?
THANK YOU.
I BET MARI TOLD YOU ABOUT *THE DANCING GIRL*.
YEAH, WELL, SHE'S GOT A COLLEGE DEGREE FROM TOKYO. YOU GOTTA EXPECT SHE'S READ A NOVEL OR TWO.
SO SHE WAS A LIT MAJOR?
YEP. SHE EVEN PUT TOGETHER THE HOTEL'S BROCHURE.
STOP BOTHERING THE GUESTS, GRAMPS.
HRUMPH!
WHAT A PLACE...
THEY GOT HOT SPRINGS, THEY GOT PRETTY GIRLS...
ADD MOUNT FUJI AND THE PLACE WOULD BE PERFECT!
TUMP
HEY GRAMPS!
HRMPH!

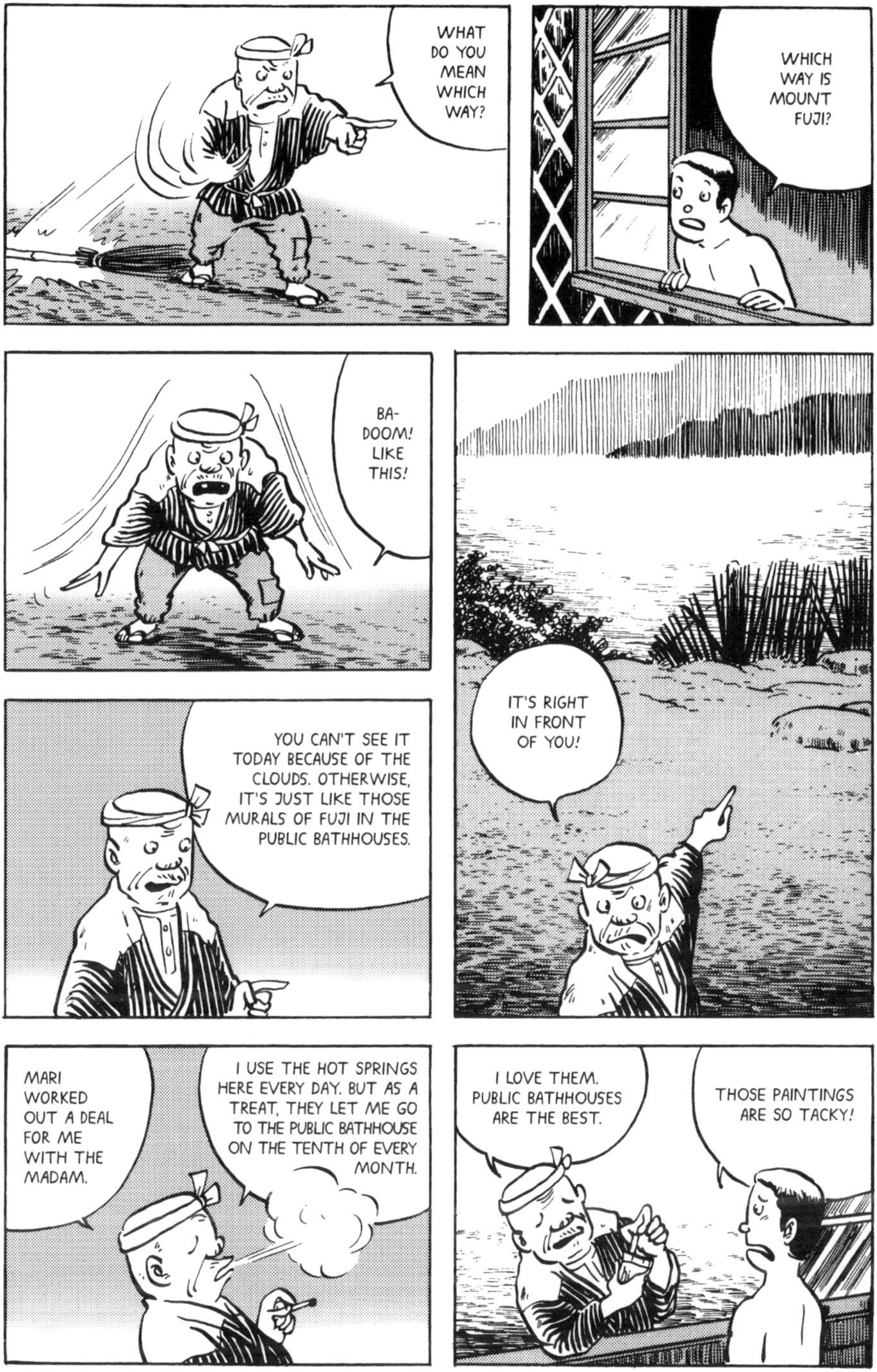
WHICH WAY IS MOUNT FUJI?
WHAT DO YOU MEAN WHICH WAY?
IT'S RIGHT IN FRONT OF YOU!
BA-DOOM! LIKE THIS!
YOU CAN'T SEE IT TODAY BECAUSE OF THE CLOUDS. OTHERWISE, IT'S JUST LIKE THOSE MURALS OF FUJI IN THE PUBLIC BATHHOUSES.
THOSE PAINTINGS ARE SO TACKY!
I LOVE THEM. PUBLIC BATHHOUSES ARE THE BEST.
I USE THE HOT SPRINGS HERE EVERY DAY. BUT AS A TREAT, THEY LET ME GO TO THE PUBLIC BATHHOUSE ON THE TENTH OF EVERY MONTH.
MARI WORKED OUT A DEAL FOR ME WITH THE MADAM.

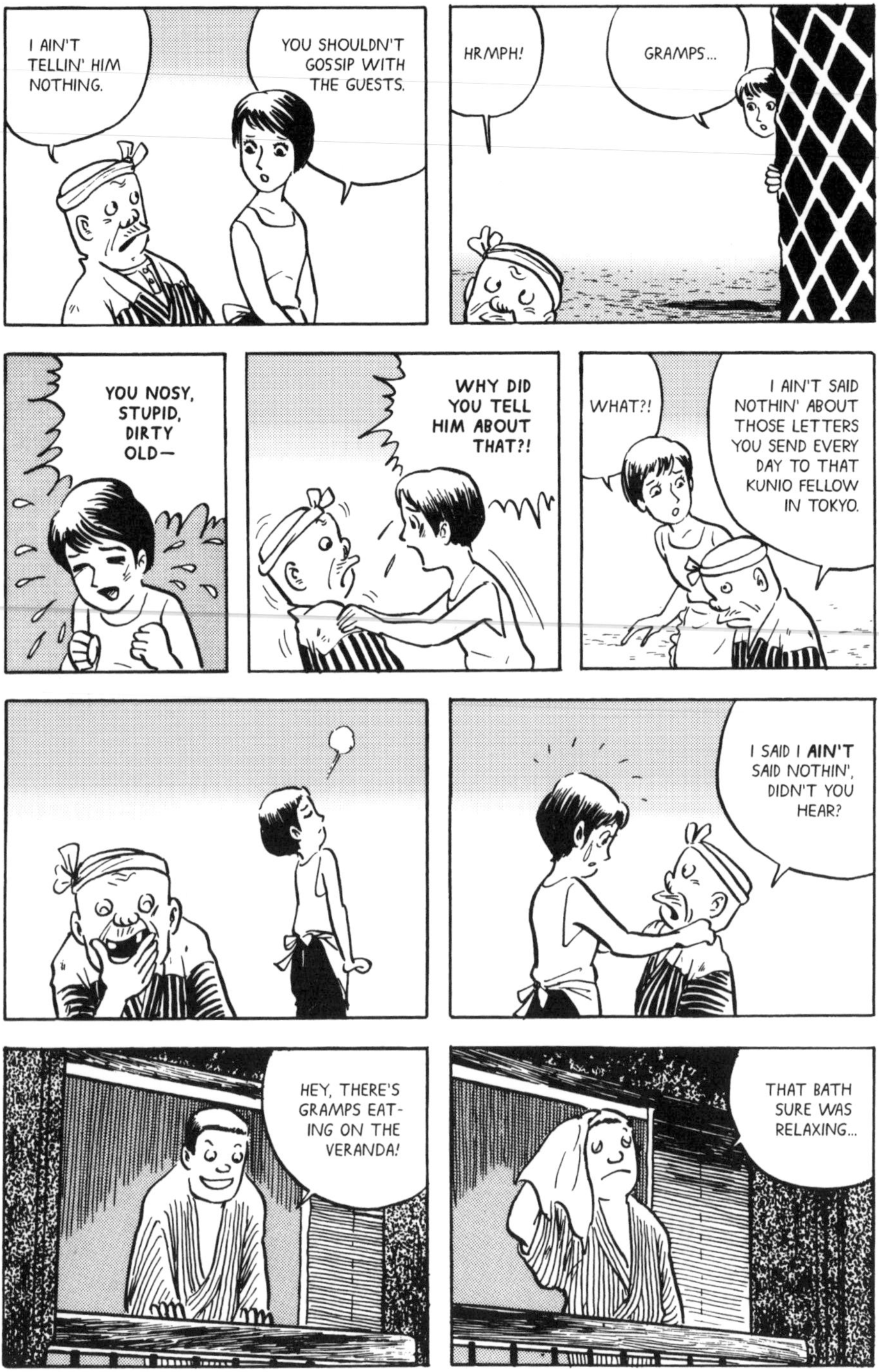
GRAMPS...
HRMPH!
YOU SHOULDN'T GOSSIP WITH THE GUESTS.
I AIN'T TELLIN' HIM NOTHING.
I AIN'T SAID NOTHIN' ABOUT THOSE LETTERS YOU SEND EVERY DAY TO THAT KUNIO FELLOW IN TOKYO.
WHAT?!
WHY DID YOU TELL HIM ABOUT THAT?!
YOU NOSY, STUPID, DIRTY OLD—
I SAID I **AIN'T** SAID NOTHIN', DIDN'T YOU HEAR?
THAT BATH SURE WAS RELAXING...
HEY, THERE'S GRAMPS EATING ON THE VERANDA!

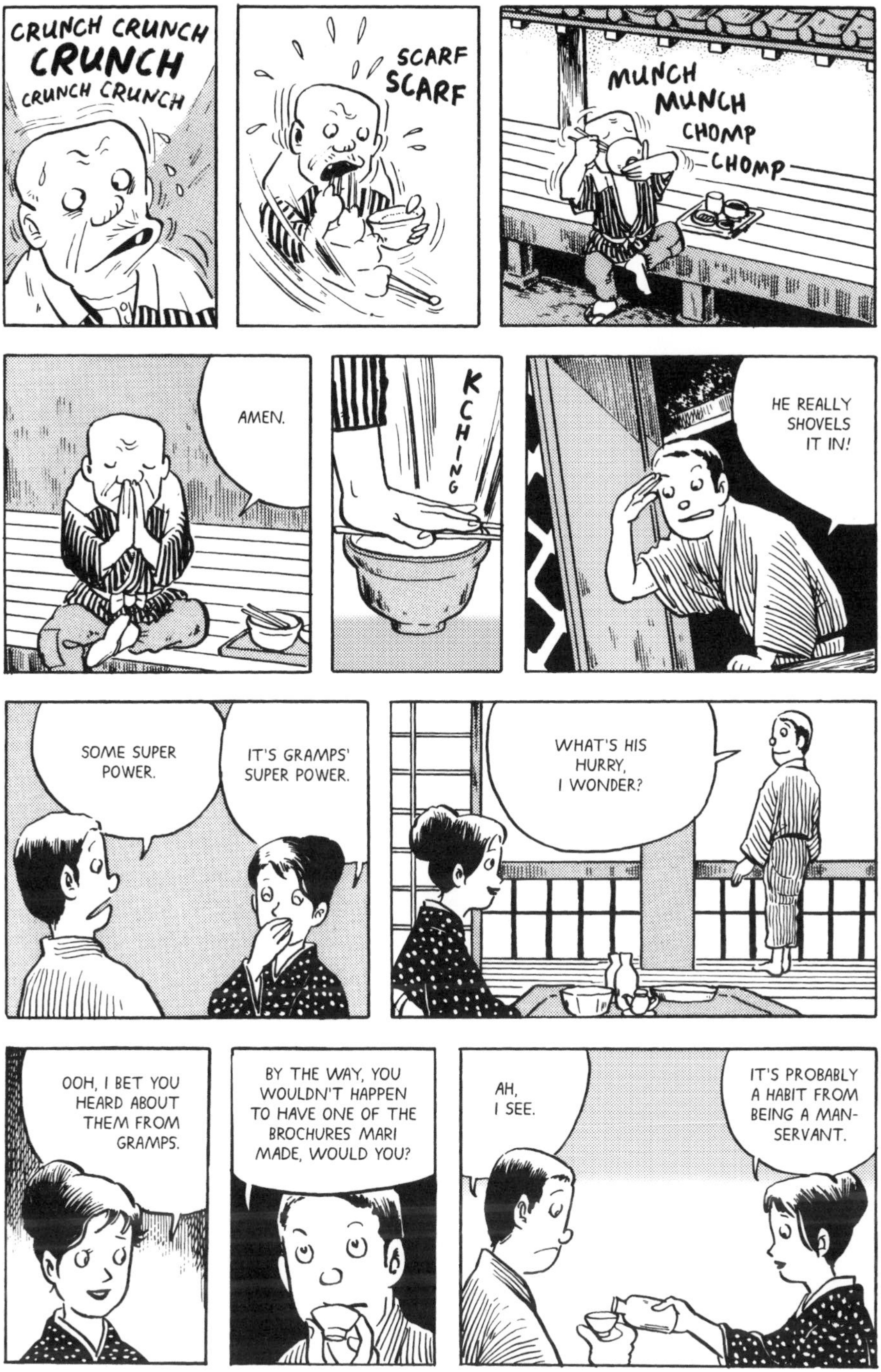
MUNCH MUNCH CHOMP CHOMP
SCARF SCARF
CRUNCH CRUNCH CRUNCH CRUNCH CRUNCH
HE REALLY SHOVELS IT IN!
KCHING
AMEN.
WHAT'S HIS HURRY, I WONDER?
IT'S GRAMPS' SUPER POWER.
SOME SUPER POWER.
IT'S PROBABLY A HABIT FROM BEING A MAN-SERVANT.
AH, I SEE.
BY THE WAY, YOU WOULDN'T HAPPEN TO HAVE ONE OF THE BROCHURES MARI MADE, WOULD YOU?
OOH, I BET YOU HEARD ABOUT THEM FROM GRAMPS.

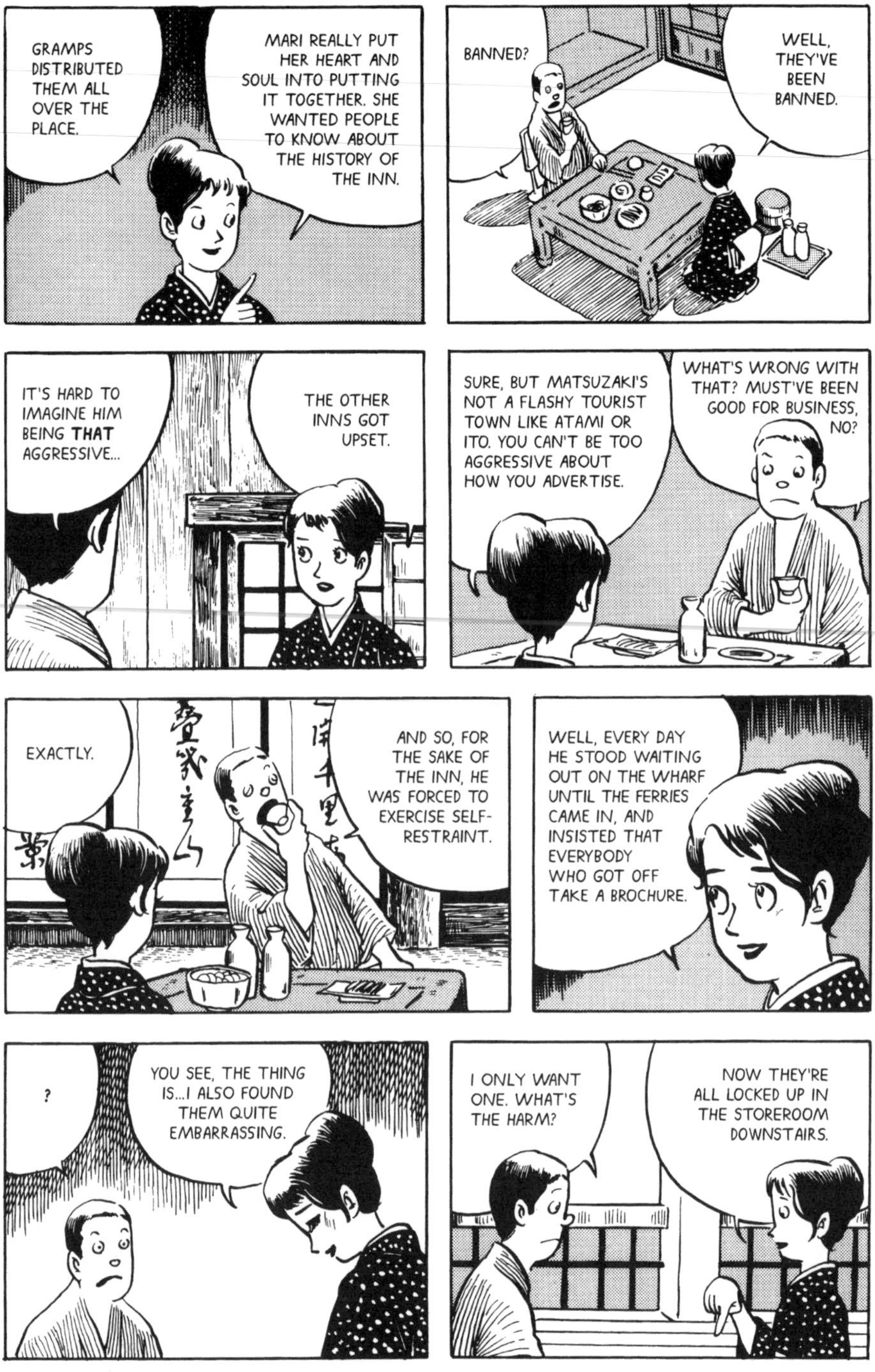
WELL, THEY'VE BEEN BANNED.
BANNED?
MARI REALLY PUT HER HEART AND SOUL INTO PUTTING IT TOGETHER. SHE WANTED PEOPLE TO KNOW ABOUT THE HISTORY OF THE INN.
GRAMPS DISTRIBUTED THEM ALL OVER THE PLACE.
WHAT'S WRONG WITH THAT? MUST'VE BEEN GOOD FOR BUSINESS, NO?
SURE, BUT MATSUZAKI'S NOT A FLASHY TOURIST TOWN LIKE ATAMI OR ITO. YOU CAN'T BE TOO AGGRESSIVE ABOUT HOW YOU ADVERTISE.
THE OTHER INNS GOT UPSET.
IT'S HARD TO IMAGINE HIM BEING **THAT** AGGRESSIVE...
WELL, EVERY DAY HE STOOD WAITING OUT ON THE WHARF UNTIL THE FERRIES CAME IN, AND INSISTED THAT EVERYBODY WHO GOT OFF TAKE A BROCHURE.
AND SO, FOR THE SAKE OF THE INN, HE WAS FORCED TO EXERCISE SELF-RESTRAINT.
EXACTLY.
NOW THEY'RE ALL LOCKED UP IN THE STOREROOM DOWNSTAIRS.
I ONLY WANT ONE. WHAT'S THE HARM?
YOU SEE, THE THING IS...I ALSO FOUND THEM QUITE EMBARRASSING.
?

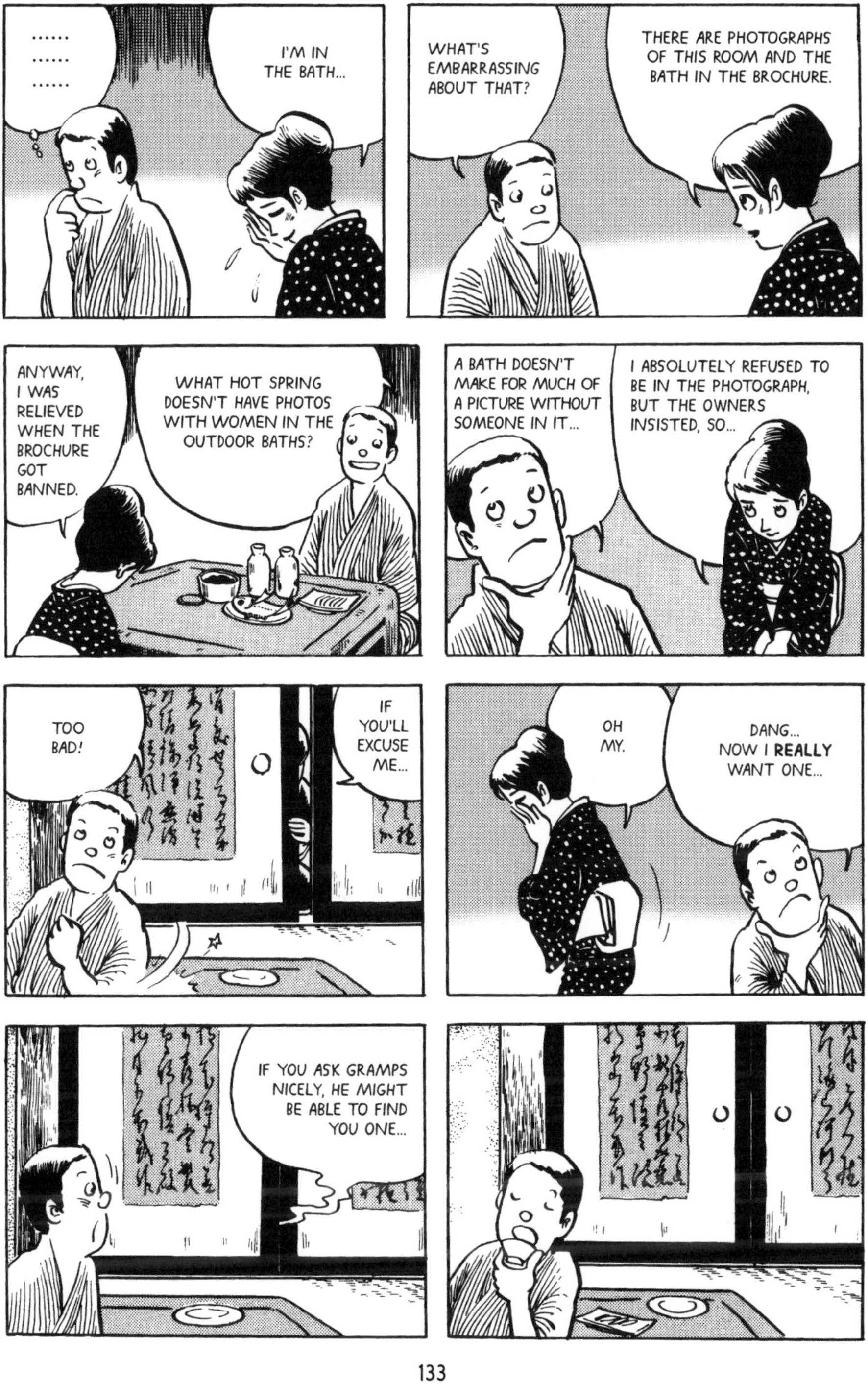
THERE ARE PHOTOGRAPHS OF THIS ROOM AND THE BATH IN THE BROCHURE.
WHAT'S EMBARRASSING ABOUT THAT?
I'M IN THE BATH...
......
......
......
I ABSOLUTELY REFUSED TO BE IN THE PHOTOGRAPH, BUT THE OWNERS INSISTED, SO...
A BATH DOESN'T MAKE FOR MUCH OF A PICTURE WITHOUT SOMEONE IN IT...
WHAT HOT SPRING DOESN'T HAVE PHOTOS WITH WOMEN IN THE OUTDOOR BATHS?
ANYWAY, I WAS RELIEVED WHEN THE BROCHURE GOT BANNED.
DANG... NOW I **REALLY** WANT ONE...
OH MY.
IF YOU'LL EXCUSE ME...
TOO BAD!
IF YOU ASK GRAMPS NICELY, HE MIGHT BE ABLE TO FIND YOU ONE...

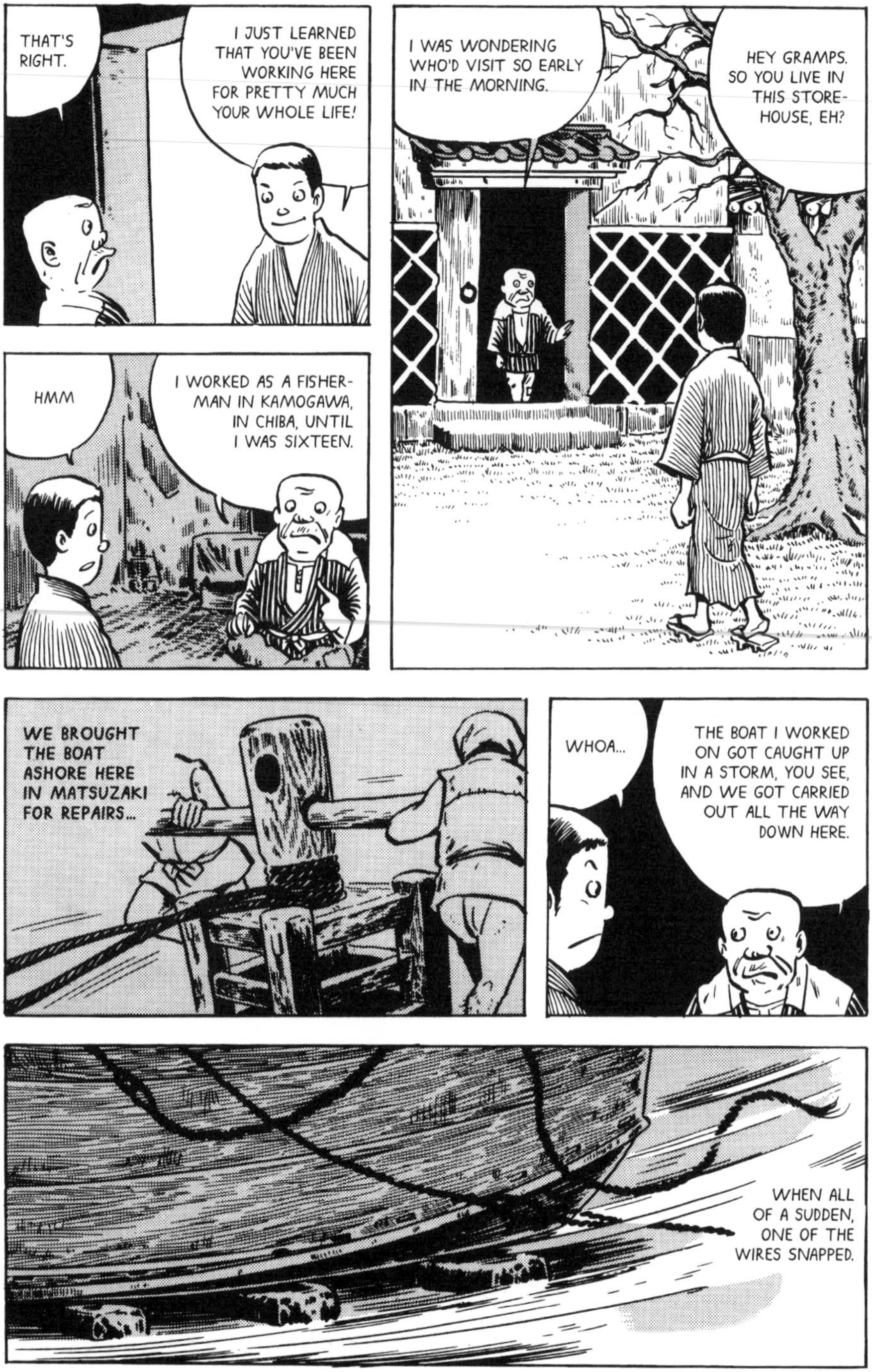
HEY GRAMPS. SO YOU LIVE IN THIS STORE-HOUSE, EH?
I WAS WONDERING WHO'D VISIT SO EARLY IN THE MORNING.
I JUST LEARNED THAT YOU'VE BEEN WORKING HERE FOR PRETTY MUCH YOUR WHOLE LIFE!
THAT'S RIGHT.
I WORKED AS A FISHER-MAN IN KAMOGAWA, IN CHIBA, UNTIL I WAS SIXTEEN.
HMM
THE BOAT I WORKED ON GOT CAUGHT UP IN A STORM, YOU SEE, AND WE GOT CARRIED OUT ALL THE WAY DOWN HERE.
WHOA...
WE BROUGHT THE BOAT ASHORE HERE IN MATSUZAKI FOR REPAIRS...
WHEN ALL OF A SUDDEN, ONE OF THE WIRES SNAPPED.

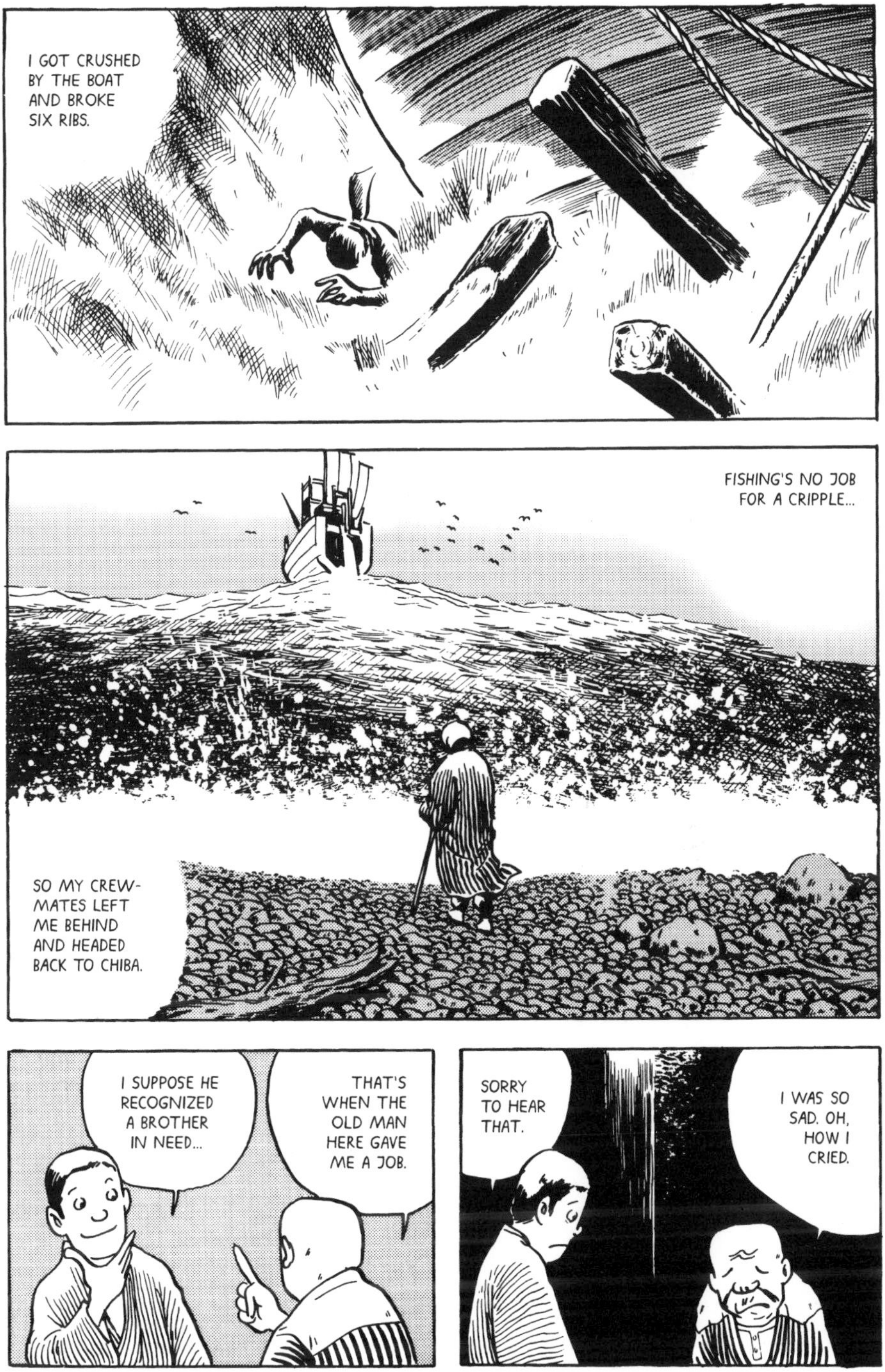
I GOT CRUSHED BY THE BOAT AND BROKE SIX RIBS.
FISHING'S NO JOB FOR A CRIPPLE...
SO MY CREW-MATES LEFT ME BEHIND AND HEADED BACK TO CHIBA.
I WAS SO SAD. OH, HOW I CRIED.
SORRY TO HEAR THAT.
THAT'S WHEN THE OLD MAN HERE GAVE ME A JOB.
I SUPPOSE HE RECOGNIZED A BROTHER IN NEED...

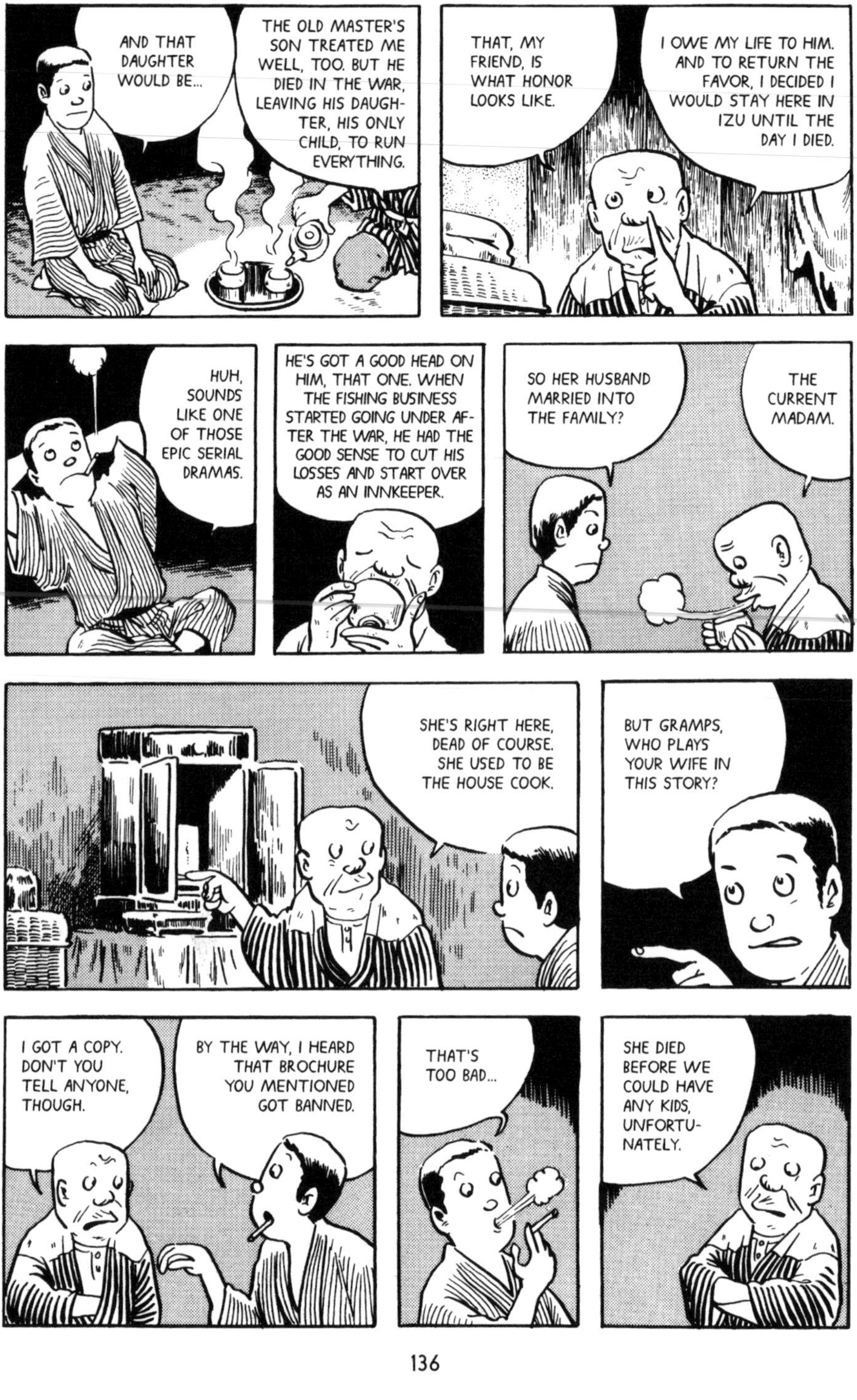
I OWE MY LIFE TO HIM. AND TO RETURN THE FAVOR, I DECIDED I WOULD STAY HERE IN IZU UNTIL THE DAY I DIED.
THAT, MY FRIEND, IS WHAT HONOR LOOKS LIKE.
THE OLD MASTER'S SON TREATED ME WELL, TOO. BUT HE DIED IN THE WAR, LEAVING HIS DAUGHTER, HIS ONLY CHILD, TO RUN EVERYTHING.
AND THAT DAUGHTER WOULD BE...
THE CURRENT MADAM.
SO HER HUSBAND MARRIED INTO THE FAMILY?
HE'S GOT A GOOD HEAD ON HIM, THAT ONE. WHEN THE FISHING BUSINESS STARTED GOING UNDER AFTER THE WAR, HE HAD THE GOOD SENSE TO CUT HIS LOSSES AND START OVER AS AN INNKEEPER.
HUH, SOUNDS LIKE ONE OF THOSE EPIC SERIAL DRAMAS.
BUT GRAMPS, WHO PLAYS YOUR WIFE IN THIS STORY?
SHE'S RIGHT HERE, DEAD OF COURSE. SHE USED TO BE THE HOUSE COOK.
SHE DIED BEFORE WE COULD HAVE ANY KIDS, UNFORTUNATELY.
THAT'S TOO BAD...
BY THE WAY, I HEARD THAT BROCHURE YOU MENTIONED GOT BANNED.
I GOT A COPY. DON'T YOU TELL ANYONE, THOUGH.

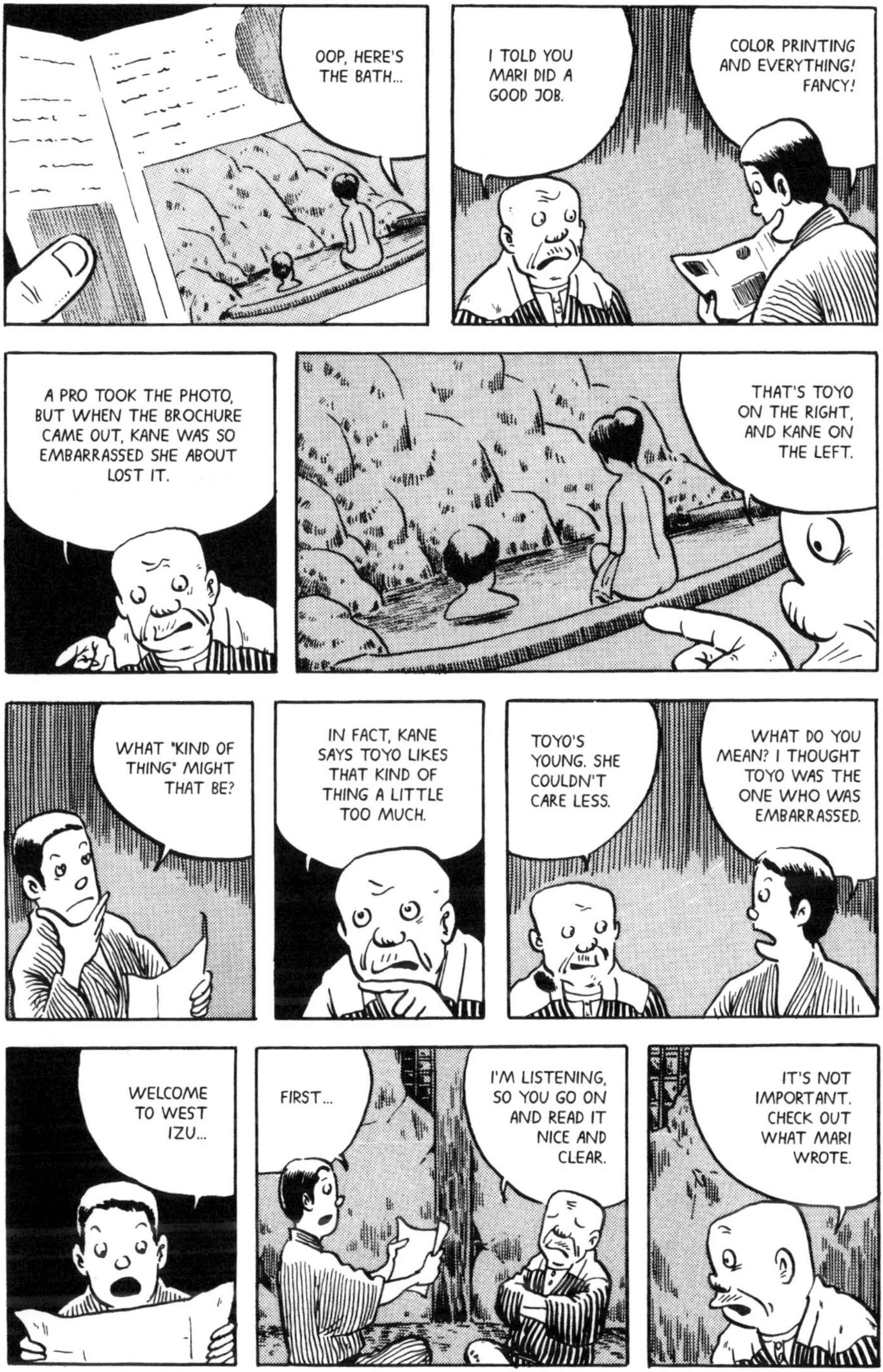
COLOR PRINTING AND EVERYTHING! FANCY!
I TOLD YOU MARI DID A GOOD JOB.
OOP, HERE'S THE BATH...
THAT'S TOYO ON THE RIGHT, AND KANE ON THE LEFT.
A PRO TOOK THE PHOTO, BUT WHEN THE BROCHURE CAME OUT, KANE WAS SO EMBARRASSED SHE ABOUT LOST IT.
WHAT DO YOU MEAN? I THOUGHT TOYO WAS THE ONE WHO WAS EMBARRASSED.
TOYO'S YOUNG. SHE COULDN'T CARE LESS.
IN FACT, KANE SAYS TOYO LIKES THAT KIND OF THING A LITTLE TOO MUCH.
WHAT "KIND OF THING" MIGHT THAT BE?
IT'S NOT IMPORTANT. CHECK OUT WHAT MARI WROTE.
I'M LISTENING, SO YOU GO ON AND READ IT NICE AND CLEAR.
FIRST...
WELCOME TO WEST IZU...

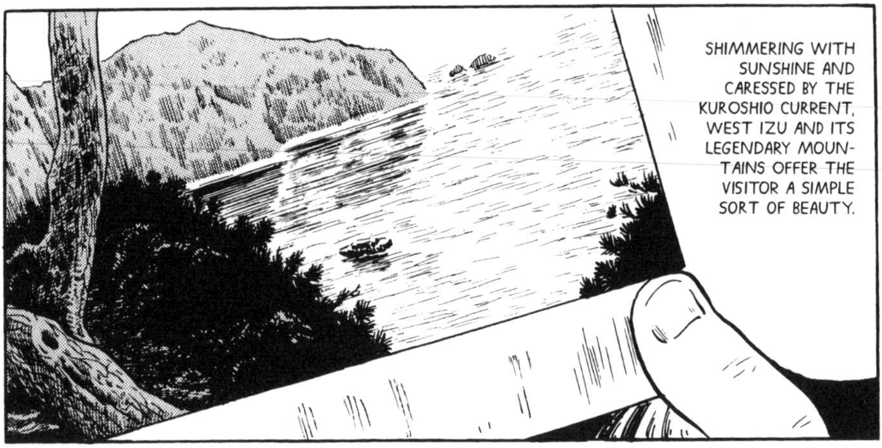
SHIMMERING WITH SUNSHINE AND CARESSED BY THE KUROSHIO CURRENT, WEST IZU AND ITS LEGENDARY MOUNTAINS OFFER THE VISITOR A SIMPLE SORT OF BEAUTY.

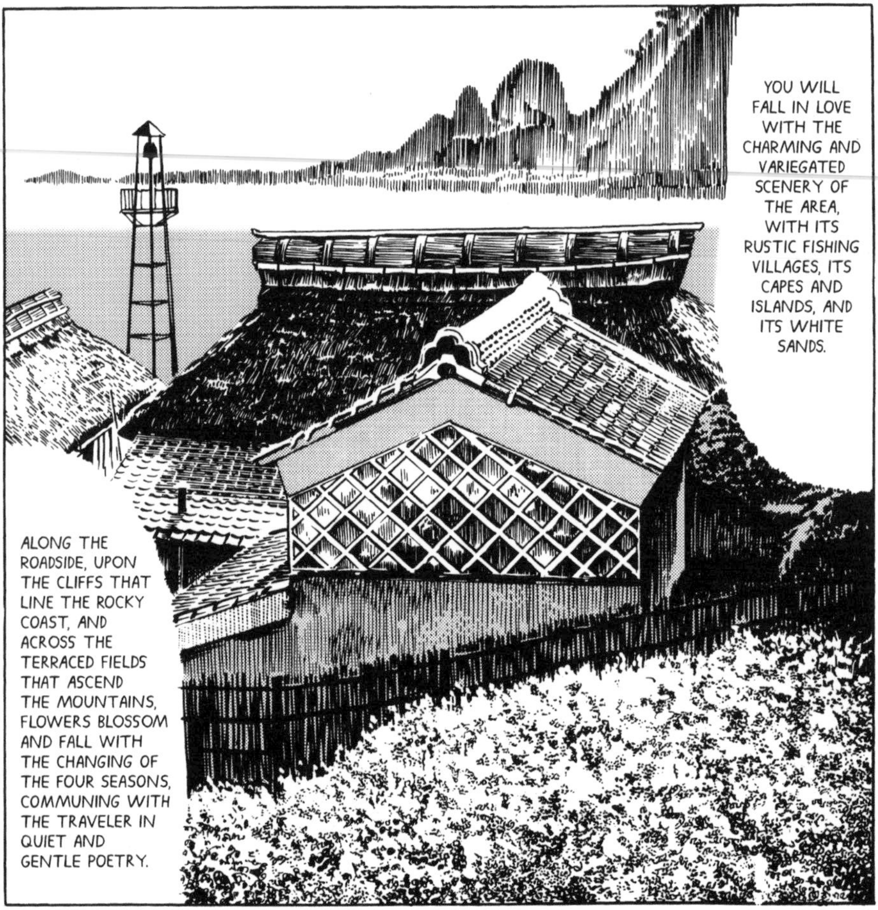
YOU WILL FALL IN LOVE WITH THE CHARMING AND VARIEGATED SCENERY OF THE AREA, WITH ITS RUSTIC FISHING VILLAGES, ITS CAPES AND ISLANDS, AND ITS WHITE SANDS.
ALONG THE ROADSIDE, UPON THE CLIFFS THAT LINE THE ROCKY COAST, AND ACROSS THE TERRACED FIELDS THAT ASCEND THE MOUNTAINS, FLOWERS BLOSSOM AND FALL WITH THE CHANGING OF THE FOUR SEASONS, COMMUNING WITH THE TRAVELER IN QUIET AND GENTLE POETRY.

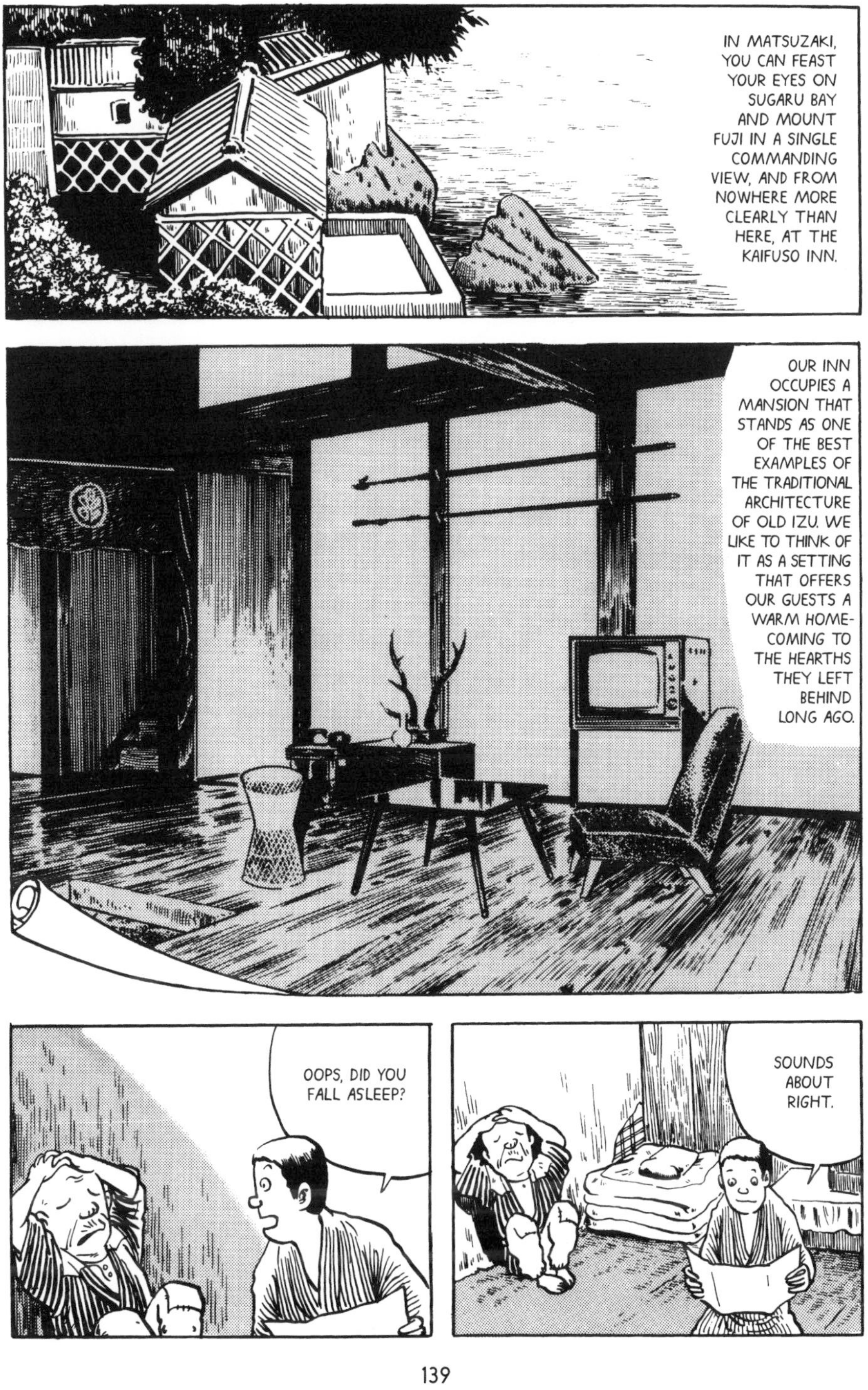
IN MATSUZAKI, YOU CAN FEAST YOUR EYES ON SUGARU BAY AND MOUNT FUJI IN A SINGLE COMMANDING VIEW, AND FROM NOWHERE MORE CLEARLY THAN HERE, AT THE KAIFUSO INN.
OUR INN OCCUPIES A MANSION THAT STANDS AS ONE OF THE BEST EXAMPLES OF THE TRADITIONAL ARCHITECTURE OF OLD IZU. WE LIKE TO THINK OF IT AS A SETTING THAT OFFERS OUR GUESTS A WARM HOME-COMING TO THE HEARTHS THEY LEFT BEHIND LONG AGO.
SOUNDS ABOUT RIGHT.
OOPS, DID YOU FALL ASLEEP?

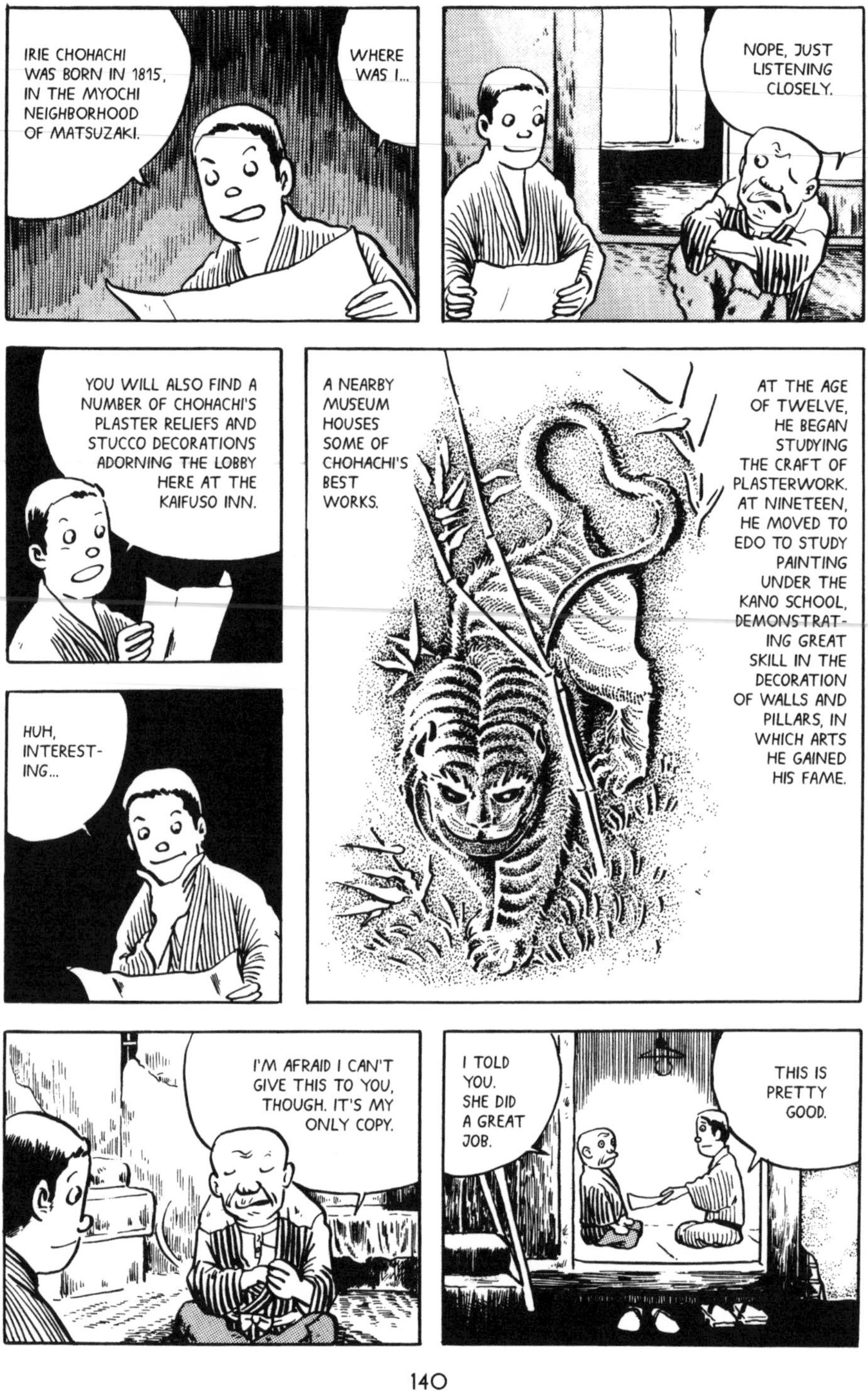
NOPE, JUST LISTENING CLOSELY.
WHERE WAS I...
IRIE CHOHACHI WAS BORN IN 1815, IN THE MYOCHI NEIGHBORHOOD OF MATSUZAKI.
AT THE AGE OF TWELVE, HE BEGAN STUDYING THE CRAFT OF PLASTERWORK. AT NINETEEN, HE MOVED TO EDO TO STUDY PAINTING UNDER THE KANO SCHOOL, DEMONSTRAT-ING GREAT SKILL IN THE DECORATION OF WALLS AND PILLARS, IN WHICH ARTS HE GAINED HIS FAME.
A NEARBY MUSEUM HOUSES SOME OF CHOHACHI'S BEST WORKS.
YOU WILL ALSO FIND A NUMBER OF CHOHACHI'S PLASTER RELIEFS AND STUCCO DECORATIONS ADORNING THE LOBBY HERE AT THE KAIFUSO INN.
HUH, INTEREST-ING...
THIS IS PRETTY GOOD.
I TOLD YOU. SHE DID A GREAT JOB.
I'M AFRAID I CAN'T GIVE THIS TO YOU, THOUGH. IT'S MY ONLY COPY.

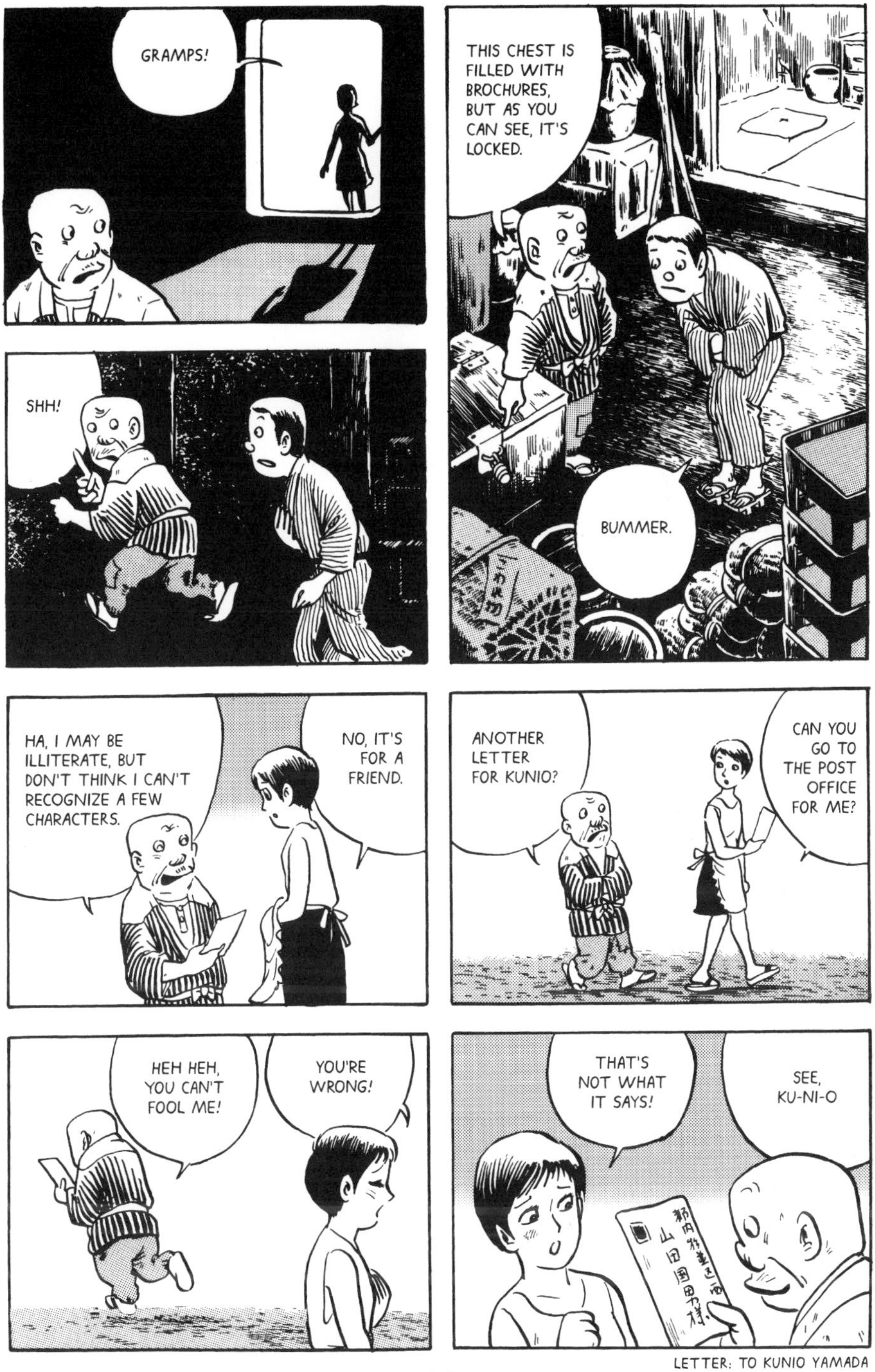
THIS CHEST IS FILLED WITH BROCHURES, BUT AS YOU CAN SEE, IT'S LOCKED.
BUMMER.
GRAMPS!
SHH!
CAN YOU GO TO THE POST OFFICE FOR ME?
ANOTHER LETTER FOR KUNIO?
NO, IT'S FOR A FRIEND.
HA, I MAY BE ILLITERATE, BUT DON'T THINK I CAN'T RECOGNIZE A FEW CHARACTERS.
SEE, KU-NI-O
THAT'S NOT WHAT IT SAYS!
YOU'RE WRONG!
HEH HEH, YOU CAN'T FOOL ME!

LETTER: TO KUNIO YAMADA

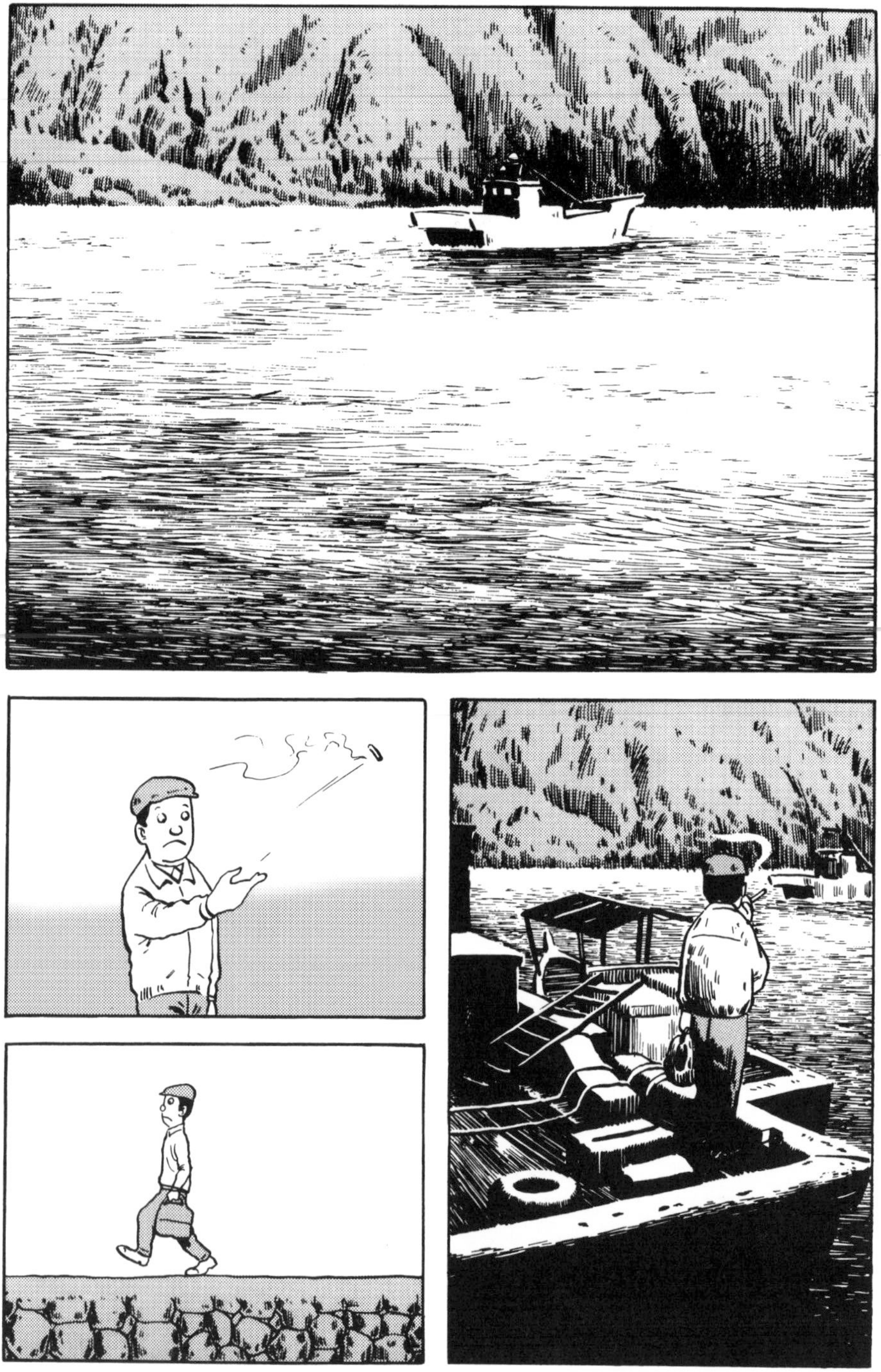

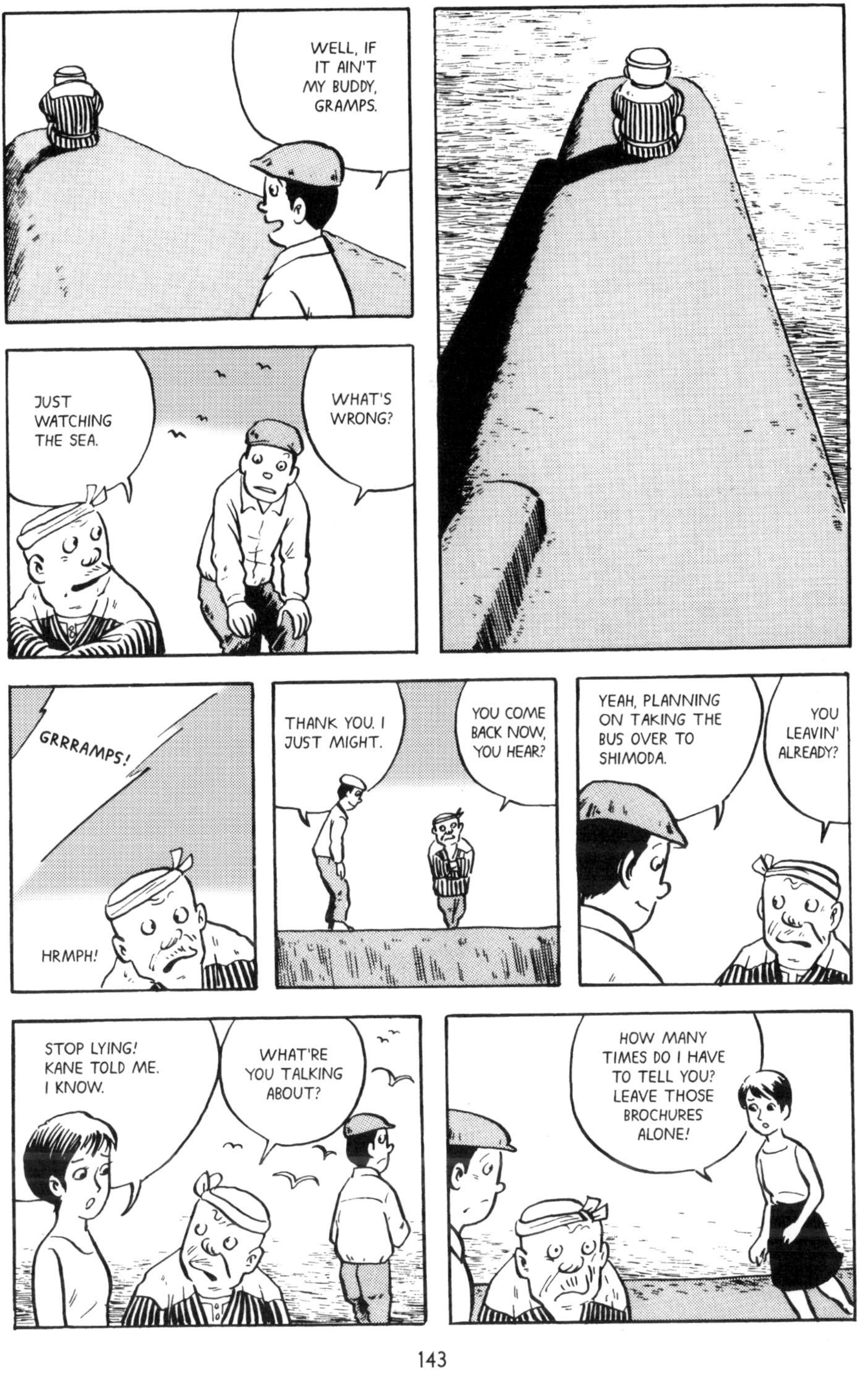
WELL, IF IT AIN'T MY BUDDY, GRAMPS.
WHAT'S WRONG?
JUST WATCHING THE SEA.
YOU LEAVIN' ALREADY?
YEAH, PLANNING ON TAKING THE BUS OVER TO SHIMODA.
YOU COME BACK NOW, YOU HEAR?
THANK YOU. I JUST MIGHT.
GRRRAMPS!
HRMPH!
HOW MANY TIMES DO I HAVE TO TELL YOU? LEAVE THOSE BROCHURES ALONE!
WHAT'RE YOU TALKING ABOUT?
STOP LYING! KANE TOLD ME. I KNOW.

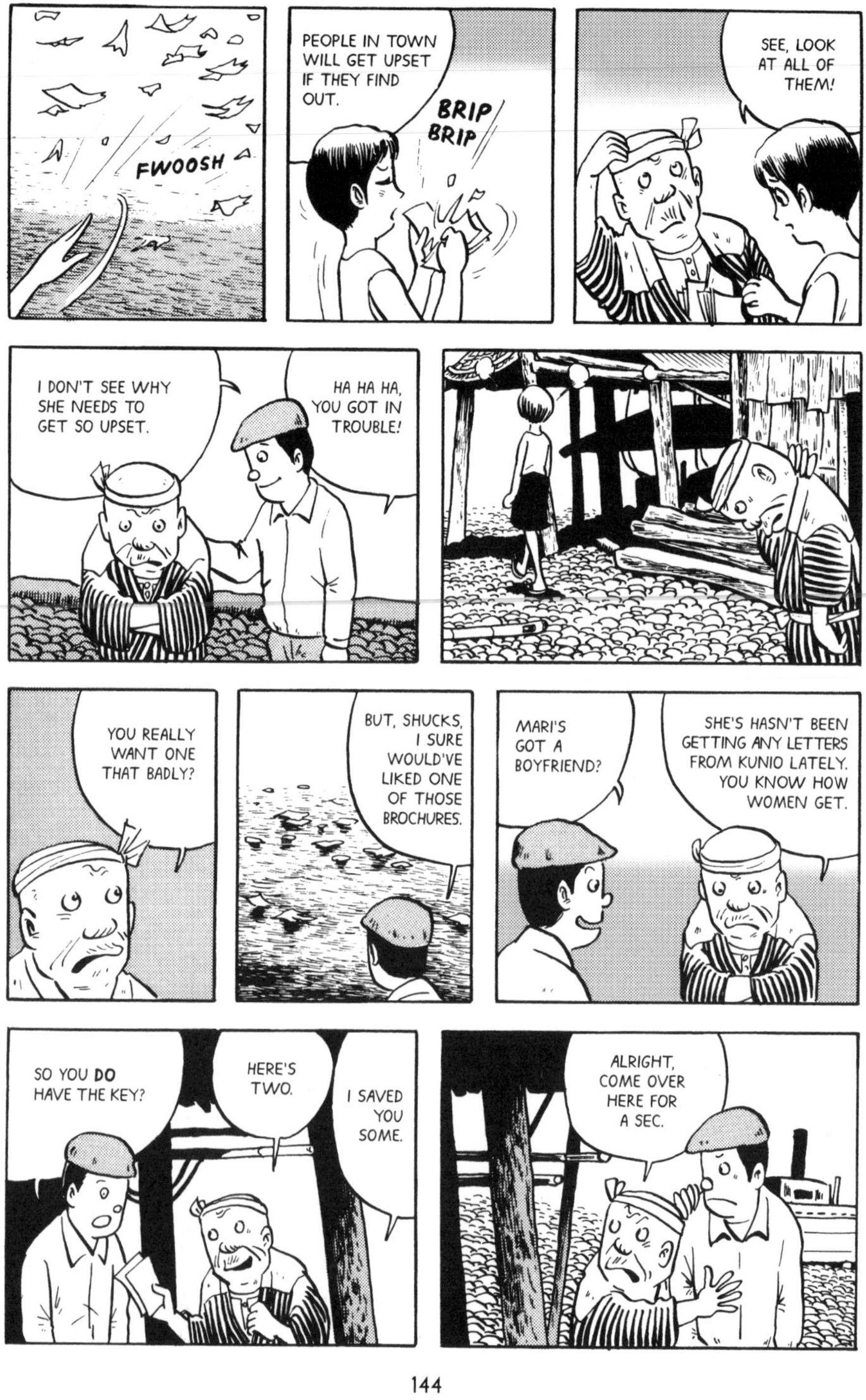
SEE, LOOK AT ALL OF THEM!
PEOPLE IN TOWN WILL GET UPSET IF THEY FIND OUT.
BRIP BRIP
FWOOSH
HA HA HA, YOU GOT IN TROUBLE!
I DON'T SEE WHY SHE NEEDS TO GET SO UPSET.
SHE'S HASN'T BEEN GETTING ANY LETTERS FROM KUNIO LATELY. YOU KNOW HOW WOMEN GET.
MARI'S GOT A BOYFRIEND?
BUT, SHUCKS, I SURE WOULD'VE LIKED ONE OF THOSE BROCHURES.
YOU REALLY WANT ONE THAT BADLY?
ALRIGHT, COME OVER HERE FOR A SEC.
I SAVED YOU SOME.
HERE'S TWO.
SO YOU **DO** HAVE THE KEY?

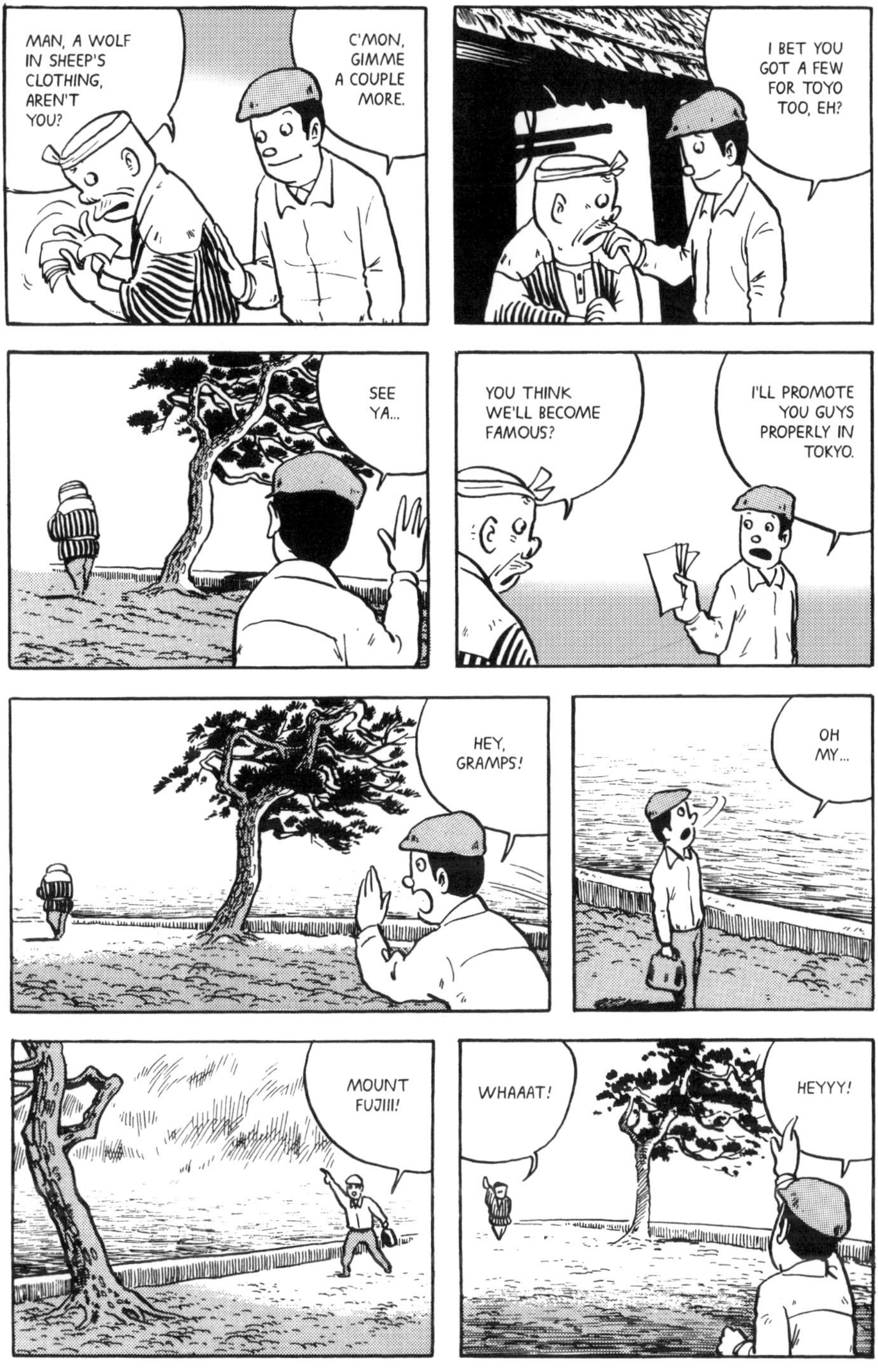
I BET YOU GOT A FEW FOR TOYO TOO, EH?
C'MON, GIMME A COUPLE MORE.
MAN, A WOLF IN SHEEP'S CLOTHING, AREN'T YOU?
I'LL PROMOTE YOU GUYS PROPERLY IN TOKYO.
YOU THINK WE'LL BECOME FAMOUS?
SEE YA...
OH MY...
HEY, GRAMPS!
HEYYY!
WHAAAT!
MOUNT FUJIII!

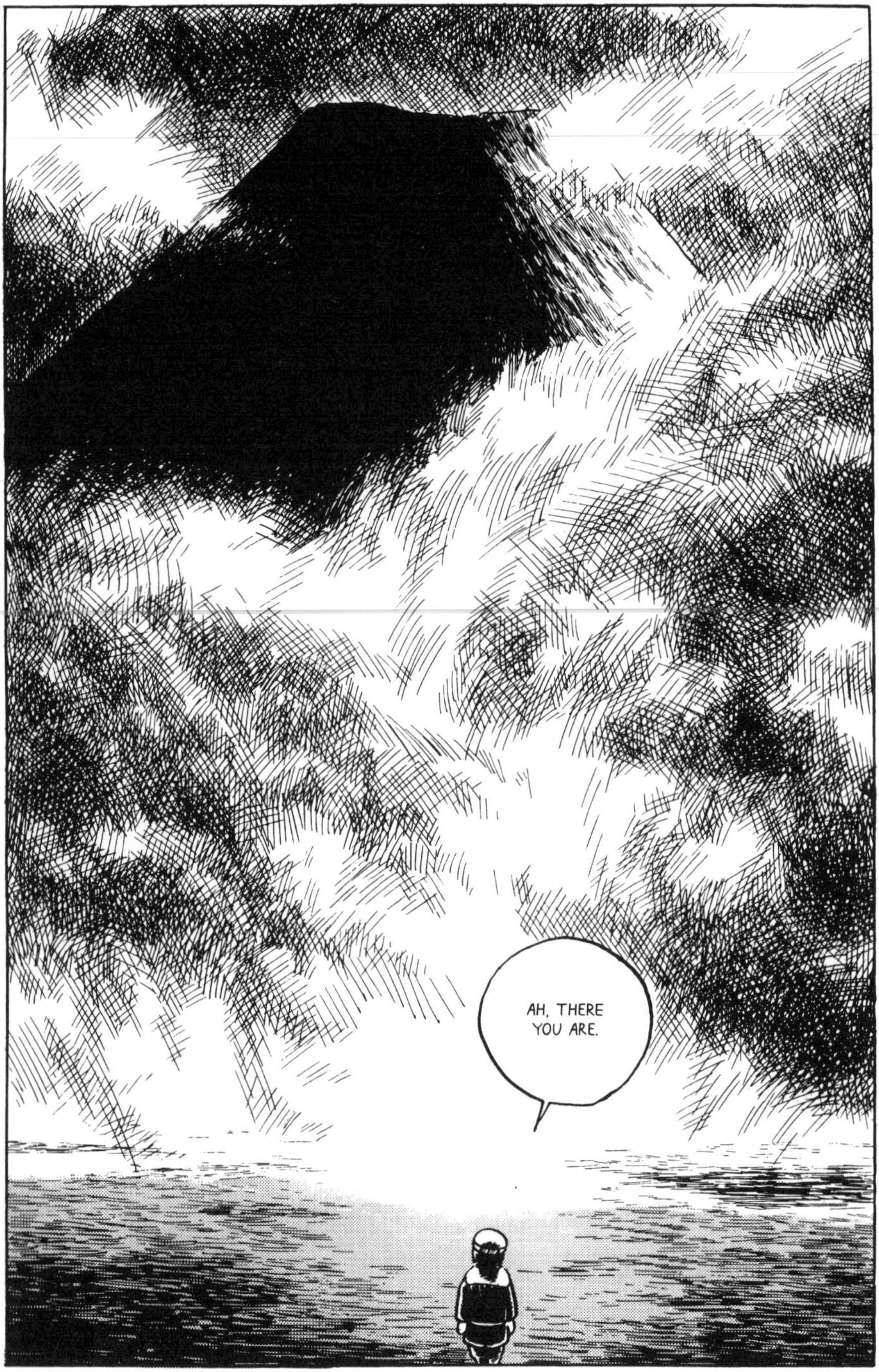
AH, THERE YOU ARE.

FUTAMATA GORGE

AS AUTUMN WOUND DOWN LAST YEAR, MY TRAVELS WERE DISRUPTED BY AN UNSEASONABLY LATE TYPHOON. SINCE I WAS DEEP IN THE MOUNTAINS OF AIZU AT THE TIME, IT WAS HARD FOR ME TO JUDGE HOW STRONG THE STORM ACTUALLY WAS. WINDS AND RAINS IN THE MOUNTAINS GIVE THE MOST TERRIFYING IMPRESSION. I THEREFORE ASSUMED THE WORST.

UPON REACHING LOWER GROUND AND WATCHING THE NEWS, HOWEVER, I WAS SURPRISED TO LEARN THAT THE DAMAGE EVERYWHERE WAS MINIMAL. EVEN WHERE I HAD BEEN IN AIZU, A LONE MONKEY WAS KILLED, THAT WAS ALL.

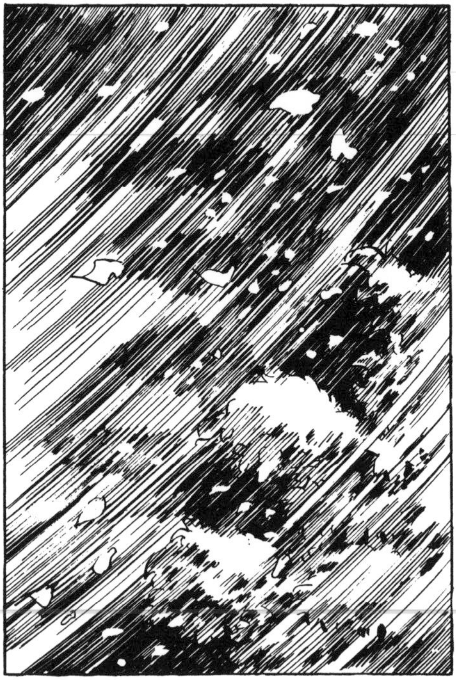

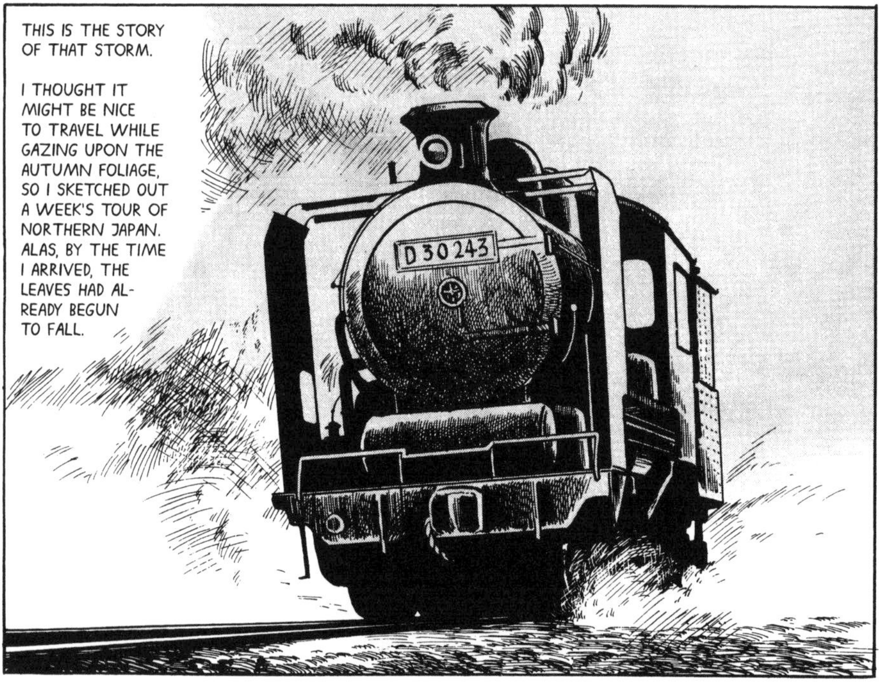
THIS IS THE STORY OF THAT STORM.
I THOUGHT IT MIGHT BE NICE TO TRAVEL WHILE GAZING UPON THE AUTUMN FOLIAGE, SO I SKETCHED OUT A WEEK'S TOUR OF NORTHERN JAPAN. ALAS, BY THE TIME I ARRIVED, THE LEAVES HAD AL-READY BEGUN TO FALL.
D30243

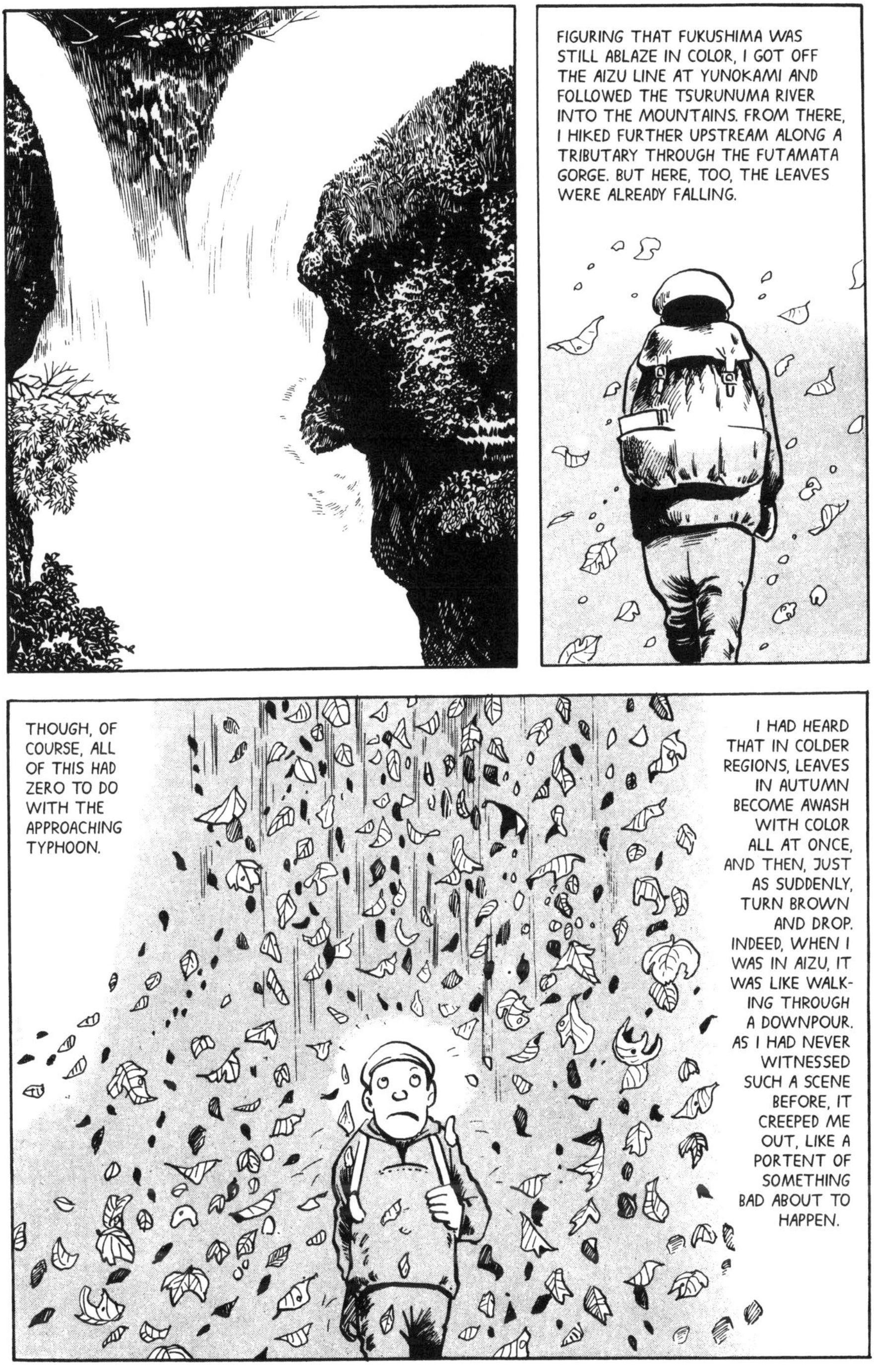
FIGURING THAT FUKUSHIMA WAS STILL ABLAZE IN COLOR, I GOT OFF THE AIZU LINE AT YUNOKAMI AND FOLLOWED THE TSURUNUMA RIVER INTO THE MOUNTAINS. FROM THERE, I HIKED FURTHER UPSTREAM ALONG A TRIBUTARY THROUGH THE FUTAMATA GORGE. BUT HERE, TOO, THE LEAVES WERE ALREADY FALLING.
I HAD HEARD THAT IN COLDER REGIONS, LEAVES IN AUTUMN BECOME AWASH WITH COLOR ALL AT ONCE, AND THEN, JUST AS SUDDENLY, TURN BROWN AND DROP. INDEED, WHEN I WAS IN AIZU, IT WAS LIKE WALKING THROUGH A DOWNPOUR. AS I HAD NEVER WITNESSED SUCH A SCENE BEFORE, IT CREEPED ME OUT, LIKE A PORTENT OF SOMETHING BAD ABOUT TO HAPPEN.
THOUGH, OF COURSE, ALL OF THIS HAD ZERO TO DO WITH THE APPROACHING TYPHOON.

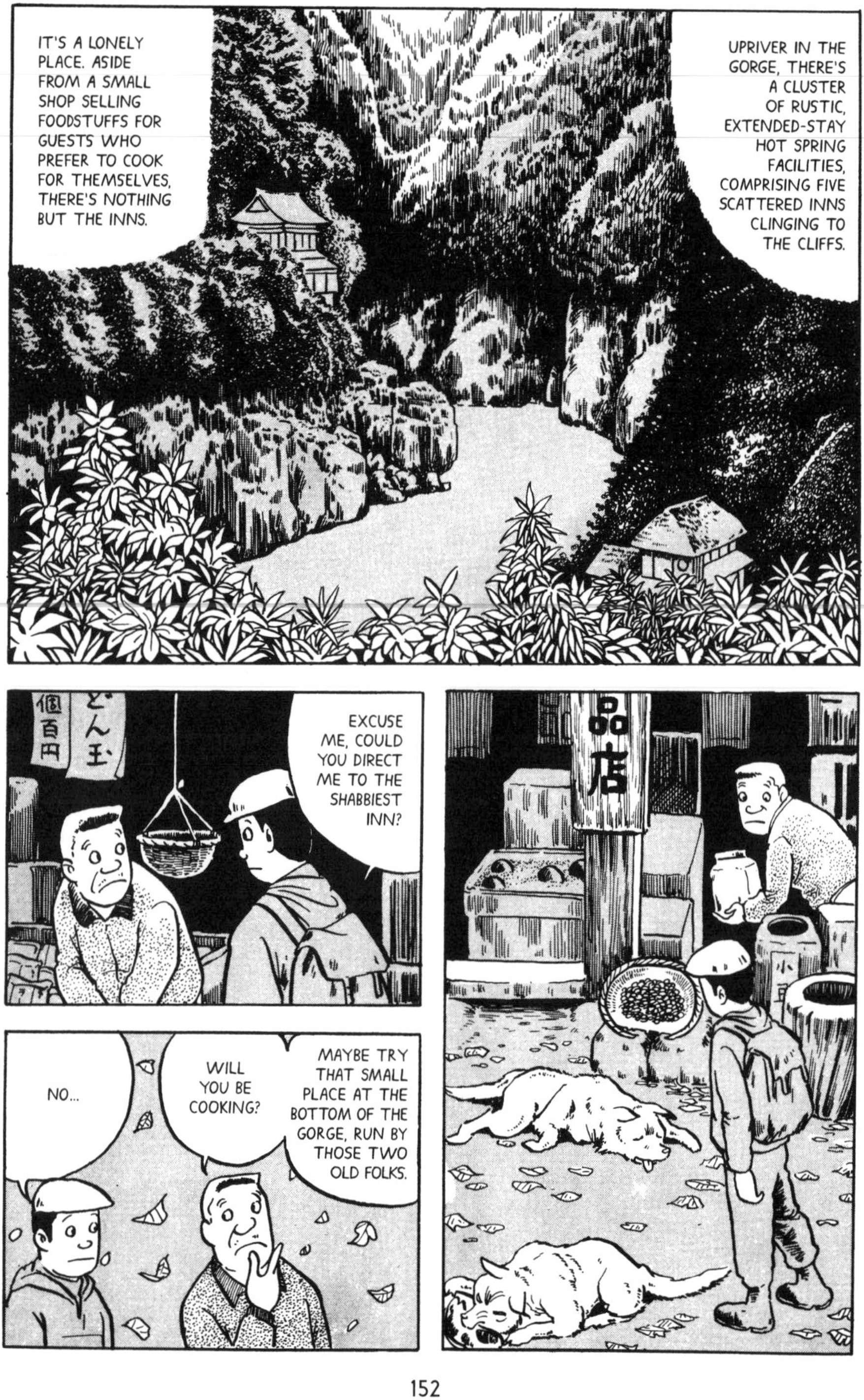
UPRIVER IN THE GORGE, THERE'S A CLUSTER OF RUSTIC, EXTENDED-STAY HOT SPRING FACILITIES, COMPRISING FIVE SCATTERED INNS CLINGING TO THE CLIFFS.
IT'S A LONELY PLACE. ASIDE FROM A SMALL SHOP SELLING FOODSTUFFS FOR GUESTS WHO PREFER TO COOK FOR THEMSELVES, THERE'S NOTHING BUT THE INNS.
品店
EXCUSE ME, COULD YOU DIRECT ME TO THE SHABBIEST INN?
MAYBE TRY THAT SMALL PLACE AT THE BOTTOM OF THE GORGE, RUN BY THOSE TWO OLD FOLKS.
WILL YOU BE COOKING?
NO...

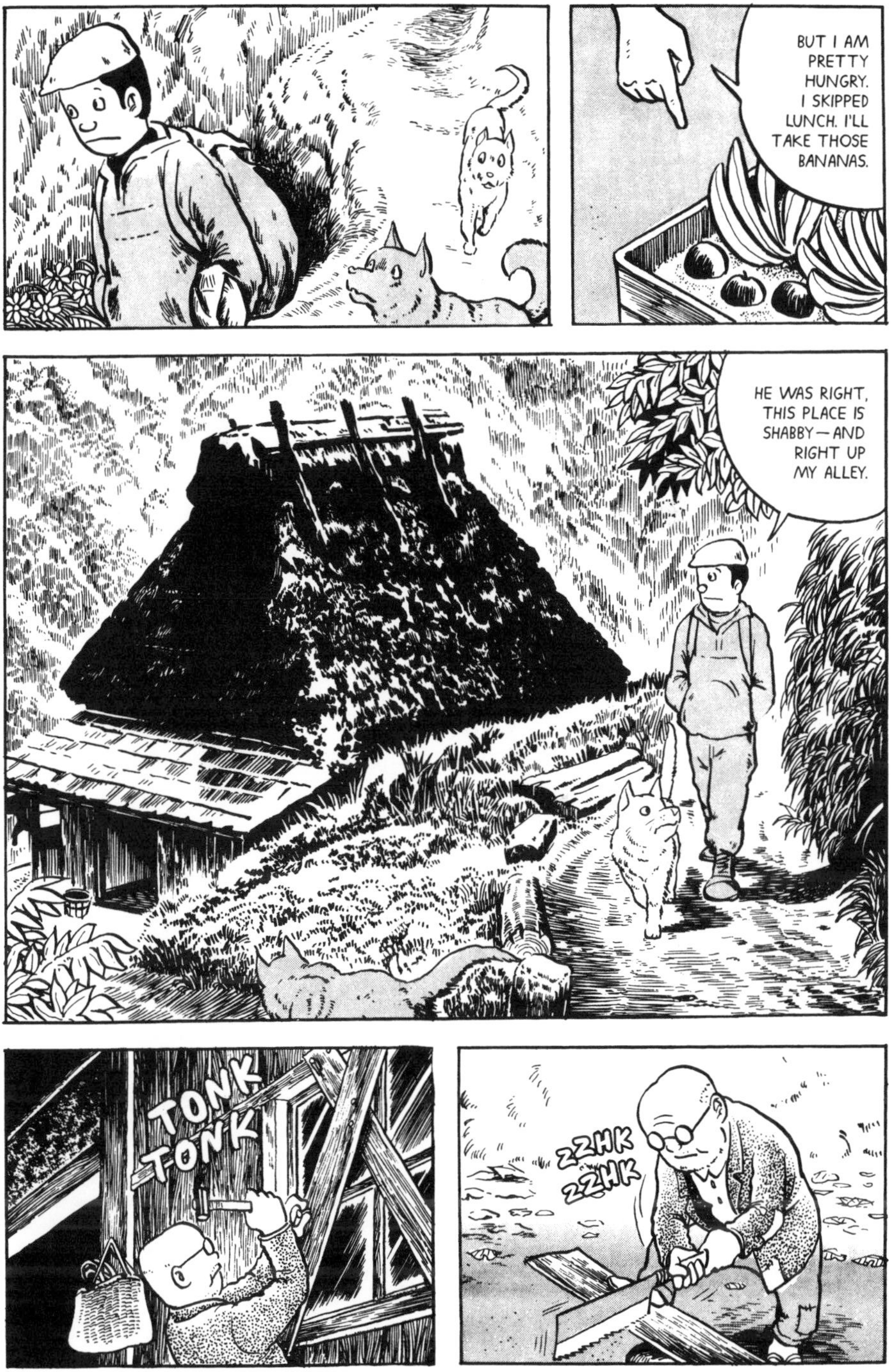
BUT I AM PRETTY HUNGRY. I SKIPPED LUNCH. I'LL TAKE THOSE BANANAS.
HE WAS RIGHT, THIS PLACE IS SHABBY—AND RIGHT UP MY ALLEY.
ZZHK ZZHK
TONK TONK

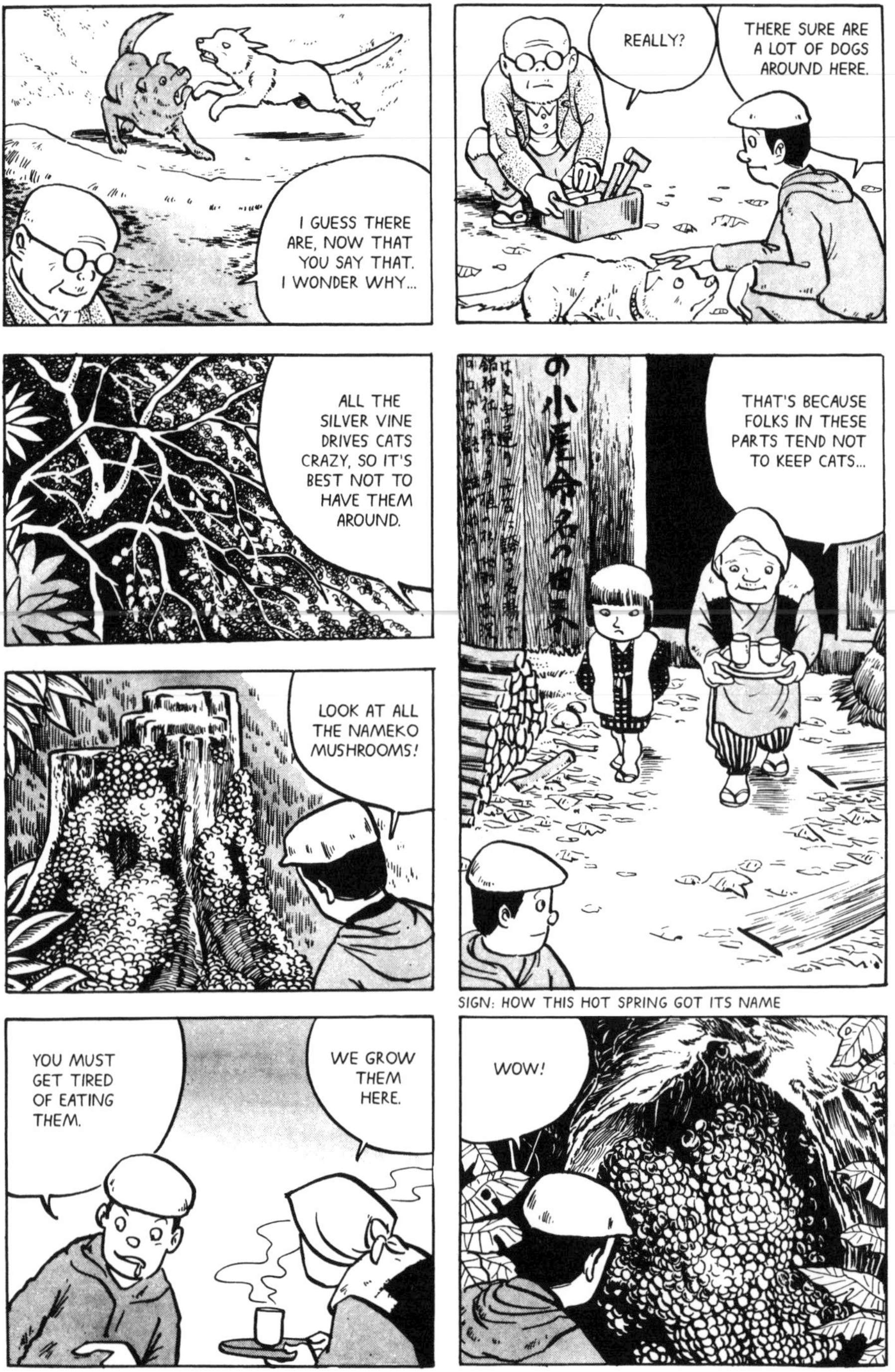
THERE SURE ARE A LOT OF DOGS AROUND HERE.
REALLY?
I GUESS THERE ARE, NOW THAT YOU SAY THAT. I WONDER WHY...
THAT'S BECAUSE FOLKS IN THESE PARTS TEND NOT TO KEEP CATS...
SIGN: HOW THIS HOT SPRING GOT ITS NAME
ALL THE SILVER VINE DRIVES CATS CRAZY, SO IT'S BEST NOT TO HAVE THEM AROUND.
LOOK AT ALL THE NAMEKO MUSHROOMS!
WOW!
WE GROW THEM HERE.
YOU MUST GET TIRED OF EATING THEM.

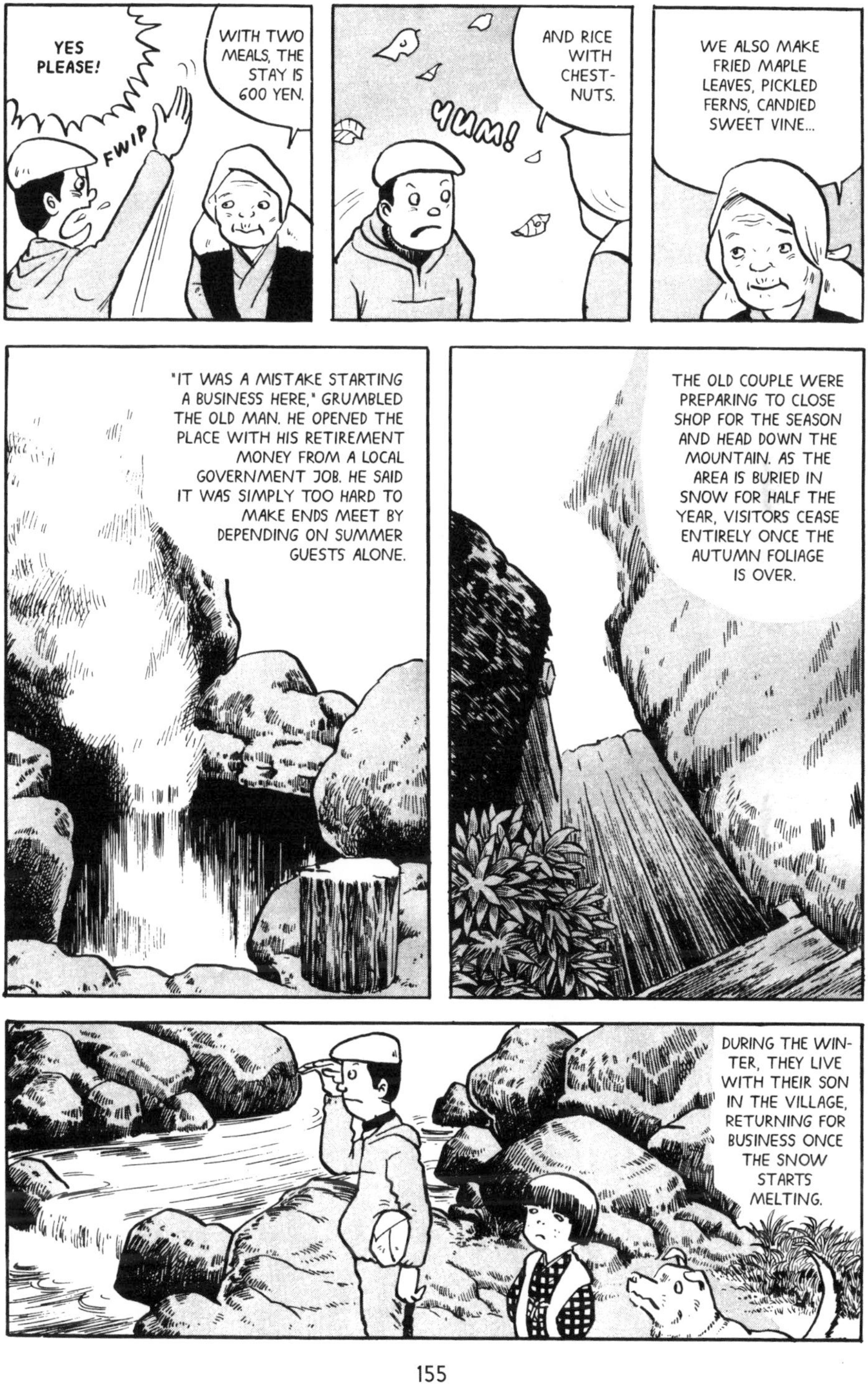
WE ALSO MAKE FRIED MAPLE LEAVES, PICKLED FERNS, CANDIED SWEET VINE...
AND RICE WITH CHEST-NUTS.
YUM!
WITH TWO MEALS, THE STAY IS 600 YEN.
YES PLEASE!
FWIP
THE OLD COUPLE WERE PREPARING TO CLOSE SHOP FOR THE SEASON AND HEAD DOWN THE MOUNTAIN. AS THE AREA IS BURIED IN SNOW FOR HALF THE YEAR, VISITORS CEASE ENTIRELY ONCE THE AUTUMN FOLIAGE IS OVER.
"IT WAS A MISTAKE STARTING A BUSINESS HERE," GRUMBLED THE OLD MAN. HE OPENED THE PLACE WITH HIS RETIREMENT MONEY FROM A LOCAL GOVERNMENT JOB. HE SAID IT WAS SIMPLY TOO HARD TO MAKE ENDS MEET BY DEPENDING ON SUMMER GUESTS ALONE.
DURING THE WIN-TER, THEY LIVE WITH THEIR SON IN THE VILLAGE, RETURNING FOR BUSINESS ONCE THE SNOW STARTS MELTING.

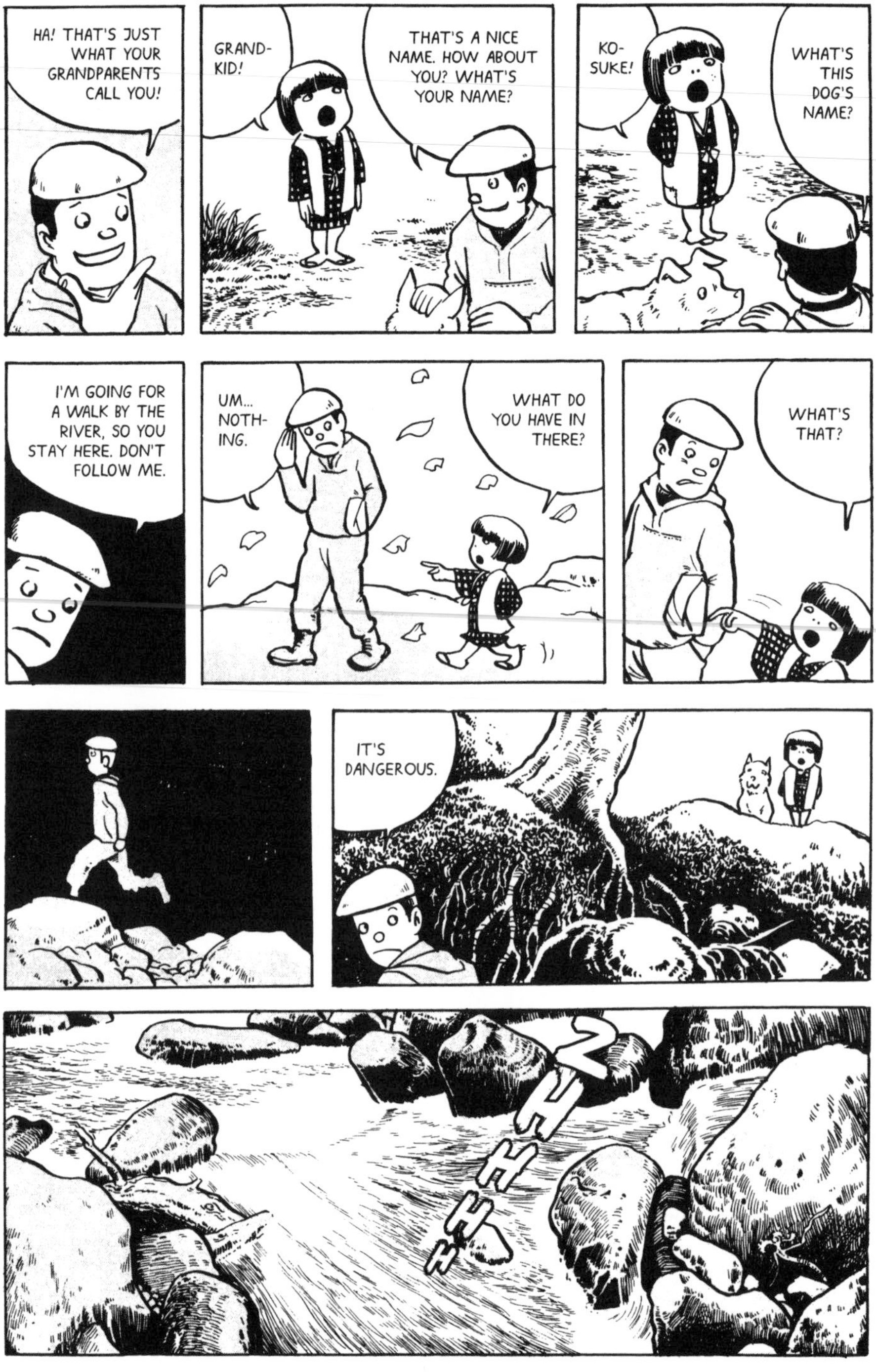
WHAT'S THIS DOG'S NAME?
KO-SUKE!
THAT'S A NICE NAME. HOW ABOUT YOU? WHAT'S YOUR NAME?
GRAND-KID!
HA! THAT'S JUST WHAT YOUR GRANDPARENTS CALL YOU!
WHAT'S THAT?
WHAT DO YOU HAVE IN THERE?
UM... NOTHING.
I'M GOING FOR A WALK BY THE RIVER, SO YOU STAY HERE. DON'T FOLLOW ME.
IT'S DANGEROUS.
ZHHHH

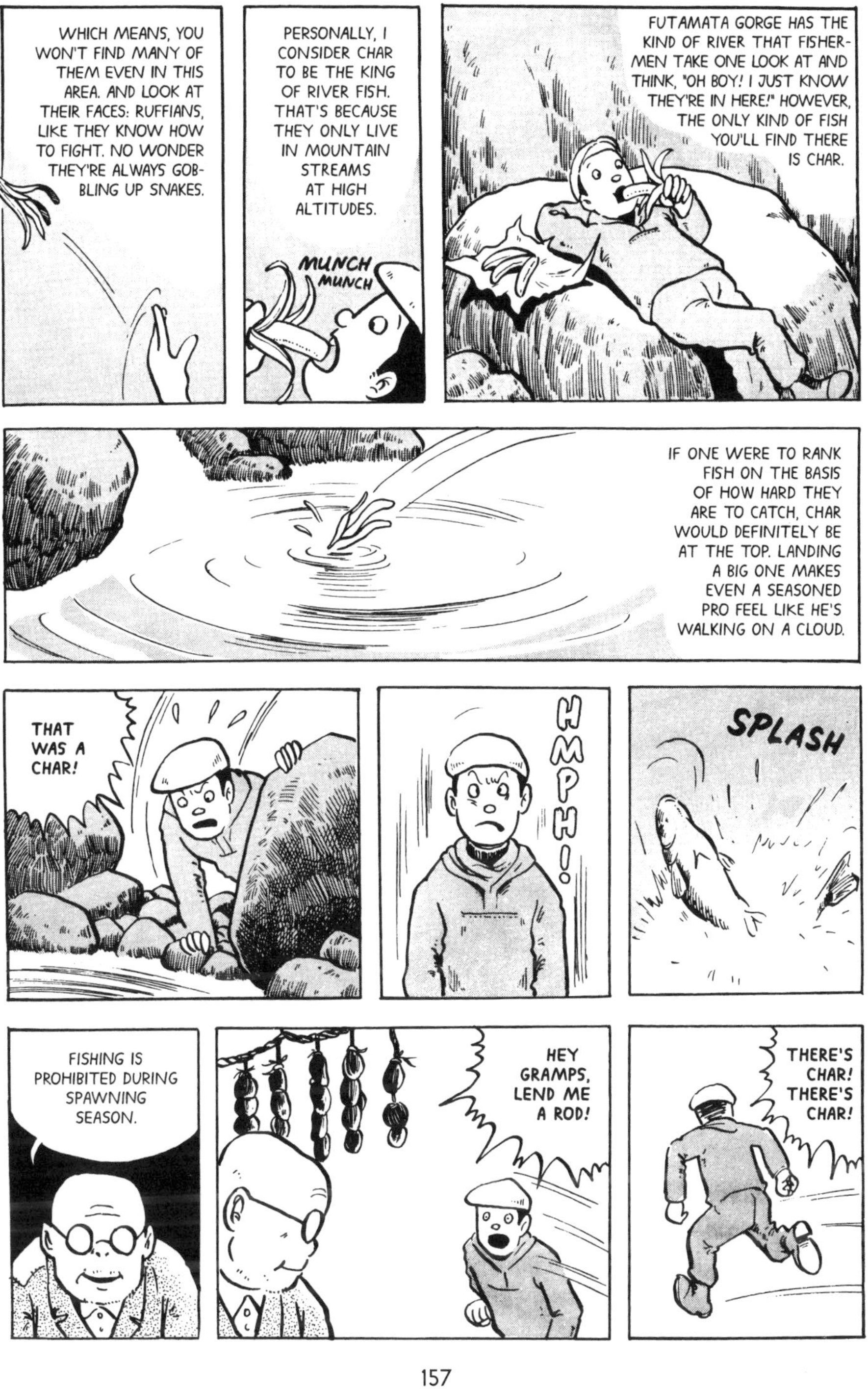
FUTAMATA GORGE HAS THE KIND OF RIVER THAT FISHERMEN TAKE ONE LOOK AT AND THINK, "OH BOY! I JUST KNOW THEY'RE IN HERE!" HOWEVER, THE ONLY KIND OF FISH YOU'LL FIND THERE IS CHAR.
PERSONALLY, I CONSIDER CHAR TO BE THE KING OF RIVER FISH. THAT'S BECAUSE THEY ONLY LIVE IN MOUNTAIN STREAMS AT HIGH ALTITUDES.
MUNCH MUNCH
WHICH MEANS, YOU WON'T FIND MANY OF THEM EVEN IN THIS AREA. AND LOOK AT THEIR FACES: RUFFIANS, LIKE THEY KNOW HOW TO FIGHT. NO WONDER THEY'RE ALWAYS GOBBLING UP SNAKES.
IF ONE WERE TO RANK FISH ON THE BASIS OF HOW HARD THEY ARE TO CATCH, CHAR WOULD DEFINITELY BE AT THE TOP. LANDING A BIG ONE MAKES EVEN A SEASONED PRO FEEL LIKE HE'S WALKING ON A CLOUD.
SPLASH
HMPH!
THAT WAS A CHAR!
THERE'S CHAR! THERE'S CHAR!
HEY GRAMPS, LEND ME A ROD!
FISHING IS PROHIBITED DURING SPAWNING SEASON.

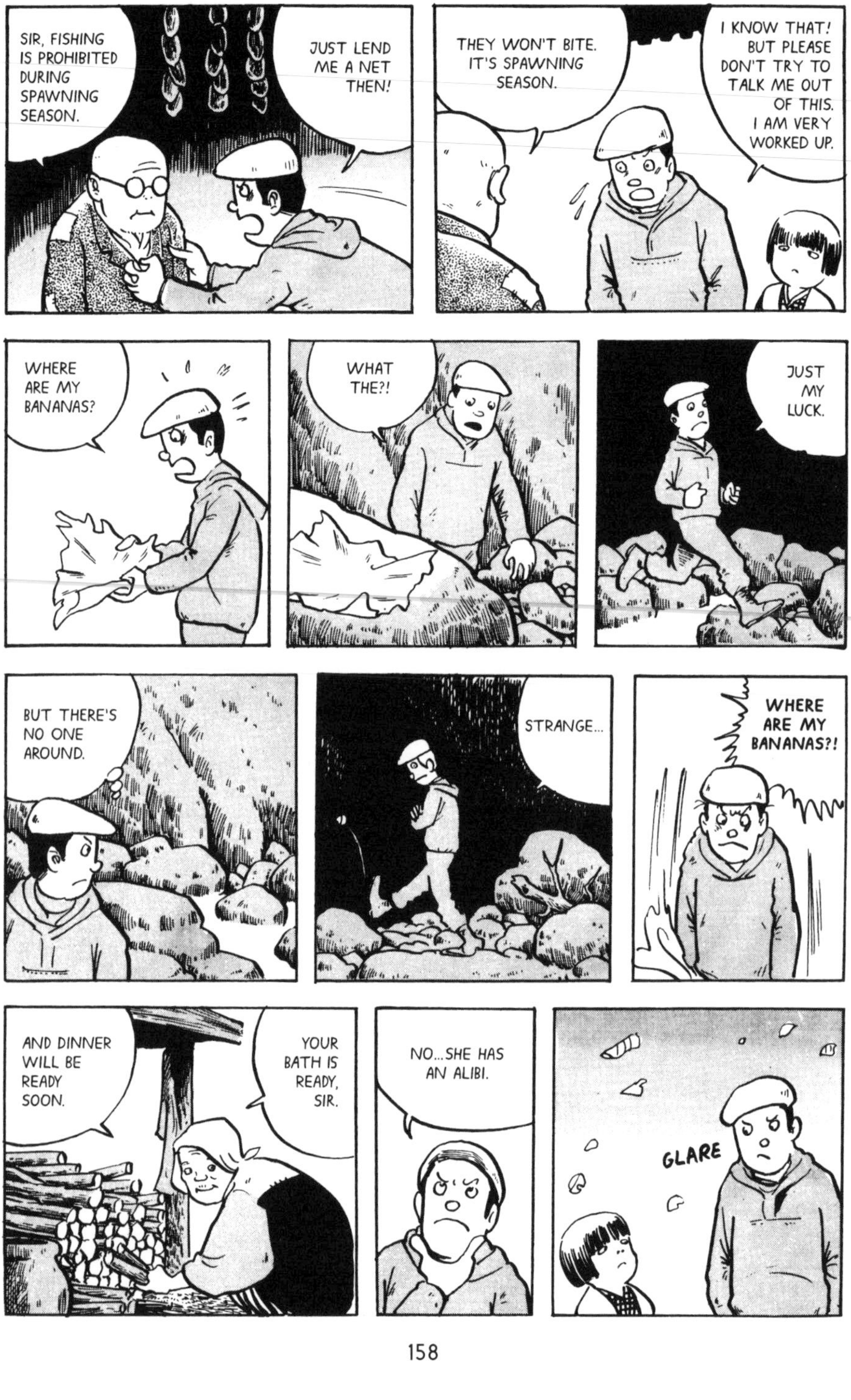
SIR, FISHING IS PROHIBITED DURING SPAWNING SEASON.
JUST LEND ME A NET THEN!
THEY WON'T BITE. IT'S SPAWNING SEASON.
I KNOW THAT! BUT PLEASE DON'T TRY TO TALK ME OUT OF THIS. I AM VERY WORKED UP.
WHERE ARE MY BANANAS?
WHAT THE?!
JUST MY LUCK.
BUT THERE'S NO ONE AROUND.
STRANGE...
WHERE ARE MY BANANAS?!
YOUR BATH IS READY, SIR.
AND DINNER WILL BE READY SOON.
NO...SHE HAS AN ALIBI.
GLARE

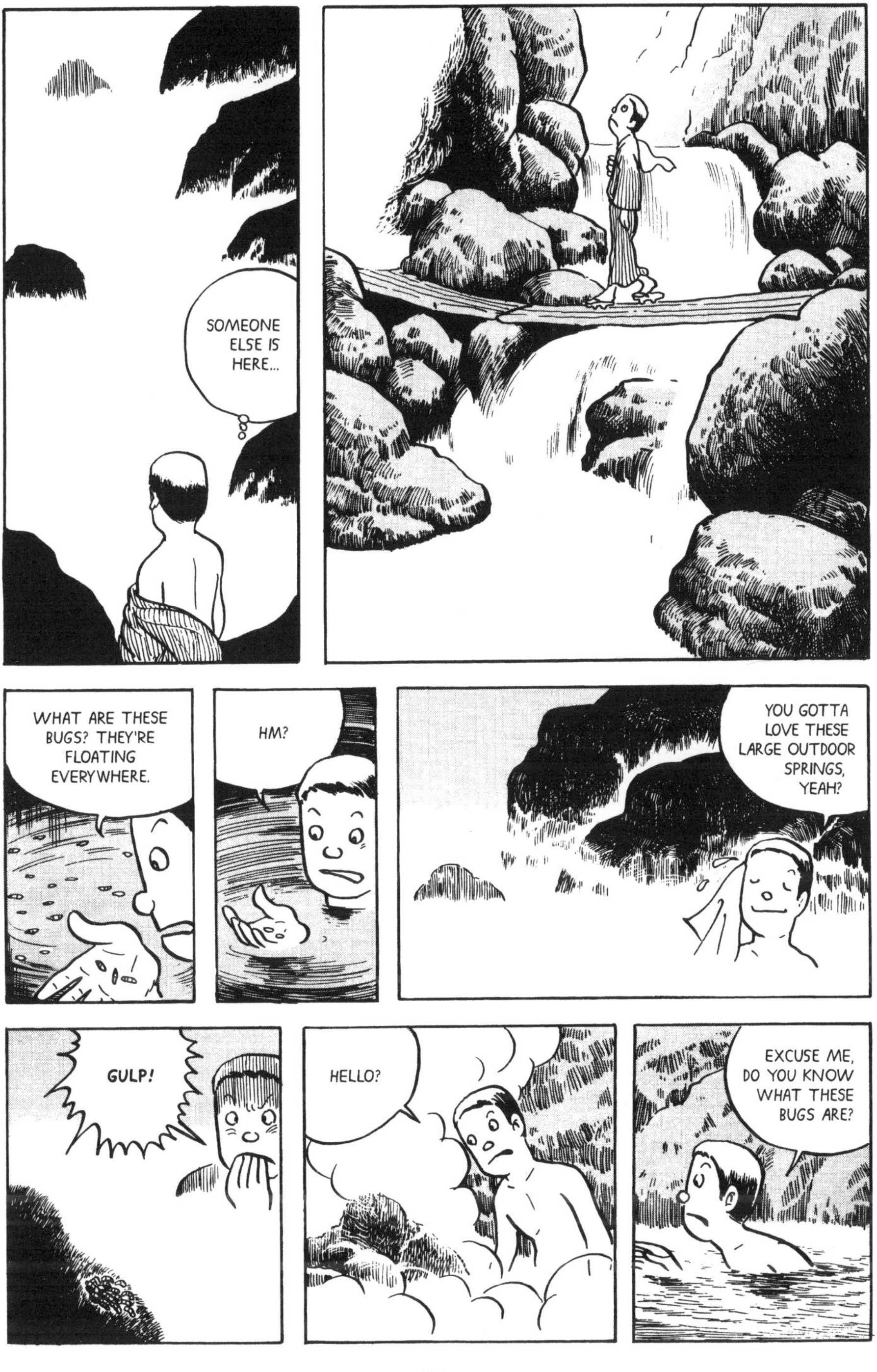
SOMEONE ELSE IS HERE...
WHAT ARE THESE BUGS? THEY'RE FLOATING EVERYWHERE.
HM?
YOU GOTTA LOVE THESE LARGE OUTDOOR SPRINGS, YEAH?
GULP!
HELLO?
EXCUSE ME, DO YOU KNOW WHAT THESE BUGS ARE?

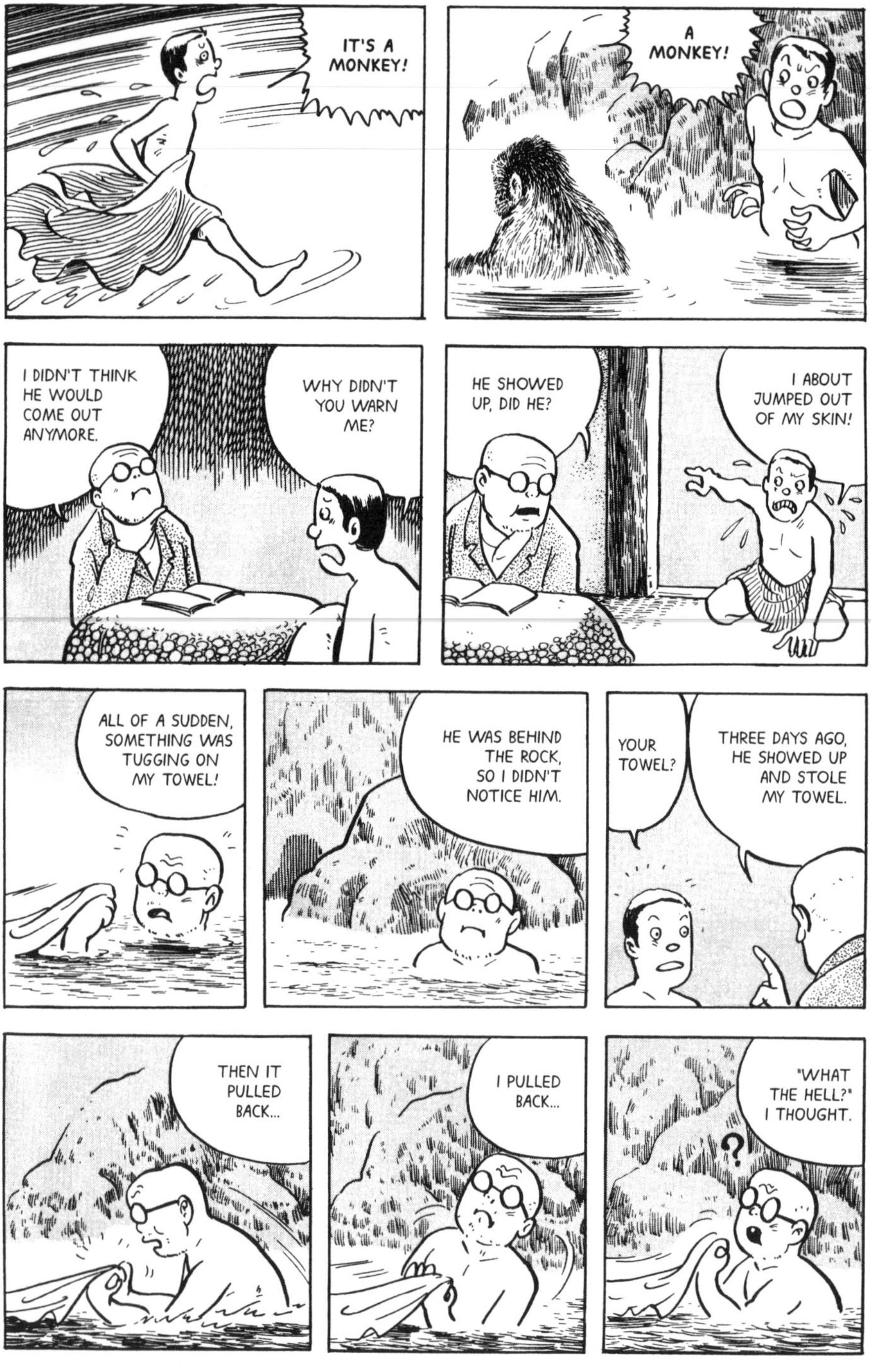
A MONKEY!
IT'S A MONKEY!
I ABOUT JUMPED OUT OF MY SKIN!
HE SHOWED UP, DID HE?
WHY DIDN'T YOU WARN ME?
I DIDN'T THINK HE WOULD COME OUT ANYMORE.
THREE DAYS AGO, HE SHOWED UP AND STOLE MY TOWEL.
YOUR TOWEL?
HE WAS BEHIND THE ROCK, SO I DIDN'T NOTICE HIM.
ALL OF A SUDDEN, SOMETHING WAS TUGGING ON MY TOWEL!
"WHAT THE HELL?" I THOUGHT.
?
I PULLED BACK...
THEN IT PULLED BACK...

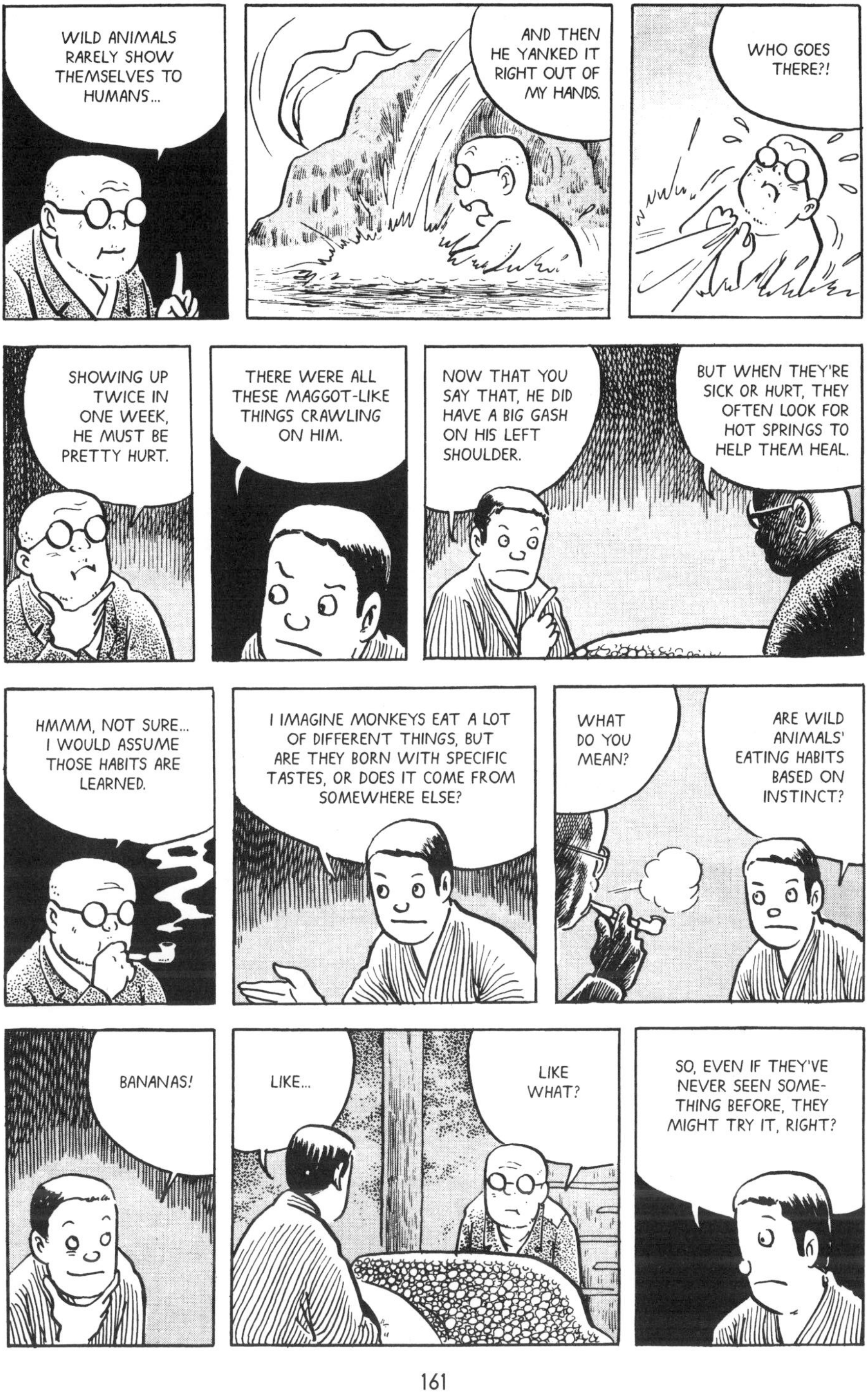
WHO GOES THERE?!
AND THEN HE YANKED IT RIGHT OUT OF MY HANDS.
WILD ANIMALS RARELY SHOW THEMSELVES TO HUMANS...
BUT WHEN THEY'RE SICK OR HURT, THEY OFTEN LOOK FOR HOT SPRINGS TO HELP THEM HEAL.
NOW THAT YOU SAY THAT, HE DID HAVE A BIG GASH ON HIS LEFT SHOULDER.
THERE WERE ALL THESE MAGGOT-LIKE THINGS CRAWLING ON HIM.
SHOWING UP TWICE IN ONE WEEK, HE MUST BE PRETTY HURT.
ARE WILD ANIMALS' EATING HABITS BASED ON INSTINCT?
WHAT DO YOU MEAN?
I IMAGINE MONKEYS EAT A LOT OF DIFFERENT THINGS, BUT ARE THEY BORN WITH SPECIFIC TASTES, OR DOES IT COME FROM SOMEWHERE ELSE?
HMMM, NOT SURE... I WOULD ASSUME THOSE HABITS ARE LEARNED.
SO, EVEN IF THEY'VE NEVER SEEN SOME-THING BEFORE, THEY MIGHT TRY IT, RIGHT?
LIKE WHAT?
LIKE...
BANANAS!

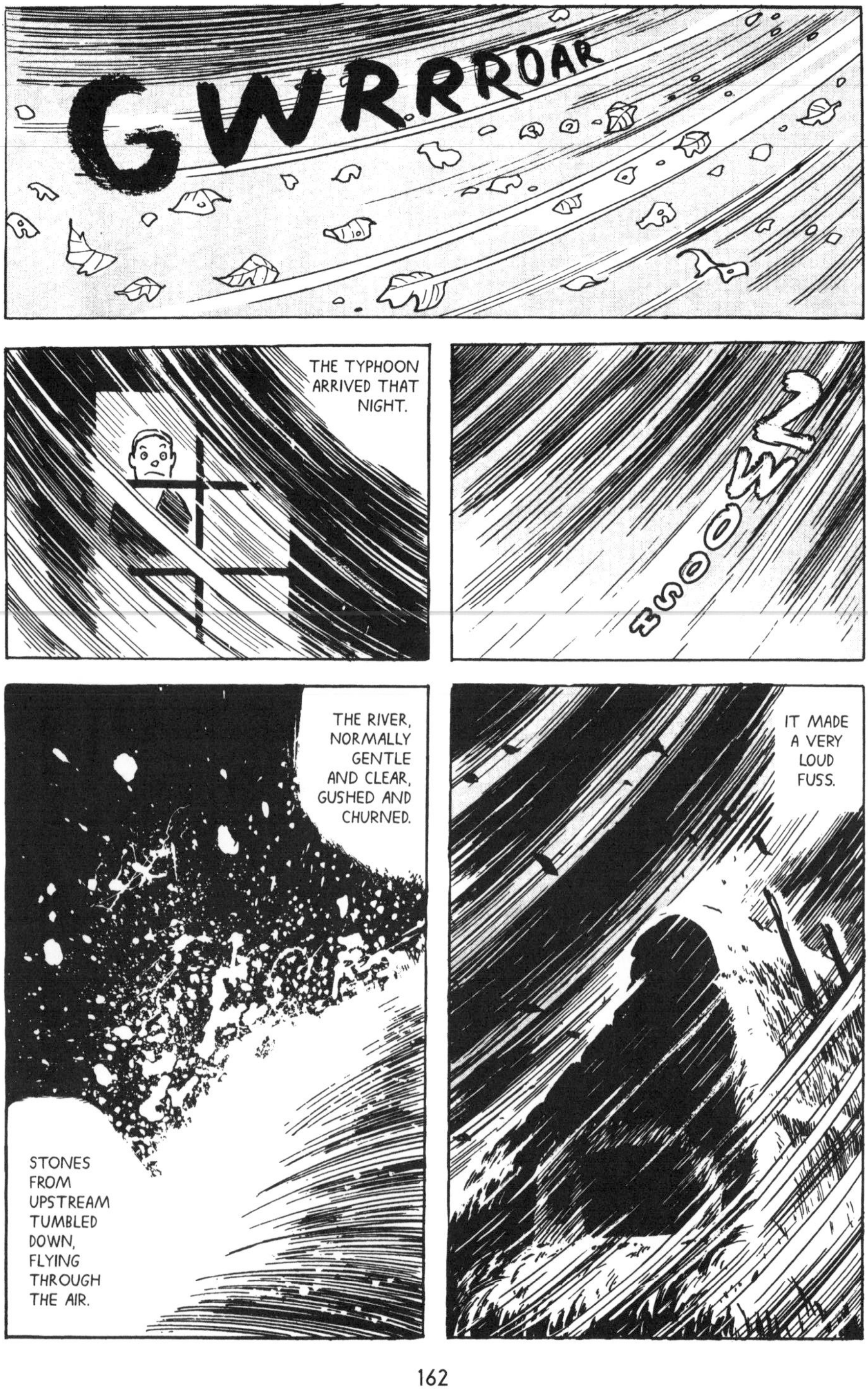
GWRRROAR
SWOOOSH
THE TYPHOON ARRIVED THAT NIGHT.
IT MADE A VERY LOUD FUSS.
THE RIVER, NORMALLY GENTLE AND CLEAR, GUSHED AND CHURNED.
STONES FROM UPSTREAM TUMBLED DOWN, FLYING THROUGH THE AIR.

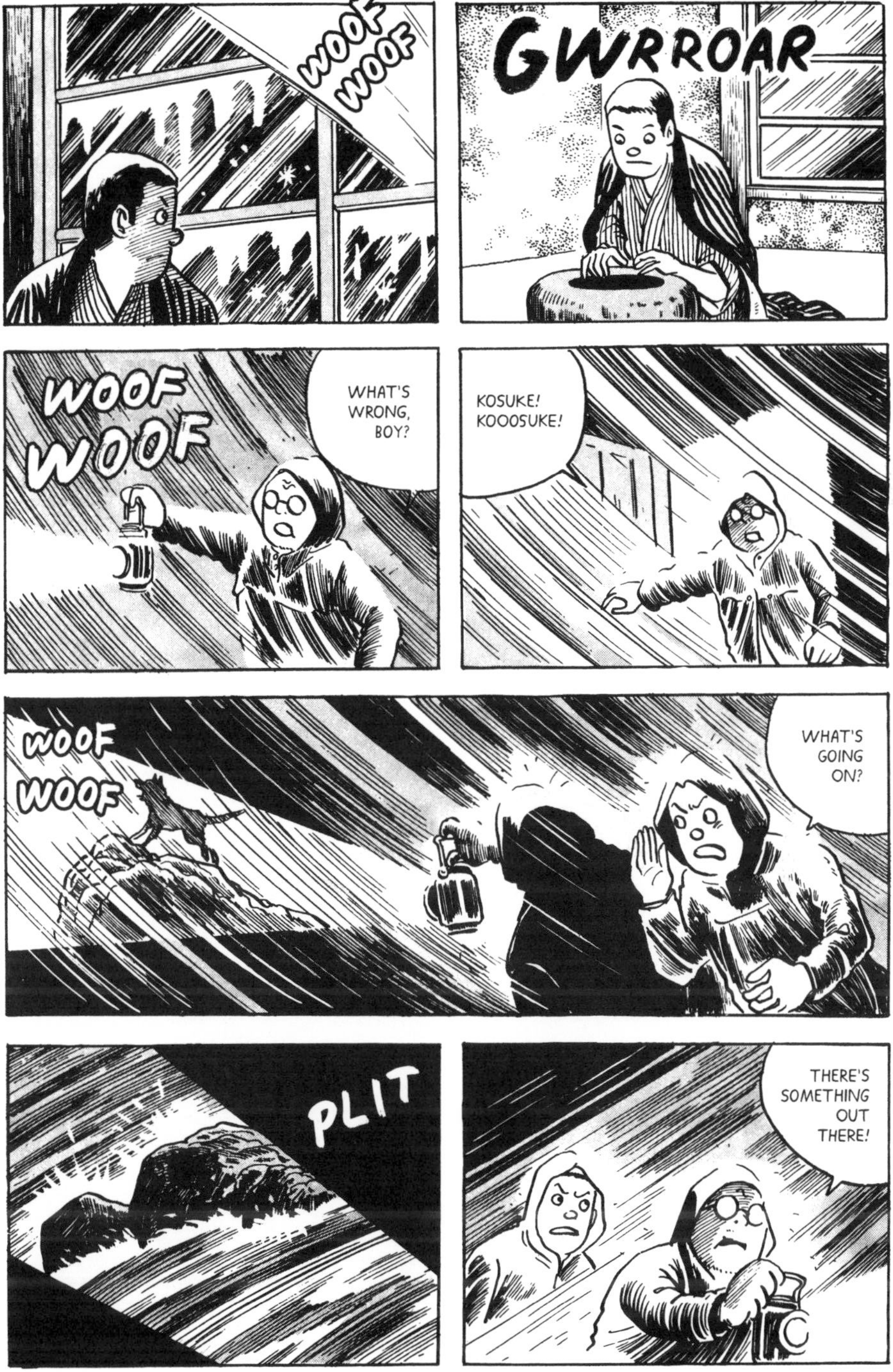
GWRROAR
WOOF WOOF
KOSUKE! KOOOSUKE!
WHAT'S WRONG, BOY?
WOOF WOOF
WHAT'S GOING ON?
WOOF WOOF
THERE'S SOMETHING OUT THERE!
PLIT

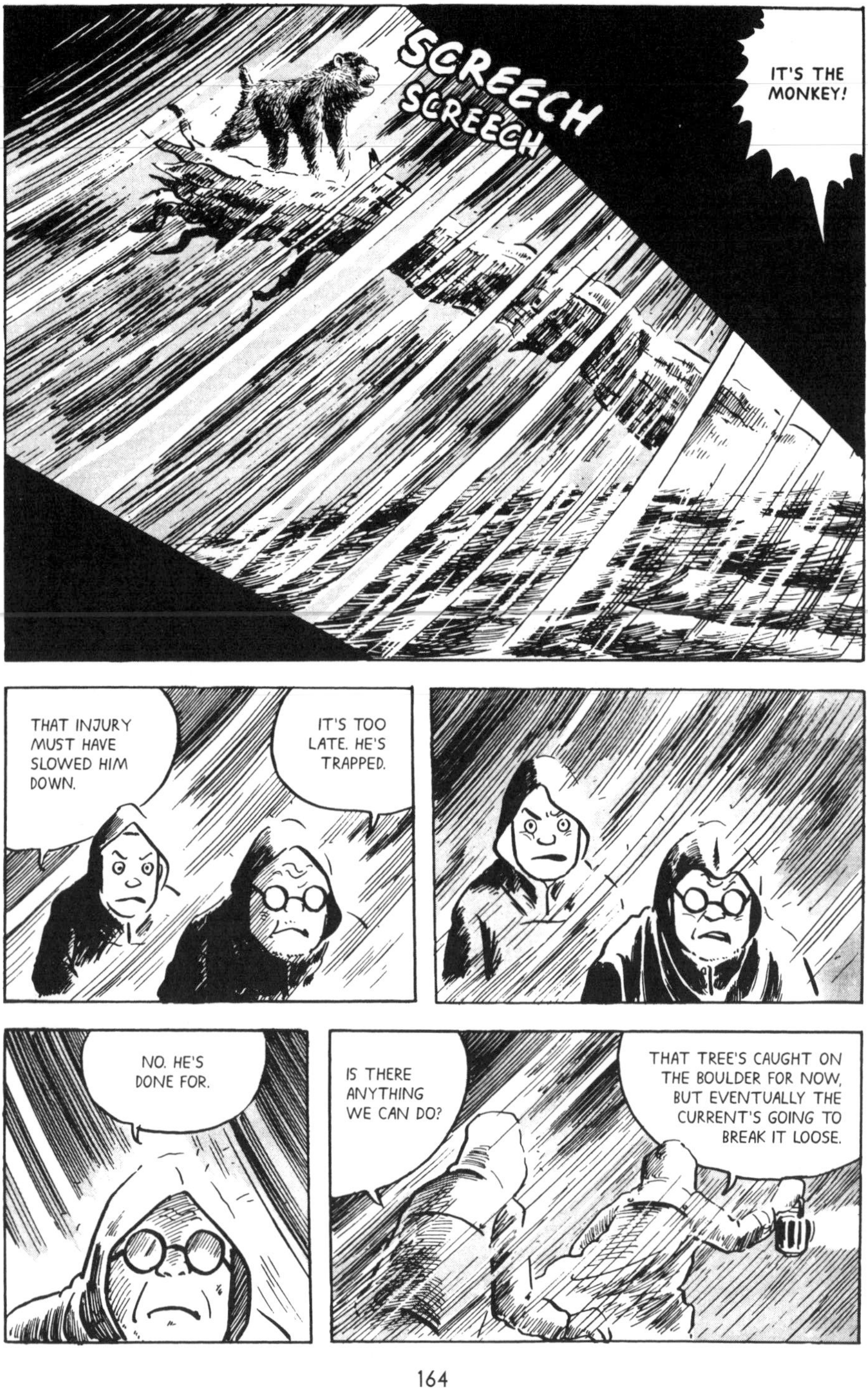
IT'S THE MONKEY!
SCREECH
SCREECH
IT'S TOO LATE. HE'S TRAPPED.
THAT INJURY MUST HAVE SLOWED HIM DOWN.
THAT TREE'S CAUGHT ON THE BOULDER FOR NOW, BUT EVENTUALLY THE CURRENT'S GOING TO BREAK IT LOOSE.
IS THERE ANYTHING WE CAN DO?
NO. HE'S DONE FOR.

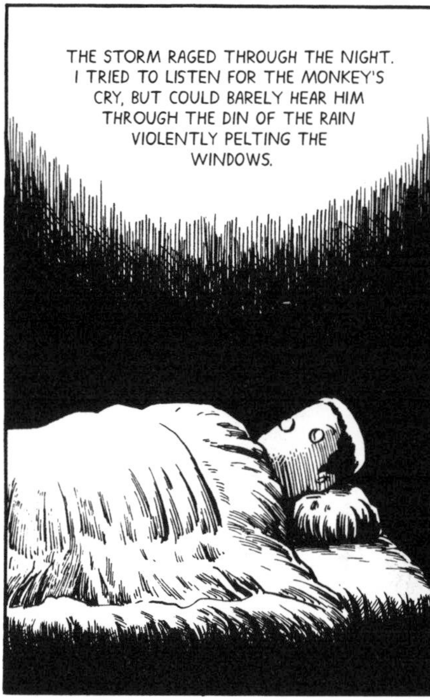
THE STORM RAGED THROUGH THE NIGHT. I TRIED TO LISTEN FOR THE MONKEY'S CRY, BUT COULD BARELY HEAR HIM THROUGH THE DIN OF THE RAIN VIOLENTLY PELTING THE WINDOWS.

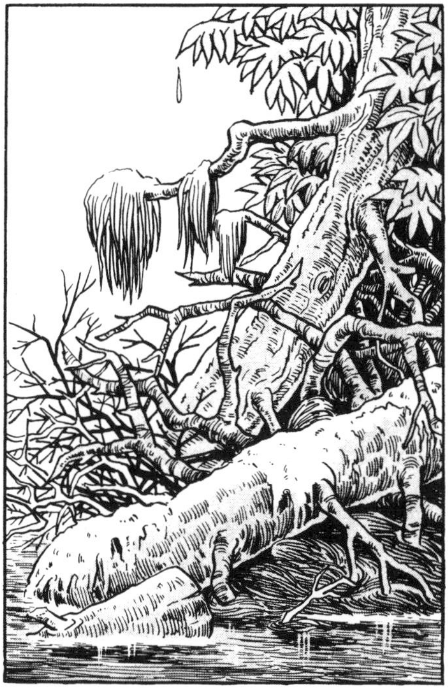

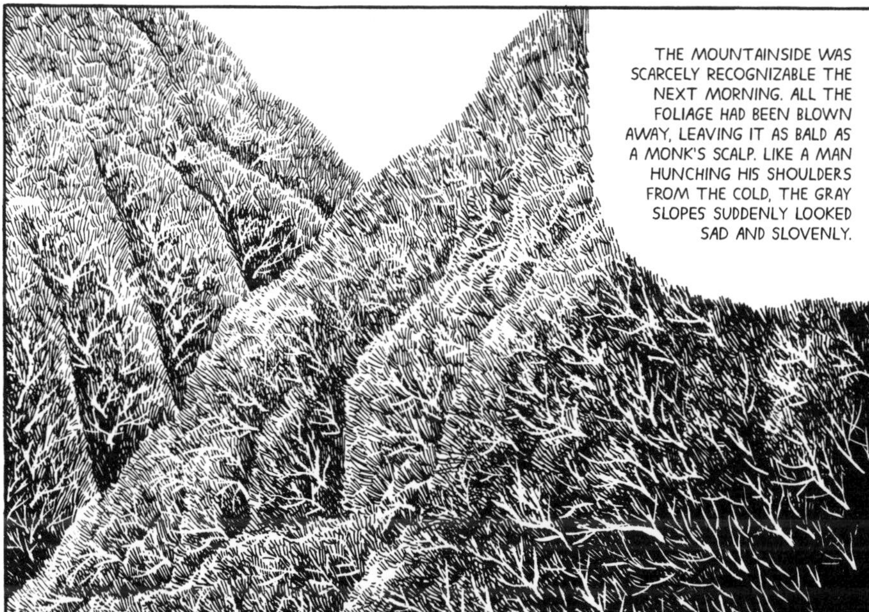
THE MOUNTAINSIDE WAS SCARCELY RECOGNIZABLE THE NEXT MORNING. ALL THE FOLIAGE HAD BEEN BLOWN AWAY, LEAVING IT AS BALD AS A MONK'S SCALP. LIKE A MAN HUNCHING HIS SHOULDERS FROM THE COLD, THE GRAY SLOPES SUDDENLY LOOKED SAD AND SLOVENLY.

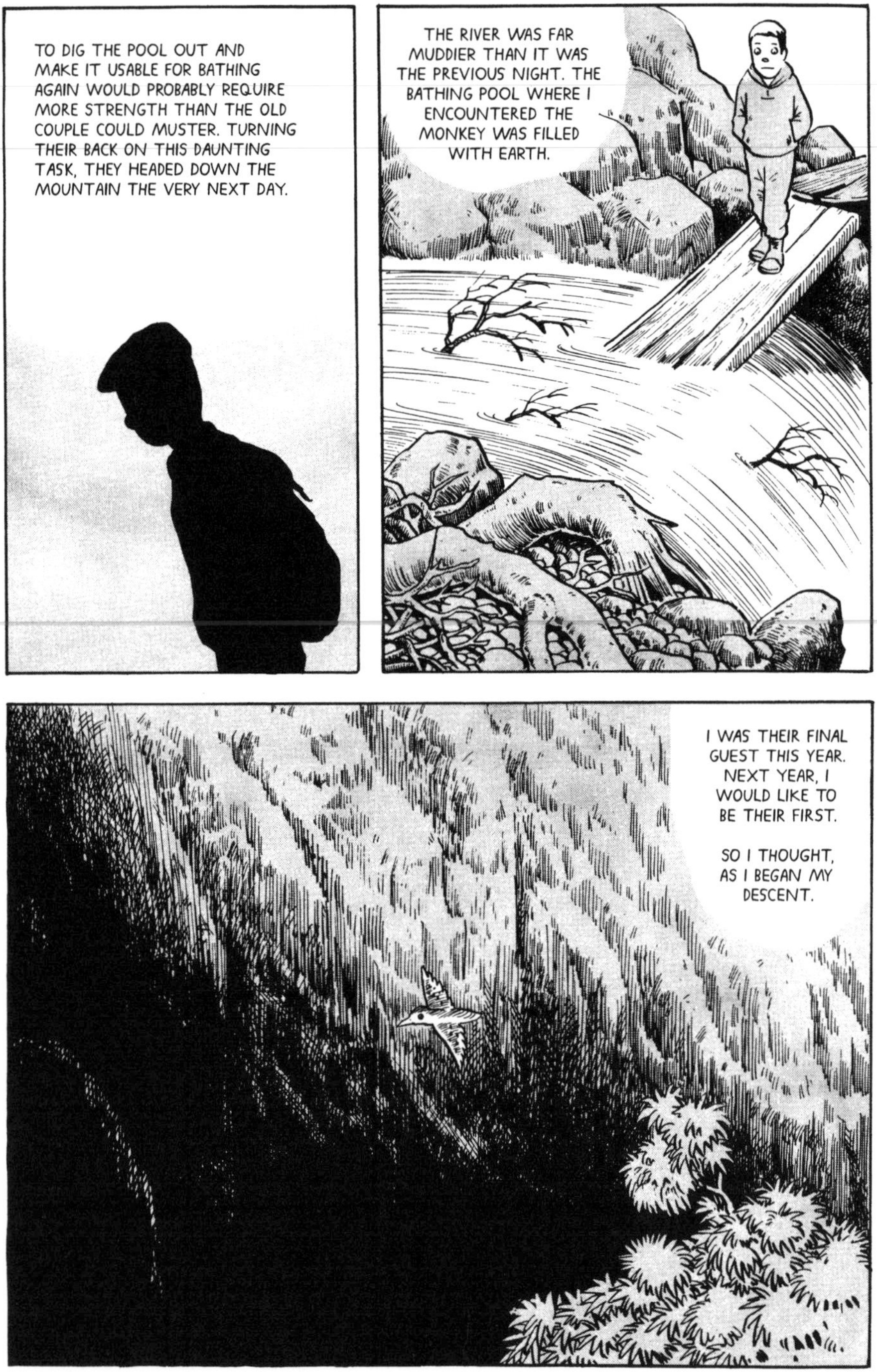
THE RIVER WAS FAR MUDDIER THAN IT WAS THE PREVIOUS NIGHT. THE BATHING POOL WHERE I ENCOUNTERED THE MONKEY WAS FILLED WITH EARTH.
TO DIG THE POOL OUT AND MAKE IT USABLE FOR BATHING AGAIN WOULD PROBABLY REQUIRE MORE STRENGTH THAN THE OLD COUPLE COULD MUSTER. TURNING THEIR BACK ON THIS DAUNTING TASK, THEY HEADED DOWN THE MOUNTAIN THE VERY NEXT DAY.
I WAS THEIR FINAL GUEST THIS YEAR. NEXT YEAR, I WOULD LIKE TO BE THEIR FIRST.
SO I THOUGHT, AS I BEGAN MY DESCENT.

THE ONDOL
SHACK

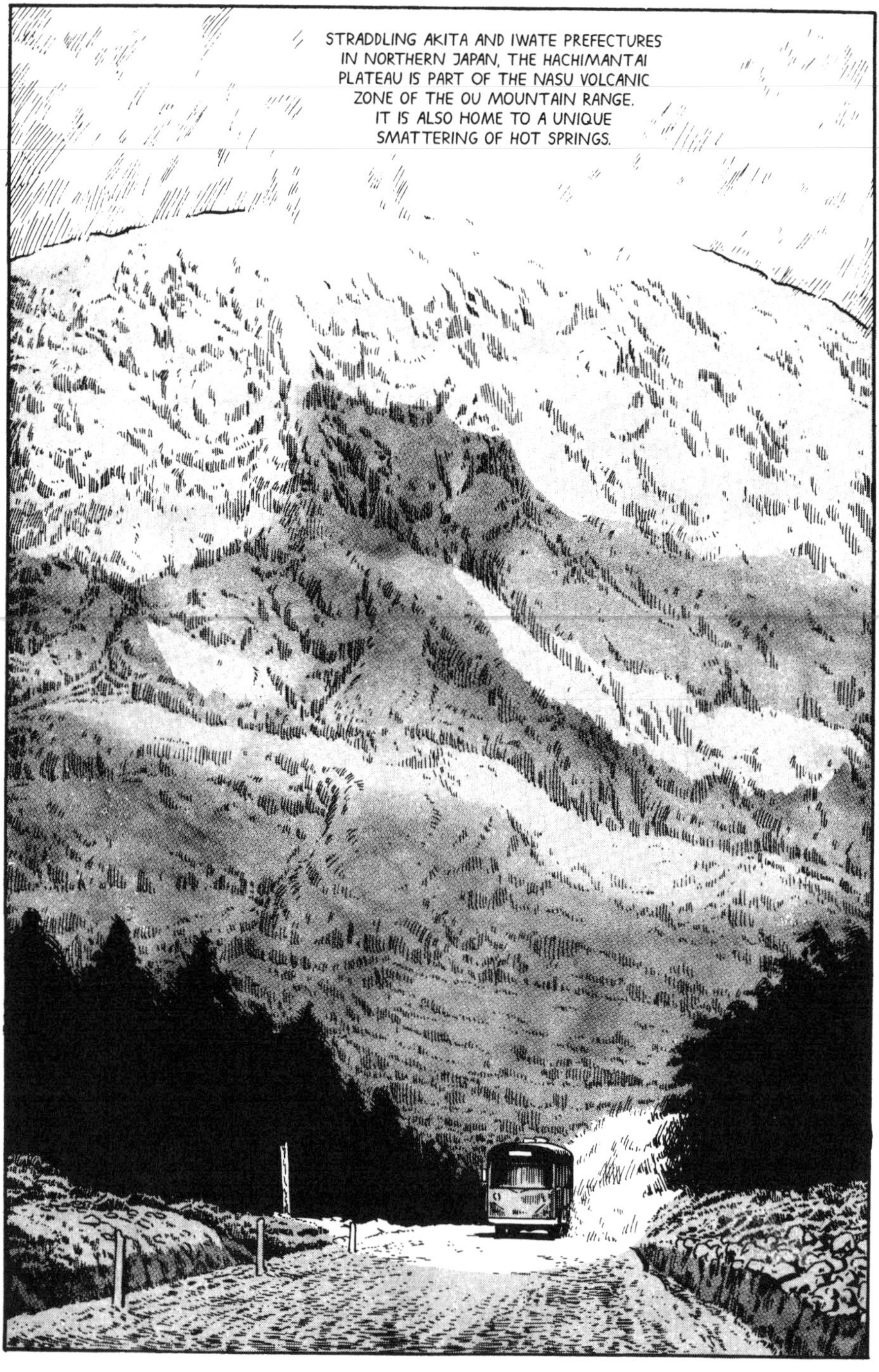
STRADDLING AKITA AND IWATE PREFECTURES IN NORTHERN JAPAN, THE HACHIMANTAI PLATEAU IS PART OF THE NASU VOLCANIC ZONE OF THE OU MOUNTAIN RANGE. IT IS ALSO HOME TO A UNIQUE SMATTERING OF HOT SPRINGS.

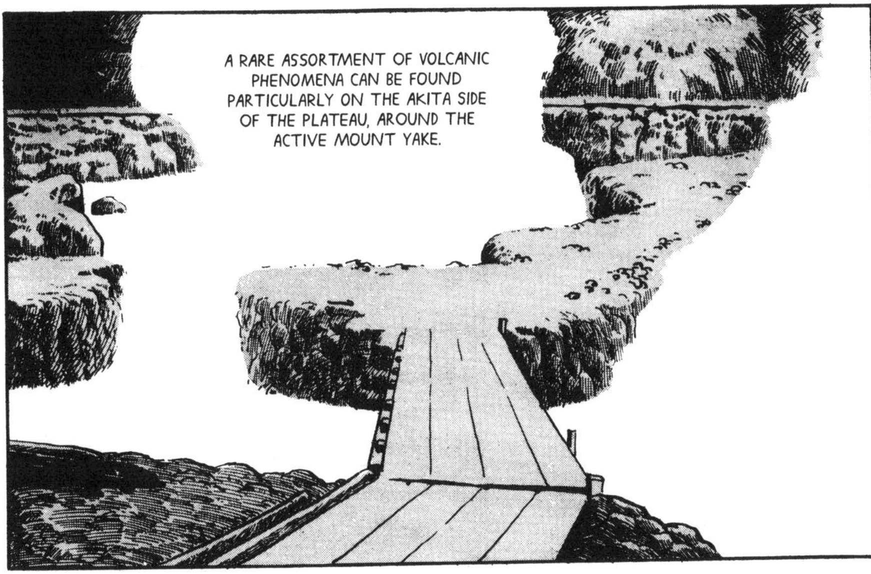
A RARE ASSORTMENT OF VOLCANIC PHENOMENA CAN BE FOUND PARTICULARLY ON THE AKITA SIDE OF THE PLATEAU, AROUND THE ACTIVE MOUNT YAKE.

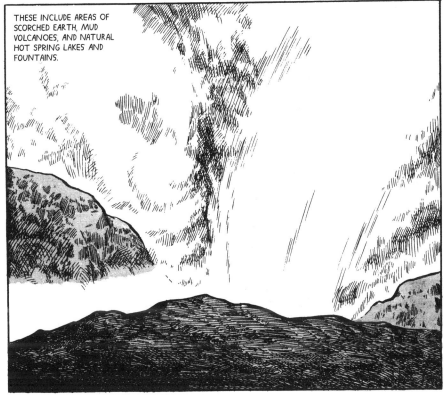

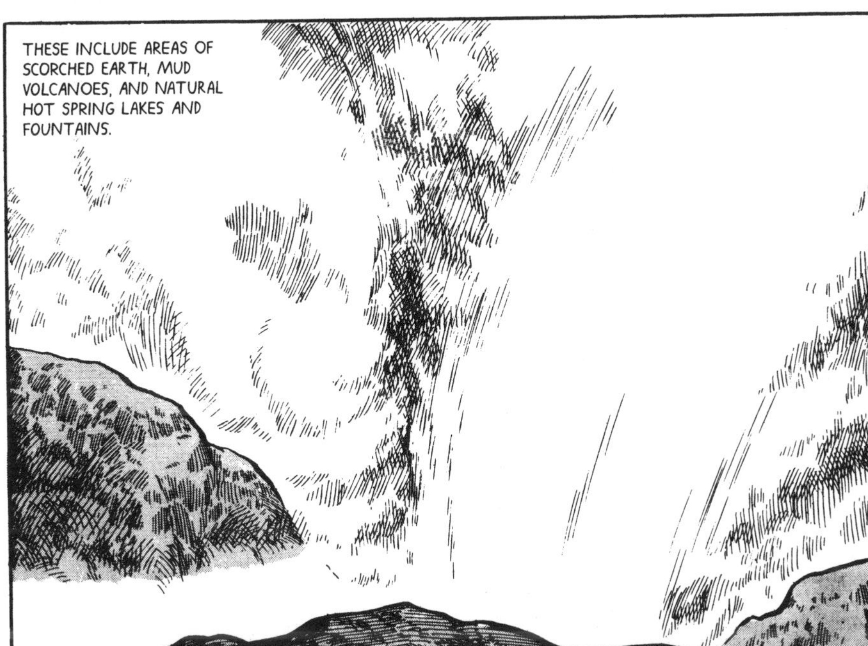
THESE INCLUDE AREAS OF SCORCHED EARTH, MUD VOLCANOES, AND NATURAL HOT SPRING LAKES AND FOUNTAINS.

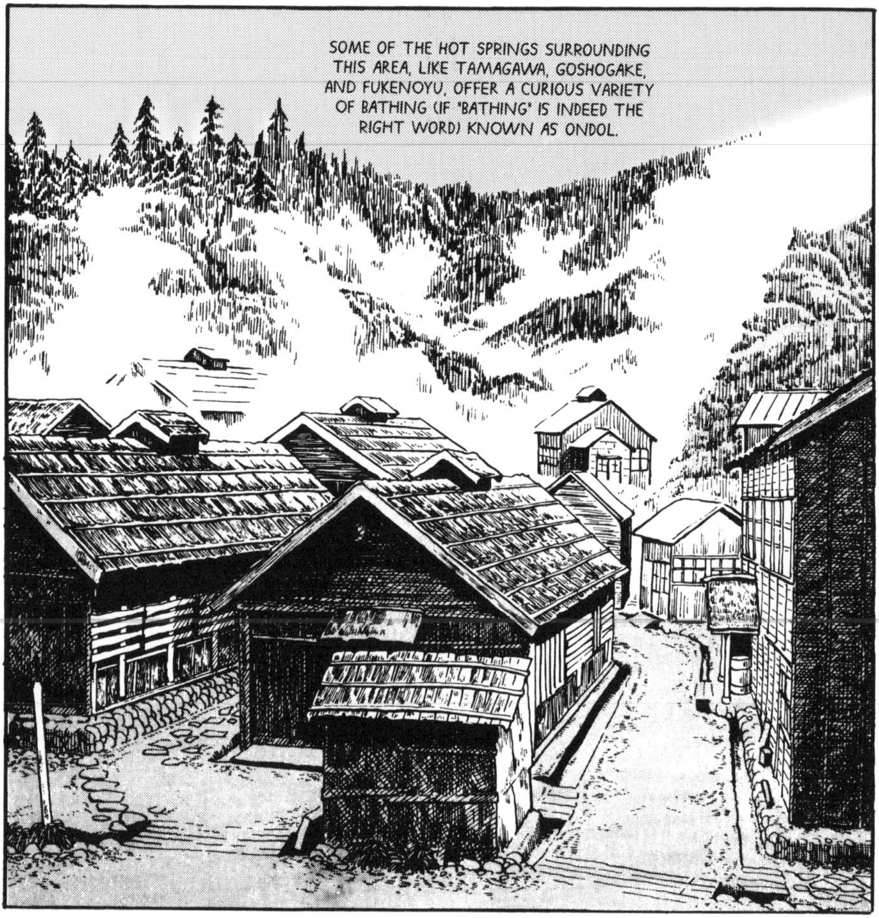
SOME OF THE HOT SPRINGS SURROUNDING THIS AREA, LIKE TAMAGAWA, GOSHOGAKE, AND FUKENOYU, OFFER A CURIOUS VARIETY OF BATHING (IF "BATHING" IS INDEED THE RIGHT WORD) KNOWN AS ONDOL.

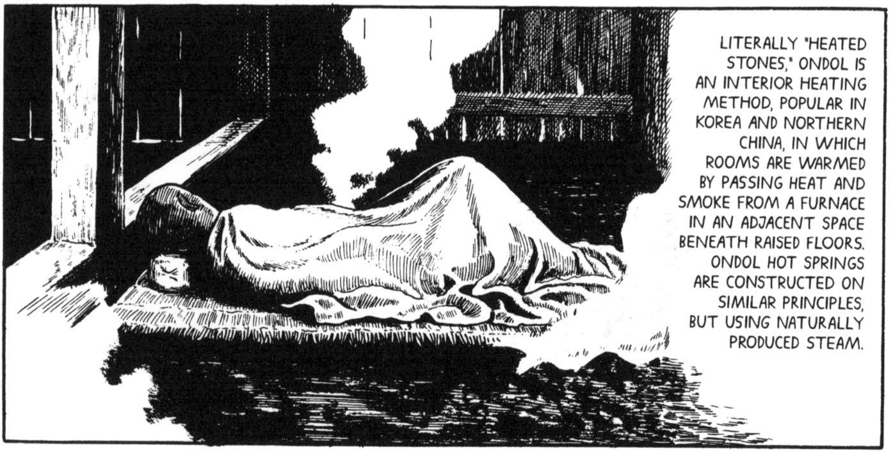
LITERALLY "HEATED STONES," ONDOL IS AN INTERIOR HEATING METHOD, POPULAR IN KOREA AND NORTHERN CHINA, IN WHICH ROOMS ARE WARMED BY PASSING HEAT AND SMOKE FROM A FURNACE IN AN ADJACENT SPACE BENEATH RAISED FLOORS. ONDOL HOT SPRINGS ARE CONSTRUCTED ON SIMILAR PRINCIPLES, BUT USING NATURALLY PRODUCED STEAM.

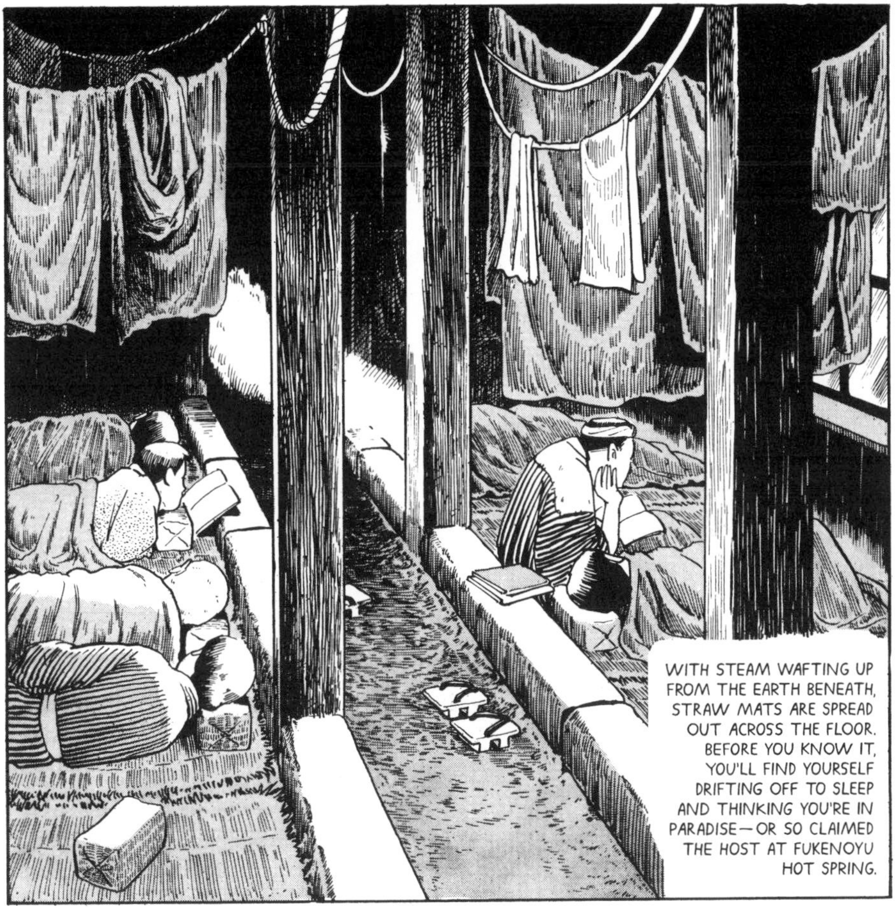
WITH STEAM WAFTING UP FROM THE EARTH BENEATH, STRAW MATS ARE SPREAD OUT ACROSS THE FLOOR. BEFORE YOU KNOW IT, YOU'LL FIND YOURSELF DRIFTING OFF TO SLEEP AND THINKING YOU'RE IN PARADISE—OR SO CLAIMED THE HOST AT FUKENOYU HOT SPRING.
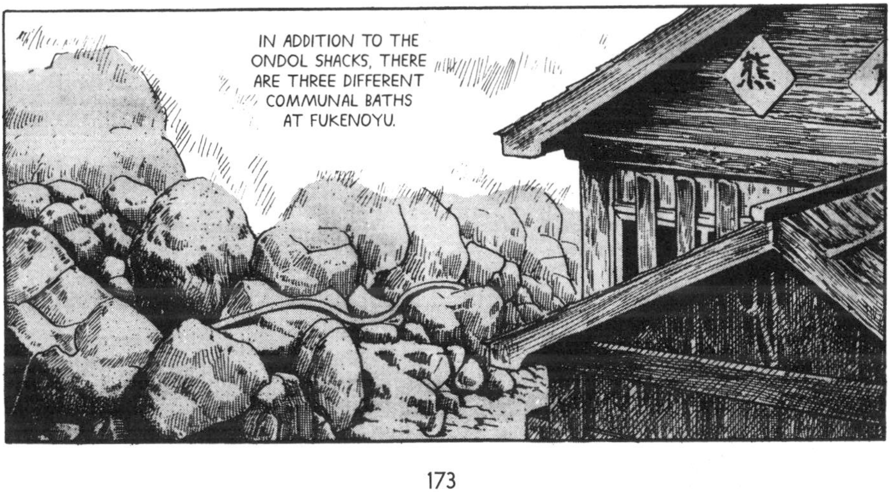
IN ADDITION TO THE ONDOL SHACKS, THERE ARE THREE DIFFERENT COMMUNAL BATHS AT FUKENOYU.

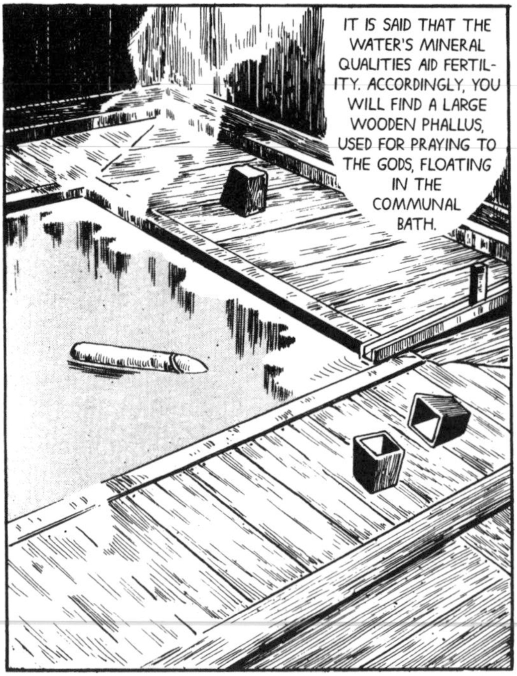
IT IS SAID THAT THE WATER'S MINERAL QUALITIES AID FERTILITY. ACCORDINGLY, YOU WILL FIND A LARGE WOODEN PHALLUS, USED FOR PRAYING TO THE GODS, FLOATING IN THE COMMUNAL BATH.

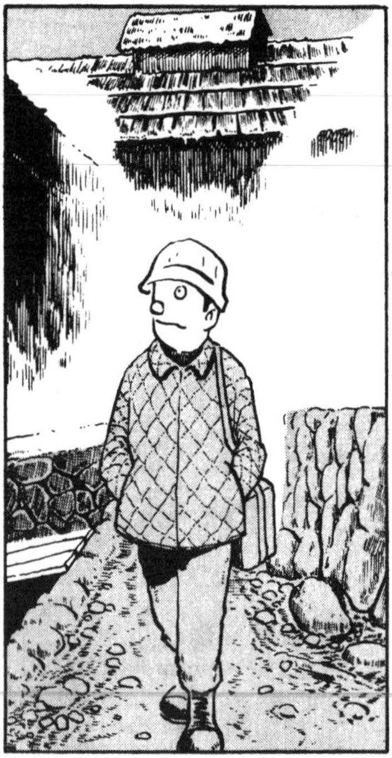

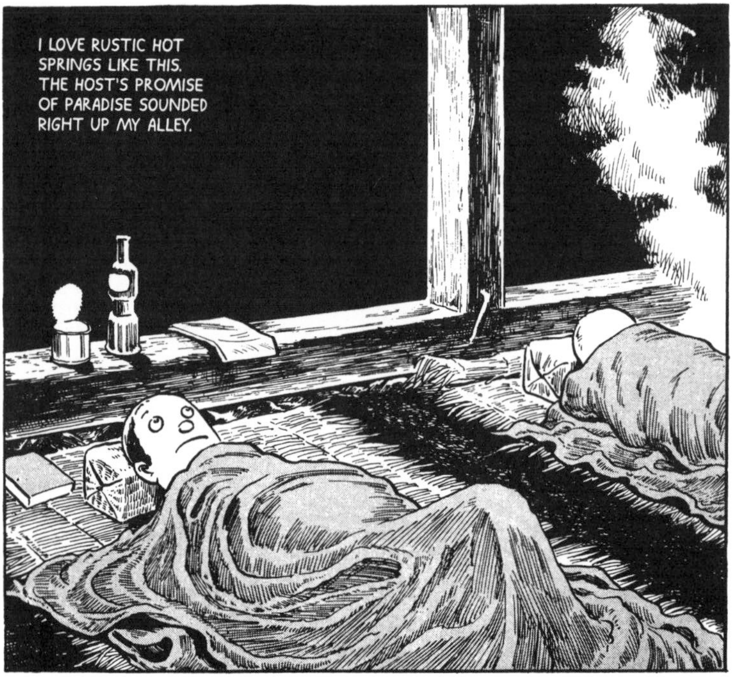
I LOVE RUSTIC HOT SPRINGS LIKE THIS. THE HOST'S PROMISE OF PARADISE SOUNDED RIGHT UP MY ALLEY.

ALAS, THERE ARE TIMES WHEN THE WRONG PEOPLE COME TO THE RIGHT PLACE—FOR THEM, IT'S PROBABLY THE WRONG PLACE—THUS SPOILING ONE'S TRAVELS. WHAT FOLLOWS IS AN ACCOUNT OF ONE SUCH DISASTER.

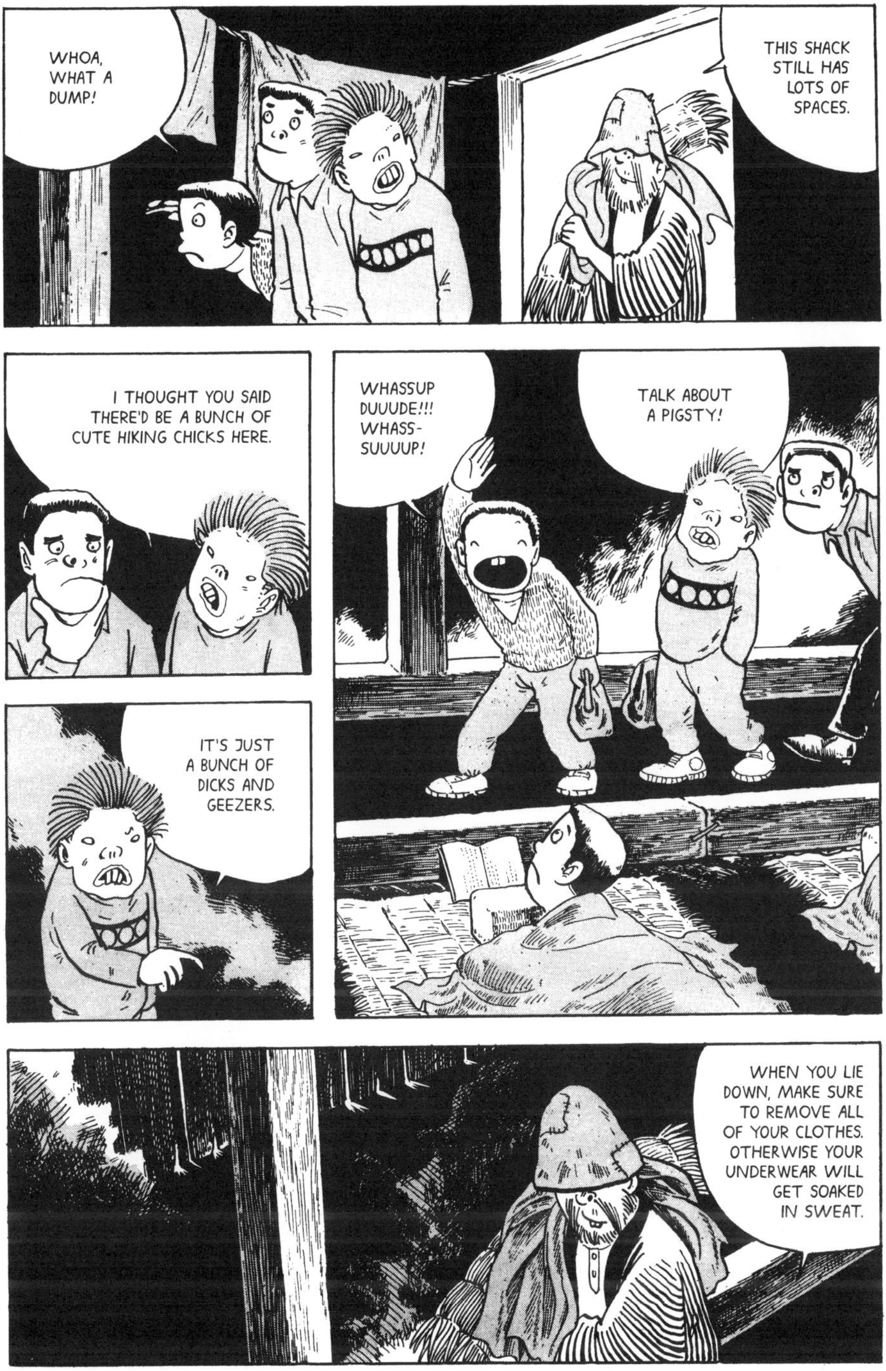
THIS SHACK STILL HAS LOTS OF SPACES.
WHOA, WHAT A DUMP!
TALK ABOUT A PIGSTY!
WHASSUP DUUUDE!!! WHASS-SUUUUP!
I THOUGHT YOU SAID THERE'D BE A BUNCH OF CUTE HIKING CHICKS HERE.
IT'S JUST A BUNCH OF DICKS AND GEEZERS.
WHEN YOU LIE DOWN, MAKE SURE TO REMOVE ALL OF YOUR CLOTHES. OTHERWISE YOUR UNDERWEAR WILL GET SOAKED IN SWEAT.

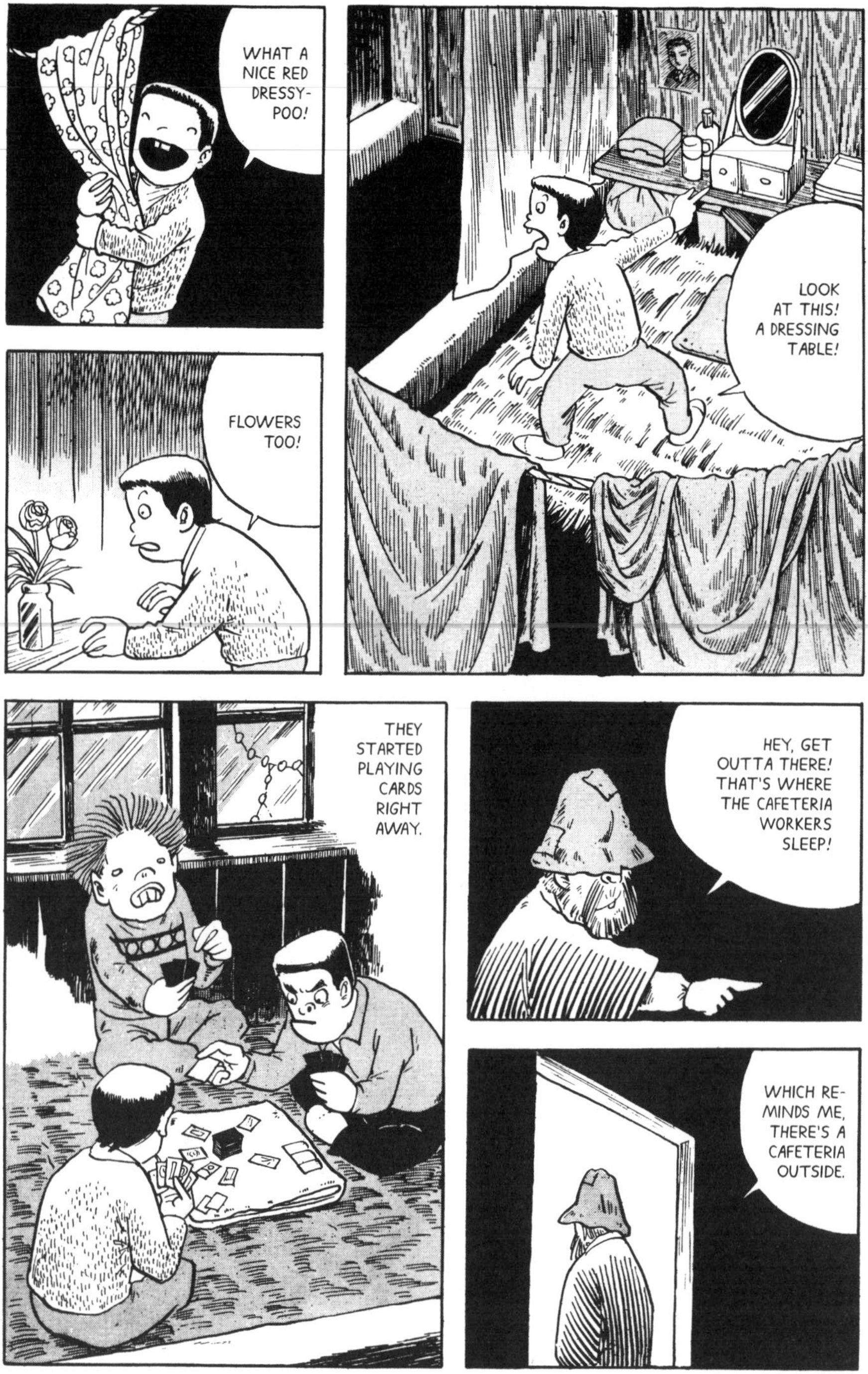
LOOK AT THIS! A DRESSING TABLE!
WHAT A NICE RED DRESSY-POO!
FLOWERS TOO!
HEY, GET OUTTA THERE! THAT'S WHERE THE CAFETERIA WORKERS SLEEP!
WHICH RE-MINDS ME, THERE'S A CAFETERIA OUTSIDE.
THEY STARTED PLAYING CARDS RIGHT AWAY.

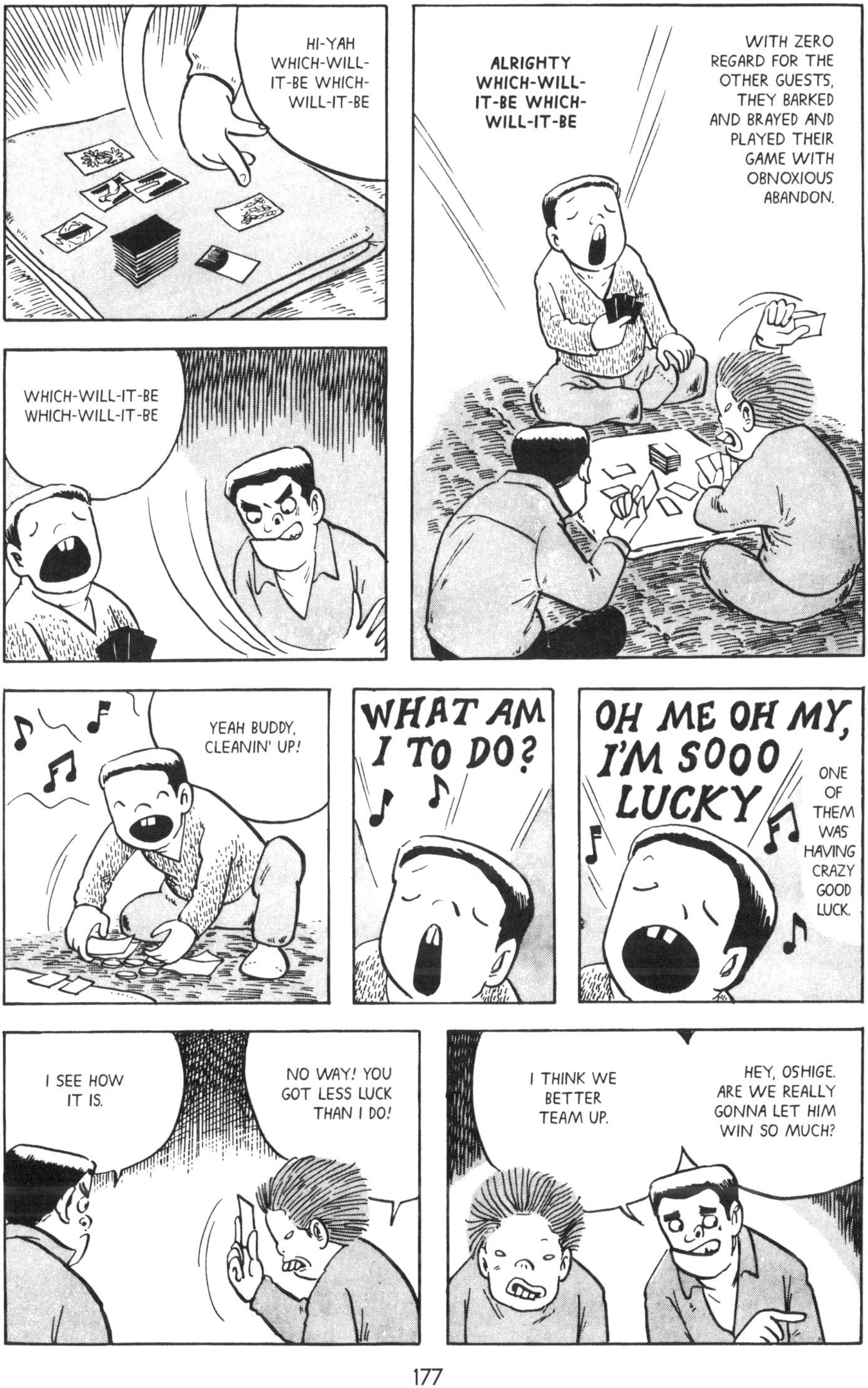
WITH ZERO REGARD FOR THE OTHER GUESTS, THEY BARKED AND BRAYED AND PLAYED THEIR GAME WITH OBNOXIOUS ABANDON.
ALRIGHTY WHICH-WILL-IT-BE WHICH-WILL-IT-BE
HI-YAH WHICH-WILL-IT-BE WHICH-WILL-IT-BE
WHICH-WILL-IT-BE WHICH-WILL-IT-BE
OH ME OH MY, I'M SOOO LUCKY
ONE OF THEM WAS HAVING CRAZY GOOD LUCK.
WHAT AM I TO DO?
YEAH BUDDY, CLEANIN' UP!
HEY, OSHIGE. ARE WE REALLY GONNA LET HIM WIN SO MUCH?
I THINK WE BETTER TEAM UP.
NO WAY! YOU GOT LESS LUCK THAN I DO!
I SEE HOW IT IS.

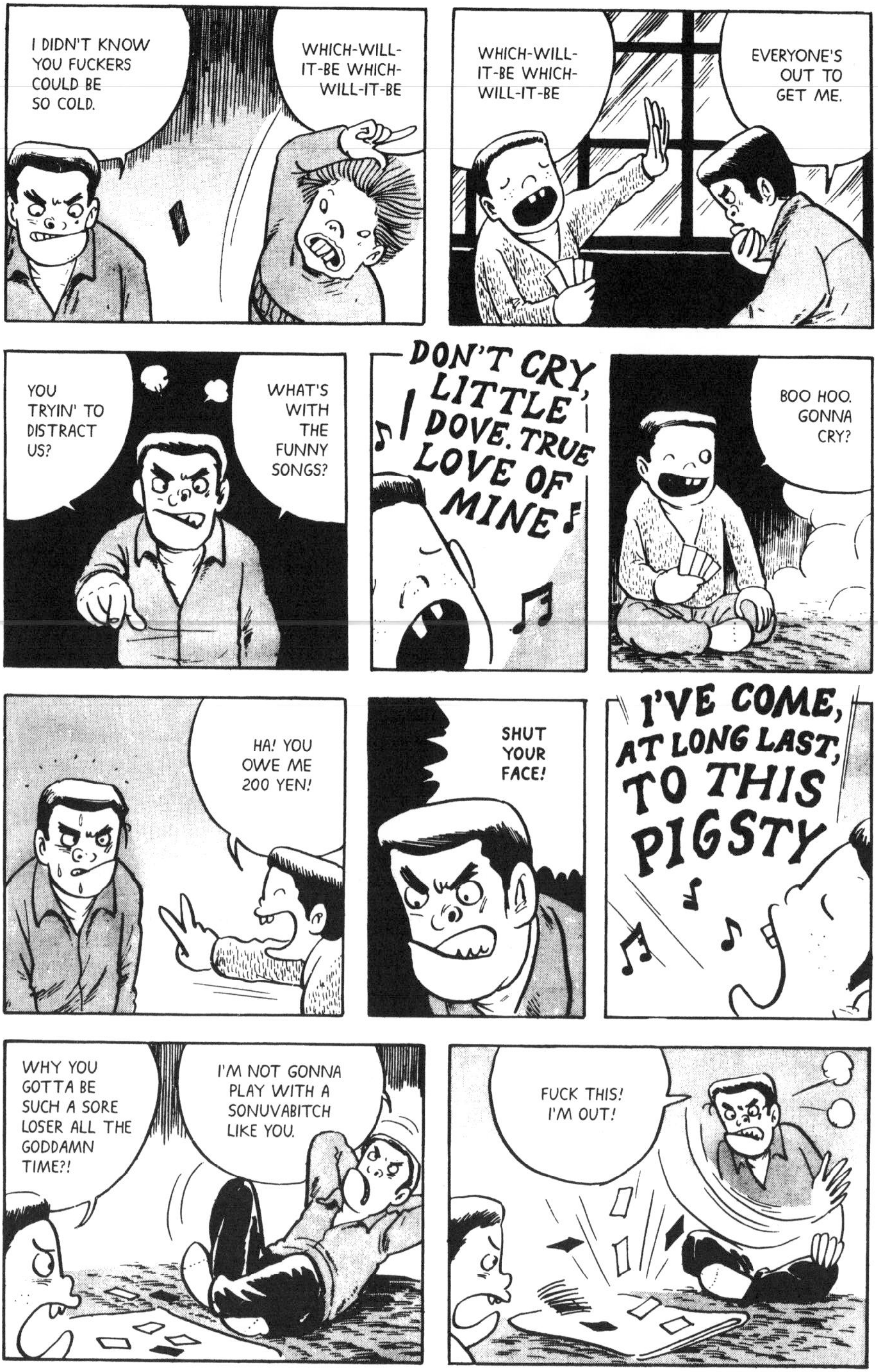
EVERYONE'S OUT TO GET ME.
WHICH-WILL-IT-BE WHICH-WILL-IT-BE
WHICH-WILL-IT-BE WHICH-WILL-IT-BE
I DIDN'T KNOW YOU FUCKERS COULD BE SO COLD.
BOO HOO. GONNA CRY?
DON'T CRY, LITTLE DOVE. TRUE LOVE OF MINE
WHAT'S WITH THE FUNNY SONGS?
YOU TRYIN' TO DISTRACT US?
I'VE COME, AT LONG LAST, TO THIS PIGSTY
SHUT YOUR FACE!
HA! YOU OWE ME 200 YEN!
FUCK THIS! I'M OUT!
I'M NOT GONNA PLAY WITH A SONUVABITCH LIKE YOU.
WHY YOU GOTTA BE SUCH A SORE LOSER ALL THE GODDAMN TIME?!

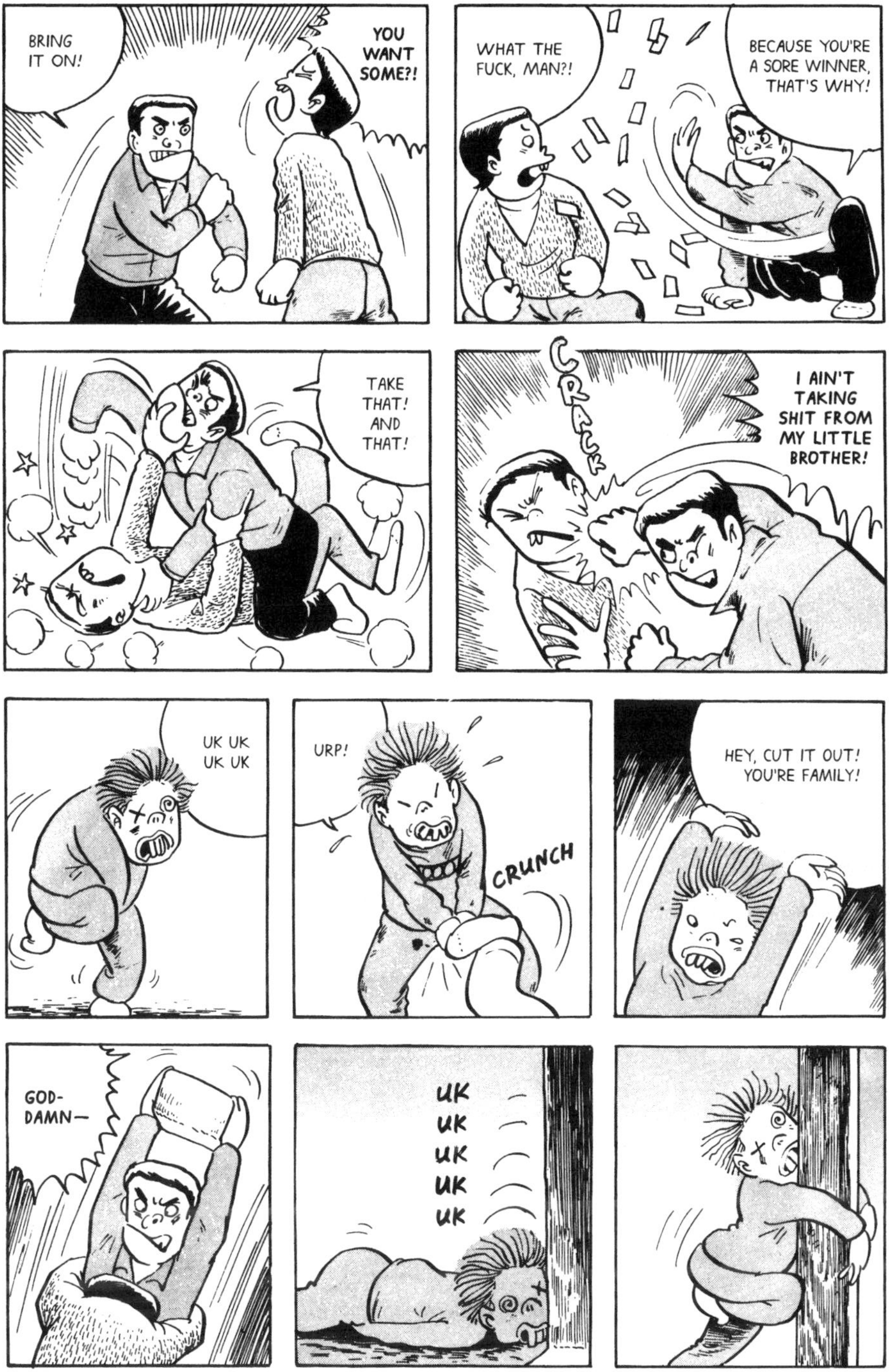
BECAUSE YOU'RE A SORE WINNER, THAT'S WHY!
WHAT THE FUCK, MAN?!
YOU WANT SOME?!
BRING IT ON!
I AIN'T TAKING SHIT FROM MY LITTLE BROTHER!
CRACK
TAKE THAT! AND THAT!
HEY, CUT IT OUT! YOU'RE FAMILY!
URP!
CRUNCH
UK UK UK UK
UK UK UK UK UK
GOD-DAMN—

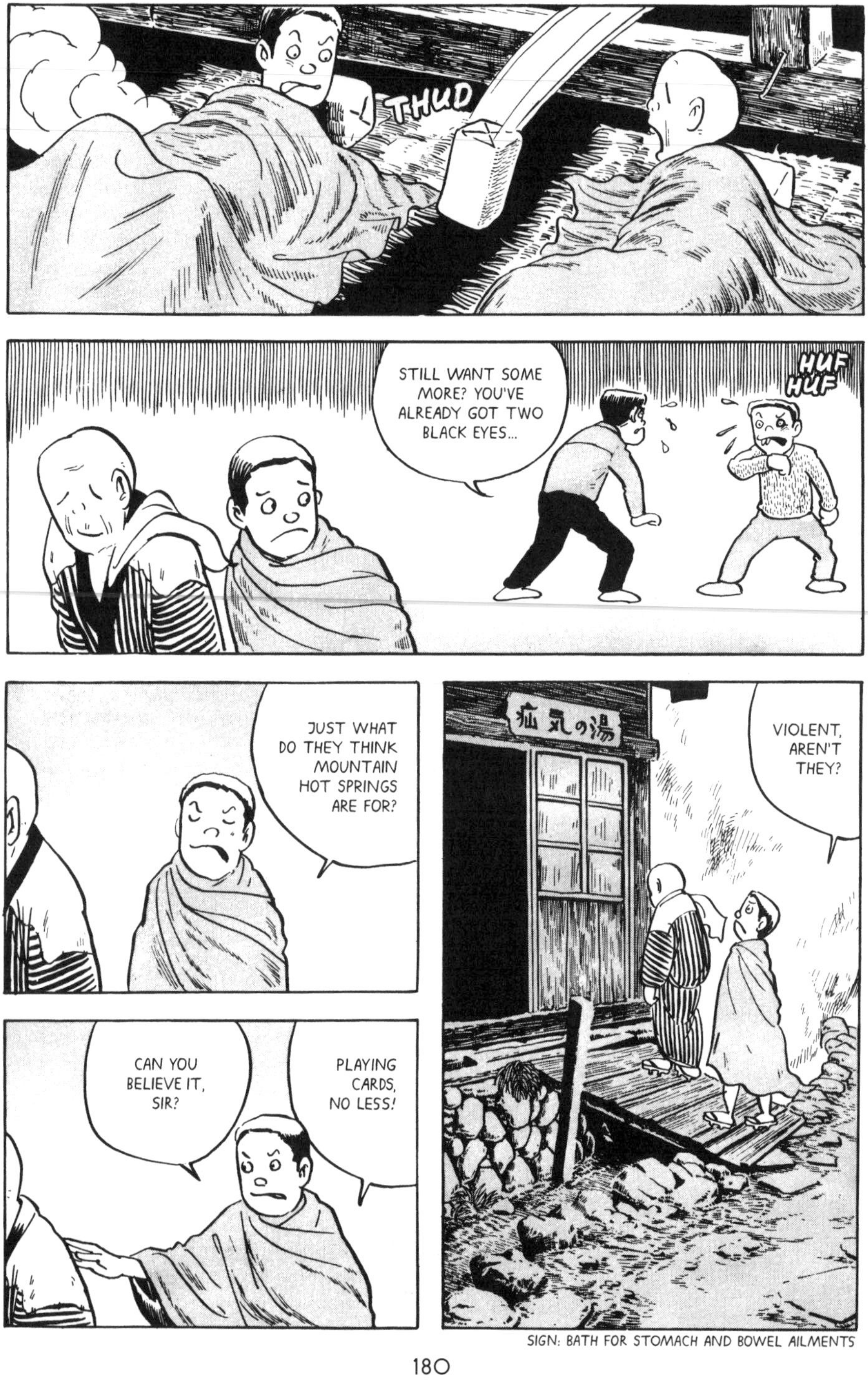
THUD
HUF HUF
STILL WANT SOME MORE? YOU'VE ALREADY GOT TWO BLACK EYES...
疝気の湯
VIOLENT, AREN'T THEY?
JUST WHAT DO THEY THINK MOUNTAIN HOT SPRINGS ARE FOR?
PLAYING CARDS, NO LESS!
CAN YOU BELIEVE IT, SIR?

SIGN: BATH FOR STOMACH AND BOWEL AILMENTS

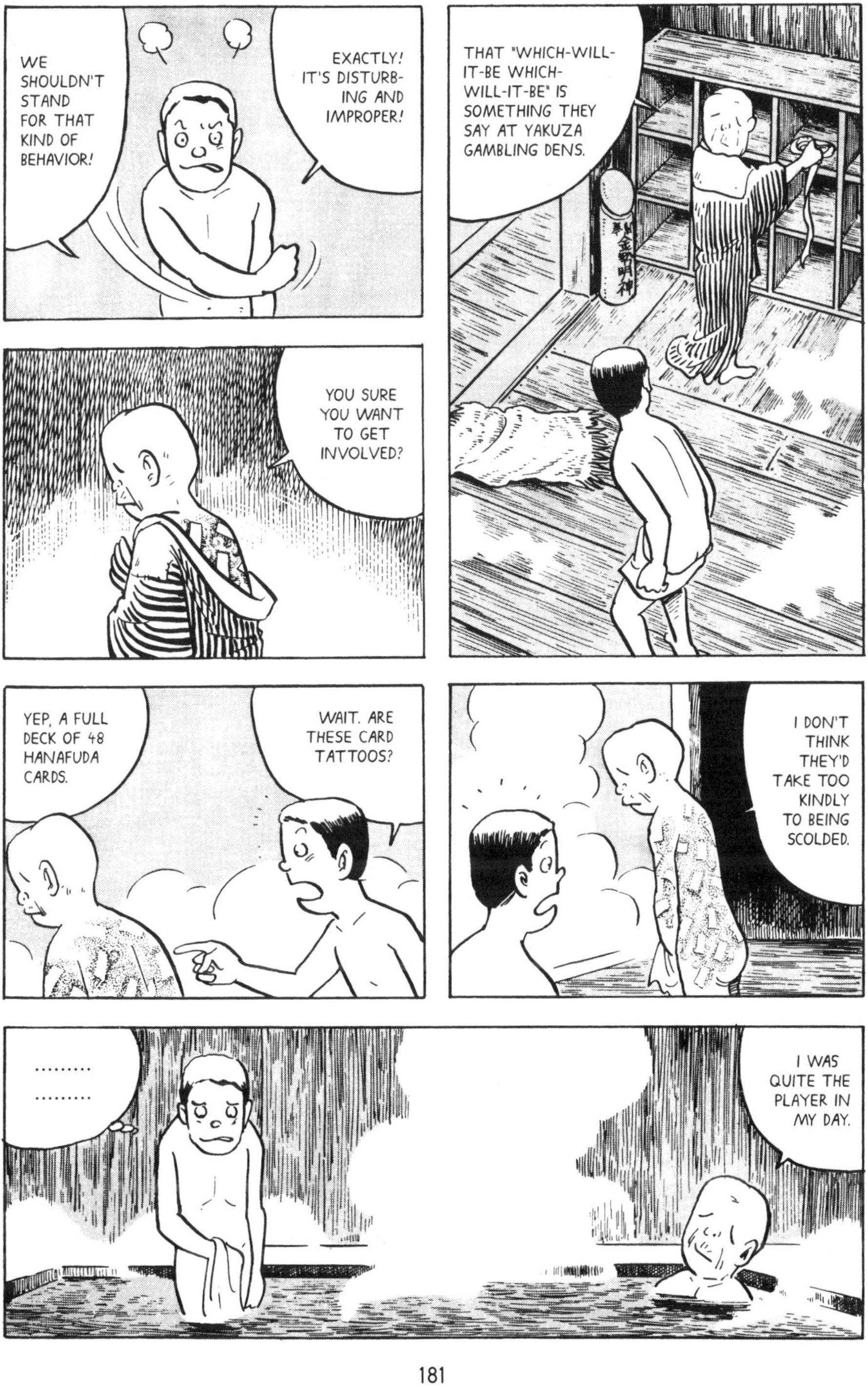
THAT "WHICH-WILL-IT-BE WHICH-WILL-IT-BE" IS SOMETHING THEY SAY AT YAKUZA GAMBLING DENS.
EXACTLY! IT'S DISTURBING AND IMPROPER!
WE SHOULDN'T STAND FOR THAT KIND OF BEHAVIOR!
YOU SURE YOU WANT TO GET INVOLVED?
I DON'T THINK THEY'D TAKE TOO KINDLY TO BEING SCOLDED.
WAIT. ARE THESE CARD TATTOOS?
YEP, A FULL DECK OF 48 HANAFUDA CARDS.
I WAS QUITE THE PLAYER IN MY DAY.
....

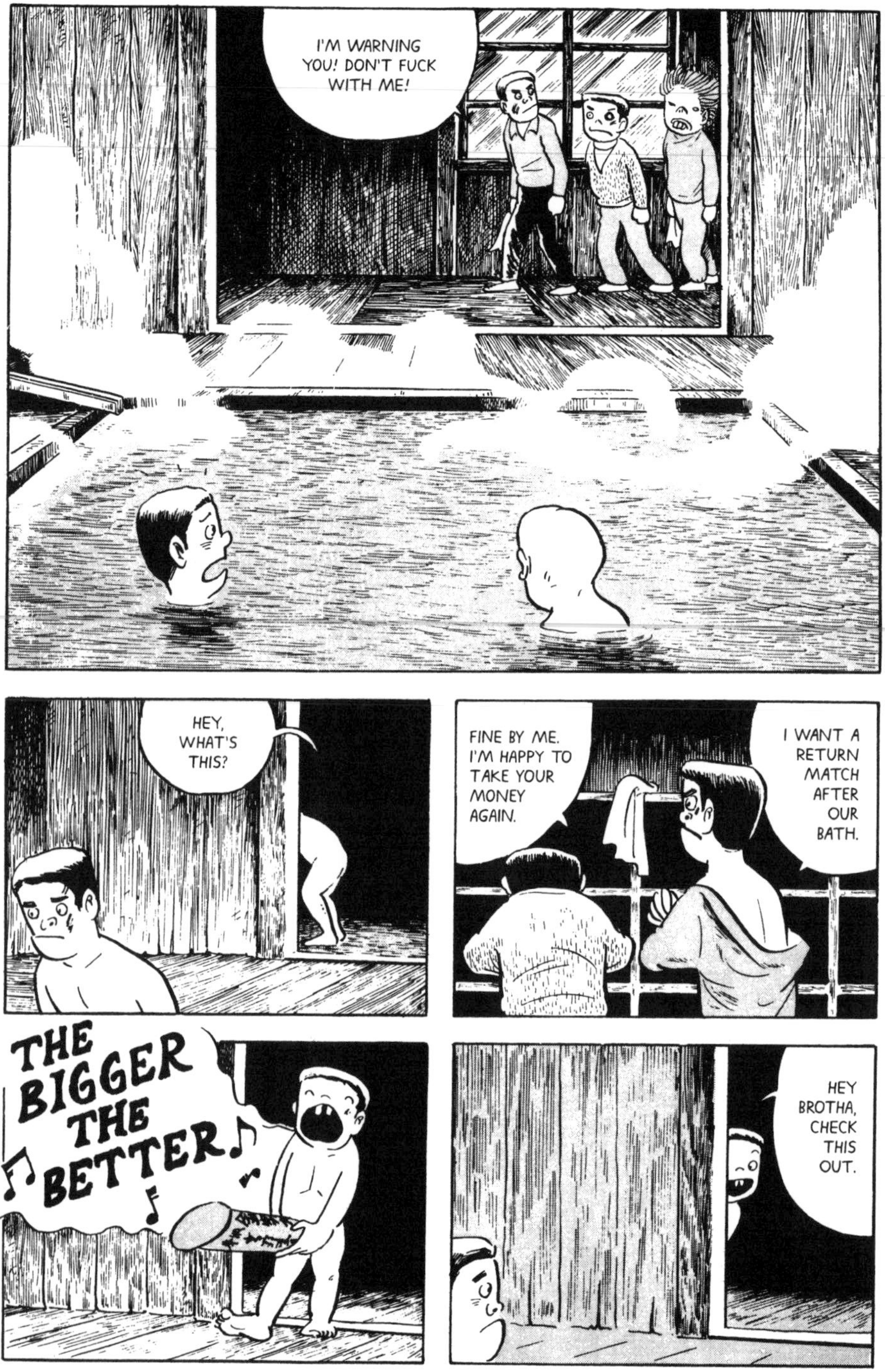
I'M WARNING YOU! DON'T FUCK WITH ME!
I WANT A RETURN MATCH AFTER OUR BATH.
FINE BY ME. I'M HAPPY TO TAKE YOUR MONEY AGAIN.
HEY, WHAT'S THIS?
HEY BROTHA, CHECK THIS OUT.
THE BIGGER THE BETTER

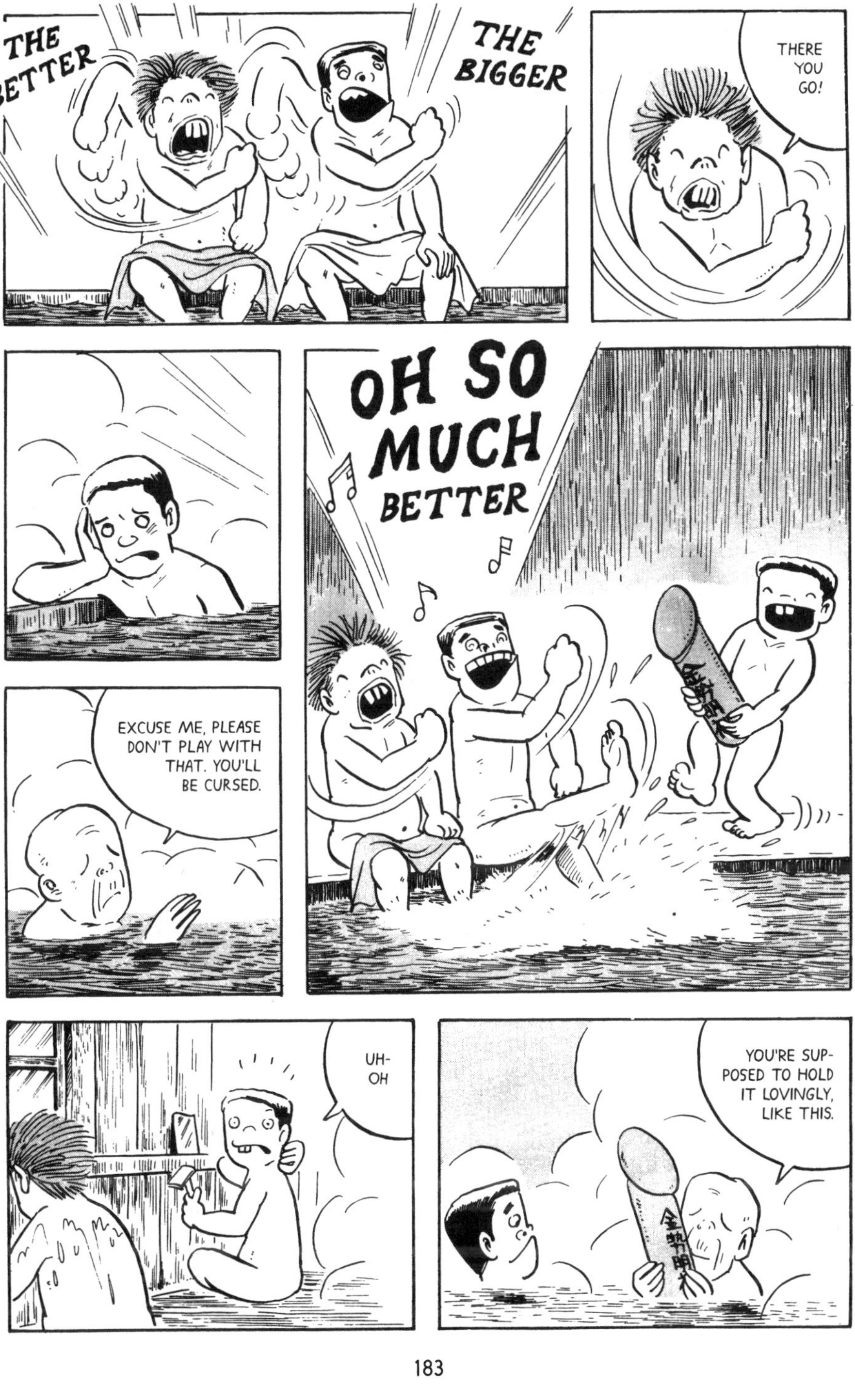
THERE YOU GO!
THE BIGGER
THE BETTER
OH SO MUCH BETTER
EXCUSE ME, PLEASE DON'T PLAY WITH THAT. YOU'LL BE CURSED.
YOU'RE SUP- POSED TO HOLD IT LOVINGLY, LIKE THIS.
UH- OH

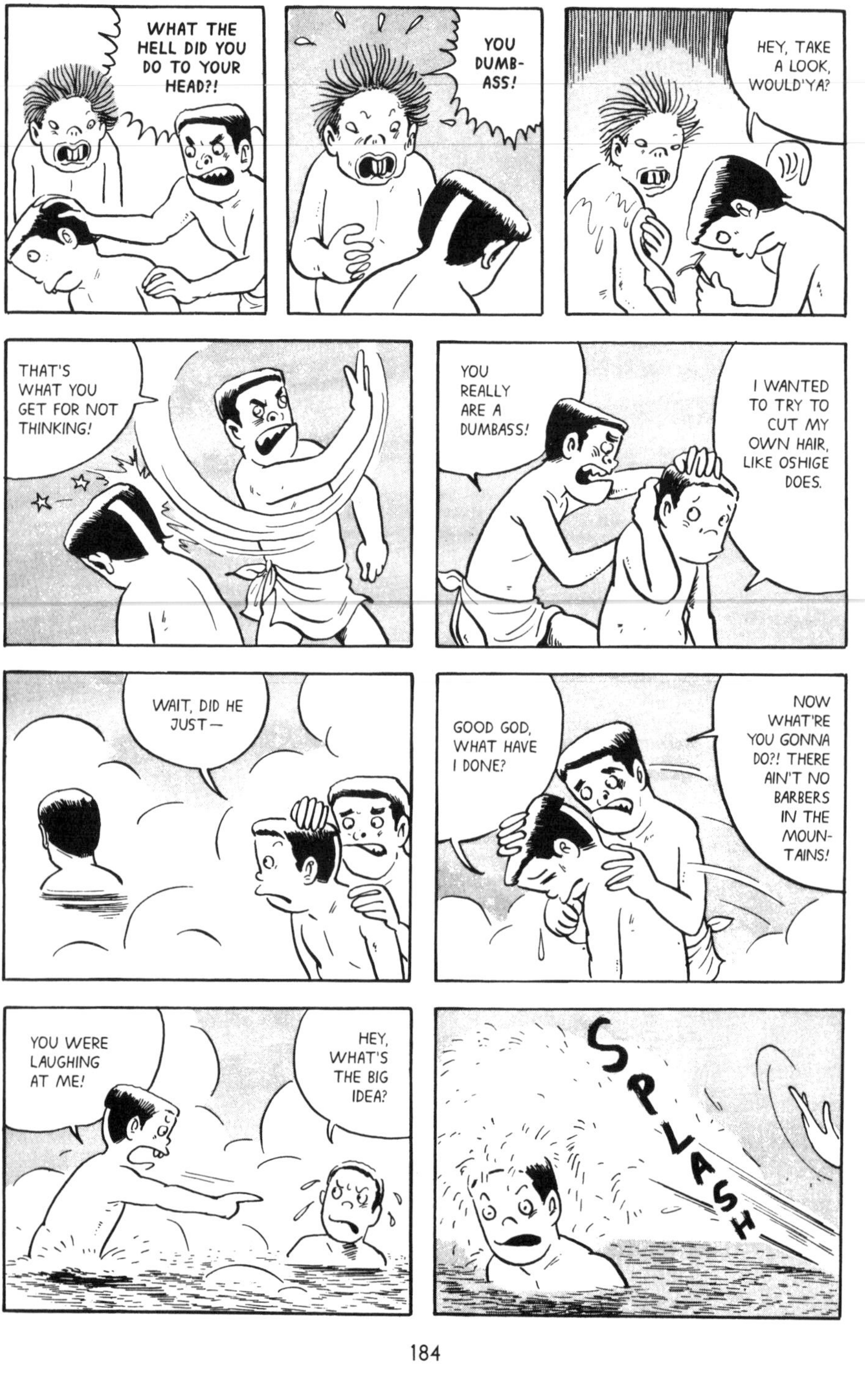
HEY, TAKE A LOOK, WOULD'YA?
YOU DUMB-ASS!
WHAT THE HELL DID YOU DO TO YOUR HEAD?!
I WANTED TO TRY TO CUT MY OWN HAIR, LIKE OSHIGE DOES.
YOU REALLY ARE A DUMBASS!
THAT'S WHAT YOU GET FOR NOT THINKING!
NOW WHAT'RE YOU GONNA DO?! THERE AIN'T NO BARBERS IN THE MOUN-TAINS!
GOOD GOD, WHAT HAVE I DONE?
WAIT, DID HE JUST—
SPLASH
HEY, WHAT'S THE BIG IDEA?
YOU WERE LAUGHING AT ME!

YOU THINK I'M STUPID?
BUT I WASN'T LAUGHING!
THEN WHY DID YOU HAVE YOUR BACK TURNED? YOU HAD YOUR BACK TURNED BECAUSE YOU THOUGHT IT WAS FUNNY!
NO I WASN'T!
IF IT'S SO FUNNY, THEN LET IT OUT ALREADY!
I KNOW HE'S AT LEAST LAUGHING ON THE INSIDE!
THIS GUY'S PISSING ME OFF!
LAUGH, DAMN IT!
LAUGH!
SHIT!
HEY, LEAVE HIM ALONE! WHO WOULDN'T LAUGH AT YOUR STUPID ASS?

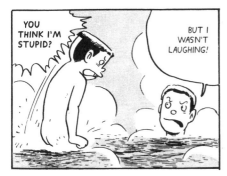

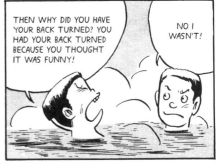

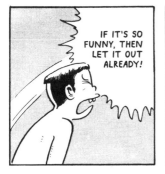

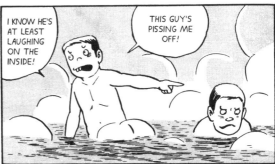

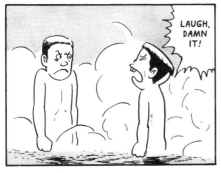

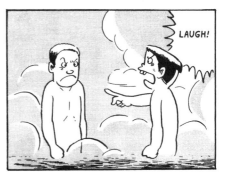

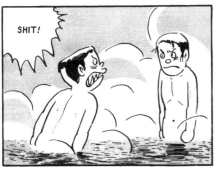

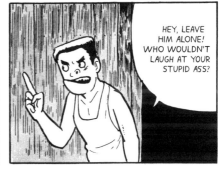

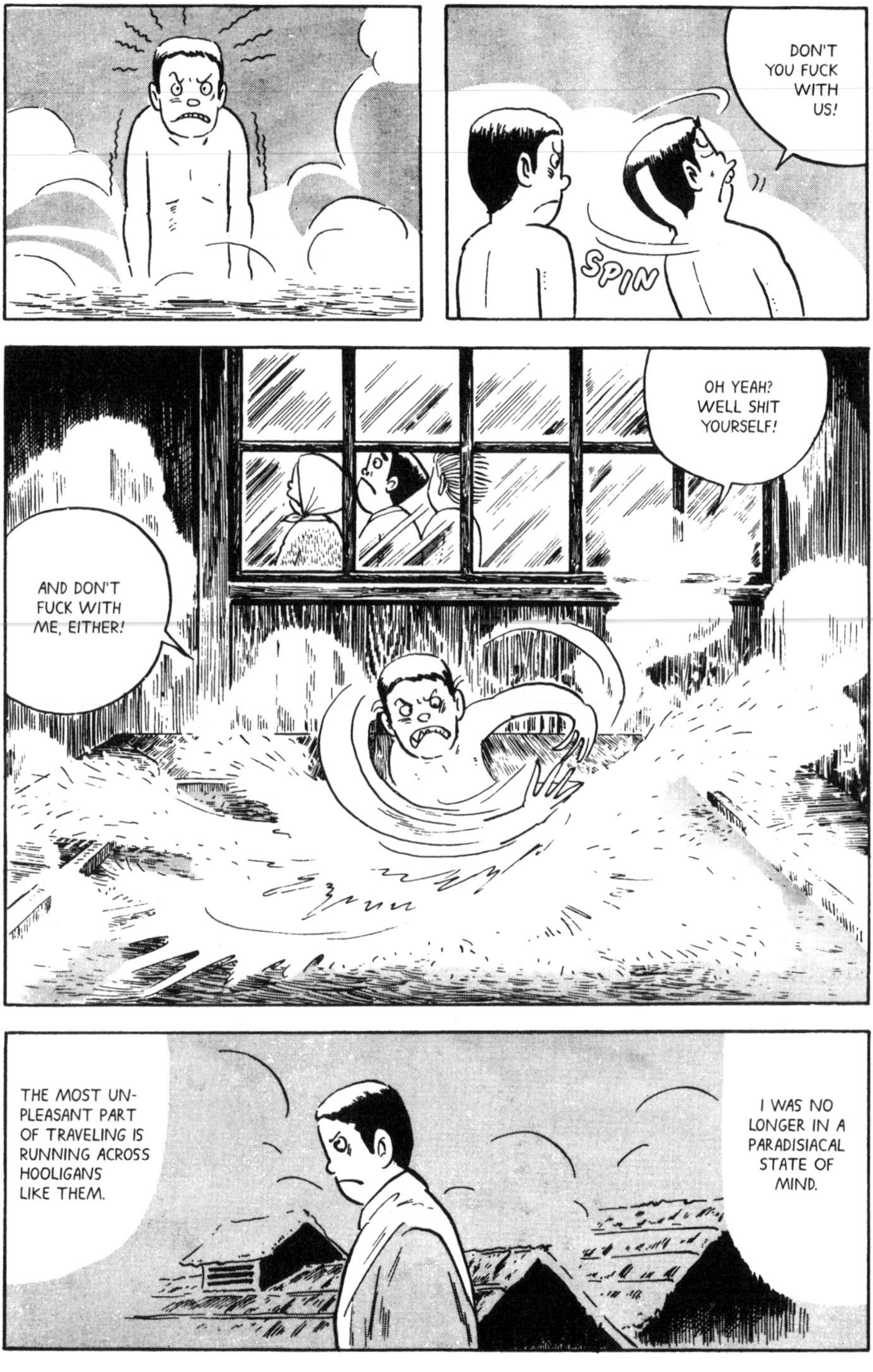
DON'T YOU FUCK WITH US!
SPIN
OH YEAH? WELL SHIT YOURSELF!
AND DON'T FUCK WITH ME, EITHER!
I WAS NO LONGER IN A PARADISIACAL STATE OF MIND.
THE MOST UN-PLEASANT PART OF TRAVELING IS RUNNING ACROSS HOOLIGANS LIKE THEM.

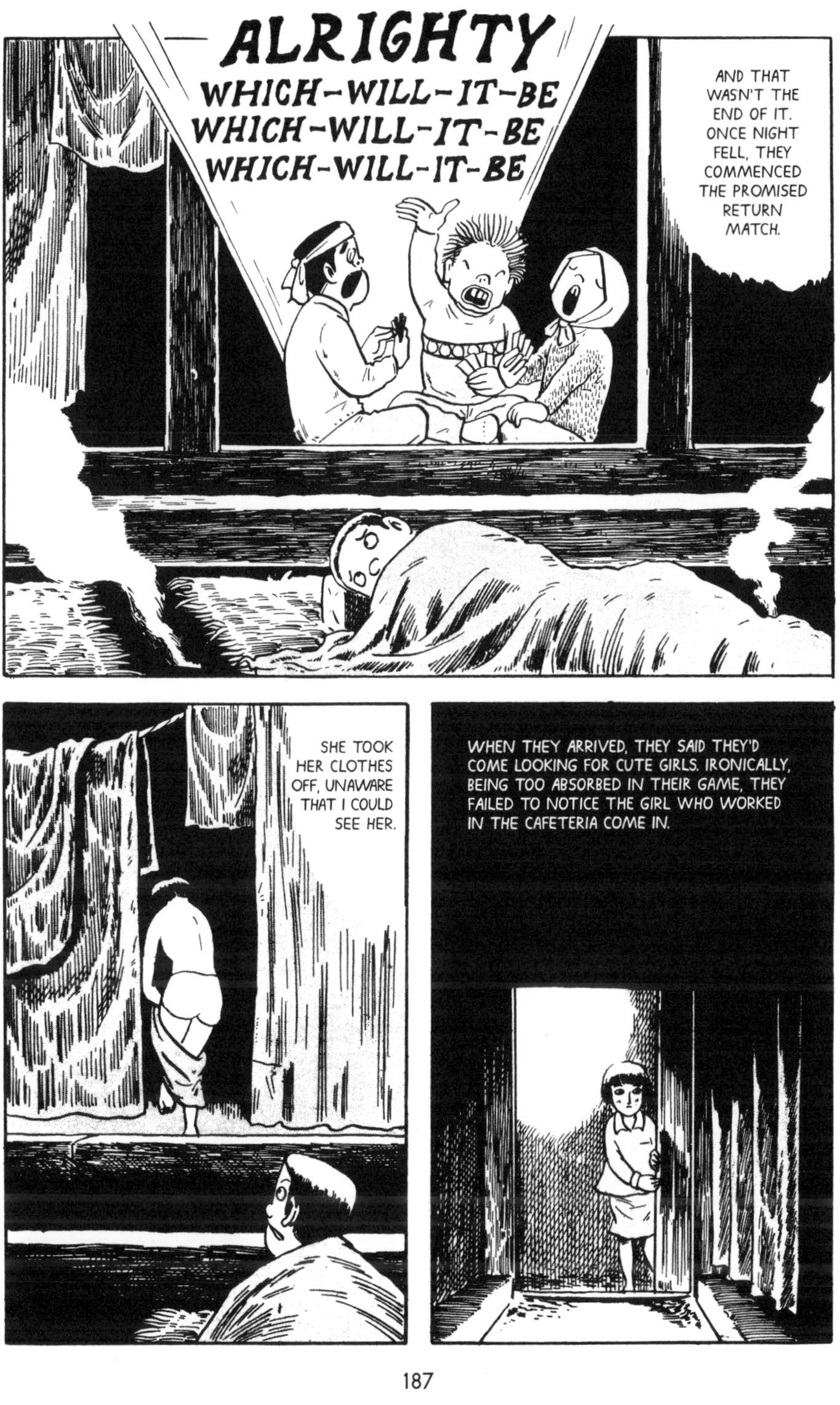
AND THAT WASN'T THE END OF IT. ONCE NIGHT FELL, THEY COMMENCED THE PROMISED RETURN MATCH.
ALRIGHTY
WHICH-WILL-IT-BE
WHICH-WILL-IT-BE
WHICH-WILL-IT-BE
WHEN THEY ARRIVED, THEY SAID THEY'D COME LOOKING FOR CUTE GIRLS. IRONICALLY, BEING TOO ABSORBED IN THEIR GAME, THEY FAILED TO NOTICE THE GIRL WHO WORKED IN THE CAFETERIA COME IN.
SHE TOOK HER CLOTHES OFF, UNAWARE THAT I COULD SEE HER.

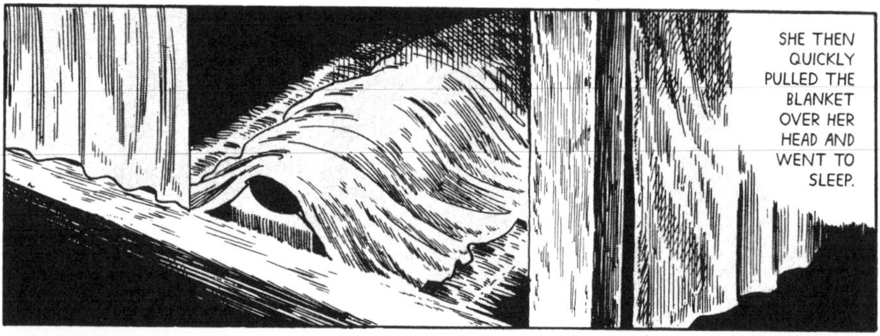
SHE THEN QUICKLY PULLED THE BLANKET OVER HER HEAD AND WENT TO SLEEP.

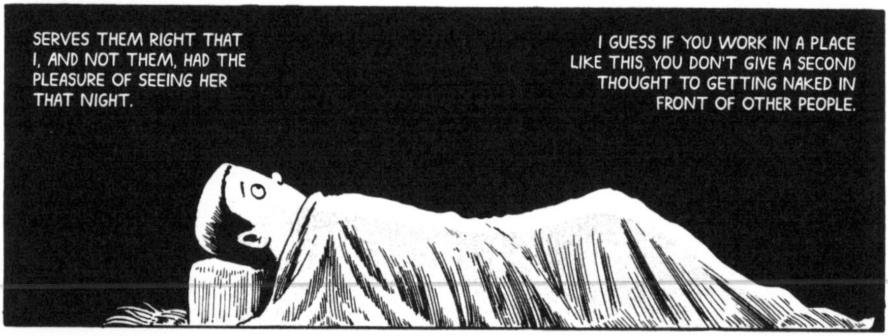
SERVES THEM RIGHT THAT I, AND NOT THEM, HAD THE PLEASURE OF SEEING HER THAT NIGHT.
I GUESS IF YOU WORK IN A PLACE LIKE THIS, YOU DON'T GIVE A SECOND THOUGHT TO GETTING NAKED IN FRONT OF OTHER PEOPLE.

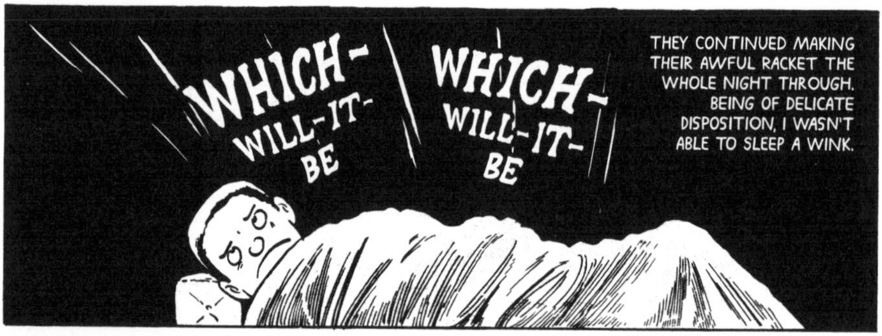
WHICH-WILL-IT-BE
WHICH-WILL-IT-BE
THEY CONTINUED MAKING THEIR AWFUL RACKET THE WHOLE NIGHT THROUGH. BEING OF DELICATE DISPOSITION, I WASN'T ABLE TO SLEEP A WINK.

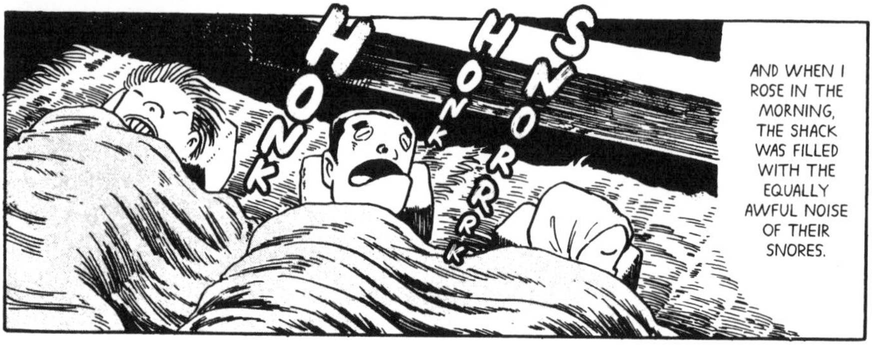
HONK
HONK
SNORRRRK
AND WHEN I ROSE IN THE MORNING, THE SHACK WAS FILLED WITH THE EQUALLY AWFUL NOISE OF THEIR SNORES.

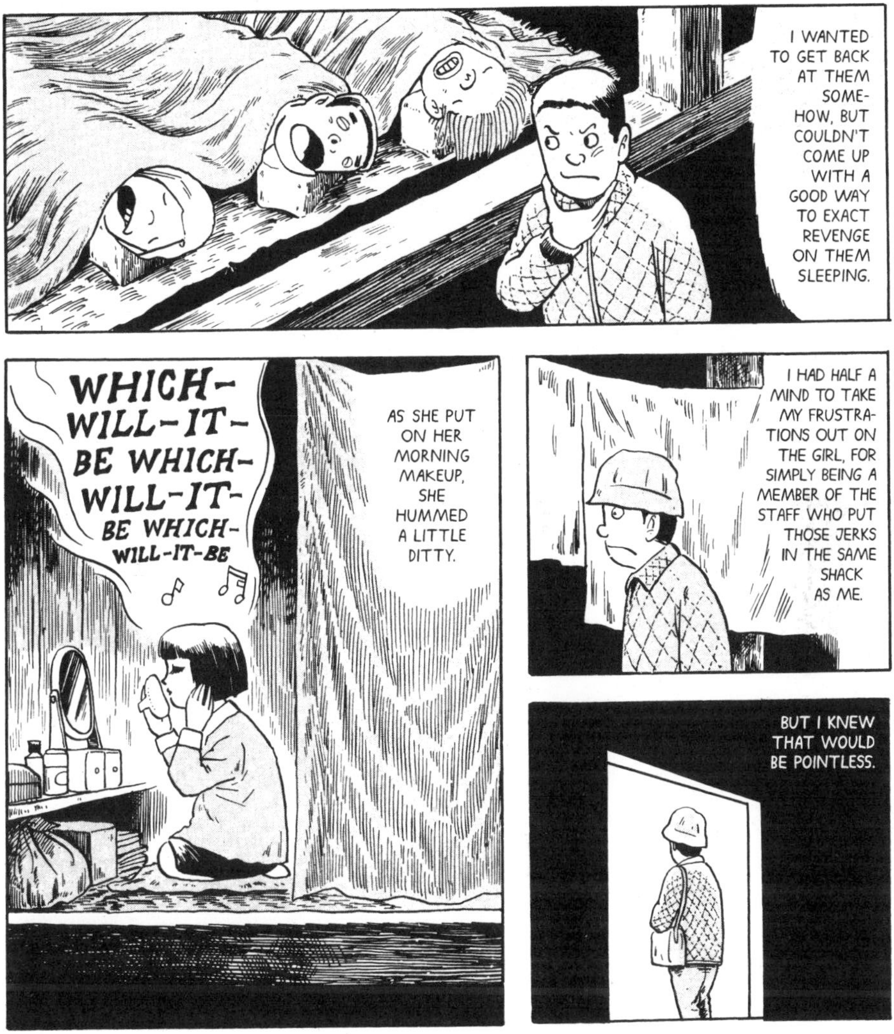
I WANTED TO GET BACK AT THEM SOME-HOW, BUT COULDN'T COME UP WITH A GOOD WAY TO EXACT REVENGE ON THEM SLEEPING.
I HAD HALF A MIND TO TAKE MY FRUSTRA-TIONS OUT ON THE GIRL, FOR SIMPLY BEING A MEMBER OF THE STAFF WHO PUT THOSE JERKS IN THE SAME SHACK AS ME.
BUT I KNEW THAT WOULD BE POINTLESS.
AS SHE PUT ON HER MORNING MAKEUP, SHE HUMMED A LITTLE DITTY.
WHICH-WILL-IT-BE WHICH-WILL-IT-BE WHICH-WILL-IT-BE

THE STRANGE THING ABOUT TRAVELING IS THAT YOU USUALLY REMEMBER ONLY THE GOOD EXPERIENCES. I'M SURE SOMEDAY I'LL LOOK BACK AT MY STAY AT THE FUKENOYU HOT SPRING AND LAUGH...

OR NOT...

JUST THE THOUGHT OF THE PLACE STILL MAKES MY BLOOD BOIL.

MISTER BEN OF THE
HONYARA CAVE

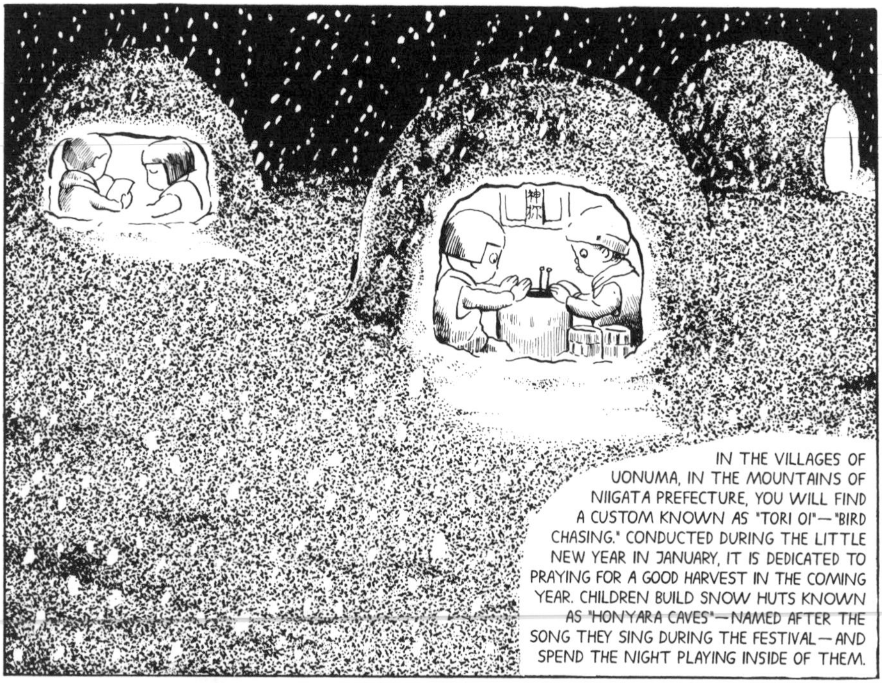
IN THE VILLAGES OF UONUMA, IN THE MOUNTAINS OF NIIGATA PREFECTURE, YOU WILL FIND A CUSTOM KNOWN AS "TORI OI"—"BIRD CHASING." CONDUCTED DURING THE LITTLE NEW YEAR IN JANUARY, IT IS DEDICATED TO PRAYING FOR A GOOD HARVEST IN THE COMING YEAR. CHILDREN BUILD SNOW HUTS KNOWN AS "HONYARA CAVES"—NAMED AFTER THE SONG THEY SING DURING THE FESTIVAL—AND SPEND THE NIGHT PLAYING INSIDE OF THEM.

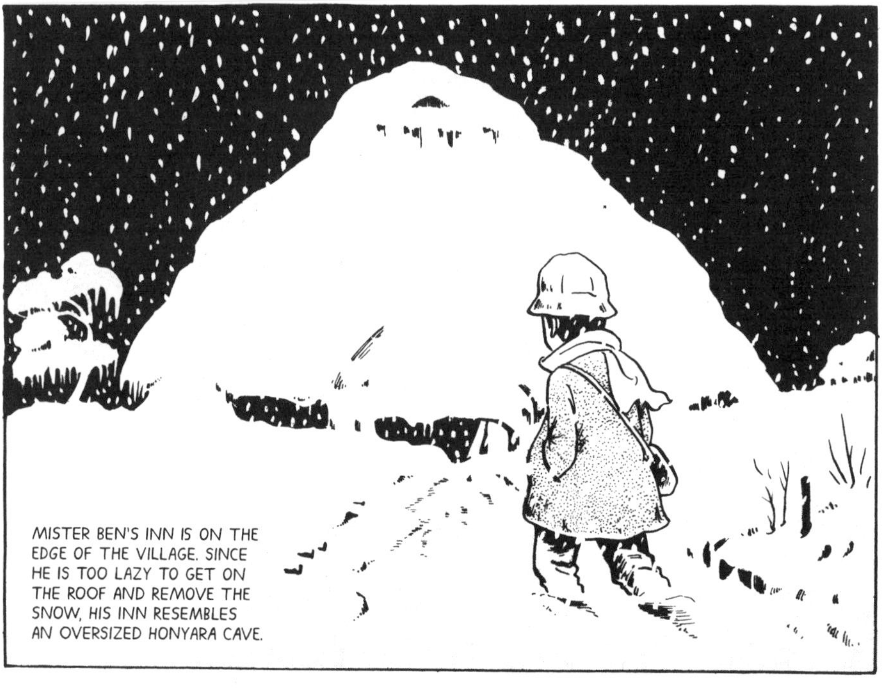
MISTER BEN'S INN IS ON THE EDGE OF THE VILLAGE. SINCE HE IS TOO LAZY TO GET ON THE ROOF AND REMOVE THE SNOW, HIS INN RESEMBLES AN OVERSIZED HONYARA CAVE.

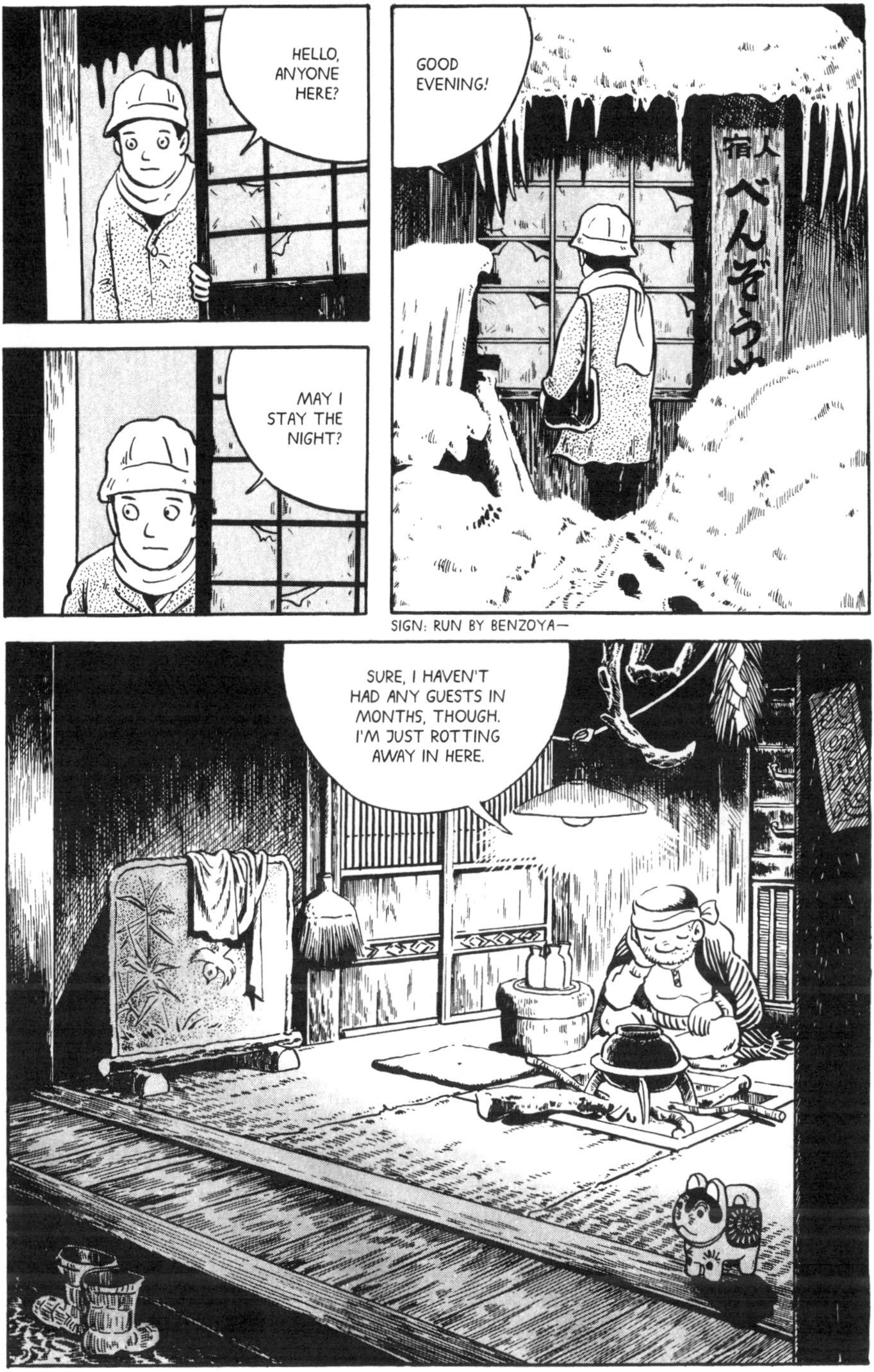
GOOD EVENING!
SIGN: RUN BY BENZOYA—
HELLO, ANYONE HERE?
MAY I STAY THE NIGHT?
SURE, I HAVEN'T HAD ANY GUESTS IN MONTHS, THOUGH. I'M JUST ROTTING AWAY IN HERE.

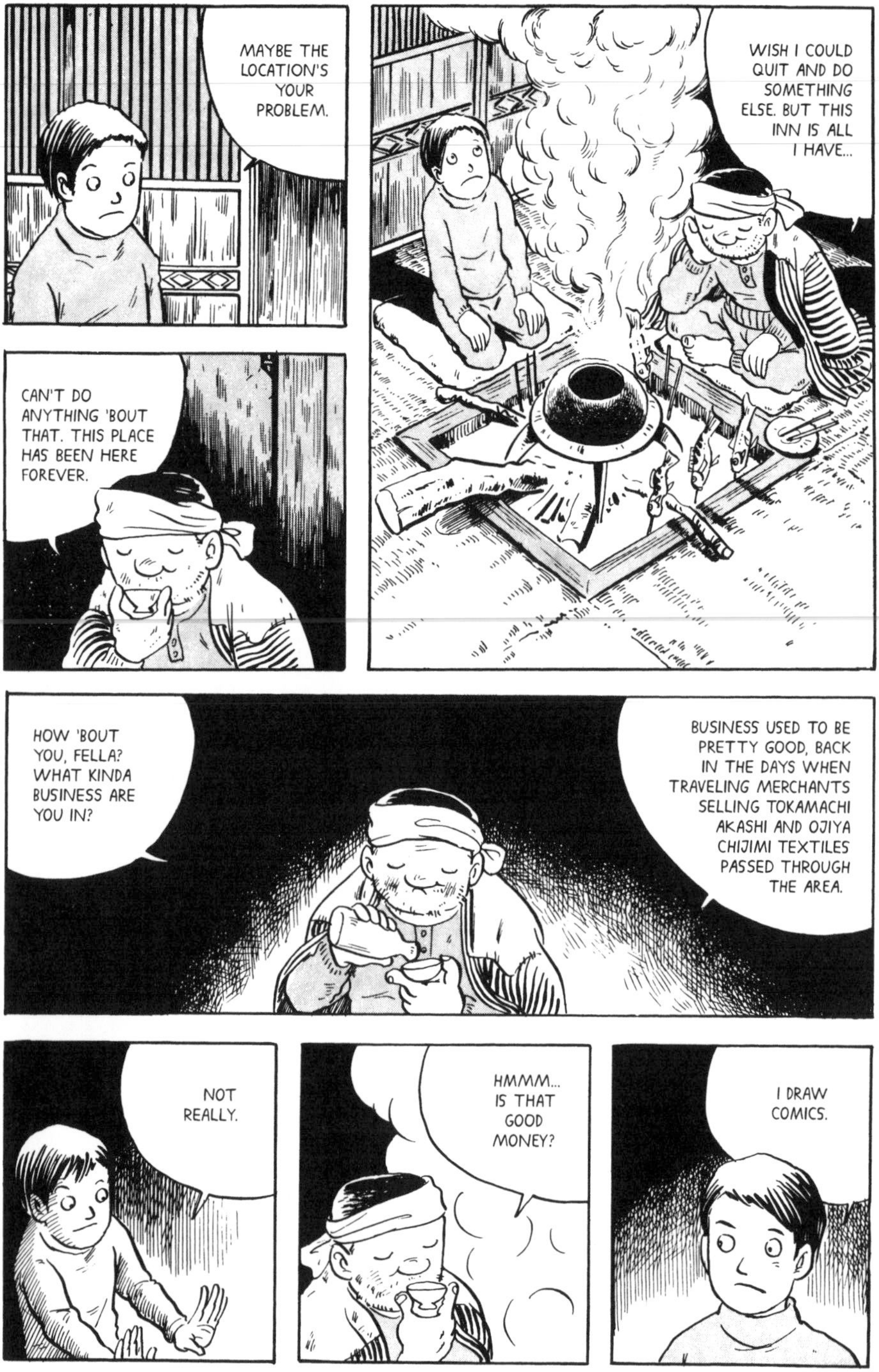
WISH I COULD QUIT AND DO SOMETHING ELSE. BUT THIS INN IS ALL I HAVE...
MAYBE THE LOCATION'S YOUR PROBLEM.
CAN'T DO ANYTHING 'BOUT THAT. THIS PLACE HAS BEEN HERE FOREVER.
BUSINESS USED TO BE PRETTY GOOD, BACK IN THE DAYS WHEN TRAVELING MERCHANTS SELLING TOKAMACHI AKASHI AND OJIYA CHIJIMI TEXTILES PASSED THROUGH THE AREA.
HOW 'BOUT YOU, FELLA? WHAT KINDA BUSINESS ARE YOU IN?
I DRAW COMICS.
HMMM... IS THAT GOOD MONEY?
NOT REALLY.

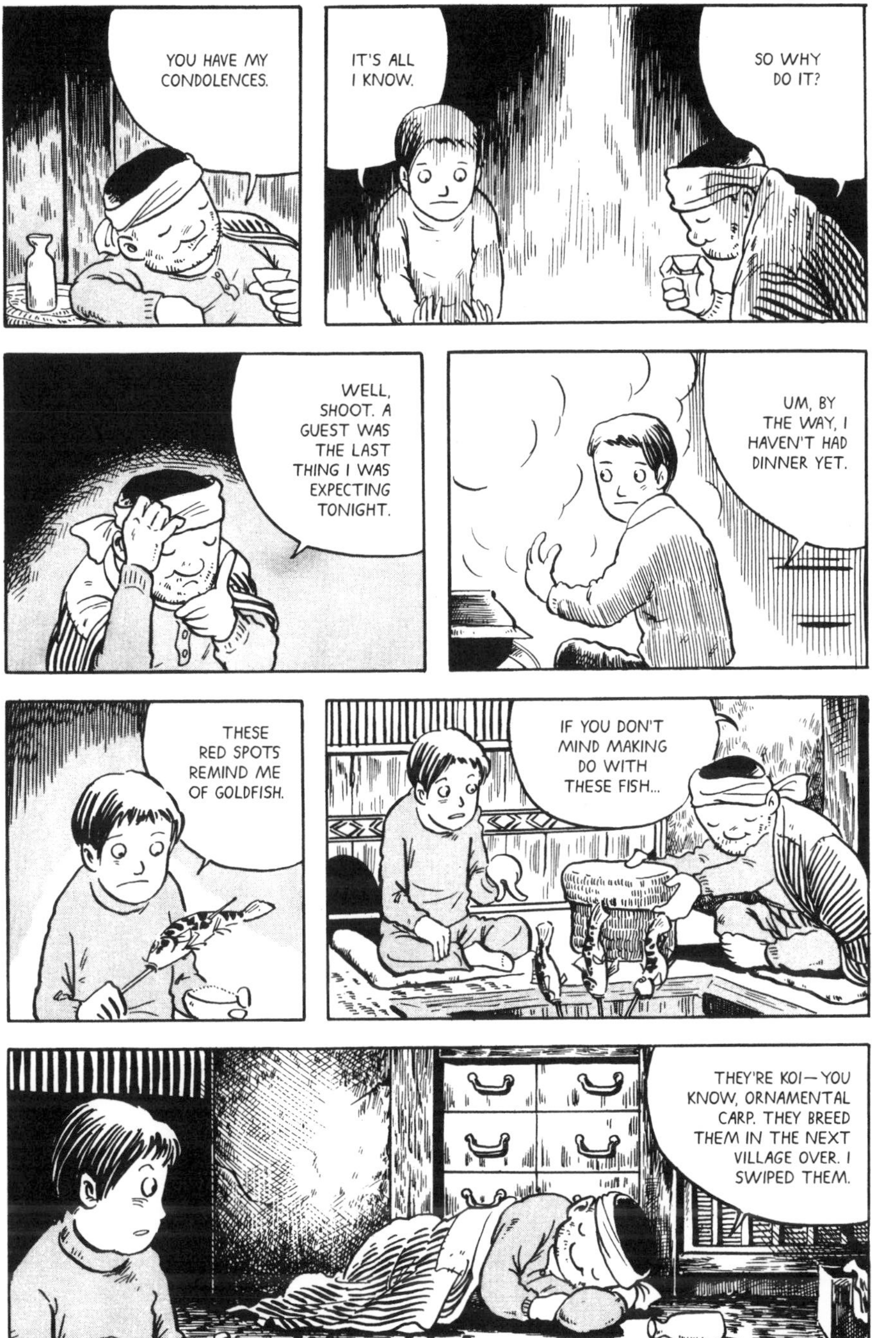
SO WHY DO IT?
IT'S ALL I KNOW.
YOU HAVE MY CONDOLENCES.
UM, BY THE WAY, I HAVEN'T HAD DINNER YET.
WELL, SHOOT. A GUEST WAS THE LAST THING I WAS EXPECTING TONIGHT.
IF YOU DON'T MIND MAKING DO WITH THESE FISH...
THESE RED SPOTS REMIND ME OF GOLDFISH.
THEY'RE KOI—YOU KNOW, ORNAMENTAL CARP. THEY BREED THEM IN THE NEXT VILLAGE OVER. I SWIPED THEM.

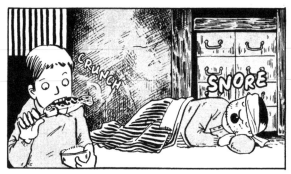

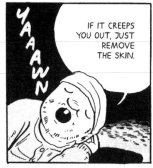

YAAAAWN
IF IT CREEPS YOU OUT, JUST REMOVE THE SKIN.
CRUNCH
SNORE
SIR, YOU CAN'T SLEEP YET.
SNORE
WHERE'S MY ROOM?
THERE'S A FUTON OVER THERE.
C'MON. LET'S SET UP THE FUTONS AND THEN YOU CAN SLEEP.
SORRY SORRY
MUST'VE DRANK TOO MUCH.

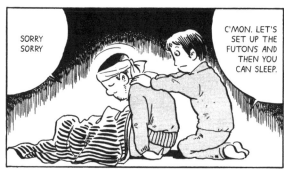

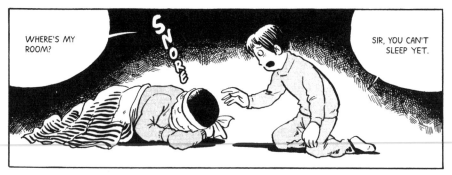

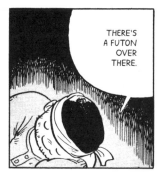

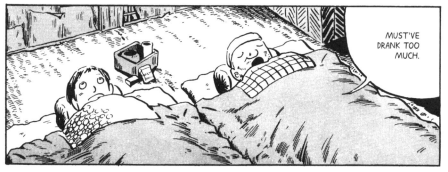

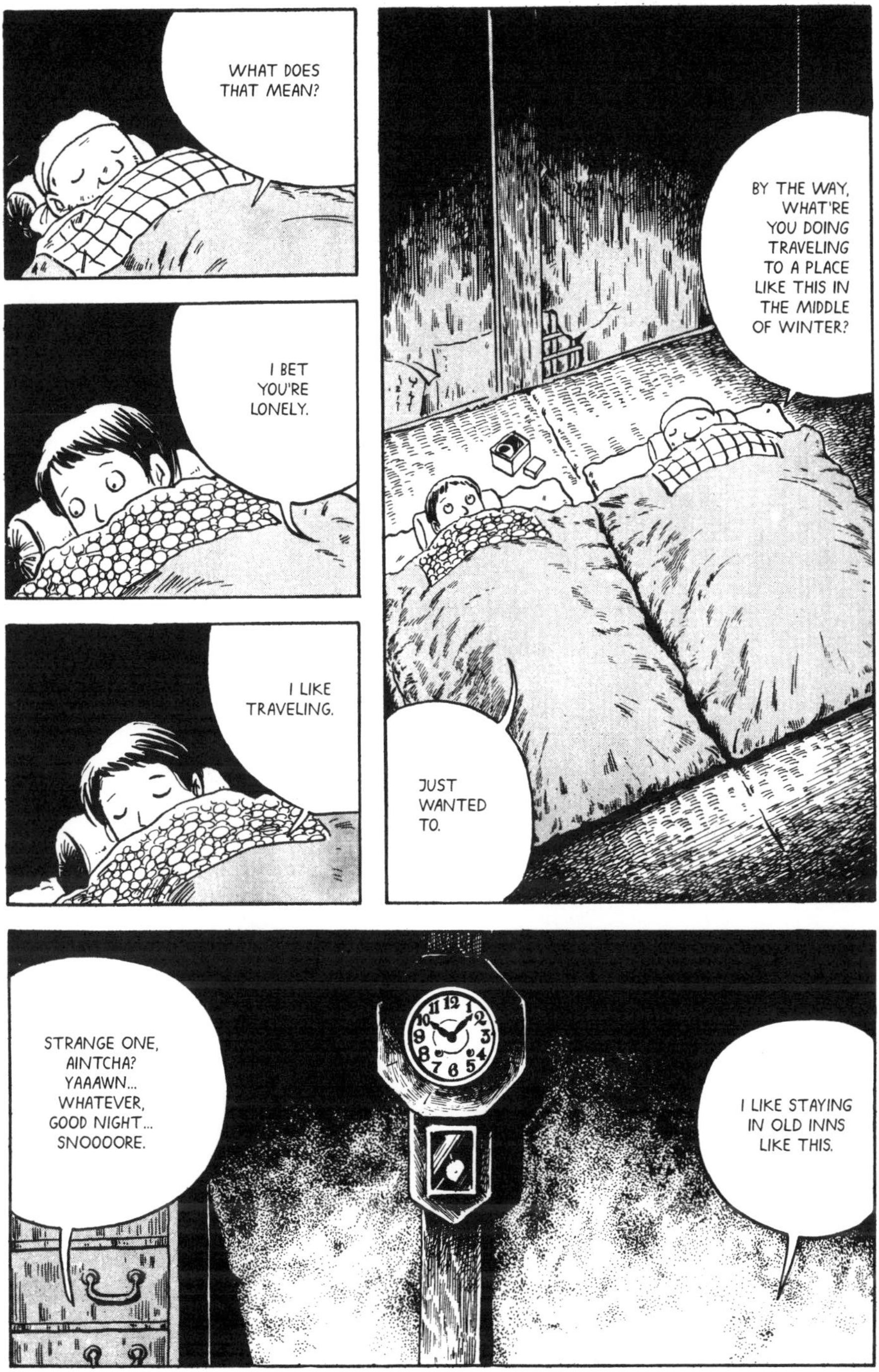
BY THE WAY, WHAT'RE YOU DOING TRAVELING TO A PLACE LIKE THIS IN THE MIDDLE OF WINTER?
JUST WANTED TO.
WHAT DOES THAT MEAN?
I BET YOU'RE LONELY.
I LIKE TRAVELING.
I LIKE STAYING IN OLD INNS LIKE THIS.
STRANGE ONE, AINTCHA? YAAAWN... WHATEVER, GOOD NIGHT... SNOOOORE.

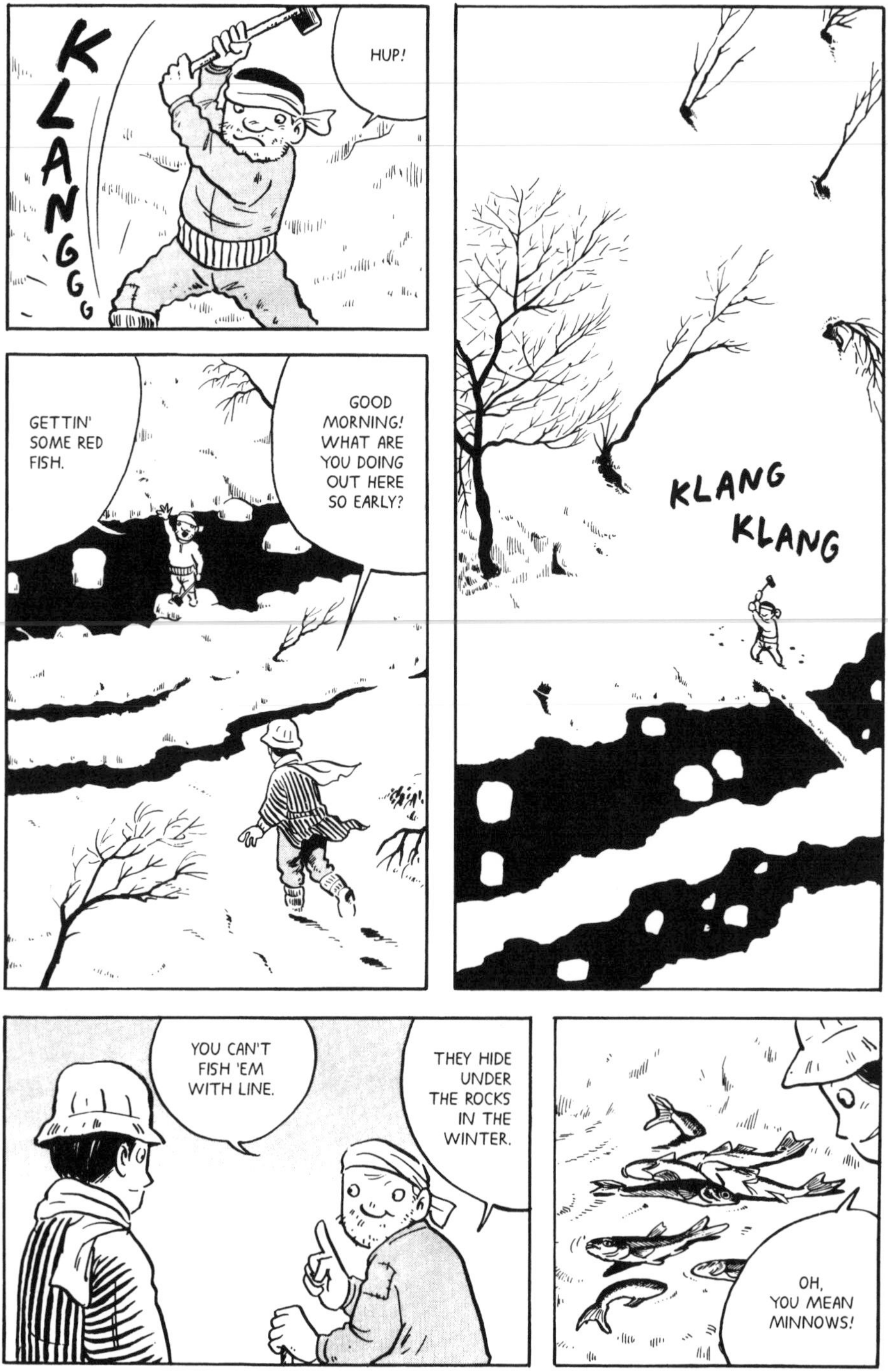
KLANG
KLANG
HUP!
KLANGGG
GOOD MORNING! WHAT ARE YOU DOING OUT HERE SO EARLY?
GETTIN' SOME RED FISH.
OH, YOU MEAN MINNOWS!
THEY HIDE UNDER THE ROCKS IN THE WINTER.
YOU CAN'T FISH 'EM WITH LINE.

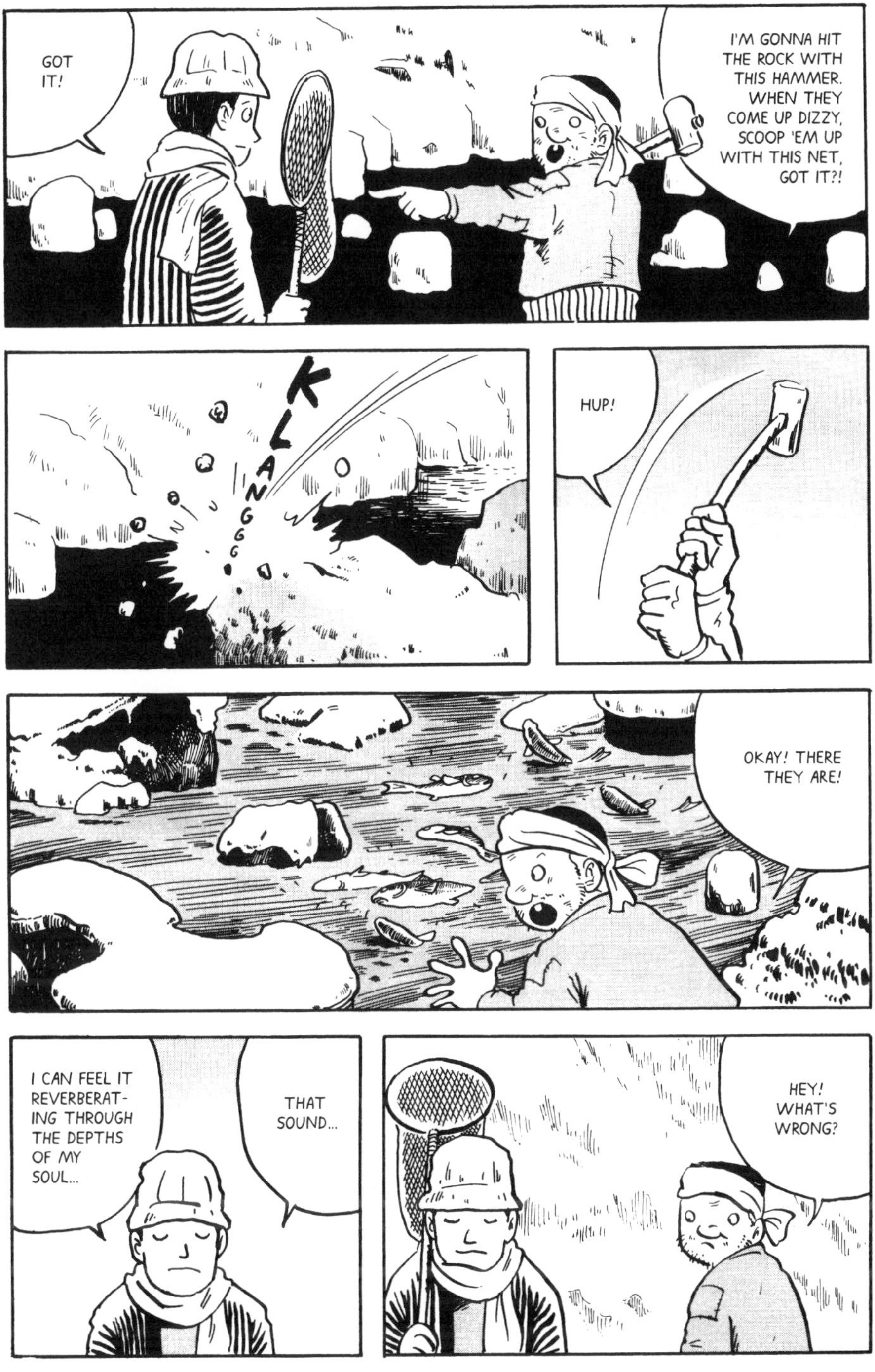
I'M GONNA HIT THE ROCK WITH THIS HAMMER. WHEN THEY COME UP DIZZY, SCOOP 'EM UP WITH THIS NET, GOT IT?!
GOT IT!
HUP!
KLANGGG
OKAY! THERE THEY ARE!
HEY! WHAT'S WRONG?
THAT SOUND...
I CAN FEEL IT REVERBERATING THROUGH THE DEPTHS OF MY SOUL...

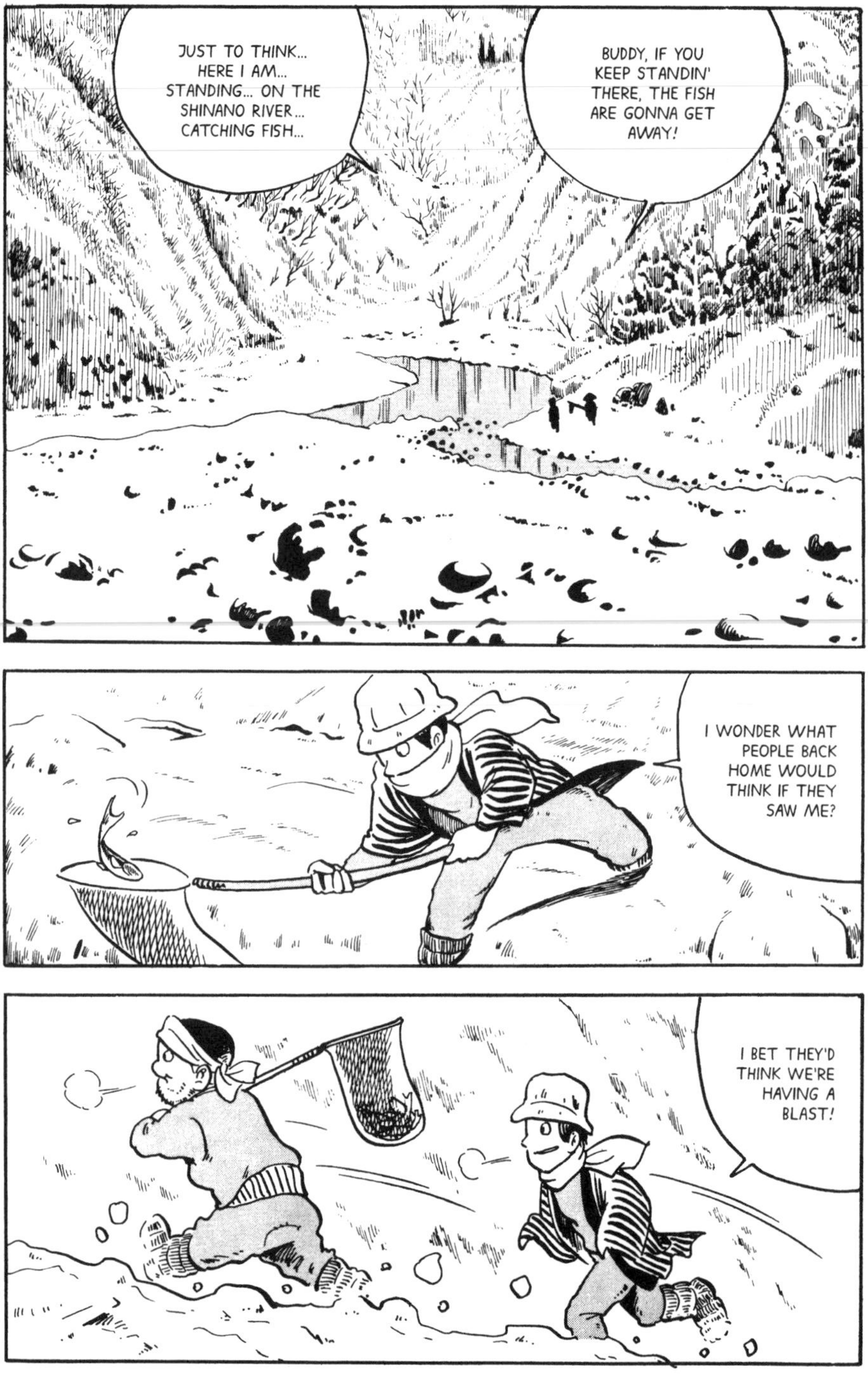
BUDDY, IF YOU KEEP STANDIN' THERE, THE FISH ARE GONNA GET AWAY!
JUST TO THINK... HERE I AM... STANDING... ON THE SHINANO RIVER... CATCHING FISH...
I WONDER WHAT PEOPLE BACK HOME WOULD THINK IF THEY SAW ME?
I BET THEY'D THINK WE'RE HAVING A BLAST!

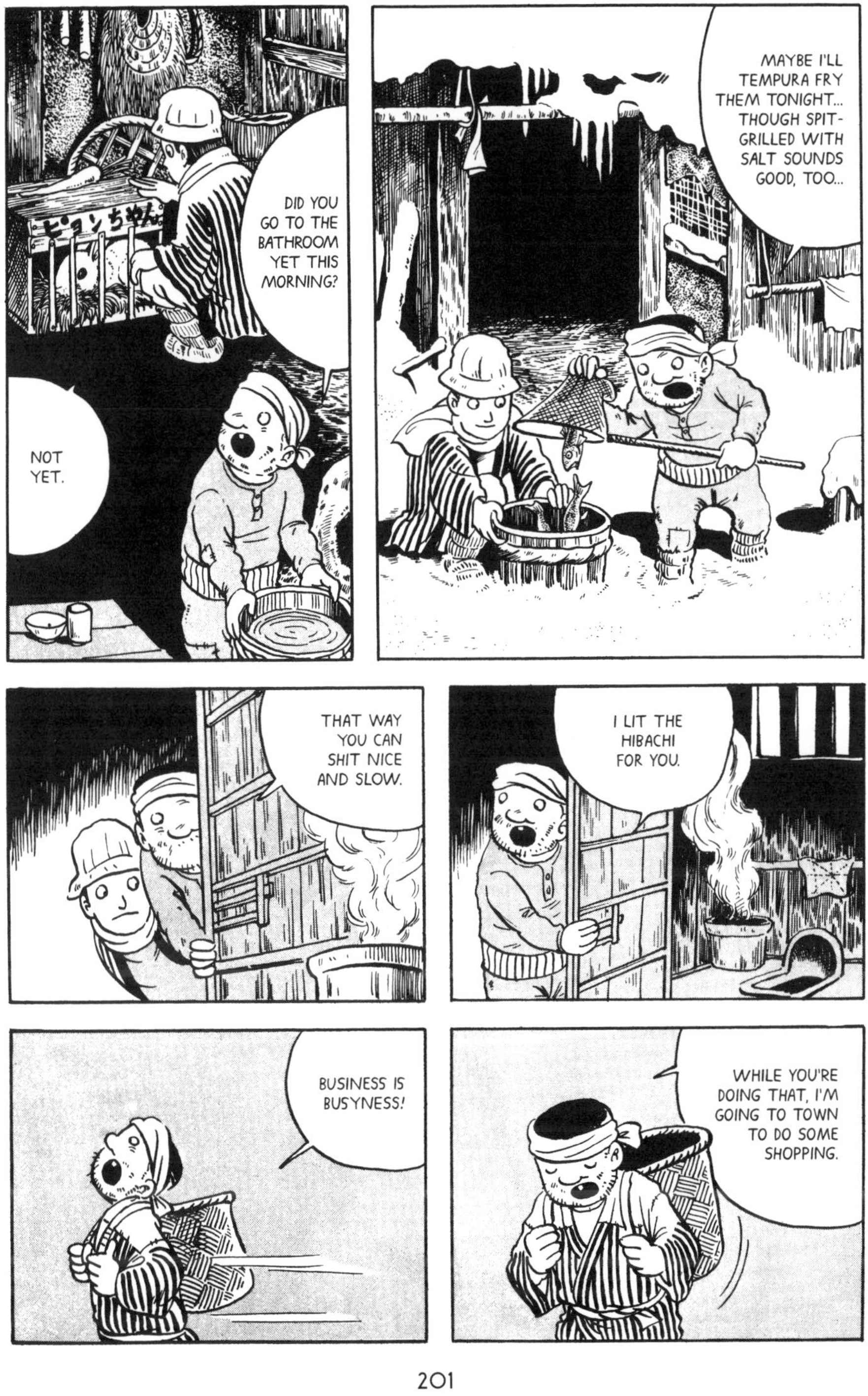
MAYBE I'LL TEMPURA FRY THEM TONIGHT... THOUGH SPIT-GRILLED WITH SALT SOUNDS GOOD, TOO...
DID YOU GO TO THE BATHROOM YET THIS MORNING?
ピョンちゃん
NOT YET.
I LIT THE HIBACHI FOR YOU.
THAT WAY YOU CAN SHIT NICE AND SLOW.
WHILE YOU'RE DOING THAT, I'M GOING TO TOWN TO DO SOME SHOPPING.
BUSINESS IS BUSYNESS!

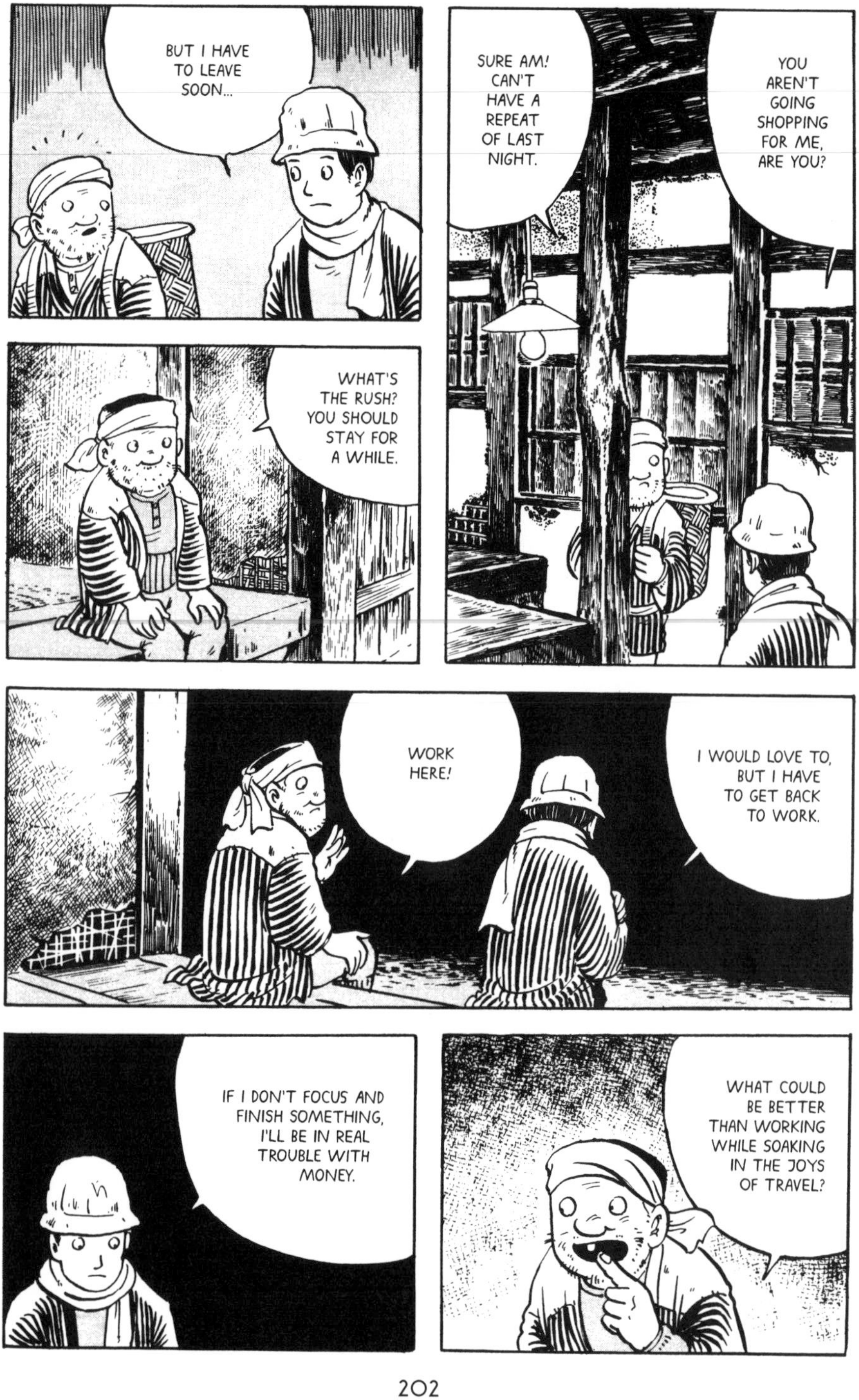
YOU AREN'T GOING SHOPPING FOR ME, ARE YOU?
SURE AM! CAN'T HAVE A REPEAT OF LAST NIGHT.
BUT I HAVE TO LEAVE SOON...
WHAT'S THE RUSH? YOU SHOULD STAY FOR A WHILE.
I WOULD LOVE TO, BUT I HAVE TO GET BACK TO WORK.
WORK HERE!
WHAT COULD BE BETTER THAN WORKING WHILE SOAKING IN THE JOYS OF TRAVEL?
IF I DON'T FOCUS AND FINISH SOMETHING, I'LL BE IN REAL TROUBLE WITH MONEY.

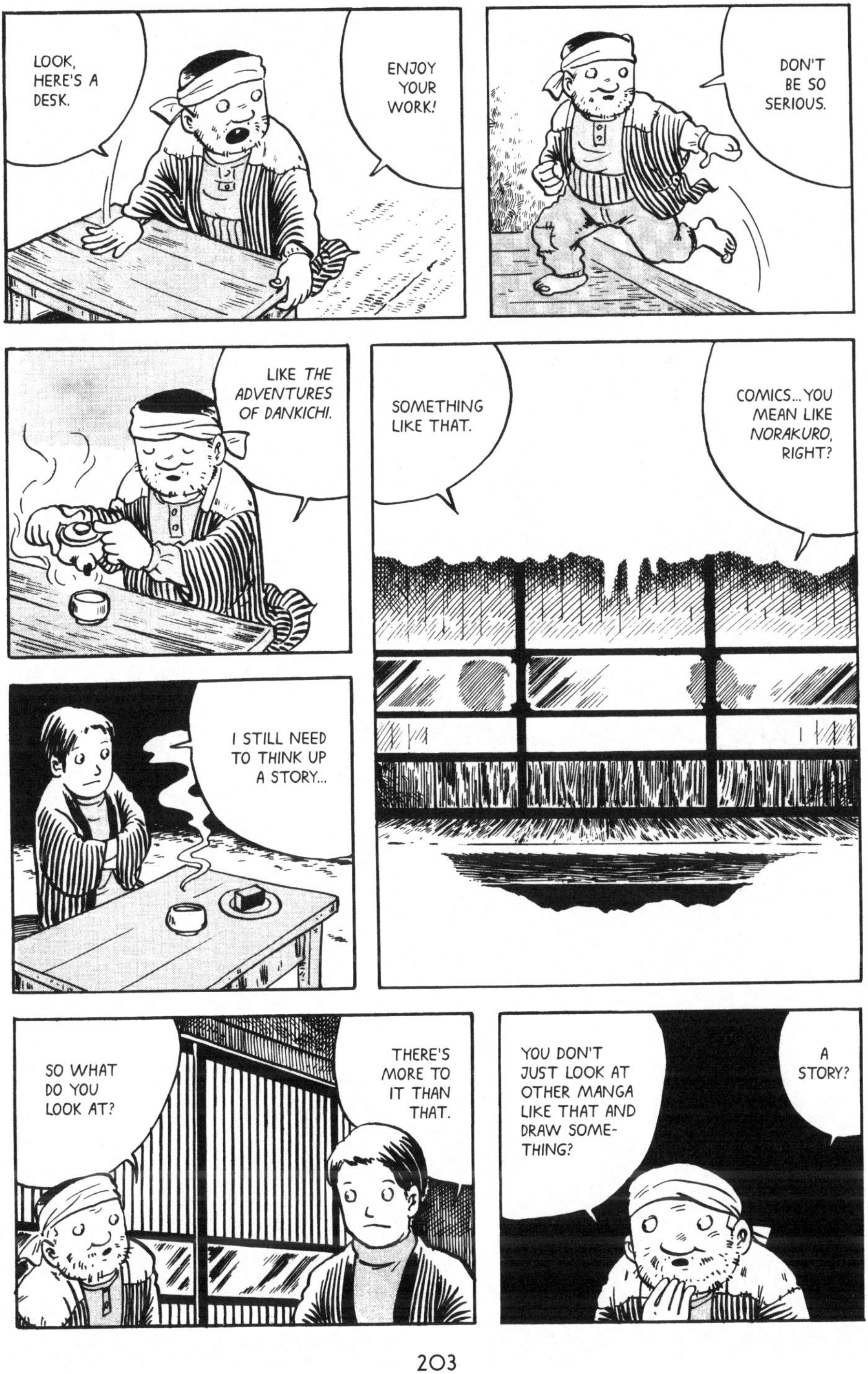
DON'T BE SO SERIOUS.
ENJOY YOUR WORK!
LOOK, HERE'S A DESK.
COMICS... YOU MEAN LIKE *NORAKURO*, RIGHT?
SOMETHING LIKE THAT.
LIKE *THE ADVENTURES OF DANKICHI*.
I STILL NEED TO THINK UP A STORY...
A STORY?
YOU DON'T JUST LOOK AT OTHER MANGA LIKE THAT AND DRAW SOME-THING?
THERE'S MORE TO IT THAN THAT.
SO WHAT DO YOU LOOK AT?

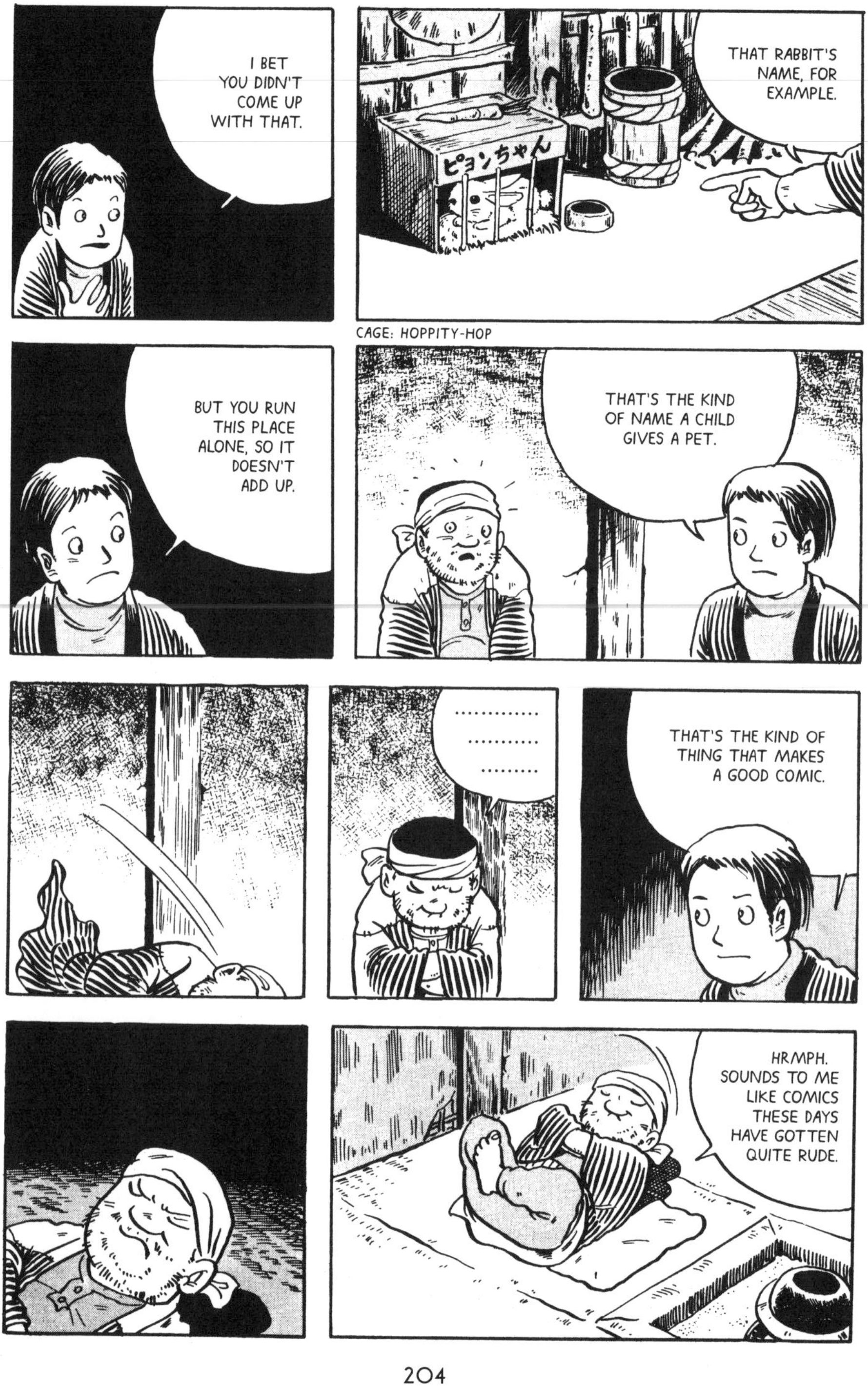
ピョンちゃん
THAT RABBIT'S NAME, FOR EXAMPLE.
CAGE: HOPPITY-HOP
I BET YOU DIDN'T COME UP WITH THAT.
THAT'S THE KIND OF NAME A CHILD GIVES A PET.
BUT YOU RUN THIS PLACE ALONE, SO IT DOESN'T ADD UP.
THAT'S THE KIND OF THING THAT MAKES A GOOD COMIC.
....
HRMPH. SOUNDS TO ME LIKE COMICS THESE DAYS HAVE GOTTEN QUITE RUDE.

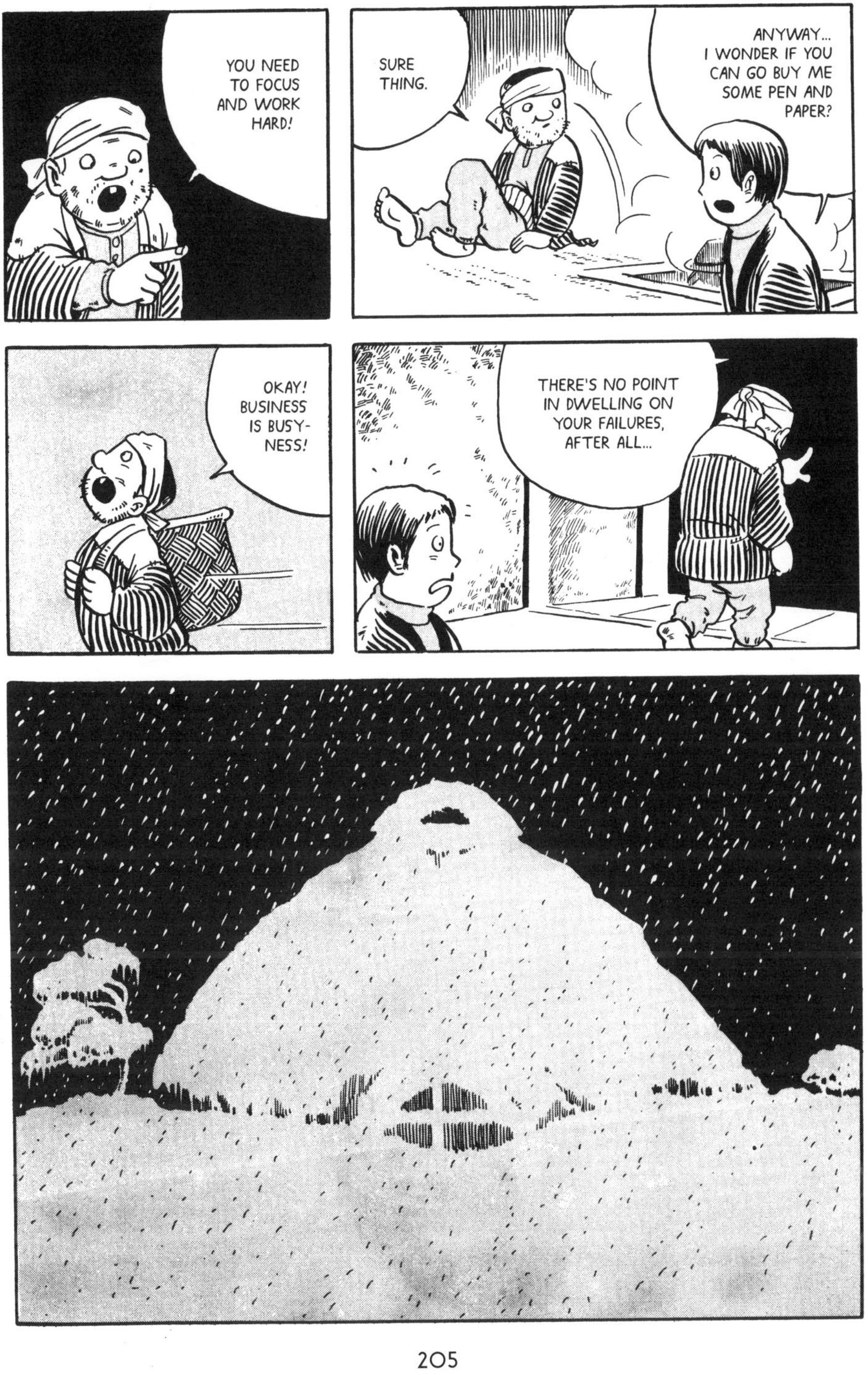
ANYWAY... I WONDER IF YOU CAN GO BUY ME SOME PEN AND PAPER?
SURE THING.
YOU NEED TO FOCUS AND WORK HARD!
THERE'S NO POINT IN DWELLING ON YOUR FAILURES, AFTER ALL...
OKAY! BUSINESS IS BUSY-NESS!

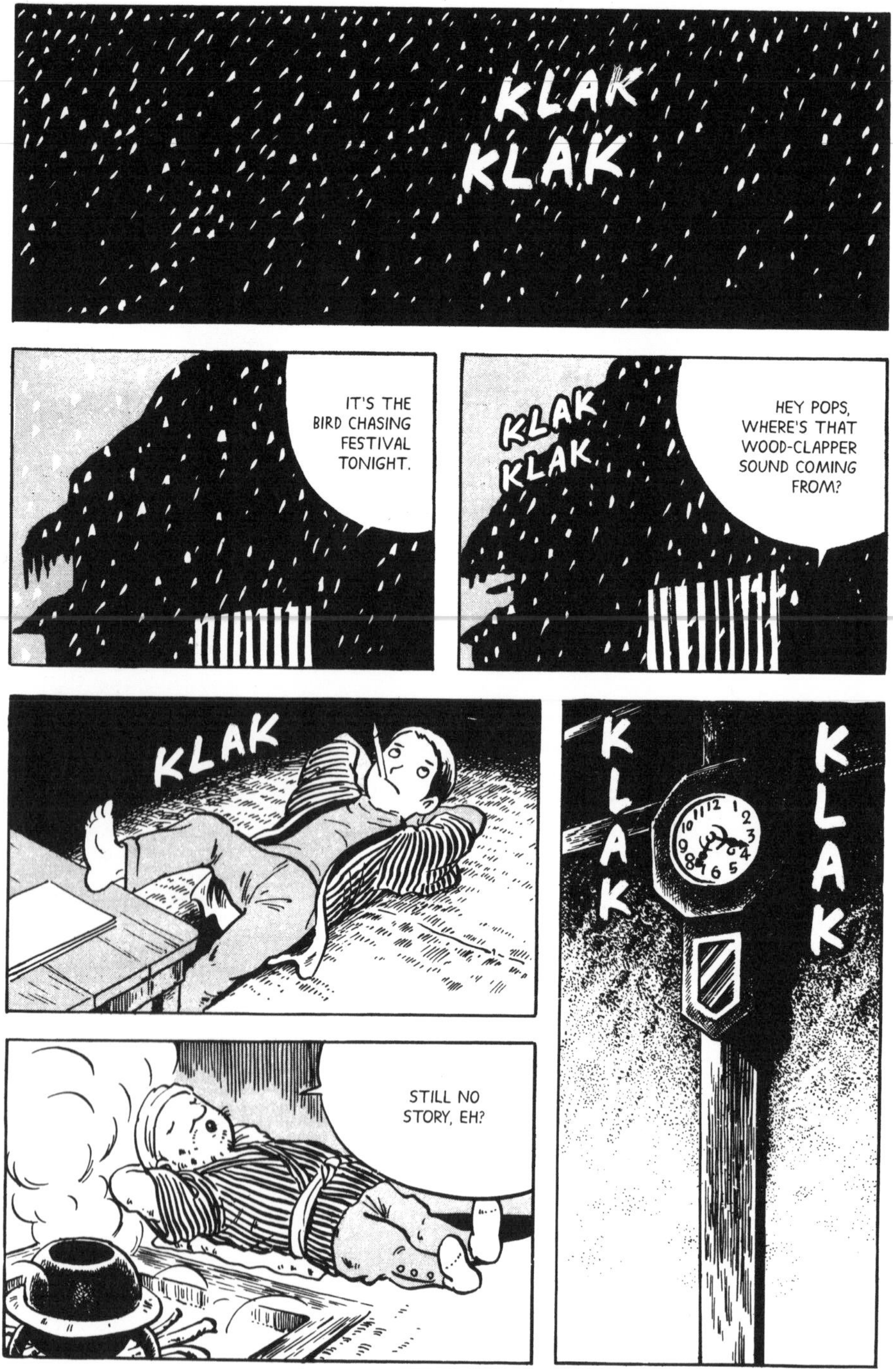
KLAK
KLAK
HEY POPS, WHERE'S THAT WOOD-CLAPPER SOUND COMING FROM?
KLAK
KLAK
IT'S THE BIRD CHASING FESTIVAL TONIGHT.
KLAK
KLAK
KLAK
STILL NO STORY, EH?

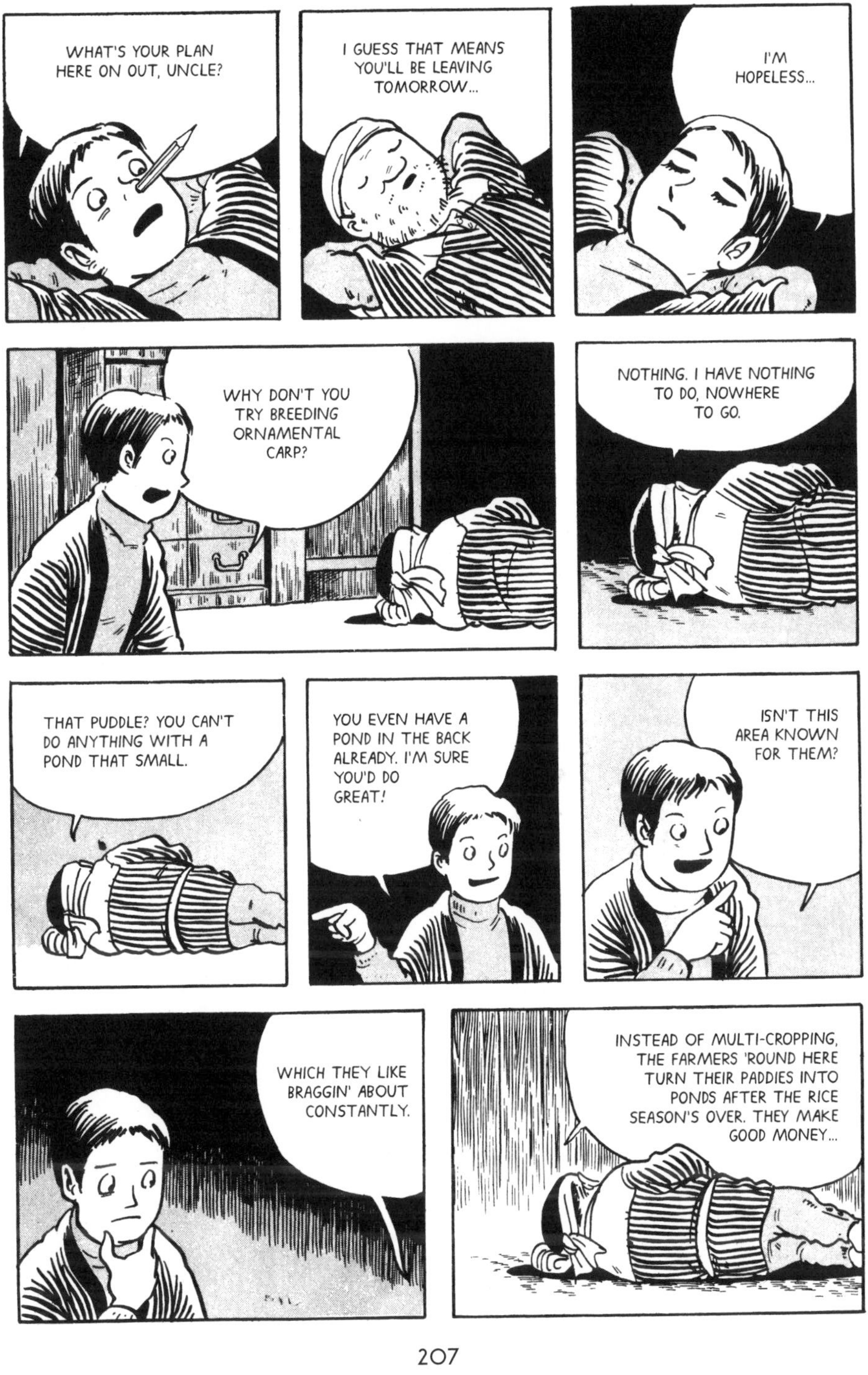
I'M HOPELESS...
I GUESS THAT MEANS YOU'LL BE LEAVING TOMORROW...
WHAT'S YOUR PLAN HERE ON OUT, UNCLE?
NOTHING. I HAVE NOTHING TO DO, NOWHERE TO GO.
WHY DON'T YOU TRY BREEDING ORNAMENTAL CARP?
ISN'T THIS AREA KNOWN FOR THEM?
YOU EVEN HAVE A POND IN THE BACK ALREADY. I'M SURE YOU'D DO GREAT!
THAT PUDDLE? YOU CAN'T DO ANYTHING WITH A POND THAT SMALL.
INSTEAD OF MULTI-CROPPING, THE FARMERS 'ROUND HERE TURN THEIR PADDIES INTO PONDS AFTER THE RICE SEASON'S OVER. THEY MAKE GOOD MONEY...
WHICH THEY LIKE BRAGGIN' ABOUT CONSTANTLY.

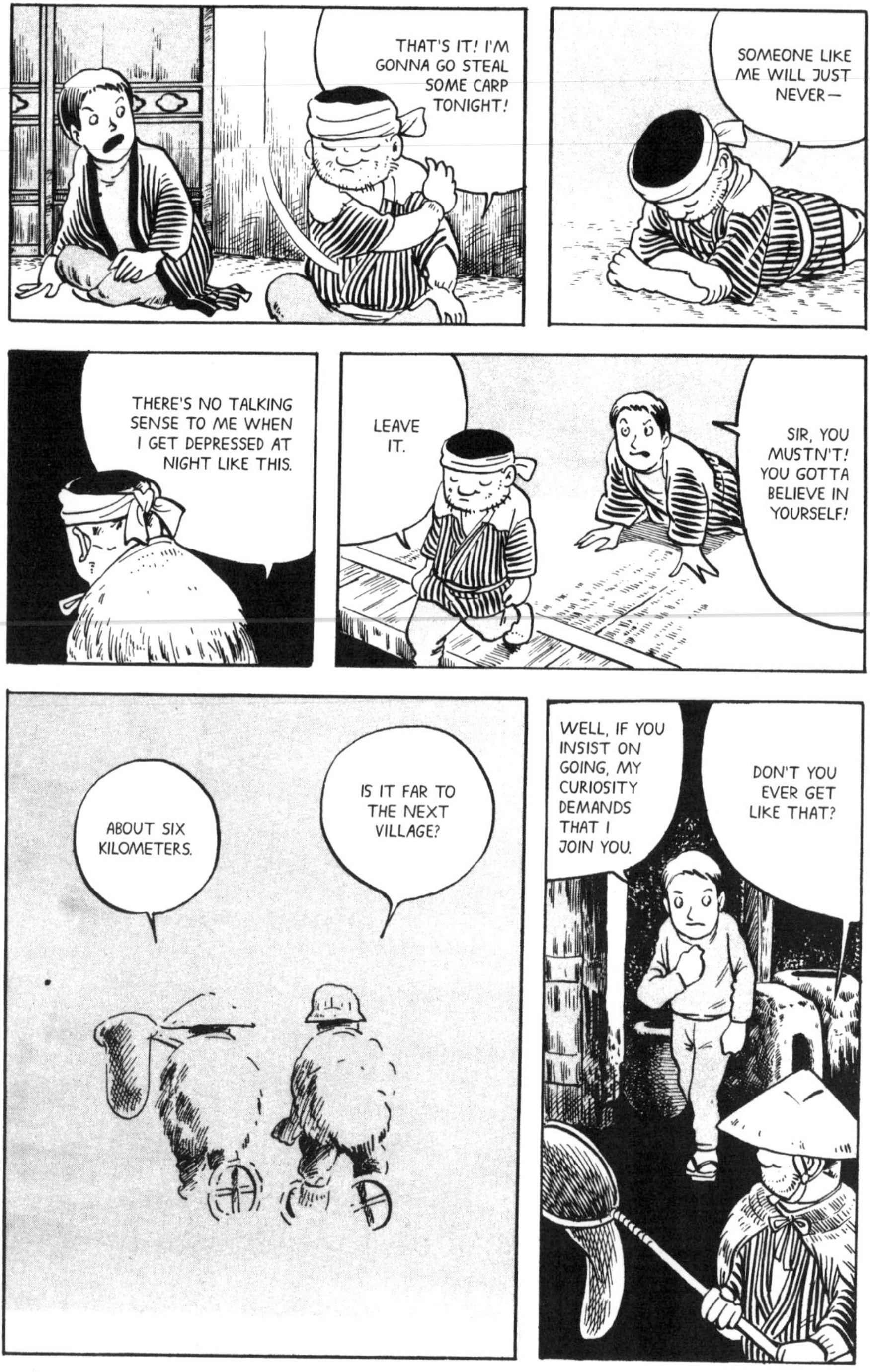
SOMEONE LIKE ME WILL JUST NEVER—
THAT'S IT! I'M GONNA GO STEAL SOME CARP TONIGHT!
SIR, YOU MUSTN'T! YOU GOTTA BELIEVE IN YOURSELF!
LEAVE IT.
THERE'S NO TALKING SENSE TO ME WHEN I GET DEPRESSED AT NIGHT LIKE THIS.
DON'T YOU EVER GET LIKE THAT?
WELL, IF YOU INSIST ON GOING, MY CURIOSITY DEMANDS THAT I JOIN YOU.
IS IT FAR TO THE NEXT VILLAGE?
ABOUT SIX KILOMETERS.

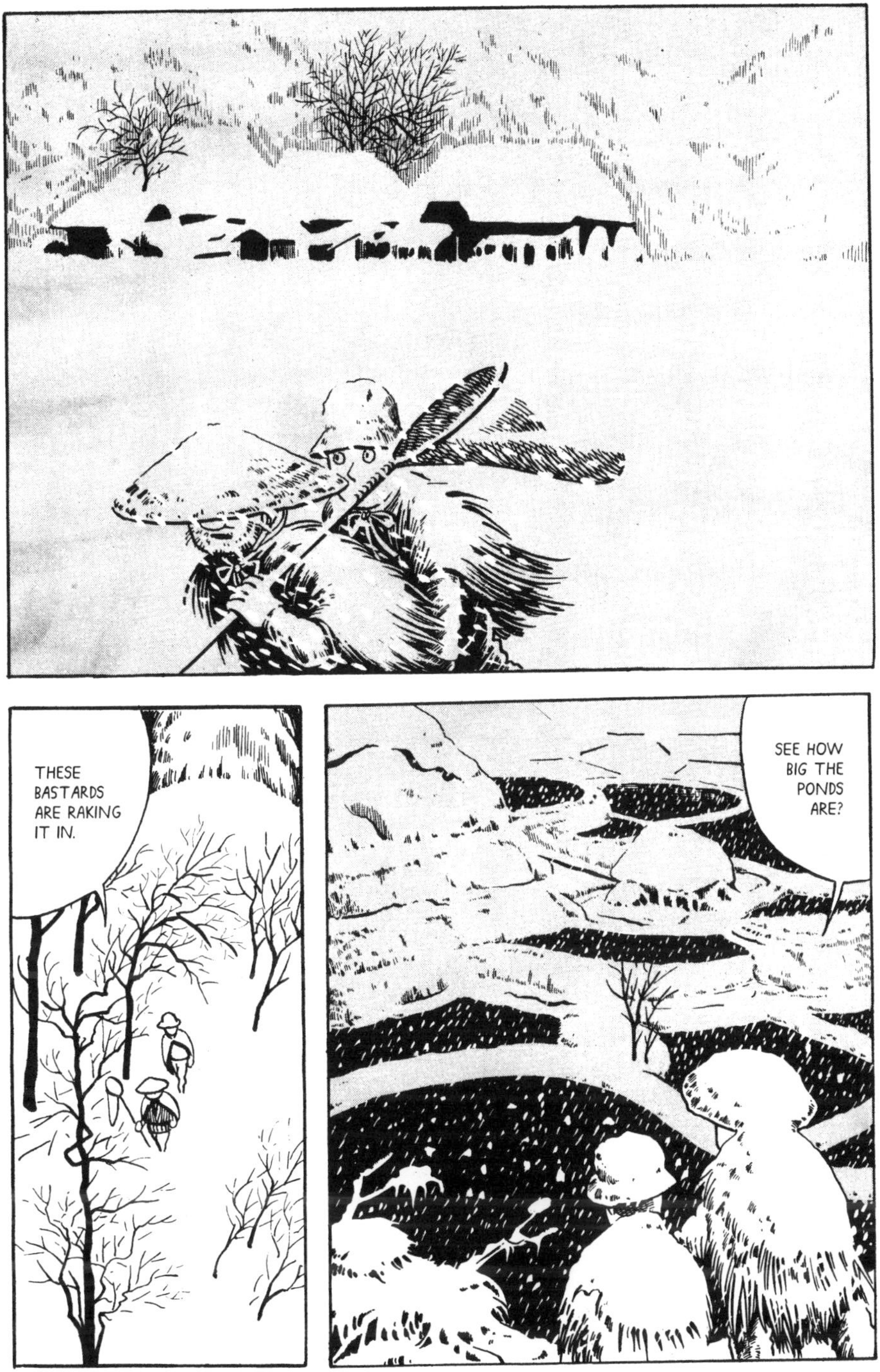
SEE HOW BIG THE PONDS ARE?
THESE BASTARDS ARE RAKING IT IN.

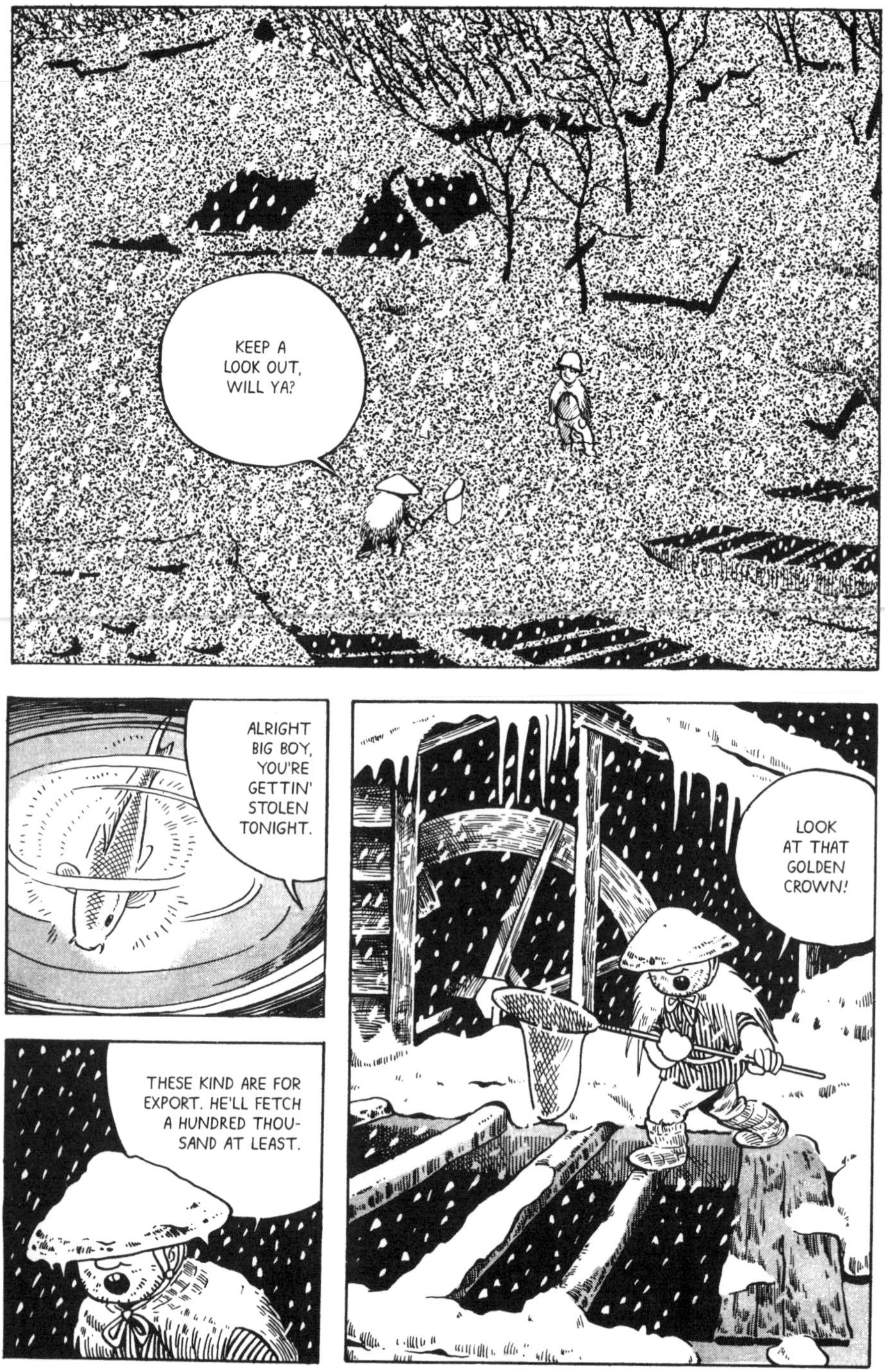
KEEP A LOOK OUT, WILL YA?
LOOK AT THAT GOLDEN CROWN!
ALRIGHT BIG BOY, YOU'RE GETTIN' STOLEN TONIGHT.
THESE KIND ARE FOR EXPORT. HE'LL FETCH A HUNDRED THOU-SAND AT LEAST.

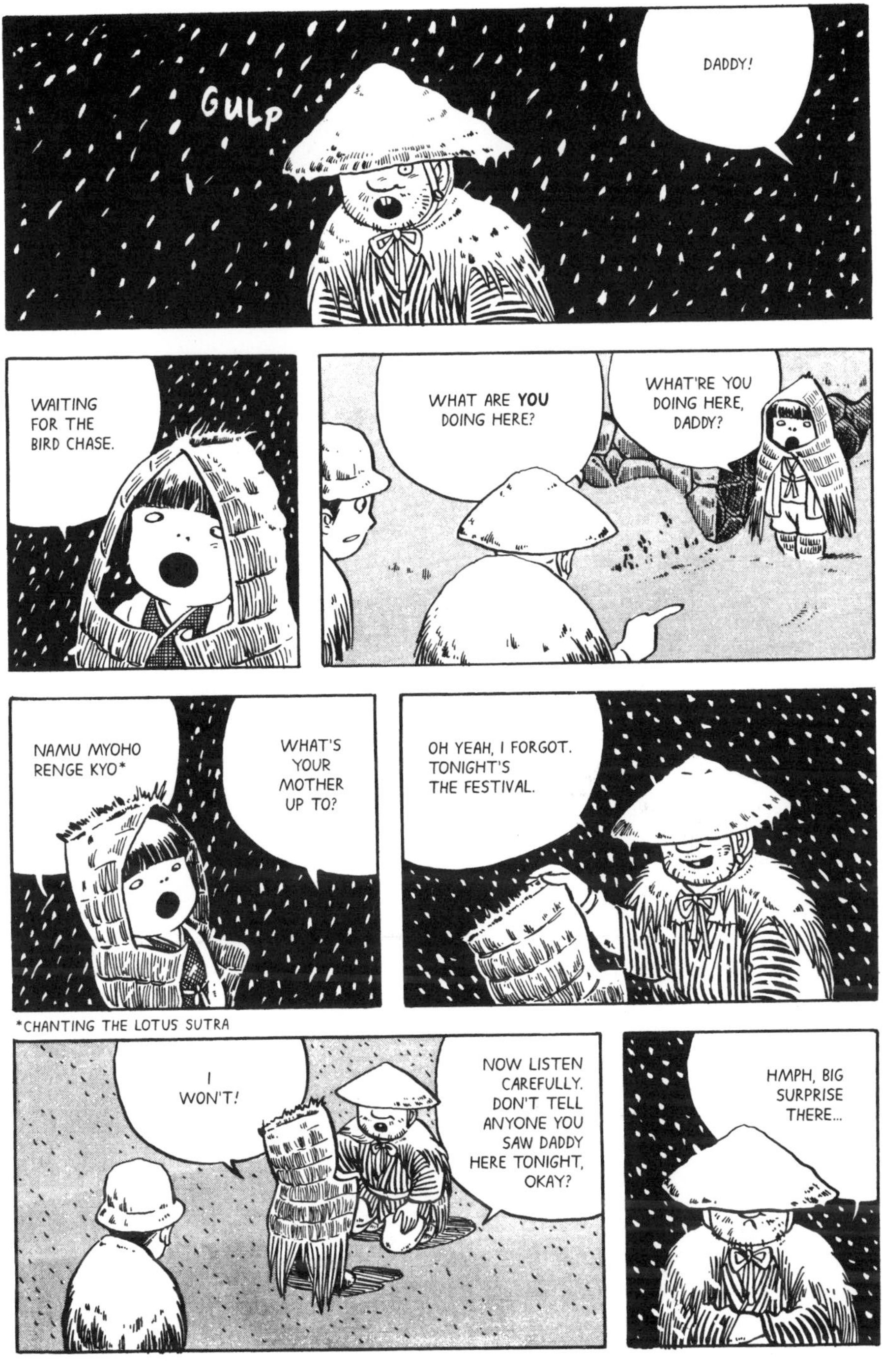
DADDY!
GULP
WHAT'RE YOU DOING HERE, DADDY?
WHAT ARE **YOU** DOING HERE?
WAITING FOR THE BIRD CHASE.
OH YEAH, I FORGOT. TONIGHT'S THE FESTIVAL.
WHAT'S YOUR MOTHER UP TO?
NAMU MYOHO RENGE KYO*
HMPH, BIG SURPRISE THERE...
NOW LISTEN CAREFULLY. DON'T TELL ANYONE YOU SAW DADDY HERE TONIGHT, OKAY?
I WON'T!

*CHANTING THE LOTUS SUTRA

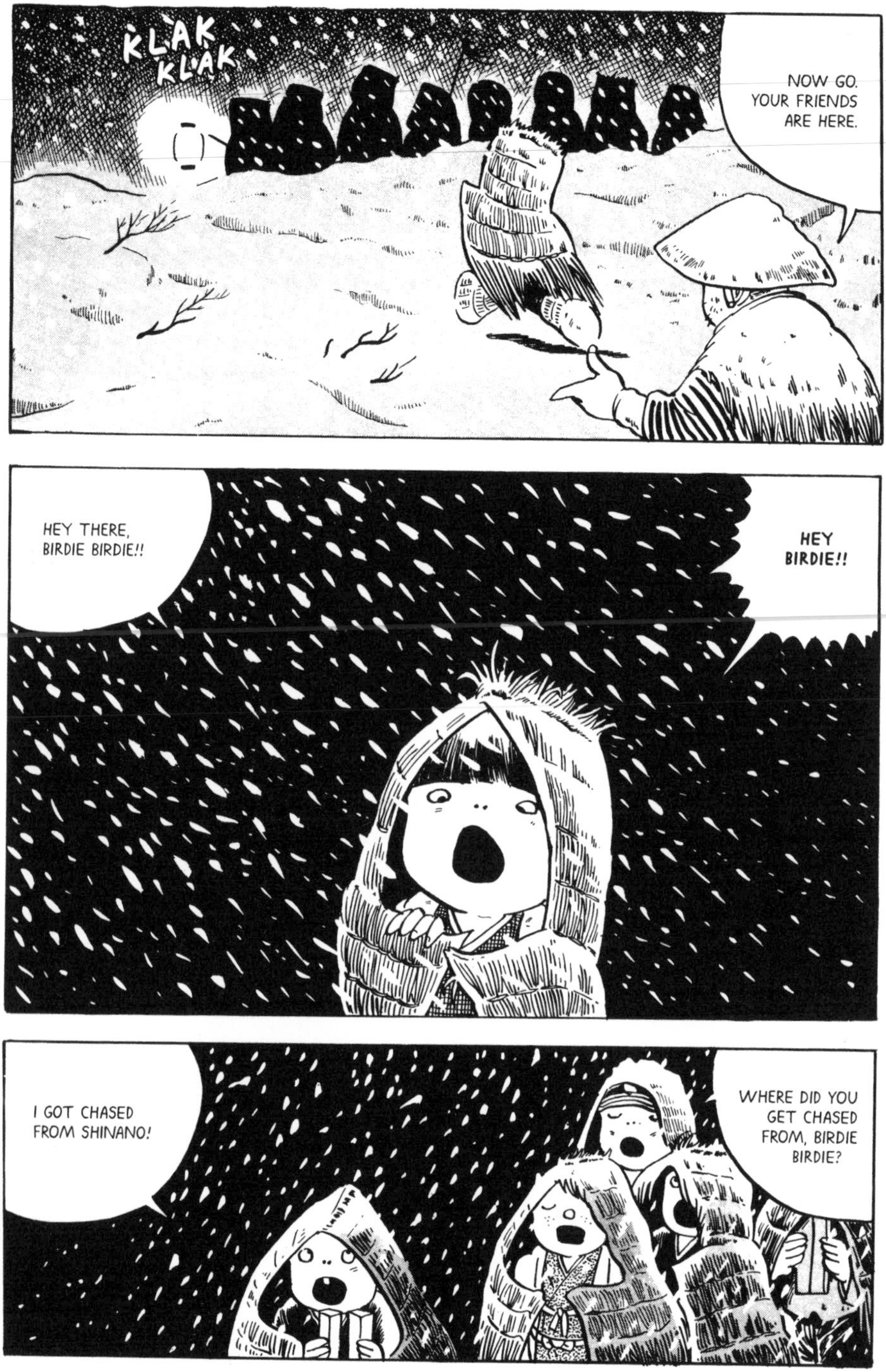
NOW GO. YOUR FRIENDS ARE HERE.
KLAK KLAK
HEY BIRDIE!!
HEY THERE, BIRDIE BIRDIE!!
WHERE DID YOU GET CHASED FROM, BIRDIE BIRDIE?
I GOT CHASED FROM SHINANO!

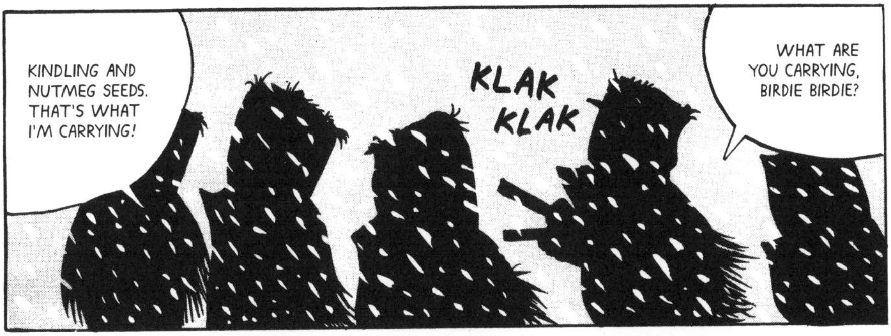
WHAT ARE YOU CARRYING, BIRDIE BIRDIE?
KLAK KLAK
KINDLING AND NUTMEG SEEDS. THAT'S WHAT I'M CARRYING!
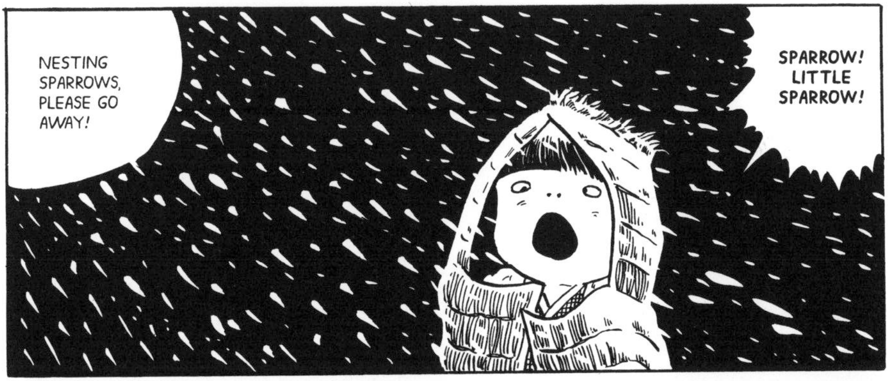
SPARROW! LITTLE SPARROW!
NESTING SPARROWS, PLEASE GO AWAY!
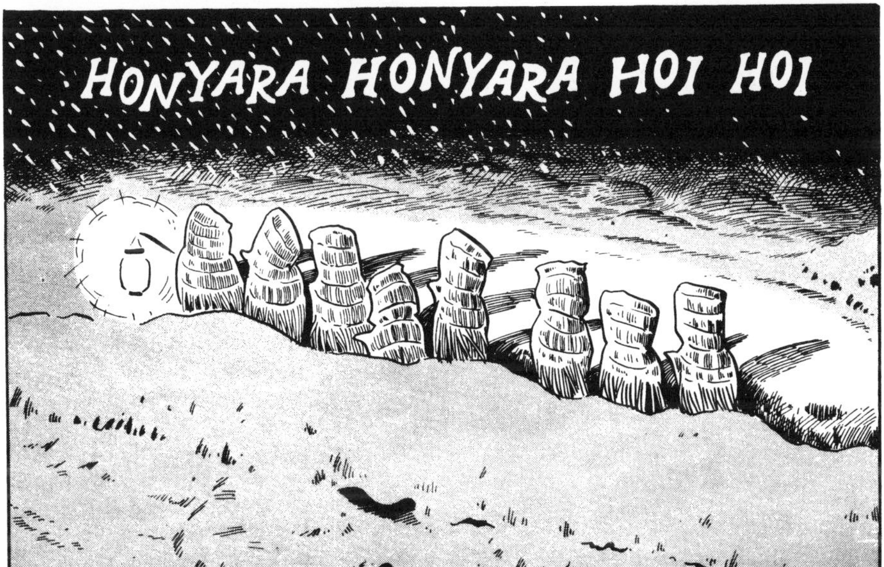
HONYARA HONYARA HOI HOI

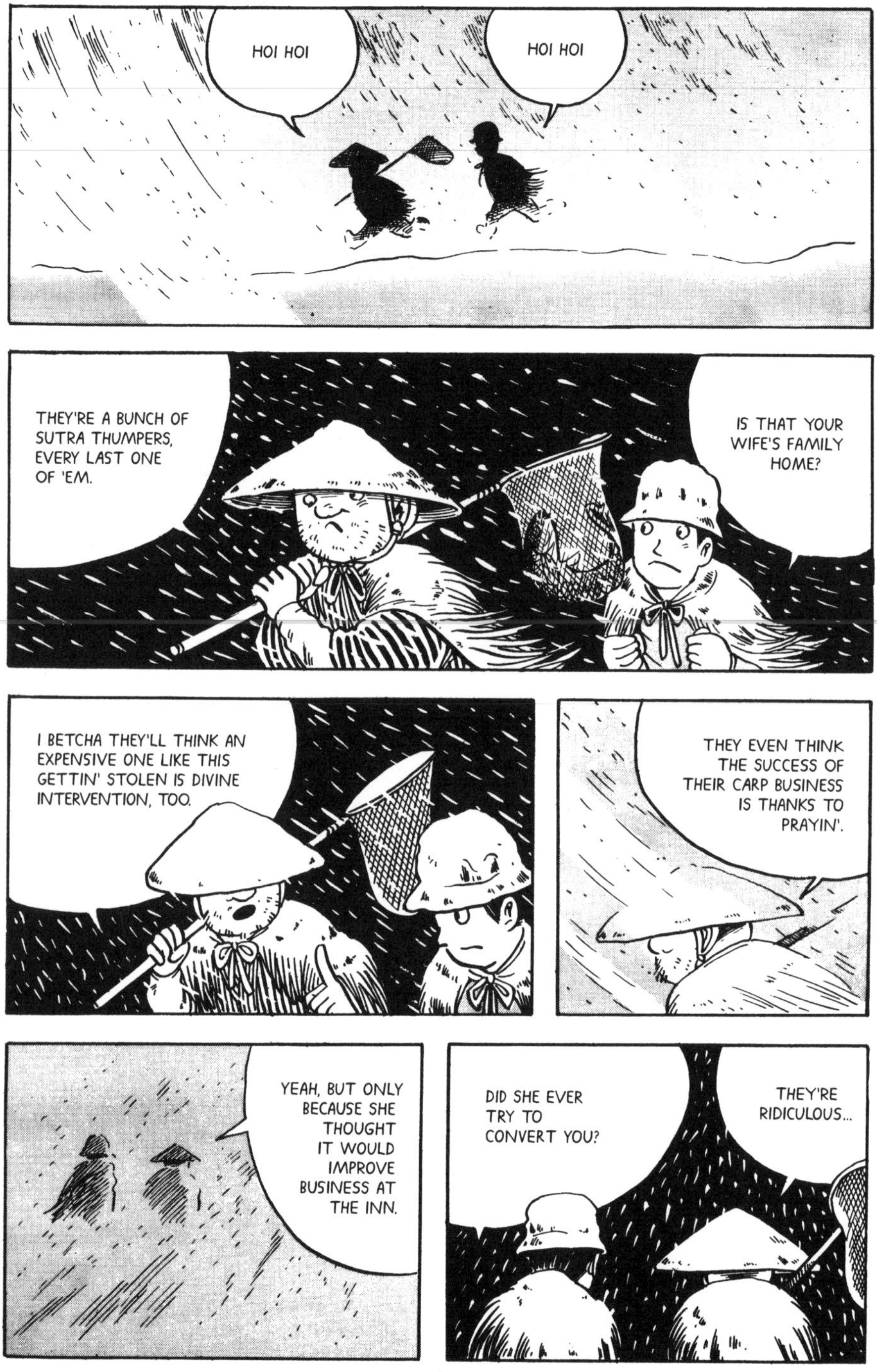
HOI HOI
HOI HOI
IS THAT YOUR WIFE'S FAMILY HOME?
THEY'RE A BUNCH OF SUTRA THUMPERS, EVERY LAST ONE OF 'EM.
THEY EVEN THINK THE SUCCESS OF THEIR CARP BUSINESS IS THANKS TO PRAYIN'.
I BETCHA THEY'LL THINK AN EXPENSIVE ONE LIKE THIS GETTIN' STOLEN IS DIVINE INTERVENTION, TOO.
THEY'RE RIDICULOUS...
DID SHE EVER TRY TO CONVERT YOU?
YEAH, BUT ONLY BECAUSE SHE THOUGHT IT WOULD IMPROVE BUSINESS AT THE INN.

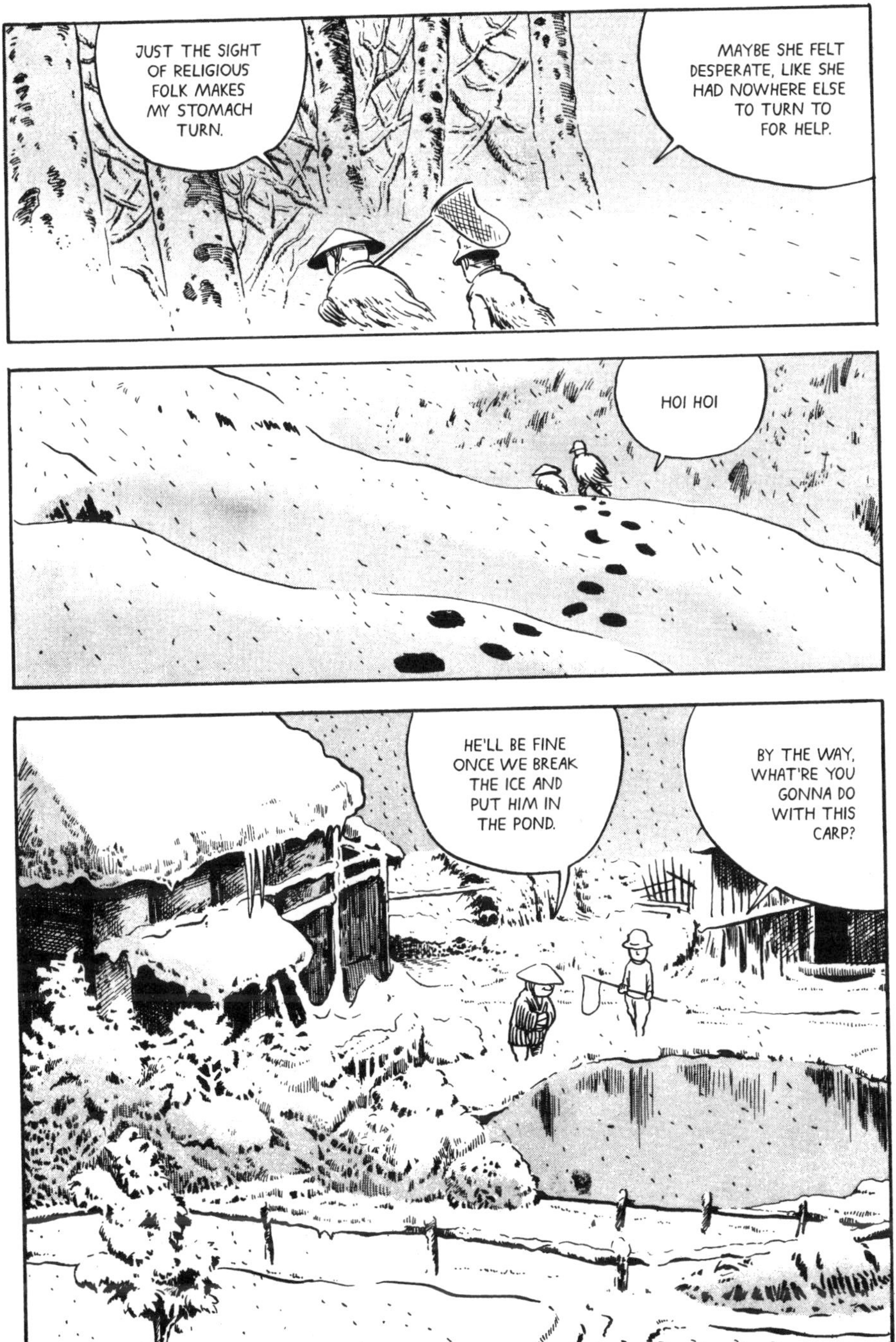
MAYBE SHE FELT DESPERATE, LIKE SHE HAD NOWHERE ELSE TO TURN TO FOR HELP.
JUST THE SIGHT OF RELIGIOUS FOLK MAKES MY STOMACH TURN.
HOI HOI
BY THE WAY, WHAT'RE YOU GONNA DO WITH THIS CARP?
HE'LL BE FINE ONCE WE BREAK THE ICE AND PUT HIM IN THE POND.

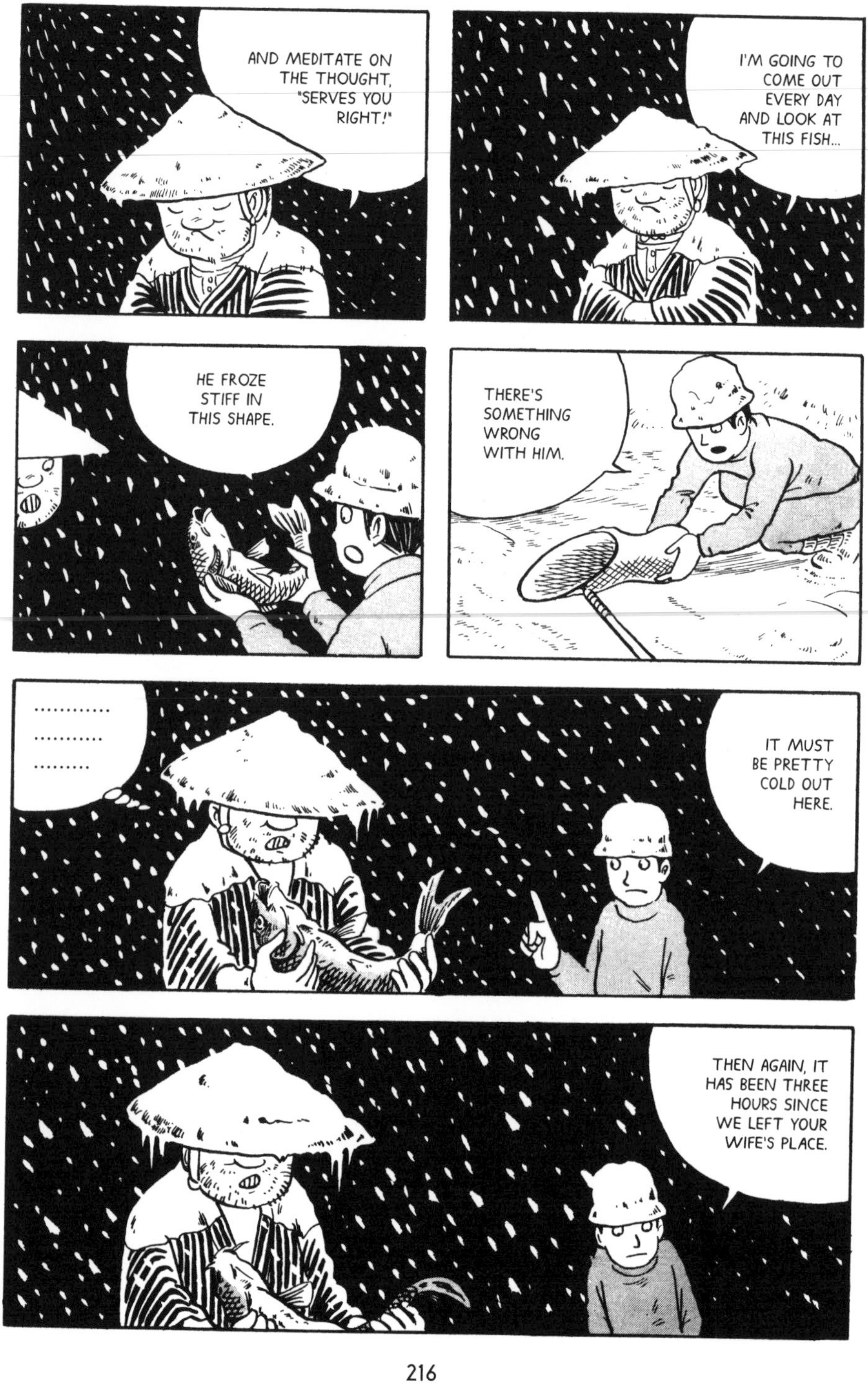
I'M GOING TO COME OUT EVERY DAY AND LOOK AT THIS FISH...
AND MEDITATE ON THE THOUGHT, "SERVES YOU RIGHT!"
THERE'S SOMETHING WRONG WITH HIM.
HE FROZE STIFF IN THIS SHAPE.
IT MUST BE PRETTY COLD OUT HERE.
....
THEN AGAIN, IT HAS BEEN THREE HOURS SINCE WE LEFT YOUR WIFE'S PLACE.

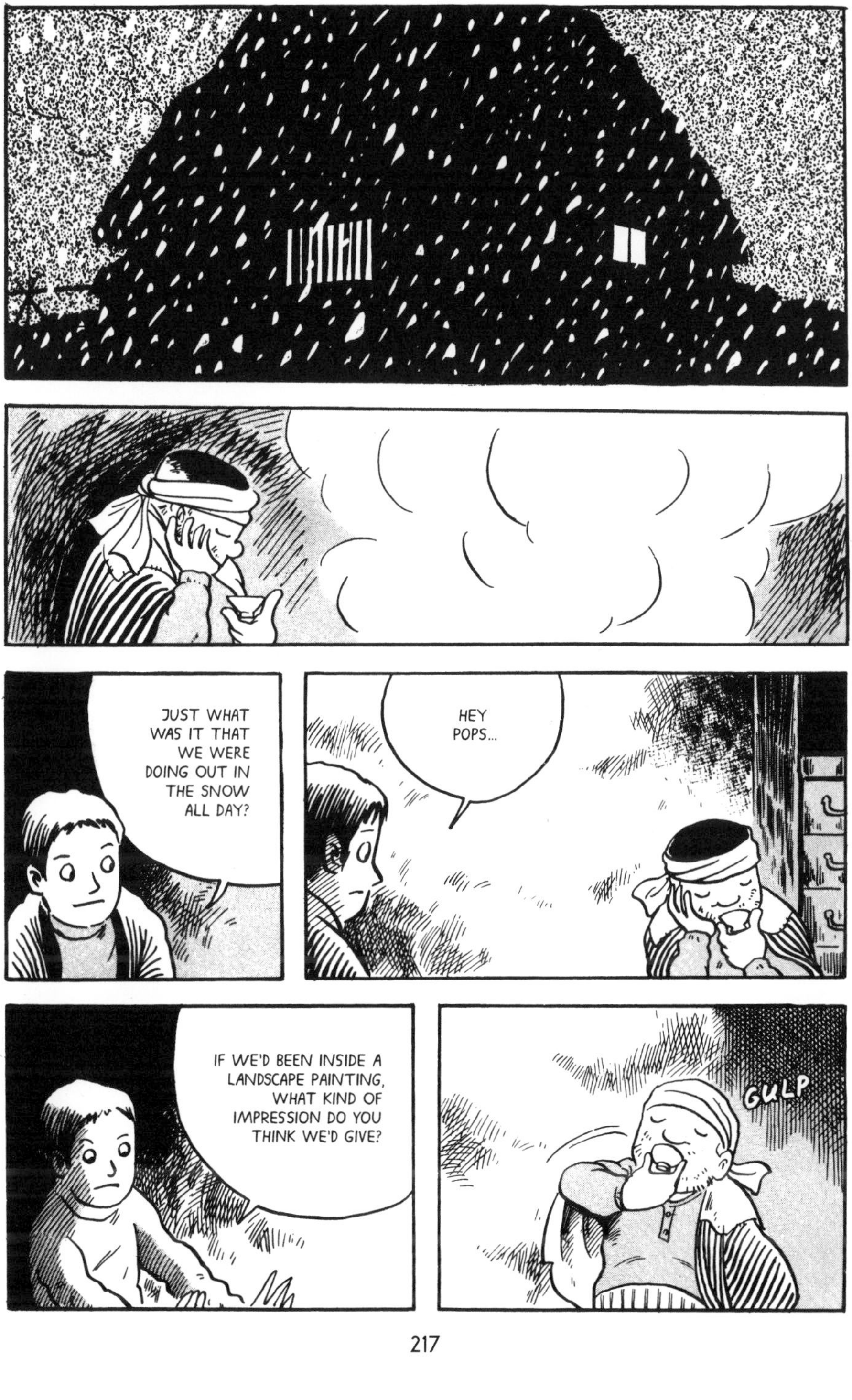
HEY POPS...
JUST WHAT WAS IT THAT WE WERE DOING OUT IN THE SNOW ALL DAY?
GULP
IF WE'D BEEN INSIDE A LANDSCAPE PAINTING, WHAT KIND OF IMPRESSION DO YOU THINK WE'D GIVE?

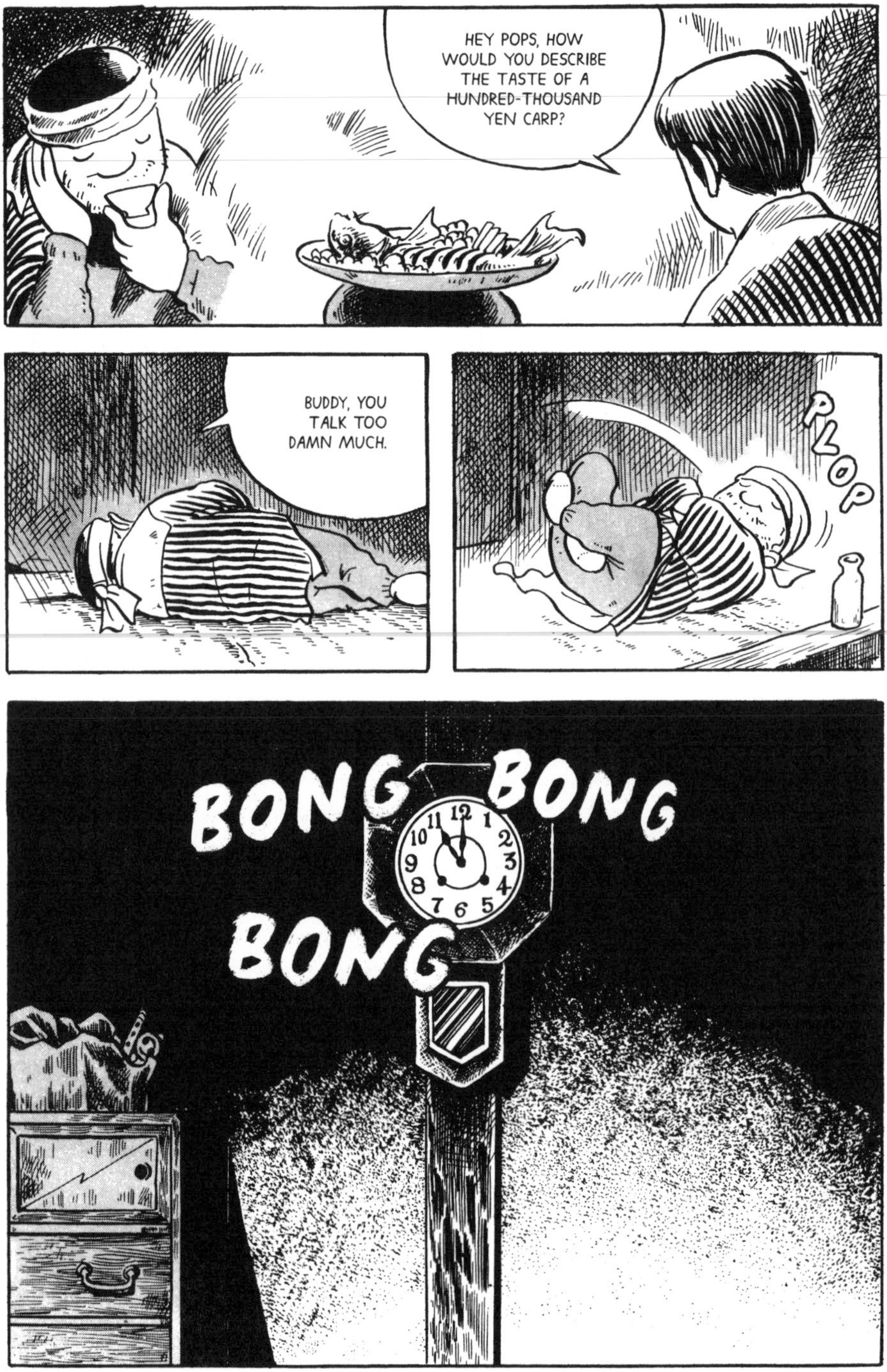
HEY POPS, HOW WOULD YOU DESCRIBE THE TASTE OF A HUNDRED-THOUSAND YEN CARP?
PLOP
BUDDY, YOU TALK TOO DAMN MUCH.
BONG BONG
BONG

THE ANTLION PIT

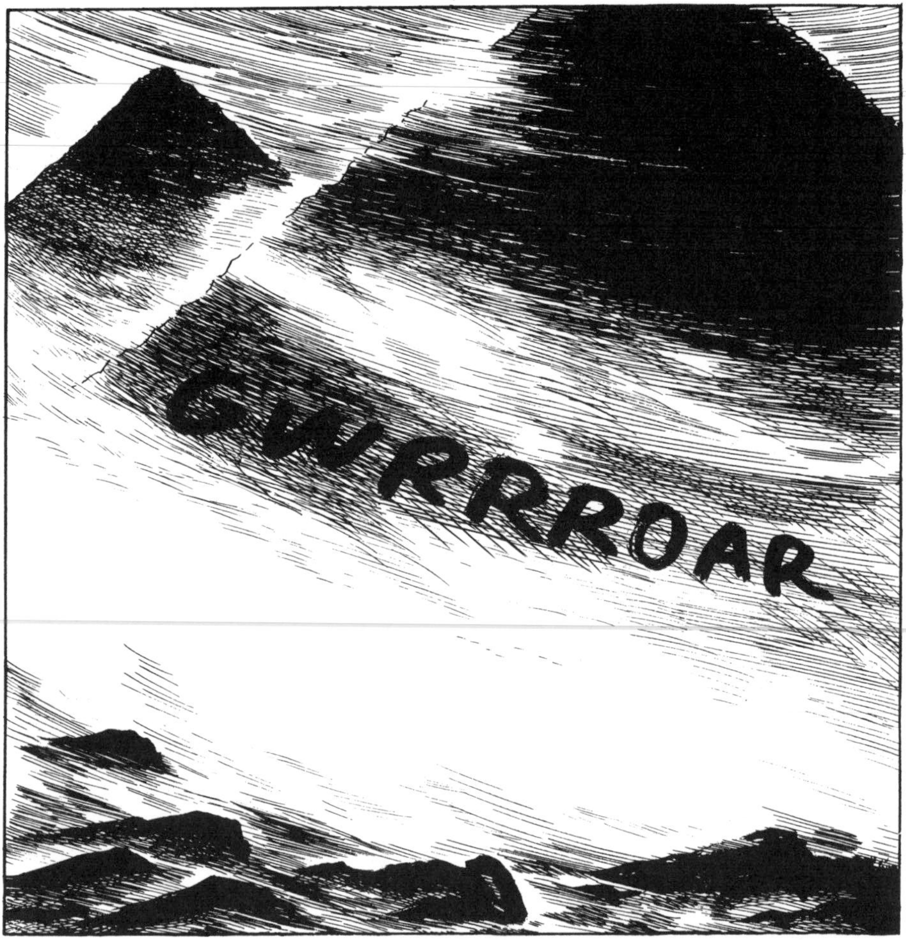
GWRRROAR
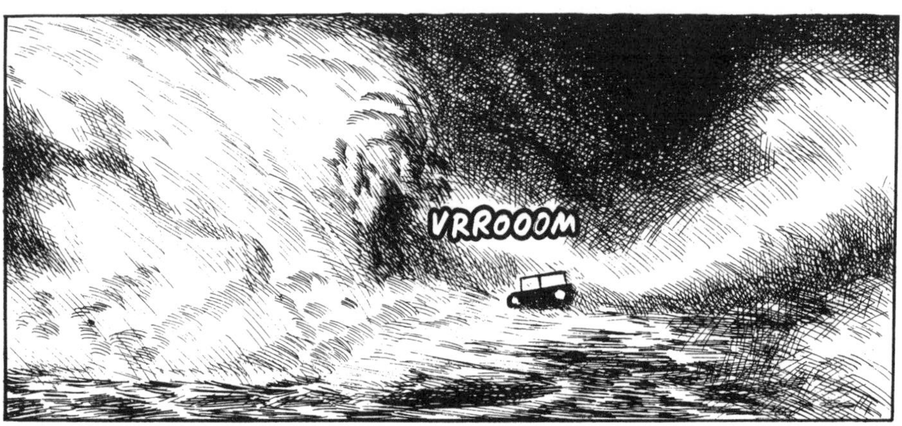
VRROOOM

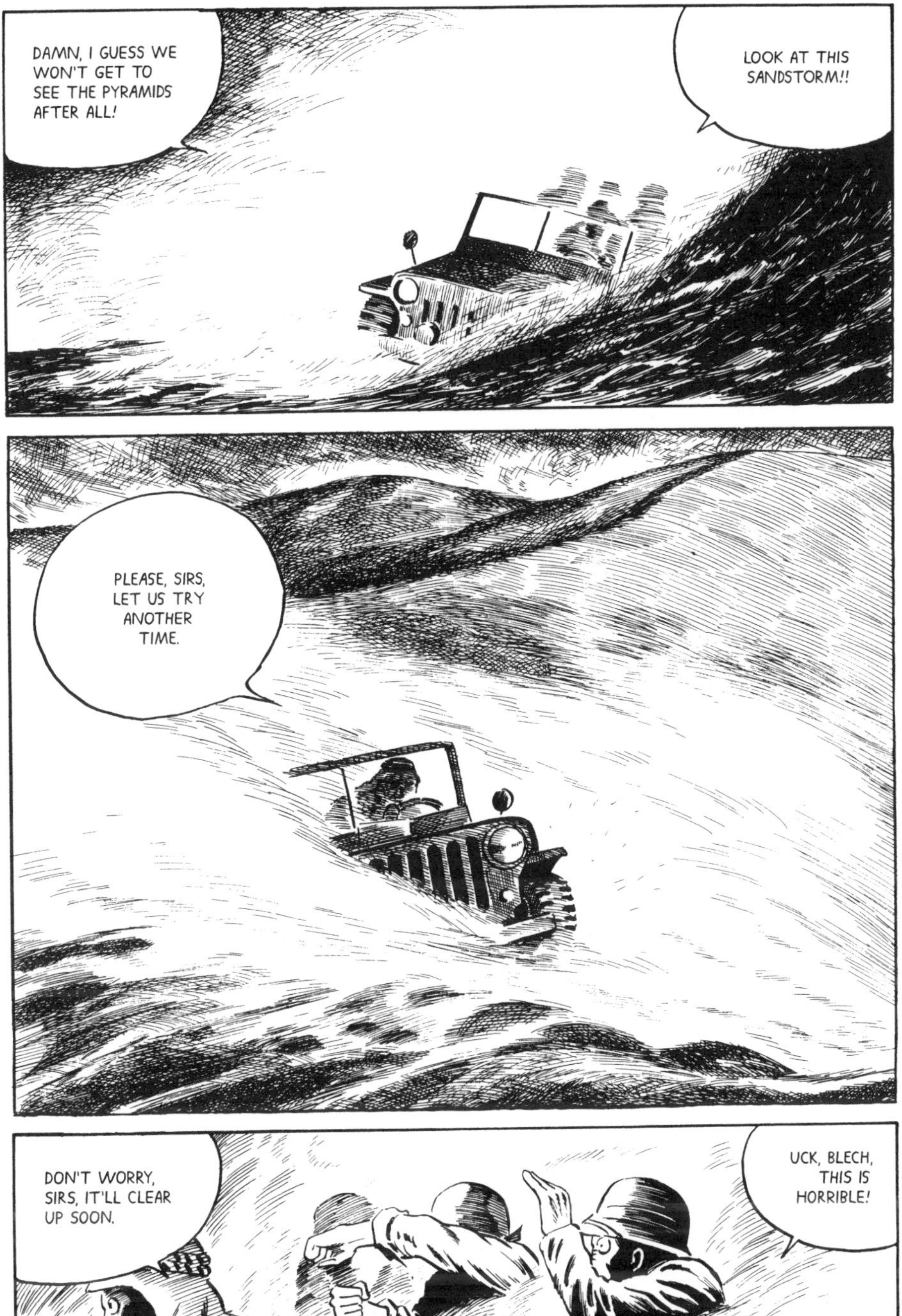
LOOK AT THIS SANDSTORM!!
DAMN, I GUESS WE WON'T GET TO SEE THE PYRAMIDS AFTER ALL!
PLEASE, SIRS, LET US TRY ANOTHER TIME.
UCK, BLECH, THIS IS HORRIBLE!
DON'T WORRY, SIRS, IT'LL CLEAR UP SOON.

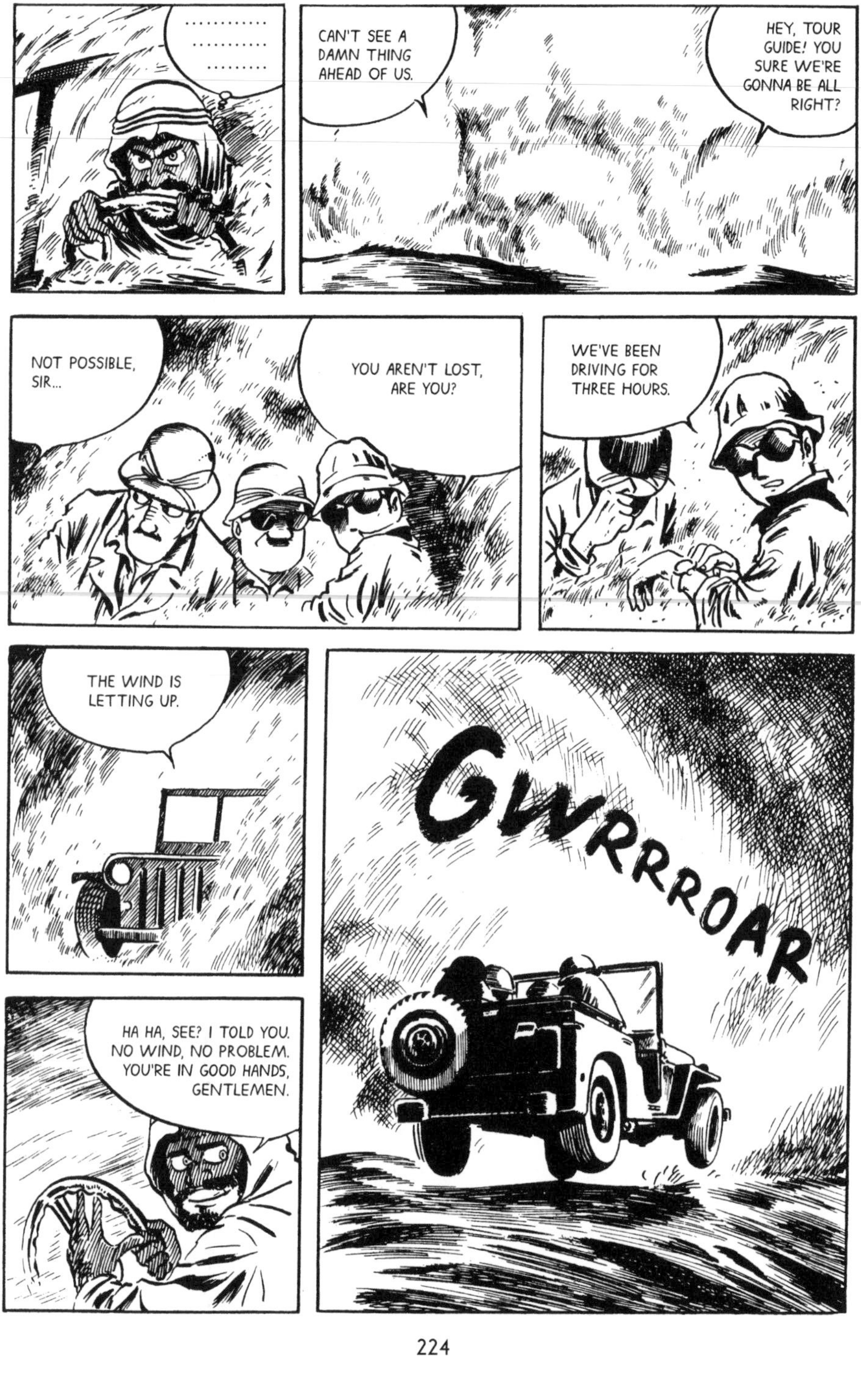
HEY, TOUR GUIDE! YOU SURE WE'RE GONNA BE ALL RIGHT?
CAN'T SEE A DAMN THING AHEAD OF US.
....
WE'VE BEEN DRIVING FOR THREE HOURS.
YOU AREN'T LOST, ARE YOU?
NOT POSSIBLE, SIR...
GWRRROAR
THE WIND IS LETTING UP.
HA HA, SEE? I TOLD YOU. NO WIND, NO PROBLEM. YOU'RE IN GOOD HANDS, GENTLEMEN.

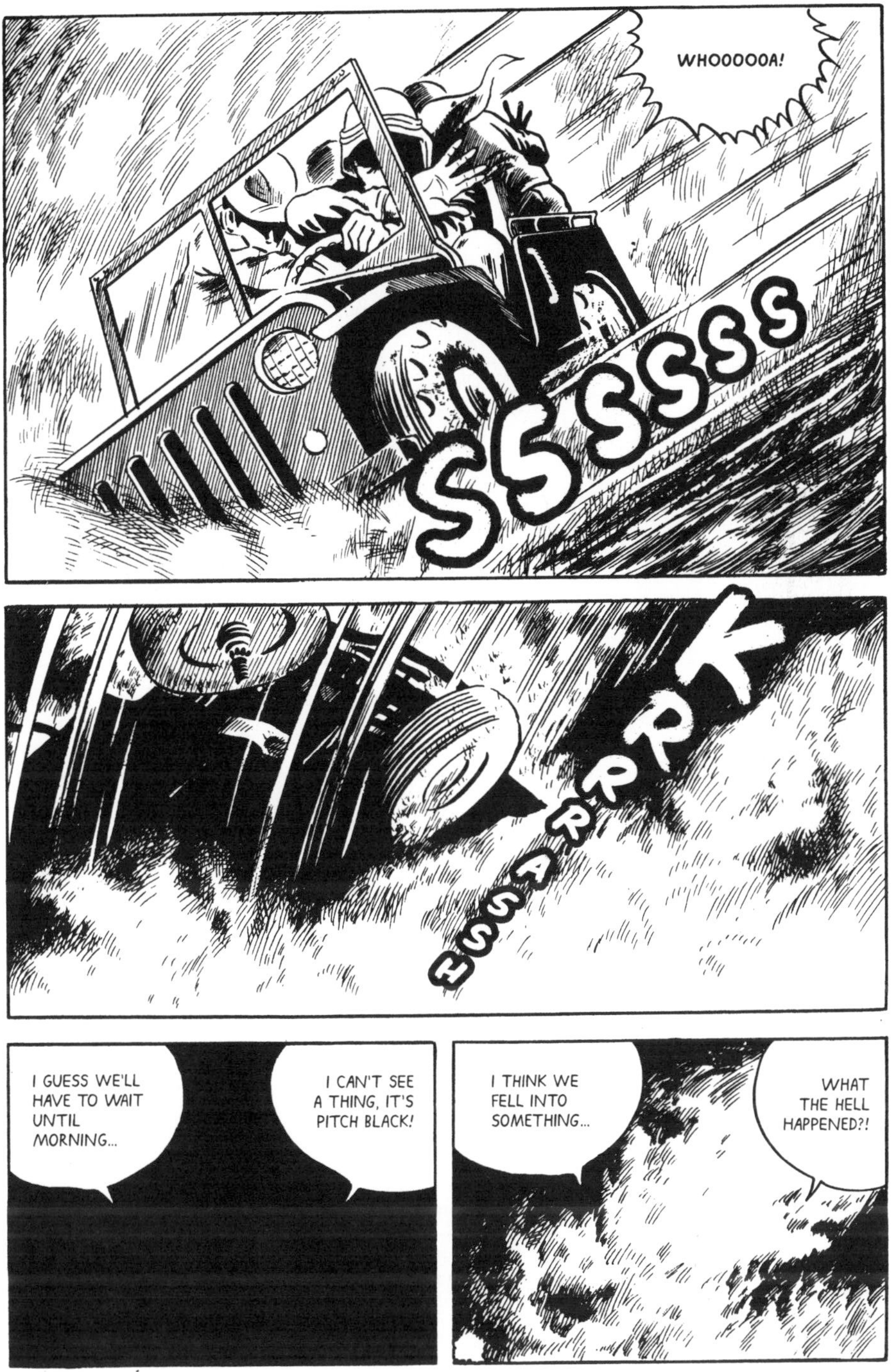
WHOOOOOA!
SSSSSSS
KRRRRASSH
WHAT THE HELL HAPPENED?!
I THINK WE FELL INTO SOMETHING...
I CAN'T SEE A THING, IT'S PITCH BLACK!
I GUESS WE'LL HAVE TO WAIT UNTIL MORNING...

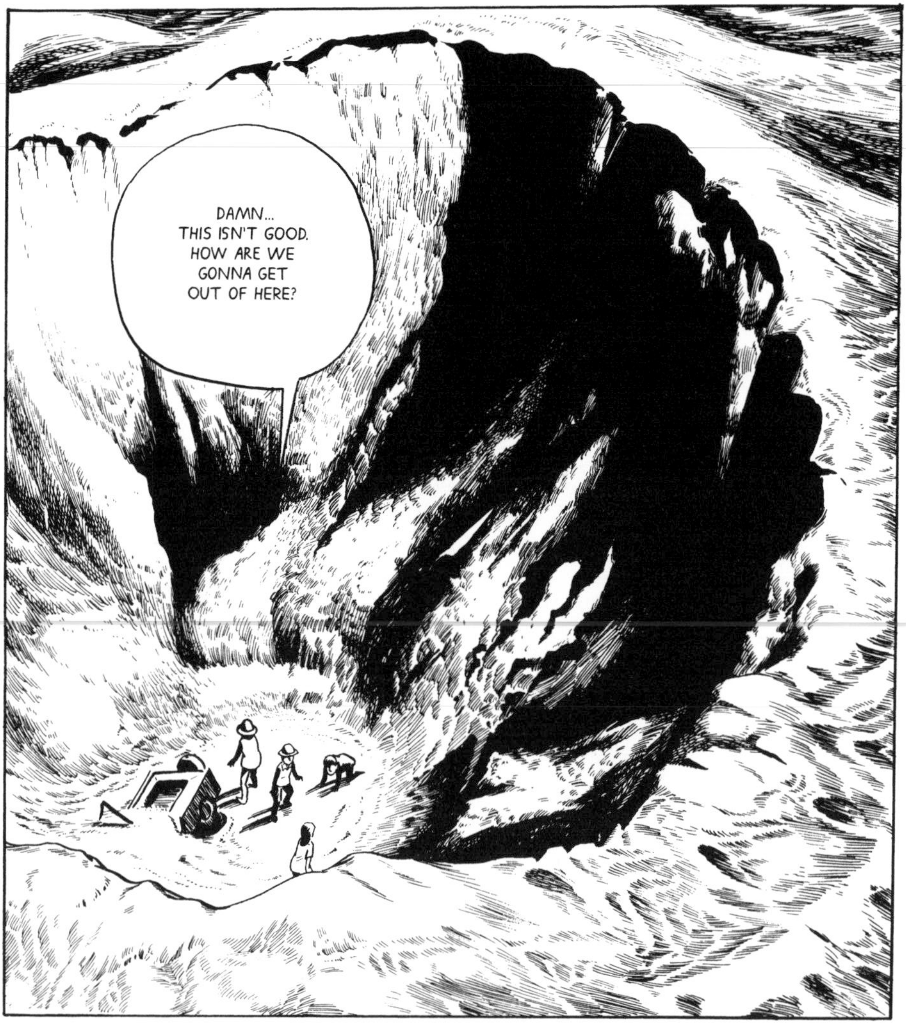
DAMN... THIS ISN'T GOOD. HOW ARE WE GONNA GET OUT OF HERE?

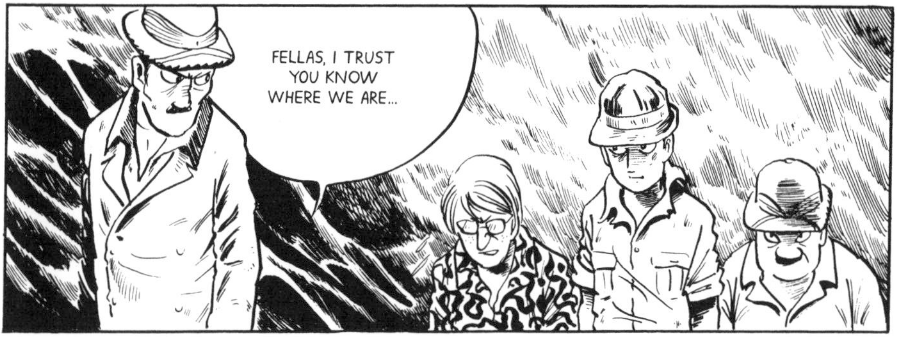
FELLAS, I TRUST YOU KNOW WHERE WE ARE...

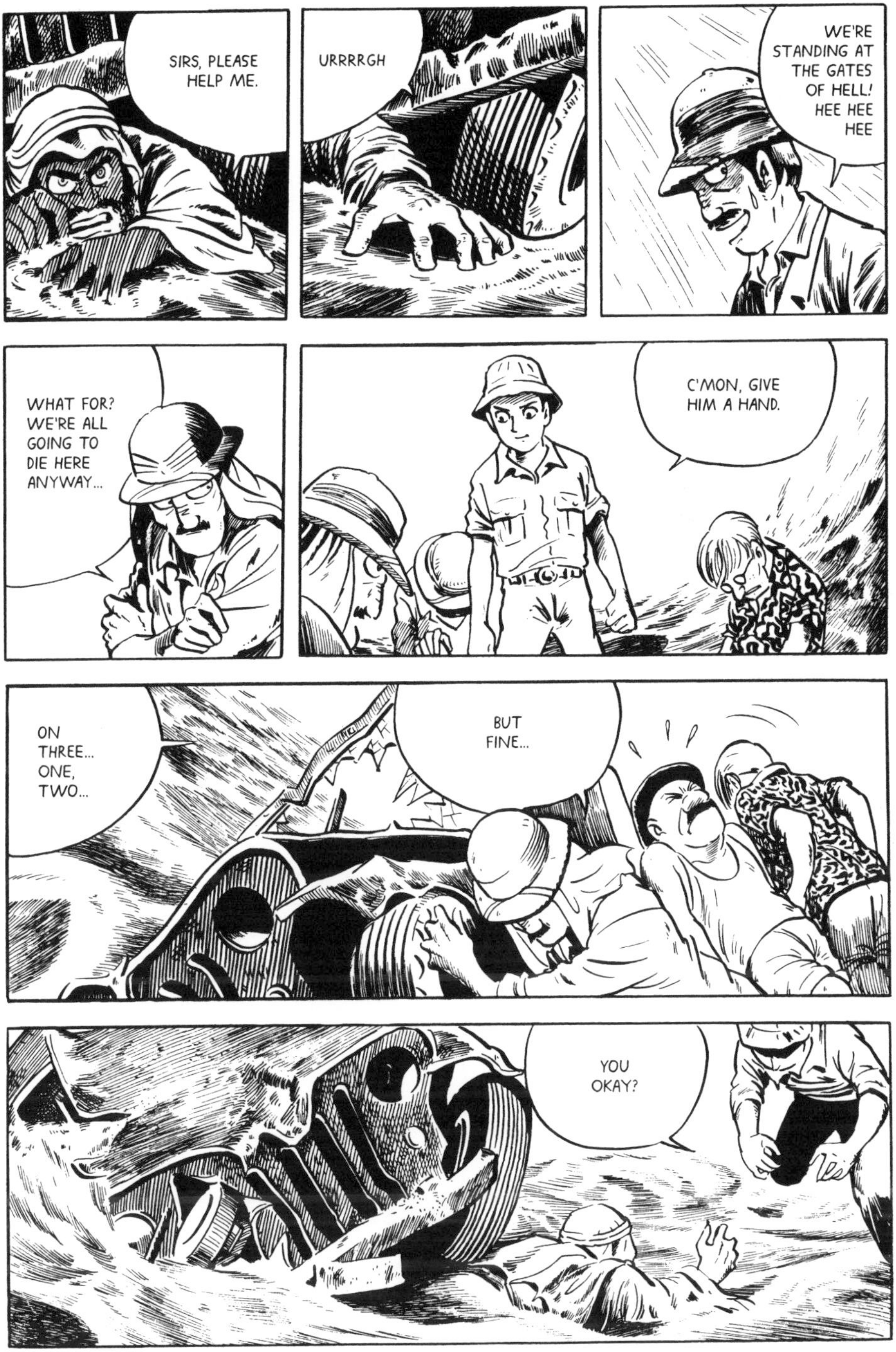
WE'RE STANDING AT THE GATES OF HELL! HEE HEE HEE
URRRRGH
SIRS, PLEASE HELP ME.
C'MON, GIVE HIM A HAND.
WHAT FOR? WE'RE ALL GOING TO DIE HERE ANYWAY...
BUT FINE...
ON THREE... ONE, TWO...
YOU OKAY?

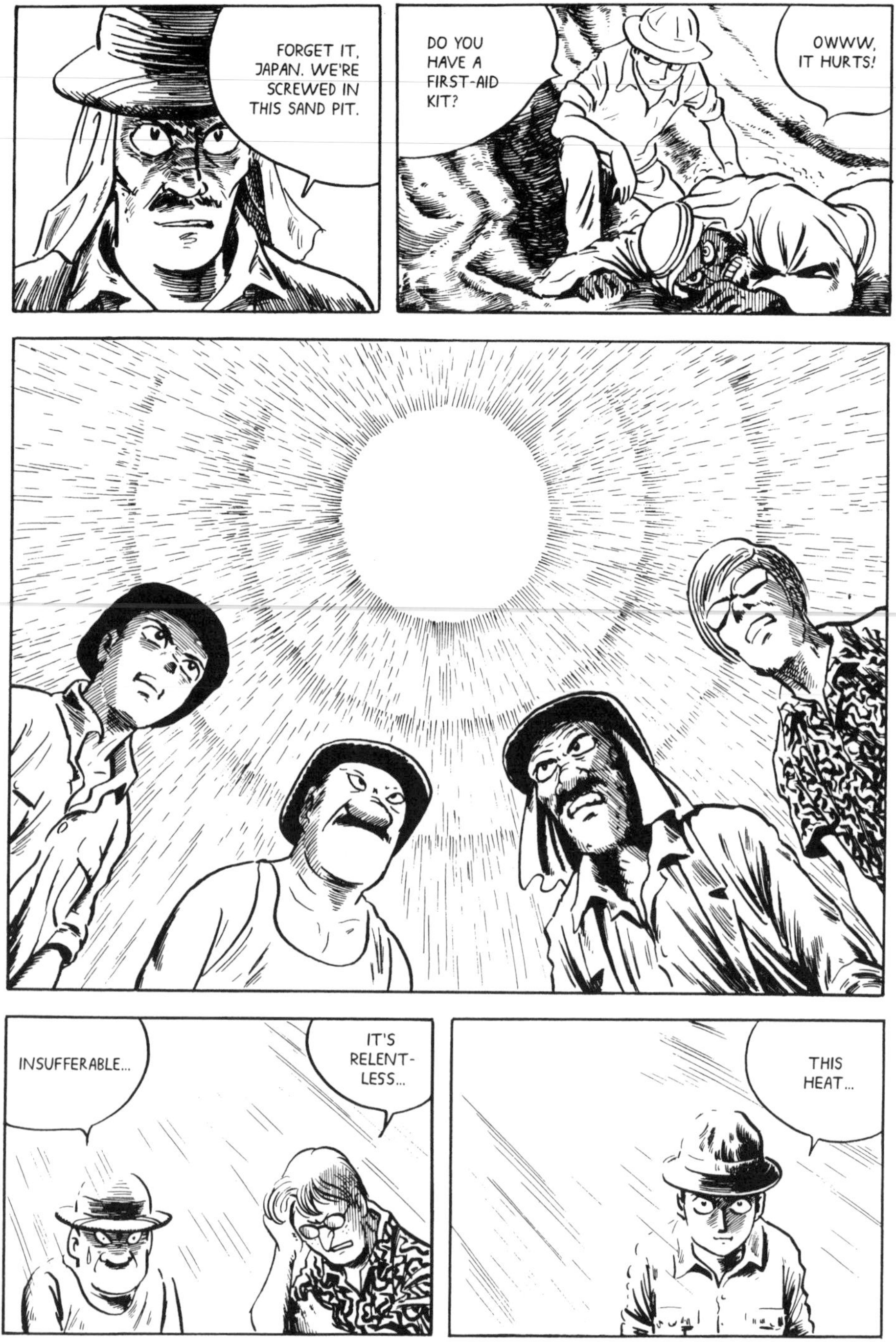
OWWW, IT HURTS!
DO YOU HAVE A FIRST-AID KIT?
FORGET IT, JAPAN. WE'RE SCREWED IN THIS SAND PIT.
THIS HEAT...
IT'S RELENT-LESS...
INSUFFERABLE...

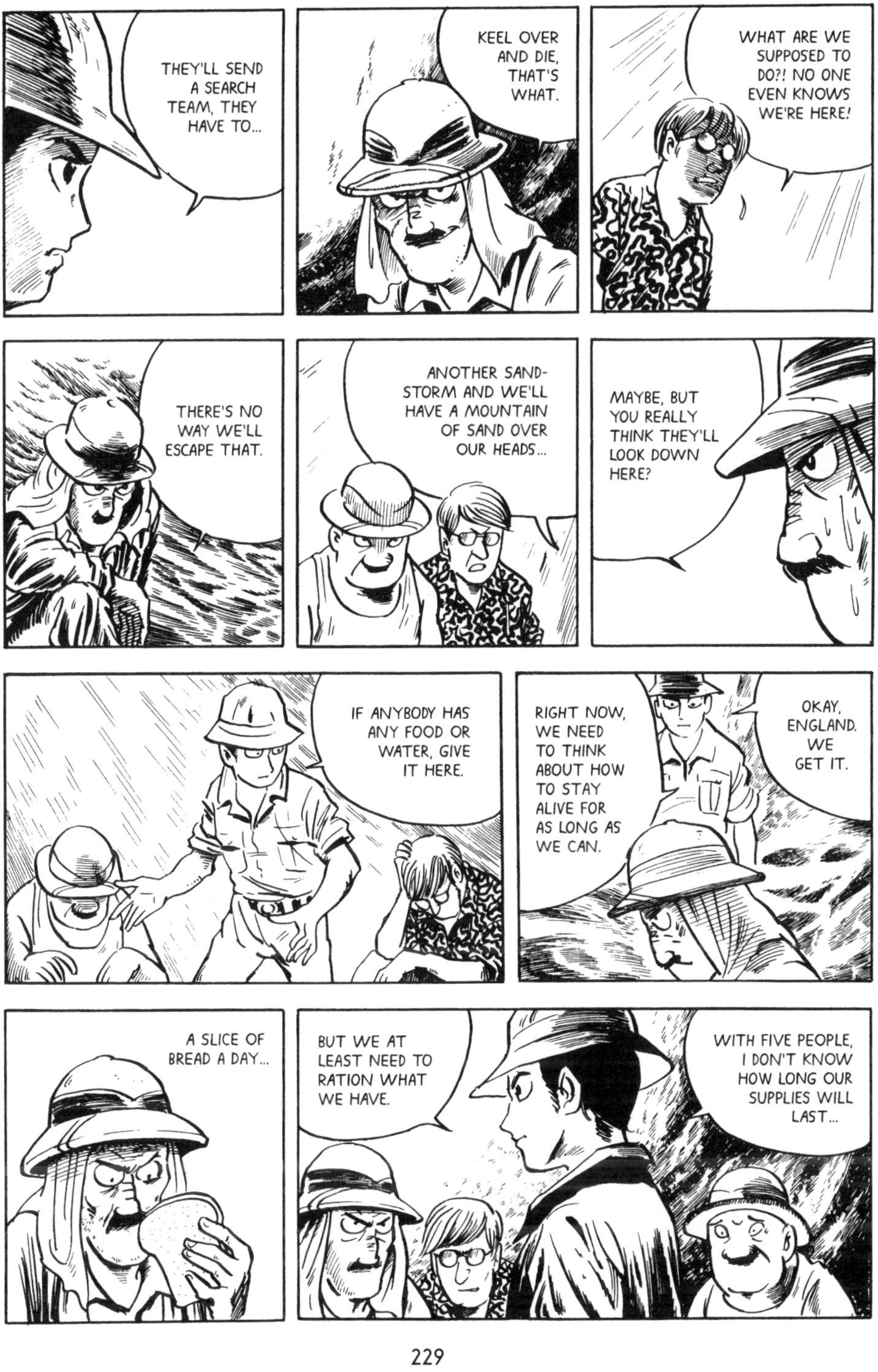
WHAT ARE WE SUPPOSED TO DO?! NO ONE EVEN KNOWS WE'RE HERE!
KEEL OVER AND DIE, THAT'S WHAT.
THEY'LL SEND A SEARCH TEAM, THEY HAVE TO...
MAYBE, BUT YOU REALLY THINK THEY'LL LOOK DOWN HERE?
ANOTHER SANDSTORM AND WE'LL HAVE A MOUNTAIN OF SAND OVER OUR HEADS...
THERE'S NO WAY WE'LL ESCAPE THAT.
OKAY, ENGLAND. WE GET IT.
RIGHT NOW, WE NEED TO THINK ABOUT HOW TO STAY ALIVE FOR AS LONG AS WE CAN.
IF ANYBODY HAS ANY FOOD OR WATER, GIVE IT HERE.
WITH FIVE PEOPLE, I DON'T KNOW HOW LONG OUR SUPPLIES WILL LAST...
BUT WE AT LEAST NEED TO RATION WHAT WE HAVE.
A SLICE OF BREAD A DAY...

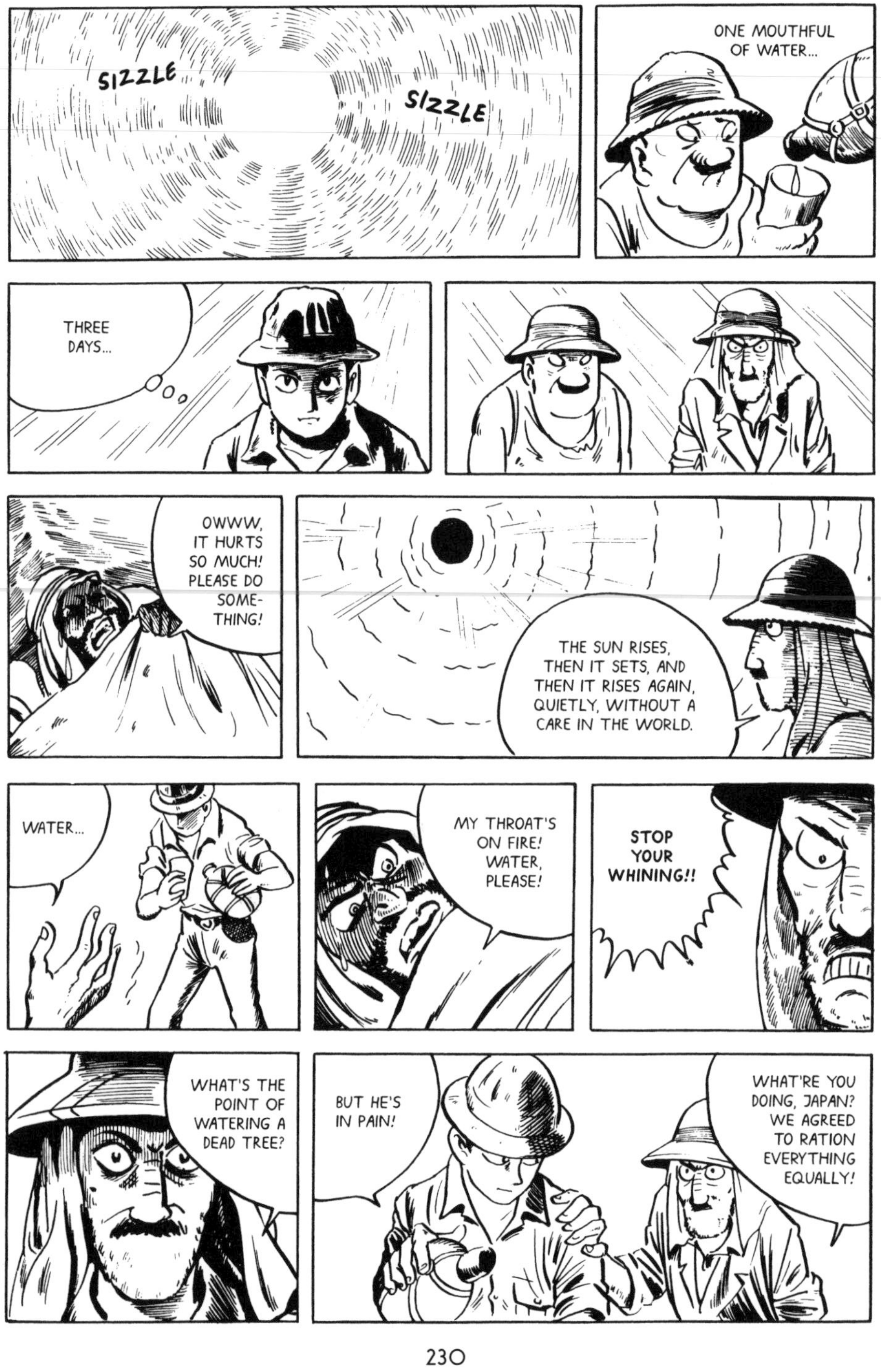
ONE MOUTHFUL OF WATER...
SIZZLE
SIZZLE
THREE DAYS...
THE SUN RISES, THEN IT SETS, AND THEN IT RISES AGAIN, QUIETLY, WITHOUT A CARE IN THE WORLD.
OWWW, IT HURTS SO MUCH! PLEASE DO SOME-THING!
STOP YOUR WHINING!!
MY THROAT'S ON FIRE! WATER, PLEASE!
WATER...
WHAT'RE YOU DOING, JAPAN? WE AGREED TO RATION EVERYTHING EQUALLY!
BUT HE'S IN PAIN!
WHAT'S THE POINT OF WATERING A DEAD TREE?

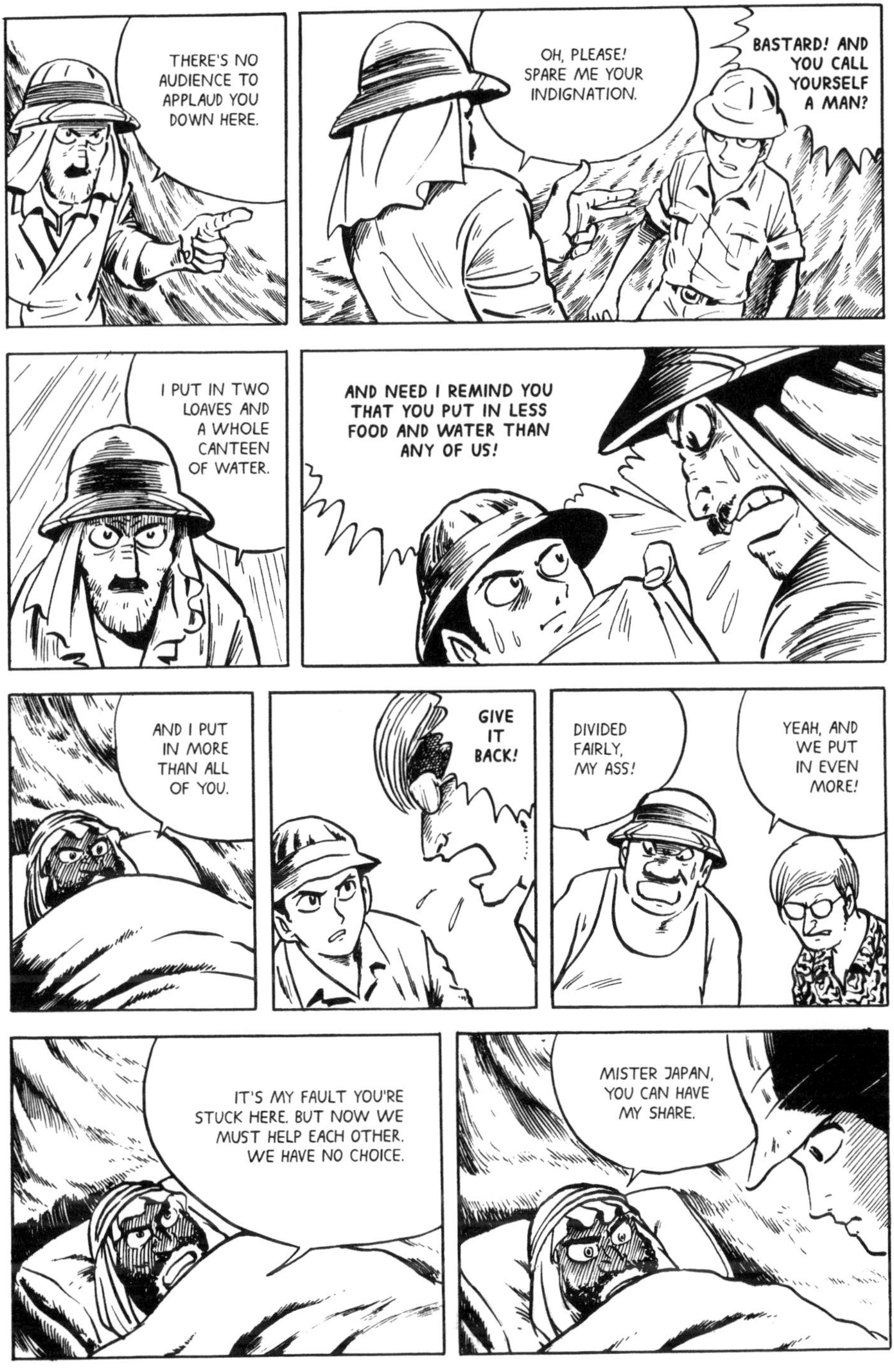
BASTARD! AND YOU CALL YOURSELF A MAN?
OH, PLEASE! SPARE ME YOUR INDIGNATION.
THERE'S NO AUDIENCE TO APPLAUD YOU DOWN HERE.
AND NEED I REMIND YOU THAT YOU PUT IN LESS FOOD AND WATER THAN ANY OF US!
I PUT IN TWO LOAVES AND A WHOLE CANTEEN OF WATER.
YEAH, AND WE PUT IN EVEN MORE!
DIVIDED FAIRLY, MY ASS!
GIVE IT BACK!
AND I PUT IN MORE THAN ALL OF YOU.
MISTER JAPAN, YOU CAN HAVE MY SHARE.
IT'S MY FAULT YOU'RE STUCK HERE. BUT NOW WE MUST HELP EACH OTHER. WE HAVE NO CHOICE.

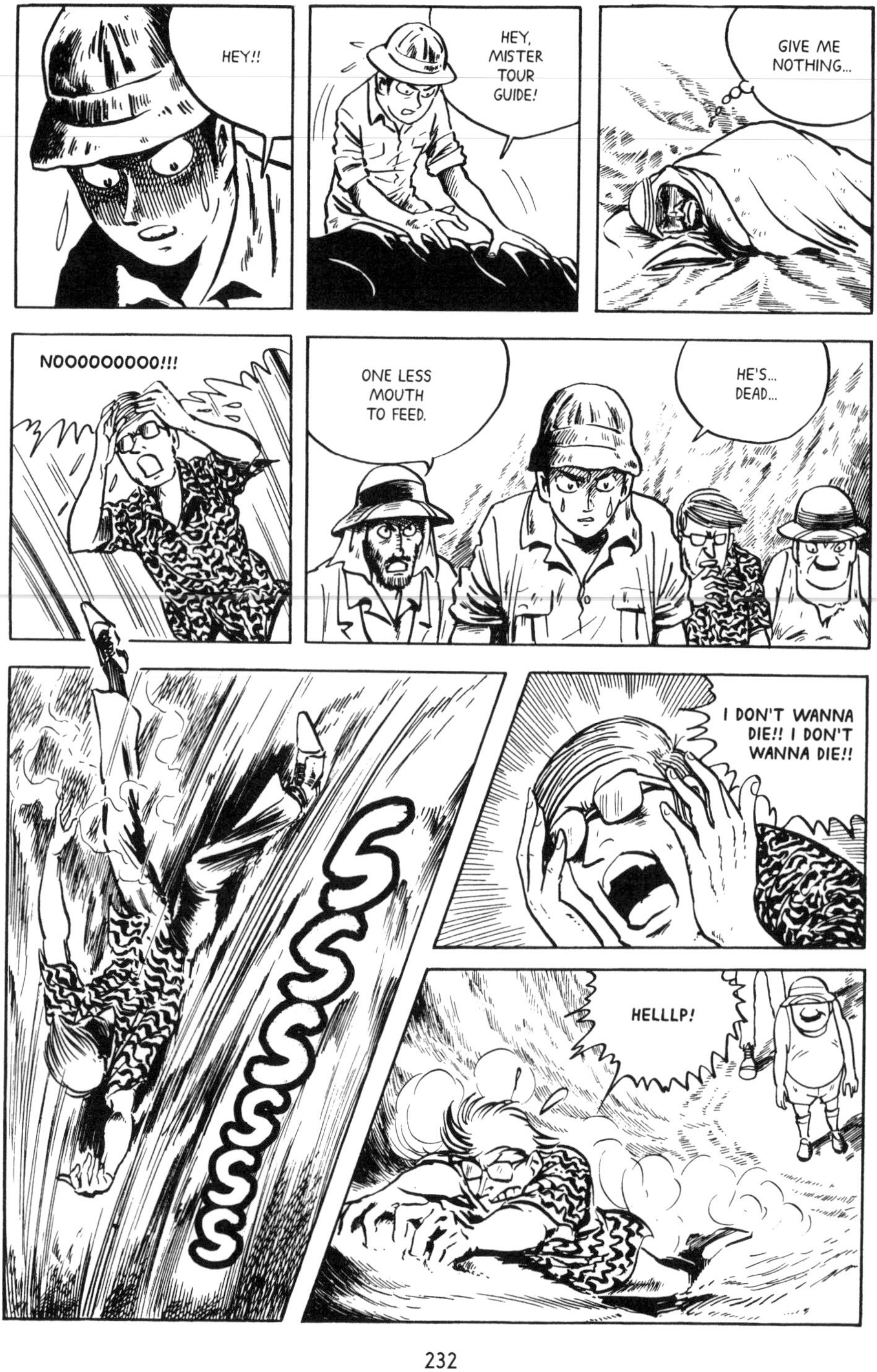
GIVE ME NOTHING...
HEY, MISTER TOUR GUIDE!
HEY!!
HE'S... DEAD...
ONE LESS MOUTH TO FEED.
NOOOOOOOOO!!!
I DON'T WANNA DIE!! I DON'T WANNA DIE!!
HELLLP!
SSSSSSS

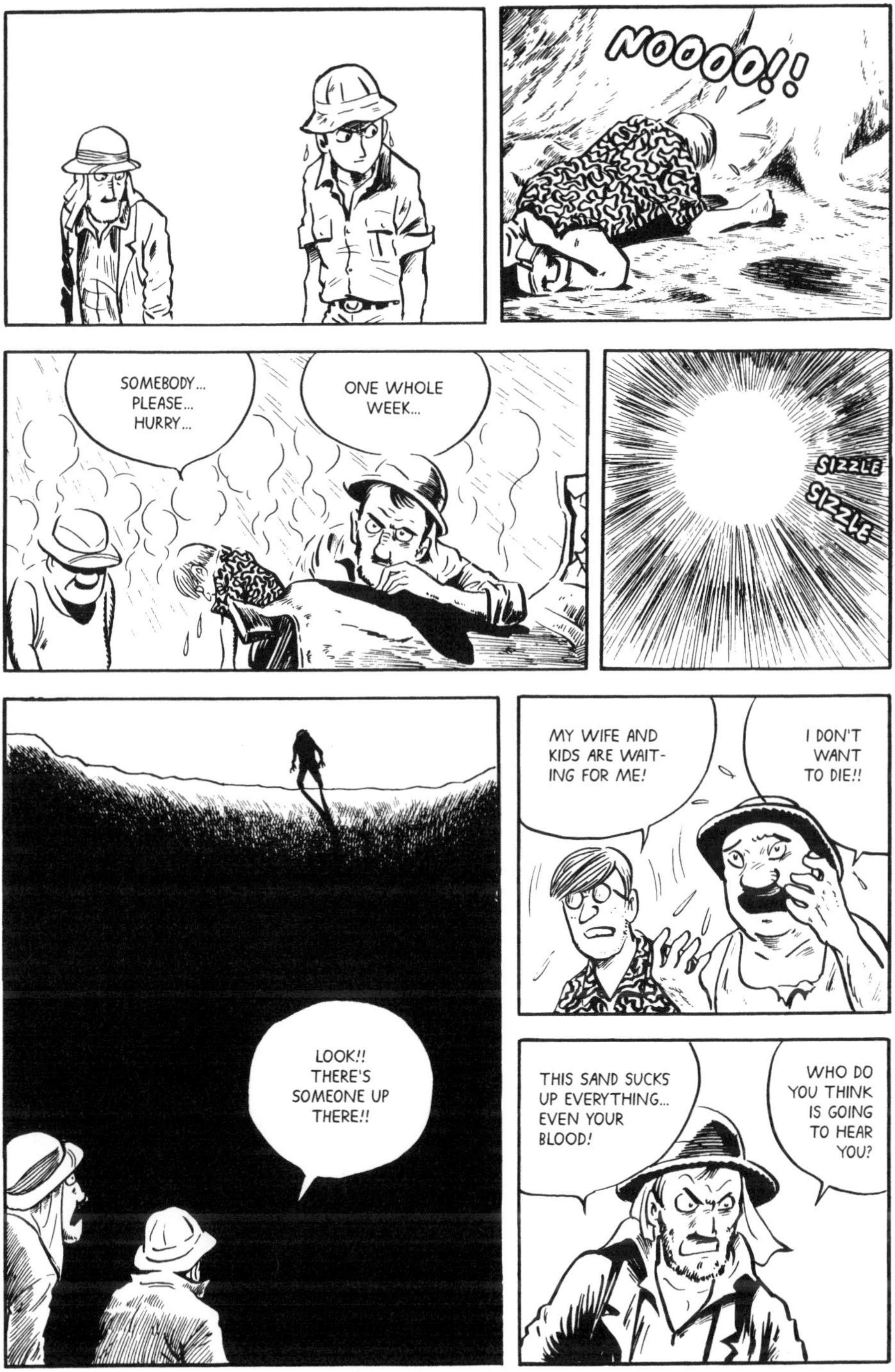
NOOOO!!
SIZZLE
SIZZLE
ONE WHOLE WEEK...
SOMEBODY... PLEASE... HURRY...
I DON'T WANT TO DIE!!
MY WIFE AND KIDS ARE WAIT-ING FOR ME!
WHO DO YOU THINK IS GOING TO HEAR YOU?
THIS SAND SUCKS UP EVERYTHING... EVEN YOUR BLOOD!
LOOK!! THERE'S SOMEONE UP THERE!!

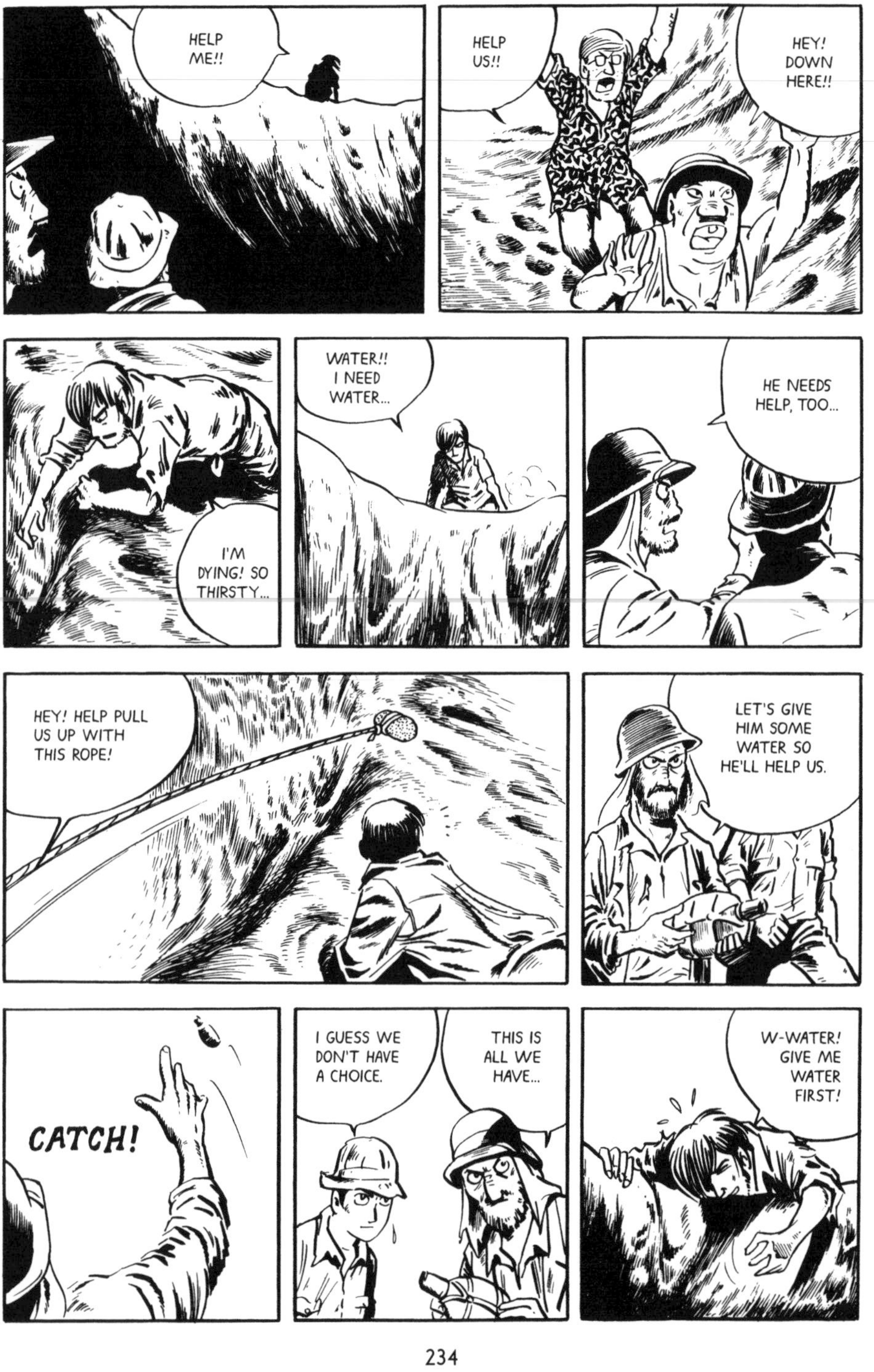
HEY! DOWN HERE!!
HELP US!!
HELP ME!!
HE NEEDS HELP, TOO...
WATER!! I NEED WATER...
I'M DYING! SO THIRSTY...
LET'S GIVE HIM SOME WATER SO HE'LL HELP US.
HEY! HELP PULL US UP WITH THIS ROPE!
W-WATER! GIVE ME WATER FIRST!
THIS IS ALL WE HAVE...
I GUESS WE DON'T HAVE A CHOICE.
CATCH!

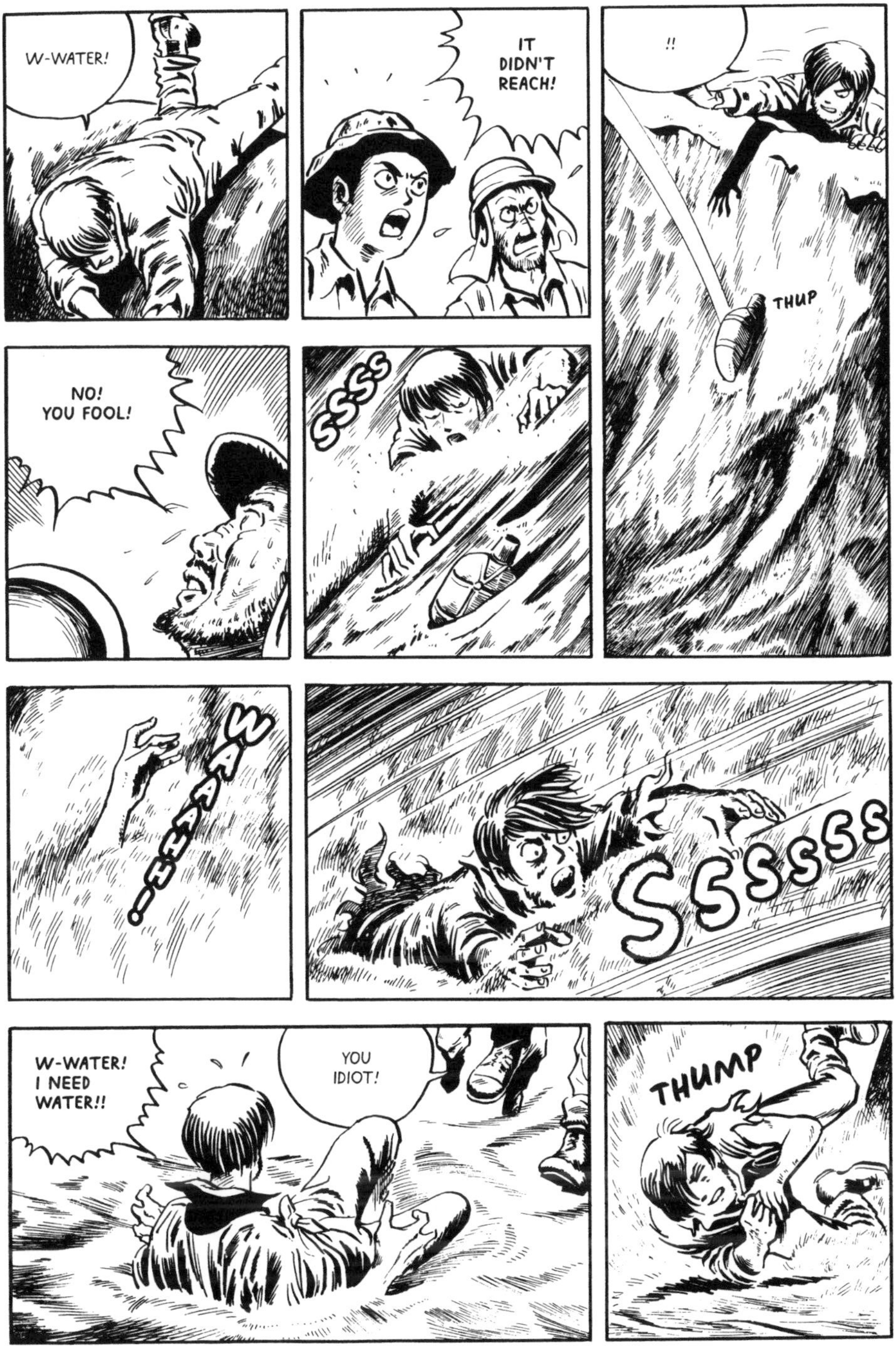
!!
THUP
IT DIDN'T REACH!
W-WATER!
SSSS
NO! YOU FOOL!
SSSSSS
WAAAHH!
THUMP
YOU IDIOT!
W-WATER! I NEED WATER!!

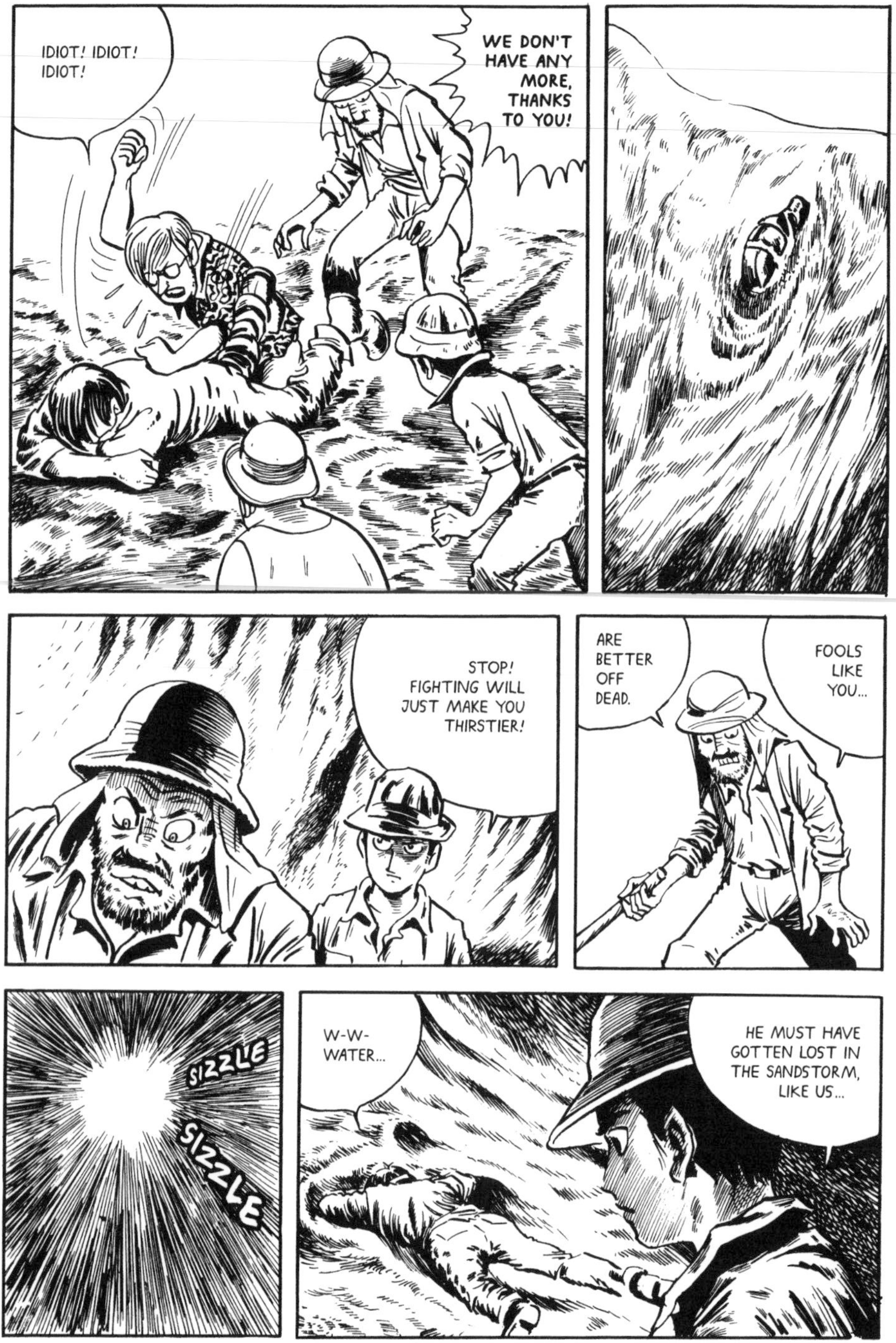
WE DON'T HAVE ANY MORE, THANKS TO YOU!
IDIOT! IDIOT! IDIOT!
FOOLS LIKE YOU...
ARE BETTER OFF DEAD.
STOP! FIGHTING WILL JUST MAKE YOU THIRSTIER!
HE MUST HAVE GOTTEN LOST IN THE SANDSTORM, LIKE US...
W-W-WATER...
SIZZLE
SIZZLE

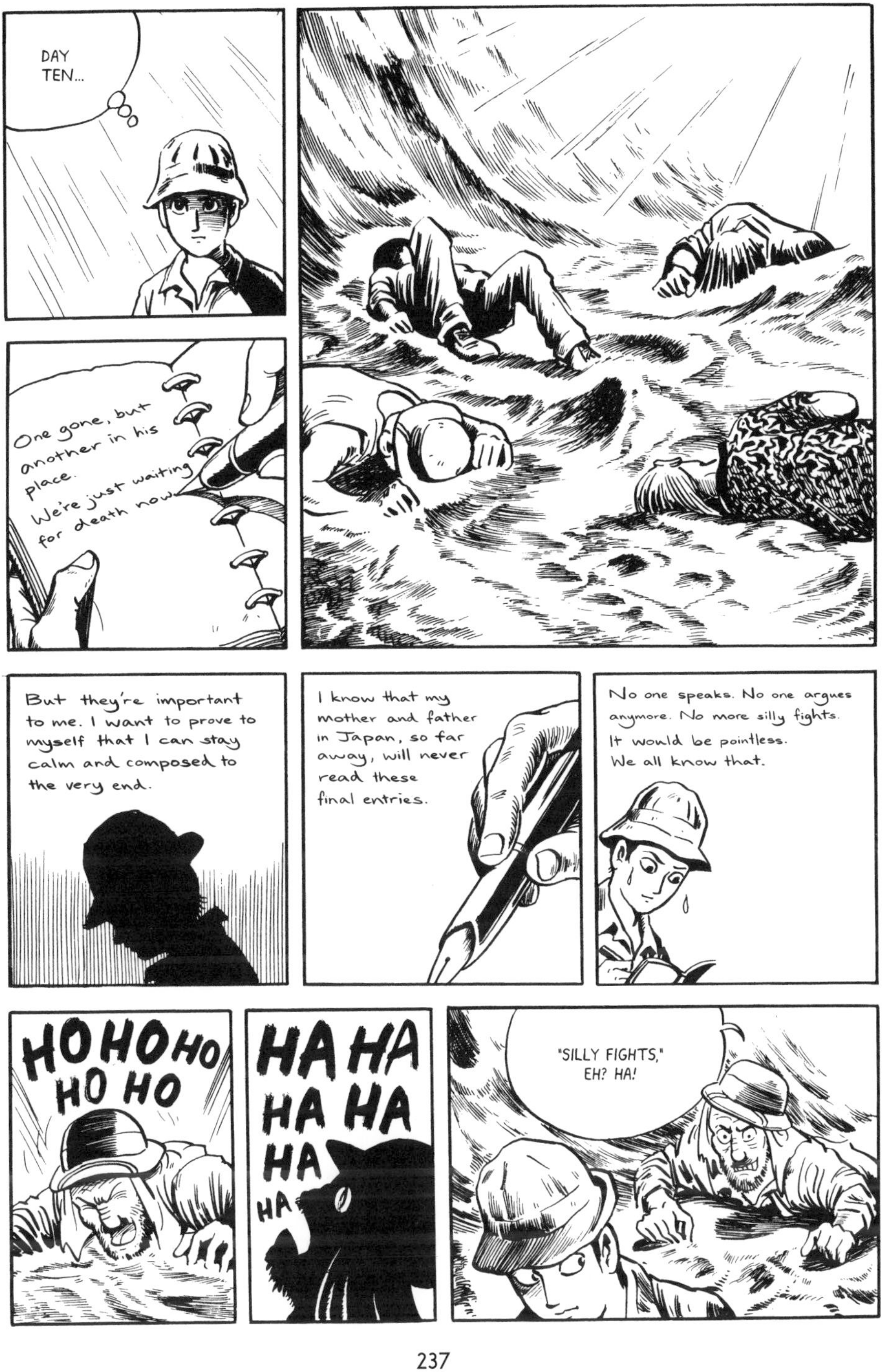
DAY TEN...
One gone, but another in his place. We're just waiting for death now.
No one speaks. No one argues anymore. No more silly fights. It would be pointless. We all know that.
I know that my mother and father in Japan, so far away, will never read these final entries.
But they're important to me. I want to prove to myself that I can stay calm and composed to the very end.
"SILLY FIGHTS," EH? HA!
HA HA HA HA HA HA
HO HO HO HO HO HO

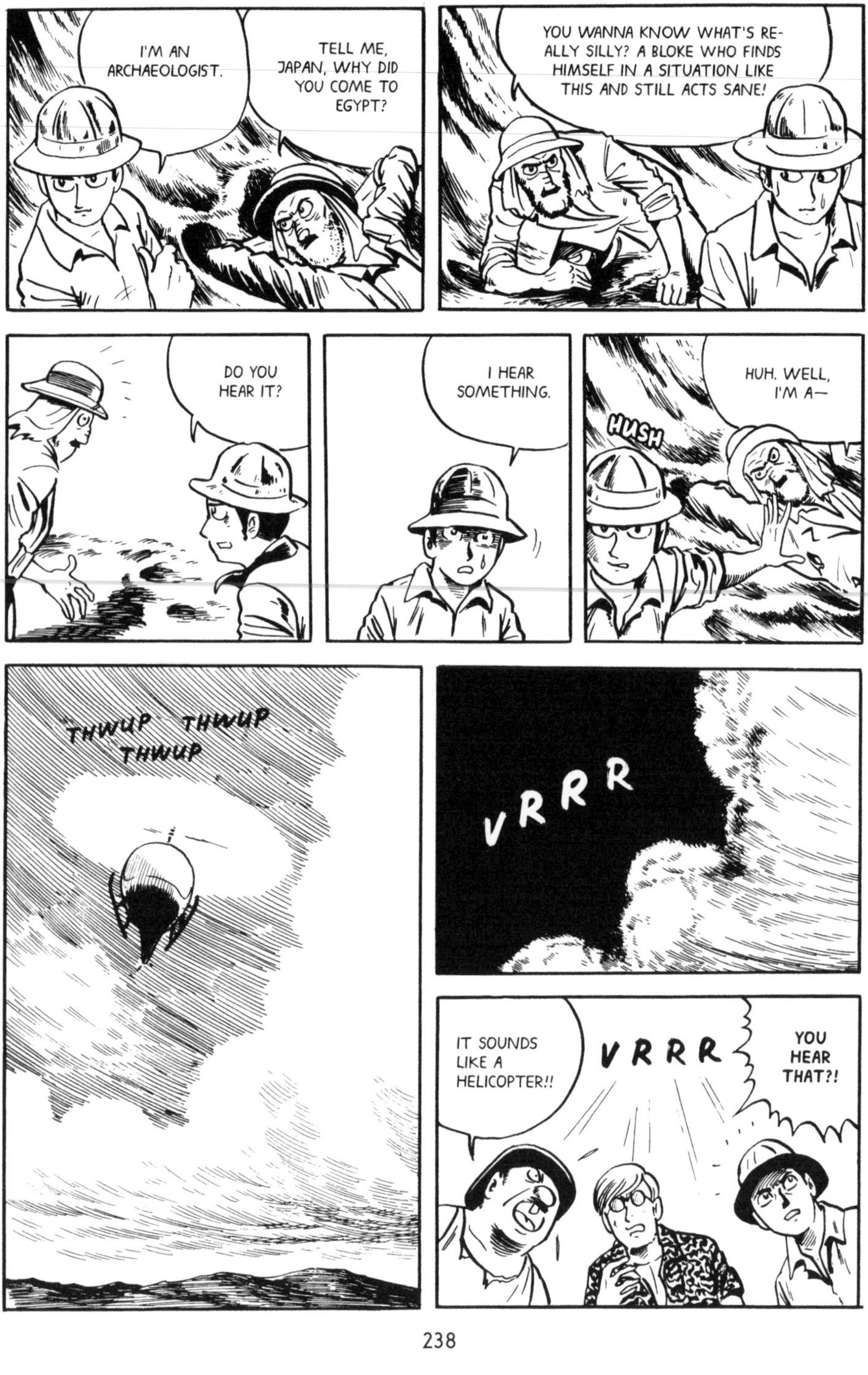

YOU WANNA KNOW WHAT'S RE-ALLY SILLY? A BLOKE WHO FINDS HIMSELF IN A SITUATION LIKE THIS AND STILL ACTS SANE!
TELL ME, JAPAN, WHY DID YOU COME TO EGYPT?
I'M AN ARCHAEOLOGIST.
HUH. WELL, I'M A—
HUSH
I HEAR SOMETHING.
DO YOU HEAR IT?
VRRR
YOU HEAR THAT?!
VRRR
IT SOUNDS LIKE A HELICOPTER!!
THWUP THWUP THWUP

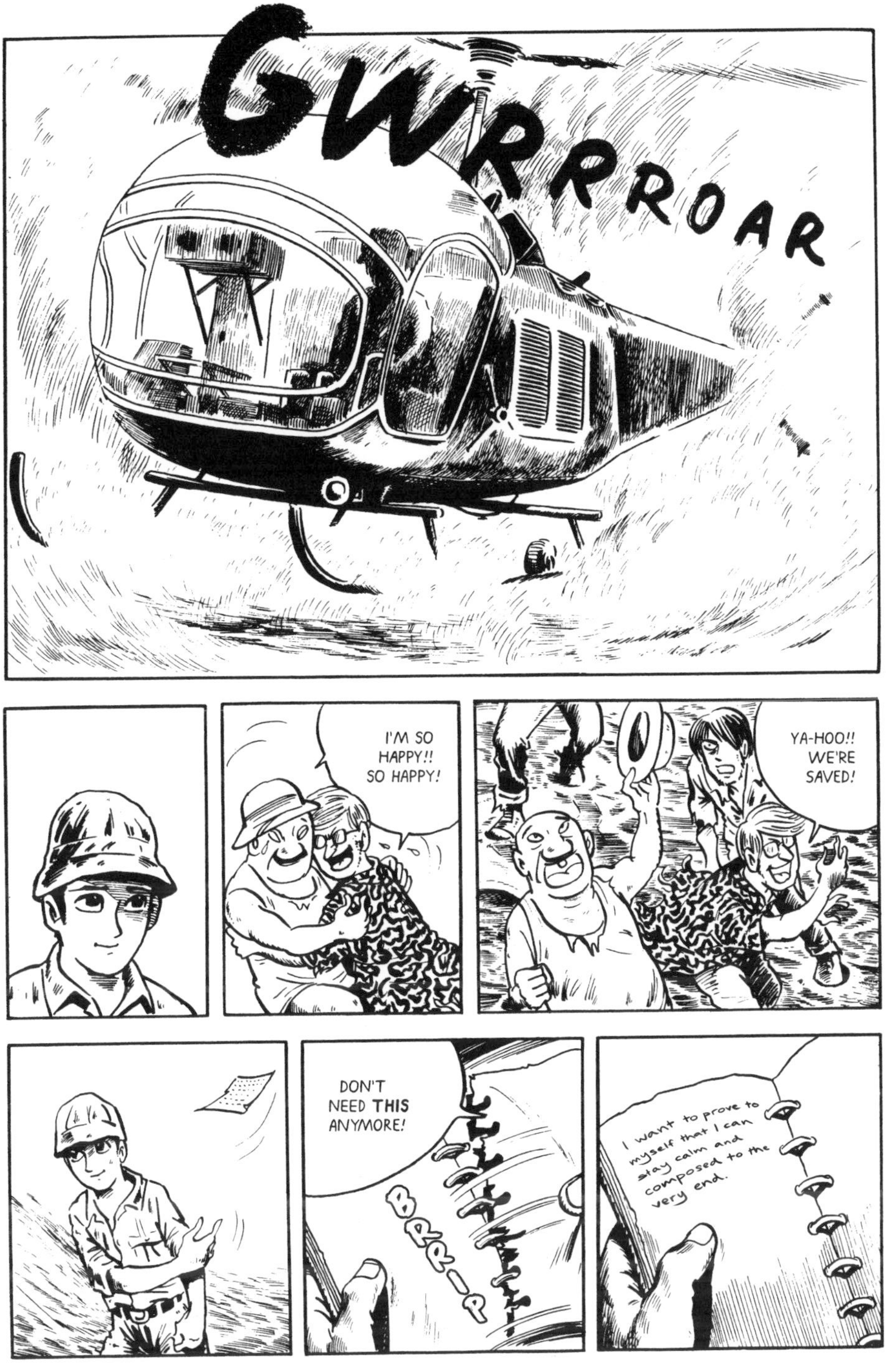
GWRRROAR
YA-HOO!! WE'RE SAVED!
I'M SO HAPPY!! SO HAPPY!
I want to prove to myself that I can stay calm and composed to the very end.
DON'T NEED **THIS** ANYMORE!
BRRIP

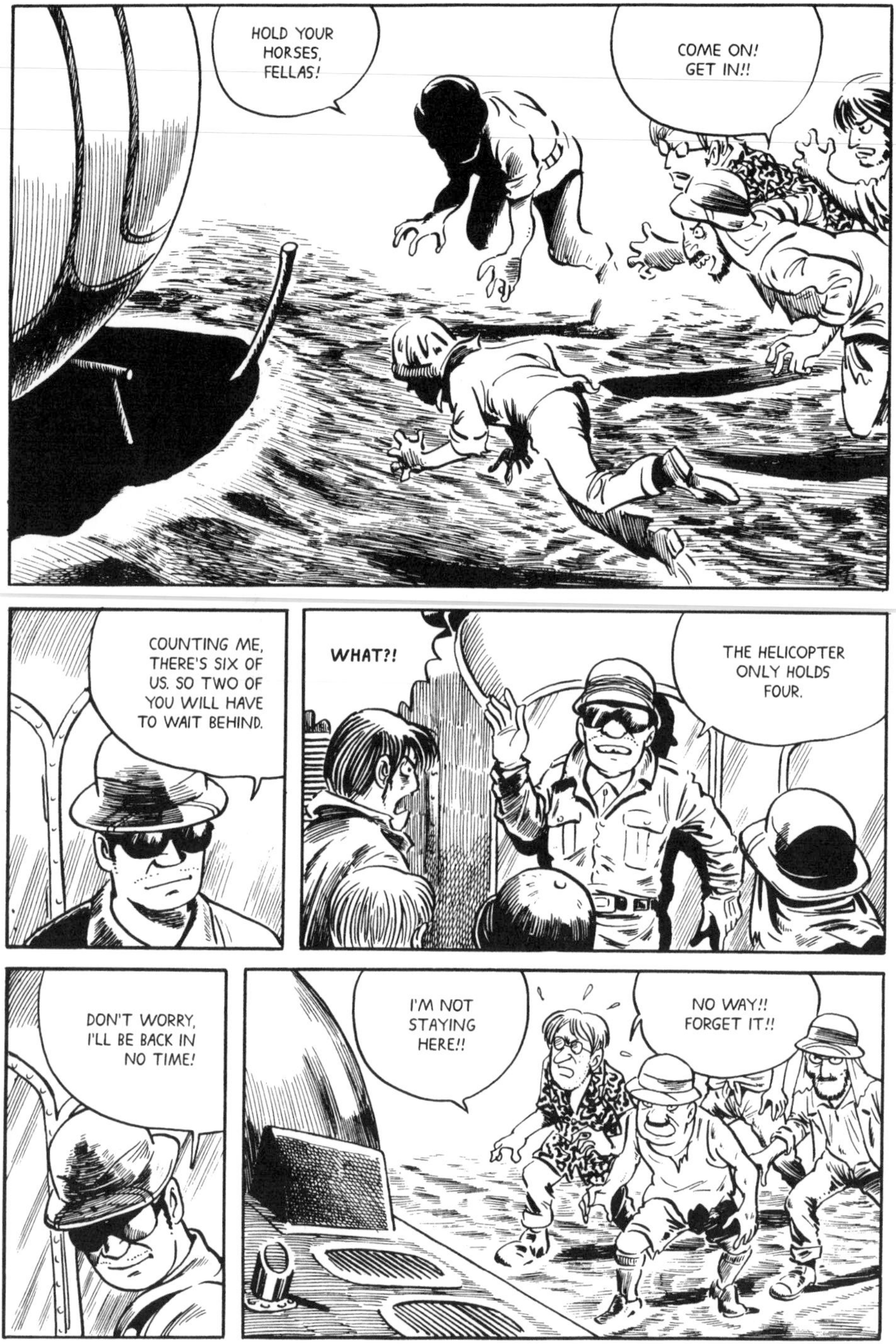
COME ON! GET IN!!
HOLD YOUR HORSES, FELLAS!
THE HELICOPTER ONLY HOLDS FOUR.
WHAT?!
COUNTING ME, THERE'S SIX OF US. SO TWO OF YOU WILL HAVE TO WAIT BEHIND.
NO WAY!! FORGET IT!!
I'M NOT STAYING HERE!!
DON'T WORRY, I'LL BE BACK IN NO TIME!

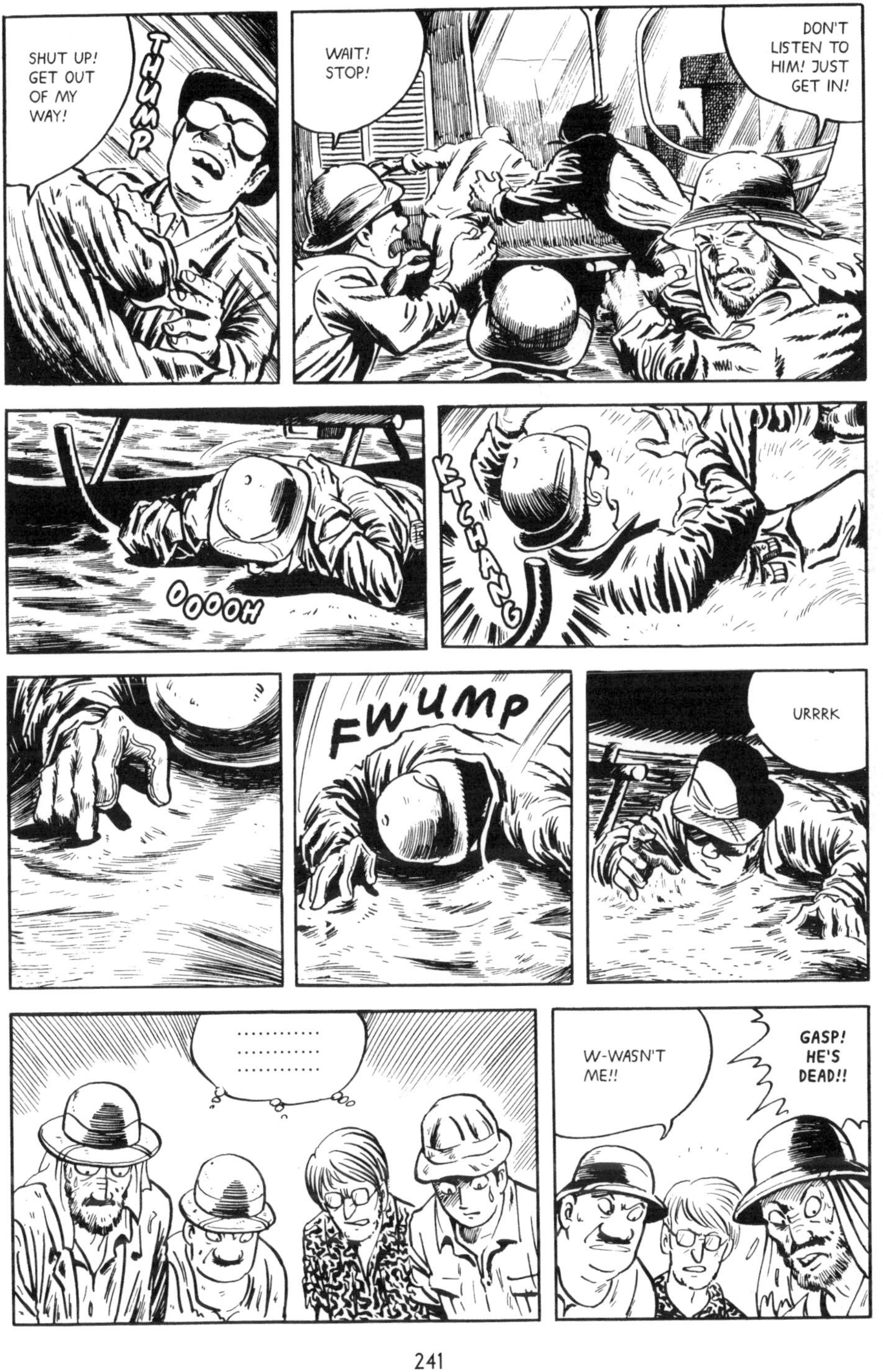

DON'T LISTEN TO HIM! JUST GET IN!
WAIT! STOP!
SHUT UP! GET OUT OF MY WAY!
THUMP
KTCHANG
OOOOH
URRRK
FWUMP
GASP! HE'S DEAD!!
W-WASN'T ME!!
....
....
....

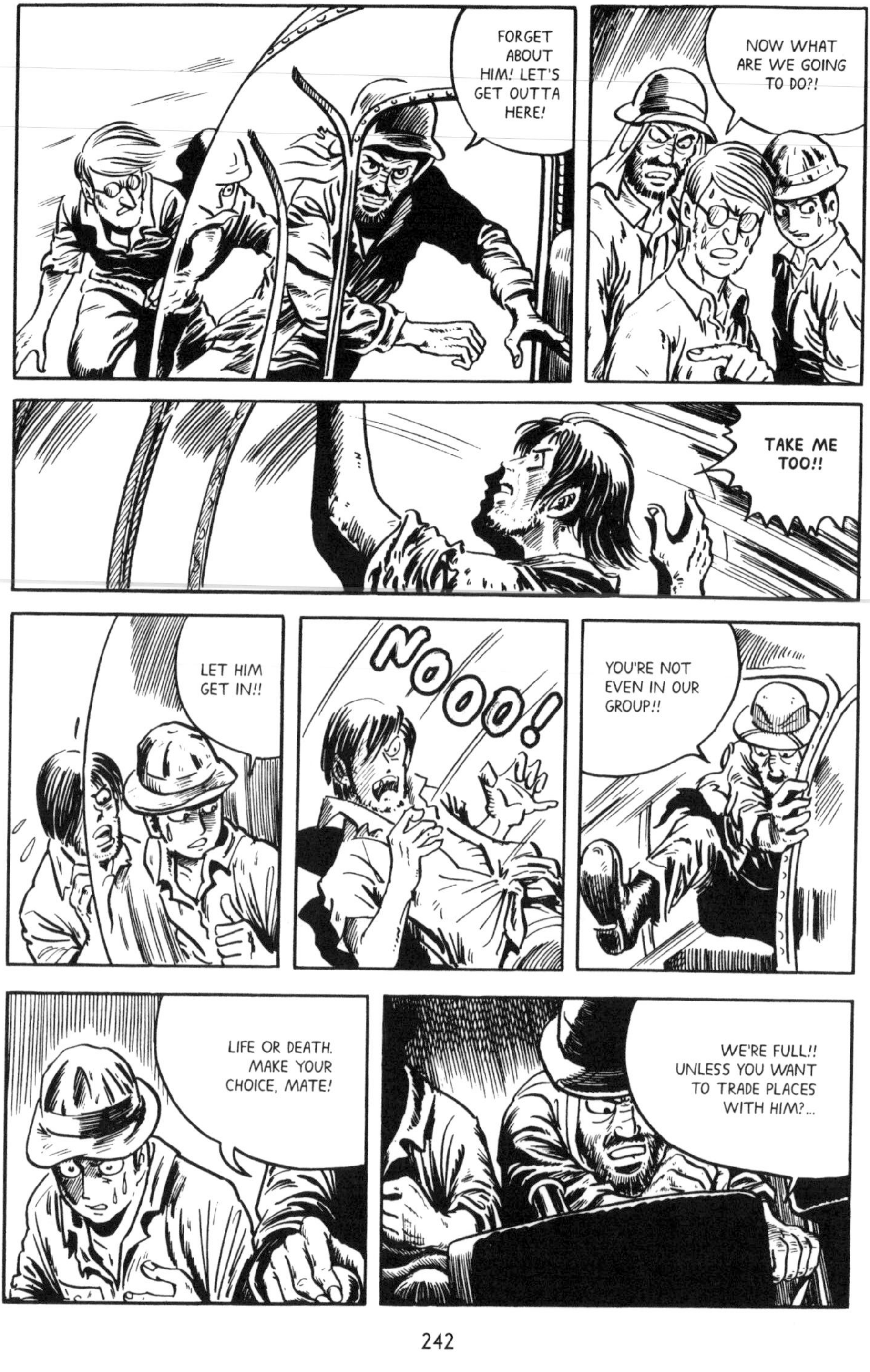
NOW WHAT ARE WE GOING TO DO?!
FORGET ABOUT HIM! LET'S GET OUTTA HERE!
TAKE ME TOO!!
YOU'RE NOT EVEN IN OUR GROUP!!
NOOOO!
LET HIM GET IN!!
WE'RE FULL!! UNLESS YOU WANT TO TRADE PLACES WITH HIM?...
LIFE OR DEATH. MAKE YOUR CHOICE, MATE!

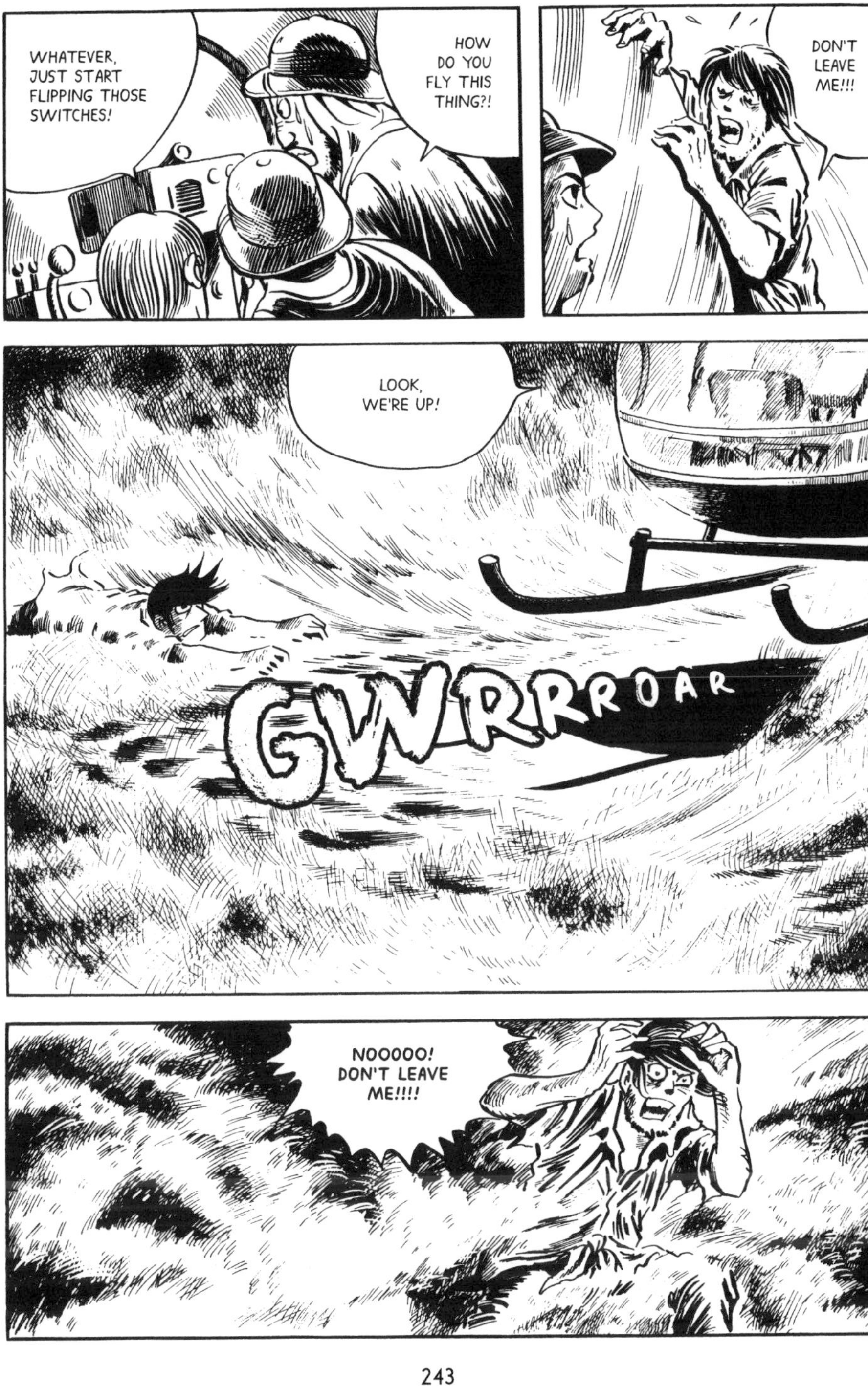
DON'T LEAVE ME!!!
HOW DO YOU FLY THIS THING?!
WHATEVER, JUST START FLIPPING THOSE SWITCHES!
LOOK, WE'RE UP!
GWRRROAR
NOOOOO! DON'T LEAVE ME!!!!

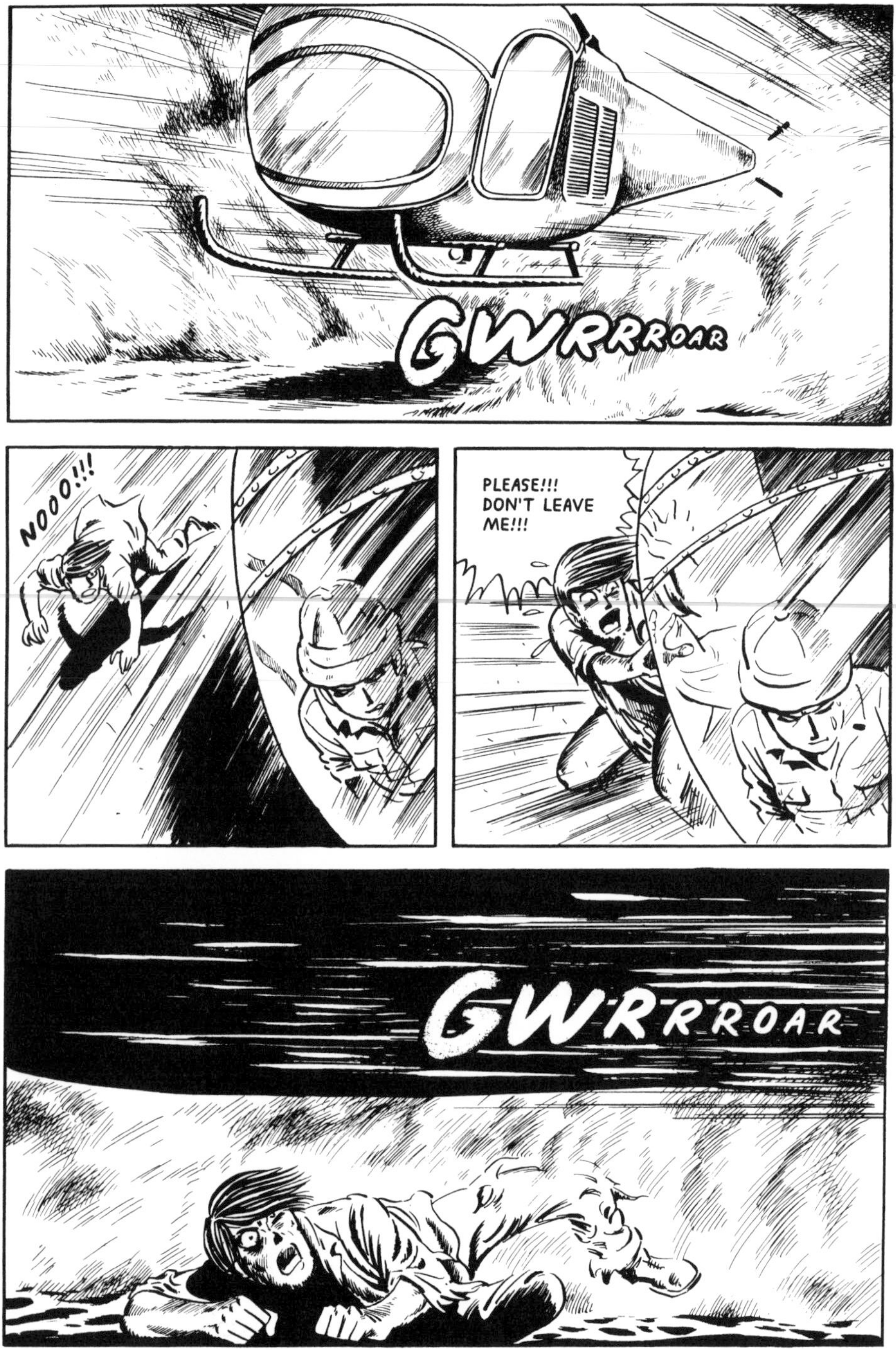
GWRRROAR
PLEASE!!! DON'T LEAVE ME!!!
NOOO!!!
GWRRROAR

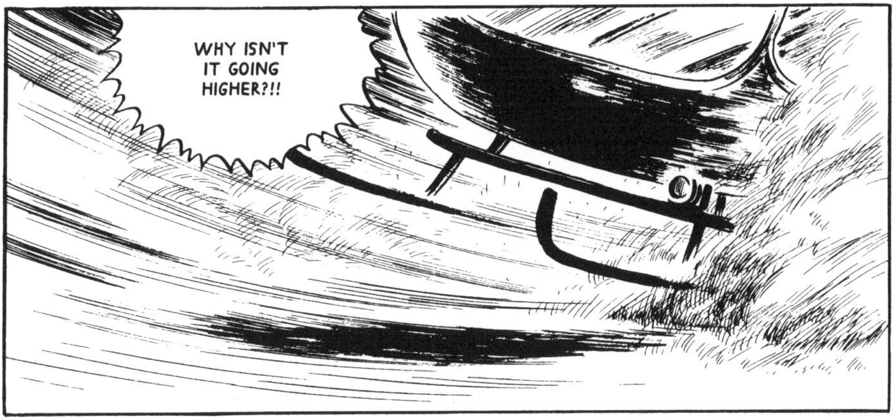
WHY ISN'T IT GOING HIGHER?!!

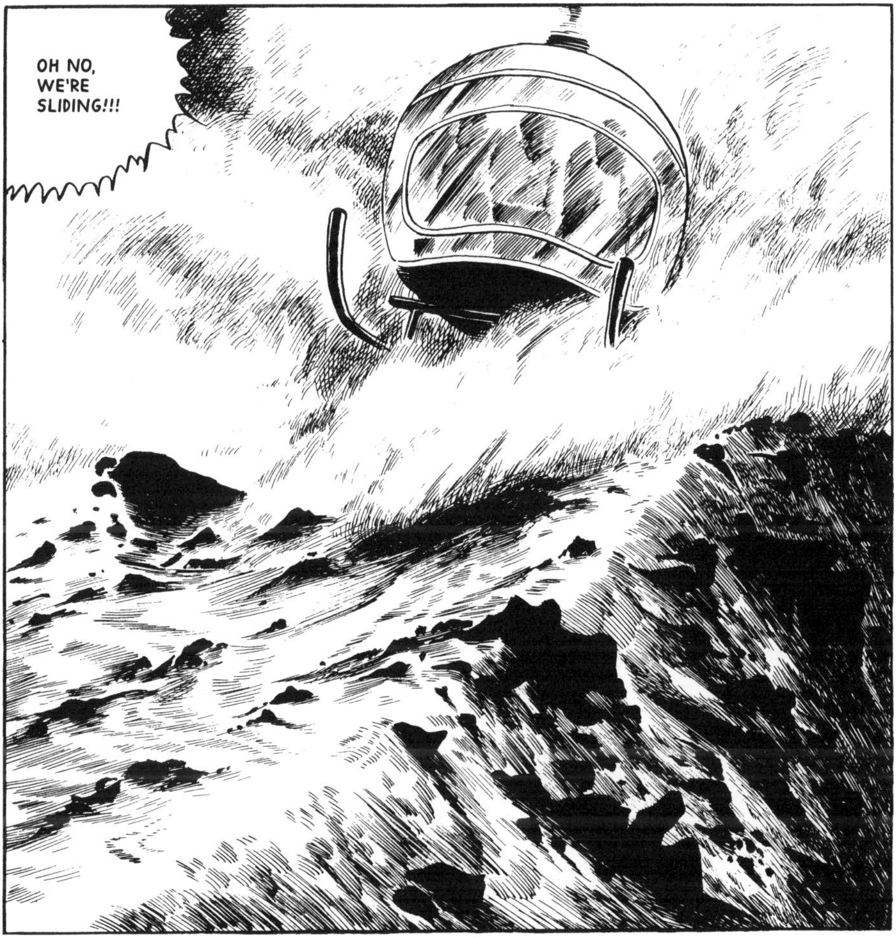
OH NO, WE'RE SLIDING!!!

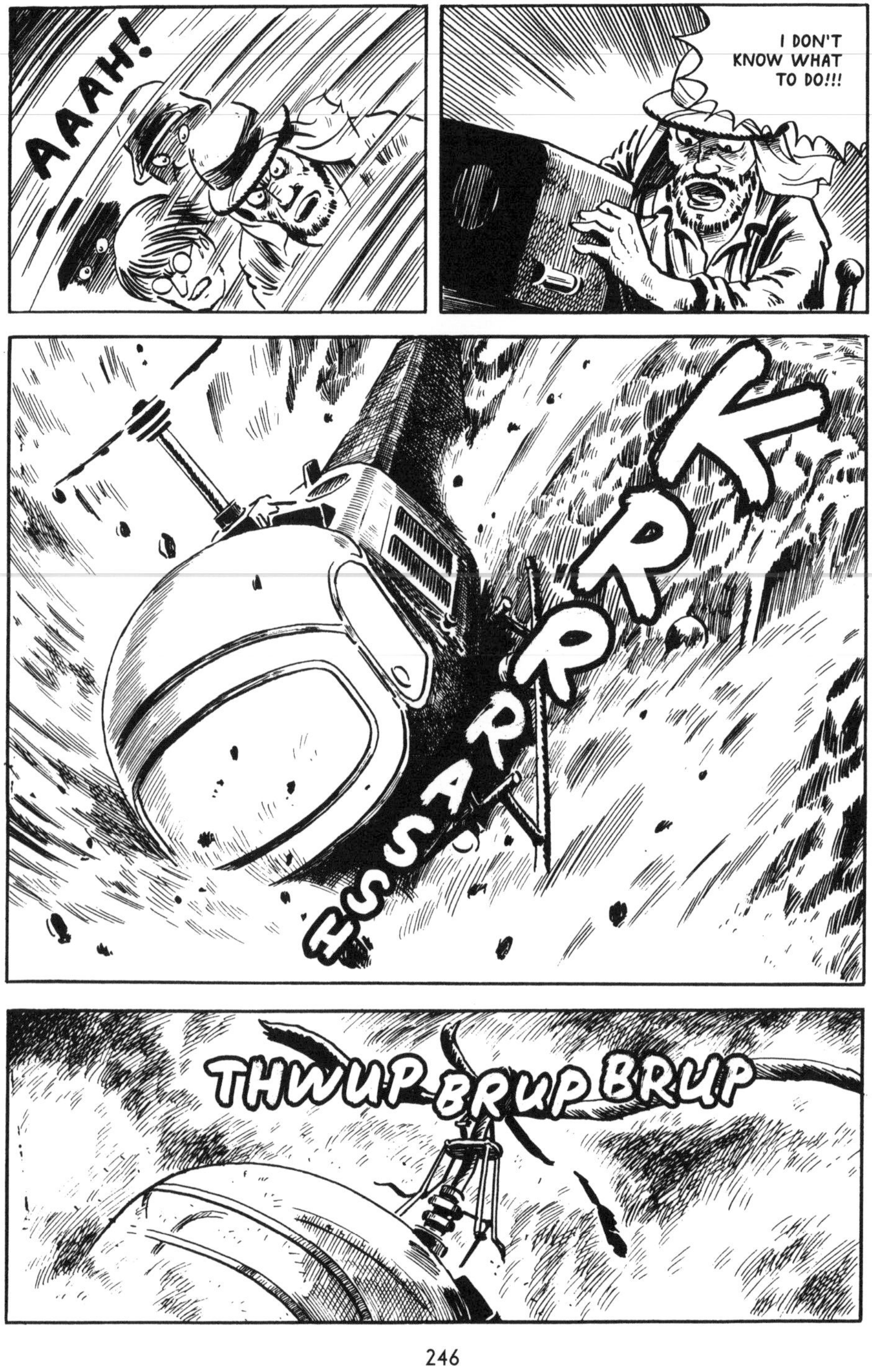
I DON'T KNOW WHAT TO DO!!!
AAAH!
KRRRASSH
THWUP BRUP BRUP

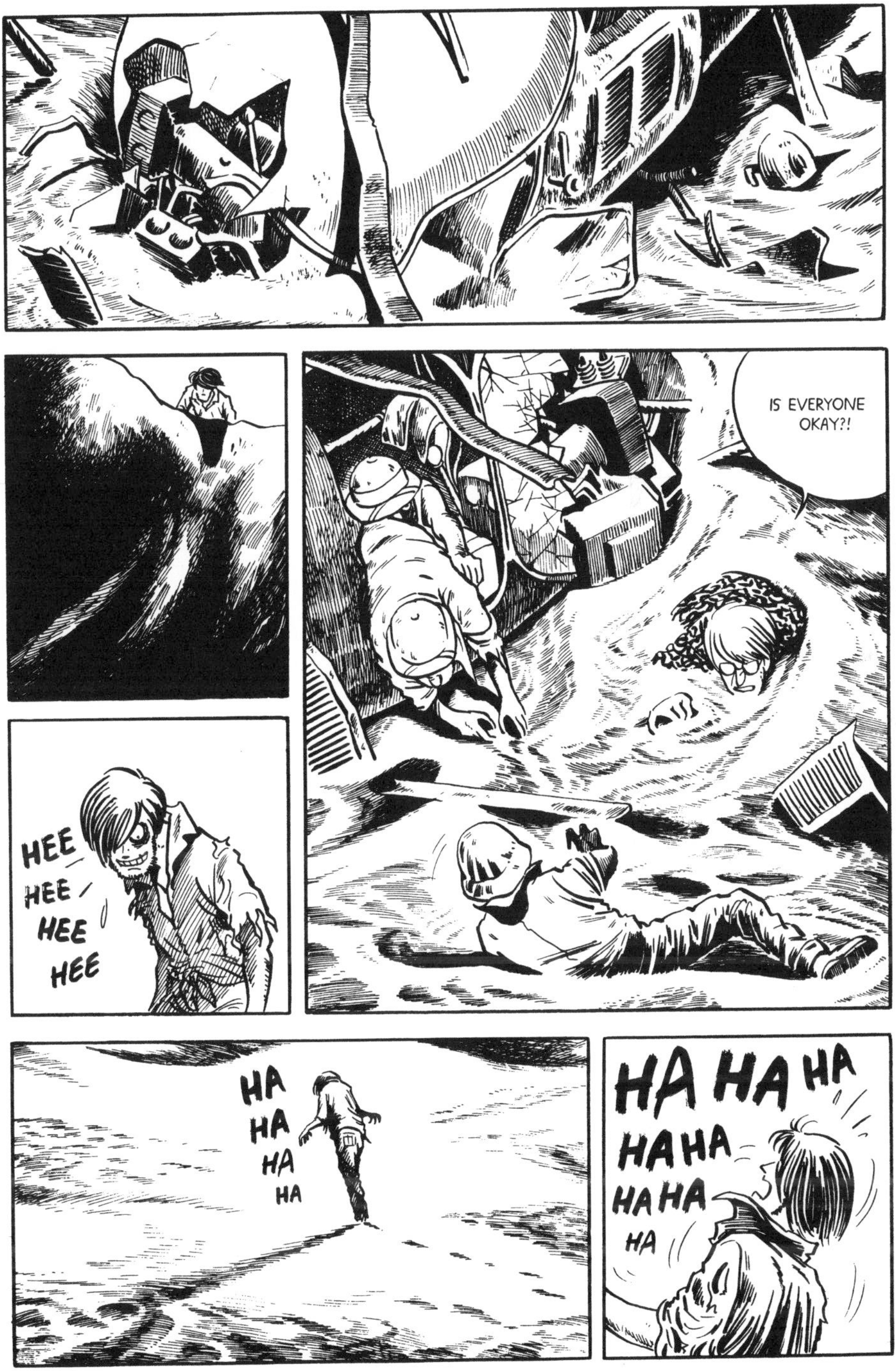

IS EVERYONE OKAY?!
HEE HEE HEE HEE
HA HA HA HAHA HAHA HA
HA HA HA HA

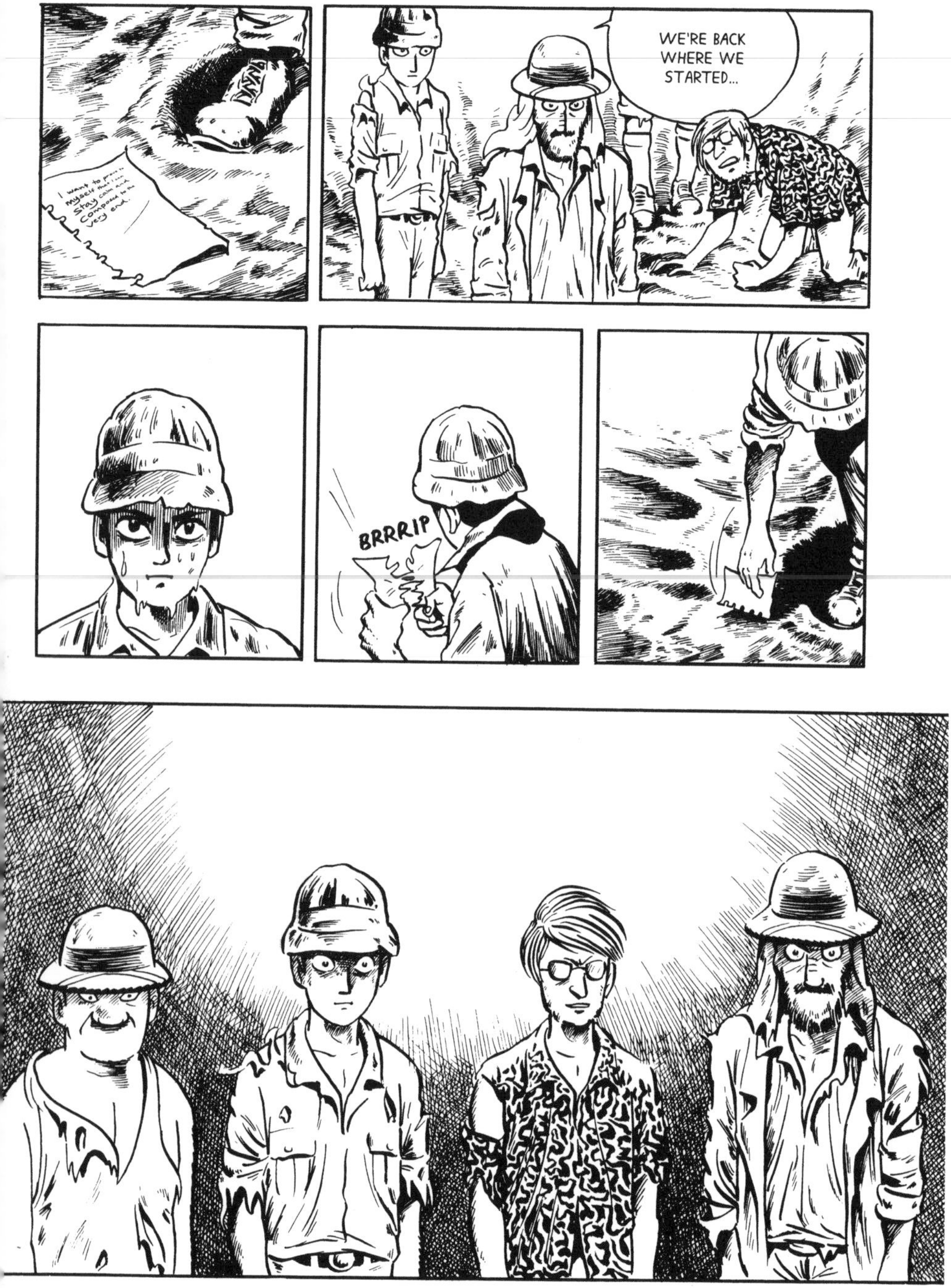
WE'RE BACK WHERE WE STARTED...
I want to prove to myself that I can stay calm and composed to the very end.
BRRRIP

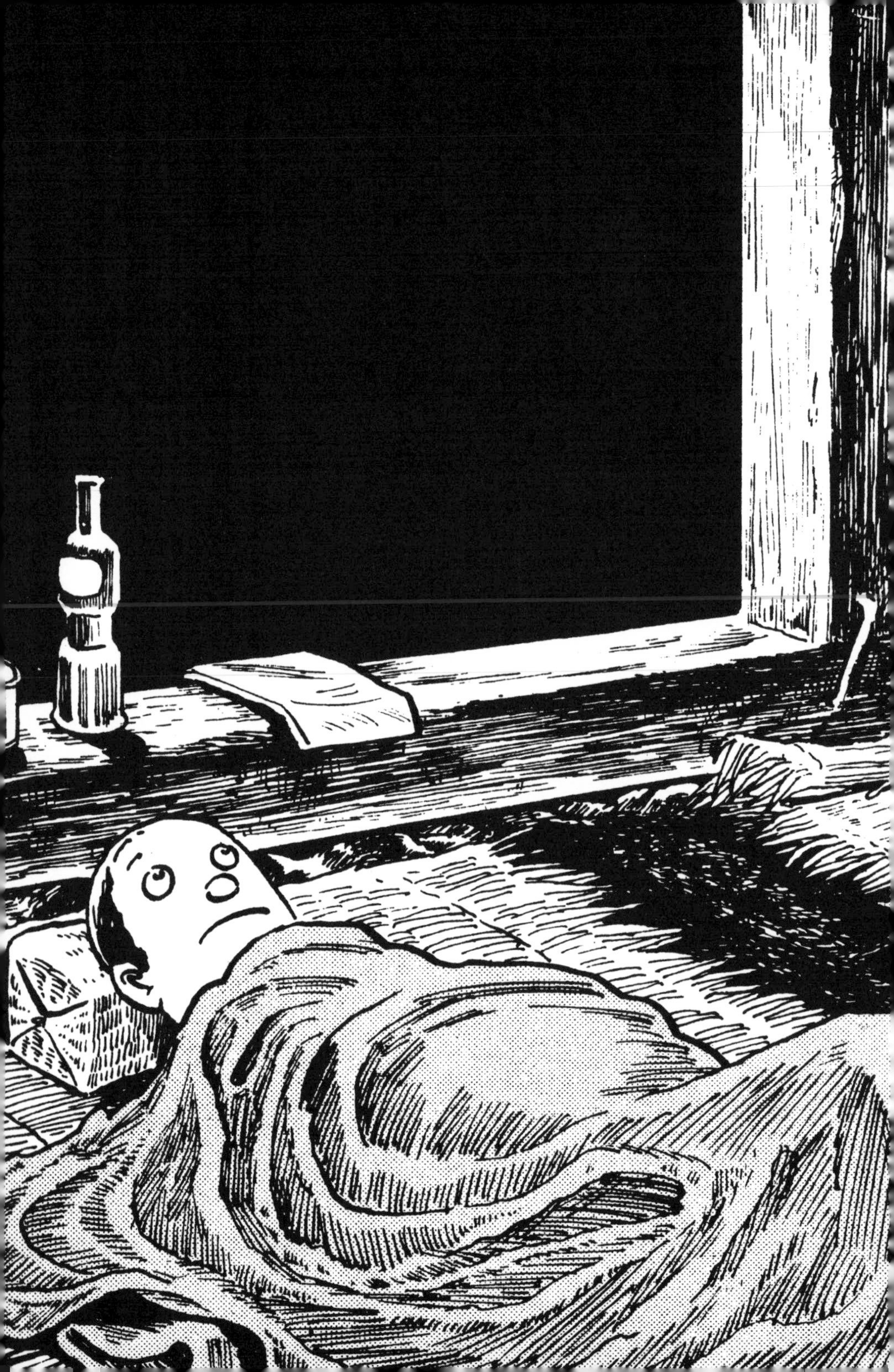

being inspired by a bus attendant at the Suehiro Inn, see "Ōtaki de no koto," *Tsuge Yoshiharu to boku*, pp. 52-4. In general, see also *Tsuge Yoshiharu mangajutsu*, vol. 2, pp. 84-92.

41 "Red Flowers," *Raw* no. 7 (1984), insert pamphlet. The crediting of the foreword and translation is based on a phone conversation with Paul Karasik in November 2020. The *Raw* translation was referenced during the production of that for the present volume.

42 Tsuge and Shimao Toshio, "Uchi ni mukau tabi," *Umi* (November 1971), p. 135; rpt. in *Uchi ni mukau tabi: Shimao Toshio taidanshū* (Tokyo: Tairyūsha, 1976).

43 "Ōtaki de no koto," p. 54.

44 On the sensitivities around buraku representation in the postwar era, especially with regards to stereotypes of insanity and violence in manga, see Ryan Holmberg, "Hirata Hiroshi and the Buraku Question: Understanding *Bloody Stumps Samurai*," and Kure Tomofusa, "The *Bloody Stumps Samurai* Incident," in Hirata Hiroshi, *Bloody Stumps Samurai* (Big Planet/Retrofit Comics, 2019), pp. 180-150.

45 *Tsuge Yoshiharu mangajutsu*, vol. 2, pp. 100-2. See also *Hinkon ryokōki*, pp. 80-7.

46 Tsuge and Suzuki Shirōyasu, "Taishū kotoba manga," *Garo* (January 1969), p. 101.

47 "Tabi nenpu," pp. 249-50. The "travel book" referred to by Tsuge is probably Yamamoto Kōtarō, *Zenkoku no mezurashii onsen annai* (Tokyo: Tōeidō, 1966).

48 *Tsuge Yoshiharu mangajutsu*, vol. 2, pp. 111-2.

49 "Tōhoku no onsen meguri," *Tsuge Yoshiharu to boku* (Tokyo: Shōbunsha, 1977), pp. 26-7.

50 "Hatago no omoide," *Hinkon ryokōki*, p. 222.

51 "Tabi nenpu," p. 250.

52 *Tsuge Yoshiharu mangajutsu*, vol. 2, p. 105.

53 "Tōhoku no onsen meguri," p. 28.

54 "Wara yane no aru fūkei," p. 48.

55 Takano, *Tsuge Yoshiharu o tabi suru*, pp. 13, 15. This book is an essential guide to the actual places behind Tsuge's manga.

56 *Mizuki kamera*, vol. 1, p. 188.

57 "Tabi nenpu," p. 250.

58 Tsuge and Fujiwara Maki, "Tokai ni kachi nanka hitotsu mo nai," *Yagyō* no. 14 (July 1985), p. 67.

59 Tsuge and Hagiwara Sakumi, "Fūkei ni deaitai," *Geijutsu kurabu* (December 1973), p. 118.

60 "Fūkei ni deaitai," p. 124.

61 *Tsuge Yoshiharu mangajutsu*, vol. 2, pp. 115-6

62 For similar thoughts on Tsuge's travel manga and landscape, see Kawakatsu Tokushige, "Tatami no me kara mita 'watakushi manga' o kangaeru," *Kakū* no. 16 (May 2017), pp. 138-40.

63 *Tsuge Yoshiharu mangajutsu*, vol. 2, pp. 118-21.

64 "Insei e no kawaranu akogare," in *Akai hana: Tsuge Yoshiharu karaa sakuhinshū* (Tokyo: Futabasha, 2013), p. 154.

22 For more on the relationship between Tsuge and Ikegami, see *Garo 1968: Zen'ei manga no shikō to kiseki* (Tokyo: Futabasha, 2018), which includes an essay on the subject by Takano Shinzō.

23 "Tsuge Yoshiharu intabyuu," *Akkusu* no. 13 (February 2000), p. 130.

24 Ibuse's "Salamander" and "Sawan on the Roof" are available in English translation in *Salamander and Other Stories*, trans. John Bester (Tokyo & New York: Kodansha International, 1981). On the influence of Ibuse on "The Swamp," see *Tsuge Yoshiharu mangajutsu*, vol. 2, pp. 28-30. The idea that "Sawan on the Roof" informed Tsuge's work was floated by Shōzu Ben, *Tsuge Yoshiharu: 'Garo' jidai* (Tokyo: Sakuhinsha, 2020), pp. 29-30.

25 On Iwasaki Minoru and *Grass*, see Onoda Shō [Asakawa Mitsuhiro], "Ei'en e no hishō 7: Kusunoki Shōhei hen 3," *Akkusu* no. 10 (August 1999), pp. 129-30.

26 "Ganso Munō no hito Tsuge Yoshiharu ni manabu," in *Munō no hito no susume* (December 1991), p. 18.

27 See Ryan Holmberg, "Where is Yoshiharu Tsuge?" in *The Man Without Talent*, trans. Holmberg (New York: New York Review Comics, 2020), pp. iii-xix.

28 Tsuge and Yaku Hiroshi, "Tsuge Yoshiharu no kojiki ron," *Munō no hito* (Tokyo: Nihon bungeisha, 1989), p. 230. For a more fleshed-out version of these thoughts, see *Tsuge Yoshiharu mangajutsu*, pp. 68-79.

29 *Tsuge Yoshiharu mangajutsu*, vol. 2, pp. 68-9.

30 Saikaku's "Mosquito Grubs" has been translated as part of "Three Stories from Saikaku," trans. Richard Lane, *Japan Quarterly* (January 1958), pp. 71-82.

31 *Tsuge Yoshiharu mangajutsu*, vol. 2, pp. 70-1.

32 Homages include: Tsugi Ateharu [Tsurita Kuniko], "Sorekara," *Garo* (September 1967); Tsurita, "Risan ichizoku" (c. 1968), first published in *Kanata e* (Tokyo: Seirinkōgeisha, 2001); Akasegawa Genpei, cover of *Manga shugi* no. 7 (August 1969); Akasegawa, "Sakura gahō, no. 32," *Garo* (June 1971); Horiguchi Kazumi, "Minasan shinjite kudasai," *Garo* (May 1972).

33 *Tsuge Yoshiharu mangajutsu*, vol. 2, p. 75.

34 *Tsuge Yoshiharu mangajutsu*, vol. 2, p. 81.

35 "Inadani no kōsenyado no mawari de, kojiki ni natte kiete ikitai," *Onsen shiki* (August 1991), p. 91.

36 See *Mizuki kamera*, vol. 1, eds. Adachi Morimasa and Fujimoto Kazuya (Uekiya, 2018), p. 179-83. This self-published and virtually impossible-to-obtain two-volume set, published as supplemental volumes to *Kuro no magajin*, a magazine dedicated to Mizuki's work, provides an exhaustive survey of Mizuki's photographic sources, with sections on Tsuge and other Mizuki Pro artists.

37 *Tsuge Yoshiharu mangajutsu*, vol. 1 (Tokyo: Waizu shuppan, 1993), pp. 170-1.

38 *Mizuki kamera*, vol. 1, p. 187.

39 Dazai's story is mentioned briefly in relation to "Red Flowers" in *Tsuge Yoshiharu mangajutsu*, p. 89. It is available in English as "Undine," in *Crackling Mountain and Other Stories*, trans. James O'Brien (Rutland, VT: Tuttle, 1989), pp. 68-79.

40 On the derivation of Sayoko's name from Ibuse, see "Shirato Sanpei ga furumatta no wa supageti ka ranchi ka? Tsuge Yoshiharu shi ni kiku," *Akkusu* no. 111 (June 2016), p. 9. On her dialogue

NOTES

1 "Yōkai hakase o tazuneta koro," *Yōkai: Mizuki Shigeru gashū* (Tokyo: Kōdansha, 2019), unpaginated. Unless otherwise noted, all sources are author/interviewee Tsuge Yoshiharu, and translated by Ryan Holmberg.

2 See *The Swamp* (Montreal: Drawn & Quarterly, 2020), p. 15.

3 Mizuki Shigeru, "Tsuge Yoshiharu to no deai," *Garo* no. 47 (June 1968), p. 28.

4 "Yōkai hakase o tazuneta koro."

5 "Seikatsujin toshite egaiteita Tatsumi san," *Akkusu* no. 104 (April 2015), p. 7.

6 See the breakdown of attributions in "Mizuki Shigeru no kimyō na sekai II: Gesuto pureeya retsuden," *Garo* (January 1993), p. 32.

7 "Yōkai hakase o tazuneta koro."

8 For example, Mizuki's version of Nurarihyon is not only clearly modeled on the way the yōkai is drawn in Sekien's *Night Parade*, but the way Mizuki describes him in the full-color yōkai features that fronted issues of *Shōnen Magazine* is thought to follow notes in Fujisawa's *A Survey of Yōkai Pictures and Tales*. See the "Gendai no Nurarihyon" section in the Japanese "Nurarihyon" Wikipedia page. This connection is also mentioned in Michael Dylan Foster, *The Book of Yōkai: Mysterious Creatures of Japanese Folklore* (University of California Press, 2015), p. 218.

9 Ikegami Ryōichi and Kondō Yōko, "Ooraka, yuumoa, kimajimesa: Mizuki Shigeru o kataru," *Akkusu* no. 109 (February 2016), p. 8.

10 "Hanzai kūfuku shūkyō" [1969], *Tsuge Yoshiharu to boku* (Tokyo: Shōbunsha, 1977), p. 174.

11 For a partial rundown of what Tsuge was reading in these years, see Tsuge and Gondō Susumu, *Tsuge Yoshiharu mangajutsu*, vol. 2 (Tokyo: Waizu shuppan, 1993), pp. 63-7. For a career-spanning overview, see "'Tsuge Yoshiharu konomi' no hon: sakka to sakuhin o fukaku shiru tame no 15 satsu," *Spectator* no. 41 (2018), pp. 217-24.

12 Gondō Susumu, *'Garo' o kizuita hitobito: manga 30 nen shishi* (Tokyo: Horupu shuppan, 1993), p. 40.

13 For more on Takano, see Holmberg, "Singing Our Own Song: Hayashi Seiichi vs. Sasaki Maki, 1969," *The Comics Journal* online (January 2016).

14 Gondō, *'Garo' o kizuita hitobito*, pp. 41-4.

15 "Tsuge Yoshiharu intabyuu," *Garo* (June 1992), p. 252.

16 "Chokkei 3 kiro ga riarizumu no moto," *Kyūjin taimusu* (November 24, 1983), p. 224.

17 *Tsuge Yoshiharu mangajutsu*, vol. 2, pp. 57-8.

18 Pu Songling, *Strange Tales from a Chinese Studio* (Penguin Books, 2006), pp. 10-4.

19 Tsuge and Takano Shinzō, "Wara yane no aru fūkei" [1997], in Takano, *Tsuge Yoshiharu o tabi suru* (Tokyo: Chikuma shobō, 2001), p. 46.

20 "Tabi nenpu" [1991], *Hinkon ryokōki* (Tokyo: Shinchōsha, 1995), pp. 46-8.

21 "Tabi nenpu," p. 247.

Diverging from the open-ended story structure he had explored in works like "The Swamp" and "The Lee Family," Tsuge's travel stories are more straightforward, with clear beginnings, carefully placed twists and climaxes, and definitive conclusions. Tsuge gained many new readers as a result, but in later years expressed regret that "Mister Ben of the Honyara Cave" in particular was too tidy, resulting in a loss of realism. In his series of interviews with Takano in 1993, the artist explained how realism as it is usually conceived within fiction left him unsatisfied. Conventional realism might offer a believable representation of the world, but such reality never became the readers' own. "I wanted to avoid that. I wanted my stories to have a reality to them which emotionally sticks with readers as an experience for years... Works that make you feel that, it doesn't matter when they were created. Even some old works achieve it. I am interested in what that quality is."[63]

While Tsuge may have thought that "Mister Ben of the Honyara Cave" failed to meet up to his own high standards as a story, there's no doubting the fineness of the drawing. Not only does the style of the scenery vary according to the needs of the story, but Tsuge's notations for how the halftones should be applied is specific to each panel, thus enlivening the snow-blanketed landscape with subtle gradations and dramatic monochromatic contrasts. "Scenes by the Seaside" is also exceptional on this count. Though so common now as to be an indispensable part of the look and production of manga, "screentones" (halftone zip-a-tone sheets) that cartoonists could affix themselves to their artwork were not widely available in the '60s. Instead, artists indicated with light blue watercolor or colored pencil which areas they would like to appear as shades of grey, with notations specifying dot density, which printshops would create by integrating halftones into the printing plates. Through 1970, almost all works in *Garo*

were created with this method. The biggest difference between artwork processed in this traditional way versus artwork using screentones is that the former is typically able to produce a greater range of gradations, resulting in a gentler, subtler, and more natural look. Since there are no screentones affixed to Tsuge's artwork from this period, the published product tends to vary with each edition, some of which veer far from the artist's intentions. For the current English edition, the halftones have been tailored to be as close as possible to the stories' *Garo* versions and thus to Tsuge's original vision.

As Tsuge became evermore intoxicated with travel in these years, he drifted further and further away from the daily rituals and social connections that keep most people grounded. At the same time, it seems that he found greater existential comfort and a new, perhaps purer sense of self as a figure in the landscapes he traveled through and depicted in his manga.

Tsuge often reflected on the ramifications of this later in life. For example, in 2013: "My creative process is definitely rooted in a desire to escape from reality. I simply do not feel comfortable in the real world, which makes me anxious... That is probably why I sought out places to flee to, dreamed about somewhere I could live in seclusion, and kept traveling to remote hot springs, wintry villages, and other out-of-the-way places. But as anxiety is an internal, psychological problem, simply changing where I was physically was never going to solve anything. That is why I eventually sought to hide, not in the real, but in the sur-real (*chōgenjitsu*), resulting in 'Nejishiki.'"[64]

That next stage, and the revolution it initiated within Tsuge's career and manga at large, as well as the ripples it created across Japanese culture, will be the subject of volume three, *Nejishiki*.

Not that I'm consciously following any rule, but I'm never satisfied with pictures drawn according to my personal preferences alone. I could draw that kind of picture if I wanted to. I could draw hot springs the way I like, I could draw trees that I like in places that I like…I could draw my idea of an ideal landscape if I really wanted to, but I suspect it would bore me. There has to be restrictions of some sort… If there was a secret to my comics, I guess that might be it…[60]

He then proceeds to denigrate traditional East Asian ink landscapes, with their "mountains, thatched houses, small boats floating on the river, maybe someone fishing," all put together just a little too neatly. One occasionally finds scenery modeled on such landscapes in Tsuge's work (see the panorama of Futamata Gorge on page 152, for example), but they are usually ironic (though not yet in the '60s), as were his references to literati pretensions in general, "The Lee Family" and *The Man Without Talent* being the most obvious such cases.

Hence, instead, the centrality of photography to Tsuge's practice. As concrete images of the real, derived directly from the real, photographs were objective enough to keep personal whim and fantasy under control, while also malleable enough for recontextualization. They were, in other words, the ideal visual substrates for making *believable fictions*. That goal underwrote Tsuge's philosophy of realism for much of the rest of his career, whether he was drawing stories based on his travels or, like *The Man Without Talent*, on his private domestic life. By the mid '70s, Tsuge may have no longer used actual photographs in his manga much, even if he continued taking them for pleasure. But note that, in *The Man Without Talent*, vintage cameras are juxtaposed against art stones (the poor man's version of East Asian scholar's rocks) as a trade capable of making at least some money (the real) versus a silly pseudo-literati fantasy.

"MISTER BEN OF THE HONYARA CAVE"

"Honyaradō no Ben san," *Garo* (June 1968), signed March 1968

The snow huts known as "Honyara caves," the *tori-oi* "bird-chasing" ceremony, and carp hatcheries are all famous sites in Niigata, the quintessential "snow country" of northern Honshū near the Japan Sea (East Sea), where this manga is set. With the story already sketched out, Tsuge traveled to Tōkamachi in the mountains of Niigata in February 1968 with the intention of taking photographs so that he could flesh out the story with accurate images. When he arrived, however, the area was so buried in snow that he was forced to stay in a hotel near the train station and leave the next day. He was able to see neither the hatcheries nor the snow huts, nor the bird-chasing festival, which anyway had come and gone the previous month. The imagery of "Mister Ben of the Honyara Cave" is thus entirely imagined, aided by photographs he found in magazines and books.[61]

Beginning with "Red Flowers," the male travelers in Tsuge's manga broadly evoke the artist himself, a fiction reinforced by first-person narration. In "Mister Ben of the Honyara Cave," the traveler is also a cartoonist and the dialogue includes meta commentary about the creative process behind the making of comics. While the manga's title frames the story as about the old man who runs the inn, equal attention is paid to the traveler's feelings and experiences. Note, in particular, the passage in which the two are standing outside in the snowy landscape netting fish (pages 199-200): the action is paused as the traveler takes in the experience aesthetically, which he then comments upon as they dash back to the inn. This is not how Ben experiences daily life in the countryside; it is how the visiting traveler processes it. That Tsuge understood travel literature as a refined, self-reflexive variety of tourist literature is evident from "Chōhachi Inn," with its emphasis on the inn's brochure.[62]

Iwase Yumoto, Fukushima prefecture. Photograph by Tsuge, October 1967

ones in nearby Iwase Yumoto (see photo above), a town which Tsuge once described as a place "where time has stopped in the Edo or Meiji period."[57] In his later travel writings, Tsuge often touched on the ways rural areas had modernized, usually to his distaste. But his manga tend to emphasize pastness, which the artist himself recognized expressed the nostalgic desires of an outsider from the city. "Call me antiquarian if you wish," Tsuge reflected in 1985, "but I do wish I could go back in time and live in that era [the early 20th century]. I know real-life traveling can never achieve that, but I want to wander with time turned back at least in my heart. I don't want to live in the present."[58]

While Tsuge's travel manga can be seen as the stirrings of an indigenous form of "comics journalism" in Japan, the artist never pretended that his stories were reportage. Over the years, he has been open about his source materials, about the fictiveness of his first-person narratives, and about how he selectively shaped observed facts to fit pre-designed stories. "Ultimately, I like telling lies," Tsuge explained about his manga in an interview for a film magazine in 1973. "I feel best about a work when I've successfully drawn a lie with it. I make images out of lies pretty often."[59]

At the same time, he was not interested in pure fantasy. He insisted on the importance of lived and objective reality as a counterpoint in the creation of realistic fiction. When asked in the same discussion about composing landscapes, he replied that he felt a strong resistance to adding elements to reference photographs he took on his travels in order to make them more picturesque.

lous number of dogs around, maybe to keep each other company when the area is buried under snow.[53] Aizu became one of the areas Tsuge frequented most over the years, with subsequent trips in 1970, 1973, and 1976. The region offered two of his favorite things, thatched roofs and hot springs, in impressive supply.[54]

Thanks to ardent Tsuge fans and hot spring afficianados, the Yunokoya Inn, where "Futamata Gorge" is set, still exists, though for the longest time was in a state of horrible disrepair. Tsuge's composite visual construction of it and the surrounding landscape provides an interesting case study of how the vaunted "realism" of Tsuge's travel manga was actually a mix of fact and fiction—of the seen, found, and imagined. Photographs taken by Takano in the mid '90s, as well as various snapshots online by recent visitors, show that Tsuge's drawing of the exterior of the bathhouse, adorned with calligraphy explaining the origins of the inn's name, are true to fact (page 154, panel 3).[55] Judging from a photo taken by Tsuge on the trip (with his brother Tadao's camera, which he then broke), the narrow bridge to the bath (pages 155 and 159) is roughly based on the actual set-up. The Yunokoya does not appear to have had a thatched roof, despite how it's depicted from the road on page 153. That iconic panel is actually a copy of a photograph of a farmhouse from a different part of Japan in a book that Mizuki frequently appropriated from, Chūji Kawashima's *A Tour of Japanese Farmhouses* (*Minka no tabi*, 1963).[56]

Thatched tops did crown other establishments in Futamata, with even more impressive

Farmhouse in Chichibu, from Chōji Kawashima, *A Tour of Japanese Farmhouses* (Jinbutsu Ōraisha, 1963)

night in a sauna. I sweated profusely, started feeling a bit dizzy, and thought I might throw up."[50]

After Hachimantai, Tsuge headed south, stopping at various hot springs along the mountainous backbone that runs down the center of Honshū—but bathing at none because he was still feeling ill. By the time he reached the Aizu region of western Fukushima prefecture, he felt better. He detrained at Yunokami, took a bus to Iwase Yumoto, and from there hiked to Futamata Gorge.

> Through the window of the bus between Yunokami and Iwase Yumoto, I could see, perched on the cliffs of the Tsurunuma River, a collection of five or six miserable-looking houses, almost like animal barns, soaked in the rain. I can recall suddenly wanting to be embraced and nestled by those ramshackle houses. I wanted to curl up in front of the warmness they exuded. I still don't know why that scene moved me so.[51]

Like the narrator in "Futamata Gorge," Tsuge had read a book about monkeys just prior to his trip, and already had that part of the story sketched out. "Once I started drawing travel manga, I wanted to learn more about the natural world," so he began reading a wide assortment of texts about animals and the natural environment.[52] Most of the other details of the manga derive from his trip, including the fact that the area was hit by a typhoon while he was there.

> I got off at Yumoto and walked into the mountains to Futamata hot springs. There were five inns along the gorge, all of which allowed you to prepare your own food. I broke my camera. Yunokoya Inn looked the most forlorn, so I decided to stay there. An old man and his wife run the place by themselves. Between November and April, they close up and relocate to Yumoto. You can catch char in the river, but fishing is banned this time of year because it's spawning season. There's a ridicu-

Yunokoya Inn, Fukushima prefecture. Photograph by Tsuge, November 1967

Fukenoyu hot springs, Akita prefecture. Photograph by Tsuge, October 1967

The cards, the singing, the fighting, and even the shaving mishap are all apparently based on actual incidents at his apartment and the local public bathhouse.[48]

Other details of the manga seem to be faithful to things Tsuge actually witnessed on his trip. This is how Fukenoyu is described in a travel essay he published in 1977, based on his diary.

> Fukenoyu really does feel like it is at the end of the road that leads to the end of the Earth. Seeing frail old people wrapped up in blankets and lying on top of straw mats like that gives the distinct impression of human life at the end of its journey. Mats and blankets for sleeping cost 20 yen apiece to rent. The mats get soaked through by the steam puffing up from the ground. A group of tourists peered in the shack, made oinking noises, saying, 'Yuck, look at those pigs,' laughed, sang loudly, then left. In the corner of the same structure, there's a place for the young woman who works in the cafeteria to sleep. To provide her some privacy, a rope is strung across the space to hang blankets and clothes from. Through a crack, however, I caught a glimpse of her undressing fully before getting into bed. Everyone does the same, as you'll sweat through your underclothes and catch a cold otherwise. I wonder if she came to work here from elsewhere in the countryside. There's a small mirror stand, too.[49]

Tsuge had planned to visit other cauldrons in the Hachimantai area, but abandoned the idea due to "bathing heat exhaustion" (*yu-atari*). "The sulfur smell of the spouting steam was strong where I stayed. It was like spending the whole

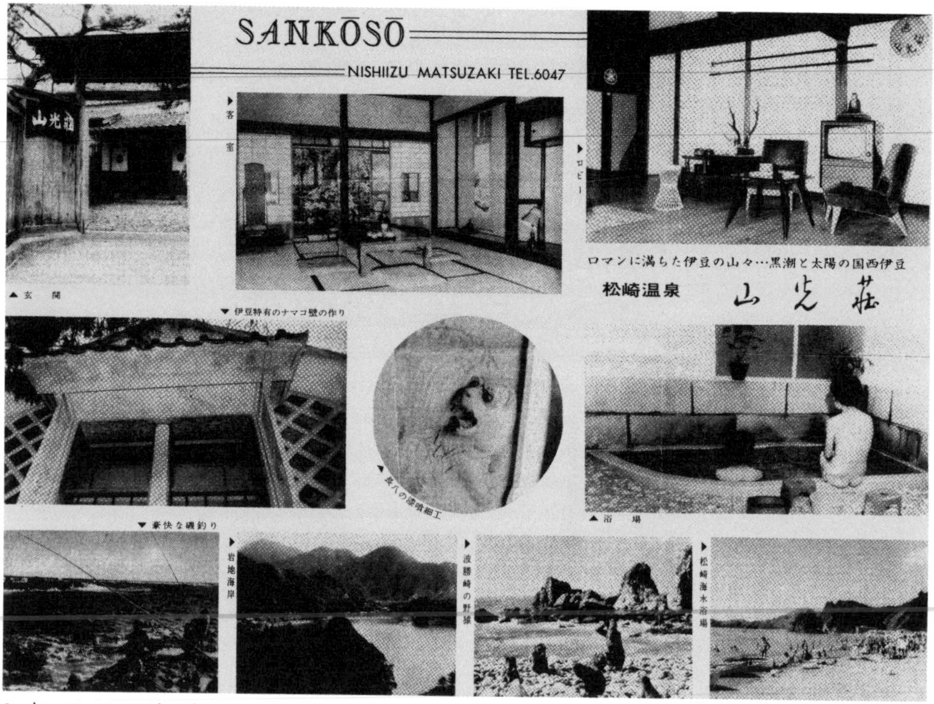
SANKŌSŌ
NISHIIZU MATSUZAKI TEL.6047
山光荘
玄関
客室
ロビー
ロマンに満ちた伊豆の山々…黒潮と太陽の国西伊豆
松崎温泉
山光荘
伊豆特有のナマコ壁の作り
長八の漆喰細工
浴場
豪快な磯釣り
岩地海岸
波勝崎の野猿
松崎海水浴場

Sankōsō Inn tourist brochure; courtesy Sankōsō Inn, Matsuzaki

der of his actual itinerary. "The Mokkiriya Tavern Girl" ("Mokkiriya no shōjo," August 1968), to be included in volume three, was also inspired by this trip. Not only was this Tsuge's first trip alone, it was also his first trip to Tōhoku, the northern hinterland of Honshū (the main island of the Japanese archipelago), a region that was regularly romanticized by artists of all mediums in the postwar period.

In a detailed "travel chronology" Tsuge composed in 1991, he recalled the transformative nature of this trip. Characteristically, the impetus was a photograph:

> In an old travel book, I saw a photograph of a *tōjiba* [extended-stay hot spring facility] in Tōhoku. I was shocked by how miserable and impoverished everything looked. I remember feeling a shudder in my chest, as if something deep inside me had been shaken. Unable to stay still, I departed on my travels.
>
> At Fukenoyu hot springs on the Hachimantai Plateau, I stayed in a shabby dorm akin to a horse shed. I felt a deep peace come over me, like I had fallen to the status of a wandering beggar, like I had been abandoned by the world. It was from that point that I became attracted to dilapidated lodgings. That self-negation underlay this feeling, that it signified liberation from the self, wasn't something I realized until many years later.[47]

That said, "The Ondol Shack" strikes an ironic tone when it comes to wanderlust and mendicant pretentions. Like *The Man Without Talent* years later, such romantic ideals are presented in the manga only to be deflated. The three obnoxious ruffians who destroy the traveler's mood were, in fact, not outsiders to Tsuge's world; they were inspired by teenagers he knew from his apartment building in slummy Kinshichō, prior to joining Mizuki Pro. "I was like that, too, back then," he admitted in 1991.

Nishibeta Village." Though Tsuge has a reputation for being unprolific, he was churning out quality stories almost monthly at this point, which is all the more impressive considering that he was also working full-time for Mizuki Pro and taking frequent trips into the countryside.

The inn in the manga actually exists. Its real name is the Sankōsō, and it is still in business today. It ranks high as a pilgrimage stop among Tsuge fans tracing the artist's footsteps, so much so that you often have to book the room in which he stayed well in advance. The detailed plaster reliefs by artist Chōhachi Irie (1815–89) still decorate the building's pillars and shutters. Nearby, there is an entire museum dedicated to Chōhachi's work. While Gramps's story of being stranded in Izu by a sea storm was inspired by a personal tale the artist's own fisherman stepgrandfather once told him, none of the other characters are based on real people—unless figures in a photograph count.[45]

Tsuge at the Sankōsō Inn, August 1967. First published in Tatsumi's *Gekiga College* (Hiro Shobō, January 1968)

Here is Tsuge in late 1968: "I've drawn a number of travel manga, but usually I already have the story thought out before going on a trip. 'Chōhachi Inn' is the only real exception. I ended up staying there [at the Sankōsō] purely by chance. One of the photographs in the pamphlet they gave me showed a woman naked [from behind] in the bathing area. She was actually one of the help. I spent the whole day looking at the pamphlet, wondering how she ended up at the inn and why she posed for that photo. That's how I came up with the story!"[46] A few of the brochure images in the manga are copied from this pamphlet.

Though the Sankōsō has since updated its brochure (and removed the nudes), it continues to distribute xerox copies of the old version to guests upon request. They also have Tsuge's manga and promotional articles about Tsuge and the inn displayed in the reception area. While many regional towns have attempted to exploit popular manga related to their locales in order to attract tourists—usually through small museums or kitschy bronze statues of manga characters on the street—the Sankōsō instead offers a case in which a work of manga has contributed materially to the historical preservation of important cultural properties by guaranteeing a stream of paying guests.

"FUTAMATA GORGE"
"Futamata keikoku," *Garo* (February 1968), signed November 1967

"THE ONDOL SHACK"
"Ondoru koya," *Garo* (April 1968), signed January 1968

In October 1967, immediately after finishing "Chōhachi Inn," Tsuge headed north, minus Tateishi, going further from Tokyo than he ever had before. Traveling by train, bus, and foot, he started in the volcanic highlands of Akita and worked his way back through Yamagata and western Fukushima. The result was not one, but two works based on what he saw, drawn in quick succession after his return, though in reverse or-half nonsense," said the artist in 1971, "we're talking about manga, so pretty much anything goes. That's why I just mixed together standard Japanese and rural dialect however I wanted."[42] Sounds like a license for liberal translation! "A new kind of literature," yes. Untranslatable poetry, no.

"THE INCIDENT AT NISHIBETA VILLAGE"

"Nishibeta mura jiken," *Garo* (December 1967), signed September 25, 1967

Nishibeta is an actual place. It's a short walk along the Isumi River from the Suehiro Inn in Ōtaki, where Tsuge first stayed with Shirato in 1965 and again with Tateishi a few months before this manga was drawn. Some of the manga's details derive from things he saw and did during his stays. "Nishibeta village is located on the opposite side of the Isumi River from the inn. There's even a mental hospital there. I went fishing near Nishibeta with Shirato pretty much every day. The part about the young man from the hospital getting his leg stuck in one of the holes left behind by dam construction was inspired by Shirato stepping into one, though he managed to pull his foot out. I made up the part about his foot tickled by the fish."[43] "My colleague S" on page 105 refers to Shirato.

In the original Japanese version, the villagers' dialogue follows regional dialect in that part of Chiba prefecture. That plus the villagers' humorous repartee and slapstick shenanigans—the whole rural comic atmosphere of the story, in fact—speaks to the magnitude of Ibuse's influence on Tsuge. The attention Tsuge pays to the lushness of the environment and the joshing affection he expresses for country folk reaffirms just how inspiring his time at Ōtaki had been. Though Tsuge had incorporated scenery and experiences from his travels before, the detailed realism of how they are presented here marks an important step toward the true dawning of Tsuge's "travel manga."

That does not mean, however, that his details are necessarily factual. Like other popular manga artists, Tsuge slightly edited his work (both the drawings and the dialogue) when it was issued in new editions over the years. While, for the most part, the present English edition follows the original *Garo* versions of these stories, there are instances in which it follows later revisions. For example, when "Nishibeta Village" was reissued in one of the first pocket paperback editions of Tsuge's work by Shōgakukan in 1976, the text in the second panel was changed to what you find on page 104. The original version read as follows: "Since locals refer to Nishibeta as a hamlet (*buraku*) even today, it probably originated as an outcast (*burakumin*) settlement long ago."

To our knowledge, there has never been an outcast community in the Ōtaki area, so Tsuge's original description is probably, first of all, inaccurate. It likely stems instead from a problematic stereotype: the association of the pariah community known as the burakumin—outcast because of their historical ties to "polluted" trades like the disposal of livestock carcasses, animal slaughter, and leatherwork—with mental illness and violent behavior, here represented by the hospital and the fugitive patient. Buraku organizations were vigilant and militant in these years, regularly confronting publishers, even manga publishers, about content they found offensive. Considering, too, that Tsuge's work was closely followed by Shirato, whose *The Legend of Kamuy* (*Kamui-den*, 1964–71), the pillar manga of early *Garo*, dealt in detail with buraku discrimination, it is somewhat surprising that "Nishibeta Village" was reprinted multiple times in various venues before this edit was made in the mid '70s, by which point most authors and publishers erred on the side of not talking about buraku issues at all.[44]

"CHŌHACHI INN"

"Chōhachi no yado," *Garo* (January 1968), signed October 1967

This story is based on a road trip to the Izu Peninsula that Tsuge made with Tateishi in August 1967, just prior to drawing "The Incident at

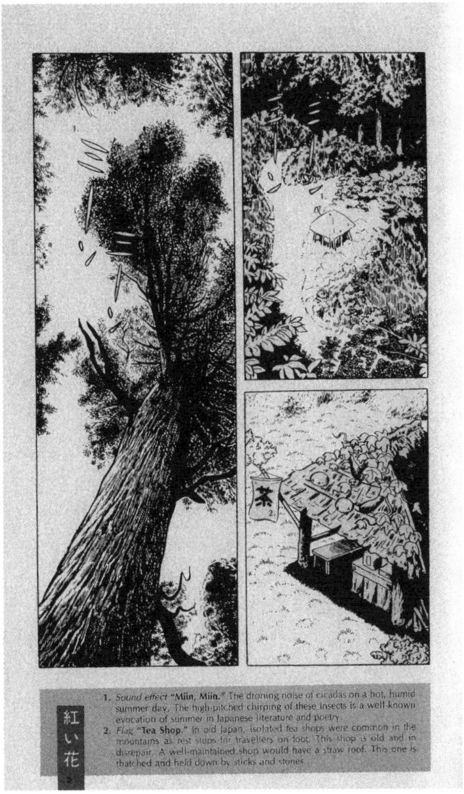
1. *Sound effect* **"Miin, Miin."** The droning noise of cicadas on a hot, humid summer day. The high-pitched chirping of these insects is a well-known evocation of summer in Japanese literature and poetry.
2. *Flag* **"Tea Shop."** In old Japan, isolated tea shops were common in the mountains as rest stops for travellers on foot. This shop is old and in disrepair. A well-maintained shop would have a straw roof. This one is thatched and held down by sticks and stones.
紅い花
2
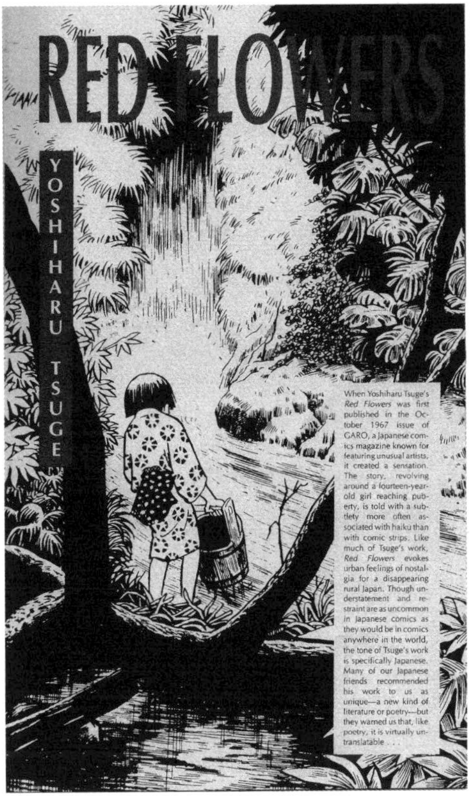
RED FLOWERS
YOSHIHARU TSUGE
When Yoshiharu Tsuge's *Red Flowers* was first published in the October 1967 issue of GARO, a Japanese comics magazine known for featuring unusual artists, it created a sensation. The story, revolving around a fourteen-year-old girl reaching puberty, is told with a subtlety more often associated with haiku than with comic strips. Like much of Tsuge's work, *Red Flowers* evokes urban feelings of nostalgia for a disappearing rural Japan. Though understatement and restraint are as uncommon in Japanese comics as they would be in comics anywhere in the world, the tone of Tsuge's work is specifically Japanese. Many of our Japanese friends recommended his work to us as unique—a new kind of literature or poetry—but they warned us that, like poetry, it is virtually untranslatable . . .

Tsuge, "Red Flowers," *Raw* no. 7 (1985), insert pamphlet

Kamimura (just to name the most obvious) all ultimately spring from this story.

On a side note, "Red Flowers" may also be the story most responsible for Tsuge not being translated until recently. One of the main reasons the artist resisted foreign editions of his work for so long was his belief that it was nigh impossible to convey the nuances of rural Japanese dialect into another language. This concern is reflected in one of the earliest editions of Tsuge's work in English, Akira Satake, Paul Karasik, and Art Spiegelman's group translation of "Red Flowers" for *Raw* no. 7 (1985), printed as an insert pamphlet. "The story, revolving around a fourteen-year-old girl reaching puberty, is told with a subtlety more often associated with haiku than with comic strips," goes the foreword, written primarily by Spiegelman. "Though understatement and restraint are as uncommon in Japanese comics as they would be in comics anywhere in the world, the tone of Tsuge's work is specifically Japanese. Many of our Japanese friends recommended his work to us as unique—a new kind of literature or poetry—but they warned us that, like poetry, it is virtually untranslatable..."[41] To this end, extensive notes are included at the bottom of each page, explaining different cicada cries, the details of the refreshment stand, and the like.

The Japanese of this manga, however, is not particularly complicated. Tsuge's country dialogue was, like Ibuse's, at least half invention, and was consciously simplified so as to be more legible for common Japanese readers, most of whom, like Tsuge, were city folk. Moreover: "Even if it's moods inspired by literary sources, snippets of made-up rural dialect, and fragmentary impressions of places he visited and people he came across, all woven into a story of his own creation, while also employing the mysterious eroticism and allusive panel breakdowns that made "The Swamp" such a watershed work.

Numerous elements of "Red Flowers" are indebted to Osamu Dazai (1909–48), an author Tsuge had been reading since 1958, at the recommendation of an acquaintance during a leisure outing to Kōfu.[37] Dazai, who committed suicide by drowning in 1948 (after multiple failed attempts in the '20s and '30s), is remembered most as an author who lived the life of bohemian decadence and alcoholic and drug-addicted desperation that he also often wrote about, especially after the war. But here, Tsuge has pulled from a different Dazai: the fantasist who reworked old fables and folktales into dark modern stories. The source is specifically one of Dazai's earliest pieces, "The Girl who Turned into a Fish" ("Gyōfukuki," 1933)—which is, interestingly, actually a retelling of an episode in *Strange Tales from a Chinese Studio*, a chapter of which inspired "The Wake." Tsuge's reinterpretation of such material (whether directly or second-hand) thus stands as an established practice with a respected lineage in modern Japanese literature.

As in "Red Flowers," one finds in Dazai's story a male traveler from the city, bewitched fishermen, a picturesque mountain landscape, a scenic pool at the base of a waterfall, and a refreshment stand run by an adolescent girl (named Suwa in Dazai), around whose coming-of-age the tale is constructed. Tsuge seems to have even appropriated specific passages. For example: "If she caught even a glimpse of any sightseers, Suwa would call out the greeting her father had taught her—'Hello! Please stop a while.'" Or: "When it rained, Suwa would crawl under a straw mat in the corner and take a nap. A large oak grew out over the tea stand, its abundant leaves providing shelter from the rain"—though the actual drawing of the towering oak (page 86) was copied from a photograph in a collection of Bokusui Wakayama's (1885–1928) poetry about travel and drink.[38]

In Dazai, the girl, after being raped by her drunk father one night, flees to the pool and turns into a fish. The story ends with her sucked down into the falls' swirling waters, like the blooms in Tsuge's manga. No sexual relationship is implied between Sayoko and her errant father in "Red Flowers," which ends at the "flowering" of the girl's womanhood. The tension between the girl and her jealous brother-in-law in "The Swamp," however, might have been informed by this part of Dazai's story.[39]

Ibuse's influence is also evident. Though this is not readily apparent in translation, the traveler in "Red Flowers" speaks standard Japanese while the girl and the boy, Masaji, speak in a rural dialect—or more precisely, a *mock* rural dialect. Effectively using different speech patterns to mark characters' social status and create innuendos and slippages between them was something Ibuse was known for. Sayoko's name comes from Ibuse's "On Words" (also a source for "The Swamp"), as does the fact that she has to skip school to supervise the refreshment stand (in Ibuse, it's an inn), and probably the Masaji character (in Ibuse, the boy wears a military-inspired school cap and carries a bugle). The girl's cries of menstrual pains, meanwhile, were inspired by the words of a young female bus attendant staying in the room next to Tsuge's at the Suehiro Inn on a subsequent trip to Ōtaki with Tateishi in April 1967. Tsuge thought he overheard her complaining about abdominal cramps (*hara ga tsupparu*, literally "my belly is stretched to bursting"), whereas she was actually saying she was irritated because her socks were ripped (*ei hara ga tatsu! tsuppatte*, "I'm so mad [literally, "my stomach is upset"]! They're busted")—a most pedestrian origin for a most influential metaphoric figure.[40] Red blooms and red other poetical vehicles in the manga of Hayashi, Katsumata, and Kazuo

Push Man and *Abandon the Old in Tokyo.* You will notice that, while many of his stories feature characters and settings similar to those in Tsuge's *Garo* work, Tatsumi still abides by the conventional dramatic principles of *kishōtenketsu*, with a clear "beginning, development, twist, and ending." Many of the stories here in *Red Flowers*, like some of those in *The Swamp*, instead end without a clear conclusion, allowing the reader greater interpretative freedom. This paved the way for the truly enigmatic works to be included in *Nejishiki*, volume three of this series. It also became a defining feature of the "*Garo*-esque" in manga, and in short-form gekiga in particular, for many years. Seiichi Hayashi, Tsurita, Tadao Tsuge, Susumu Katsumata, Shin'ichi Abe, Ōji Suzuki—in fact, almost all of the artists associated with early *Garo* except Shirato and Mizuki—experimented with elliptical, tableaux-esque last pages in the wake of Tsuge.

"SCENES FROM THE SEASIDE"
"Umibe no jokei," *Garo* (September 1967), signed June 30, 1967

Take the train two hours east from Tokyo, to the eastern side of the Bōsō Peninsula in Chiba prefecture. Get off at Ōhara station, and walk fifteen minutes to the ocean. You will have arrived at where this story is set: Ōhara Beach in the town of Isumi—though where the beach is now is north of where it used to be.

From the ages of four to five, Tsuge lived in Ōhara with his mother and his two brothers, while his father worked as a cook at an elite restaurant in Tokyo. The scenery depicted in this manga was a stone's throw from their house. The high promontory from which the fisherman loses his catch is called Hachiman Cape, named after the Hachiman Shrine (dedicated to the Shinto god of war) on its landward side. The sweetened, red algae snack the young man and woman share in the rain, known as *tokoroten*, is a local specialty that Tsuge had eaten numerous times as a kid, and again on a trip with his mother to visit family

around 1965.[34] Even the male lead's boasting that he's a strong swimmer derives from the artist's life. "Though I've never really been into sports, I am a pretty good swimmer," Tsuge stated in 1991. "Good enough, in fact, that I could probably coach kids! When I was young, I even used to swim in the rivers of the working class parts of Tokyo."[35]

The romantic element, on the other hand, is completely invented. When Tsuge drew "Scenes from the Seaside," he was not only single, but also profoundly lonely. After being dumped by his live-in girlfriend in 1961 (experiences of which informed "Chirpy"), Tsuge was utterly heartbroken. It was one of the reasons he attempted suicide the following year. He would not have another serious relationship until he met his future wife, actress Maki Fujiwara (1941–99), in 1969. "Scenes from the Seaside" is thus a highly personal work informed by multiple strains of nostalgia and longing. That notwithstanding, some of the beach scenery is sourced from photos in issues of *Asahi Camera* and other photography magazines, most likely from the scrapbooks housed at Mizuki Pro—none of which depict Ōhara.[36] This foregrounding of the concrete and personal to subsume the found and invented would become a core feature of Tsuge's realism, more about which below.

"RED FLOWERS"
"Akai hana," *Garo* (October 1967), signed July 28, 1967

Tsuge is much celebrated for his travel stories (*tabimono*), the earliest of which are collected in the present volume. Though "The Swamp" was inspired by his time in Ōtaki, it evokes the countryside in only broad strokes. "Red Flowers" is likewise not set in any specific locale. But by this point, Tsuge was taking trips into the countryside practically every month, usually with his friend Tateishi—the influence of which is palpable in the care with which this story, one of Tsuge's most famous, was put together.

A harbinger of the true travel stories to come, "Red Flowers" blends various elements Tsuge had been experimenting with previously: motifs and detail about Tsuge's relationship to Zainichi Koreans (people of Korean descent who live in Japan). Suffice to say, having grown up in the working class slums of Tokyo, he had lived around Koreans pretty much his whole life. He had Korean friends, Korean bosses, and a Korean roommate. So, however one feels about "The Lee Family," it is important to remember that it comes from an ally's perspective. In 1981, Tsuge would detail the abject living conditions and vulnerability of the Korean squatter settlement along the Tamagawa River in Chōfu in his story "Neighborhood Scenery" ("Kinjo no keshiki"). In the present volume, even "The Ondol Shack" might be said to have a Zainichi subtext, with its careful description of a type of sauna modeled on traditional Korean technology.

In its time, "The Lee Family" was most famous, however, because of its last page. Part of the reason the story closes in the open-ended way that it does is that Tsuge intended to write a sequel. Alas, it would be more than two years before he actually drew one, in the form of "The Crab" ("Kani") for *Manga Story* (January 1970). Meanwhile, a number of artists were so seduced by "The Lee Family" that they spontaneously drew their own parodic sequels, among them fellow *Garo* contributors Kuniko Tsurita and Genpei Akasegawa.[32] This speaks to the charming nature of Tsuge's characters and scenarios, but also to the power of the hanging endings he had been actively experimenting with since "The Swamp," if not earlier with kashihon stories like "Ghost Chimneys" ("Obake entotsu," 1958). Knowing that he had hit on something new, Tsuge was planning on writing a theory of comics storytelling around the time of "The Lee Family," but sadly never carried through with the idea.[33]

For contrast, look at Yoshihiro Tatsumi's work from this period, in D&Q collections like

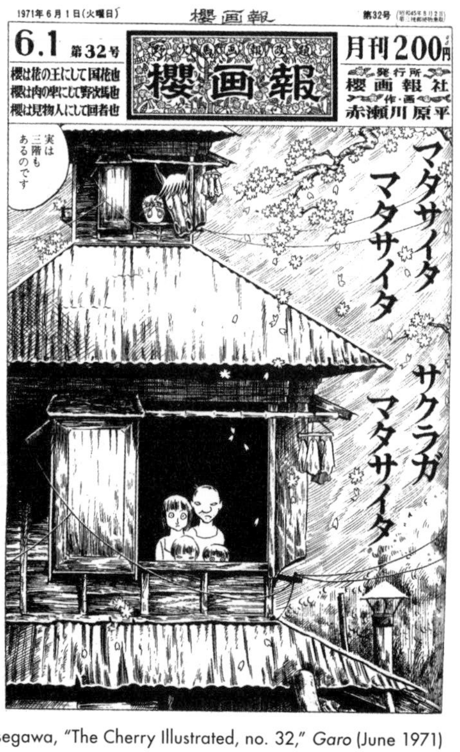
1971年6月1日(火曜日)
櫻画報
第32号
6.1 第32号
櫻は花の王にして国花也
櫻画報
月刊200円
発行所
櫻画報社
作・画
赤瀬川原平
実は三階もあるのです
マタサイタ
マタサイタ
サクラガ
マタサイタ

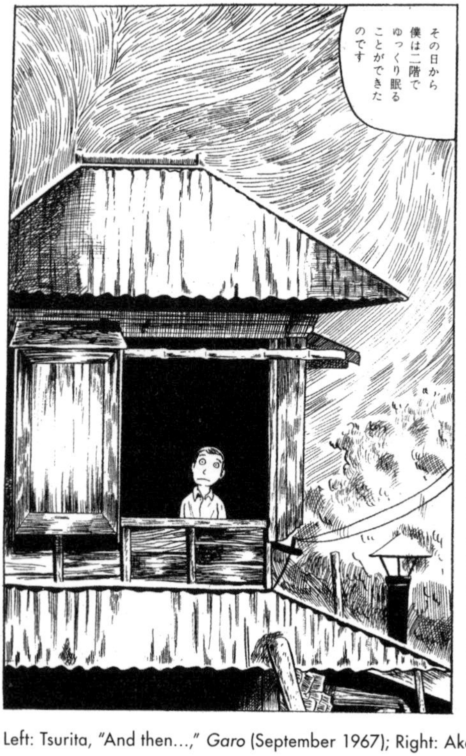
その日から僕は二階でゆっくり眠ることができたのです

Left: Tsurita, "And then...," *Garo* (September 1967); Right: Akasegawa, "The Cherry Illustrated, no. 32," *Garo* (June 1971)

theme of self-marginalized and rootless men. As Tsuge explained on the occasion of the first book edition of *The Man Without Talent* in 1989, both stories were directly inspired by Karaki's text.

What moved me most about the book was the part about a monk named Kyōshin [786–886], who Karaki presents as one of the progenitors of useless men. One day, Kyōshin simply disappeared. Stories about him come up often in various classical texts. For example, that after vanishing, he married and had a kid, or lived as a farmhand, or pretended that he was a coolie while quietly chanting the Buddha's name, or took to begging. He died curled up in the corner of his garden, letting dogs feast on his corpse. His family, unable to afford a proper funeral, could only look on and weep... Also well known is the story of Chōzō, a monk from Mount Hiei who gave up his high position at the temple and vanished into thin air. Years later, someone finally discovered him living as a beggar. They tried to drag him to the temple, but he broke free and disappeared again, eventually dying while praying westward [toward the Buddhist Pure Land] deep in the mountains somewhere. The bit about the monk dying at Prayer Pass in 'The Dog from Prayer Pass' comes from that. It's a playful reference to Chōzō.[28]

Over time, travel for Tsuge became less about simply enjoying the rusticity of rural Japan and more about escaping one's daily life and personal anxieties—about escaping the self. Thus, while the traveling merchant in "The Dog from Prayer Pass" clearly reflects Tsuge's own increasing peregrinations, it is significant that the manga's titular subject is instead the dog: a worthless, pitiable soul whose migrant identity is defined by where he happens to lodge himself at any point in time.

In Karaki's *Men of No Use*, there are many stories about monks, aristocrats, and merchants rejecting lives of comfort for the path of pauperism. Among them is the inspiration behind Mister Lee of "The Lee Family": a character from Saikaku Ihara's *Parting Gifts* (*Okimiyage*, 1693), a series of comic short stories about playboys who waste their fortunes on booze and women, by one of the most popular authors of the Edo period. It was specifically the story titled "Mosquito Grubs" ("Bōfura," which also means "worthless person" in Japanese) that stirred Tsuge's imagination.[29] There, the fallen rake has been reduced to digging up and selling mosquito larvae as food to goldfish sellers in Ueno. When old friends spot him in this sad station, he is overjoyed, buys what little sake he can afford, and invites them to his home to reminisce about the good old days. Waiting at his "shack" of a home are his wife (the former courtesan responsible for his fall) and their little boy. "Papa's come back with the money!" the child cries through the window, upon spotting his father approaching across the overgrown farm plot that separates their house from the street. They heat their house with chopped-up Buddhist altar doors—a terrible taboo—while their child lies shivering naked under a patchwork quilt. Upon leaving, his friends try to slip him money, but he throws it back at them with the full force of undiminished pride.[30]

There are a number of similarities between the two stories: morning glories in the garden, a pitiful child (two in "The Lee Family"), a sensual wife, a derelict abode, a need to trespass through unkempt property to get there. But the most curious is Tsuge's decision to interpret Saikaku's dissipated but good-natured "human grub" as Korean. "There's this common image of Koreans as not being able to get jobs because they're Korean, of always bumming around (*furōsha*)," Tsuge explained in 1993. "Unlike the larvae-seller [in Saikaku], however, they don't choose to drop out of society on their own accord. They are pushed out, they are forcibly cut off from society. Having your existence negated like that is trying, but it can also be liberating. It's probably similar to the self-abandonment (*jiko hōge*) they talk about in religion."[31] There is no space here to go into mimeographed literary magazine titled *Grass* (*Kusa*) with other members of Akame Pro. He had previously been an editor at Sanyōsha, the kashihon publisher run by Nagai before he founded Seirindō, which published a number of important Shirato, Mizuki, and Tsuge titles between 1959 and 1962. Iwasaki was, in other words, well-positioned to guide Tsuge on his transition from genre-based kashihon gekiga to something more aligned with "high literature." Other artists associated with *Garo*, like Ikegami, Kuniko Tsurita, and Shōhei Kusunoki (who worked at Akame Pro and contributed to *Grass*), would soon aspire to the same.[25]

It is also important to think about how Tsuge's work from this period relates to the identity of *Garo* as a new breed of manga magazine. "The Salamander," for example, is about a creature that lives in the sewer, cut off from society. Shirato's ninjas and poor peasants, like Mizuki's yōkai, are outsiders who move about in society's margins. We might even call them "underground," and their existence and community "alternative." That is precisely the territory Shirato sought to occupy and develop for *Garo*, both in terms of subject matter and artistic techniques. As visionary an editor as he was an artist, Shirato pushed for Mizuki and Tsuge's inclusion not only because he recognized their talents and promise (neither were stars when he brought them aboard), but also how each could contribute in his own idiosyncratic way to the creation of a strong and rounded "alternative" within manga and society. Like the creature in "The Salamander," the artists and readers of early *Garo* found in that subterranean realm new currents of existing and creating—which proved to be so powerful that more and more people were drawn into *Garo*'s dark but magical cave.

"THE LEE FAMILY"

"Li san ikka," *Garo* (June 1967), signed March 27, 1967

"THE DOG FROM PRAYER PASS"

"Tōge no inu," *Garo* (August 1967), signed May 30, 1967

"Life has always been hard for me. For as long as I remember, I've never felt comfortable with the world around me, which has always made me anxious about who I am. Most people find ways to adapt, right? That I am incapable of doing so makes me worry about myself, about whether there might be something wrong with me. I've lived with that feeling of instability my whole life." So wrote Tsuge in 1991, a middle-aged man of fifty-four.[26]

Readers of *The Man Without Talent*, a semi-autobiographical graphic novel about a cartoonist whose psychological inability to draw and obsession with frivolous pursuits nearly sinks his family, should be familiar with the centrality of these sentiments within the life and legend of Yoshiharu Tsuge.[27] The artist suffered from acute social phobias since childhood. In 1962, beset by poverty, self-doubt, and heartbreak, he attempted suicide. His first years at Mizuki Pro were among his most stable, and the comics he drew while there eventually assured him lifelong solvency. But even at the height of his success, Tsuge remained attuned to the fragility of his own existence. By late 1968 (not long after the timeframe covered by the present volume), he started disappearing for weeks at a time.

Yet, there is also an artistic element to Tsuge's expressions of alienation, and this, too, was strongly shaped by the books he read while at Mizuki Pro. Most important here is a scholarly work, Junzō Karaki's *A Lineage of Men of No Use* (*Muyōmono no keifu*, 1960), a survey of tropes of exile and self-abnegation in Japanese literature from the Heian to Edo periods, by an author best known for his writings about the centrality of the Buddhist idea of *mujō* (impermanence) within Japanese culture. Without Karaki's *Men of No Use*, there would be no *The Man Without Talent*. There might not even be a "Yoshiharu Tsuge"—that is, the mercurial, ethereal, dropout persona through which the artist is primarily known and marketed.

"The Lee Family" and "The Dog from Prayer Pass" are the first of Tsuge's many stories on the fix what the work is about...I wasn't comfortable with that. I wanted to allow readers to read the work freely."[23]

While the sewer setting and dialogue is original, "The Salamander" borrows many core features (including its title) from one of the best-known and influential short stories in the history of modern Japanese literature: Masuji Ibuse's (1898–1993) "Salamander" (1929), about a giant salamander (*Andrias japonicus*) stuck inside a riverine cave and philosophizing about his predicament. Readers may recognize Ibuse's name as the author of *Black Rain* (*Kuroi ame*, 1965–66), probably the world's most famous novel about Hiroshima in the aftermath of the atomic bombing. He was also one of the central figures in the development of the short story form in Japan in the '20s and '30s, working through the influences of Tolstoy, Dostoevsky, and especially Chekhov. In fact, his "Salamander" was inspired by Chekhov's "The Bet" (1889), about a young man who spends fifteen years in solitary confinement to win a bet. By the late '30s, Ibuse was lauded for his sensitive depictions of rural Japanese life, enlivened with folksy humor and snappy dialogue. He also wrote pithy travelogues, think pieces on rural life and dialect, and even tracts about fishing—all of which seem "Tsuge-esque" in retrospect.

Tsuge's interest in Ibuse predates his joining Mizuki Pro. As described in *The Swamp*, in August 1965, Tsuge was invited by Shirato to spend time with him and members of his studio, Akame Pro, in Ōtaki, in the hills of Chiba prefecture. The verdant surroundings made such an impression on the city boy that he began drawing with a new vigor, and with a new attention to rural settings. "The Swamp," about a hunter who encounters an exotic young woman in the hills, was the first direct product of this experience. That groundbreaking story, which otherwise represents an evolution of gekiga mystery and samurai rōnin tropes, is also the first by Tsuge to borrow directly from Ibuse. Parts of the girl's speech and her

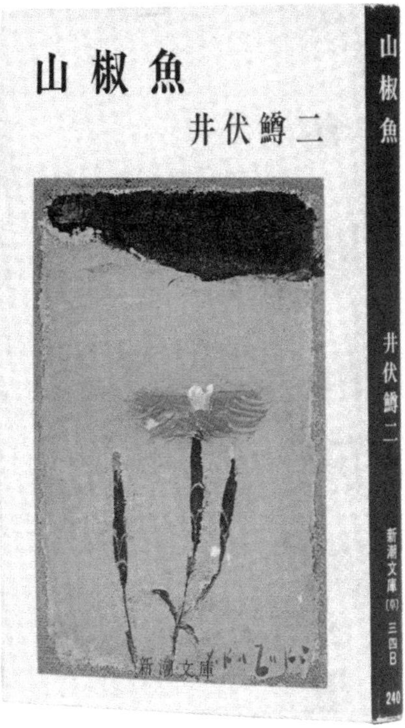
山椒魚
井伏鱒二
山椒魚
井伏鱒二
新潮文庫
240

Masuji Ibuse, *Salamander* (Shinchōsha, 1953)

abrupt invitation to spend the night were adapted from a travel essay by Ibuse focusing on rural dialect, "On Words" ("Kotoba ni tsuite," 1933), while the introductory image of the shot bird derives from Ibuse's story "Sawan on the Roof" ("Yane no ue no sawan," 1929), as probably does the manga's central theme of entrapment and escape.[24] Both of these items, along with "Salamander," are included in the most popular paperback edition of Ibuse's short stories, *Salamander*, published by Shinchōsha in 1953. Given its impact on Tsuge, this slim volume (which remains in print) is arguably the single-most important book in the formation of literary manga.

Again, Shirato played an essential role here. It was his manager, Minoru Iwasaki (1937–n.d.), who introduced Tsuge to Ibuse's work, if not while in Ōtaki then soon after. Iwasaki was, in fact, so passionate about literature that he created a

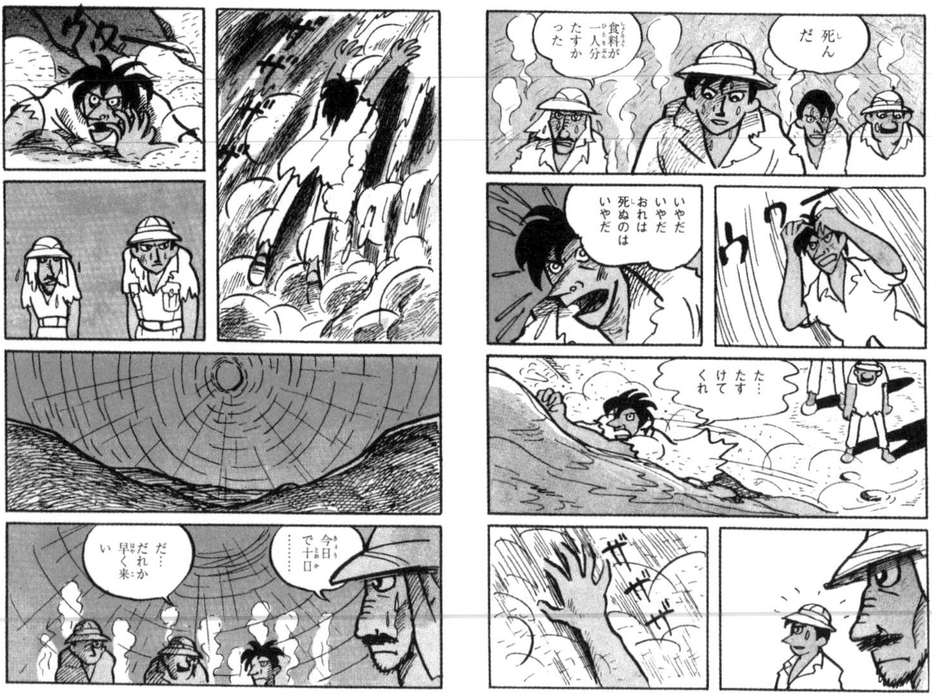

死んだ
食料が一人分たすかった
ウワー
いやだ いやだ おれは死ぬのは いやだ
た…たすけてくれ
ザザザ
ザザザ
ウワー
今日で十日……
だ…だれか早く来い

Tsuge, "Beneath the Blazing Sun," *Meiro bessatsu* (April 1960)

a number of the stories included in *The Swamp*, "Antlion Pit" is a redraw of a work Tsuge originally created for a kashihon venue: "Beneath the Blazing Sun" ("Shakunetsu no taiyō no shita ni"), published in *Meiro bessatsu* (April 1960).

It was rare for Tsuge to publish anywhere but in *Garo* at this point. This particular exception came about as a result of working at Mizuki Pro. Editors of magazines from big publishing houses frequently came knocking at Mizuki's door, to pick up promised work or commission something new. Among them was Shōnen Gahōsha, publisher of the monthly *Shōnen King*. Such visits might have been a headache for Mizuki, who was already overloaded with deadlines. But they could be a blessing for his staff, looking for lucrative assignments and break-out opportunities of their own.

Considering that *Shōnen King* paid 3,000 yen per page—versus *Garo*'s rate of 800 yen—there's little wonder why Tsuge, who had only recently pulled himself out of poverty, jumped at the opportunity. However, as Tsuge himself was too busy with Mizuki Pro duties, the inking of "Antlion Pit" was largely executed by another member of Mizuki's staff, Ryōichi Ikegami, who also helped with the backgrounds of "The Salamander."[22]

"THE SALAMANDER"

"Sanshōuo," *Garo* (May 1967), signed February 18, 1967

Traditionally, the title pages of manga feature characters in some sort of dramatic pose and/or evocative scenery, overlaid with ornately rendered titles and scintillating verbiage. In contrast, from "The Salamander" forward, Tsuge's are as simple as can be: just the story's title and the artist's name in unadorned typography. This soon became standard among *Garo*'s contributors due to Tsuge's influence. "There's no deep reason why I did that," he once explained, "except that, if you put a picture on the title page, it tends to in "The Wake"?) into the faces of three of the men, the fourth fleeing to the safety of a Buddhist temple.[18] Tsuge's story is constructed to leave open the question of whether the "corpse" is actually dead or not—turning the *qiguai* of ghosts and the undead into an irreverent modern debunking of the otherworldly and unseen.

Notice the close attention paid to architectural details like ratty thatched roofing, weathered wooden doors and walls, and tattered floor mats. Such images, clearly informed by the Mizuki Pro style, signal Tsuge's growing interest in a stereotypically "Japanese" aesthetic. "I am attracted to poor, rusticated, and forlorn landscapes, ones that look like they have been abandoned by the world, like ruins," he offered in 1998.[19] One doesn't usually think of manga as a medium with connections to *wabi-sabi*—that quintessential, Buddhism-inspired, Japanese passion for the imperfect and impermanent—but thanks to Tsuge it gradually became one, even if only in a marginal way. Mizuki's work also clings to the lonely and derelict, but typically as part of his singular investment in the haunted and phantasmagorical. For Tsuge, in contrast (though this is not yet the case with "The Wake"), these aesthetic qualities gradually become reflections of the traveler-protagonist's own sense of abandonment and mortality.

Behind this, and perhaps behind the motif of the three travelers looking for a place to stay, was Tsuge's recent awakening to the joys of travel to remote and rural places. In August 1966, he and his friend Tateishi drove to Kazuma, in the village of Hinohara, in the mountains about as far west as you can go in greater Tokyo (fifty-plus miles from the capitol) before you get to Yamanashi prefecture. It is a fairly secluded place even today, and was poorly served by public transportation back then. "We stayed at the Yamazakiya, a mountain inn with a straw-thatched roof. Mountains, gorges, a worn-down village, unassuming lodgings—it was a simple outing and we only stayed one night," recalled Tsuge in 1991. "Still, everything felt fresh and inspiring, probably also because it was my first time going

somewhere like that. I had never experienced such feelings while traveling before. It turned me on to the charm of travel, with which I have been obsessed ever since."[20] While the popular image of Tsuge is of the solitary male traveler, at this early juncture he always traveled with Tateishi, with the two reportedly goofing off and making a ruckus wherever they went, though not as boorishly as the ruffians in "The Wake."

Also in August, Tsuge and Tateishi took a trip on Tateishi's motorcycle around the Bōsō Peninsula (the east arm of Tokyo Bay) with the goal of swimming in the ocean and enjoying the summer air. But they got lost on the way, and ended up staying in a type of old traveler's inn called a *hatago*—piquing Tsuge's lifelong interest in Edo period inns and waystations. In September, they drove north with no particular destination in mind, tooling around Ishikawa prefecture, where they checked out fishing villages, temples, and promontories along the Japan Sea (East Sea), then entering the winding roads of the mountains of Gifu, stopping in Shirakawagō to see its famous "prayer hand" *gasshō-zukuri* farmhouses (so-called because of the high-pitched angles of their thatched roofs, like hands in prayer), before heading back to Tokyo via Nagano. Today, parts of this route are overrun by tourists; not so in the '60s, when domestic tourism had yet to boom and road infrastructure had yet to be overhauled by the rural construction frenzy of the '70s. At certain spots, Tsuge and Tateishi even had to push Tateshi's jalopy microcar through steeply graded tunnels and turn back because of washouts.[21] Similar such incidents supplied some of the dramatic and comedic material for Tsuge's later travel manga, where concrete, offbeat happenings (both experienced and invented) are a central node in Tsuge's distinctive brand of realism.

"ANTLION PIT"

"Ari jigoku," *Bessatsu Shōnen King* (April 1967), signed December 1966

Though this story has been placed at the end of this volume, chronologically it belongs second. Like

It was thus that "The Wake," the first story in the present volume, was created in December 1966 and published in the March 1967 issue of *Garo*. It was the artist's first new work in eleven months, since "Mushroom Hunting" the previous April. "They told me I could draw whatever I wanted, however I wanted," remembered Tsuge. "The ideas burst forth all at once. Whatever energy I'd been holding back wasn't going to be so anymore."[16]

March 1967 also marked the publication of the inaugural issue of *Manga-ism* (*Manga shugi*), a quarterly of comics criticism edited and self-published by Takano and three other writers who believed in comics as a respectable art form: art historian and critic Junzō Ishiko, film critic Asajirō Kikuchi (née Sadao Yamane), and editor and critic Jun Kajii. The first issue featured four articles about Tsuge's work; many more followed in subsequent issues. That October, Seirindō published a pamphlet titled *The World of Garo* (*Garo no sekai*), collecting articles about *Garo* artists, especially Shirato and Mizuki, from various sources, including intellectual journals and college newspapers. Positive appraisals of Tsuge's work also started appearing in the reader's column of *Garo* around this time.

Which is all to say, the year 1967 was a truly revolutionary one in manga history, marking not just Tsuge's renaissance—which would change the face of Japanese comics as we know it—but also the consolidation of manga criticism as a sustained and focused practice, likewise around Tsuge and *Garo*. Shirato had created, funded, and led *Garo* through its earliest years. But by the end of the period covered in the present volume—that is, the summer of 1968—it was becoming known more as Tsuge's magazine, thus marking the transfer of the torch of "alternative manga" from the left-wing commitments that Shirato upheld to the apolitical, literary, introspective turn pioneered by Tsuge.

Because of their paramount importance, it is worth looking at each story from this era in detail, with special attention paid to the textual and visual influences, as well as the personal experiences, that contributed to Tsuge's invention of a new kind of graphic literature.

"THE WAKE"
"Tsuya," *Garo* (March 1967), signed December 17, 1966

Between "The Swamp" and "Chirpy" being published in *Garo* in early 1966, and when Tsuge began drawing "The Wake" toward the end of that same year, the readership of *Garo* seems to have shifted from elementary and middle school to high school and college students. Since its first issue in September 1964, *Garo* had sported the words "Junior Magazine" on its cover. That disappeared with the May 1966 issue. Likewise, the use of syllabic kana glosses (*rubi*) to help young readers decipher kanji (Chinese characters) became progressively less common in 1967, until there were practically none after the May issue. "The Wake" was the last Tsuge story with *rubi* glosses in its original published version.

In a series of detailed interviews with Takano in 1993, Tsuge stated that the general "mood" of the story was inspired by his voracious consumption of classical Japanese and Chinese tales of the supernatural and strange. Among the titles he names are Japanese anthologies of short Buddhist-inspired stories like *Tales from Times Past* (*Konjaku monogatari*, mid-late twelfth century) and *A Record of Miraculous Events in Japan* (*Nihon ryōiki*, 787–824), and Pu Songling's *Strange Tales from a Chinese Studio* (*Liaozhai zhiyi*, 1740), which is filled with magical foxes, ghosts, zombies, homunculi, and other Mizuki-esque beings. Tsuge claimed that the story itself was "completely my invention."[17] However, the basic conceit and humor of "The Wake" bears a close resemblance to a chapter in Pu's frequently comical anthology, titled "The Living Dead" in Penguin's English edition. Four travelers ask to be put up for the night at a roadside tavern. They are told that the only room available is occupied by the landlord's recently deceased daughter-in-law, lying in wait until her coffin is made. At night, the corpse comes alive, breathing death (like farts in the summer of 1966, with them usually going into the countryside by car or motorcycle, and often sleeping outdoors. It was Tateishi, a bibliophile, who lent Tsuge a copy of Fujisawa's *A Survey of Yōkai Pictures and Tales*, which Tsuge then lent to Mizuki. Tateishi was also the original "man without talent" in Tsuge's life: the broke layabout who somehow thrives. When Tsuge first met him in the late '50s, he made a living from questionable commissions using his hazmat license to sign off as a guarantor for other people's businesses. Later, he opened a used bookstore, regularly ignoring customers and sleeping on the job, and inspiring the lazy bookseller, Yamai, in *The Man Without Talent* (*Munō no hito*, 1985–86).

On the more intellectual side, Mizuki's new obsession with yōkai probably inspired Tsuge to hit the books more seriously himself. He began devouring folklore collections and ethnographically-sensitive travel writing (Yanagita and Tsuneichi Miyamoto, in particular), Chinese and Japanese classics of the supernatural and bizarre, academic studies about Japanese literature and Buddhist philosophy, and encyclopedias of Japanese cultural geography. He also familiarized himself with existentialist writings by the likes of Kafka, Sartre, and Camus, though claims not to have been that interested in Western authors. This wide-ranging bibliography complemented the novelists Tsuge had been reading since before joining Mizuki Pro, most of all Masuji Ibuse and Osamu Dazai, as well as those he started reading after, like Toshio Shimao, Rinzō Shiina, and Haruo Umezaki—all of whom belong to what Japanese call "pure literature" (*junbungaku*) versus popular genre fiction (*taishū bungaku*), which Tsuge also read avidly as an author of mystery and samurai/ninja comics in the '50s and early '60s.[11] How this combination of travel and literature revolutionized Tsuge's work will be explained below.

Just as Tsuge started thinking he might as well live out his life comfortably as Mizuki's employee, *Garo* hired a new editor who, thankfully, disrupted his plans: Shinzō Takano (b. 1940), known to manga history better by his pen name, Susumu Gondō (or Shin Gondō). "I wanted to join the staff of Seirindō ... simply to have the opportunity to talk leisurely with Tsuge," recalled Takano. Bowled over by "The Swamp," "Chirpy," and "Mushroom Hunting," Takano started thinking that "comics deserved to be appreciated as an artistic medium on par with painting, literature, and music."[12] Previously, as a reporter with *Japan Reader's News* (*Nihon dokusho shinbun*), Takano had interviewed and written about Sanpei Shirato (b. 1932) and Mizuki in 1965, when it was still rare to find positive appraisals of cartoonists, especially those working in the kashihon market, anywhere in the press.[13] Shirato's *The Legend of Kagemaru* (*Ninja bugeichō*, 1959–62), published by Sanyōsha, had been heralded as a timely political masterpiece by prominent left-leaning intellectuals. But otherwise, kashihon manga, including Shirato's work, were typically denounced as violent, vulgar trash.

"If you don't hire me, I'll burn the company down," Takano told Seirindō at his interview. A few weeks later, he got a phone call. It was Nagai, Seirindō's president: "You can start on Monday." And so he did, in September 1966. At the time, Tsuge was not producing new work—only redraws of old kashihon stories for *Garo* and other venues (collected in *The Swamp*). Nonetheless, Takano had ample opportunity to meet and talk with Tsuge during visits to Mizuki Pro to fetch artwork from Mizuki, on which occasions he tried to cajole the dormant genius into tapping his own creative fount again.[14] It worked. "When I met Takano, I told him about story ideas I had," recalled Tsuge in 1992. "He said they sounded really interesting, so I figured I'd try to draw them. In that sense, it was Takano's encouragement that got me drawing again after I had stopped for about a year."[15] This was the beginning of a close working relationship that continued into the '90s, and a friendship that continues to the present day.

Mizuki's popularity skyrocketed. Soon, hundreds of pages of manga were being commissioned from Mizuki Pro every month. To cope with the proliferating deadlines, Mizuki hired more staff, among them the future gekiga star Ryōichi Ikegami (b. 1944), who joined in November 1966 and stayed until March 1968. In a 2016 interview, Ikegami provided a glimpse of just how important Tsuge was to Mizuki Pro, not just as an ink pusher, but also as part of the studio's brain trust. "Each installment of *Kitarō* took us three days to draw. We worked through the night on day two. Sometimes, the following morning, we still weren't able to come up with a good way to end the story. Mizuki would get really stressed out, tapping his foot and chain-smoking. Then, as the sun started to come up, he'd turn to me and say, 'Hey, Ikegami, go get Tsuge,' and so I'd go over to his place. Tsuge never looked happy to see me! But he'd come to the studio anyway, and he and Mizuki would start quietly exchanging ideas."[9] The grueling schedule took its toll. By May 1967,

Tsuge was suffering from acute tenosynovitis. Considering that he was not only drawing pretty much full-time for Mizuki, but had also begun producing his own comics again, one wonders how he lasted for so long or managed to persevere through.

Mizuki Pro opened up new horizons for Tsuge, as well. The money helped, of course. "They told me the daily wage would be 2,000 yen. As I could fill my stomach on 300 yen a day back then, this was a dream come true."[10] Not only was Tsuge able to pay back what he owed his former landlord in Kinshichō, he even had enough to buy a car off of an old buddy of his in February 1967: a beat-up Daihatsu Fellow (a.k.a. Daihatsu 360), a kei-class microcar. In a manga-worthy twist, he was unable to drive it, however. Though he passed the written exam for his driver's license, he failed the driving test. He thus appointed the very same friend from whom he bought the car, Shintarō Tateishi (1937–2004), to be his informal chauffeur. It was Tateishi, in fact, who first got Tsuge into recreational travel

Mizuki Pro in 1967; left to right: Mizuki, Kitagawa Yoshikazu, Tsuge, and Ikegami

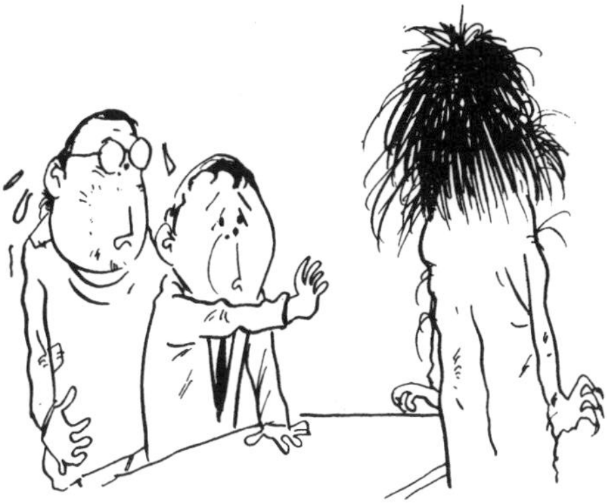

Mizuki's impression of Tsuge when they first met at Sanyōsha in the early '60s, with Nagai in the middle, *Garo* (June 1968), special Tsuge issue

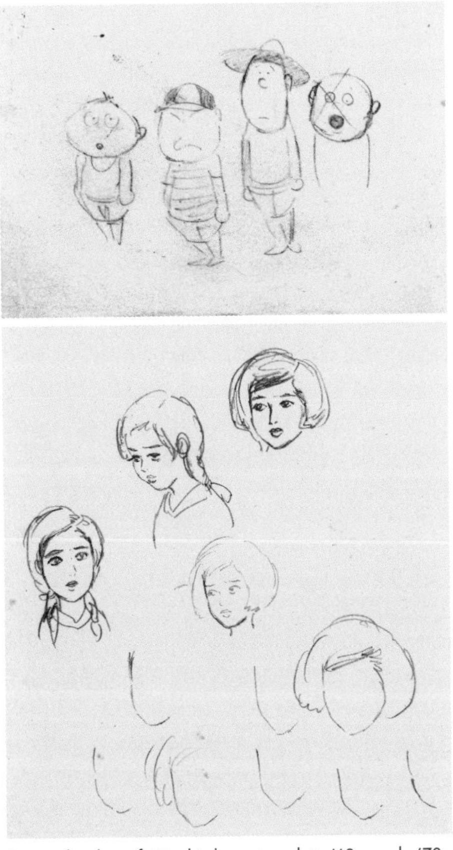

Tsuge, sketches of Mizuki characters, late '60s–early '70s

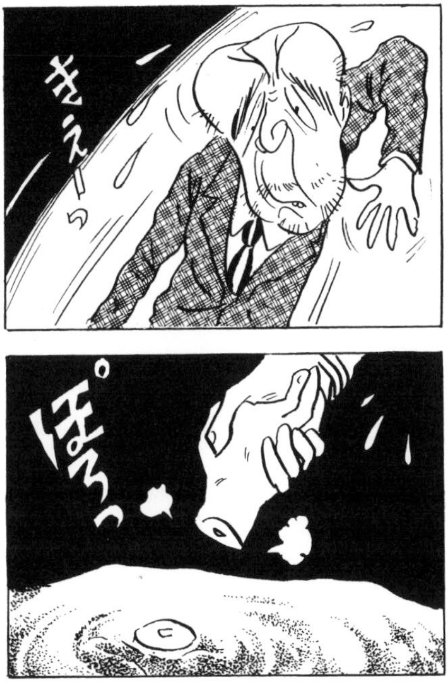
きえーっ
ぽろっ

Mizuki, "Nurarihyon," *Shōnen Magazine* (October 1, 1967)

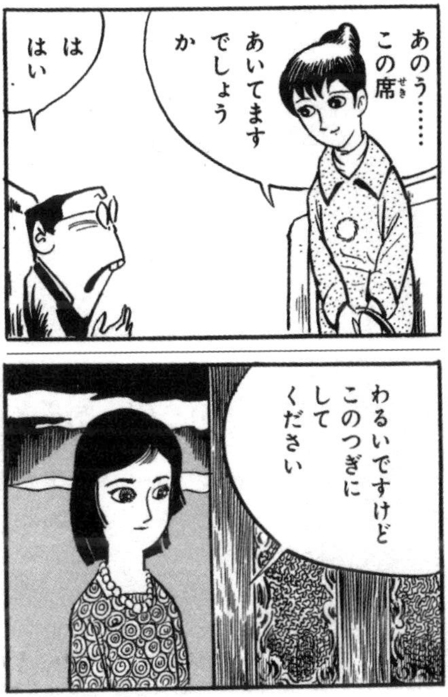
あのう……この席あいてますでしょうか
は はい
わるいですけど このつぎにしてください

Top: Mizuki, "The Man Who Peered into the Future," *Garo* (May 1966); Bottom: Mizuki, "The Haunted Mansion," *Devil Boy*, *Shōnen Magazine* (March 5, 1967)

kashihon years. Once I joined Mizuki Pro, I began using greater detail and a greater sense of spatial depth, reflecting the influence of Mizuki's work on my own infrequent contributions to *Garo*. The practice of using photographs and other materials to draw detailed backgrounds was also something I picked up from him."[4] In addition, Tsuge's sound effects got more Mizuki-esque. Some of the slapstick, like that in "The Ondol Shack," feels shaped by Mizuki's relentless wisecracking. Even small figurative traits: "The hardest thing about drawing Mizuki's characters were the hands," explained Tsuge in 2015. "His fingers are crazy. If you draw them properly, it doesn't look like Mizuki."[5] You can find Mizuki's tenticular digits in a number of the stories in the present volume: "The Wake" (page 11), "The Lee Family" (page 37), and "Red Flowers" (page 97, panel 7), for example. For comparison, see the panels from Mizuki's "Nurarihyon" (*Shōnen Magazine*, October 1, 1967) on the next page, showing Mizuki's "crazy" hands literally going rogue.

The influence went the other way, too. It is fairly easy to identify characters drawn by Tsuge in Mizuki's comics during his years at Mizuki Pro, between 1966 and 1970. The most obvious are the young female figures. Mizuki struggled drawing pretty girls. Then suddenly, you find many slender *bishōjo* in Mizuki's work, some of which look straight out of Tsuge's own comics. Look at the young woman in the panels on the next page from Mizuki's "The Man Who Peered into the Future" ("Mirai o nozoku otoko," *Garo*, May 1966), which, given the date, must have been drawn immediately after Tsuge joined the studio: It's the artist's girlfriend from "Chirpy." The mysterious, snake-eyed girl from "The Swamp" appears in "The Haunted Mansion" ("Maboroshi no kan") storyline of Mizuki's *Devil Boy* for *Shōnen Magazine* in March 1967. Later, the more distressed and realistic female faces Tsuge began deploying in mid 1968 appear in various Mizuki titles, especially those for adult

magazines, including *Kitarō's Vietnam War Tales* (*Kitarō no betonamu senki*, 1968) and *The Korpokkur's Pillow* (*Koropokkuru no makura*, 1970).[6]

Of greater significance is the largely overlooked likelihood that Mizuki's emergence as Japan's most prominent yōkai-ologist was facilitated by Tsuge. Both artists had been interested in folklore and popular religion for many years. According to Tsuge, when he joined Mizuki Pro, conversation naturally turned to Kunio Yanagita (compiler of the *The Legends of Tōno*, the locus classicus of Japanese folklore studies) and Shinobu Orikuchi, as well as lesser known writers, including Morihiko Fujisawa (1885–1967), a prolific historian of Japanese folk legends, popular music, and children's culture. Mizuki was much impressed by a book about "folk religion" (*minkan shinkō*) by Fujisawa that Tsuge had lent him, so much so that the two artists called on the octogenarian scholar together at his book-crammed home.[7] As confirmed in a recent interview with the artist, the book in question was from Fujisawa's multi-volume *A Survey of Yōkai Pictures and Tales* (*Yōkai gadan zenshū*, 1929). The Japanese volume contains numerous images from Sekien Toriyama's *The Illustrated Night Parade of One Hundred Demons* (*Gazu hyakki yagyō*, 1776), which is widely recognized as a major influence on Mizuki's work, not only in terms of how various monsters, spirits, and demons look, but also where they reside and what they do.[8] As Mizuki's work does not reflect knowledge of Sekien or Fujisawa's glosses prior to Tsuge joining his studio—in fact, it is only really in 1966–67 that Japanese and Chinese yōkai started outnumbering vampires, zombies, giant monsters, and other creatures derived from American comics and movies in Mizuki's manga and illustrations—one might go as far as to say that, without Tsuge, there would have been no yōkai boom, in Japan or globally. Mizuki didn't even regularly use the word "yōkai" for Japanese supernatural creatures before that point, preferring the more general "*bakemono*," roughly "monsters."

Tsuge's stories with a depth of realistic humanity rare among his contemporaries in manga. Details of time and place, meanwhile, paint a vivid picture of regions in Japan that few readers, especially back in the '60s, had ever been to.

"In my opinion," stated Tsuge recently, "what makes a work of gekiga capable of standing the test of time is whether the panels can move viewers as independent pictures in their own right, while also functioning as necessary pieces of the story."[1] He was talking about Mizuki's work, but the description befits his own comics more. This essay aims to pick up where volume one, *The Swamp*, left off, and narrate in greater detail Tsuge's transformation from a struggling artist for the *kashihon* (rental book) market to one of the most influential and celebrated Japanese artists of the 20th century.

As described in *The Swamp*, 1966 was a transitional year for Tsuge. Though "The Swamp" (February 1966) and "Chirpy" (March 1966) broke new ground, they were poorly received when they were first published. The artist, still only twenty-eight at the time, seriously considered quitting comics.

Fortunately, Tsuge was kept in the industry by a well-timed invitation from Shigeru Mizuki (1922–2015). His new studio, Mizuki Pro, was bombarded with deadlines due to the sudden success of *Devil Boy* (*Akuma kun*) and *Kitarō* in the mainstream market, and he needed help. Through *Garo*, word was passed on to Tsuge, who, penurious, uncertain about his own artistic prospects, and thinking about seeking work at a printshop, quickly said yes. He joined Mizuki Pro that April, ditching his derelict apartment in Kinshichō, on the dense, working class, east side of Tokyo, for Chōfu, a suburb twenty miles to the west, where Mizuki Pro is located. Tsuge still lives in Chōfu today.

The two cartoonists' relationship was truly unique. Tsuge went to work for Mizuki, not as an assistant, per se, but as a respected colleague and reliable handyman. Though fifteen years younger than Mizuki, Tsuge debuted as a cartoonist four years before Mizuki: Tsuge in 1954, at the age of seventeen, Mizuki in 1958, at a ripe thirty-five. The measure of seniority that usually governed the Japanese workplace—where greater age almost always meant greater experience and greater authority—did not apply here.

The artists had been fans of each other's work for years. Tadao Tsuge, when he was still dabbling with the idea of becoming a cartoonist in the early '60s, recalled his brother strongly recommending that he read Mizuki's *Yokai Chess Necronomicon* (*Yōkai shi'ninchō*), a kashihon manga published in 1962. Staring out from the peanut gallery in "The Phony Warrior" (August 1965), Tsuge's debut work for *Garo*, one finds Mizuki's Nezumi Otoko (Rat Man), famous as a character from *Kitarō*, but also a regular in Mizuki's short parables for *Garo*.[2] In the opening scene of "Chirpy," one of the books by the artist's side says "Shigeru Mizuki" on its cover. Mizuki particularly liked the tightly-crafted mystery stories Tsuge drew for mainstream youth monthlies and his wry ninja stories for the kashihon periodical *Ninpū* (1960–61). Both artists had published numerous books with Sanyōsha, co-run by Katsuichi Nagai (1921–96), the future proprietor of Seirindō, *Garo*'s publisher. They first crossed paths in Sanyōsha's offices in the early '60s, and again briefly at an event in 1965, where Mizuki recalled Tsuge looking malnourished and homeless "in the way that genius poets often do." They never really talked to one another, however, until Tsuge began working at Mizuki Pro.[3]

Tsuge's hiring galvanized both of their work. In Tsuge's case, "Soon after I started drawing for *Garo*, I felt like I wanted to get away from conventional storytelling in manga. My drawing style also hadn't changed much since my

A NEW KIND OF LITERATURE:
THE AWAKENING OF YOSHIHARU TSUGE, 1967–68

Mitsuhiro Asakawa and Ryan Holmberg

It is no exaggeration to say that the volume you hold in your hands contains some of the most important works in Japanese comics history—nay, in Japanese cultural history. It represents the beginnings of what we might call "literary manga."

Japanese cartoonists, of course, had long been influenced by prose narratives. The swordsmen, virtuous outlaws, and magical ninja of popular kōdan tales were a prime influence upon early adventure manga in the late 1920s and '30s. The gekiga movement in the '50s, in which Yoshiharu Tsuge (b. 1937) cut his teeth, aimed to translate the suspense and shock of mystery movies and novels, and the epic settings and drama of period genre fiction, into comics form. Also in the '50s, publishers big and small issued countless comicalizations of world literature, in an attempt to affirm the cultural legitimacy of the medium as it was taking off commercially as entertainment. But when it came to "high literature" of recent vintage, for the most part, cartoonists limited themselves to off-hand citations and comedic retellings. That changed with Tsuge in the mid '60s, with numerous cartoonists following in his footsteps and a wide range of cultural practitioners—from poets and professors, to playwrights and photographers—beginning to see comics as a serious art form in Japan.

To be more precise, "literary" in Tsuge's case means: an adoption of the modern short story form as it was popularized in Japan in the '20s and '30s; a distancing from the genres (mystery, action, romance, comedy, sci-fi, and samurai/ninja) that dominated manga; a foregrounding of the author's fictive self through first-person narration, supported by the incorporation of autobiographical elements (central features of the so-called "I-novel," or *shishōsetsu*); and an investment in travel, folklore, and cultural geography, which had been an integral part of Japanese letters for decades if not centuries. It also entailed bringing together disparate traditions in the visual arts: the suspenseful, image-driven breakdowns of gekiga, as developed by Masahiko Matsumoto and Yoshihiro Tatsumi in the '50s; the prominent use of photographic sources, as popularized by Shigeru Mizuki in the '60s, to create a distinct form of realism; a quasi-documentary attention to the details of rural landscape, buildings, and peoples, aided by a proliferation of photography publications on related topics and the rise of a domestic tourist industry; and an interest in the rusticated and forlorn akin to the classical aesthetic of *wabi-sabi*.

Like all watershed cultural moments, Tsuge's "invention" of literary manga thus creatively wove together a wide range of influences. When examined at a granular level, as this essay aims to do, there are times when Tsuge's pioneering work may sound like little more than skillful pastiche. However, as anyone who has read the manga translated in the present volume can attest, Tsuge's work is far more than the sum of its parts. The storytelling is tight, with nary a panel wasted, yet leaving much room for the imagination. The characters are rounded and personable. The scenery holds the eye and transports the viewer. The comedic passages make us smile, while also providing

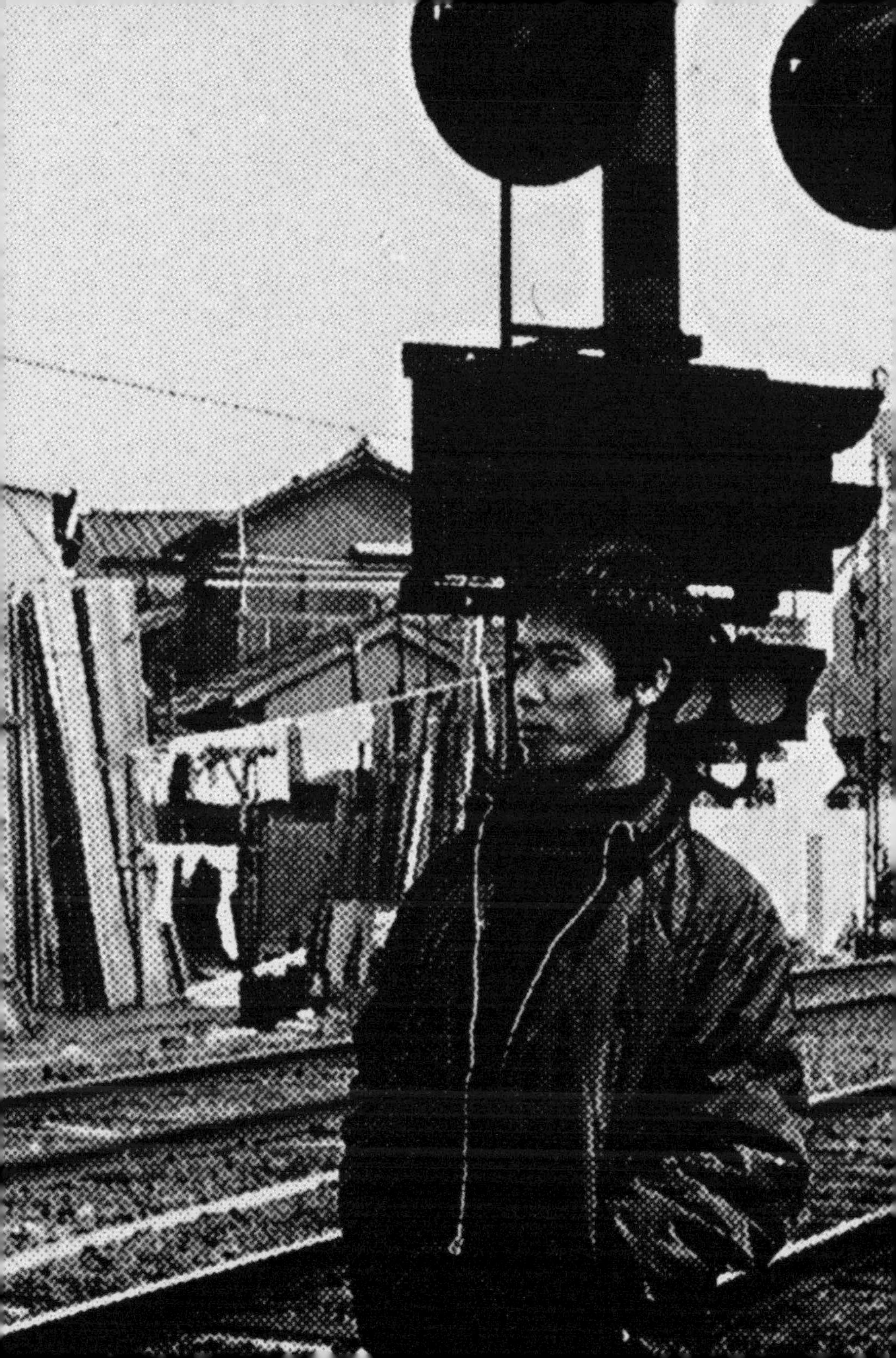

YOSHIHARU TSUGE was born in Tokyo in 1937. Influenced by the adventure comics of Osamu Tezuka and the gritty mystery manga of Yoshihiro Tatsumi and Masahiko Matsumoto, he began making his own comics in the mid '50s. He also assisted Shigeru Mizuki during his explosion of popularity in the '60s. In 1968, Tsuge published the groundbreaking surrealistic story "Nejishiki" in the legendary alternative manga magazine *Garo*. This story cemented Tsuge's position as an influential *manga-ka*, as well as a major figure within Japan's artistic counterculture at large. He is considered the originator and greatest practitioner of the semi-autobiographical "I-novel" genre of comics-making. In 2017, a survey of his work, *A World of Dreams and Travel*, won the Japan Cartoonists Association Grand Award, and in 2020, he was honored for his career achievements at Angoulême International.

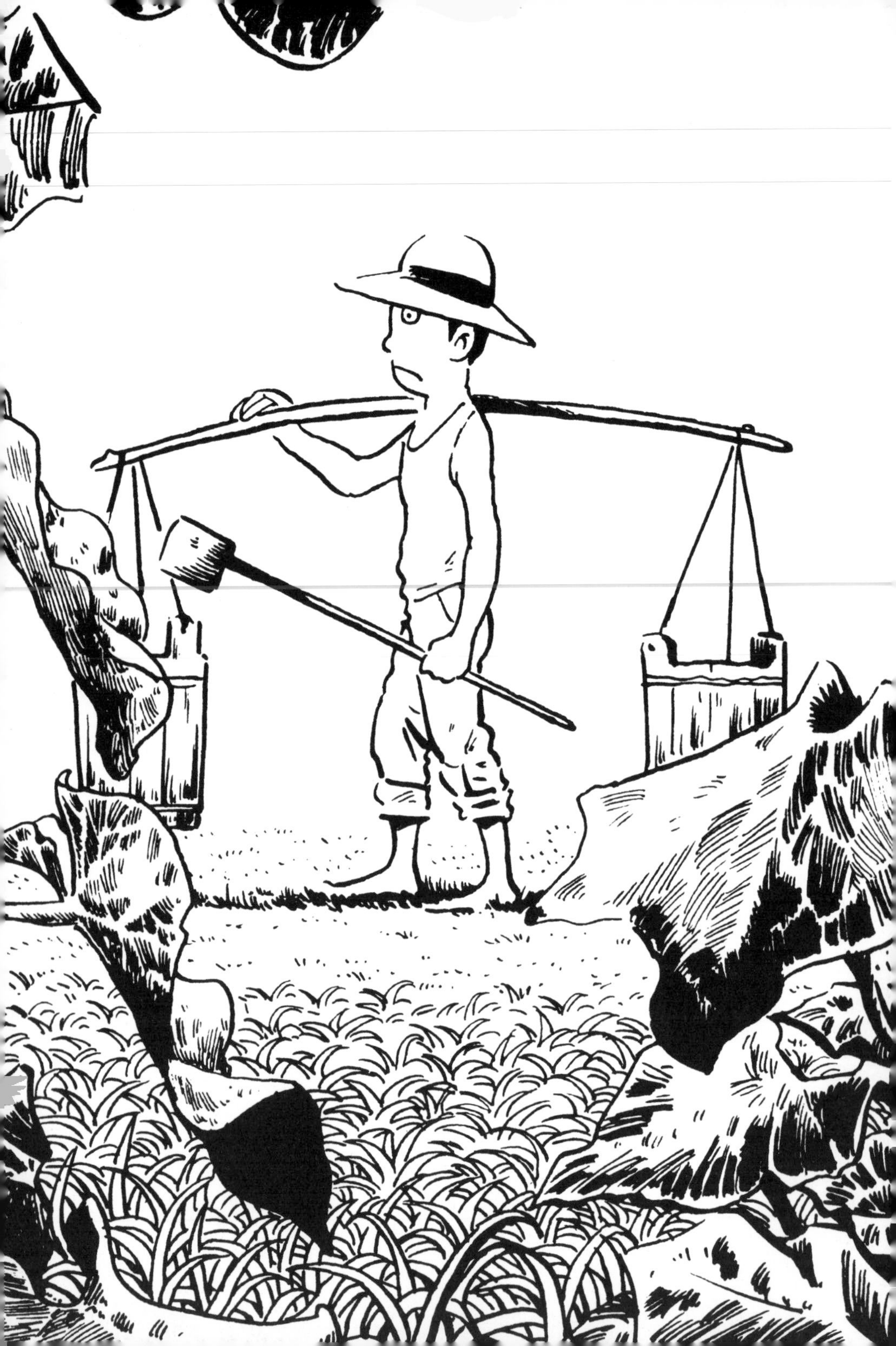

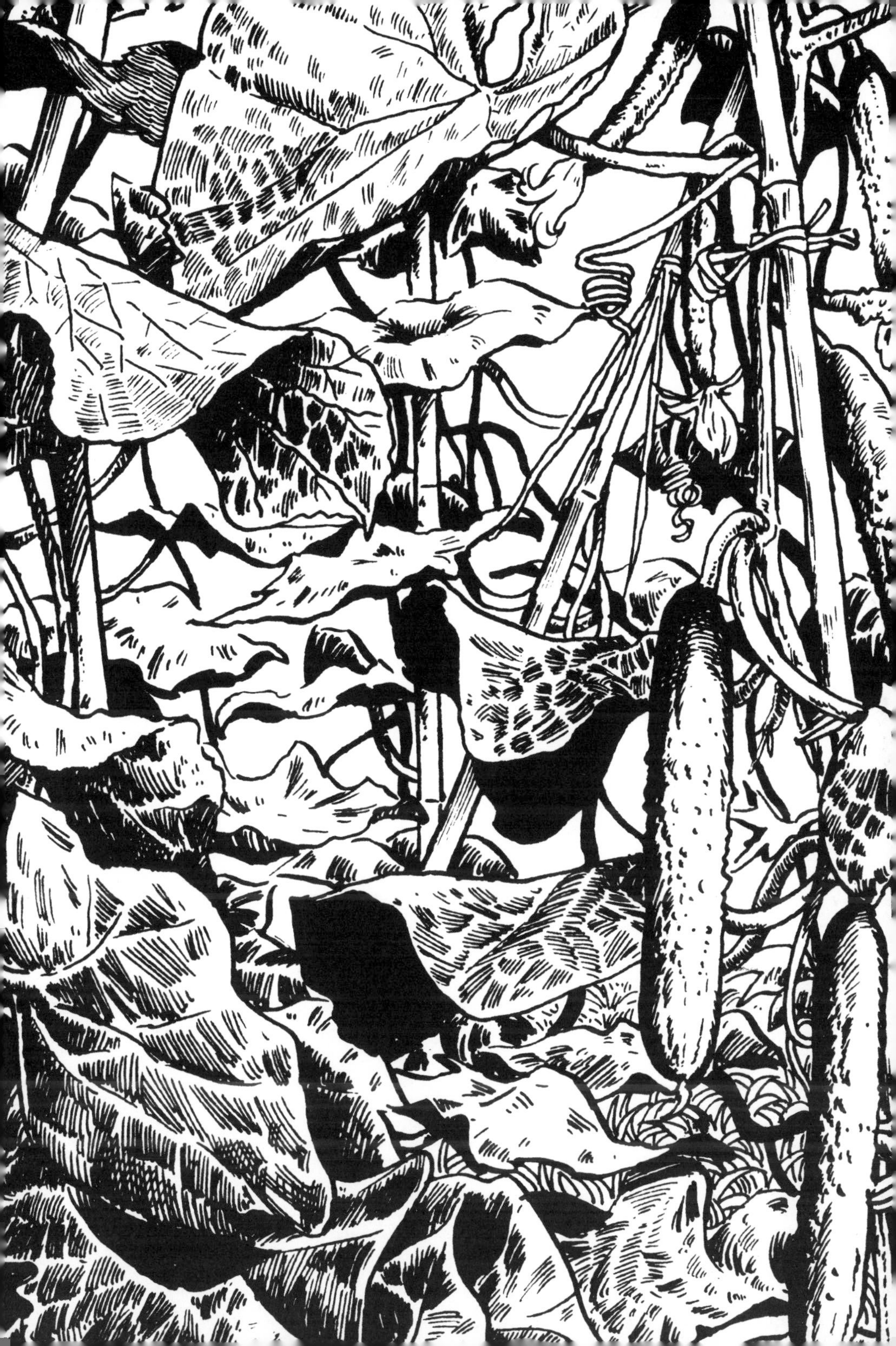

This book is presented in the traditional Japanese manner and is meant to be read from right to left. The cover at the opposite end is considered the front of the book.

To begin reading the manga, please flip the book over and start at the other end. For the historical essay, turn this page and read from left to right.

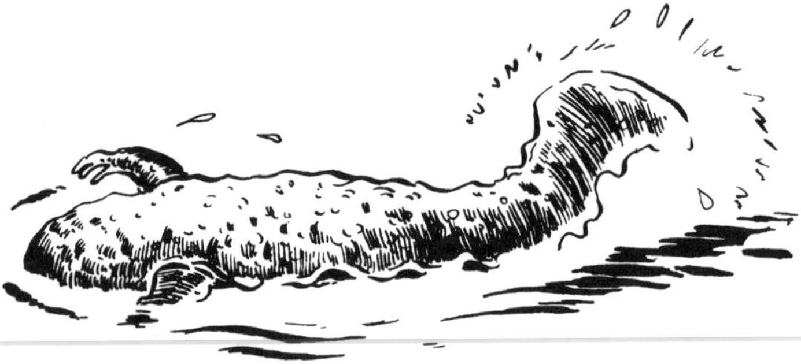

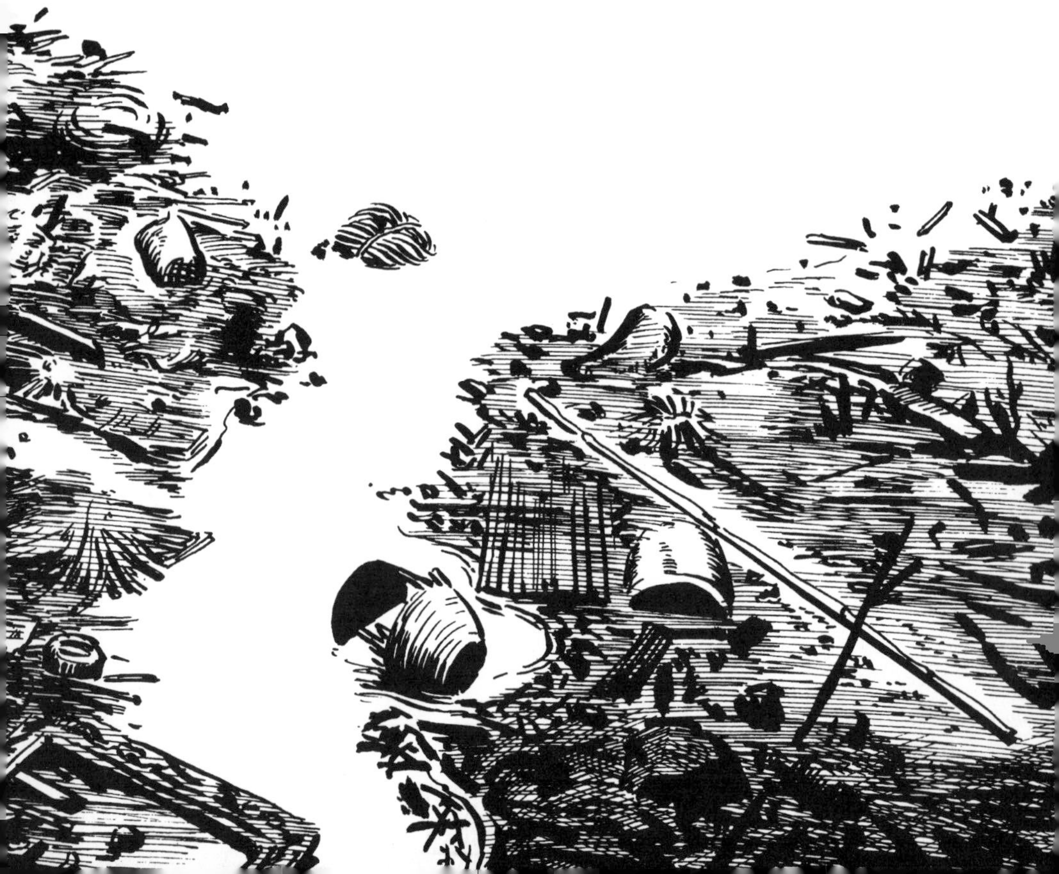

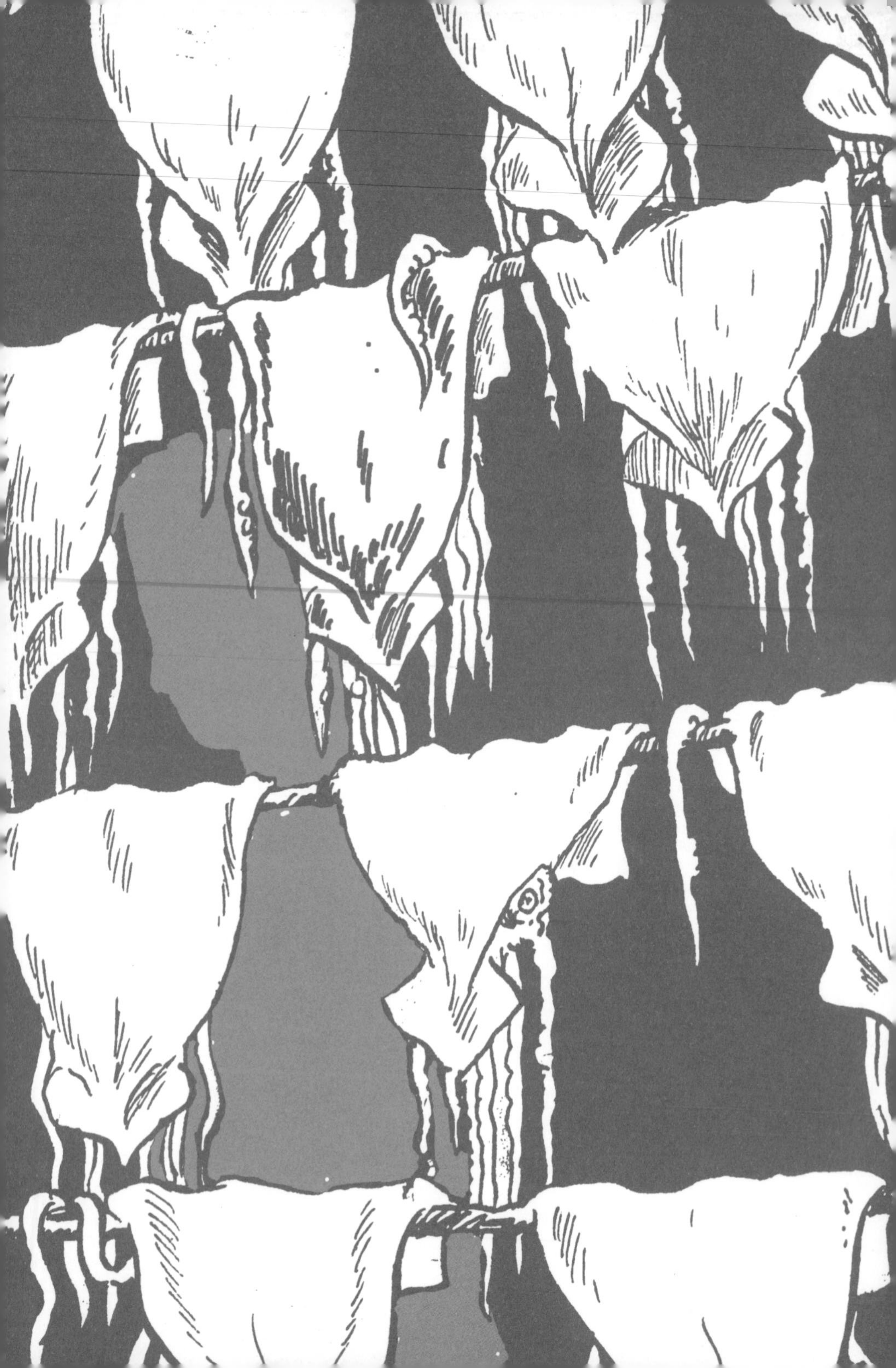